NOISY INFORMATION AND COMPUTATIONAL COMPLEXITY

NOISY INFORMATION AND COMPUTATIONAL COMPLEXITY

Leszek Plaskota

Institute of Applied Mathematics and Mechanics
University of Warsaw
Warsaw, Poland

CAMBRIDGE
UNIVERSITY PRESS

CAMBRIDGE UNIVERSITY PRESS
Cambridge, New York, Melbourne, Madrid, Cape Town, Singapore, São Paulo, Delhi

Cambridge University Press
The Edinburgh Building, Cambridge CB2 8RU, UK

Published in the United States of America by Cambridge University Press, New York

www.cambridge.org
Information on this title: www.cambridge.org/9780521553681

First published 1996

A catalogue record for this publication is available from the British Library

ISBN 978-0-521-55368-1 hardback

Transferred to digital printing 2009

*To
my wife
Aleksandra,
and our daughters
Kinga,
Klaudia,
and Ola.*

Contents

Preface

In the modern world, the importance of information can hardly be overestimated. Information also plays a prominent role in scientific computations. A branch of computational complexity which deals with problems for which information is partial, noisy and priced is called *information-based complexity*.

In a number of information-based complexity books, the emphasis was on partial and exact information. In the present book, the emphasis is on *noisy* information. We consider deterministic and random noise. The analysis of noisy information leads to a variety of interesting new algorithms and complexity results.

The book presents a theory of computational complexity of continuous problems with noisy information. A number of applications is also given. It is based on results of many researchers in this area (including the results of the author) as well as new results not published elsewhere.

This work would not have been completed if I had not received support from many people. My special thanks go to H. Woźniakowski who encouraged me to write such a book and was always ready to offer his help. I appreciate the considerable help of J.F. Traub. I would also like to thank M. Kon, A. Werschulz, E. Novak, K. Ritter and other colleagues for their valuable comments on various portions of the manuscript.

I wish to express my thanks to the Institute of Applied Mathematics and Mechanics at the University of Warsaw, where the book was almost entirely written. Some parts of the book were prepared in the Mathematical Institute of the Erlangen-Nuremberg University, and in the Columbia University Computer Science Department.

And finally, I am pleased to acknowledge the substantial support of my wife Aleksandra, my daughters Kinga, Klaudia and Ola, as well as my whole family, who patiently waited for completion of this work.

List of symbols

$$S : F \to G \qquad \text{solution operator}$$

$$g = S(f) \qquad \text{exact solution}$$

$$E \subset F \qquad \text{set of problem elements}$$

$$\mu \qquad \text{a priori distribution (measure) on } F$$

$$N : F \to Y \qquad \text{exact information operator}$$

$$N(f) \qquad \text{exact information about } f$$

$$\Delta \qquad \text{precision vector}$$

$$\Sigma \qquad \text{correlation matrix}$$

$$\mathbb{N} : F \to 2^Y, \mathbb{N} = \{N, \Delta\} \qquad \text{(noisy) information operator}$$

$$\mathbb{III} = \{\pi_f\}_f, \mathbb{III} = \{N, \Sigma\} \qquad \text{information distribution}$$

$$y \in \mathbb{N}(f) \qquad \text{information about } f \text{ (deterministic)}$$

$$y \sim \pi_f \qquad \text{information about } f \text{ (random)}$$

$$x = y - N(f) \qquad \text{information noise}$$

$$\delta, \sigma^2 \qquad \text{noise level (bound and variance)}$$

$$\varphi : Y \to G \qquad \text{algorithm}$$

$$\varphi(y) \qquad \text{approximate solution (approximation)}$$

$$e^{\text{wor}}(\mathbb{N}, \varphi), e^{\text{wor}}(\mathbb{N}, \varphi; E) \qquad \text{worst case error of the algorithm } \varphi$$

$$e^{\text{ave}}(\mathbb{III}, \varphi), e^{\text{ave}}(\mathbb{III}, \varphi; \mu) \qquad \text{average error of } \varphi$$

$$e^{\text{w}-\text{a}}(\mathbb{III}, \varphi), e^{\text{w}-\text{a}}(\mathbb{III}, \varphi; E) \qquad \text{worst-average error of } \varphi$$

$$e^{\text{a}-\text{w}}(\mathbb{N}, \varphi), e^{\text{a}-\text{w}}(\mathbb{N}, \varphi; \mu) \qquad \text{average-worst error of } \varphi$$

$$\text{rad}^{\text{wor}}(\mathbb{N}), \text{rad}^{\text{wor}}(\mathbb{N}; E) \qquad \text{worst case radius of information } \mathbb{N}$$

$$\text{rad}^{\text{ave}}(\mathbb{III}), \text{rad}^{\text{ave}}(\mathbb{III}; \mu) \qquad \text{average radius of information } \mathbb{III}$$

$\mathrm{diam}(\mathbb{N})$	diameter of information
Λ	class of permissible functionals
$\mathcal{N}_n$	a class of exact information
$r_n^{\mathrm{wor}}(\delta), r_n^{\mathrm{wor}}(\Delta)$	minimal radius (worst case)
$r_n^{\mathrm{ave}}(\sigma^2), r_n^{\mathrm{ave}}(\Sigma)$	minimal radius (average case)
$\mathbf{c}(\delta), \mathbf{c}(\sigma^2)$	cost function
$\mathbf{g}$	cost of operations in G
$\mathrm{R}(T)$	Tth minimal radius
$\mathcal{P}$	program
$\mathrm{cost}^{\mathrm{wor}}(\mathcal{P}), \mathrm{cost}^{\mathrm{ave}}(\mathcal{P})$	cost of executing $\mathcal{P}$
$\mathrm{comp}^{\mathrm{wor}}(\mathbb{N}, \varphi)$	worst case complexity of φ using $\mathbb{N}$
$\mathrm{comp}^{\mathrm{ave}}(\mathbb{II}, \varphi)$	average complexity of φ using $\mathbb{II}$
$\mathrm{IC}^{\mathrm{non}}(\varepsilon)$	(nonadaptive) information ε-complexity
$\mathrm{Comp}^{\mathrm{wor}}(\varepsilon), \mathrm{Comp}^{\mathrm{ave}}(\varepsilon)$	ε-complexity (of a problem)
$\mathbb{R}$	reals
A^*	adjoint operator to A
App	approximation problem
Int	integration problem
$R(\cdot, \cdot)$	reproducing kernel (covariance kernel)
G_N	Gram matrix for exact information N
$\mathrm{tr}(\cdot)$	trace of an operator
$\{H, F\}$	abstract Wiener space
w, w_r	classical and r-fold Wiener measure
$C_\mu : F^* \to F$	correlation operator of the measure μ
$\mu_2(\cdot|y)$	conditional distribution on F
W_r^0	r-fold square integrable functions
C_r^0	r-fold continuous functions
$\mathcal{N}(\cdot, \cdot)$	Gaussian (normal) distribution on $\mathbb{R}^n$
$a_n \asymp b_n$	weak equivalence of sequences
$a(\varepsilon) \asymp b(\varepsilon)$	weak equivalence functions
$a_n \approx b_n$	strong equivalence of sequences
$a(\varepsilon) \approx b(\varepsilon)$	strong equivalence of functions

1

Overview

In the process of doing scientific computations we always rely on some *information*. In practice, this information is typically *noisy*, i.e., contaminated by error. Sources of noise include

- previous computations,
- inexact measurements,
- transmission errors,
- arithmetic limitations,
- an adversary's lies.

Problems with noisy information have always attracted considerable attention from researchers in many different scientific fields, e.g., statisticians, engineers, control theorists, economists, applied mathematicians. There is also a vast literature, especially in statistics, where noisy information is analyzed from different perspectives.

In this monograph, noisy information is studied in the context of the computational complexity of solving mathematical problems.

Computational complexity focuses on the intrinsic difficulty of problems as measured by the minimal amount of time, memory, or elementary operations necessary to solve them. *Information-based complexity* (IBC) is a branch of computational complexity that deals with problems for which the available information is

- *partial,*
- *noisy,*
- *priced.*

Information being *partial* means that the problem is not uniquely determined by the given information. Information is *noisy* since it may be contaminated by error. Information is *priced* since we must pay for

1

getting it. These assumptions distinguish IBC from *combinatorial complexity*, where information is complete, exact, and free.

Since information about the problem is partial and noisy, only approximate solutions are possible. Approximations are obtained by *algorithms* that use this information. One of the main goals of IBC is to find the ε-*complexity* of the problem, i.e., the intrinsic cost of computing an approximation with the accuracy ε.

Partial, noisy and priced information is typical of many problems arising in different scientific fields. These include, for instance, signal processing, control theory, computer vision, and numerical analysis. As a rule, a digital computer is used to perform scientific computations. A computer can only use a finite set of numbers. Usually, these numbers cannot be entered exactly into the computer's memory. Hence problems described by infinitely many parameters can be 'solved' only by using partial and noisy information.

The theory of optimal algorithms for solving problems with partial information has a long history. It can be traced back to the pioneering papers of Sard (1949), Nikolskij (1950), and Kiefer (1953). A systematic and unified approach to such problems was first presented by J.F. Traub and H. Woźniakowski in the monograph *A General Theory of Optimal Algorithms*, Academic Press, 1980. This was an important stage in the development of the theory of IBC.

The monograph was followed by *Information, Uncertainty, Complexity*, Addison-Wesley, 1983, and *Information-based Complexity*, Academic Press, 1988, both authored by J.F. Traub, G.W. Wasilkowski, and H. Woźniakowski. Computational complexity of approximately solved problems is also studied in *Problem Complexity and Method Efficiency in Optimization* by A.S. Nemirovski and D.B. Yudin, Wiley and Sons, 1983, *Deterministic and Stochastic Error Bounds in Numerical Analysis* by E. Novak, Springer Verlag, 1988, and *The Computational Complexity of Differential and Integral Equations* by A.G. Werschulz, Oxford University Press, 1991.

Relatively few IBC papers study noisy information. One reason is the technical difficulty of its analysis. A second reason is that even if we are primarily interested in noisy information, the results on exact information establish a benchmark. Negative results for exact information are usually applicable for the noisy case. On the other hand, it is not clear whether positive results for exact information have a counterpart for noisy information.

In the mathematical literature, the word 'noise' is used mainly by statisticians to mean random error that contaminates experimental observations. We also want to study deterministic error. Therefore by noise we mean random or deterministic error. Moreover, in our model, the source of the information noise is not important. We may say that 'information is observed' or that it is 'computed'.

We also stress that the case of exact information is not excluded, either in the model or in most results. Exact information is obtained as a special case by setting the noise level to zero. This permits us to study the dependence of the results on the noise level, and to compare the noisy and exact information cases.

The general IBC model covers a large variety of problems. In this monograph, we are mainly interested in *linear problems*, i.e., problems which can be described in terms of approximating a linear operator from noisy information about values of some linear functionals. Examples include function approximation and integration, where information is given by noisy function values.

For linear problems, many effective algorithms are already known. Among them, algorithms based on smoothing splines and regularization, or the least squares algorithm, are some of the most frequently used in computations. We shall see that effectiveness of these algorithms can be confirmed in the IBC model.

In general, optimal algorithms and problem complexity depend on the *setting*. The setting is specified by the way the error and cost of algorithms are defined. In this monograph we study:

- *worst case setting*,
- *average case setting*,
- *worst-average case setting*,
- *average-worst case setting*,
- *asymptotic setting*.

In the worst case setting, the error and cost are defined by their worst performance. In the average case setting, we consider the average error and cost. The mixed worst-average and average-worst case settings are obtained by combining the worst and average cases. In the asymptotic setting, we are interested in the asymptotic behavior of algorithms. Other settings such as probabilistic or randomized settings are also important and will be involved in topics of future research.

Despite the differences, the settings have certain features in common. For instance, smoothing spline, regularization and least squares algorithms possess optimality properties, independent of the setting. This shows that these algorithms are universal and robust.

Most of the research presented in this monograph has been done over the last six to seven years by different people, including the author. Some of the results have not been previously reported. The references to the original results are given in Notes and Remarks at the end of each section. Clearly, the author does not pretend to cover the whole subject of noisy information in one monograph. Only those topics are presented that are typical of IBC, or are needed for the complexity analysis. Many problems are still open. Some of these are indicated in the text.

The monograph consists of six chapters. We start with the worst case setting in Chapter 2. Chapter 3 deals with the average case setting. Each of these two settings is studied following the same scheme. We first look for the best algorithms that use fixed information. Then we allow the information to vary and seek optimal information. We also analyze adaptive information and the problem adaption versus nonadaption. Finally, complexity concepts are introduced and complexity results are presented for some particular problems. Chapters 4 and 5 deal with the mixed settings, and Chapter 6 with the asymptotic setting.

Each subsequent chapter consists of several sections, most followed by Notes and Remarks, and Exercises. A preview of the results is presented in the introduction to each chapter.

2

Worst case setting

2.1 Introduction

In this chapter we study the worst case setting. We shall present results
already known as well as showing some new results. As already mentioned in the Overview, precise information about what is known and
what is new can be found in the Notes and Remarks.

Our major goal is to obtain tight complexity bounds for the approximate solution of linear continuous problems that are defined on infinite
dimensional spaces. We first explain what is to be approximated and
how an approximation is obtained. Thus we carefully introduce the
fundamental concepts of solution operator, noisy information and algorithm. Special attention will be devoted to information, which is most
important in our analysis. Information is, roughly speaking, what we
know about the problem to be solved. A crucial assumption is that
information is *noisy*, i.e., it is given not exactly, but with some error.

Since information is usually partial (i.e., many elements share the same
information) and noisy, it is impossible to solve the problem exactly. We
have to be satisfied with only approximate solutions. They are obtained
by algorithms that use information as data. In the worst case setting, the
error of an algorithm is given by its worst performance over all problem
elements and possible information. A sharp lower bound on the error
is given by a quantity called *radius of information*. We are obviously
interested in algorithms with the minimal error. Such algorithms are
called *optimal*.

In Sections 2.4 to 2.6 we study optimal algorithms and investigate
whether they can be linear or affine. In many cases the answer is affir-
mative. This is the case for approximation of linear functionals and approximation of operators that act between spaces endowed with Hilbert

5

seminorms, assuming that information is linear with noise bounded in a Hilbert seminorm. The optimal linear algorithms are based on the well known smoothing splines. This confirms a common opinion that smoothing splines are a very good practical tool for constructing approximations. We show that in some special cases smoothing splines are closely related to the least squares and regularization algorithms.

When using smoothing splines or regularization, we need to know how to choose the smoothing or regularization parameters. Often, special methods, such as cross-validation, are developed to find them. We show how to choose the smoothing and regularization parameters optimally in the worst case setting, and how this choice depends on the noise level and the domain of the problem. It turns out that in some cases, the regularization parameter is independent of the noise level, provided that we have a sufficiently small bound on the noise.

In Sections 2.7 and 2.8 we allow not only algorithms but also information to vary. We assume that information is obtained by successive noisy observations (or computations) of some functionals. The choice of functionals and noise bounds depends on us. We stress that we do not exclude the case where errors coming from different observations are correlated. This also allows us to model information where the noise of information is bounded, say, in a Hilbert norm.

With varying information, it is important to know whether adaption can lead to better approximations than nonadaption. We give sufficient conditions under which adaption is not better than nonadaption. These conditions are satisfied, for instance, if we use linear information whose noise is bounded in some norm.

Then we study the optimal choice of observations with given precision. This is in general a difficult problem. Therefore we establish complete results only for two classes of problems. The first class consists of approximating compact operators acting between Hilbert spaces where the noise is bounded in a weighted Euclidean norm. In particular, it turns out that in this case the error of approximation can be arbitrarily reduced by using observations of fixed precision. This does not hold for noise bounded in the supremum norm. When using this norm, to decrease the error of approximation, we have to perform observations with higher precision. We stress that observations with noise bounded in the supremum norm seem to be most often used in practice. Exact formulas for the minimal errors are in this case obtained for approximating Lipschitz functions based on noisy function values.

In Section 2.9 we present the model of computation and define the ε-complexity of a problem as the minimal cost needed to obtain an approximation with the (worst case) error at most ε. In the worst case setting, the cost of approximation is measured by the worst performance of an algorithm over all problem elements. In general, the cost of successive observations depends on their precisions. However, the model also covers the case when only observations with a given, fixed precision are allowed.

The complexity results are obtained using previously established results on optimal algorithms, adaption and optimal information. We first give tight general bounds on the ε-complexity. It turns out that if the optimal algorithms are linear (or affine) then in many cases the cost of combining information is much less than the cost of gaining it. In such a case, the problem complexity is roughly equal to the *information complexity*, which is defined as the minimal cost of obtaining information that guarantees approximation within error ε. This is the reason why we are so interested in the existence of optimal linear or affine algorithms.

In the last section we specialize the general complexity results to some specific problems. First, we consider approximation of compact operators in Hilbert spaces, where the information is linear with noise bounded in a weighted Euclidean norm. We obtain sharp upper and lower complexity bounds. We also investigate how the complexity depends on the cost assigned to each precision.

Next, we derive the ε-complexity for approximating and integrating Lipschitz functions. For a fixed positive bound on the noise, the complexity is infinite for sufficiently small ε. To make the complexity finite for all positive ε, we have to allow observations with arbitrary precision. Then the ε-complexity is roughly attained by information that uses observations of function values at equidistant points with the same precision, proportional to ε.

Finally, we consider approximation of smooth multivariate functions in a Banach space. We assume that the noise of successive observations is bounded in the absolute or relative sense. We show that in either case, the ε-complexity is roughly the same and is achieved by polynomial interpolation based on data about function values at equispaced points with noise bounds proportional to ε.

2.2 Information, algorithms, approximation

Let F be a linear space and G a normed space, both over the reals. Let

$$S : F \to G$$

be a mapping, called a *solution operator*. We are mainly interested in linear S. However, for the general presentation of the basic concepts we do not have to put any restrictions on S. We wish to approximate $S(f)$ for f belonging to a given set

$$E \subset F$$

of *problem elements*. An approximation is constructed based *only* on some information about f. We now explain precisely what we mean by information and how the approximations are obtained.

An *information operator* (or simply *information*) is a mapping

$$\mathbb{N} : F \to 2^Y ,$$

where Y is a set of finite real sequences, $Y \subset \bigcup_{n=1}^{\infty} \mathbb{R}^n$. That is, $\mathbb{N}(f)$ is a subset of Y. We assume that $\mathbb{N}(f)$ is nonempty for all $f \in F$. Any element $y \in \mathbb{N}(f)$ will be called *information about f*. Note that knowing y, we conclude that f is a member of the set $\{ f_1 \in F \mid y \in \mathbb{N}(f_1) \}$. This yields some information about the element f and justifies the names for $\mathbb{N}$ and y.

If the set $\mathbb{N}(f)$ has exactly one element for all $f \in F$, information $\mathbb{N}$ is called *exact*. In this case, $\mathbb{N}$ will be identified with the operator $N : F \to Y$, where $N(f)$ is the unique element of $\mathbb{N}(f)$. If there exists f for which $\mathbb{N}(f)$ has at least two elements, we say that $\mathbb{N}$ is *noisy*.

Knowing the information y about f, we combine it to get an *approximation*. More precisely, the approximation is produced by an *algorithm* which is given as a mapping

$$\varphi : Y \to G.$$

The algorithm takes the information obtained as data. Hence the approximation to $S(f)$ is $\varphi(y)$, where y is information about f. The *error of approximation* is defined by the distance $\|S(f) - \varphi(y)\|$ where $\| \cdot \|$ is the norm in the space G.

We illustrate the concepts of noisy information and algorithm by three simple examples.

Example 2.2.1 Suppose we want to approximate a real number (parameter) f based on its perturbed value y, $|y - f| \leq \delta$. This corresponds to $F = G = \mathbb{R}$ and $S(f) = f$. The information is of the form

$$\mathbb{N}(f) = \{ y \in \mathbb{R} \mid |y - f| \leq \delta \}$$

with $Y = \mathbb{R}$. For $\delta = 0$, we have exact information, $N(f) = f$, and for $\delta > 0$ we have noisy information. An algorithm is a mapping $\varphi : \mathbb{R} \to \mathbb{R}$. For instance, it may be given as $\varphi(y) = y$.

Example 2.2.2 Suppose we want to approximate a smooth function based on noisy function values at n points. This can be modeled as follows.

Let F be the space of twice continuously differentiable real functions $f : [0,1] \to \mathbb{R}$. We approximate $f \in F$ in the norm of the space $G = \mathcal{L}_2(0,1)$. That is, $S(f) = f$. For $t_i \in [0,1]$, the information operator is given by

$$\mathbb{N}(f) = \left\{ y \in \mathbb{R}^n \mid \sum_{i=1}^{n} (y_i - f(t_i))^2 \leq \delta^2 \right\}.$$

Knowing y corresponds to n noisy observations of $f(t_i)$, $1 \leq i \leq n$. An example of the algorithm is provided by a smoothing spline. For a given parameter $\gamma \geq 0$, this is defined as the function $\varphi_\gamma(y)$ which minimizes the functional

$$\Gamma_\gamma(f, y) = \gamma \cdot \int_0^1 (f''(t))^2 \, dt + \sum_{i=1}^{n} (y_i - f(t_i))^2$$

over all $f \in F$.

Example 2.2.3 Let F be as in Example 2.2.2 or another 'nice' class of smooth functions. The problem now is to approximate the integral of f based on noisy function values $f(t_i)$ with different precisions. That is, the solution operator is given as

$$S(f) = \int_0^1 f(t) \, dt,$$

and information is defined as

$$\mathbb{N}(f) = \{ y \in \mathbb{R}^n \mid |y_i - f(t_i)| \leq \delta_i, 1 \leq i \leq n \}.$$

An example of the algorithm is a quadrature formula $\varphi(y) = \sum_{i=1}^{n} a_i \, y_i$.

In all the above examples, information operators belong to a common class. This class is defined in the following way.

An *extended seminorm* in a linear space X is a functional $\| \cdot \|_X$: $X \to [0, +\infty]$, such that the set $X_1 = \{ x \in X \mid \|x\|_X < +\infty \}$ is a linear subspace, and $\| \cdot \|_X$ is a seminorm on X_1. That is,

(a) $\|\alpha x\|_X = |\alpha| \|x\|_X, \qquad \forall \alpha \in \mathbb{R}, \forall x \in X_1,$
(b) $\|x_1 + x_2\|_X \leq \|x_1\|_X + \|x_2\|_X, \qquad \forall x_1, x_2 \in X_1.$

We shall say that an information operator N is *linear with uniformly bounded noise*, iff it is of the form

$$N(f) = \{ y \in \mathbb{R}^n \mid \|y - N(f)\|_Y \leq \delta \}, \qquad \forall f \in F, \qquad (2.1)$$

where $N : F \to Y = \mathbb{R}^n$ is a linear operator, $\| \cdot \|_Y$ is an extended seminorm in $\mathbb{R}^n$, and $\delta \geq 0$. That is, information y about f is a noisy value of exact (linear) information $N(f)$, and the *noise* $x = y - N(f)$ is bounded by δ in the extended seminorm $\| \cdot \|_Y$.

For instance, in Example 2.2.2 we have

$$N(f) = [f(t_1), f(t_2), \ldots, f(t_n)].$$

As the extended seminorm $\| \cdot \|_Y$ we may take the Euclidean norm, $\|x\|_Y = \|x\|_2 = (\sum_{i=1}^n x_i^2)^{1/2}$. In Example 2.2.3, the operator N is as above and

$$\|x\|_Y = \max_{1 \leq i \leq n} \frac{|x_i|}{\delta_i}$$

(with the convention that $a/(+\infty) = 0$, $a/0 = +\infty$, $0/0 = 0$), and $\delta = 1$.

Observe that for any linear information with uniformly bounded noise, the extended seminorm $\| \cdot \|_Y$ and the parameter δ are not determined uniquely. In particular, replacing $\| \cdot \|_Y$ for $\delta > 0$ by $\|x\|_Y' = \|x\|_Y/\delta$, and for $\delta = 0$ by

$$\|x\|_Y' = \begin{cases} 0 & \|x\|_Y = 0, \\ +\infty & \|x\|_Y > 0, \end{cases}$$

we can always set δ to be 1. However, we prefer to have a parameter δ (and the norm independent of δ) since it can often be interpreted as a *noise level*. The smaller δ, the smaller the noise. If $\| \cdot \|_Y$ is a norm and δ goes to zero, then noisy information approaches exact information.

We now characterize linear information with uniformly bounded noise. Suppose that a subset B of a linear space X is convex (i.e., $x, y \in B$

implies $\alpha x + (1 - \alpha)y \in B$ for all $\alpha \in [0,1]$), and balanced (i.e., $x \in B$ iff $-x \in B$). Let

$$p_B(x) = \inf\{t > 0 \mid x/t \in B\}, \qquad x \in X.$$

Lemma 2.2.1 *The functional p_B is an extended seminorm on X.*

Proof Indeed, let $p_B(x), p_B(y) < +\infty$ and $\alpha \in \mathbb{R}$. Then for $\alpha = 0$ we have $p_B(\alpha x) = 0 = \alpha p_B(x)$, and for $\alpha \neq 0$ we have

$$\begin{aligned} p_B(\alpha x) &= \inf\{t > 0 \mid \alpha x/t \in B\} \\ &= \inf\{|\alpha|\,t > 0 \mid x/t \in B\} = |\alpha|\,p_B(x). \end{aligned}$$

We now check the triangle inequality. If $x/t, y/u \in B$, then from the convexity of B we obtain

$$\frac{x+y}{t+u} = \frac{t}{t+u} \cdot \frac{x}{t} + \frac{u}{t+u} \cdot \frac{y}{u} \in B.$$

Hence

$$\begin{aligned} p_B(x) + p_B(y) &= \inf\{t > 0 \mid x/t \in B\} + \inf\{u > 0 \mid y/u \in B\} \\ &\geq \inf\{t + u > 0 \mid (x+y)/(t+u) \in B\} \\ &= p_B(x+y). \end{aligned}$$

Thus the set $X_1 = \{x \in X \mid p_B(x) < \infty\}$ is a linear subspace, on which p_B is a seminorm, which means that p_B is an extended seminorm on X. □

We also observe that

$$\{x \in X \mid p(x) < 1\} \subset B \subset \{x \in X \mid p(x) \leq 1\}.$$

Moreover, if B is a closed [1] subset of $\mathbb{R}^n$ then $B = \{x \in \mathbb{R}^n \mid p(x) \leq 1\}$.

Now let the set $B \subset \mathbb{R}^n$ be convex, balanced and closed. Consider the information operator

$$\mathbb{N}(f) = \{y \in \mathbb{R}^n \mid y - N(f) \in B\}, \tag{2.2}$$

where $N : F \to \mathbb{R}^n$ is a linear mapping. Then, setting $\|x\|_Y = \delta\,p(x)$ (with $\delta > 0$), we have that $\mathbb{N}$ is linear with noise bounded uniformly by δ in the extended seminorm $\|\cdot\|_Y$. On the other hand, if information $\mathbb{N}$ is of the form (2.1) then it can be expressed by (2.2) with $B = \{x \in \mathbb{R}^n \mid \|x\|_Y \leq \delta\}$. Thus we have proved the following fact.

---

[1] Recall that in $\mathbb{R}^n$ all norms are equivalent. Therefore, if B is closed with respect to a particular norm, then B is also closed with respect to all norms in $\mathbb{R}^n$.

Corollary 2.2.1 *The classes of information (2.2) and linear information with uniformly bounded noise are equivalent.*

Clearly, not all information operators of interest can be expressed by
(2.1).

Example 2.2.4 Suppose we have a vector $f = (f_1, f_2, \ldots, f_n) \in \mathbb{R}^n$
with $|f_i| \leq 1$, $\forall i$, which we store in computer memory using floating
point representation with t mantissa bits. Then the difference between
the exact f_i and stored data y_i satisfies $|y_i - f_i| \leq 2^{-t}|f_i|$. The vector
y can be interpreted as noisy information about f where

$$\mathbb{N}(f) = \{ y \in \mathbb{R}^n \mid |y_i - f_i| \leq 2^{-t}|f_i|, \ 1 \leq i \leq n \}.$$

In this case, $\mathbb{N}(0) = \{0\}$ is a singleton, which is not true for $\mathbb{N}(f)$ with
$f \neq 0$. Hence the noise of information is *not* uniformly bounded.

Notes and remarks

NR 2.2.1 A more general concept of solution operator may be found in
Traub *et al.* (1983).

NR 2.2.2 For the exact information case, the formulation presented here
corresponds to the formulation given in Traub *et al.* (1988). The concept of
noisy information is, however, slightly different from that given in Traub *et
al.* (1988, Chap. 12).

NR 2.2.3 The problem of approximating an operator $S : F \to G$ by noisy or
exact information can be formulated in terms of approximating multi-valued
operators by single-valued operators. Indeed, let the multi-valued operator be
given as $\tilde{S} : Y_0 \to 2^G$ with $Y_0 = \bigcup_{f \in E} \mathbb{N}(f)$ and

$$\tilde{S}(y) = \{ S(f) \mid f \in E, \ y \in \mathbb{N}(f) \}.$$

Then $\tilde{S}(y)$ is approximated by $\varphi(y)$, where $\varphi : Y_0 \to G$ is an arbitrary
single-valued operator. This approach is presented in, e.g., Arestov (1990)
or Magaril-Il'yaev and Osipenko (1991).

NR 2.2.4 The functional $p_B(x)$ is called the Minkowski functional (or gauge
function) corresponding to the set B, see e.g. Wilansky (1978).

2.3 Radius and diameter of information

Let $\mathbb{N} : F \to 2^Y$ be a given information operator. The *worst case error*
(or simply *error*) of an algorithm $\varphi : Y \to G$ that uses information
$y \in \mathbb{N}(f)$ is defined as

$$e^{\mathrm{wor}}(\mathbb{N}, \varphi) = \sup_{f \in E} \ \sup_{y \in \mathbb{N}(f)} \|S(f) - \varphi(y)\|. \tag{2.3}$$

Our aim is to minimize the error (2.3) with respect to all algorithms φ. An algorithm φ_{opt} for which

$$e^{\mathrm{wor}}(\mathbb{N}, \varphi_{\mathrm{opt}}) = \inf_{\varphi} e^{\mathrm{wor}}(\mathbb{N}, \varphi)$$

is called *optimal*.

It turns out that the problem of an optimal algorithm is closely related to the concepts of the radius and center of a set. We recall that the *radius* of a set $A \subset G$ is given as

$$r(A) = \inf_{g \in G} \sup_{a \in A} \|a - g\|.$$

If for some $g_A \in G$ we have $\sup_{a \in A} \|a - g_A\| = r(A)$, then g_A is called a *center* of A. [1]

Denote $Y_0 = \bigcup_{f \in E} \mathbb{N}(f)$. For $y \in Y_0$, let

$$E(y) = \{ f \in E \mid y \in \mathbb{N}(f) \}$$

be the set of all elements f which are in E and share the same information y. Finally, let

$$A(y) = \{ S(f) \mid f \in E(y) \}$$

be the set of solution elements with information y. The *(worst case) radius of information* $\mathbb{N}$ is defined as

$$\mathrm{rad}^{\mathrm{wor}}(\mathbb{N}) = \sup_{y \in Y_0} r(A(y)).$$

Clearly, the radius $\mathrm{rad}^{\mathrm{wor}}(\mathbb{N})$ (and error $e^{\mathrm{wor}}(\mathbb{N}, \varphi)$) depends not only on the information $\mathbb{N}$ (and algorithm φ) but also on the other parameters of the problem such as the solution operator S or the set of problem elements E. If necessary, we will indicate this dependence and write, for instance, $\mathrm{rad}^{\mathrm{wor}}(\mathbb{N}; E)$ (or $e^{\mathrm{wor}}(\mathbb{N}, \varphi; E)$).

It turns out that the radius of information is the minimal error among all algorithms using such information.

Theorem 2.3.1 *For any information operator* $\mathbb{N}$,

$$\inf_{\varphi} e^{\mathrm{wor}}(\mathbb{N}, \varphi) = \mathrm{rad}^{\mathrm{wor}}(\mathbb{N}).$$

An optimal algorithm exists if and only if $r(A(y)) = \mathrm{rad}^{\mathrm{wor}}(\mathbb{N})$ *implies*

---

[1] The element g_A is also called a *Chebyshev center*.

that $A(y)$ has a center. In particular, if for every y there exists a center g_y of the set $A(y)$, then the algorithm

$$\varphi_{\mathrm{ctr}}(y) = g_y$$

is optimal.

Proof For any algorithm φ, its error can be rewritten as

$$
\begin{aligned}
e^{\mathrm{wor}}(\mathbb{N}, \varphi) &= \sup_{y \in Y_0} \sup_{f \in E(y)} \|S(f) - \varphi(y)\| \\
&= \sup_{y \in Y_0} \sup_{g \in A(y)} \|g - \varphi(y)\|.
\end{aligned}
$$

Hence, using the definition of the radius of a set, we obtain

$$
e^{\mathrm{wor}}(\mathbb{N}, \varphi) \geq \sup_{y \in Y_0} r(A(y)) = \mathrm{rad}^{\mathrm{wor}}(\mathbb{N}),
$$

and consequently

$$
\inf_{\varphi} e^{\mathrm{wor}}(\mathbb{N}, \varphi) \geq \mathrm{rad}^{\mathrm{wor}}(\mathbb{N}).
$$

To prove the reverse inequality, it suffices to observe that for any $\varepsilon > 0$ it is possible to select elements $\varphi_\varepsilon(y)$, $y \in Y_0$, such that

$$
\sup_{f \in E(y)} \|S(f) - \varphi_\varepsilon(y)\| \leq r(A(y)) + \varepsilon.
$$

For the algorithm φ_ε we have

$$
e^{\mathrm{wor}}(\mathbb{N}, \varphi_\varepsilon) \leq \mathrm{rad}^{\mathrm{wor}}(\mathbb{N}) + \varepsilon.
$$

Since ε is arbitrary, $\inf_{\varphi} e^{\mathrm{wor}}(\mathbb{N}, \varphi) \leq \mathrm{rad}^{\mathrm{wor}}(\mathbb{N})$.

To prove the second part of the theorem, suppose that each set $A(y)$ with $r(A(y)) = \mathrm{rad}^{\mathrm{wor}}(\mathbb{N})$ has a center g_y. Then for any $y \in Y_0$ we can choose an element $\tilde{g}_y \in G$ such that

$$
\sup_{a \in A(y)} \|a - \tilde{g}_y\| \leq \mathrm{rad}^{\mathrm{wor}}(\mathbb{N})
$$

(if $r(A(y)) = \mathrm{rad}^{\mathrm{wor}}(N)$ then $\tilde{g}_y = g_y$). The optimal algorithm is given by $\varphi_{\mathrm{opt}}(y) = \tilde{g}_y$.

On the other hand, if for some $y_0 \in Y_0$ we have $r(A(y_0)) = \mathrm{rad}^{\mathrm{wor}}(\mathbb{N})$ and the set $A(y_0)$ has no center, then for any algorithm we have

$$
\begin{aligned}
e^{\mathrm{wor}}(\mathbb{N}, \varphi) &\geq \sup_{f \in E(y_0)} \|S(f) - \varphi(y_0)\| \\
&> r(A(y_0)) = \mathrm{rad}^{\mathrm{wor}}(\mathbb{N}).
\end{aligned}
$$

This shows that an optimal algorithm does not exist. $\qquad\square$

The algorithm φ_{ctr} defined in the above theorem is called *central*. A central algorithm (if it exists) has even stronger properties than a 'usual' optimal algorithm. Indeed, φ_{ctr} is optimal not only with respect to the set E, but also with respect to each $E(y)$. That is, for any $y \in Y_0$ we have

$$e^{\mathrm{wor}}(\mathbb{N}, \varphi_{\mathrm{ctr}}; E(y)) = \inf_{\varphi} e^{\mathrm{wor}}(\mathbb{N}, \varphi; E(y)) = r(A(y)).$$

Together with the notion of a radius, it is convenient to introduce the notion of a diameter of information $\mathbb{N}$. Recall first that the *diameter* of a set A is given as

$$d(A) = \sup_{a_{-1}, a_1 \in A} \|a_1 - a_{-1}\|.$$

We also recall that for any set A we have

$$r(A) \leq d(A) \leq 2 \cdot r(A). \tag{2.4}$$

Example 2.3.1 Let a set $A \subset G$ be centrosymmetric. That is, there exists an element $a^* \in G$ such that the condition $a \in A$ implies $2a^* - a \in A$. Then a^* is a center of A and

$$d(A) = 2 \cdot r(A) = 2 \cdot \sup \{ \|a - a^*\| \mid a \in A \}.$$

Indeed, using the triangle inequality we obtain

$$
\begin{aligned}
r(A) &\geq \inf_{g \in G} \sup_{a \in A} \tfrac{1}{2} (\|g - a\| + \|g - (2a^* - a)\|) \\
&\geq \inf_{g \in G} \sup_{a \in A} \|a - a^*\| = \sup_{a \in A} \|a - a^*\|,
\end{aligned}
$$

which shows that a^* is a center. To prove the remaining equality, observe that

$$d(A) \geq \sup_{a \in A} \|a - (2a^* - a)\| = 2 \sup_{a \in A} \|a - a^*\|.$$

The *diameter of information* $\mathbb{N}$ is defined as

$$\mathrm{diam}(\mathbb{N}) = \sup_{y \in Y_0} d(A(y)).$$

Observe that in view of the equality

$$d(A(y)) = \sup\{\|S(f_1) - S(f_{-1})\| \mid f_{-1}, f_1 \in F_0, y \in \mathbb{N}(f_{-1}) \cap \mathbb{N}(f_1)\},$$

the diameter of information can be rewritten as

$$\mathrm{diam}(\mathbb{N}) = \sup \|S(f_1) - S(f_{-1})\|,$$

where the supremum is taken over all $f_{-1}, f_1 \in E$ such that $\mathbb{N}(f_{-1}) \cap \mathbb{N}(f_1) \neq \emptyset$. Thus diam($\mathbb{N}$) measures the largest distance between two elements in $S(E)$ which cannot be distinguished with respect to the information.

The diameter of information is closely related to the radius, though its definition is independent of the notion of an algorithm. That is, in view of (2.4), we have the following fact.

Theorem 2.3.2 *For any information* $\mathbb{N}$,

$$\mathrm{diam}(\mathbb{N}) \; = \; c \cdot \mathrm{rad}^{\mathrm{wor}}(\mathbb{N})$$

where $c = c(\mathbb{N}) \in [1, 2]$.

In general, c depends on the information, the solution operator and the set E. However, in some cases it turns out to be an absolute constant.

Example 2.3.2 Let S be a functional, i.e., let the range space $G = \mathbb{R}$. Then for any set $A \subset \mathbb{R}$ we have $d(A) = 2\,r(A)$ and the center of A is $(\sup A + \inf A)/2$. Hence for any information $\mathbb{N}$ the constant c in Theorem 2.3.2 is equal to 2.

The relation between the radius and diameter of information allows us to show 'almost' optimality of an important class of algorithms. An algorithm φ_{itp} is called *interpolatory* iff for all $y \in Y_0$

$$\varphi_{\mathrm{itp}}(y) \; = \; S(f_y),$$

for an element $f_y \in E(y)$.

Since $S(f_y)$ is a member of $A(y)$, for any $f \in E(y)$ we have

$$\|S(f) - \varphi_{\mathrm{itp}}(y)\| \; = \; \|S(f) - S(f_y)\| \; \leq \; d(A(y)) \; \leq \; \mathrm{diam}(\mathbb{N}).$$

This yields the following fact.

Corollary 2.3.1 *For any interpolatory algorithm* φ_{itp} *we have*

$$e^{\mathrm{wor}}(\mathbb{N}, \varphi_{\mathrm{itp}}) \; \leq \; 2 \cdot \mathrm{rad}^{\mathrm{wor}}(\mathbb{N}).$$

In some important cases, the diameter of information can be expressed in a simple way. For a set $A \subset F$, let

$$\mathrm{bal}(A) \; = \; (A - A)/2 \; = \; \{\, (a_1 - a_{-1})/2 \mid \; a_{-1}, a_1 \in A \,\}.$$

Observe that the set bal(A) is balanced, i.e., it is centrosymmetric with center zero. It is also convex for convex A. Obviously, $\mathrm{bal}(A) = A$ for convex and balanced A.

Lemma 2.3.1 *Let the solution operator S be linear. Let $\mathbb{N}$ be an information operator with $Y = \mathbb{R}^n$ satisfying*

$$\mathbb{N}(f_1) \cap \mathbb{N}(f_{-1}) \neq \emptyset, \ f_{-1}, f_1 \in E \implies 0 \in \mathbb{N}((f_1 - f_{-1})/2) \quad (2.5)$$

and

$$h \in \mathrm{bal}(E), \ 0 \in \mathbb{N}(h) \implies \exists f_{-1}, f_1 \in E, \ s.t. \ h = (f_1 - f_{-1})/2,$$
$$\mathbb{N}(f_1) \cap \mathbb{N}(f_{-1}) \neq \emptyset. \quad (2.6)$$

Then

$$\mathrm{diam}(\mathbb{N}) = 2 \cdot \sup \{ \, \|S(h)\| \mid \ h \in \mathrm{bal}(E), \ 0 \in \mathbb{N}(h) \, \}. \quad (2.7)$$

If, in addition, the set E is convex and balanced, then

$$\begin{aligned} \mathrm{diam}(\mathbb{N}) &= 2 \cdot \sup \{ \, \|S(h)\| \mid \ h \in E, \ 0 \in \mathbb{N}(h) \, \} \\ &= d(A(0)) = 2 \cdot r(A(0)), \end{aligned} \quad (2.8)$$

where $A(0) = \{ S(h) \mid h \in E, \ 0 \in \mathbb{N}(h) \}$.

Proof The first part of the lemma follows directly from (2.5), (2.6), and linearity of S. The assumption (2.5) yields the upper bound and (2.6) yields the lower bound on $\mathrm{diam}(\mathbb{N})$ in (2.7). Since for a convex and balanced set E we have $\mathrm{bal}(E) = E$, the first equality in (2.8) is also valid.

To prove the remaining two equalities in (2.8), we first show that the set $A(0)$ is balanced. Indeed, let $h \in E$, $0 \in \mathbb{N}(h)$. Then from (2.6) we have $h = (f_1 - f_{-1})/2$, where $f_{-1}, f_1 \in E$ and $\mathbb{N}(f_{-1}) \cap \mathbb{N}(f_1) \neq \emptyset$. Using (2.5) we get $0 \in \mathbb{N}((f_{-1} - f_1)/2) = \mathbb{N}(-h)$. Hence $S(h) \in A(0)$ implies $-S(h) = S(-h) \in A(0)$.

To complete the proof it suffices to observe that the set $A(0)$ is centrosymmetric with center zero and use the fact proven in Example 2.3.1. □

Lemma 2.3.1 yields the following theorem which is the main result of this section.

Theorem 2.3.3 *Suppose that the solution operator S is linear, information $\mathbb{N}$ is linear with uniformly bounded noise,*

$$\mathbb{N}(f) = \{ y \in \mathbb{R}^n \mid \ \|y - N(f)\|_Y \leq \delta \},$$

and the set E of problem elements is convex. Then

$$\operatorname{diam}(\mathbb{N}) \;=\; 2 \cdot \sup\{\, \|S(h)\| \mid\ h \in \operatorname{bal}(E),\ \|N(h)\| \le \delta \,\}.$$

Proof It suffices to check the assumptions of Lemma 2.3.1. If $\|y - N(f_i)\|_Y \le \delta$, for $i = -1, 1$, then also $\|0 - N(f_1 - f_{-1})/2\|_Y \le \delta$, which shows (2.5). To show (2.6), let $h = (f_1 - f_{-1})$ with $f_1, f_{-1} \in E$ and $0 \in \mathbb{N}(h)$, i.e., $\|N(f_1 - f_{-1})/2\|_Y \le \delta$. Then for $y = N(f_{-1} + f_1)/2$ we have $\|y - N(f_i)\|_Y \le \delta$, as claimed.   □

A larger class of information for which Lemma 2.3.1 holds consists of information operators $\mathbb{N} : F \to 2^Y$ such that $Y = \mathbb{R}^n$ and the graph of $\mathbb{N}$,

$$\operatorname{gr}(\mathbb{N}; E) \;=\; \{(f, y) \in F \times \mathbb{R}^n \mid\ f \in E,\ y \in \mathbb{N}(f)\},$$

is a convex and balanced set. This fact is left as E 2.3.8.

Notes and remarks

NR 2.3.1   Abstractly, the concept of an optimal algorithm can be introduced as follows. Let R be a relation defined on the Cartesian product of algorithms. For two algorithms we write $\varphi_1 \prec \varphi_2$ iff $(\varphi_1, \varphi_2) \in R$ and say that φ_1 is *not worse* than φ_2 (or that φ_2 is *not better* than φ_1). An algorithm φ_{opt} is *optimal* iff

$$\varphi_{\mathrm{opt}} \prec \varphi, \qquad \forall \varphi.$$

In this chapter we use the (worst case) error criterion. It corresponds to the relation

$$\varphi_1 \prec \varphi_2 \quad \Longleftrightarrow \quad e^{\mathrm{wor}}(\mathbb{N}, \varphi_1) \le e^{\mathrm{wor}}(\mathbb{N}, \varphi_2).$$

If the relation is defined as

$$\varphi_1 \prec \varphi_2 \quad \Longleftrightarrow \quad e^{\mathrm{wor}}(\mathbb{N}, \varphi_1; E(y)) \le e^{\mathrm{wor}}(\mathbb{N}, \varphi_2; E(y)), \quad \forall y \in Y_0,$$

then only a central algorithm (if it exists) turns out to be optimal.

NR 2.3.2   The notions of the radius and diameter of information were introduced in Traub and Woźniakowski (1980). The formula for $\operatorname{diam}(\mathbb{N})$ in the case of a convex and balanced set E, and linear information with noise bounded in a seminorm, was first shown by Micchelli and Rivlin (1977). They used the fact that the radius of noisy information is equal to the radius of some appropriately chosen exact information; see also E 2.3.7.

Exercises

E 2.3.1   Give an example of information $\mathbb{N}$ and a set E for which:
1. An optimal algorithm does not exist.
2. An optimal algorithm does exist, but a central algorithm does not.

E 2.3.2 Show that the set of all optimal algorithms is convex.

E 2.3.3 Prove the inequalities

$$r(A) \leq d(A) \leq 2 \cdot r(A),$$

for an arbitrary bounded set A.

E 2.3.4 Let $1 \leq c \leq 2$.
1. Find a set A for which $d(A) = cr(A)$, with $r(A) \in (0, +\infty)$.
2. Find information $\mathbb{N}$ and a set E, such that

$$\text{diam}(\mathbb{N}) = c \cdot \text{rad}^{\text{wor}}(\mathbb{N})$$

and $r(\mathbb{N}) \in (0, +\infty)$.

E 2.3.5 Let $S : F \to G$ be an arbitrary solution operator. Show that for any information operator $\mathbb{N}$ and any convex set $E \subset F$ we have

$$\text{rad}^{\text{wor}}(\mathbb{N}; E) = c \cdot \sup_{f_1, f_2 \in E} \text{rad}^{\text{wor}}(\mathbb{N}; [f_1, f_2]),$$

where $c \in [1, 2]$. Moreover, if S is a functional then $c = 1$. (Here $[f_1, f_2] = \{\alpha f_1 + (1 - \alpha) f_2 \mid 0 \leq \alpha \leq 1\}$.)

E 2.3.6 Let the solution operator $S : F \to G$ be linear. Let E be a balanced and convex set, and information $\mathbb{N}$ be linear with noise bounded uniformly in a norm $\|\cdot\|_Y$. Suppose there exists an operator $A : Y \to F$ such that for any $f \in E$ and $y \in \mathbb{N}(f)$ we have $f - A(y) \in \{h \in E \mid \|\mathbb{N}(h)\|_Y \leq \delta\}$. Show that then the algorithm $\varphi(y) = S(A(y))$ is optimal.

E 2.3.7 Let the solution operator $S : F \to G$, information $\mathbb{N} : F \to 2^Y$ with $Y = \mathbb{R}^n$, and set E be given. Define the space $\tilde{F} = F \times Y$, solution operator $\tilde{S} : \tilde{F} \to G$, exact information operator $\tilde{N} : \tilde{F} \to Y$, and set $\tilde{E} \subset \tilde{F}$ as

$$
\begin{aligned}
\tilde{S}(f, y) &= S(f), \\
\tilde{N}(f, y) &= y, \\
\tilde{E} &= \{(f, y) \mid f \in E, \ y \in \mathbb{N}(f)\}.
\end{aligned}
$$

Show that for any algorithm $\varphi : Y \to G$ we have

$$e^{\text{wor}}(\mathbb{N}, \varphi; S, E) = \tilde{e}^{\text{wor}}(\tilde{N}, \varphi; \tilde{S}, \tilde{E})$$

where the second quantity stands for the error of φ over $\tilde{E}$, in approximating $\tilde{S}(f, y)$ based on exact information $y = \tilde{N}(f)$.

E 2.3.8 Show that information whose graph $\text{gr}(N; E)$ is convex and balanced satisfies the conditions (2.5) and (2.6) of Lemma 2.3.1.

E 2.3.9 Let

$$\mathbb{N}(f) = \{y \in \mathbb{R}^n \mid (y - N(f)) \in B\},$$

where $N : F \to \mathbb{R}^n$ is linear and B is a given set of $\mathbb{R}^n$. Show that if both the sets B and E are convex (and balanced), then the graph $\text{gr}(\mathbb{N}; E)$ is convex (and balanced).

2.4 Affine algorithms for linear functionals

We start the study of problems with the case of the solution operator S being a linear operator. In this section, we assume that

- S is a linear functional.

We are especially interested in finding optimal linear or affine algorithms.

2.4.1 Existence of optimal affine algorithms

Since now the space $G = \mathbb{R}$, we have

$$\mathrm{diam}(\mathbb{N}) \;=\; 2 \cdot \mathrm{rad}^{\mathrm{wor}}(\mathbb{N}) \;=\; \sup_{y \in Y_0} \left(\sup A(y) - \inf A(y) \right),$$

where $Y_0 = \bigcup_{f \in E} \mathbb{N}(f)$, $A(y) = \{ S(f) \mid f \in E, \, y \in \mathbb{N}(f) \}$. The algorithm $\varphi(y) = (\sup A(y) + \inf A(y))/2$ is optimal and also central. We now ask if there exists an optimal algorithm which is linear or affine. It is easily seen that, in general, this is not true.

Example 2.4.1 Let $F = \mathbb{R}^2$ and

$$E \;=\; \{\, f = (f_1, f_2) \in \mathbb{R}^2 \mid \quad f_2 = f_1^3, \; |f_1| \leq 1 \,\}.$$

Then the set E is balanced but not convex. Let $S(f) = f_2$ and $\mathbb{N}(f) = \{f_1\}$. In this case the problem can be solved exactly. However, the only optimal algorithm, $\varphi_{\mathrm{opt}}(y) = y^3$, is nonlinear.

Restricting the class of problems properly, it is, however, possible to show the positive result. In what follows, we assume that $Y = \mathbb{R}^n$ and $\mathrm{rad}^{\mathrm{wor}}(\mathbb{N}) < +\infty$.

Theorem 2.4.1 *Let S be a linear functional. If the graph $\mathrm{gr}(\mathbb{N}; E)$ of the information operator $\mathbb{N}$ is convex, then there exists an optimal affine algorithm. If, in addition, $\mathrm{gr}(\mathbb{N}, E)$ is balanced then any optimal affine algorithm is linear.*

Proof Suppose first that $\mathrm{gr}(\mathbb{N}, E)$ is a convex set. Let $r = \mathrm{rad}^{\mathrm{wor}}(\mathbb{N})$. If $r = 0$ then each set $A(y)$, $y \in Y_0$, has exactly one element which we denote by a_y. Let $y_0 \in Y_0$. The functional $\varphi_1(y) = a_{y+y_0} - a_{y_0}$ is linear on its convex domain $Y_0 - y_0$ and can be extended to a linear functional φ_2 defined on Y. Letting $\varphi(y) = \varphi_2(y - y_0) + a_{y_0}$ we obtain an optimal affine algorithm.

Let $r > 0$. Consider the set

$$A = \{(y, S(f)) \in \mathbb{R}^{n+1} \mid f \in E, y \in \mathbb{N}(f)\}.$$

Since $\mathrm{gr}(\mathbb{N}, E)$ is convex, A is also convex. Then the set $A_1 = \mathrm{bal}(A) = (A - A)/2$ is convex and balanced. Let

$$p(u) = \inf\{t > 0 \mid u/t \in A_1\}, \qquad u \in \mathbb{R}^{n+1}.$$

We show that for $u = (0, g) \in A_1$, $g > 0$, we have $p(u) = g/r$. Indeed, Lemma 2.3.1 yields

$$\begin{aligned} r &= \sup\{|S(h)| \mid h \in \mathrm{bal}(E), 0 \in \mathbb{N}(h)\} \\ &= \sup\{\alpha \in \mathbb{R} \mid (0, \alpha) \in A_1\}. \end{aligned}$$

Hence the infimum over all $t > 0$ such that $(0, g/t) \in A_1$ is equal to g/r.

Recall that $p(u)$ is a seminorm on the space $P = \{u \in \mathbb{R}^{n+1} \mid p(u) < +\infty\}$. Let $P_0 = \{u \in \mathbb{R}^{n+1} \mid p(u) = 0\}$ and $P_1 = \{(0, g) \in \mathbb{R}^{n+1} \mid g \in \mathbb{R}\}$. Since $P_1 \cap P_0 = \{0\}$, P can be decomposed as $P = P_0 \oplus P_0^\perp$ where $P_1 \subset P_0^\perp$. Define on P_1 the linear functional ξ_1 as $\xi_1(u) = p(u) = g/r$ where $u = (0, g)$. Since $p(u)$ is a norm on $P_0^\perp$, from the classical Hahn-Banach theorem it follows that ξ_1 can be extended to a functional ξ_2 which is defined on $P_0^\perp$ and satisfies $\xi_2(u) = \xi_1(u)$ for $u \in P_1$, and $\xi_2(u) \leq p(u)$ for all $u \in P_0^\perp$.

For $u = u_0 + u_0^\perp \in P$ with $u_0 \in P_0$, $u_0^\perp \in P_0^\perp$, we now define $\xi(u) = \xi_2(u_0^\perp)$. We claim that the functional ξ has two properties:

(i) $\xi(u) = p(u)$, $\forall u \in P_1$,

(ii) $\xi(u) \leq p(u)$, $\forall u \in P$.

As (i) is obvious, it remains to show (ii). Let $u = u_0 + u_0^\perp$ and $t > 0$ be such that $u/t \in A_1$. Let $0 < \alpha < 1$ and $\beta = -\alpha/(1 - \alpha)$. Since $p(u_0) = 0$, we have $\beta u_0/t \in A_1$, and from the convexity of A_1 it follows that $\alpha u_0^\perp/t = \alpha u/t + (1 - \alpha)\beta u_0/t \in A_1$. Since t and α can be arbitrarily close to $p(u)$ and 1, respectively, we obtain $p(u_0^\perp) \leq p(u)$. Hence $\xi(u) = \xi_2(u_0^\perp) \leq p(u_0^\perp) \leq p(u)$, and (ii) follows.

For $(y, g) \in P$, $y \in \mathbb{R}^n$, $g \in \mathbb{R}$, the functional ξ can be represented as $\xi(y, g) = \varphi_1(y) + \gamma(g)$ where $\varphi_1(y) = \xi(y, 0)$ and $\gamma(g) = \xi(0, g) = g/r$. As $u \in A_1$ yields $p(u) \leq 1$, we have $A_1 \subset P$. Hence, for any $f_i \in E$, $y_i \in \mathbb{N}(f_i)$, $i = -1, 1$,

$$\begin{aligned} &\xi\left(\frac{y_1 - y_{-1}}{2}, \frac{S(f_1) - S(f_{-1})}{2}\right) \\ &= \varphi_1\left(\frac{y_1 - y_{-1}}{2}\right) + \frac{1}{2r}(S(f_1) - S(f_{-1})) \leq 1. \end{aligned}$$

Setting $\varphi_2 = -r\varphi_1$ we get from the last inequality that

$$S(f_1) - \varphi_2(y_1) - r \leq S(f_{-1}) - \varphi_2(y_{-1}) + r.$$

It now follows that there exists a number $a \in \mathbb{R}$ such that for all f_i and $y_i \in \mathbb{N}(f_i)$, $i = -1, 1$, we have

$$S(f_1) - \varphi_2(y_1) - r \leq a \leq S(f_{-1}) - \varphi_2(y_{-1}) + r.$$

Setting $\varphi_{\mathrm{aff}}(y) = \varphi_2(y) + a$ we finally obtain

$$|S(f) - \varphi_{\mathrm{aff}}(y)| \leq r, \qquad f \in E, \ y \in \mathbb{N}(f).$$

Thus the affine algorithm φ_{aff} is optimal.

Suppose now that $\mathrm{gr}(\mathbb{N}, E)$ is not only convex but also balanced. Then from Lemma 2.3.1 we have $\mathrm{rad}^{\mathrm{wor}}(\mathbb{N}) = r(A(0))$. Since in this case the set $A(0)$ is balanced, its center is zero and for any optimal algorithm φ we have $\varphi(0) = 0$. Hence any optimal affine algorithm is linear. □

The fact that S is a functional together with Theorem 2.4.1 yields an interesting property of the radius of information. Assume that the set E of problem elements is convex and the information is linear with noise bounded uniformly in a norm $\|\cdot\|_Y$,

$$\mathbb{N}(f) = \{y \in \mathbb{R}^n \mid \|y - N(f)\|_Y \leq \delta\}.$$

Let $r(\delta)$ be the radius of $\mathbb{N}$.

Lemma 2.4.1 *The function $K(\delta)$ defined by*

$$K(\delta) = \frac{r(\delta) - r(0)}{\delta}, \qquad \delta > 0,$$

is nonincreasing and bounded. In particular, the derivative $r'(0^+)$ exists.

Proof We first show that $K(\delta)$ is nonincreasing. Let $0 < \gamma < \delta$. For $\varepsilon > 0$, let $h_0, h_\delta \in \mathrm{bal}(E)$ be such that $N(h_0) = 0$, $S(h_0) \geq r(0) - \varepsilon$, and $\|N(h_\delta)\|_Y \leq \delta$, $S(h_\delta) \geq r(\delta) - \varepsilon$. Let $h_\gamma = h_0 + (\gamma/\delta)(h_\delta - h_0)$. Then $h_\gamma \in \mathrm{bal}(E)$ and $\|N(h_\gamma)\|_Y \leq \gamma$. Hence

$$r(\gamma) \geq S(h_\gamma) = S(h_0) + \frac{\gamma}{\delta}\left(S(h_\delta) - S(h_0)\right)$$

$$\geq r(0) + \gamma\frac{r(\delta) - r(0)}{\delta} - \varepsilon\left(1 + \frac{\gamma}{\delta}\right).$$

Letting $\varepsilon \to 0$, we obtain the desired inequality $K(\gamma) \geq K(\delta)$.

We now prove that $K(\delta)$ is bounded. To this end, let φ_{aff} be the optimal affine algorithm for $\delta = 0$. Then $\varphi_{\text{lin}}(y) = \varphi_{\text{aff}}(y) - \varphi_{\text{aff}}(0)$ is a linear functional whose norm

$$\|\varphi_{\text{lin}}\|_Y = \sup_{\|x\|_Y \leq 1} |\varphi_{\text{lin}}(x)|$$

is finite. For any $f \in E$ and $y \in \mathbb{N}(f)$ we have

$$
\begin{aligned}
|S(f) - \varphi_{\text{aff}}(y)| &\leq |S(f) - \varphi_{\text{aff}}(N(f))| + |\varphi_{\text{aff}}(y) - \varphi_{\text{aff}}(N(f))| \\
&\leq r(0) + \delta \|\varphi_{\text{lin}}\|_Y.
\end{aligned}
$$

Taking the supremum over f and y we get $K(\delta) \leq \|\varphi_{\text{lin}}\|_Y$. $\square$

Observe now that if $r'(0^+) = 0$ then $r(\delta) \equiv$ const. In this case information is useless, $r(\delta) = \sup\{ S(h) \,|\, h \in \text{bal}(E)\}$, and the optimal algorithm is constant. This and Lemma 2.4.1 yield the following theorem.

Theorem 2.4.2 *For an arbitrary linear functional S and noise bounded uniformly in a norm by δ, the radius $r(\delta)$ of noisy information either is constant or converges linearly to the radius $r(0)$ of exact information in $\delta \to 0^+$, i.e.,*

$$r(\delta) = r(0) + \delta \cdot r'(0^+) + o(\delta).$$

2.4.2 The case of Hilbert noise

We now construct all optimal affine algorithms for an important class of problems. That is, we assume that the set E is convex and information is linear with noise uniformly bounded in a Hilbert norm, i.e.,

$$\mathbb{N}(f) = \{y \in \mathbb{R}^n \,|\, \|y - N(f)\|_Y \leq \delta \} \qquad (2.9)$$

where $\delta > 0$ and the norm $\|\cdot\|_Y$ is induced by an inner product $\langle \cdot, \cdot \rangle_Y$. Clearly, in this case the graph $\text{gr}(\mathbb{N}, E)$ is convex and an optimal affine algorithm exists.

We also assume that the radius $r = \text{rad}^{\text{wor}}(\mathbb{N})$ is finite and is attained. That is, there exists $h^* = (f_1^* - f_{-1}^*)/2 \in \text{bal}(E)$ with $f_{-1}^*, f_1^* \in E$ such that $\|N(h^*)\|_Y \leq \delta$ and $r = S(h^*)$. We shall see later that the latter assumption is not restrictive.

For two elements $f_{-1}, f_1 \in F$, let $I = I(f_{-1}, f_1)$ denote the interval $I = \{\alpha f_{-1} + (1 - \alpha)f_1 \,|\, 0 \leq \alpha \leq 1\}$. It is clear that if $f_{-1}, f_1 \in E$ then $I(f_{-1}, f_1) \subset E$ and $\text{rad}^{\text{wor}}(\mathbb{N}; I) \leq \text{rad}^{\text{wor}}(\mathbb{N}; E)$. In words, this means that any one dimensional subproblem is at least as difficult as the original problem. Furthermore, for $I^* = I(f^*_{-1}, f^*_1)$ we have

$$\mathrm{rad}^{\mathrm{wor}}(\mathbb{N}; E) = \mathrm{rad}^{\mathrm{wor}}(\mathbb{N}; I^*)$$

(compare with E 2.3.5). Hence the problem of approximating $S(f)$ for f belonging to the one dimensional subset $I^* \subset E$ is as difficult as the problem of approximating $S(f)$ for $f \in E$. We shall say, for brevity, that I^* is the *hardest one dimensional subproblem* contained in E. In particular, we have that any algorithm which is optimal for E is also optimal for I^*.

The latter observation yields a method of finding *all* optimal affine algorithms. That is, it suffices to find all such algorithms for I^* and then check which of them do not increase the error when taken over the whole set E. In the sequel, we follow this approach.

Observe first that if $\|N(h^*)\|_Y < \delta$ then the only optimal affine algorithm is constant, $\varphi(y) = S(f_0)$ where $f_0 = (f^*_1 + f^*_{-1})/2$. Indeed, let $y = N(f_0) + x$ where $\|x\|_Y \leq \delta - \|N(h^*)\|_Y$. Then y is noisy information for any $f \in I^*$ and therefore $\varphi_{\mathrm{aff}}(y) = S(f_0)$. Hence φ_{aff} is constant on a nontrivial ball. Its unique affine extension on $\mathbb{R}^n$ is $\varphi_{\mathrm{aff}} \equiv S(f_0)$.

In what follows, we assume that $\|N(h^*)\|_Y = \delta$.

Lemma 2.4.2 *For the one dimensional subproblem $I^* = [f^*_{-1}, f^*_1]$, all optimal affine algorithms are given as*

$$\varphi_{\mathrm{aff}}(y) = S(f_0) + d \cdot \langle y - N(f_0), w \rangle_Y, \qquad (2.10)$$

where $w = N(h^*)/\|N(h^*)\|_Y$ and $d = cr/\delta$, for any $c \in [0,1]$.

Proof Let $y_0 = N(f_0)$ and $w^* = N(h^*)$. For $y_\alpha = y_0 + \alpha w^*$, $\alpha \in \mathbb{R}$, the set of all elements which are in the interval $S(I^*)$ and cannot be distinguished with respect to the information y_α is given as $S(I^*) \cap B(S(f_0) + \alpha r, r)$, where $B(a, \tau)$ is the ball with center a and radius τ. From this it follows that for any optimal affine algorithm φ_{aff} we have

$$\varphi_{\mathrm{aff}}(y_\alpha) = S(f_0) + c\alpha r \qquad (2.11)$$

where $0 \leq c \leq 1$. Since $\alpha = \langle y_\alpha - y_0, w \rangle_Y/\delta$, (2.11) can be rewritten as

$$\varphi_{\mathrm{aff}}(y_\alpha) = S(f_0) + c \cdot \frac{r}{\delta} \cdot \langle y_\alpha - y_0, w \rangle_Y. \qquad (2.12)$$

We now show that for any $c \in [0,1]$, the formula (2.12) is valid, not only for y_α, but for all $y \in \mathbb{R}^n$. To this end, it is enough to show that for any $y = y_0 + x$, where $\|x\|_Y \le \delta$, $\langle x, w \rangle_Y = 0$, we have $\varphi_{\text{aff}}(y) = \varphi_{\text{aff}}(y_0) = S(f_0)$. Indeed, let $\varphi_{\text{aff}}(y) = S(f_0) + a$ where (without loss of generality) $a > 0$. Then $\varphi_{\text{aff}}(y_0 + \varepsilon x) = S(f_0) + \varepsilon a$. Since $y_0 + \varepsilon x$ is noisy information for $f_\varepsilon = f_0 - h^*\sqrt{1 - \varepsilon^2\|x\|_Y^2/\delta^2}$, we obtain

$$
\begin{aligned}
e^{\text{wor}}(\mathbb{N}, \varphi_{\text{aff}}; I^*) &\ge \varphi_{\text{aff}}(y_0 + \varepsilon x) - S(f_\varepsilon) \\
&= \varepsilon a + r\sqrt{1 - \varepsilon^2\|x\|_Y^2/\delta^2}.
\end{aligned}
$$

For small $\varepsilon > 0$, the last expression is greater than r, which contradicts the assumption that the algorithm φ_{aff} is optimal, and completes the proof. □

So the affine algorithm (2.10) is optimal for the hardest one dimensional subproblem I^*. We now wish to find the values of d for which (2.10) is an optimal algorithm for the original problem E.

To this end, we first evaluate the error $e^{\text{wor}}(\mathbb{N}, \varphi_{\text{aff}}; E)$ of the algorithm (2.10). For any $f \in E$ and $y = N(f) + x \in \mathbb{N}(f)$ we have

$$
\begin{aligned}
S(f) - \varphi_{\text{aff}}(y) &= S(f) - S(f_0) - d\langle N(f) - y_0, w \rangle_Y - d\langle x, w \rangle_Y \\
&= S(f) - \varphi_{\text{aff}}(N(f)) - d\langle x, w \rangle_Y.
\end{aligned}
$$

Hence

$$
\sup_{\|x\|_Y \le \delta} |S(f) - \varphi_{\text{aff}}(y)| = |S(f) - \varphi_{\text{aff}}(N(f))| + d\delta. \tag{2.13}
$$

We also have

$$
S(f_1^*) - \varphi_{\text{aff}}(N(f_1^*)) = -(S(f_{-1}^*) - \varphi_{\text{aff}}(N(f_{-1}^*))) = r - d\delta. \tag{2.14}
$$

From (2.13) and (2.14) it follows that the necessary and sufficient condition for the algorithm (2.10) to be optimal for the set E is that for all $f \in E$

$$
S(f_{-1}^*) - \varphi_{\text{aff}}(N(f_{-1}^*)) \le S(f) - \varphi_{\text{aff}}(N(f)) \le S(f_1^*) - \varphi_{\text{aff}}(N(f_1^*)).
$$

Using the formula for φ_{aff} these two inequalities can be rewritten as

$$
\begin{aligned}
S(f_1^*) - S(f) &\ge d \cdot \langle N(f_1^*) - N(f), w \rangle_Y, \tag{2.15} \\
S(f_{-1}^*) - S(f) &\le d \cdot \langle N(f_{-1}^*) - N(f), w \rangle_Y. \tag{2.16}
\end{aligned}
$$

We now show that (2.15) and (2.16) are equivalent to

$$
S(h^*) - S(h) \ge d \cdot \langle N(h^*) - N(h), w \rangle_Y, \qquad \forall h \in \text{bal}(E). \tag{2.17}
$$

Indeed, let (2.15) and (2.16) hold. Then for any $h = (f_1 - f_{-1})/2$, $f_i \in E$, we have

$$
\begin{aligned}
S(h^*) - S(h) &= \tfrac{1}{2}\left((S(f_1^*) - S(f_1)) - (S(f_{-1}^*) - S(f_{-1}))\right) \\
&\geq \tfrac{1}{2}d\left(\langle N(f_1^* - f_1), w\rangle_Y - \langle N(f_{-1}^* - f_{-1}), w\rangle_Y\right) \\
&= d\langle N(h^*) - N(h), w\rangle_Y.
\end{aligned}
$$

Suppose now that (2.17) holds. Let $f \in E$. Then, for $h = (f - f_{-1}^*)/2 \in$ bal(E) we have

$$
\begin{aligned}
S(f_1^*) - S(f) &= 2\left(S(h^*) - S(h)\right) \geq 2d\langle N(h^*) - N(h), w\rangle_Y \\
&= d\langle N(f_1^*) - N(f), w\rangle_Y,
\end{aligned}
$$

which shows (2.15). Similarly, taking $h = (f_1^* - f)/2$ we obtain (2.16).

Thus the number d should be chosen in such a way that (2.17) holds. This condition has a nice geometrical interpretation. That is, for $\gamma > 0$, let

$$
r(\gamma) = \sup\{S(h) \mid h \in \text{bal}(E), \|N(h)\|_Y \leq \gamma\}
$$

be the radius of information $\mathbb{N}$ with the noise level δ replaced by γ.

Lemma 2.4.3 *The condition (2.17) holds if and only if the line with slope d passing through $(\delta, r(\delta))$ lies above the graph of $r(\gamma)$, i.e.,*

$$
r(\gamma) \leq r(\delta) + d(\gamma - \delta), \qquad \forall \gamma > 0. \tag{2.18}
$$

Proof Observe first that (2.18) can be rewritten as

$$
S(h^*) - S(h) \geq d(\|N(h^*)\|_Y - \|N(h)\|_Y), \qquad \forall h \in \text{bal}(E). \tag{2.19}
$$

Indeed, if (2.18) holds then for any $h \in \text{bal}(E)$, $\gamma = \|N(h)\|_Y$, we have

$$
\begin{aligned}
S(h^*) - S(h) &\geq r(\delta) - r(\gamma) \geq d(\delta - \gamma) \\
&= d(\|N(h^*)\|_Y - \|N(h)\|_Y).
\end{aligned}
$$

Let (2.19) hold. Then for any $\gamma > 0$ and $\varepsilon > 0$ there is $h_\varepsilon \in \text{bal}(E)$ such that $\|N(h_\varepsilon)\|_Y \leq \gamma$ and $S(h_\varepsilon) \geq r(\gamma) - \varepsilon$. Hence

$$
\begin{aligned}
r(\delta) &= S(h^*) \geq S(h_\varepsilon) + d(\|N(h^*)\|_Y - \|N(h_\varepsilon)\|_Y) \\
&\geq r(\gamma) - \varepsilon + d(\delta - \gamma).
\end{aligned}
$$

Letting $\varepsilon \to 0^+$ we get (2.18).

Thus it suffices to show that (2.17) is equivalent to (2.19). Indeed, since

$$\langle N(h^*) - N(h), w \rangle_Y = \|N(h^*)\|_Y - \frac{\langle N(h), N(h^*) \rangle_Y}{\|N(h^*)\|_Y}$$
$$\geq \|N(h^*)\|_Y - \|N(h)\|_Y,$$

the condition (2.17) implies (2.19).

We now show that (2.17) follows from (2.19). Let $h \in \text{bal}(E)$,

$$S(h^*) - S(h) = d \langle N(h^*) - N(h), w \rangle_Y + a. \tag{2.20}$$

For $0 < \tau \leq 1$, let $h_\tau = (1 - \tau)h^* + \tau h = h^* - \tau(h^* - h)$. Then $h_\tau \in \text{bal}(E)$ and from (2.20) we have

$$S(h^*) - S(h_\tau) = \tau \left(S(h^*) - S(h) \right) = \tau d \langle N(h^*) - N(h), w \rangle_Y + \tau a. \tag{2.21}$$

We also have

$$\|N(h_\tau)\|_Y^2 = \|N(h^*) - \tau(N(h^*) - N(h))\|_Y^2$$
$$= \left(\|N(h^*)\|_Y - \tau \langle N(h^*) - N(h), w \rangle_Y \right)^2 + O(\tau^2),$$

as $\tau \to 0^+$. Hence

$$\|N(h^*)\|_Y - \|N(h_\tau)\|_Y = \tau \langle N(h^*) - N(h), w \rangle_Y + O(\tau^2). \tag{2.22}$$

Combining (2.21) and (2.22) with (2.19) we now obtain $\tau a \geq O(\tau^2)$, which means that a is nonnegative. This together with (2.20) proves (2.17). $\qquad\square$

We summarize our analysis in the following theorem.

Theorem 2.4.3 *Let $\mathbb{N}$ be information (2.9) with noise level $\delta > 0$. Let $h^* = (f_1^* - f_{-1}^*)/2$, $f_1^*, f_{-1}^* \in E$, be an element such that*

$$S(h^*) = \sup \{ S(h) \mid h \in \text{bal}(E), \|N(h)\| \leq \delta \}.$$

Then all optimal affine algorithms are given by

$$\varphi_{\text{aff}}(y) = g_0 + d \cdot \langle y - y_0, w \rangle_Y,$$

where $g_0 = S(f_1^* + f_{-1}^*)/2$, $y_0 = N(f_1^* + f_{-1}^*)/2$, $w = N(h^*)/\|N(h^*)\|_Y$ (or $w = 0$ for $N(h^*) = 0$), and d satisfies

$$r(\gamma) \leq r(\delta) + d(\gamma - \delta), \qquad \forall \gamma \geq 0.$$

We stress that Theorem 2.4.3 gives *all* optimal affine algorithms. In particular, another choice of h^* leads to the same optimal affine algorithms. Note also that if $\|N(h^*)\|_Y < \delta$ then $d = 0$ and $\varphi_{\text{aff}} \equiv S(f_0)$.

We now briefly discuss the case when the hardest one dimensional subproblem does not exist. Then we can extract a sequence $\{h_i\} \subset \text{bal}(E)$ such that $\|N(h_i)\|_Y \le \delta$, $\forall i$, and $\lim_{i \to \infty} S(h_i) = r(\delta)$. Since $\{N(h_i)\}$ is a bounded set of $\mathbb{R}^n$, it has an attraction point w^*.

Suppose first that $\|w^*\|_Y = \delta$. In this case we let $w = w^*/\delta$ and d be as in Theorem 2.4.3. Using the technique from the proof of Lemma 2.4.3 and some approximation arguments, we can show that for all $h \in \text{bal}(E)$,

$$r(\delta) - S(h) \ge d \cdot (\delta - \langle N(h), w \rangle_Y), \quad \forall h \in \text{bal}(E),$$

which corresponds to inequality (2.17). Hence $S(h) - d\langle N(h), w \rangle_Y \le r(\delta) - \delta d$, or equivalently,

$$S(f_{-1}) - d\langle N(f_{-1}), w \rangle_Y - r(\delta) \le S(f_1) - d\langle N(f_1), w \rangle_Y + r(\delta),$$

for all $f_{-1}, f_1 \in E$. Letting $g = \sup_{f \in E}(S(f) - d\langle N(f), w \rangle_Y) - r(\delta)$, we obtain $|S(f) - d\langle y, w \rangle_Y - g| \le r(\delta)$, $\forall f \in E$, $y \in N(f)$. This means that the algorithm

$$\varphi_{\text{aff}}(y) = g + d \cdot \langle y, w \rangle_Y$$

is optimal.

If $\|w^*\|_Y < \delta$ then $r(\gamma)$ is constant for $\gamma > \|w^*\|_Y$. Hence the optimal affine algorithm is also constant, $\varphi_{\text{aff}} \equiv \sup_{f \in E} S(f) - r(\delta)$.

So far we have not covered the exact information case $\delta = 0$. It turns out, however, that exact information can be treated as the limiting case. Indeed, let $\varphi_\delta = g_\delta + d_\delta \langle \cdot, w_\delta \rangle_Y$ be the optimal affine algorithm for $\delta > 0$. Let w_0 be an attraction point of $\{w_\delta\}$ as $\delta \to 0^+$. As $\lim_{\delta \to 0} d_\delta = r'(0^+)$ and

$$S(h) - d_\delta \langle N(h), w_\delta \rangle_Y \le r(\delta) - \delta d_\delta, \quad \forall h \in \text{bal}(E),$$

letting $\delta \to 0^+$ we obtain

$$S(h) - r'(0^+) \langle N(h), w_0 \rangle_Y \le r(0), \quad \forall h \in \text{bal}(E).$$

Hence, for $g_0 = \sup_{f \in E}(S(f) - r'(0^+)\langle N(f), w_0 \rangle_Y) - r(0)$, we have

$$|S(f) - r'(0^+)\langle N(f), w_0 \rangle_Y - g_0| \le r(0), \quad \forall f \in E,$$

and the algorithm

$$\varphi_0(y) = r'(0^+) \cdot \langle y, w_0 \rangle_Y + g_0$$

is optimal. (See also E 2.4.8 for another construction.)

We end this section with a simple illustration of Theorem 2.4.3.

Example 2.4.2 Let F be a linear space of Lipschitz functions $f :$ $[0,1] \to \mathbb{R}$ that satisfy $f(0) = f(1)$, i.e., f are 1-periodic. Let

$$E = \{ f \in F \mid |f(x_1) - f(x_2)| \le |x_1 - x_2|, \, \forall x_1, x_2 \}.$$

We want to approximate the integral of f, i.e.,

$$S(f) = \int_0^1 f(t) \, dt.$$

Noisy information is given by perturbed evaluations of function values at equidistant points, $y = [y_1, \ldots, y_n] \in \mathbb{R}^n$, where $y_i = f(i/n) + x_i$, $1 \le i \le n$, and the noise $\|x\|_2 = (\sum_{i=1}^n x_i^2)^{1/2} \le \delta$.

Since S is a functional and the set E is convex and balanced, Theorem 2.3.3 yields

$$\text{rad}^{\text{wor}}(\mathbb{N}) = \sup \left\{ \int_0^1 f(t) \, dt \,\middle|\, f \in E, \, \sum_{i=1}^n f^2(i/n) \le \delta^2 \right\}.$$

The last supremum is attained for

$$h^*(t) = \frac{\delta}{\sqrt{n}} + \frac{1}{2n} - \left| t - \frac{2i-1}{2n} \right|, \qquad \frac{i-1}{n} \le t \le \frac{i}{n}, \, 1 \le i \le n,$$

and

$$\text{rad}^{\text{wor}}(\mathbb{N}) = r(\delta) = \frac{\delta}{\sqrt{n}} + \frac{1}{4n}.$$

(Compare this with Theorem 2.4.2.) Hence $w = n^{-1/2}(1, 1, \ldots, 1)$ and $d = n^{-1/2}$. The unique optimal linear algorithm is the well known arithmetic mean

$$\varphi_{\text{lin}}(y) = \frac{1}{n} \sum_{i=1}^n y_i.$$

Note that in this case the optimal linear algorithm is independent of the noise level δ. However, its error does depend on δ.

Notes and remarks

NR 2.4.1 The problem of the existence of optimal linear or affine algorithms for approximating linear functionals has a long history. The first positive result on this subject is due to Smolyak (1965) who considered exact information and a convex and balanced set E; see also Bakhvalov (1971). His results were then generalized by Sukharev (1986) to the case of only a convex set E. The noisy case was considered by, e.g., Marchuk and Osipenko (1975), Micchelli and Rivlin (1977). The proof of Theorem 2.4.1 is taken from Magaril-Il'yaev and Osipenko (1991) where an even more general result is given; see E 2.4.2.

NR 2.4.2 We want to stress that Theorem 2.4.1 does not hold when the solution operator S is linear but not a functional. Examples (for exact information) are provided by Micchelli and Rivlin (1977), Packel (1986), Werschulz and Woźniakowski (1986); see also Traub *et al.* (1988, Sect. 5.5 of Chap. 4).

NR 2.4.3 The dependence of the radius on the noise level δ was studied in Kacewicz and Kowalski (1995a) for linear functionals S, and in Kacewicz and Kowalski (1995b) for arbitrary linear S. They showed, in particular, that if E is the unit ball with respect to a Hilbert norm and S is a functional, then $r(\delta) = r(0) + \delta\, r'(0^+) + O(\delta^2)$. The general result of Theorem 2.4.2 is, however, new.

NR 2.4.4 Optimality of the affine algorithms defined in Theorem 2.4.3 was shown by Donoho (1994). The idea of using in the proof the hardest one dimensional subproblems belongs to him. We additionally showed that those are the only optimal affine algorithms. The results in the case when the radius is not attained, as well as the formulas for the optimal affine algorithm in the exact information case, are new.

The concept of the hardest one dimensional subproblem will also be used in other settings to derive optimal algorithms.

NR 2.4.5 Optimal algorithms for noise bounded in the sup-norm rather than in the Hilbert norm are in general unknown. We mention one special result which has been recently obtained by Osipenko (1994).

Let F be a separable Hilbert space with a complete orthonormal system $\{e_i\}_{i\geq 1}$. For $f \in F$, let $f_j = \langle f, e_j \rangle_F$ be the ith Fourier coefficient of f. Consider the problem of approximating a functional $S = \langle \cdot, s \rangle_F$ for f from the unit ball of F, based on noisy values of the Fourier coefficients, $y_i = f_i + x_i$, where $|x_i| \leq \delta_i$, $1 \leq i \leq n$. Osipenko showed, in particular, that the optimal linear algorithm φ_{opt} is in this case given as follows. Let $\lambda \in (0, \|s\|_F)$ be the solution of

$$\|s\|_F^2 - \sum_{j=1}^{n}(|s_j|^2 - \lambda^2\delta_j^2)_+ - \lambda^2 = 0.$$

Then

$$\varphi_{\mathrm{opt}}(y) = \sum_{j=1}^{n}(1 - \lambda\delta_j|s_j|^{-1})_+ s_j y_j,$$

and the radius is

$$\mathrm{rad}^{\mathrm{wor}}(\mathbb{N}) = \lambda + \sum_{j=1}^{n}\delta_j(|s_j| - \lambda\delta_j)_+.$$

Exercises

E 2.4.1 Show that an optimal affine (linear) algorithm for a functional S exists if the set

$$\tilde{A} = \{ (y, S(f)) \mid y \in \mathbb{N}(f),\ f \in E \}$$

is convex (convex and balanced).

E 2.4.2 (Magaril-Il'yaev and Osipenko, 1991) Let $c(A)$ ($cb(A)$) be the smallest convex (convex and balanced) set which contains A. Show that an optimal affine (linear) algorithm exists iff

$$\text{rad}^{\text{wor}}(c(\mathbb{N}), c(E)) = \text{rad}^{\text{wor}}(\mathbb{N}; E)$$
$$(\text{rad}^{\text{wor}}(cb(\mathbb{N}), cb(E)) = \text{rad}^{\text{wor}}(\mathbb{N}; E)).$$

E 2.4.3 Suppose that the radius is attained for two elements $h_1^*, h_2^* \in \text{bal}(E)$ such that $N(h_1^*) \neq N(h_2^*)$. Show that then the only optimal affine algorithm is constant, $\varphi_{\text{aff}} \equiv (\sup_{f \in E} S(f) + \inf_{f \in E} S(f))/2$. Use this result to show the formula for h^* in Example 2.4.2.

E 2.4.4 Consider the problem of estimating a real parameter f from the interval $I = [-\tau, \tau] \subset \mathbb{R}$, based on the data y such that $|y - f| \leq \delta$. Show that in this case the radius is equal to $\min\{\tau, \delta\}$ and the optimal affine algorithm is given as

$$\varphi_{\text{aff}}(y) = \begin{cases} y & \delta < \tau, \\ cy & \delta = \tau \quad (0 \leq c \leq 1), \\ 0 & \delta > \tau. \end{cases}$$

E 2.4.5 Let $\mathbb{N}$ be linear information with noise bounded uniformly by $\delta \geq 0$ in a Hilbert space norm. Let $f_{-1}, f_1 \in F$ be such that $\|N(f_1 - f_{-1})\|_Y > 2\delta$. Show that for the interval $I = [f_{-1}, f_1]$ we have

$$\text{rad}^{\text{wor}}(\mathbb{N}; I) = \frac{|S(f_1) - S(f_{-1})|}{\|N(f_1) - N(f_{-1})\|_Y} \cdot \delta$$

and the only optimal affine algorithm is given as

$$\varphi_{\text{aff}}(y) = S(f_0) + \frac{S(f_1) - S(f_{-1})}{\|N(f_1) - N(f_{-1})\|_Y} \cdot \langle y - N(f_0), w \rangle_Y,$$

where $f_0 = (f_{-1} + f_1)/2$ and $w = (N(f_1) - N(f_{-1}))/\|N(f_1) - N(f_{-1})\|_Y$.

E 2.4.6 Let E be a convex set. Show that the radius

$$r(\delta) = \sup\{ S(h) \mid h \in \text{bal}(E),\ \|N(h)\|_Y \leq \delta \}$$

is a concave and subadditive function of δ.

E 2.4.7 Why does the number d in Theorem 2.4.3 exist? For $0 \leq a \leq b < +\infty$, give an example where the set of all such d forms the closed interval $[a, b]$.

E 2.4.8 (Bakhvalov, 1971) Let E be a convex and balanced set. Consider approximation of a linear functional S for $f \in E$, based on *exact* linear information $y = [L_1(f), \ldots, L_n(f)]$ where the functionals L_i are linearly independent on span E. Let

$$r_k(x) = \sup\{ S(h) \mid h \in E,\ L_k(h) = x,\ L_j(h) = 0,\ i \neq k \}.$$

Assuming that the derivatives $r'_k(0)$ exist for all $1 \leq k \leq n$, show that $\varphi(y) = \sum_{j=1}^{n} r'_j(0) \, y_j$ is the unique optimal linear algorithm.

E 2.4.9 Give an example showing that if the solution operator S is linear but not a functional, then the assertion of Thorem 2.4.2 is no longer true.

E 2.4.10 Find an example of a balanced but *not* convex set E such that for some linear functional S and some linear information N with noise bounded uniformly in a Hilbert norm we have $\mathrm{rad}^{\mathrm{wor}}(N) = 0$, but the error of any affine algorithm is infinite.

E 2.4.11 Find an optimal linear algorithm for the integration problem of Example 2.4.2, in which the function values are observed at arbitrary, not necessarily equidistant, points.

2.5 Optimality of spline algorithms

In this section we assume that:

- S is an arbitrary linear operator,
- E is the unit ball in an extended seminorm $\| \cdot \|_F$,

$$E = \{ f \in F \mid \| f \|_F \leq 1 \},$$

- information is linear with uniformly bounded noise,

$$N(f) = \{ y \in \mathbb{R}^n \mid \| y - N(f) \|_Y \leq \delta \}, \qquad \delta > 0.$$

As explained in Section 2.2, the second assumption is roughly equivalent to assuming that E is a convex and balanced set. The assumption $\delta > 0$ is not restrictive. If $\delta = 0$ then by changing the extended seminorm $\| \cdot \|_Y$ properly we can make δ positive.

Owing to Theorem 2.3.3, in this case we have

$$\mathrm{diam}(N) = 2 \cdot \sup \{ \| S(h) \| \mid \| h \|_F \leq 1, \ \| N(h) \|_Y \leq \delta \}. \qquad (2.23)$$

Optimal or almost optimal algorithms can be now constructed using splines. We shall see that sometimes spline algorithms turn out to be not only optimal but also linear.

2.5.1 Splines and smoothing splines

Let $\rho \geq 1$. For information $y \in \{ N(f) + x \mid f \in F, \| x \|_Y \leq \delta \}$, an *(ordinary) spline* is an element $\mathbf{s}_o(y) \in F$ defined by the following two conditions:

(i) $y \in N(\mathbf{s}_o(y))$,
(ii) $\| \mathbf{s}_o(y) \|_F \leq \rho \cdot \inf \{ \| f \|_F \mid y \in N(f) \}$.

Hence $s_o(y)$ is the element whose extended seminorm does not exceed ρ times the minimal value of $\|f\|_F$ among all f that share the same information y. Note that for $\rho > 1$, a spline $s_o(y)$ always exists, but is not determined uniquely.

An *(ordinary) spline algorithm* is given as

$$\varphi_o(y) = S(s_o(y)).$$

Theorem 2.5.1 *For the spline algorithm φ_o, we have*

$$\|S(f) - \varphi_o(y)\| \leq c(f) \cdot \operatorname{diam}(\mathbb{N}), \qquad \forall f \in F, \forall y \in \mathbb{N}(f),$$

where $c(f) = \max\{1, (1 + \rho)\|f\|_F/2\}$. Hence

$$e^{\mathrm{wor}}(\mathbb{N}, \varphi_o) \leq \tfrac{1}{2}(1 + \rho) \cdot \operatorname{diam}(\mathbb{N}).$$

Proof For $f \in F$ and information y such that $\|y - N(f)\|_Y \leq \delta$, we have $\|N(f - s_o(y))\|_Y \leq \|N(f) - y\|_Y + \|y - N(s_o(y))\|_Y \leq 2\delta$. Hence, for $\|f - s_o(y)\|_F \leq 2$, we get from (2.23) that

$$\|S(f) - \varphi_o(y)\| = \|S(f - s_o(y))\| \leq \operatorname{diam}(\mathbb{N}).$$

On the other hand, for $\|f - s_o(y)\|_F > 2$, we have

$$
\begin{aligned}
\|S(f) - \varphi_o(y)\| &= \|f - s_o(y)\|_F \cdot \left\| S\left(\frac{f - s_o(y)}{\|f - s_o(y)\|_F}\right) \right\| \\
&\leq \tfrac{1}{2}(\|f\|_F + \|s_o(y)\|_F) \cdot \operatorname{diam}(\mathbb{N}) \\
&\leq \tfrac{1}{2}(1 + \rho)\|f\|_F \cdot \operatorname{diam}(\mathbb{N}).
\end{aligned}
$$

Combining both cases and the fact that $f \in E$ gives $\|f\|_F \leq 1$, we obtain the desired inequalities. $\qquad\square$

Thus the error of the spline algorithm with $\rho \cong 1$ is, roughly speaking, at most twice as large as the optimal error. This is not very surprising since φ_o is nearly an interpolatory algorithm. For arbitrary ρ, an additional advantage of φ_o is that it is the spline algorithm for any set $E_b = \{f \in F \mid \|f\|_F \leq b\}$, $b > 0$. Indeed, the definition of φ_o is independent of b. Hence φ_o preserves almost optimal properties for any such set. Unfortunately, as illustrated below, the ordinary spline algorithm is usually not linear, even when $\|\cdot\|_F$ and $\|\cdot\|_Y$ are Hilbert norms.

Example 2.5.1 Consider the problem of approximating a real parameter $f \in E = [-a, a]$ from information $y \in \mathbb{N}(f) = \{f + x \mid |x| \leq \delta\}$.

Then the ordinary spline algorithm with $\rho = 1$ is given as

$$\varphi_0(y) = \left\{ \begin{array}{ll} y - \delta & y > \delta, \\ 0 & |y| \le \delta, \\ y + \delta & y < -\delta. \end{array} \right.$$

For $\delta > 0$, this is *not* a linear algorithm.

We now turn to smoothing spline algorithms. The idea is to minimize not only the norm of f in the definition of a spline element, but also the noise $y - N(f)$. In general, a smoothing spline algorithm φ_* is given in the following way.

Let $\|(\cdot, \cdot)\|_*$ be an extended seminorm in the linear space $F \times \mathbb{R}^n$, and let $\rho \ge 1$. A *smoothing spline* is an element $\mathbf{s}_*(y) \in F$ satisfying

$$\| (\mathbf{s}_*(y), y - N(\mathbf{s}_*(y))) \|_* \le \rho \cdot \inf_{f \in F} \| (f, y - N(f)) \|_*.$$

Then

$$\varphi_*(y) = S(\mathbf{s}_*(y))$$

is a *smoothing spline algorithm*.

Consider first the case when the extended seminorm $\|(\cdot, \cdot)\|_*$ is given as

$$\|(f, x)\|_* = \max \{ \|f\|_F, \|x\|_Y / \delta \}, \qquad f \in F, \ x \in \mathbb{R}^n.$$

In this case, we write $\|(\cdot, \cdot)\|_* = \|(\cdot, \cdot)\|_\infty$ and $\varphi_* = \varphi_\infty$.

Theorem 2.5.2 *For the smoothing spline algorithm φ_∞, we have*

$$\|S(f) - \varphi_\infty(y)\| \le \tfrac{1}{2}(1 + \rho) \cdot \max \{ \|f\|_F, \|y - N(f)\|_Y / \delta \} \cdot \operatorname{diam}(\mathbb{N}),$$

for all $f \in F$ and $y \in N(f)$. Hence

$$e^{\mathrm{wor}}(\mathbb{N}, \varphi_\infty) \le \tfrac{1}{2}(1 + \rho) \cdot \operatorname{diam}(\mathbb{N}).$$

Proof Let $f \in F$ and $y \in \mathbb{R}^n$ be such that $\|y - N(f)\|_Y \le \delta$. Consider first the case when $\|f - \mathbf{s}_\infty(y)\|_F = 0$ and $\|N(f - \mathbf{s}_\infty(y))\|_Y = 0$. Then for any c we have $f_c = c(f - \mathbf{s}_\infty(y)) \in E$ and zero is noisy information for f_c. Since also $\|S(f_c) - \varphi_\infty(0)\| = |c| \cdot \|S(f - \mathbf{s}_\infty(y))\|$, we obtain $\|S(f) - \varphi_\infty(y)\| = 0$, or $\operatorname{diam}(\mathbb{N}) = +\infty$. In both cases the theorem holds.

Assume now that $\max\{\|f - s_\infty(y)\|_F, \|N(f - s_\infty(y))\|_Y\} > 0$. Then

$$
\begin{aligned}
\|S(f) - \varphi_\infty(y)\| &= \|(f - s_\infty(y), N(f - s_\infty(y)))\|_\infty \\
&\times \left\| S\left(\frac{f - s_\infty(y)}{\|(f - s_\infty(y), N(f - s_\infty(y)))\|_\infty} \right) \right\| \\
&\le \left(\|(f, y - N(f))\|_\infty + \|(s_\infty(y), y - N(s_\infty(y)))\|_\infty \right) \\
&\times \sup_{\|(h, N(h))\|_\infty \le 1} \|S(h)\| \\
&\le \tfrac{1}{2}(1 + \rho)\, \|(f, y - N(f))\|_\infty \, \mathrm{diam}(N).
\end{aligned}
$$

Since for $f \in E$ and $y \in \mathbb{N}(f)$ we have $\max\{\|f\|_F, \|y - N(f)\|_Y/\delta\} \le 1$, the smoothing spline algorithm φ_∞ is almost interpolatory and the upper bounds on the errors $e(\mathbb{N}, \varphi_\infty)$ and $e(\mathbb{N}, \varphi_o)$ are the same. This completes the proof. $\qquad\square$

The advantage of smoothing spline algorithms is that in some cases the extended seminorm $\|(\cdot, \cdot)\|_*$ can be chosen in such a way that φ_* becomes not only (almost) optimal, but also linear. This holds when F and Y are Hilbert spaces. Because of its importance, we devote special attention to this case.

2.5.2 α-smoothing splines

We now additionally assume that

- $\|\cdot\|_F$ and $\|\cdot\|_Y$ are Hilbert extended seminorms.

This means that on the linear subspaces $F' = \{f \in F \mid \|f\|_F < +\infty\}$ and $Y' = \{y \in \mathbb{R}^n \mid \|y\|_Y < +\infty\}$, the functionals $\|\cdot\|_F$ and $\|\cdot\|_Y$ are seminorms induced by some semi–inner–products $\langle\cdot, \cdot\rangle_F$ and $\langle\cdot, \cdot\rangle_Y$, respectively. Moreover, F' and Y' are complete with respect to $\|\cdot\|_F$ and $\|\cdot\|_Y$.

Let $0 \le \alpha \le 1$. For $f \in F$ and $y \in \mathbb{R}^n$, define

$$
\Gamma_\alpha(f, y) = \alpha \cdot \|f\|_F^2 + (1 - \alpha) \cdot \delta^{-2} \|y - N(f)\|_Y^2.
$$

(We use above the convention that $a\,(+\infty) = +\infty, \ \forall\, a \ge 0$.) Observe that $\Gamma_\alpha(f, y)$ represents a trade-off between the seminorm of f and the fidelity of $N(f)$ to the data y. This trade-off is controlled by the parameter α. Let

$$
\Gamma_\alpha(y) = \inf_{f \in F} \Gamma_\alpha(f, y).
$$

Then the set Y_1 of all y for which $\Gamma_\alpha(y) < +\infty$ is a linear subspace of $\mathbb{R}^n$, and

$$Y_1 = \{\, y = N(f) + x \mid \|f\|_F < +\infty,\ \|x\|_Y < +\infty \,\}.$$

Also, $\Gamma_\alpha(y) \leq 1$ iff y is noisy information for some $f \in E$.

An α-*smoothing spline* is an element $\mathbf{s}_\alpha(y) \in F$ for which

$$\Gamma_\alpha(\mathbf{s}_\alpha(y), y) = \Gamma_\alpha(y).$$

Observe that an α-smoothing spline is a special instance of a smoothing spline (with $\rho = 1$) when the extended seminorm $\|(\cdot, \cdot)\|_* = \|(\cdot, \cdot)\|_\alpha$ in the space $F \times \mathbb{R}^n$ is induced by the semi–inner–product

$$\langle (f_1, x_1), (f_2, x_2) \rangle_\alpha = \alpha \langle f_1, f_2 \rangle_F + (1 - \alpha)\, \delta^{-2} \langle x_1, x_2 \rangle_Y.$$

An α-*smoothing spline algorithm* is defined as

$$\varphi_\alpha(y) = S(\mathbf{s}_\alpha(y)).$$

We first give a sufficient condition for existence of α-smoothing splines. In addition, we characterize some of their useful properties.

Theorem 2.5.3   *Assume that the operator N is closed, i.e., $\|f_i\|_F \to 0$ and $\|N(f_i) - y\|_Y \to 0$ imply $y = 0$.*

(i) An α-smoothing spline exists for any $y \in \mathbb{R}^n$.

(ii) Let $y \in Y_1$. Then $\mathbf{s}_\alpha(y)$ is an α-smoothing spline for y if and only if $\Gamma_\alpha(\mathbf{s}_\alpha(y), y) < +\infty$ and

$$\alpha \langle \mathbf{s}_\alpha(y), f \rangle_F + (1 - \alpha)\, \delta^{-2} \langle N(\mathbf{s}_\alpha(y)) - y, N(f) \rangle_Y = 0, \qquad (2.24)$$

for all $f \in F$ for which $\Gamma_\alpha(f, 0) < +\infty$.

(iii) For all $y \in Y_1$, the α-smoothing spline is defined uniquely if and only if

$$\Gamma_\alpha(f, N(f)) > 0, \qquad \forall f \neq 0.$$

(iv) There exist smoothing splines $\mathbf{s}_\alpha(y)$, such that $y \mapsto \mathbf{s}_\alpha(y)$, $y \in \mathbb{R}^n$, is a linear mapping.

Proof   In the proof we write, for brevity, f_y instead of $\mathbf{s}_\alpha(y)$.

(i)   If $\Gamma_\alpha(y) = +\infty$ then any element of F is a smoothing spline. Assume that $\Gamma_\alpha(y) < +\infty$. Then $f_y \in F$ is an α-smoothing spline iff $(f_y, N(f_y))$ is the element of $V = \{(f, N(f)) \mid f \in F\} \subset F \times \mathbb{R}^n$, closest to $(0, y)$ with respect to the extended seminorm $\|\cdot\|_\alpha$. Hence for an α-smoothing spline to exist, it suffices to show that the subspace V

is closed with respect to $\|(\cdot,\cdot)\|_\alpha$. Indeed, if $(f_i, N(f_i)) \to (f, y)$ then $\|f_i - f\|_F \to 0$ and $\|N(f_i) - y\|_Y \to 0$. Since N is closed, we obtain $y = N(f)$ which means that $(f, y) = (f, N(f)) \in V$.

(ii) If $\|(\cdot,\cdot)\|_\alpha$ is a Hilbert norm then the element $(f_y, N(f_y)) - (0, y)$ is orthogonal to V. This means that

$$\alpha \langle f_y, f \rangle_F + (1 - \alpha) \delta^{-2} \langle N(f_y) - y, N(f) \rangle_Y = 0,$$

for all $f \in F$. We can easily convince ourselves that the same holds for the case of $\|(\cdot,\cdot)\|_\alpha$ an extended seminorm. (The proof goes exactly as for the Hilbert norm.) We add the condition $\Gamma_\alpha(f, 0) = \|(f, N(f))\|_\alpha^2 < +\infty$ only to make the semi–inner–product in (2.24) well defined.

Suppose now that $\Gamma_\alpha(f_y, y) < +\infty$ and (2.24) both hold. Let f be such that $\Gamma_\alpha(f, y) < +\infty$. Then $\|(f_y, N(f_y)) - y\|_\alpha < +\infty$ and $\|(f, N(f)) - y\|_\alpha < +\infty$, which forces the element $(f - f_y, N(f - f_y)) = (f, N(f)) - y) - (f_y, N(f_y) - y)$ also to have finite extended seminorm $\|\cdot\|_\alpha$, or equivalently, $\Gamma_\alpha(f - f_y, 0) < +\infty$. Since, in addition, this element is in V, from the orthogonality condition (2.24) we obtain

$$\begin{aligned}
\Gamma_\alpha(f, y) &= \|(f, N(f) - y)\|_\alpha^2 \\
&= \|(f_y, N(f_y) - y) + (f - f_y, N(f - f_y))\|_\alpha^2 \\
&= \|(f_y, N(f_y) - y)\|_\alpha^2 + \|(f - f_y, N(f - f_y))\|_\alpha^2 \\
&\geq \Gamma_\alpha(f_y, y).
\end{aligned}$$

This means that f_y is an α-smoothing spline.

(iii) The orthogonal projection on V is determined uniquely iff $\|\cdot\|_\alpha$ is an extended norm on V. This in turn is equivalent to $\Gamma_\alpha(f, N(f)) > 0$, for $f \neq 0$, as claimed.

(iv) From (2.24) it follows that smoothing splines are linear on the subspace Y_1. That is, if $s_\alpha(y_1)$, $s_\alpha(y_2)$ are α-smoothing splines for $y_1, y_2 \in Y_1$, then $\gamma_1 s_\alpha(y_1) + \gamma_2 s_\alpha(y_2)$ is an α-smoothing spline for $\gamma_1 y_1 + \gamma_2 y_2$. Hence, $s_\alpha(y)$ can be chosen in such a way that the mapping $y \to s_\alpha(y)$, $y \in \mathbb{R}^n$, is linear. $\qquad\square$

We now turn to the error of the α-smoothing spline algorithm.

Lemma 2.5.1 *For any $f \in E$ and $y \in \mathbb{N}(f)$*

$$\|S(f) - \varphi_\alpha(y)\| \leq \sqrt{1 - \Gamma_\alpha(y)} \qquad (2.25)$$
$$\times \sup \{\, \|S(h)\| \mid \ \alpha \|h\|_F^2 + (1 - \alpha) \delta^{-2} \|N(h)\|_Y^2 \leq 1 \}.$$

In particular, if $\alpha \in (0,1)$ then

$$e^{\text{wor}}(\mathbb{N}, \varphi_\alpha) \leq c(\alpha) \cdot \text{rad}^{\text{wor}}(\mathbb{N}),$$

where $c(\alpha) = \max\{\alpha^{-1/2}, (1-\alpha)^{-1/2}\}$.

Proof Theorem 2.5.3(ii) yields

$$\begin{aligned}
\|(f, N(f)) - (0, y)\|_\alpha^2 &= \|(f, N(f)) - (s_\alpha(y), N(s_\alpha(y)))\|_\alpha^2 \\
&\quad + \|(s_\alpha(y), N(s_\alpha(y))) - (0, y)\|_\alpha^2 \\
&= \alpha\|f - s_\alpha(y)\|_F^2 + (1-\alpha)\delta^{-2}\|N(f - s_\alpha(y))\|_Y^2 + \Gamma_\alpha(y).
\end{aligned}$$

We also have

$$\|(f, N(f)) - (0, y)\|_\alpha^2 = \alpha\|f\|_F^2 + (1-\alpha)\delta^{-2}\|y - N(f)\|_Y^2 \leq 1.$$

Hence, setting $h = f - s_\alpha(y)$, we obtain

$$\alpha\|h\|_F^2 + (1-\alpha)\delta^{-2}\|N(h)\|_Y^2 \leq 1 - \Gamma_\alpha(y)$$

and (2.25) follows.

To show the second inequality of the lemma, observe that the condition $\alpha\|h\|_F^2 + (1-\alpha)\delta^{-2}\|N(h)\|_Y^2 \leq 1$ implies $\|h\|_F \leq \alpha^{-1/2}$ and $\|N(h)\|_Y \leq \delta(1-\alpha)^{-1/2}$. Hence

$$\begin{aligned}
\sup\{\,\|S(h)\| \mid \alpha\|h\|_F^2 + (1-\alpha)\delta^{-2}\|N(h)\|_Y^2 \leq 1\} \\
\leq c(\alpha) \cdot \sup\{\,\|S(h)\| \mid \|h\|_F \leq 1, \|N(h)\|_Y \leq \delta\,\}.
\end{aligned}$$

The last supremum is equal to half the diameter of the information $\mathbb{N}$ on the set E. The lemma now follows from the fact that $(1/2)\text{diam}(\mathbb{N}) \leq \text{rad}^{\text{wor}}(\mathbb{N})$. $\qquad\square$

Thus the error of the α-spline algorithm is at most $c(\alpha)$ times as large as the minimal error. In particular, one can take $\min_\alpha c(\alpha) = c(1/2) = \sqrt{2}$. Then

$$e^{\text{wor}}(\mathbb{N}, \varphi_{1/2}) \leq \sqrt{2} \cdot \text{rad}^{\text{wor}}(\mathbb{N}).$$

In some cases, the parameter α can be chosen in such a way that the α-smoothing spline algorithm is strictly optimal. Clearly, this is true if $\text{rad}^{\text{wor}}(\mathbb{N}) = +\infty$. For $\text{rad}^{\text{wor}}(\mathbb{N}) = 0$, it follows from Lemma 2.5.1 that the algorithm φ_α is optimal for any $0 < \alpha < 1$.

Assume that $\text{rad}^{\text{wor}}(\mathbb{N}) \in (0, +\infty)$. Let $\text{conv}(A)$ be the convex hull of A. For $a = (a_1, a_2, \ldots, a_m) \in \mathbb{R}^m$, let $\|a\|_\infty = \max_{1 \leq i \leq m} |a_i|$. Then we have the following theorem.

Theorem 2.5.4 *Let* $\text{rad}^{\text{wor}}(\mathbb{N}) \in (0, +\infty)$. *Let the set*

$$A = \left\{ \left(\|h\|_F^2, \delta^{-2}\|N(h)\|_Y^2 \right) \in \mathbb{R}^2 \mid h \in F, \|S(h)\| \geq 1 \right\}$$

satisfy

$$\inf_{a \in A} \|a\|_\infty = \inf_{a \in \text{conv}(A)} \|a\|_\infty. \qquad (2.26)$$

Then

$$\begin{aligned}
\text{rad}^{\text{wor}}(\mathbb{N}) &= \tfrac{1}{2} \cdot \text{diam}(\mathbb{N}) \\
&= \sup \left\{ \|S(h)\| \mid \|h\|_F \leq 1, \|N(h)\|_Y \leq \delta \right\},
\end{aligned}$$

and there exists $0 \leq \alpha^* \leq 1$ *such that the* α^**-smoothing spline algorithm is optimal. Furthermore,*

$$\|S(f) - \varphi_{\alpha^*}(y)\| \leq \sqrt{1 - \Gamma_{\alpha^*}(y)} \cdot \text{rad}^{\text{wor}}(\mathbb{N}), \quad \forall f \in E, \forall y \in \mathbb{N}(f).$$

Proof For $r = \sup \{ \|S(h)\| \mid \|h\|_F \leq 1, \|N(h)\|_Y \leq 1 \}$ we have $r \in (0, +\infty)$. Since $r = (1/2)\text{diam}(\mathbb{N}) \leq \text{rad}^{\text{wor}}(\mathbb{N})$, it follows from (2.25) that a sufficient condition for the α-smoothing spline algorithm to be optimal is that

$$r \geq \sup \{ \|S(h)\| \mid \alpha\|h\|_F^2 + (1-\alpha)\delta^{-2}\|N(h)\|_Y^2 \leq 1 \},$$

or equivalently

$$\begin{aligned}
&\inf_{\|S(h)\| \geq r} \max \{ \|h\|_F^2, \delta^{-2}\|N(h)\|_Y^2 \} \\
&\leq \inf_{\|S(h)\| \geq r} \alpha \|h\|_F^2 + (1 - \alpha) \delta^{-2}\|N(h)\|_Y^2. \qquad (2.27)
\end{aligned}$$

For $a = (a_1, a_2)$, $b = (b_1, b_2) \in \mathbb{R}^2$, let $\langle a, b \rangle_2 = a_1 b_1 + a_2 b_2$ be the Euclidean inner product in $\mathbb{R}^2$. Then (2.27) can be rewritten as

$$\inf_{a \in A} \|a\|_\infty \leq \inf_{a \in A} \langle \beta, a \rangle_2 \qquad (2.28)$$

where $\beta = \beta(\alpha) = (\alpha, 1 - \alpha)$.

We now show that there exists $\alpha = \alpha^*$ for which (2.28) is an equality. Assume first that the set A is convex. Let $\gamma = \inf_{a \in A} \|a\|_\infty$ and $a^* = (a_1^*, a_2^*) \in \overline{A}$ be a point for which $\|a^*\|_\infty = \gamma$. Clearly, a^* is a boundary point of $\overline{A}$. It follows from convex analysis that there exists a line $\langle \beta, a \rangle_2 = c$ passing through a^* and separating A from the convex set $\{ a \in \mathbb{R}^2 \mid \|a\|_\infty \leq \gamma \}$ (which is disjoint from the interior of A). That is, $\langle \beta, a^* \rangle = c$ and $\langle \beta, a \rangle_2 \geq c$ for $a \in A$, $\langle \beta, a \rangle_2 \leq c$ for $\|a\|_\infty \leq \gamma$. Observe that β_1, β_2 and c can all be chosen nonnegative. Let β be normalized so that $\beta_1 + \beta_2 = 1$. Then $c = \gamma$. Indeed, this is clear if $a_1^* = a_2^* = \gamma$. For $a_1^* < a_2^* = \gamma$ (or $a_2^* < a_1^* = \gamma$) it is enough to note that then $\beta = (0,1)$ (or $\beta = (1,0)$). Hence we have obtained that $\inf_{a \in A} \langle \beta, a \rangle_2 \geq \gamma$ and (2.28) follows with $\alpha^* = \beta_1$.

If the set A is not convex, we take β constructed as above for the convex set $\text{conv}(A)$. From the condition (2.26) we obtain

$$
\begin{aligned}
\inf_{a \in A} \|a\|_\infty &= \inf_{a \in \text{conv}(A)} \|a\|_\infty \\
&\leq \inf_{a \in \text{conv}(A)} \langle \beta, a \rangle_2 \leq \inf_{a \in A} \langle \beta, a \rangle_2,
\end{aligned}
$$

as claimed. The proof of the theorem is complete. $\square$

Theorem 2.5.4 applies whenever the range space G of the solution operator S is a Hilbert space. Indeed, this follows from the following lemma.

Lemma 2.5.2 *Let* $\| \cdot \|_i$, $i = 0, 1, 2$, *be three extended Hilbert semi-norms on the same linear space* X. *Then the set*

$$
A = \left\{ \, (\|x\|_1^2, \|x\|_2^2) \in \mathbb{R}^2 \mid \ 1 \leq \|x\|_0^2 < +\infty \right\}
$$

satisfies

$$
\inf_{a \in A} \|a\|_\infty = \inf_{a \in \text{conv}(A)} \|a\|_\infty.
$$

Proof For $x \in X$, we write $a(x) = (\|x\|_1^2, \|x\|_2^2)$. Let $\gamma = \inf_{a \in A} \|a\|_\infty$.

Suppose that the lemma is not true. Then there exist two different points $a(x), a(y) \in A$ such that $\|x\|_0 = \|y\|_0 = 1$, and for some u from the interval $[a(x), a(y)]$ we have $\|u\|_\infty < \gamma$. We show that this is impossible. More precisely, we show that there exists a continuous curve $C \subset A$ joining $a(x)$ with $a(y)$ and passing through the interval $[0, u]$ at some u'. Then $u' \in A$ and $\|u'\|_\infty \leq \|u\|_\infty < \inf_{a \in A} \|a\|_\infty$, which is a contradiction.

Since $a(x) = a(-x)$, we can assume that $\langle x, y \rangle_0 \geq 0$. Let $L = \{ a \in \mathbb{R}^2 \mid \langle w, a \rangle = c \}$ be the line passing through $a(x)$ and $a(y)$. (Here $\langle \cdot, \cdot \rangle$ is the Euclidean inner product.) Since $\|u\|_\infty < \min\{\|a(x)\|_\infty, \|a(y)\|_\infty\}$, the line L passes through the half-lines $\{(t, 0) \mid t \geq 0\}$ and $\{(0, t) \mid t \geq 0\}$. We consider two cases.

1. $\|x - y\|_0 > 0$.

Write $x(t) = t\,x + (1-t)\,y$ and $u(t) = a(\,x(t)/\|x(t)\|_0\,)$. Since $\langle x, y \rangle_0 \geq 0$, the 0-seminorm of $x(t)$ is positive. Then $\{\, u(t) \mid\ -\infty < t < +\infty \}$ is a continuous curve in A with $\lim_{t \to \pm\infty} u(t) = a((x - y)/\|x - y\|_0) \in A$.

Since the quadratic polynomial $Q(t) = \|x(t)\|_0^2(\langle w, u(t)\rangle_2 - c)$ vanishes for $t = 0, 1$, the line L divides the curve into two curves that lie on opposite sides of L and join $a(x)$ with $a(y)$. One of them passes through $[0, u]$.

2. $\|x - y\|_0 = 0$.

In this case $\|x(t)\|_0 = 1$, for all $t \in \mathbb{R}$. Hence $\lim_{t \to \pm\infty}(u(t)/t^2) = a(x - y) \neq 0$. Using this and the previous argument about the zeros of the polynomial $Q(t)$, we conclude that the curve $\{u(t) \mid 0 \le t \le 1\}$ passes through $[0, u]$. □

We have shown that there exists an optimal linear smoothing spline algorithm provided that $\|\cdot\|_F$, $\|\cdot\|_Y$ and $\|\cdot\|$ are all Hilbert extended seminorms. This was a consequence of the fact that for some α we have the equality

$$\sup\{\,\|S(h)\| \mid \ \|h\|_F \le 1, \|N(h)\|_Y \le \delta\,\}$$
$$= \ \sup\{\,\|S(h)\| \mid \ \alpha\|h\|_F^2 + (1 - \alpha)\delta^{-2}\|N(h)\|_Y^2 \le 1\,\}.$$

In particular, α should be chosen in such a way that the right hand side of this equality is minimal. The value of α with this property will be called *optimal* and denoted by α^*. Thus we have the following corollary.

Corollary 2.5.1 *The optimal value of α is given as*

$$\alpha^* = \arg \min_{0 \le \alpha \le 1} \sup\{\,\|S(h)\| \mid \ \alpha\|h\|_F^2 + (1 - \alpha)\delta^{-2}\|N(h)\|_Y^2 \le 1\,\}.$$

The same ideas can be used to prove optimality of smoothing spline algorithms in another case. As before, we assume that $\|\cdot\|_F$ is a Hilbert seminorm, but relax this requirement for the seminorm $\|\cdot\|_Y$. That is, we let

$$\mathbb{N}(f) = \{\,y = [y_1, \ldots, y_n] \in \mathbb{R}^n \mid \ |y_i - L_i(f)| \le \delta_i,\ 1 \le i \le n\,\},$$

where the L_i are linear functionals and $0 \le \delta_i \le +\infty$, $1 \le i \le n$. We also assume that the solution operator S is a linear functional.

For $\beta = (\beta_1, \ldots, \beta_{n+1}) \in \mathbb{R}^{n+1}$ such that $\beta_i \ge 0$ and $\sum_{i=1}^{n+1} \beta_i = 1$, we define

$$\Gamma_\beta(f, y) = \beta_{n+1}\|f\|_F^2 + \sum_{i=1}^{n} \beta_i \delta_i^{-2} |y_i - L_i(f)|^2.$$

A *β-smoothing spline algorithm* is then $\varphi_\beta(y) = S(\mathbf{s}_\beta(y))$ where $\mathbf{s}_\beta(y)$ minimizes $\Gamma_\beta(f, y)$ over all $f \in F$.

Owing to Theorem 2.4.1, an optimal linear algorithm exists. It turns out that it can be interpreted as a β-smoothing spline algorithm.

Theorem 2.5.5 *If S is a linear functional then*

$$\operatorname{rad}^{\operatorname{wor}}(\mathbb{N}) = \sup\{\, S(h) \mid \|h\| \leq 1,\ |L_i(h)| \leq \delta_i,\ 1 \leq i \leq n \,\}$$

and there exists β^* such that the β^*-smoothing spline algorithm is optimal. Furthermore, for any $f \in F$ and $y \in \mathbb{N}(f)$

$$|S(f) - \varphi_{\beta^*}(y)| \leq \sqrt{1 - \Gamma_{\beta^*}(y)} \cdot \operatorname{rad}^{\operatorname{wor}}(\mathbb{N}).$$

Proof As in the proof of Lemma 2.5.1 we can show that

$$|S(f) - \varphi_\beta(y)| \leq \sqrt{1 - \Gamma_\beta(y)}$$

$$\times \sup\left\{\, S(h) \,\middle|\, \beta_{n+1}\|h\|_F^2 + \sum_{i=1}^n \beta_i\, \delta_i^{-2}|L_i(h)|^2 \leq 1 \right\}.$$

Repeating the corresponding part of the proof of Theorem 2.5.4 we obtain a sufficient condition for the β-smoothing spline algorithm to be optimal. That is, the set

$$B = \{\, (\|x\|_1^2, \ldots, \|x\|_{n+1}^2) \in \mathbb{R}^{n+1} \mid S(x) \geq 1 \,\},$$

where $\|x\|_i = |L_i(x)|/\delta_i$ for $1 \leq i \leq n$ and $\|x\|_{n+1} = \|x\|_F$, must satisfy

$$\inf_{b \in B} \|b\|_\infty = \inf_{b \in c(B)} \|b\|_\infty. \tag{2.29}$$

But (2.29) follows from the fact that for any $b \in c(B)$ there exists $\tilde{b} \in B$ with all $n+1$ components not greater than the corresponding components of b. Indeed, if $b = \sum_{j=1}^m c_j b_j$, where $b_j = (\|x_j\|_i^2,\ 1 \leq i \leq n+1) \in B$, $\sum_{j=1}^m c_j = 1$, and $c_j \geq 0$, then one can take $\tilde{b} = (\|\sum_{j=1}^m c_j x_j\|_i^2,\ 1 \leq i \leq n+1)$. Direct calculations show that

$$\left\| \sum_{j=1}^m c_j\, x_j \right\|_i^2 \leq \sum_{j=1}^m c_j\, \|x_j\|_i^2, \qquad 1 \leq i \leq n+1.$$

$\square$

Notes and remarks

NR 2.5.1 The names 'splines' and 'smoothing splines' have been adopted from the theory of polynomial splines in function spaces. In this case, the norm $\|f\|_F$ usually represents the smoothness of f in the usual sense. Polynomial splines are studied in Subsection 2.6.3.

NR 2.5.2 A general approach to spline algorithms in the worst case setting with exact information, and most relations between splines and optimal error algorithms, were presented in Traub and Woźniakowski (1980, Chap. 4). The general definition of smoothing splines and Theorem 2.5.2 seem to be new.

NR 2.5.3 Optimality of ordinary splines in the worst case setting was shown by Kacewicz and Plaskota (1991), while optimality of α-smoothing splines was proved by Melkman and Micchelli (1979). The proof of Theorem 2.5.5 is based on the latter paper (see also Micchelli, 1993). However, Theorems 2.5.3 and 2.5.5 seem to be new.

NR 2.5.4 For optimality of the α-smoothing spline algorithm, it is essential that G be a Hilbert space; see Melkman and Micchelli (1979) for a counterexample.

Exercises

E 2.5.1 Give an example of an (ordinary) spline algorithm for which the estimate $e^{\text{wor}}(\mathbb{N}, \varphi_o) \leq (1/2)(1+\rho)\text{diam}(\mathbb{N})$ in Theorem 2.5.1 is sharp.

E 2.5.2 Show that the definitions of the ordinary spline $s_o(y)$ for $\rho = 1$ and α-smoothing spline $s_\alpha(y)$ with $0 < \alpha < 1$ coincide, if the information $\mathbb{N}$ is exact and linear.

E 2.5.3 Let $\|(\cdot, \cdot)\|_*$ be an extended seminorm on the space $F \times \mathbb{R}^n$ such that for some $0 < d_1 \leq d_2 < +\infty$ we have
$$d_1 \|(f, x)\|_\infty \leq \|(f, x)\|_* \leq d_2 \|(f, x)\|_\infty, \quad \forall f \in F, \, x \in \mathbb{R}^n.$$
Show that then for the smoothing spline algorithm φ_* we have
$$e^{\text{wor}}(\mathbb{N}, \varphi_*) \leq \frac{1+\rho}{2} \frac{d_2}{d_1} \text{diam}(\mathbb{N}).$$

E 2.5.4 Let $\text{rad}^{\text{wor}}(\mathbb{N}) < +\infty$ and $0 < \alpha < 1$. Show that then $S(f_1) = S(f_2)$, for any α-smoothing splines f_1, f_2 corresponding to information y such that $\Gamma_\alpha(y) < +\infty$. That is, the α-smoothing spline algorithm is defined uniquely on the subspace $\{ y \in \mathbb{R}^n \mid \Gamma_\alpha(y) < +\infty \}$.

E 2.5.5 Let $\| \cdot \|_0$ and $\| \cdot \|_1$ be two extended seminorms on a linear space, and let $0 < r_0, r_1 < +\infty$. Show that
$$\sup_{\|h\|_1 \leq r_1} \|h\|_0 = r_0 \quad \Longleftrightarrow \quad \inf_{\|h\|_0 \geq r_0} \|h\|_1 = r_1.$$

E 2.5.6 Prove that the set A in Lemma 2.5.2 is convex.

E 2.5.7 Let $\| \cdot \|_F$ and $\| \cdot \|_Y$ be Hilbert extended seminorms, and let $0 < \alpha < 1$. Define the set
$$E = \{ f \in F \mid \|f\|_F^2 \leq 1/\alpha \},$$
and the information operator
$$\mathbb{N}(f) = \left\{ y \in \mathbb{R}^n \mid \|y - N(f)\|_Y^2 \leq \frac{1 - \alpha \|f\|_F^2}{1 - \alpha} \right\},$$

where $N : F \to \mathbb{R}^n$ is a linear operator. Show that in this case the α-smoothing spline algorithm is optimal for any linear solution operator S, and

$$\text{rad}^{\text{wor}}(\text{N}) = \sup \{ \|S(h)\| \mid \alpha \|h\|_F^2 + (1 - \alpha) \|N(h)\|_Y^2 \le 1 \}.$$

E 2.5.8 Suppose that the solution operator S in Theorem 2.5.5 is not a functional. Show that then there exists a linear algorithm with error not larger than $\sqrt{n+1} \cdot \text{rad}^{\text{wor}}(\text{N})$, where n is the number of functionals in N.

E 2.5.9 Give an example of a problem for which the smoothing spline element does not exist.

2.6 Special splines

In this section we consider several special cases. We first show explicit formulas for the α-smoothing spline and the optimal choice of α in the case when F is a Hilbert space. Then we prove that regularization and classical polynomial splines lead to algorithms that are optimal in the worst case setting. Finally, we consider splines in reproducing kernel Hilbert spaces.

2.6.1 The Hilbert case with optimal α

Let F and G be separable Hilbert spaces and $S : F \to G$ a continuous linear operator. Let E be the unit ball in F. Suppose that for an (unknown) element $f \in E$ we observe data

$$y = N(f) + x,$$

where $N : F \to Y = \mathbb{R}^n$ is a continuous linear operator,

$$N = [\langle \cdot, f_1 \rangle_F, \langle \cdot, f_2 \rangle_F, \ldots, \langle \cdot, f_n \rangle_F],$$

and $f_i \in F$, $1 \le i \le n$. The noise x is bounded in an extended Hilbert norm of $\mathbb{R}^n$, $\|x\|_Y \le \delta$ with $\delta > 0$. That is, $\| \cdot \|_Y$ is given by $\|x\|_Y = \sqrt{\langle x, x \rangle_Y}$,

$$\langle x_1, x_2 \rangle_Y = \begin{cases} \langle \Sigma^{-1} x_1, x_2 \rangle_2 & x_1, x_2 \in \Sigma(\mathbb{R}^n), \\ +\infty & \text{otherwise}, \end{cases}$$

where the operator (matrix) $\Sigma : \mathbb{R}^n \to \mathbb{R}^n$ is symmetric and nonnegative definite, $\Sigma = \Sigma^* \ge 0$. Note that $\langle \cdot, \cdot \rangle_Y$ is a well defined inner product on $\Sigma(\mathbb{R}^n)$ since $\Sigma y_1 = \Sigma y_2 = x_1$ implies $\langle y_1, x_2 \rangle_2 = \langle y_2, x_2 \rangle_2$, for all $x_1, x_2 \in \Sigma(\mathbb{R}^n)$.

We first show formulas for the α-smoothing spline. For $\alpha = 1$ we obviously have $\mathbf{s}_\alpha \equiv 0$.

Lemma 2.6.1 *Let $0 \le \alpha < 1$. The quantity $\Gamma_\alpha(y) = \inf_{f \in F} \Gamma_\alpha(f, y)$ is finite if and only if $y \in Y_1 = N(F) + \Sigma(\mathbb{R}^n)$. For $y \in Y_1$, the α-smoothing spline is given as*

$$s_\alpha(y) = \sum_{j=1}^n z_j f_j,$$

where $z \in Y_1$ is the solution of the linear system

$$(\gamma \Sigma + G_N) z = y,$$

with the Gram matrix

$$G_N = \{\langle f_i, f_j \rangle_F\}_{i,j=1}^n$$

and $\gamma = \alpha(1-\alpha)^{-1}\delta^2$. Moreover, $\Gamma_\alpha(y) = \Gamma_\alpha(s_\alpha(y), y) = \langle y, z \rangle_2$. For $\alpha > 0$ and $y \in Y_1$, the α-smoothing spline is defined uniquely.

Proof If $y \notin Y_1$ then for all $f \in F$ we have $y - N(f) \notin \Sigma(\mathbb{R}^n)$ and $\|y - N(f)\|_Y = +\infty$. Hence $\Gamma_\alpha(f, y) = +\infty$.

Assume that $y \in Y_1$. Then any $f \in F$ can be decomposed as $f = \sum_{j=1}^n \beta_j f_j + f^\perp$, where $f^\perp$ is orthogonal to span$\{f_1, \ldots, f_n\}$. (Note that this decomposition need not be unique.) We have $\|f\|_F^2 = \langle G_N\beta, \beta \rangle_2 + \|f^\perp\|_F^2$ and $\|y - N(f)\|_Y^2 = \langle \Sigma^{-1}(y - G_N\beta), (y - G_N\beta) \rangle_2$. Hence

$$\Gamma_\alpha(y) = \inf_\beta \left(\gamma \langle G_N\beta, \beta \rangle_2 + \langle \Sigma^{-1}(y - G_N\beta), (y - G_N\beta) \rangle_2 \right).$$

Denoting by P the orthogonal projection in $\mathbb{R}^n$ onto the subspace $\Sigma(\mathbb{R}^n)$ with respect to $\langle \cdot, \cdot \rangle_2$, we obtain

$$\begin{aligned} &\gamma \langle G_N\beta, \beta \rangle_2 + \langle \Sigma^{-1}(y - G_N\beta), (y - G_N\beta) \rangle_2 \\ &= \gamma \langle G_N\beta, \beta \rangle_2 + \langle \Sigma^{-1}P(y - G_N\beta), (y - G_N\beta) \rangle_2 \\ &= \langle A\beta, \beta \rangle_2 - 2\langle b, \beta \rangle_2 + c, \end{aligned}$$

where

$$A = G_N\left(\gamma I + \Sigma^{-1}PG_N\right), \quad b = G_N\Sigma^{-1}Py, \quad c = \langle \Sigma^{-1}Py, y \rangle_2.$$

Clearly, $A = A^* > 0$. It is well known that $\langle A\beta, \beta \rangle_2 - 2\langle b, \beta \rangle_2$ is minimized for any β satisfying $A\beta = b$, i.e.,

$$G_N\left(\gamma I + \Sigma^{-1}PG_N\right)\beta = G_N\Sigma^{-1}Py. \tag{2.30}$$

In particular, (2.30) holds for $\beta = z$. Furthermore, for $f_y = \sum_{j=1}^n z_j f_j$ we have $\Gamma_\alpha(f_y, y) = \langle z, y \rangle_2$.

To prove the uniqueness of s_α in the case $\alpha \neq 0$, it suffices to show that if (2.30) holds for two different $\beta^{(1)}$ and $\beta^{(2)}$, then $f^{(1)} = f^{(2)}$ where $f^{(1)} = \sum_{j=1}^{n} \beta_j^{(1)} f_j$ and $f^{(2)} = \sum_{j=1}^{n} \beta_j^{(2)} f_j$. Indeed, let $\beta = \beta^{(1)} - \beta^{(2)}$. Then $A\beta = 0$ and

$$\langle A\beta, \beta \rangle_2 = \gamma \langle G_N \beta, \beta \rangle_2 + \langle G_N \Sigma^{-1} P G_N \beta, \beta \rangle_2 = 0.$$

Since the matrix $G_N \Sigma^{-1} P G_N$ is nonnegative definite, $\langle G_N \beta, \beta \rangle_2 = \|f^{(1)} - f^{(2)}\|_F^2 = 0$ which means that $f^{(1)} = f^{(2)}$, as claimed. $\qquad\square$

We note that Lemma 2.6.1 says, in particular, that the smoothing spline is in the space spanned by the elements f_i which form the information N. To find s_α it suffices to solve a linear system of equations with the Gram matrix G_N.

Corollary 2.6.1 *For $0 \le \alpha < 1$, the α-smoothing spline algorithm is given as*

$$\varphi_\alpha(y) = \sum_{j=1}^{n} z_j S(f_j), \qquad y \in Y_1,$$

where $z \in Y_1$ satisfies $(\gamma \Sigma + G_N)z = y$ and $\gamma = \alpha(1-\alpha)^{-1}\delta^2$.

We pass to the optimal choice of α. Recall that the algorithm φ_α with $\alpha = 1/2$ gives error at most $\sqrt{2}$ times as large as the minimal error, and that there exists α^* for which φ_{α^*} is optimal.

Consider first the case when Σ is positive definite, $\Sigma > 0$. Then $\|\cdot\|_Y$ is a Hilbert norm and there exists the operator N^* adjoint to N with respect to the inner product $\langle \cdot, \cdot \rangle_Y$ in $\mathbb{R}^n$. That is,

$$\langle N(f), y \rangle_Y = \langle f, N^*(y) \rangle_F, \qquad \forall f \in F, y \in \mathbb{R}^n.$$

Lemma 2.6.2 *Let $\Sigma > 0$. Then the optimal parameter α^* is given as*

$$\alpha^* = \arg \min_{0 \le \alpha \le 1} \max \left\{ \lambda \,\middle|\, \lambda \in \mathrm{Sp}(S A_\alpha^{-1} S^*) \right\},$$

where

$$A_\alpha = \alpha I + \delta^{-2}(1 - \alpha) N^* N$$

and $\mathrm{Sp}(\cdot)$ is the spectrum of an operator. Furthermore,

$$\begin{aligned}
e^{\mathrm{wor}}(\mathbb{N}, \varphi_{\alpha^*}) &= \mathrm{rad}^{\mathrm{wor}}(\mathbb{N}) \\
&= \max \left\{ \sqrt{\lambda} \,\middle|\, \lambda \in \mathrm{Sp}(S A_{\alpha^*}^{-1} S^*) \right\}.
\end{aligned}$$

Note that for $\alpha = 0$, the operator $A_\alpha = \delta^{-2} N^* N$ may not be one-to-one. In this case, if $\ker N \not\subset \ker S$ then we formally set $\max\{\lambda \mid \lambda \in \mathrm{Sp}(SA_0^{-1}S^*)\} = +\infty$. If $\ker N \subset \ker S$ then we treat $A_0 = \delta^{-2} N^* N$ as an operator acting in the space $V = (\ker N)^\perp$. Since $S(\ker N) = \{0\}$, we have $S^*(V) \subset V$ and $SA_0^{-1}S^* : V \to V$ is a well defined self-adjoint nonnegative definite operator.

Proof Owing to Corollary 2.5.1, the optimal $\alpha = \alpha^*$ minimizes

$$\sup \{\, \|Sh\| \mid \; \alpha \|h\|_F^2 + \delta^{-2}(1 - \alpha) \|Nh\|_Y^2 \le 1 \,\}, \qquad (2.31)$$

and $\mathrm{rad}^{\mathrm{wor}}(\mathbb{N})$ is equal to the minimal value of (2.31). In our case, (2.31) can be rewritten as

$$\begin{aligned}
&\sup \{\, \|SA_\alpha^{-1/2}(A_\alpha^{1/2} h)\| \mid \; \|A_\alpha^{1/2} h\|_F \le 1 \,\} \\
=\;& \sup \{\, \|SA_\alpha^{-1/2} h\| \mid \; \|h\|_F \le 1 \,\} \\
=\;& \max \{\, \sqrt{\lambda} \mid \; \lambda \in \mathrm{Sp}(SA_\alpha^{-1}S^*) \,\}
\end{aligned}$$

(this also holds for $\alpha = 0$), which completes the proof. $\square$

From Lemma 2.6.2 we can derive the following more specific theorem about α^*.

Theorem 2.6.1 *Let $\{\xi_j\}$ be a complete orthonormal basis of eigenelements of the operator $N^* N$. Let η_j be the corresponding eigenvalues,*

$$N^* N \xi_j \;=\; \eta_j \xi_j, \qquad j \ge 1.$$

Then the optimal α^* is the minimizer of

$$\psi(\alpha) \;=\; \sup_{\|g\|=1} \sum_{j \ge 1} \frac{\langle S(\xi_j), g \rangle^2}{\alpha + \delta^{-2}\eta_j(1 - \alpha)}, \qquad 0 \le \alpha \le 1,$$

and $\mathrm{rad}^{\mathrm{wor}}(\mathbb{N}) = \sqrt{\psi(\alpha^*)}$. In particular, if S is a functional then

$$\psi(\alpha) \;=\; \sum_{j \ge 1} \frac{S^2(\xi_j)}{\alpha + \delta^{-2}\eta_j(1 - \alpha)}.$$

Proof Owing to Lemma 2.6.2, the optimal α^* minimizes the inner product $\langle SA_\alpha^{-1}S^* g, g \rangle$ over all g with $\|g\| = 1$. Observe that

$$A_\alpha^{-1} \xi_j \;=\; (\alpha + \delta^{-2}\eta_j(1 - \alpha))^{-1} \xi_j$$

and $S^*g = \sum_{j \geq 1} \langle S\xi_j, g \rangle \xi_j$. This and the orthonormality of $\{\xi_j\}$ yield

$$\langle SA_\alpha^{-1}S^*g, g \rangle = \langle A_\alpha^{-1}S^*g, S^*g \rangle_F = \sum_{j \geq 1} \frac{\langle S\xi_j, g \rangle^2}{\alpha + \delta^{-2}\eta_j(1-\alpha)}.$$

If S is a functional then $g \in \{-1, 1\}$ and $\langle S\xi_j, g \rangle^2 = S^2\xi_j$, which completes the proof. $\square$

For singular Σ, Lemma 2.6.2 and Theorem 2.6.1 should be modified as follows. Let $F_1 = \{f \in F \mid N(f) \in \Sigma(\mathbb{R}^n)\}$. Let $S_1 : F_1 \to G$ and $N_1 : F_1 \to \Sigma(\mathbb{R}^n)$ be defined by $S_1(f) = f$ and $N_1(f) = N(f)$, $f \in F_1$. Since $\|\cdot\|_Y$ is a Hilbert norm in $\Sigma(\mathbb{R}^n)$, the adjoint operator $N_1^* : \Sigma(\mathbb{R}^n) \to F_1$ exists. Lemma 2.6.2 and Theorem 2.6.1 hold with S and N replaced by S_1 and N_1. For instance, if information is exact then $\Sigma \equiv 0$, $F_1 = \ker N$, $N_1^*N_1 \equiv 0$, and $A_\alpha = \alpha I$. The optimal α is then $\alpha^* = 1$. That is, $\mathbf{s}_{\alpha^*}(y)$ is the element of the set $\{f \in F \mid N(f) = y\}$ with minimal norm, and

$$\mathrm{rad}^{\mathrm{wor}}(\mathbb{N}) = e^{\mathrm{wor}}(\mathbb{N}, \varphi_{\alpha^*}) = \sup\{\|S(h)\| \mid h \in \ker N, \|h\| \leq 1\}.$$

We now specialize the formulas for the optimal α^*, for $\gamma^* = \alpha^*(1 - \alpha^*)^{-1}\delta^2$, and for $\mathrm{rad}^{\mathrm{wor}}(\mathbb{N})$, assuming that S is a compact operator and S^*S and N^*N possess a common orthonormal basis of eigenvectors. That is, we assume that there exists in F an orthonormal basis $\{\xi_i\}_{i=1}^d$ ($d = \dim F \leq +\infty$) such that

$$S^*S\xi_i = \lambda_i\xi_i \qquad \text{and} \qquad N^*N\xi_i = \eta_i\xi_i,$$

where $\lambda_1 \geq \lambda_2 \geq \ldots \geq 0$ are the eigenvalues of S^*S and η_i are the eigenvalues of N^*N. (If $d < +\infty$ then we formally set $\lambda_i = \eta_i = 0$ for $i > d$.)

In this case, $\{S\xi_i/\|S\xi_i\| \mid \xi_i \notin \ker S\}$ is an orthonormal basis in $S(F)$ of eigenelements of the operator $SA_\alpha^{-1}S^*$, and the corresponding eigenvalues are

$$\tilde{\lambda}_i(\alpha) = \frac{\lambda_i}{\alpha + \delta^{-2}\eta_i(1-\alpha)}, \qquad i \geq 1.$$

Hence, to find the optimal α and the radius of $\mathbb{N}$, we have to minimize $\max_{i \geq 1} \tilde{\lambda}_i(\alpha)$ over all $\alpha \in [0, 1]$.

Let $1 = p_1 < p_2 < \cdots < p_k$ be the finite sequence of integers defined (uniquely) by the following condition. For any i, p_{i+1} is the smallest integer such that $p_{i+1} > p_i$ and $\lambda_{p_i}\eta_{p_i}^{-1} < \lambda_{p_{i+1}}\eta_{p_{i+1}}^{-1}$ (here $a0^{-1} = +\infty$

for $a > 0$ and $00^{-1} = 0$). If such a p_{i+1} does not exist then $k = i$. It is easy to see that for any α

$$\max_{i \geq 1} \tilde{\lambda}_i(\alpha) = \max_{1 \leq i \leq k} \tilde{\lambda}_{p_i}(\alpha).$$

Next, let

$$P_1 = \{p_i \mid 1 \leq i \leq k, \, \delta^2 < \eta_{p_i}\}, \tag{2.32}$$

$$P_2 = \{p_i \mid 1 \leq i \leq k, \, \delta^2 \geq \eta_{p_i}\}. \tag{2.33}$$

Observe that for any $i \in P_1$, $\tilde{\lambda}_i(\alpha)$ is an increasing function of α, while for $j \in P_2$ it is nonincreasing. Hence in the case $P_1 = \emptyset$ we have $\alpha^* = 1$ and $\mathrm{rad}^{\mathrm{wor}}(\mathbb{N}) = \sqrt{\lambda_1}$, while for $P_2 = \emptyset$ we have $\alpha^* = 0$ and $\mathrm{rad}^{\mathrm{wor}}(\mathbb{N}) = \delta\sqrt{\max_i(\lambda_i/\eta_i)}$.

Suppose that both the sets P_1 and P_2 are nonempty. Then

$$\min_{0 \leq \alpha \leq 1} \max_{1 \leq j \leq k} \tilde{\lambda}_{i_j}(\alpha) = \max_{i \in P_1, j \in P_2} \beta_{ij},$$

where $\beta_{ij} = \tilde{\lambda}_i(\alpha_{ij})$ and the α_{ij} are such that $\tilde{\lambda}_i(\alpha_{ij}) = \tilde{\lambda}_j(\alpha_{ij})$. The optimal $\alpha^* = \alpha_{st}$, where s, t are chosen in such a way that β_{st} minimizes β_{ij} over $i \in P_1$ and $j \in P_2$. Furthermore, $\mathrm{rad}^{\mathrm{wor}}(\mathbb{N}) = \sqrt{\beta_{st}}$.

Noting that

$$\alpha_{ij} = \frac{\lambda_j \eta_i - \lambda_i \eta_j}{\lambda_i(\delta^2 - \eta_j) + \lambda_j(\eta_i - \delta^2)}$$

and

$$\beta_{ij} = \lambda_j + \left(\frac{\delta^2 - \eta_j}{\eta_i - \eta_j}\right)(\lambda_i - \lambda_j),$$

we obtain the following corollary.

Corollary 2.6.2 *Suppose that the operators S^*S and N^*N have a common basis of eigenelements with the corresponding eigenvalues $\{\lambda_i\}$ and $\{\eta_i\}$. Let the sets P_1 and P_2 be defined by (2.32) and (2.33).*
 (i) If $P_1 = \emptyset$ then $\alpha^* = 1$ and $\mathrm{rad}^{\mathrm{wor}}(\mathbb{N}) = \sqrt{\lambda_1}$.
 (ii) If $P_2 = \emptyset$ then $\alpha^* = 0$ and

$$\mathrm{rad}^{\mathrm{wor}}(\mathbb{N}) = \delta \cdot \sqrt{\max_{i \geq 1} \frac{\lambda_i}{\eta_i}}.$$

 (iii) If both P_1 and P_2 are nonempty then

$$\alpha^* = \frac{\lambda_t \eta_s - \lambda_s \eta_t}{\lambda_s(\delta^2 - \eta_t) + \lambda_t(\eta_s - \delta^2)}$$

and

$$\text{rad}^{\text{wor}}(\mathbb{N}) = \sqrt{\lambda_t + \left(\frac{\delta^2 - \eta_t}{\eta_s - \eta_t}\right)(\lambda_s - \lambda_t)},$$

where

$$(s,t) = \arg \max_{(i,j) \in P_1 \times P_2} \left(\lambda_j + \left(\frac{\delta^2 - \eta_j}{\eta_i - \eta_j}\right)(\lambda_i - \lambda_j)\right).$$

Suppose now that δ is small,

$$0 < \delta \leq \max_{1 \leq i \leq t} \sqrt{\eta_i},$$

where $t = \min\{\, i \geq 1 \mid \eta_i = 0 \,\}$. Let $s = \arg \max_{1 \leq i \leq t-1}(\eta_i^{-1}(\lambda_i - \lambda_t))$. Then Corollary 2.6.2 yields the following formulas:

$$\alpha^* = \frac{\lambda_t}{\lambda_t + \delta^2 \eta_s^{-1}(\lambda_s - \lambda_t)}$$

and

$$\text{rad}^{\text{wor}}(\mathbb{N}) = \sqrt{\lambda_t + \frac{\delta^2}{\eta_s}(\lambda_s - \lambda_t)}.$$

Observe that $\alpha^* \to 1$ as $\delta \to 0^+$. For $\alpha^* \neq 1$ (which holds when $\lambda_s > \lambda_t$) the parameter

$$\gamma^* = \frac{\eta_s \lambda_t}{\lambda_s - \lambda_t}$$

is constant. This means that the optimal algorithm is independent of the noise level, provided that δ is small. (The same algorithm is also optimal for exact information, see E 2.6.3.) This nice property is, however, not preserved in general, as shown in E 2.6.4.

2.6.2 Least squares and regularization

Consider the Hilbert case of Subsection 2.6.1 with $\|\cdot\|_Y$ a Hilbert norm. In this case, as an approximation to $S(f)$ one can take

$$\varphi_{\text{ls}}(y) = S(u_{\text{ls}}(y)),$$

where $u_{\text{ls}}(y)$ is the solution of the *least squares* problem. This is defined by the equation

$$\|y - N(u_{\text{ls}}(y))\|_Y = \min_{f \in F} \|y - N(f)\|_Y,$$

or equivalently, $N(u_{ls}(y)) = P_N y$ where $P_N : \mathbb{R}^n \to \mathbb{R}^n$ is the orthogonal projection of y onto $Y_N = N(F)$ (with respect to the inner product $\langle \cdot, \cdot \rangle_Y$). This is in turn equivalent to the condition that $u_{ls}(y)$ is the solution of the normal equations

$$N^* N f = N^* y. \tag{2.34}$$

Indeed, if (2.34) holds then $\langle y - Nf, Nf \rangle_Y = \langle N^* y - N^* Nf, f \rangle_F = 0$, which means that $Nf = P_N y$. On the other hand, since $N^*(Y_N^\perp) = \{0\}$, for any solution h of the least squares problem we have $N^* N h = N^* P_N y = N^* y$, as claimed.

The algorithm φ_{ls} is called the *(generalized) least squares algorithm*. For finite dimensional problems with small noise level, the least squares algorithm turns out to be optimal, as we see in the following theorem.

Theorem 2.6.2 *Let* $\dim F = \dim N(F) = d < +\infty$. *Let* $\bar{g} \in G$ *be such that* $\|\bar{g}\| = 1$ *and*

$$\|S(N^* N)^{-1} S^* \bar{g}\| = \|S(N^* N)^{-1} S^*\|.$$

Let δ *be chosen so that*

$$\delta^2 \left\langle S(N^* N)^{-2} S^* \bar{g}, \bar{g} \right\rangle \le \|S(N^* N)^{-1} S^*\|. \tag{2.35}$$

Then the (generalized) least squares algorithm φ_{ls} *is optimal. Furthermore,*

$$\mathrm{rad}^{\mathrm{wor}}(\mathbb{N}) = \mathrm{e}^{\mathrm{wor}}(\mathbb{N}, \varphi_{ls}) = \delta \sqrt{\|S(N^* N)^{-1} S^*\|}.$$

Proof We can assume that $\|S(N^* N)^{-1} S^*\| > 0$ since otherwise $S \equiv 0$ and the theorem is trivially true. Let $\bar{h} = (N^* N)^{-1} S^* \bar{g}$ and $h = \bar{h}/\|\bar{h}\|_F$. Observe that then $\|S(\bar{h})\| = \|S(N^* N)^{-1} S^*\|$ and

$$\begin{aligned}
\|N(\bar{h})\|_Y &= \langle N(N^* N)^{-1} S^* \bar{g}, N(N^* N)^{-1} S^* \bar{g} \rangle_Y^{1/2} \\
&= \langle S(N^* N)^{-1} S^* \bar{g}, \bar{g} \rangle^{1/2} = \|S(N^* N)^{-1} S^*\|^{1/2}.
\end{aligned}$$

Hence the condition (2.35) gives $\delta \le \|N(h)\|_Y$, and consequently

$$\begin{aligned}
\mathrm{rad}^{\mathrm{wor}}(\mathbb{N}; E) &\ge \mathrm{rad}^{\mathrm{wor}}(\mathbb{N}, [-h, h]) \\
&= \sup \{ \|S(f)\| \mid f \in [-h, h], \|N(f)\|_Y \le \delta \} \\
&= \delta \frac{\|S(h)\|}{\|N(h)\|} = \delta \|S(N^* N)^{-1} S^*\|^{1/2}.
\end{aligned}$$

On the other hand, for any f, the least squares algorithm gives

$$\sup_{\|x\|_Y \le \delta} \|S(f) - \varphi_{ls}(N(f) + x)\| = \sup_{\|x\|_Y \le \delta} \|SN^{-1}P_N x\|$$

$$= \delta \|SN^{-1}P_N\| = \delta \|S(N^*N)^{-1}S^*\|^{1/2},$$

and the theorem follows. $\qquad\qquad\qquad\qquad\qquad\qquad\qquad\qquad\square$

Example 2.6.1 Consider the case where $F = G$ and S is the identity operator, $S = I$. That is, we want to approximate f from the unit ball of F. In this case, the condition (2.35) takes the form $\delta \le \lambda_{\min}^{1/2}$ where $\lambda_{\min}$ is the minimal eigenvalue of N^*N. For such δ we have $\mathrm{rad}^{\mathrm{wor}}(\mathbb{N}) = \delta \lambda_{\min}^{-1/2}$. On the other hand, for $\delta \ge \lambda_{\min}^{1/2}$ we have $\mathrm{rad}^{\mathrm{wor}}(\mathbb{N}) \ge \delta$ and the error δ is achieved by the zero algorithm. Hence

$$\mathrm{rad}^{\mathrm{wor}}(\mathbb{N}) = \min\left\{1, \frac{\delta}{\sqrt{\lambda_{\min}}}\right\}.$$

For small noise level, $\delta \le \lambda_{\min}^{1/2}$, the least squares algorithm is optimal. Otherwise information is useless—zero is the best approximation.

We also note that if the unit ball E is replaced by the whole space F, then φ_{ls} is optimal for any $\delta \ge 0$.

Unfortunately, in general, the least squares algorithm can be arbitrarily bad. For instance, for the one dimensional problem of Example 2.5.1 we have $\varphi_{ls}(y) = y$. Hence the error of φ_{ls} equals $e^{\mathrm{wor}}(\mathbb{N}, \varphi_{ls}) = \delta$, while $\mathrm{rad}^{\mathrm{wor}}(\mathbb{N}) = \min\{a, \delta\}$. Consequently,

$$\frac{e^{\mathrm{wor}}(\mathbb{N}, \varphi_{ls})}{\mathrm{rad}^{\mathrm{wor}}(\mathbb{N})} \to +\infty \qquad \text{as} \qquad \frac{a}{\delta} \to 0.$$

Observe also that the solution of (2.34) is in general not unique and therefore the least squares algorithm φ_{ls} is not uniquely determined.

A simple modification of the least squares algorithm relies on *regularization* of the normal equations (2.34). That is, instead of (2.34) we solve 'perturbed' linear equations

$$(\omega I + N^*N)f = N^*y, \qquad\qquad\qquad (2.36)$$

where $I : F \to F$ is the identity operator and $\omega > 0$ is a *regularization parameter*. Then the solution $u_\omega(y)$ of (2.36) exists and is unique for any y. Moreover, it turns out that for a properly chosen parameter ω the *regularization algorithm* $S(u_\omega(y))$ is optimal. Indeed, we have the following fact.

Lemma 2.6.3 *For $0 < \alpha < 1$, the α-smoothing spline is the regularized solution, i.e.,*

$$\mathbf{s}_\alpha(y) \;=\; u_\omega(y) \;=\; (\,\omega I + N^* N\,)^{-1} N^* y$$

where $\omega = \alpha\,(1-\alpha)^{-1}\delta^2$. Or, equivalently, u_ω is the α-smoothing spline with $\alpha = \omega(\omega + \delta^2)^{-1}$.

Proof Let $\alpha \in (0,1)$. Define the Hilbert space $\tilde{F} = F \times \mathbb{R}^n$ with the extended norm

$$\|(f,y)\|^2 \;=\; \omega\,\|f\|_F^2 + \|y\|_Y^2,$$

where $\omega = \alpha(1 - \alpha)^{-1}\delta^2$. We know from Theorem 2.5.3 that $\mathbf{s}_\alpha(y)$ is the α-smoothing spline iff

$$\|(0,y) - (\mathbf{s}_\alpha(y))\| \;=\; \min_{f \in F} \|(0,y) - (f, N(f))\|.$$

As in (2.34) we can show that $\mathbf{s}_\alpha(y)$ is the solution of

$$\tilde{N}^* \tilde{N} f \;=\; \tilde{N}^* \tilde{y},$$

where the information operator $\tilde{N} : F \to \tilde{F}$ is defined by $\tilde{N}(f) = (f, N(f))$, and $\tilde{y} = (0, y)$. Since $\tilde{N}^* \tilde{y} = N^* y$ and $\tilde{N}^* \tilde{N} = \omega I + N^* N$, the lemma follows. $\qquad\square$

Thus the well known technique of regularization leads to the smoothing spline algorithms. Observe that the optimal value of the regularization parameter ω is the same as the γ in Lemma 2.6.1.

Example 2.6.2 Let $F = G$ with the complete orthonormal basis $\{\xi_i\}_{i\geq 1}$. Let

$$S(f) \;=\; \sum_{i=1}^{\infty} \beta_i \langle f, \xi_i \rangle_F \xi_i,$$

with $\beta_1 \geq \beta_2 \geq \cdots \geq 0$, and information consist of noisy evaluations of the Fourier coefficients, i.e.,

$$N(f) \;=\; [\,\langle f, \xi_1 \rangle_F, \dots, \langle f, \xi_n \rangle_F\,]$$

and $\mathbb{N}(f) = \{N(f) + x \mid \|x\|_2 \leq \delta\}$ (where $\|\cdot\|_2$ stands for the Euclidean norm). We also assume, for simplicity, that $\delta \leq 1$. In view of Corollary 2.6.2, the optimal α is in this case

$$\alpha^* \;=\; \frac{\beta_{n+1}^2}{\beta_{n+1}^2 + \delta^2(\beta_1^2 - \beta_{n+1}^2)}.$$

Hence for $\beta_1 = \beta_{n+1}$ the zero algorithm is optimal, while for $\beta_{n+1} = 0$ we obtain optimality of the least squares algorithm. Let $\beta_1 > \beta_{n+1} > 0$. Then the regularization algorithm with the parameter

$$\omega^* = \frac{\beta_{n+1}}{\beta_1 - \beta_{n+1}}$$

is an optimal algorithm.

Observe that for $\delta \to 0^+$ we have $\alpha^* \to 1$. However, the regularization parameter ω^* is constant. This seems to contradict the intuition that ω^* decreases with δ.

Clearly, we can always apply the algorithm $\varphi_\omega(y) = S(u_\omega(y))$ with $\omega = \delta^2$. Then $\omega \to 0^+$ as $\delta \to 0^+$ and $e^{\text{wor}}(\mathbb{N}, \varphi_\omega) \le \sqrt{2}\,\text{rad}^{\text{wor}}(\mathbb{N})$.

2.6.3 Polynomial splines

In this subsection we recall the classical result that for an appropriately chosen space F, polynomial splines are also α-smoothing splines.

Let $a < b$ and knots $a \le t_1 < t_2 < \cdots < t_m \le b$ be given. A *polynomial spline* of order $r \ge 1$ corresponding to the knots t_i is a function $\mathbf{p} : [a, b] \to \mathbb{R}$ satisfying the following conditions:

(a) $\mathbf{p} \in \Pi_{2r-1}$ on each subinterval $[a, t_1]$, $[t_m, b]$, and $[t_i, t_{i+1}]$ for $1 \le i \le m - 1$,

(b) $\mathbf{p}$ has continuous $(2r - 2)$nd derivative on $[a, b]$.

(Here Π_k is the space of polynomials of degree at most k.) A polynomial spline is called *natural* if, in addition,

(c) $\mathbf{p}^{(i)}(a) = 0 = \mathbf{p}^{(i)}(b)$ for $r \le i \le 2r - 2$, and also $\mathbf{p}^{2r-1}(a) = 0$ if $a < t_1$, and $\mathbf{p}^{2r-1}(b) = 0$ if $t_m < b$.

If instead of (c) we have

(d) $\mathbf{p}^{(i)}(a) = \mathbf{p}^{(i)}(b)$ for $1 \le i \le 2r - 2$, and also $\mathbf{p}^{(2r-1)}(a) = \mathbf{p}^{(2r-1)}(b)$ in the case $a < t_1$, $t_m < b$,

then the polynomial spline is called *periodic*.

Let $W_r(a, b)$ be the Sobolev space of functions f defined on $[a, b]$ that have absolutely continuous $(r-1)$st derivative and square integrable rth derivative,

$$W_r(a, b) = \{\, f : [a, b] \to \mathbb{R} \mid f^{(r-1)} \text{ is abs. cont.}, \ f^{(r)} \in \mathcal{L}_2(a, b) \,\}.$$

Similarly, let $\tilde{W}_r(a, b)$ be the space of functions from $W_r(a, b)$ that can be extended to $(b-a)$-periodic functions on $\mathbb{R}$ with $r-1$ continuous derivatives,

$$\tilde{W}_r(a,b) = \{ f \in W_r(a,b) \mid f^{(i)}(a) = f^{(i)}(b),\ 0 \le i \le r-1 \}.$$

Note that natural and periodic polynomial splines belong to $W_r(a,b)$ and $\tilde{W}_r(a,b)$, respectively. They are also α-smoothing splines in these spaces, provided that information is given by noisy function values at t_is. This fact follows from the following two well known lemmas. For completeness, we add the proofs.

Lemma 2.6.4 *If a function $f \in W_r(a,b)$ (or $f \in \tilde{W}_r(a,b)$) vanishes at t_i,*

$$f(t_i) = 0, \qquad 1 \le i \le m,$$

then for any natural (periodic) polynomial spline $\mathbf{p}$ of order r we have

$$\int_a^b f^{(r)}(x)\mathbf{p}^{(r)}(x)\,dx = 0.$$

Proof Integrating by parts we get

$$\int_a^b f^{(r)}(x)\mathbf{p}^{(r)}(x)\,dx = f^{(r-1)}(x)\mathbf{p}^{(r)}(x)\Big|_a^b - \int_a^b f^{(r-1)}(x)\mathbf{p}^{(r+1)}(x)\,dx.$$

Observe that $f^{(r-1)}(x)\mathbf{p}^{(r)}(x)\big|_a^b = 0$, no matter whether we have the periodic or the nonperiodic case. Proceeding in this way we obtain

$$\int_a^b f^{(r)}(x)\mathbf{p}^{(r)}(x)\,dx = -\int_a^b f^{(r-1)}(x)\mathbf{p}^{(r+1)}(x)\,dx$$

$$= \cdots = (-1)^i \int_a^b f^{(r-i)}(x)\mathbf{p}^{(r+i)}(x)\,dx$$

$$= \cdots = \int_a^b f'(x)\mathbf{p}^{(2r-1)}(x)\,dx. \qquad (2.37)$$

The function $\mathbf{p}^{(2r-1)}$ is piecewise constant. Write $t_0 = a$, $t_{m+1} = b$, and let p_i denote the value of $\mathbf{p}^{(2r-1)}$ on the interval (t_i, t_{i+1}) for $0 \le i \le m$ (for $a = t_1$ we set $p_0 = p_1$, and for $t_m = b$ we set $p_m = p_{m-1}$). Then (2.37) is equivalent to

$$\sum_{i=0}^m p_i\left(f(t_{i+1}) - f(t_i) \right) = p_m f(b) - p_0 f(a) = 0,$$

as claimed. $\qquad\square$

Lemma 2.6.5 *Let $f \in W_r(a,b)$ (or $f \in \tilde{W}_r(a,b)$). Then there exists a natural (periodic) polynomial spline $\mathbf{p}_f$ of order r such that*

$$\mathbf{p}_f(t_i) = f(t_i), \qquad 1 \le i \le m.$$

The spline $\mathbf{p}_f$ is determined uniquely for all $m \ge r$ (or for all $m \ge 1$). Moreover,

$$\int_a^b (\mathbf{p}_f^{(r)}(x))^2 \, dx \le \int_a^b (f^{(r)}(x))^2 \, dx.$$

Proof In the nonperiodic case with $m < r$ we can take as $\mathbf{p}_f$ any polynomial p of degree at most $r - 1$ satisfying $p(t_i) = f(t_i)$, $\forall i$. Therefore we can assume in the nonperiodic case that $m \ge r$.

We first show that $\mathbf{p} = 0$ is the unique spline that vanishes at t_i, $1 \le i \le m$. Indeed, if for a natural (periodic) spline we have $\mathbf{p}(t_i) = 0$, $\forall i$, then by Lemma 2.6.4 with $f = \mathbf{p}$ we have $\int_a^b (\mathbf{p}^{(r)}(x))^2 dx = 0$. Thus we have $\mathbf{p}^{(r)} = 0$, and $\mathbf{p}$ is a polynomial of degree at most $r-1$ that vanishes at m different points. In the nonperiodic case we have $m \ge r$ which means that $\mathbf{p} = 0$. In the periodic case, $\mathbf{p}$ satisfies $\mathbf{p}^{(i)}(a) = \mathbf{p}^{(i)}(b)$, $0 \le i \le r - 1$. Then it must be of the form

$$\mathbf{p}(x) = \sum_{i=0}^{r-1} \beta_i (x - a)^i = \sum_{i=0}^{r-1} \beta_i (x - b)^i.$$

This in turn means that $\mathbf{p}$ is a constant polynomial that vanishes at at least one point. Hence $p = 0$, as claimed.

Observe now that to find all the coefficients of the (natural or periodic) spline that interpolates f, we have to solve a system of linear equations with the number of unknowns equal to the number of equations. The necessary and sufficient condition for the system to have a unique solution is that zero must be the only solution of the homogeneous system. However, this is the case since the homogeneous system corresponds to $f = 0$.

To show the second part of the lemma, observe that by Lemma 2.6.4 (with f replaced by $f - \mathbf{p}_f$) we have $\int_a^b \mathbf{p}_f^{(r)}(x)(f^{(r)}(x) - \mathbf{p}_f^{(r)}(x)) \, dx = 0$. Hence

$$\int_a^b (f^{(r)}(x))^2 dx = \int_a^b (\mathbf{p}_f^{(r)}(x))^2 dx + \int_a^b (f^{(r)}(x) - \mathbf{p}_f^{(r)}(x))^2 dx$$

$$\ge \int_a^b (\mathbf{p}_f^{(r)}(x))^2 dx,$$

which completes the proof. $\qquad\qquad\qquad\qquad\qquad\qquad\qquad\qquad \square$

Now let $F = W_r(a, b)$ (or $F = \tilde{W}_r(a, b)$) with the seminorm $\| \cdot \|_F$ which is generated by the semi–inner–product

$$\langle f_1, f_2 \rangle_F = \int_a^b f_1^{(r)}(x) \, f_2^{(r)}(x) \, dx.$$

We consider the problem with an arbitrary linear solution operator S : $F \to G$ and information $\mathbb{N}$ of the form

$$\mathbb{N}(f) = \{ y \in \mathbb{R}^n \mid \| y - N(f) \|_Y \le \delta \},$$

where

$$N(f) = [\underbrace{f(t_1), \ldots, f(t_1)}_{k_1}, \ldots, \underbrace{f(t_m), \ldots, f(t_m)}_{k_m}],$$

$\sum_{i=1}^m k_i = n$, and $\| \cdot \|_Y$ is a Hilbert norm in $\mathbb{R}^n$.

Theorem 2.6.3 *Let $\mathbf{p}_y$ be the natural (periodic) polynomial spline of order r minimizing*

$$\Gamma_\alpha(\mathbf{p}, y) = \alpha \int_a^b (\mathbf{p}^{(r)}(x))^2 \, dx + \delta^{-2}(1 - \alpha) \| y - N(\mathbf{p}) \|_Y^2.$$

Then $\mathbf{p}_y$ is the α-smoothing spline.

Proof It follows from Theorem 2.5.3(i) that the α-smoothing spline $\mathbf{s}_\alpha(y)$ exists. We choose $\mathbf{p}$ to be the natural (periodic) polynomial spline of order r satisfying $\mathbf{p}(t_i) = \mathbf{s}_\alpha(y)(t_i)$, $1 \le i \le m$. By Lemma 2.6.5 we have $\| \mathbf{p} \|_F \le \| \mathbf{s}_\alpha(y) \|_F$. This means that $\Gamma_\alpha(\mathbf{p}, y) \le \Gamma_\alpha(\mathbf{s}_\alpha(y), y)$ and $\mathbf{p}$ is the α-smoothing spline. $\qquad \square$

Thus the search for the α-smoothing spline can be restricted to the (finite dimensional) subspace of polynomial splines.

We conclude that for $\alpha = 1/2$ the algorithm $\varphi_{1/2}(y) = S(\mathbf{p}_y)$ is at most $\sqrt{2}$ times worse than optimal. If G is a Hilbert space then

$$\mathrm{rad}^{\mathrm{wor}}(\mathbb{N})$$
$$= \sup \left\{ \| S(f) \| \, \Big| \, \int_a^b (f^{(r)}(x))^2 \, dx \le 1, \ \| y - N(f) \|_Y \le \delta \right\}.$$

However, the optimal value of α is in this case not explicitly known, even for as simple a problem as integration.

2.6.4 Splines in r.k.h.s.

In this subsection we consider smoothing splines in function spaces where function evaluations are continuous functionals. Such spaces have a nice characterization which we briefly recall.

Let $\mathcal{T}$ be a given set of indices, e.g., $\mathcal{T} = [0, 1]$, and $R : \mathcal{T} \times \mathcal{T} \to \mathbb{R}$ a symmetric and nonnegative definite function [1]. It is known that there exists a uniquely determined Hilbert space H_R of functions $f : \mathcal{T} \to \mathbb{R}$ such that for any $t \in \mathcal{T}$, $f \mapsto f(t)$ is a continuous linear functional whose representer in H_R is $L_t = R(\cdot, t)$. That is,

$$f(t) = \langle f, L_t \rangle_R, \qquad f \in H_R,$$

where $\langle \cdot, \cdot \rangle_R$ is the inner product in H_R.

The space H_R is called a *reproducing kernel Hilbert space* with *reproducing kernel* R, or r.k.h.s. with r.k. R, for brevity. It consists of all linear combinations of the functions L_t, $t \in \mathcal{T}$, and their limits with respect to the norm $\| \cdot \|_R = \sqrt{\langle \cdot, \cdot \rangle_R}$, where

$$\left\langle \sum_{i=1}^{n} \alpha_i L_{t_i}, \sum_{j=1}^{k} \beta_j L_{s_j} \right\rangle_R = \sum_{i=1}^{n} \sum_{j=1}^{k} \alpha_i \beta_j R(t_i, s_j).$$

On the other hand, with any Hilbert space H of functions $f : \mathcal{T} \to \mathbb{R}$ possessing the property that the functionals $f \mapsto f(t)$ are continuous, we can associate a uniquely determined r.k. R such that $H = H_R$ is an r.k.h.s., namely,

$$R(s, t) = \langle L_s, L_t \rangle_H, \qquad s, t \in \mathcal{T},$$

where $L_t \in H$ is the representer of function evaluation at t. Hence there exists a one-to-one correspondence between symmetric nonnegative functions and Hilbert spaces in which function evaluations are continuous functionals.

Example 2.6.3 Let $a < b$ and $r \geq 1$. Define the separable Hilbert space $W_r^0(a, b)$ as

$$W_r^0(a, b) = \{ f : [a, b] \to \mathbb{R} \mid f^{(r-1)} \text{ is abs. cont.},$$
$$f^{(i)}(a) = 0, \, 0 \leq i \leq r - 1, \, f^{(r)} \in \mathcal{L}_2(a, b) \},$$

with inner product $\langle f_1, f_2 \rangle_{W_r} = \int_a^b f_1^{(r)}(u) f_2^{(r)}(u) \, du$. Then $W_r^0(a, b)$ is

---

[1] This means that for any $n \geq 1$ and $t_i \in \mathcal{T}$, $1 \leq i \leq n$, the matrix $\{R(t_i, t_j)\}_{i,j=1}^{n}$ is symmetric and nonnegative definite.

an r.k.h.s. with r.k.

$$R(s,t) = R_{r-1}(s,t) = \int_a^b G_{r-1}(s,u)\, G_{r-1}(t,u)\, du,$$

where

$$G_{r-1}(t,u) = \frac{(t-u)_+^{r-1}}{(r-1)!}$$

and $x_+ = \max\{x, 0\}$.

Indeed, applying the formula $f(t) = \int_a^t f'(u)\, du$ r times we obtain

$$f(t) = \int_a^b \frac{(t-u)_+^{r-1}}{(r-1)!}\, f^{(r)}(u)\, du = \int_a^b G_{r-1}(t,u)\, f^{(r)}(u)\, du. \quad (2.38)$$

Hence $f \mapsto f(t)$ is a continuous functional with

$$|f(t)| \leq \sqrt{\int_a^b |G_{r-1}(t,u)|^2 du} \cdot \|f\|_{W_r}.$$

Letting $f = L_t$ (the representer of evaluation at t) in (2.38), we get that $L_t^{(r)}(u) = G_{r-1}(t,u)$ and

$$R_{r-1}(s,t) = \langle L_s, L_t \rangle_{W_r} = \int_a^b G_{r-1}(t,u)\, G_{r-1}(s,u)\, du,$$

as claimed.

In particular, for $r = 1$ we have $R_0(s,t) = \min\{s,t\}$.

The fact that any r.k.h.s. is determined by its r.k. R allows us to write the formulas for the α-smoothing spline in terms of R. That is, using Lemma 2.6.1 we immediately obtain the following theorem.

Theorem 2.6.4 *Let $F = H$ be an r.k.h.s. with r.k. $R : T \times T \to \mathbb{R}$. Let information $y = N(f) + x$, where*

$$N(f) = [f(t_1), f(t_2), \dots, f(t_n)],$$

for $t_i \in T$, $1 \leq i \leq n$, and $\|x\|_2 \leq \delta$. Define the matrix

$$R_{t_1 \dots t_n} = \{R(t_i, t_j)\}_{i,j=1}^n.$$

Then the α-smoothing spline is given as

$$\mathbf{s}_\alpha(y) = \sum_{j=1}^n z_j R(t_j, \cdot),$$

where $(\gamma I + R_{t_1 \dots t_n})z = y$ and $\gamma = \alpha(1 - \alpha)^{-1}\delta^2$.

Observe that the values of $s_\alpha(y)$ at t_i, $1 \le i \le n$, are equal to $N(s_\alpha(y)) = R_{t_1 \dots t_n} z = y - \gamma z$. Hence the spline is the function from span$\{R(t_i, \cdot)\}_{1 \le i \le n}$ that interpolates data $\{t_i, w_i\}_{i=1}^n$, where $w_i = y_i - \gamma z_i$ are obtained by smoothing the original data y.

Finally, we discuss the case when $H = W_r^0 = W_r^0(0,1)$ is the r.k.h.s. of Example 2.6.3. Since we now have $L_t^{(r)}(s) = G_{r-1}(t,s)$, the representer of evaluation at t is a polynomial spline,

$$L_t(s) = (-1)^r \frac{(t-s)_+^{2r-1}}{(2r-1)!} + \sum_{j=0}^{r-1} (-1)^j \frac{t^{r+j} s^{r-j-1}}{(r+j)!(r-j-1)!}.$$

We have that $s_\alpha(y)$ is the unique polynomial spline of order r corresponding to the knots t_i, $1 \le i \le n$, that satisfies the linear boundary conditions $s_\alpha^{(i)}(0) = 0$ for $0 \le i \le r-1$, and $s_\alpha^{(r)}(1) = 0$, and interpolates data $\{t_i, w_i\}_{i,j=1}^n$.

Notes and remarks

NR 2.6.1 The theory of polynomial splines can be traced back to the paper of Schoenberg (1946) who introduced these functions. The minimal norm properties of polynomial splines presented in Subsection 2.6.3 were first discovered by Holladay (1957). Since that time splines have become well known and have been studied from different viewpoints in approximation theory, numerical analysis and statistics. A partial list of contributions includes Golomb and Weinberger (1959), Greville (1969), Schoenberg (1964a, 1964b), and Schoenberg and Greville (1965). A thorough study and history of the field may be found in the monographs Schoenberg (1973) and Schumaker (1981). See also Steckin and Subbotin (1976).

NR 2.6.2 Smoothing splines and, in particular, polynomial splines are commonly studied in numerical analysis and statistics in the context of smoothing experimental data. Continuous as well as discrete problems are considered. The main question there is how to choose the smoothing (regularization) parameter. To this end, special methods have been developed. They include the discrepancy principle, ordinary and generalized cross-validation, and methods based on the so-called L-curve, see e.g. Golub et al. (1979), Hansen (1992), Morozow (1984), Wahba (1990) and references there. We note that most of those methods are based on the assumption that the noise level δ is unknown. Consequently, the choice of the smoothing (regularization) parameter depends also on the data y, and the resulting algorithms for approximating $S(f)$ are usually nonlinear in y. Moreover, in the sense of the worst case setting they can be far from optimal; see E 2.6.7.

NR 2.6.3 The formulas for the smoothing spline $s_\alpha(y)$ are well known for specific assumptions on the space F. Results on the optimal choice of the parameter α of Subsection 2.6.1 are new.

NR 2.6.4 The worst case optimality of the least squares algorithm in the case when $F = G = \mathbb{R}^n$, $S = I$ and E is the whole space, $E = \mathbb{R}^n$, was shown by Kacewicz *et al.* (1986). The more general Theorem 2.6.2 is, however, new.

Readers interested in numerical realization of the least squares algorithm are referred to Björck (1990), Kiełbasiński and Schwetlick (1988), or Lawson and Hanson (1974).

NR 2.6.5 Regularization was originally proposed by Tikhonov as a method of 'solving' ill-posed problems, see e.g. Tikhonov (1963) and Tikhonov and Arsenin (1979). We note that ill-posed problems in the worst case setting were studied by Werschulz (1987) (see also Werschulz, 1991). He proved, in particular, that if the solution operator S is unbounded then it cannot be approximated with finite error.

The relation between regularization and smoothing splines given in Lemma 2.6.3 seems to be new.

NR 2.6.6 Reproducing kernel Hilbert spaces are studied, e.g., in Aronszajn (1950), Parzen (1962, 1963), Vakhania *et al.* (1987), Wahba (1990).

NR 2.6.7 In the multivariate case, r.k.h.s.'s can be defined as tensor products of r.k.h.s.'s in the univariate case. More precisely, let H_i be the r.k.h.s. of functions $f : [a_i, b_i] \to \mathbb{R}$, and R_i be its r.k., $1 \leq i \leq d$. Then the tensor product H of the H_is, $H = \bigotimes_{i=1}^{d} H_i$, is the r.k.h.s. of functions

$$f : [a_1, b_1] \times \cdots \times [a_d, b_d] \to \mathbb{R}$$

with r.k. $R(s, t) = \prod_{i=1}^{d} R_i(s_i, t_i)$, $s = (s_1, \ldots, s_d), t = (t_1, \ldots, t_d) \in [0, 1]^d$.

For instance, if H_i is the space $W_{r_i}^0 = W_{r_i}^0(0, 1)$ of Example 2.6.3, then the tensor product space H is given as follows. Let

$$D^{i_1 \cdots i_d} f = \frac{\partial^{i_1 + \cdots + i_d}}{\partial x_1^{i_1} \ldots \partial x_d^{i_d}} f.$$

Then

$$
\begin{aligned}
H = W_{r_1 \cdots r_d}^{0 \ldots 0} = \{ &f : [0, 1]^d \to \mathbb{R} \mid \\
&D^{r_1 - 1 \cdots r_d - 1} f \text{ abs. cont.}, D^{r_1 \cdots r_d} f \in \mathcal{L}_2((0, 1)^d), \\
&D^{i_1 \cdots i_d} f(t) = 0, \ 0 \leq i_j \leq r_j - 1, \ 1 \leq j \leq d, \\
&\text{when one of the components of } t \text{ is zero} \}
\end{aligned}
$$

with inner product

$$\langle f_1, f_2 \rangle_{W_{r_1 \cdots r_d}} = \int_{[0,1]^d} (D^{r_1 \cdots r_d} f_1)(t)(D^{r_1 \cdots r_d} f_2)(t) \, dt.$$

Exercises

E 2.6.1 Suppose one approximates a vector $f \in E \subset \mathbb{R}^n$ based on information $y = f + x$, where $x \in B$ and $B \subset \mathbb{R}^n$ is a convex, balanced and bounded set. Let $h \in \mathbb{R}^n$ be such that $h \in \overline{B}$ and

$$\|h\|_2 = r(B) = \sup_{x \in B} \|x\|_2.$$

Show that if the interval $[-h, h]$ is a subset of $\overline{B}$ then the identity algorithm, $\varphi(y) = y$, is optimal and its error equals $r(B)$.

E 2.6.2 One can consider a modified least squares algorithm, $\varphi_{\mathrm{md}}(y) = S(\mathsf{s}_{\mathrm{md}}(y))$, where $\mathsf{s}_{\mathrm{md}}(y) \in E$ and

$$\|y - N(\mathsf{s}_{\mathrm{md}}(y))\|_Y = \inf_{f \in E} \|y - N(f)\|_Y,$$

i.e., the minimization is taken over the set E instead of the whole space F. Show that

$$e^{\mathrm{wor}}(\mathbb{N}, \varphi_{\mathrm{md}}) \leq 2 \cdot \mathrm{rad}^{\mathrm{wor}}(\mathbb{N}),$$

but that this algorithm is in general not linear.

E 2.6.3 Consider the problem of Corollary 2.6.2 with $\lambda_s > \lambda_t$. Show that if the information is exact ($\delta = 0$), then the algorithm $\varphi_\gamma(y) = \sum_{j=1}^n z_j S(f_j)$, where $(\gamma \Sigma + G_N) z = y$, is optimal for any

$$\gamma \in \left[0, \frac{\eta_s \lambda_t}{\lambda_s - \lambda_t} \right].$$

E 2.6.4 Let S and N be linear functionals on $F = \mathbb{R}^2$, i.e., $S = \langle \cdot, s \rangle_2$ and $N = \langle \cdot, v \rangle_2$ for some $s, v \in \mathbb{R}^2$. Consider approximation of $S(f)$ for f from the unit ball based on information $y = N(f) + x$ with $|x| \leq \delta$. What is the optimal value of the regularization parameter γ^* in this case? In particular, show that if s and v are linearly independent and not orthogonal, then γ^* is positive, but tends to zero linearly as $\delta \to 0^+$.

E 2.6.5 Let F be a Hilbert space with inner product $\langle \cdot, \cdot \rangle_F$. Let the set E be the ellipsoid

$$E = \{ f \in F \mid \langle Bf, f \rangle_F \leq 1 \},$$

where $B : F \to F$ is a self-adjoint and positive definite operator. Let the information operator be defined as

$$\mathbb{N}(f) = \{ N(f) + x \mid \|Dx\|_2 \leq \delta \},$$

where $N : F \to \mathbb{R}^n$ and $D : \mathbb{R}^n \to \mathbb{R}^n$ are continuous linear operators. Show that then the α-smoothing spline (if it exists) is the solution of the linear system

$$(\omega B + N^* D^* D N) f = N^* D^* y$$

where $\omega = \alpha(1 - \alpha)^{-1} \delta^2$.

E 2.6.6 Show that if the operator B in the previous exercise is compact then the α-smoothing spline does not necessarily exist.

E 2.6.7 The smoothing parameter α_{cv} given by (ordinary) cross-validation is determined by the following condition:

$$\alpha_{\mathrm{cv}} = \alpha_{\mathrm{cv}}(y) = \arg \min_{0 \leq \alpha \leq 1} \|y - N(\mathsf{s}_\alpha(y))\|_Y.$$

Show that the algorithm $\varphi_{\mathrm{cv}}(y) = S(\mathsf{s}_{\alpha_{\mathrm{cv}}})(y)$ is in general not optimal and that the ratio $e^{\mathrm{wor}}(\mathbb{N}, \varphi_{\mathrm{cv}})/\mathrm{rad}^{\mathrm{wor}}(\mathbb{N})$ can be arbitrarily large.

E 2.6.8 Show that natural (periodic) polynomial splines are also ordinary splines for the problem of Theorem 2.6.3.

E 2.6.9 Find the natural (periodic) polynomial spline of order 1 that minimizes $\Gamma_\alpha(\mathbf{p}, y)$ in the case when $\alpha = 1/2$ and $\|\cdot\|_Y$ is the Euclidean norm.

E 2.6.10 Let $\mathcal{T} \subset \mathbb{R}$. Find the r.k.h.s. H_R for $R(s,t) = \delta_{st}$, $s, t \in \mathcal{T}$.

E 2.6.11 Show that in an r.k.h.s. the functionals $f \mapsto f(t_i)$, $1 \le i \le n$, are linearly dependent iff $\det\{R(t_i, t_j)\}_{i,j=1}^n = 0$.

E 2.6.12 Let H be an r.k.h.s. with positive r.k. R. Show that then the interpolation problem of finding $f \in \mathrm{span}\{R(t_1, \cdot), \ldots, R(t_n, \cdot)\}$ such that $f(t_i) = y_i$, $1 \le i \le n$, has a unique solution.

E 2.6.13 Show that the following functions are reproducing kernels:

$$
\begin{aligned}
R(s,t) &= 1 - |s - t|, & s, t \in [0,1], \\
R(s,t) &= \exp\{-|s-t|\}, & s, t \in [0,1], \\
R(s,t) &= (\,\|s\|_2 + \|t\|_2 - \|s - t\|_2\,)/2, & s, t \in [0,1]^d.
\end{aligned}
$$

E 2.6.14 Let the functions $R_i : [0,1] \times [0,1] \to \mathbb{R}$, $1 \le i \le d$, be symmetric and nonnegative definite. Show that then the function $R : [0,1]^d \times [0,1]^d \to \mathbb{R}$, $R(s,t) = \prod_{i=1}^d R_i(s_i, t_i)$ is also symmetric and nonnegative definite.

E 2.6.15 Let $0 < t_1 < t_2 < \cdots < t_n$ and $M = \{\min\{t_i, t_j\}\}_{i,j=1}^n$. Show that $M = M^* > 0$ and that the inverse M^{-1} is given as

$$
\begin{bmatrix}
\frac{1}{t_1} + \frac{1}{t_2 - t_1} & \frac{-1}{t_2 - t_1} & & & \\
\frac{-1}{t_2 - t_1} & \frac{1}{t_2 - t_1} + \frac{1}{t_3 - t_2} & \frac{-1}{t_3 - t_2} & & 0 \\
& \frac{-1}{t_3 - t_2} & \frac{1}{t_3 - t_2} + \frac{1}{t_4 - t_3} & \ddots & \\
& & \ddots & \ddots & \frac{-1}{t_n - t_{n-1}} \\
0 & & & \frac{-1}{t_n - t_{n-1}} & \frac{1}{t_n - t_{n-1}}
\end{bmatrix}
$$

2.7 Varying information

So far the information operator $\mathbb{N}$ has been regarded as given and we have been looking for the optimal algorithm. In this section, we assume that not only the algorithm but also the information operator can vary.

2.7.1 Nonadaptive and adaptive information

Let Λ be a given class of functionals over the space F. We assume that we can collect information about f only by noisy observations of functionals from Λ. Each such observation is performed with some precision which can also vary.

More specifically, a (noisy) *nonadaptive* information operator $\mathbb{N}$ is determined by an exact information operator $N : F \to \mathbb{R}^n$ of the form

$$
N(f) = [L_1(f), L_2(f), \ldots, L_n(f)], \qquad \forall f \in F,
$$

where the $L_i : F \to \mathbb{R}$ belong to the class Λ of *permissible functionals*, and by a *precision vector*

$$\Delta = [\delta_1, \delta_2, \ldots, \delta_n],$$

where $\delta_i \geq 0$, $1 \leq i \leq n$. When using N and Δ we obtain information $y = N(f) + x$, where the noise x is known to belong to a given set $B = B(\Delta, N(f))$ of $\mathbb{R}^n$. That is, the nonadaptive information operator $\mathbb{N}$ is identified with the pair $\{N, \Delta\}$,

$$\mathbb{N} = \{N, \Delta\},$$

and it is formally given as $\mathbb{N} : F \to 2^Y$, where $Y = \mathbb{R}^n$ and

$$\mathbb{N}(f) = \{y \in \mathbb{R}^n \mid x = (y - N(f)) \in B(\Delta, N(f))\}. \qquad (2.39)$$

We may consider, for instance,

$$B(\Delta, N(f)) = B(\Delta) = \{x \in \mathbb{R}^n \mid |x_i| \leq \delta_i, 1 \leq i \leq n\}, \qquad (2.40)$$

which means that for each i the value of $L_i(f)$ is observed with error δ_i, $|y_i - L_i(f)| \leq \delta_i$, or that the noise is bounded in a 'weighted' sup-norm. This definition of $B(\Delta, N(f))$ seems to be the most natural. However, we may also have a more complicated dependence of the noise on the precision vector, namely,

$$B(\Delta, N(f)) = B(\Delta) = \left\{ x \in \mathbb{R}^n \mid \sum_{i=1}^{n} \frac{x_i^2}{\delta_i^2} \leq 1 \right\}, \qquad (2.41)$$

which corresponds to noise bounded in the weighted Euclidean norm, or more generally,

$$B(\Delta, N(f))) = B(\Delta) = \left\{ x \in \mathbb{R}^n \mid \sum_{i=1}^{n} \frac{|x_i|^p}{\delta_i^p} \leq 1 \right\}, \quad p \geq 1. \qquad (2.42)$$

Contrary to (2.40), the bound on the noise x_i coming from the ith observation now depends on $x_1, \ldots, x_{i-1}$, since $|x_i| \leq (1 - \sum_{j=1}^{i-1} (|x_j|/\delta_j)^p)^{1/p}$. In particular, if $|x_1| = \delta_1$ then the next observations are performed exactly, $x_2 = \cdots = x_n = 0$.

In (2.40) to (2.42) the noise is independent of the exact information $N(f)$. The noise depends on $N(f)$ when, for instance, the relative error is considered. In this case,

$$B(\Delta, N(f)) = \{x \in \mathbb{R}^\infty \mid |x_i| \leq \delta_i |L_i(f)|, 1 \leq i \leq n\}. \qquad (2.43)$$

In general, we assume that the sets $B(\Delta, z)$, for $\Delta, z \in \mathbb{R}^n$ and $n \geq 1$, satisfy the following conditions.

(i) $B(0, z) = \{0\}$.
(ii) If $0 \leq \delta_i \leq \delta_i'$, $1 \leq i \leq n$, then

$$B([\delta_1, \ldots, \delta_n], z) \subset B([\delta_1', \ldots, \delta_n'], z).$$

(iii) Let $z^n = [z_1, \ldots, z_n]$, $\Delta^n = [\delta_1, \ldots, \delta_n]$, and $z^{n+1} = [z^n, z_{n+1}]$, $\Delta^{n+1} = [\Delta^n, \delta_{n+1}]$. Then

$$B(\Delta^n, z^n) = \{x \in \mathbb{R}^n \mid \exists a \in \mathbb{R} : [x, a] \in B(\Delta^{n+1}, z^{n+1})\}. \tag{2.44}$$

The first condition means that the zero precision vector corresponds to exact information. The second condition says that we decrease the noise by decreasing the precisions δ_i. The third condition indicates a relation between the noise of successive observations. It states that from the nth observation we can pass to the $(n + 1)$st observation. Indeed, suppose that there is a noise vector $x^n = (y^n - N^n(f)) \in B(\Delta^n, N^n(f))$ that cannot be extended to $[x^n, a] \in B(\Delta^{n+1}, N^{n+1}(f))$. This means that the noisy observation of $L_{n+1}(f)$ is impossible. Similarly, suppose that for some $x^{n+1} = (y^{n+1} - N^{n+1}(f)) \in B(\Delta^{n+1}, N^{n+1}(f))$ we have $x^n = (y^n - N^n(f)) \notin B(\Delta^n, N^n(f))$. Then y^n is not information about f, although this vector comes from the first n observations.

We leave it as an exercise to show that all three conditions are satisfied by the noises defined by (2.40) to (2.43).

We also admit a more general class of adaptive information where decisions about successive observations are made based on previously obtained values y_i. The effect of adaption can be obtained by adaptive choice of

• information functionals L_i, or
• precisions δ_i, or
• the number n of observations.

Formally, a (noisy) *adaptive* information operator $\mathbb{N} : F \to 2^Y$ is determined by a family $N = \{N_y\}_{y \in Y}$ of exact information operators of the form

$$N_y = [L_1(\cdot), L_2(\cdot; y_1), \ldots, L_{n(y)}(\cdot; y_1, \ldots, y_{n(y)-1})],$$

where the functionals $L_i(\cdot; y_1, \ldots, y_{i-1}) \in \Lambda$, and a family $\Delta = \{\Delta_y\}_{y \in Y}$

of precision vectors,

$$\Delta_y = [\delta_1, \delta_2(y_1), \ldots, \delta_{n(y)}(y_1, \ldots, y_{n(y)-1})].$$

Here, $n(y)$ is the length of y, i.e., $y = [y_1, \ldots, y_{n(y)}]$. We also assume that the set Y (the range of $\mathbb{N}$) satisfies the following condition:

for any $(y_1, y_2, \ldots) \in \mathbb{R}^\infty$ there exists exactly one index n

such that $(y_1, \ldots, y_n) \in Y$.   (2.45)

Hence the functionals $L_i(\cdot; y_1, \ldots, y_{i-1})$ and precisions $\delta_i(y_1, \ldots, y_i)$ are defined for $(y_1, \ldots, y_i)$ such that $(y_i, \ldots, y_j) \notin Y_j$, $1 \leq j \leq i-1$.

For the noisy adaptive information operator $\mathbb{N} = \{N, \Delta\}$ we have

$$\mathbb{N}(f) = \{ y \in Y \mid x = (y - N_y(f)) \in B(\Delta_y, N_y(f)) \}.$$

The essence of the definition above is as follows. At the ith step of gaining information, we observe a noisy value y_i of $L_i(f; y_1, \ldots, y_{i-1})$ with precision $\delta_i(y_1, \ldots, y_{i-1})$. Then we check whether the condition $[y_1, \ldots, y_i] \in Y$ is satisfied[1]. If the answer is 'yes', the observations are terminated and $[y_1, \ldots, y_i]$ is noisy information about f. Otherwise we proceed to the $(i+1)$st step. Note that (2.45) ensures that the observations will be terminated after a finite number of steps. The resulting information y about f satisfies $(y - N_y(f)) \in B(\Delta_y, N_y(f))$, as though we had used nonadaptive information $\{N_y, \Delta_y\}$.

Clearly, any nonadaptive information $\mathbb{N} = \{N, \Delta\}$ of the form (2.39) can be considered as adaptive since then $Y = \mathbb{R}^n$, $N_y = N$, and $\Delta_y = \Delta$, $\forall y \in Y$.

To stress what kind of information we are dealing with, we sometimes add the superscripts 'ad' and 'non', and write $\mathbb{N}^{\mathrm{ad}}$ and $\mathbb{N}^{\mathrm{non}}$ for adaptive and nonadaptive information, respectively.

2.7.2 When does adaption not help?

It is clear that adaptive information has a much richer structure than nonadaptive information. So we might expect that it should lead to better approximations. This is, however, not always true. We shall give a sufficient condition under which adaption does not help much.

For an (in general adaptive) information operator $\mathbb{N} : F \to 2^Y$, let

---

[1] This is what in computational practice is often called a *termination criterion* or *stopping rule*.

$Y_0 = \bigcup_{f \in E} \mathbb{N}(f) \subset Y$ be the set of all possible information values. For $y \in Y_0$, let

$$A_\mathbb{N}(y) = \{ S(f) \mid f \in E, \ y \in \mathbb{N}(f) \}.$$

We shall say that $f^* \in E$ is a κ-*hard element* iff for any nonadaptive information operator $\mathbb{N} = \{N, \Delta\}$ of the form (2.39) we have

$$\mathrm{rad}^{\mathrm{wor}}(\mathbb{N}) \leq \kappa \cdot r(A_\mathbb{N}(N(f^*))).$$

(Recall that $r(B)$ is the usual radius of the set B, see Section 2.3.) Note that if f^* is a κ-hard element then it is also a κ_1-hard element for all $\kappa_1 > \kappa$.

Suppose that the κ-hard element f^* exists. Let $\mathbb{N}^{\mathrm{ad}}$ be an arbitrary adaptive information operator corresponding to a set Y, a family

$$N_y = [L_1(\cdot), L_2(\cdot; y_1), \ldots, L_{n(y)}(\cdot; y_1, \ldots, y_{n(y)-1})],$$

and precisions Δ_y, $y \in Y$. Let $y^* \in Y$ be given as $y_1^* = L_1(f^*)$ and $y_i^* = L_i(f^*; y_1^*, \ldots, y_{i-1}^*)$ for $2 \leq i \leq n^*$, where n^* is the length of y^*, i.e., the minimal n for which $[y_1^*, \ldots, y_n^*] \in Y$. Define a nonadaptive information operator $\mathbb{N}^{\mathrm{non}} = \{N^{\mathrm{non}}, \Delta^{\mathrm{non}}\}$ where

$$N^{\mathrm{non}} = N_{y^*} = [L_1(\cdot), L_2(\cdot; y_1^*), \ldots, L_{n^*}(\cdot; y_1^*, y_2^*, \ldots, y_{n^*-1}^*)]$$

and

$$\Delta^{\mathrm{non}} = \Delta_{y^*} = [\delta_1, \delta_2(y_1^*), \ldots, \delta_{n^*}(y_1^*, \ldots, y_{n^*-1}^*)].$$

It turns out that nonadaptive information $\mathbb{N}^{\mathrm{non}}$ is almost as good as adaptive information $\mathbb{N}^{\mathrm{ad}}$.

Theorem 2.7.1

$$\mathrm{rad}^{\mathrm{wor}}(\mathbb{N}^{\mathrm{non}}) \leq \kappa \cdot \mathrm{rad}^{\mathrm{wor}}(\mathbb{N}^{\mathrm{ad}}).$$

Proof Observe that $A_{\mathbb{N}^{\mathrm{non}}}(y^*) = A_{\mathbb{N}^{\mathrm{ad}}}(y^*)$. Hence

$$\begin{aligned}
\mathrm{rad}^{\mathrm{wor}}(\mathbb{N}^{\mathrm{non}}) &\leq \kappa \cdot r(A_{\mathbb{N}^{\mathrm{non}}}(y^*)) \\
&= \kappa \cdot r(A_{\mathbb{N}^{\mathrm{ad}}}(y^*)) \leq \kappa \cdot \mathrm{rad}^{\mathrm{wor}}(\mathbb{N}^{\mathrm{ad}}),
\end{aligned}$$

as claimed. $\qquad\qquad\square$

The meaning of Theorem 2.7.1 is evident when the information uses only an adaptive choice of functionals, and the precision vector Δ and the number n of functionals are fixed. Then the existence of a κ-hard element suffices for the adaptive information to be no more than κ times as good as some nonadaptive information that uses the same number n of functionals and the same precision Δ.

A κ-hard element exists for some important problems. Consider first the case of a linear solution operator S with a convex and balanced set $E \subset F$. We assume that the class Λ consists of some linear functionals, and that the set $B(\Delta, z)$ is the unit ball in an extended seminorm $\|\cdot\|_\Delta$ (which can depend on Δ),

$$B(\Delta, z) = B(\Delta) = \{x \in \mathbb{R}^n \mid \|x\|_\Delta \leq 1\}, \quad \Delta, z \in \mathbb{R}^n, n \geq 1. \tag{2.46}$$

Observe that then any nonadaptive information is linear with noise bounded uniformly in an extended seminorm. Lemma 2.3.1 and Theorem 2.3.3 yield that for any nonadaptive information $\mathbb{N}$ using n observations we have

$$\mathrm{rad}^{\mathrm{wor}}(\mathbb{N}) \leq 2 \cdot r\big(A_\mathbb{N}(\underbrace{0,\ldots,0}_{n})\big).$$

Hence the zero element of F is the κ-hard element with $\kappa = 2$. If S is a functional, or if E is a ball in a Hilbert extended seminorm, $\|\cdot\|_\Delta$ is a Hilbert extended seminorm, and G is a Hilbert space, then we can even take $\kappa = 1$, since in these cases $\mathrm{diam}(\mathbb{N}) = 2 \cdot \mathrm{rad}^{\mathrm{wor}}(\mathbb{N})$. We summarize these observations as

Corollary 2.7.1 *Suppose that the set E of problem elements is convex and balanced, the solution operator S is linear, the class Λ consists of linear functionals, and $B(\Delta, z)$ is of the form (2.46). Then for any adaptive information $\mathbb{N}^{\mathrm{ad}} = \{N_y, \Delta_y\}_{y \in Y}$ we have*

$$\mathrm{rad}^{\mathrm{wor}}(\mathbb{N}^{\mathrm{non}}) \leq 2 \cdot \mathrm{rad}^{\mathrm{wor}}(\mathbb{N}^{\mathrm{ad}}),$$

where $\mathbb{N}^{\mathrm{non}}$ is the nonadaptive information constructed as in Theorem 2.7.1 for $f^* = 0$. If, additionally, S is a linear functional or if we have the Hilbert case, then $\mathrm{rad}^{\mathrm{wor}}(\mathbb{N}^{\mathrm{non}}) \leq \mathrm{rad}^{\mathrm{wor}}(\mathbb{N}^{\mathrm{ad}})$.

We now give an example in which f^* exists and is not zero, although E is a convex and balanced set. Let F be a normed space and E the unit ball in F. Consider a nonadaptive linear information operator with noise bounded in the relative sense,

$$\mathbb{N}(f) = \{y \in \mathbb{R}^n \mid |y_i - L_i(f)| \leq \delta_i |L_i(f)|, 1 \leq i \leq n\}, \tag{2.47}$$

where $0 \leq \delta_i < 1$ and $\|L_i\|_F \leq 1$, $1 \leq i \leq n$. Then for any linear solution operator S and any f with $\|f\|_F \leq 1$, we have

$$r(A_N(N(f))) \geq \tfrac{1}{2} d(A_N(N(f)))$$
$$\geq \tfrac{1}{2} \sup \{ \|S(f+h) - S(f-h)\| \mid \|h\|_F \leq 1 - \|f\|_F,$$
$$|L_i(h)| \leq \delta_i |L_i(f \pm h)|, \, 1 \leq i \leq n \}$$
$$\geq \sup \{ \|S(h)\| \mid \|h\| \leq 1 - \|f\|,$$
$$|L_i(h)| \leq \delta_i(1 + \delta_i)^{-1} L_i(f)|, \, 1 \leq i \leq n \}$$
$$\geq \min \{ 1 - \|f\|_F, \, a(f)/2 \}$$
$$\times \sup \{ \|S(h)\| \mid \|h\|_F \leq 1, \, |L_i(h)| \leq \delta_i, \, 1 \leq i \leq n \},$$

where $a(f) = \min_{1 \leq i \leq n} |L_i(f)|$. The last supremum is equal to half of the diameter of the same linear information, but with noise bounded in the absolute sense. Since $\|L_i\|_F \leq 1$, the inequality $|y_i - L_i(f_1)| \leq \delta_i |L_i(f_1)|$ implies $|y_i - L_i(f_1)| \leq \delta_i$. Hence the diameter of information with noise bounded in the absolute sense is not smaller than the diameter of information with noise bounded in the relative sense. We obtain

$$r(A_N(N(f))) \geq \tfrac{1}{2} \cdot \min \{ 1 - \|f\|_F, \, a(f)/2 \} \cdot \mathrm{rad}^{\mathrm{wor}}(\mathbb{N}).$$

Suppose now that F is the space of functions $f : [0,1] \to \mathbb{R}$ with continuous rth derivatives. Let

$$\|f\|_F = \max_{1 \leq i \leq r} \sup_{0 \leq t \leq 1} |f^{(i)}(t)|. \tag{2.48}$$

The class Λ consists of functionals of the form $L(f) = f(t)$, for some $t \in [0,1]$. Then taking $f^* = 2/3$ we have $(1/2) \cdot \min\{1 - \|f^*\|_F, \, a(f^*)/2\} = 1/6$. Hence f^* is a 6-hard element and adaption cannot be much better than nonadaption. That is,

$$\mathrm{rad}^{\mathrm{wor}}(\mathbb{N}^{\mathrm{non}}) \leq 6 \cdot \mathrm{rad}^{\mathrm{wor}}(\mathbb{N}^{\mathrm{ad}})$$

with $\mathbb{N}^{\mathrm{non}} = \{N_{2/3}, \Delta_{2/3}\}$.

We leave it to the reader to verify that in this case zero is not a κ-hard element for any finite κ; see E 2.7.3.

Notes and remarks

NR 2.7.1 In the case of exact information, the result of Corollary 2.7.1 was proven in Bakhvalov (1971) and Gal and Micchelli (1980) for approximating linear functionals, and in Traub and Woźniakowski (1980, Sect. 7 of Chap. 2) for arbitrary linear S. A similar general model with varying noisy information, but with fixed noise level, is considered in Traub *et al.* (1983, Chap. 4). The method of showing when adaption does not help is adopted from that book.

NR 2.7.2 We have shown that for a convex and balanced set E, and for linear information with noise bounded in an extended seminorm, adaptive information can be at most twice as good as nonadaptive information. It had long been an open problem whether adaption helps at all. An example of a problem (with exact information) where adaption helps only a little was given by Kon and Novak (1989, 1990).

NR 2.7.3 Korneichuk (1994) and Novak (1993, 1995a) considered the problem of adaption (and n-widths) for convex but nonbalanced sets. For such sets adaptive information can be significantly better than nonadaptive information. An example is given in E 2.7.4.

A recent survey on 'adaption versus nonadaption' may be found in Novak (1995c).

NR 2.7.4 The fact that adaption may be not much better than nonadaption in the case of relative perturbations was noticed by Kacewicz and Plaskota (1990).

NR 2.7.5 Adaptive information is also frequently called sequential or active, while nonadaptive information is called parallel or passive, respectively.

Exercises

E 2.7.1 Show that if $B(\Delta, N(f)) = B(\Delta)$ is the unit ball in an extended seminorm $\|\cdot\|_\Delta$, then (2.44) is equivalent to the following condition. Let $\Delta = [\delta_1, \ldots, \delta_n]$ and $\Delta' = [\Delta, \delta_{n+1}]$. Then

$$\|x\|_\Delta = \min_{a \in \mathbb{R}} \|[x, a]\|_{\Delta'}, \qquad \forall x \in \mathbb{R}^n.$$

E 2.7.2 Show that for any information operators N^n, $N^{n+1} = [N^n, L_{n+1}]$, and precision vectors Δ^n, $\Delta^{n+1} = [\Delta^n, \delta_{n+1}]$, we have

$$\mathrm{rad}^{\mathrm{wor}}(N^{n+1}, \Delta^{n+1}) \leq \mathrm{rad}^{\mathrm{wor}}(N^n, \Delta^n).$$

E 2.7.3 Let F be the space of functions $f : [0, 1] \to \mathbb{R}$ with continuous rth derivative and the norm (2.48). Let E be the unit ball in F. Give an example of a solution operator such that the following holds: for any finite κ there is information N of the form (2.47) such that $\mathrm{rad}^{\mathrm{wor}}(N) > \kappa \cdot r(A_N(0))$.

E 2.7.4 (Novak, 1993) Let

$$E = \left\{ f \in \mathbb{R}^\infty \;\middle|\; f_k \geq 0, \; \sum_{i=1}^\infty f_i \leq 1, \; f_k \geq \max\{f_{2k}, f_{2k+1}\} \right\}.$$

Consider the approximation of $f \in E$ in the l_∞-norm from exact information of the form $N(f) = [f_{j_1}, \ldots, f_{j_n}]$.

1. Show that the radius of nonadaptive information using n observations is minimal for $N_n(f) = [f_1, \ldots, f_n]$, and

$$\mathrm{rad}^{\mathrm{wor}}(N_n) \approx \frac{1}{\log_2 n} \qquad \text{as} \quad n \to \infty.$$

2. Find adaptive information N_n^{ad} that uses exactly n observations of f_j for which

$$\text{rad}^{\text{wor}}(N_n^{\text{ad}}) \leq \frac{1}{n}.$$

2.8 Optimal nonadaptive information

Suppose that n and the precision vector $\Delta = [\delta_1, \delta_2, \ldots, \delta_n]$ are given. Then it makes sense to ask for the minimal error that can be achieved when noisy observations of n functionals from the class Λ with precisions δ_i are used. We formalize this issue in the following way.

Let $\mathcal{N}_n$ be the class of exact information operators consisting of n functionals, i.e., $N \in \mathcal{N}_n$ iff

$$N = [L_1, L_2, \ldots, L_n],$$

for some $L_i \in \Lambda$, $1 \leq i \leq n$. Let $\text{rad}^{\text{wor}}(N, \Delta)$ denote the radius of noisy information $\mathbb{N}$ corresponding to N and precision vector Δ.

The *minimal radius* corresponding to the precision vector Δ is given as

$$r_n^{\text{wor}}(\Delta) = \inf_{N \in \mathcal{N}_n} \text{rad}^{\text{wor}}(N, \Delta).$$

If for some $N_\Delta \in \mathcal{N}_n$ we have

$$r_n^{\text{wor}}(\Delta) = \text{rad}^{\text{wor}}(N_\Delta, \Delta),$$

then N_Δ is called *optimal information*.

We shall find the minimal radius and optimal information in two special cases: for linear problems defined in Hilbert spaces, and for approximation and integration of Lipschitz functions.

2.8.1 Linear problems in Hilbert spaces

We assume that F and G are separable Hilbert spaces and the solution operator $S : F \to G$ is compact. The set E of problem elements is the unit ball in F. The class Λ of permissible information functionals consists of all linear functionals with norm bounded by 1,

$$\Lambda = \left\{ \text{ linear functionals } L \ \middle| \ \|L\|_F = \sup_{\|f\|_F = 1} |L(f)| \leq 1 \right\}.$$

We also assume that the observation noise is bounded in the weighted Euclidean norm. That is, for $\Delta = [\delta_1, \ldots, \delta_n]$ and $N = [L_1, \ldots, L_n] \in$

$\mathcal{N}_n$, a sequence $y \in \mathbb{R}^n$ is noisy information about $f \in F$ iff

$$\sum_{i=1}^{n} \delta_i^{-2} \left(y_i - L_i(f) \right)^2 \leq 1.$$

To cover the case where some $L_i(f)$s are obtained exactly ($\delta_i = 0$), we use above the convention that $0^{-2}a^2 = +\infty$ for $a \neq 0$, and $0^{-2}0^2 = 0$. Note that if all δ_is are equal, $\delta_i = \delta$, then $\sum_{i=1}^{n}(y_i - L_i(f))^2 \leq \delta^2$, i.e., the noise is bounded by δ in the Euclidean norm.

Before stating a theorem about optimal information, we first introduce some necessary notation. Let $d = \dim F \leq +\infty$. Let $\{\xi_i\}_{i=1}^{d}$ be a complete F-orthonormal system of eigenelements of the operator S^*S. Let λ_i be the corresponding eigenvalues,

$$S^*S\,\xi = \lambda_i\,\xi_i.$$

Since S is compact, we can assume without loss of generality that the λ_is are ordered, $\lambda_1 \geq \lambda_2 \geq \ldots \geq 0$. We consider the sequence $\{\lambda_i\}$ to be infinite by letting, if necessary, $\lambda_i = 0$ for $i > d$. Similarly, $\xi_i = 0$ for $i > d$. Obviously, we have $\lim_{i \to \infty} \lambda_i = 0$.

We also need the following important lemma.

Lemma 2.8.1 *Let the nonincreasing sequences $\beta_1 \geq \beta_2 \geq \cdots \geq \beta_n \geq 0$ and $\eta_1 \geq \eta_2 \geq \cdots \geq \eta_n \geq 0$ be such that*

$$\sum_{i=r}^{n} \eta_i \leq \sum_{i=r}^{n} \beta_i, \qquad 1 \leq r \leq n,$$

and $\sum_{i=1}^{n} \eta_i = \sum_{i=1}^{n} \beta_i$. Then there exists a real matrix $W = \{w_{ij}\}_{i,j=1}^{n}$ for which

$$\sum_{s=1}^{n} w_{is}^2 = \beta_i \qquad and \qquad \sum_{s=1}^{n} w_{si}w_{sj} = \eta_i \delta_{ij},$$

for all $1 \leq i, j \leq n$ (δ_{ij} stands for the Kronecker delta).

Proof   We shall construct the matrix W using induction on n. For $n = 1$ we obviously have $\eta_1 = \beta_1$ and $w_{11} = \sqrt{\eta_1}$. Let $n \geq 2$. If $\eta_i = \beta_i$, $1 \leq i \leq n$, then $W = \text{diag}\{\sqrt{\eta_1}, \ldots, \sqrt{\eta_n}\}$. Otherwise there is an index s, $1 \leq s \leq n-1$, such that $\eta_s > \beta_s \geq \eta_{s+1}$. Set $\bar{\eta} = \eta_s + \eta_{s+1} - \beta_s > 0$. Let $U = \{u_{ij}\}_{i,j=1}^{n-1} \in \mathbb{R}^{(n-1) \times (n-1)}$ be the required matrix for the sequences $\beta_1 \geq \cdots \geq \beta_{s-1} \geq \beta_{s+1} \geq \cdots \geq \beta_n$ and

$\eta_1 \geq \cdots \geq \eta_{s-1} \geq \bar{\eta} \geq \eta_{s+2} \geq \cdots \geq \eta_n$. Let

$$a = \left(\frac{\eta_{s+1}(\eta_s - \beta_s)}{\bar{\eta}(\eta_s - \eta_{s+1})} \right)^{1/2}, \qquad b = (1-a^2)^{1/2},$$

$$c = \left(\frac{\eta_s(\beta_s - \eta_{s+1})}{(\eta_s - \eta_{s+1})} \right)^{1/2}, \qquad d = -(1-c^2)^{1/2}.$$

Elementary calculations show that as W we can take the matrix $W = \{w_{ij}\}_{i,j=1}^n$ with the coefficients given as follows. For $1 \leq i \leq n-1$

$$w_{i,j} = \begin{cases} u_{i,j} & 1 \leq j \leq n-1, \\ au_{i,s} & j = s, \\ bu_{i,s} & j = s+1, \\ u_{i,j-1} & s+2 \leq j \leq n, \end{cases}$$

and for $i = n$

$$w_{n,j} = \begin{cases} 0 & j \neq s, s+1, \\ c & j = s, \\ d & j = s+1. \end{cases}$$

□

We assume without loss of generality that the components of the precision vector $\Delta = [\delta_1, \ldots, \delta_n]$ are nondecreasing,

$$0 = \delta_1 = \cdots = \delta_{n_0} < \delta_{n_0+1} \leq \cdots \leq \delta_n.$$

(If all δ_is are positive then $n_0 = 0$.) It turns out that the following minimization problem plays a crucial role in finding the optimal information N_Δ.

Problem (MP)   *Minimize*

$$\Omega(\alpha; \eta_{n_0+1}, \ldots, \eta_n) = \max_{n_0+1 \leq i \leq n+1} \frac{\lambda_i}{\alpha + (1-\alpha)\eta_i}$$

over all $0 \leq \alpha \leq 1$ *and* $\eta_{n_0+1} \geq \cdots \geq \eta_{n+1} = 0$ *satisfying*

$$\sum_{i=r}^n \eta_i \leq \sum_{i=r}^n \delta_i^{-2}, \qquad n_0 + 1 \leq r \leq n, \qquad (2.49)$$

and $\sum_{i=n_0+1}^n \eta_i = \sum_{i=n_0+1}^n \delta_i^{-2}$ *(as before, $a/0 = +\infty$ for $a > 0$, and $0/0 = 0$, by convention).*

Theorem 2.8.1 *Let α^* and $\eta^*_{n_0+1} \geq \cdots \geq \eta^*_n$ be the solution of* (MP). *Then the minimal radius is given by*

$$r_n^{\mathrm{wor}}(\Delta) = \sqrt{\Omega(\alpha^*; \eta^*_{n_0+1}, \ldots, \eta^*_n)}.$$

Furthermore, the optimal information is given by

$$N_\Delta = [\langle \cdot, \xi_1 \rangle_F, \ldots, \langle \cdot, \xi_{n_0} \rangle_F, \langle \cdot, \xi^\Delta_{n_0+1} \rangle_F, \ldots, \langle \cdot, \xi^\Delta_n \rangle_F],$$

where

$$\xi^\Delta_{n_0+i} = \delta_{n_0+i} \sum_{j=1}^{n-n_0} w_{ij} \xi_{n_0+j}$$

and $W = \{w_{ij}\}_{i,j=1}^{n-n_0}$ is the matrix from Lemma 2.8.1 with

$$\eta_i = \eta^*_{n_0+i} \qquad and \qquad \beta_i = \delta^{-2}_{n_0+i},$$

$1 \leq i \leq n - n_0$.

Proof Consider first the case when all δ_is are positive, i.e., $n_0 = 0$. Let

$$N = [\langle \cdot, f_1 \rangle_F, \langle \cdot, f_2 \rangle_F, \ldots, \langle \cdot, f_n \rangle_F],$$

with $\|f_i\|_F \leq 1$, be an arbitrary information operator. In fact, we can assume that $\|f_i\|_F = 1, 1 \leq i \leq n$, since by multiplying f_i by a constant larger than one we can only increase the accuracy of noisy information. Using Lemma 2.6.2, the radius of N is the minimal norm of the operator $SA_\alpha^{-1/2}$ over all $\alpha \in [0,1]$. In our case,

$$A_\alpha = \alpha I + (1-\alpha) N^* N,$$

where $N^* : Y \to F$, $N^*(y) = \sum_{i=1}^n (y_i f_i / \delta_i^2)$. Then

$$\| SA_\alpha^{-1/2} \|^2 = \sup_{h \neq 0} \frac{\| SA_\alpha^{-1/2} h \|^2}{\|h\|_F^2} = \sup_{h \neq 0} \frac{\langle S^* S h, h \rangle_F}{\langle A_\alpha h, h \rangle_F}.$$

Taking $h = \xi_i, 1 \leq i \leq n$, we obtain

$$\| SA_\alpha^{-1/2} \|^2 \geq \max_{1 \leq i \leq n} \frac{\lambda_i}{\langle A_\alpha \xi_i, \xi_i \rangle_F}. \tag{2.50}$$

For $d > n$, we get an additional lower bound. That is, since the operator N is at most n dimensional, there exists a nonzero element $h_0 \in \mathrm{span}\{\xi_1, \ldots, \xi_{n+1}\}$ such that $N(h_0) = 0$. Hence

$$\| SA_\alpha^{-1/2} \|^2 \geq \frac{\langle S^* S h_0, h_0 \rangle_F}{\langle A_\alpha h_0, h_0 \rangle_F} \geq \frac{\lambda_{n+1}}{\alpha}. \tag{2.51}$$

Let $\eta_1 \geq \eta_2 \geq \ldots \geq \eta_n \geq 0 = \eta_{n+1}$ be the eigenvalues of N^*N. Then the η_i are also eigenvalues of the operator $NN^* : Y \to Y$ whose matrix (in the basis $\{e_i\}$) is

$$M = \left\{ \delta_j^{-2} \langle f_i, f_j \rangle_F \right\}_{i,j=1}^n .$$

Since the $\tilde{e}_i = \delta_i e_i$, $1 \leq i \leq n$, are an orthonormal basis in Y, for $1 \leq r \leq n$ we have, see NR 2.8.6,

$$\sum_{i=r}^n \eta_i \leq \sum_{i=r}^n \langle M\tilde{e}_i, \tilde{e}_i \rangle_Y = \sum_{i=r}^n \delta_i^{-2}, \tag{2.52}$$

and $\sum_{i=1}^n \eta_i = \sum_{i=1}^n \delta_i^{-2}$.

Taking (2.50), (2.51) and (2.52) together, we obtain the following lower bound on $r_n^{\mathrm{wor}}(\Delta)$:

$$(r_n^{\mathrm{wor}}(\Delta))^2 \geq \min \max_{1 \leq i \leq n+1} \frac{\lambda_i}{\alpha + (1 - \alpha)\,\eta_i}, \tag{2.53}$$

where the minimum is taken over all $\alpha \in [0, 1]$ and η_is satisfying (2.49). To complete the proof of the lower bound, observe that the minimum in (2.53) is attained for some η_i^*s satisfying $\eta_1^* \geq \cdots \geq \eta_n^*$.

We now show that the lower bound (2.53) is attained for the information operator N_Δ. To this end, it suffices to show that all the ξ_is are the eigenelements of the operator $N_\Delta^* N_\Delta$ and the corresponding eigenvalues are the η_i^*. Indeed, we have

$$
\begin{aligned}
N_\Delta^* N_\Delta \, \xi_i &= \sum_{s=1}^n \delta_s^{-2} \, \langle \xi_i, \xi_s^\Delta \rangle_F \xi_s^\Delta \\
&= \sum_{s=1}^n \Big\langle \xi_i, \sum_{t=1}^n w_{st}\xi_t \Big\rangle_F \Big(\sum_{j=1}^n w_{sj}\xi_j \Big) \\
&= \sum_{s=1}^n \sum_{j=1}^n w_{si} w_{sj} \xi_j = \sum_{j=1}^n \Big(\sum_{s=1}^n w_{si} w_{sj} \Big) \xi_j \\
&= \sum_{j=1}^n \eta_i^* \delta_{ij} \xi_j = \eta_i^* \, \xi_i .
\end{aligned}
$$

Since

$$\| \langle \cdot, \xi_i^\Delta \rangle \|_F = \| \xi_i^\Delta \|_F^2 = \delta_i^2 \sum_{j=1}^n w_{ij}^2 = 1,$$

N_Δ is also a permissible information operator, $N_\Delta \in \mathcal{N}_n$. This completes the proof of the case $n_0 = 0$.

Suppose now that not all δ_is are positive, $n_0 \geq 1$. Then for any $N = [L_1, \ldots, L_n] \in \mathcal{N}_n$ we have

$$
\begin{aligned}
\mathrm{rad}^{\mathrm{wor}}(N, \Delta) &= \sup\{\,\|S(h)\| \mid \|h\|_F \leq 1, \ \|N(h)\|_Y \leq 1\} \\
&= \sup\{\,\|S_1(h)\| \mid \|h\|_F \leq 1, \ \|N_1(h)\|_{Y_1} \leq 1\},
\end{aligned}
$$

where $F_1 = \{f \in F \mid L_i(f) = 0, 1 \leq i \leq n_0\}$, $S_1 : F_1 \to G$ is the restriction of S to the space F_1, $S_1 = S|_{F_1}$, the information operator $N_1 = [L_{n_0+1}, \ldots, L_n]$, and $\|\cdot\|_{Y_1}$ is the extended seminorm on $\mathbb{R}^{n-n_0}$ defined by $\|x\|_{Y_1} = \|[0, x]\|_Y$. It is known that the dominating eigenvalues $\lambda_1' \geq \lambda_2' \geq \ldots$ of the operator $S_1^* S_1 : F_1 \to F_1$ satisfy $\lambda_i' \geq \lambda_{n_0+i}$, $\forall\, i \geq 1$. Moreover, for $L_j = \langle \cdot, \xi_j \rangle_F$, $1 \leq i \leq n_0$, we have $\lambda_i' = \lambda_{n_0+i}$, $\forall\, i \geq 1$. Hence we obtain the desired result by reducing our problem to that of finding optimal $N_1 \in \mathcal{N}_{n-n_0}$ for approximating S_1 from data $y \in \mathbb{R}^{n-n_0}$ satisfying $\|y - N_1(f)\|_{Y_1} \leq 1$. □

Thus, to construct the optimal information N_Δ, we have first to solve the minimization problem (MP) and then to find the matrix W. The solution of (MP) will be given below. The matrix W can be found by following the construction from the proof of Lemma 2.8.1. Note that the optimal approximation φ_Δ is given by the α^*-smoothing spline where α^* comes from the solution of (MP).

We now show how to solve the problem (MP). For $0 \leq \alpha \leq 1$ and $n_0 \leq q \leq r \leq n$, define the following two auxiliary problems:

Problem $P_\alpha(q, r)$ *Minimize*

$$
\Omega_{qr}^\alpha(\eta_{q+1}, \ldots, \eta_r) = \max_{q+1 \leq i \leq r} \frac{\lambda_i}{\alpha + (1 - \alpha)\eta_i}
$$

over all $\eta_{q+1} \geq \cdots \geq \eta_r \geq 0$ *satisfying* $\sum_{i=q+1}^r \eta_i = \sum_{i=q+1}^r \delta_i^{-2}$.

Problem $P(q)$ *Minimize*

$$
\Omega_q(\alpha; \eta_{q+1}, \ldots, \eta_n) = \max_{q+1 \leq i \leq n+1} \frac{\lambda_i}{\alpha + (1 - \alpha)\eta_i}
$$

over all $0 \leq \alpha \leq 1$ *and* $\eta_{q+1} \geq \cdots \geq \eta_{n+1} = 0$ *satisfying* $\sum_{i=q+1}^n \eta_i = \sum_{i=q+1}^n \delta_i^{-2}$.

Consider first the problem $P_\alpha(q, r)$. If $\alpha = 1$ then $\Omega_\alpha \equiv \lambda_1$. Let $0 \leq \alpha < 1$. Then the solution $\eta^* = (\eta_{q+1}^*, \ldots, \eta_r^*)$ of $P_\alpha(q, r)$ can be obtained as follows. Let $\gamma = \gamma(\alpha) = \alpha/(1 - \alpha)$. Let $k = k(\alpha; q, r)$ be the largest integer satisfying $q + 1 \le k \le r$ and

$$\lambda_k \ge \frac{\gamma \sum_{j=q+1}^{k} \lambda_j}{\gamma (k - q) + \sum_{j=q+1}^{r} \delta_j^{-2}} . \tag{2.54}$$

Then

$$\eta_i^* = \frac{\gamma (k - q) + \sum_{j=q+1}^{r} \delta_j^{-2}}{\sum_{j=q+1}^{k} \lambda_j} \lambda_i - \gamma, \qquad q + 1 \le i \le k, \tag{2.55}$$

and $\eta_i^* = 0$ for $k + 1 \le i \le r$. Furthermore,

$$\Omega_{qr}^{\alpha}(\eta^*) = \frac{\sum_{j=q+1}^{k} \lambda_j}{\alpha (k - q) + (1 - \alpha) \sum_{j=q+1}^{r} \delta_j^{-2}} . \tag{2.56}$$

We now pass to the solution of $P(q)$. Let α_i, $i \ge q + 1$, be defined in such a way that we have equality in (2.54) when k and γ are replaced by i and $\gamma_i = \alpha_i / (1 - \alpha_i)$, respectively. Such an α_i exists only for $i \ge s = \min\{ j \mid \lambda_j < \lambda_{q+1} \}$. Then $\alpha_i = \gamma_i / (1 + \gamma_i)$, where

$$\gamma_i = \frac{\lambda_i \sum_{j=q+1}^{n} \delta_j^{-2}}{\sum_{j=q+1}^{i-1} (\lambda_j - \lambda_i)} .$$

Letting $\alpha_i = 1$ for $i < s$, we have $1 = \alpha_{q+1} \ge \alpha_{q+2} \ge \cdots$ and the solution η^i of the problem $P_\alpha(q, r)$ with $r = n$ satisfies $\eta_{q+1}^i \ge \cdots \ge \eta_i^i = 0$. Since in addition the right hand side of (2.56) is a monotone function of α, we obtain

$$\min_{\alpha, \eta} \Omega_q(\alpha; \eta) = \min_{q+1 \le i \le n+1} \Omega_q(\alpha_i, \eta^i).$$

After some further calculations we finally arrive at the following formulas for the solution (α^*, η^*) of $P(q)$. Let

$$k = k(q) = \min \left\{ n, q + \left\lfloor \sum_{j=q+1}^{n} \delta_j^{-2} \right\rfloor \right\}. \tag{2.57}$$

If $\lambda_{q+1} = \lambda_{k+1}$ then $\alpha^* = 1$ and $\Omega_q(\alpha^*; \cdot) \equiv \lambda_{q+1}$. If $\lambda_{q+1} > \lambda_{k+1}$ then $\alpha^* = \gamma^* / (1 + \gamma^*)$, where

$$\gamma^* = \frac{\lambda_{k+1} \sum_{j=q+1}^{n} \delta_j^{-2}}{\sum_{j=q+1}^{k} (\lambda_j - \lambda_{k+1})}$$

and η^* is given by (2.55) with $\gamma = \gamma^*$. Furthermore,

$$\Omega_q(\alpha^*; \eta^*) = \lambda_{k+1} + \frac{\sum_{j=q+1}^{k} (\lambda_j - \lambda_k)}{\sum_{j=q+1}^{n} \delta_j^{-2}} .$$

We shall say that the solution $\eta^* = (\eta^*_{q+1}, \ldots, \eta^*_r)$ of $P_\alpha(q, r)$ is acceptable iff

$$\sum_{j=s}^r \eta^*_j \le \sum_{j=s}^r \delta_j^{-2}, \qquad \text{for } q+1 \le s \le r. \tag{2.58}$$

Similarly, the solution (α^*, η^*) of $P(q)$ is acceptable iff (2.58) holds with $r = n$.

Let the number p, $0 \le p < n$, and the sequence $n = n_{p+1} > n_p > \cdots > n_0 \ge 0$ be (uniquely) defined by the conditions

$$n_p = \min\{s \ge n_0 \,|\, \text{solution of P}(s) \text{ is acceptable}\}, \tag{2.59}$$
$$n_i = \min\{s \ge n_0 \,|\, \text{solution of P}_{\alpha^*}(s, n_{i+1}) \text{ is acceptable}\}, \tag{2.60}$$

$0 \le i \le p - 1$, where α^* comes from the solution of $P(n_p)$.

Theorem 2.8.2 *Let p, the sequence $n_0 < n_1 < \cdots < n_{p+1} = n$ and α^* be defined by (2.59) and (2.60). Then the solution of the problem (MP) is given by α^* and*

$$\eta^* = (\eta^{(0)}, \eta^{(1)}, \ldots, \eta^{(p)}),$$

where $\eta^{(p)}$ and $\eta^{(i)}$ are solutions of $P(n_p)$ and $P_{\alpha^*}(n_i, n_{i+1})$, $0 \le i \le p - 1$, respectively.

Proof Let $k = k(n_p)$. Using the definition of n_i we have $\eta^*_1 \ge \cdots \ge \eta^*_k \ge \eta^*_{k+1} = 0$ and the maximal value of $\lambda_j / (\alpha^* + (1 - \alpha^*) \eta^*_j)$, $n_0 + 1 \le j \le n$, is attained for $j = n_p + 1$. The definition of n_p yields in turn that the $\eta^{(p)}$ are the last $(n - n_p)$ components of the solution of (MP) and that α^* is optimal. This completes the proof. □

As a consequence of this theorem we obtain the following corollary.

Corollary 2.8.1 *Let n_p and $k = k(n_p)$ be defined by (2.59) and (2.57), respectively. Then*

$$r_n^{\text{wor}}(\Delta) = \sqrt{\lambda_{k+1} + \frac{\sum_{j=n_p+1}^k (\lambda_j - \lambda_{k+1})}{\sum_{j=n_p+1}^n \delta_j^{-2}}}.$$

Observe that we always have $\sqrt{\lambda_{n+1}} \le r_n^{\text{wor}}(\Delta) \le \sqrt{\lambda_1}$. The lower bound is achieved if, for instance, the δ_i's are zero, i.e., if we are dealing with exact information. The upper bound, $r_n^{\text{wor}}(\Delta) = \sqrt{\lambda_1}$, is achieved if for instance $\sum_{i=1}^{n} \delta_i^{-2} \leq 1$, see also E 2.8.4. In this case, the information is useless.

Let us now consider the case when all δ_is are constant, $\delta_i = \delta$, and $0 < \delta \leq 1$. That is, noisy information satisfies

$$\sqrt{\sum_{i=1}^{n} (y_i - L_i(f))^2} \leq \delta.$$

Then the solution of P(0) is acceptable and $k = k(0) = n$. Hence the formula for the radius reduces to

$$r_n^{\text{wor}}(\Delta) = r_n^{\text{wor}}(\delta) = \sqrt{\lambda_{n+1} + \frac{\delta^2}{n} \sum_{j=1}^{n} (\lambda_j - \lambda_{n+1})}. \qquad (2.61)$$

If $\lambda_1 = \cdots = \lambda_{n+1}$ then $r_n^{\text{wor}}(\Delta) = \sqrt{\lambda_1}$ and the zero approximation is optimal. For $\lambda_1 > \lambda_{n+1}$ we have $\gamma^* = \delta^{-2}\gamma^{**}$ where

$$\gamma^{**} = \frac{n \lambda_{n+1}}{\sum_{j=1}^{n} (\lambda_j - \lambda_{n+1})},$$

and the optimal η_i^*s are $\eta_i^* = \delta^{-2}\eta_i^{**}$ with

$$\eta_i^{**} = \frac{n (\lambda_i - \lambda_{n+1})}{\sum_{j=1}^{n} (\lambda_j - \lambda_{n+1})}, \qquad 1 \leq i \leq n.$$

The optimal information $N_n = [\langle \cdot, \xi_1^* \rangle_F, \dots, \langle \cdot, \xi_n^* \rangle_F]$ is given by Theorem 2.8.1 with the matrix W constructed for $\eta_i = \eta_i^{**}$ and $\beta_i = 1$, $1 \leq i \leq n$. The optimal algorithm is $\varphi_n(y) = \sum_{j=1}^{n} z_j S(f_j)$ where $(\gamma_n I + G_{N_n}) z = y$ and the parameter $\gamma_n = \gamma^{**}$. We stress that neither the optimal information nor the optimal algorithm depends on the noise level δ.

We now comment on the minimal radius $r_n^{\text{wor}}(\delta)$. If we fix n and let the noise level δ tend to zero, then $r_n^{\text{wor}}(\delta)$ approaches the minimal radius of exact information, $r_n^{\text{wor}}(0) = \sqrt{\lambda_{n+1}} \geq 0$. For $r_n^{\text{wor}}(0) > 0$ we have

$$r_n^{\text{wor}}(\delta) - r_n^{\text{wor}}(0) \approx \frac{\delta^2}{2 n \sqrt{\lambda_{n+1}}} \sum_{j=1}^{n} (\lambda_j - \lambda_{n+1}),^{[1]}$$

---

[1] The symbol '$\approx$' denotes here the *strong* equivalence of sequences. We write $a_n \approx b_n$ iff $\lim_{n \to \infty} (a_n / b_n) = 1$.

while for $r_n^{\mathrm{wor}}(0) = 0$ we have

$$r_n^{\mathrm{wor}}(\delta) - r_n^{\mathrm{wor}}(0) = r_n^{\mathrm{wor}}(\delta) = \delta \sqrt{\frac{1}{n} \sum_{j=1}^{n} \lambda_j}.$$

Hence for $r_n^{\mathrm{wor}}(0) > 0$ the convergence is quadratic, and for $r_n^{\mathrm{wor}}(0) = 0$ it is linear in δ.

Consider now the case where the noise level δ is fixed and $n \to +\infty$. The formula (2.61) can be rewritten as

$$r_n^{\mathrm{wor}}(\delta) = \sqrt{\lambda_{n+1}(1 - \delta^2) + \frac{\delta^2}{n} \sum_{j=1}^{n} \lambda_j}.$$

The compactness of S^*S implies $\lim_j \lambda_j = 0$. Hence λ_{n+1} as well as $n^{-1} \sum_{j=1}^{n} \lambda_j$ converges to zero with n, and consequently,

$$\lim_{n \to +\infty} r_n^{\mathrm{wor}}(\delta) = 0.$$

This result should not be a surprise since for noise bounded in the Euclidean norm we can obtain the value of any functional L at f with arbitrarily small error. Indeed, repeating observations of $L(f)$ we obtain information $y_1, \ldots, y_k$ such that $\sum_{i=1}^{k}(y_i - L(f))^2 \le \delta^2$. Hence for large k most of the y_is are very close to $L(f)$, and for $\|f\|_F \le 1$ the least squares approximation, $k^{-1} \sum_{i=1}^{k} y_i$, converges uniformly to $L(f)$.

Observe also that $r_n^{\mathrm{wor}}(\delta) \ge \delta \lambda_1 / \sqrt{n}$. Thus for $S \not\equiv 0$ the radius cannot tend to zero faster than $\delta / \sqrt{n}$.

To see more precisely how $r_n(\delta)$ depends on the eigenvalues λ_j, suppose that

$$\lambda_j \asymp \left(\frac{\ln^s j}{j} \right)^p \qquad \text{as} \quad j \to +\infty,[1]$$

where $p > 0$ and $s \ge 0$. Such behavior of the eigenvalues is typical of some multivariate problems defined in tensor product spaces; see NR 2.8.4. In this case, for $\delta > 0$ we have

$$r_n^{\mathrm{wor}}(\delta) \asymp \begin{cases} \delta \left(\ln^s n / n \right)^{p/2} & 0 < p < 1, \\ \delta \left(\ln^{s+1} n / n \right)^{1/2} & p = 1, \\ \delta \left(1/n \right)^{1/2} & p > 1, \end{cases} \qquad (2.62)$$

---

[1] For two sequences, we write $a_n \asymp b_n$ iff there exist constants $0 < c_1 \le c_2 < +\infty$ such that for all sufficiently large n, $c_1 a_n \le b_n \le c_2 a_n$. Such sequences are said to be *weakly* equivalent.

where the constants in the '$\asymp$' notation do not depend on δ. Since

$$r_n^{\text{wor}}(0) \asymp \left(\frac{\ln^s n}{n} \right)^{p/2},$$

we conclude that for $p < 1$ the radius of noisy information essentially behaves as the radius of exact information, while for $p > 1$ the radius of noisy information essentially behaves as $\delta/\sqrt{n}$. Hence, in the presence of noise, the best convergence rate is $\delta/\sqrt{n}$.

2.8.2 Approximation and integration of Lipschitz functions

In this subsection we deal with noise bounded in the sup-norm. We assume that F is the space of Lipschitz functions $f : [0,1] \to \mathbb{R}$, and consider the following two solution operators on F:

• *Function approximation.*

This is defined as App : $F \to C([0,1])$,

$$\text{App}(f) = f, \qquad f \in F,$$

where $C([0,1])$ is the space of continuous functions $f : [0,1] \to \mathbb{R}$ with the norm

$$\|f\| = \|f\|_\infty = \max_{0 \le t \le 1} |f(t)|.$$

• *Integration.*

The solution operator is given as Int : $F \to \mathbb{R}$,

$$\text{Int}(f) = \int_0^1 f(t)\,dt.$$

The set $E \subset F$ of problem elements consists of functions for which the Lipschitz constant is 1,

$$E = \{\, f : [0,1] \to \mathbb{R} \mid |f(t_1) - f(t_2)| \le |t_1 - t_2|,\ 0 \le t_1, t_2 \le 1 \,\}.$$

Observe that E is the unit ball of F with respect to the seminorm

$$\|f\|_F = \sup_{0 \le t_1 < t_2 \le 1} \frac{|f(t_1) - f(t_2)|}{|t_1 - t_2|}.$$

Information $y \in \mathbb{R}^n$ about $f \in F$ is obtained by noisy observations of the function values at some points $t_i \in [0,1]$, and

$$|y_i - f(t_i)| \le \delta_i, \qquad 1 \le i \le n.$$

That is, exact information is now of the form

$$N(f) = [f(t_1), f(t_2), \ldots, f(t_n)], \qquad f \in F, \qquad (2.63)$$

and the noise $x = y - N(f)$ belongs to the set $B(\Delta, z) = B(\Delta) = \{\, x \in \mathbb{R}^n \mid |x_i| \le \delta_i, 1 \le i \le n \,\}$. Hence the noise is bounded uniformly in the 'weighted' sup-norm.

For a given precision vector $\Delta = [\delta_1, \ldots, \delta_n] \in \mathbb{R}^n$, we want to choose the t_is in such a way as to minimize the radius $r_n^{\mathrm{wor}}(S; N, \Delta)$, for $S \in \{\mathrm{App}, \mathrm{Int}\}$. We assume without loss of generality that

$$0 \le \delta_1 \le \delta_2 \le \cdots \le \delta_n.$$

We have the following theorem.

Theorem 2.8.3   *Let k be the largest integer such that $1 \le k \le n$ and*

$$\delta_k \le \frac{1}{k}\left(\frac{1}{2} + \sum_{j=1}^{k} \delta_j\right).$$

Then the minimal radius satisfies

$$r_n^{\mathrm{wor}}(\mathrm{App}; \Delta) = \frac{1}{k}\left(\frac{1}{2} + \sum_{j=1}^{k} \delta_j\right)$$

and

$$r_n^{\mathrm{wor}}(\mathrm{Int}; \Delta) = \frac{1}{k}\left(\frac{1}{2} + \sum_{j=1}^{k} \delta_j\right)^2 - \sum_{j=1}^{k} \delta_j^2.$$

Furthermore, the optimal points t_i^* are for both problems given as

$$t_i^* = \frac{2i-1}{k}\left(\frac{1}{2} + \sum_{j=1}^{k} \delta_j\right) - 2\left(\sum_{j=1}^{i-1} \delta_j\right) - \delta_i, \qquad for\ 1 \le i \le k,$$

with t_i^* arbitrary for $k+1 \le i \le n$.

Proof   Consider first the approximation problem, $S = \mathrm{App}$. Let an exact information operator N of the form (2.63) be given. We claim that

$$\mathrm{rad}^{\mathrm{wor}}(\mathrm{App}; N, \Delta) = \tfrac{1}{2}\,\mathrm{diam}(\mathrm{App}; N, \Delta)$$
$$= \sup\{\,\|f\|_\infty \mid |f(t_i)| \le \delta_i, 1 \le i \le n\,\}. \qquad (2.64)$$

Indeed, for $y \in \bigcup_{f \in E} N(f)$, define the functions

$$
\begin{aligned}
f_y^+(t) &= \sup \{ f(t) \mid f \in E, \ |y_i - f(t_i)| \le \delta_i, \ 1 \le i \le n \} \\
&= \min_{1 \le i \le n} (y_i + \delta_i + |t - t_i|),
\end{aligned}
$$

$$
\begin{aligned}
f_y^-(t) &= \inf \{ f(t) \mid f \in E, \ |y_i - f(t_i)| \le \delta_i, \ 1 \le i \le n \} \\
&= \max_{1 \le i \le n} (y_i - \delta_i - |t - t_i|).
\end{aligned}
$$

Then $f_y^+, f_y^- \in E$ and for any $t \in [0,1]$ and $f_1, f_2 \in E$ such that $y \in N(f_1) \cap N(f_2)$, we have $|f_1(t) - f_2(t)| \le f_y^+(t) - f_y^-(t)$. Hence $f_y = (f_y^+ + f_y^-)/2 \in E$ is the center of the set $A_N(y)$ of functions from E that share the information y, and $r(A_N(y)) = (1/2)d(A_N(y))$. Consequently, $\mathrm{rad}^{\mathrm{wor}}(\mathrm{App}; N, \Delta) = (1/2)\mathrm{diam}(\mathrm{App}; N, \Delta)$. The second equality in (2.64) follows from the definition of the diameter.

The formula for f_y^+ with $y = 0$ yields

$$
\mathrm{rad}^{\mathrm{wor}}(\mathrm{App}; N, \Delta) = \|f_0^+\|_\infty = \max_{0 \le t \le 1} \min_{1 \le i \le n} (\delta_i + |t - t_i|).
$$

Since $\mathrm{rad}^{\mathrm{wor}}(\mathrm{App}; N, \Delta)$ is a continuous function of $t_1, \ldots, t_n$ defined on a compact set $[0,1]^n$, the minimal radius $r_n^{\mathrm{wor}}(\mathrm{App}; \Delta)$ is attained. Using some geometrical arguments we get that $r_n^{\mathrm{wor}}(\mathrm{App}; \Delta)$ is attained for t_is satisfying the following system of equations:

$$
\begin{aligned}
A &= t_1 + \delta_1, \\
A &= (t_i - t_{i-1})/2 + (\delta_{i-1} + \delta_i)/2, \qquad 2 \le i \le m, \\
A &= \delta_m + (1 - t_m),
\end{aligned}
$$

where $A = \mathrm{rad}^{\mathrm{wor}}(\mathrm{App}; N, \Delta)$ and m is the largest integer such that $1 \le m \le n$ and $\delta_m \le A$. Solving this system we obtain the desired result.

We now turn to the integration problem, $S = \mathrm{Int}$. Since Int is a functional, we have

$$
\mathrm{rad}^{\mathrm{wor}}(\mathrm{Int}; N, \Delta)
$$

$$
= \sup \left\{ \left. \int_0^1 f(t)\,dt \ \right| \ f \in E, \ |f(t_i)| \le \delta_i, \ 1 \le i \le n \right\}.
$$

Using geometrical arguments as above we obtain that the optimal t_is are the same as for function approximation. Hence the formulas for integration can be obtained by integrating the function f_0^+ constructed for $t_i = t_i^*$, which is given by

$$
f_0^+(t) = \delta_i + |t - t_i^*|, \qquad |t - t_i^*| \le A - \delta_i, \ 1 \le i \le k.
$$

This completes the proof.   □

Assume now that all observations are performed with the same precision, $\Delta = \underbrace{[\delta, \ldots, \delta]}_{n}$. Then the formulas of Theorem 2.8.3 take the following form:

$$r_n^{\text{wor}}(\text{App}; \Delta) = r_n^{\text{wor}}(\text{App}; \delta) = \frac{1}{2n} + \delta \qquad (2.65)$$

and

$$r_n^{\text{wor}}(\text{Int}; \Delta) = r_n^{\text{wor}}(\text{Int}; \delta) = \frac{1}{4n} + \delta. \qquad (2.66)$$

The optimal points are $t_i^* = (2i - 1)/(2n)$, $1 \le i \le n$. The reader can also check that for $S \in \{\text{App}, \text{Int}\}$, the optimal algorithm is in this case given by $\varphi(y) = S(\mathbf{p}(y))$, where $\mathbf{p}(y)$ is the natural spline of degree 1 such that $\mathbf{p}(t_i^*) = y_i$, $1 \le i \le n$.

For both problems we have $r_n^{\text{wor}}(\delta) = r_n^{\text{wor}}(0) + \delta$. Thus the error of any algorithm is always greater than δ, no matter how many observations have been performed. This is not a coincidence. Problems with noise bounded in the sup-norm cannot be approximated with arbitrarily small error. More precisely, consider a general problem with linear S, the set E being the unit ball in a seminorm $\| \cdot \|_F$, and the noise satisfying $|x_i| \le \delta$, $\forall\, i$.

Lemma 2.8.2 *Suppose there exists $h^* \in F$ such that $h^* \notin \ker S$ and*

$$|L(h^*)| \le 1, \qquad \forall\, L \in \Lambda.$$

Then for any $n \ge 1$ we have

$$r_n^{\text{wor}}(\delta) \ge \min\{\delta, \|h^*\|_F^{-1}\} \cdot \|S(h^*)\|$$

(1/0 = +∞).

Proof For

$$h_\delta = \begin{cases} \delta\, h^* & \delta \le 1/\|h^*\|_F, \\ h^*/\|h^*\|_F & \delta > 1/\|h^*\|_F, \end{cases}$$

we have $\|h_\delta\|_F \le 1$ and $|L(h_\delta)| \le \delta$, $\forall\, L \in \Lambda$. Hence, for any exact information $N = [L_1, \ldots, L_n]$ with $L_i \in \Lambda$, $1 \le i \le n$,

$$\text{rad}^{\text{wor}}(N, \underbrace{[\delta, \ldots, \delta]}_{n}) \ge \tfrac{1}{2} \operatorname{diam}(N, \underbrace{[\delta, \ldots, \delta]}_{n})$$

$$= \sup\{\, \|S(h)\| \mid h \in E, |L_i(h)\| \le \delta, 1 \le i \le n\}$$

$$\geq \quad \|S(h_\delta)\| \ = \ \min\{\, \delta, \, \|h^*\|_F^{-1}\} \, \|S(h^*)\|,$$

as claimed. □

For the problems App and Int, the lemma holds with $h^* \equiv 1$. Then $\|h^*\|_F = 0$ and $r_n^{\mathrm{wor}}(\delta,) \geq \delta$. The formulas (2.65) and (2.66) show that this is the 'worst' possible choice of h^*. (Actually, we have $r_n^{\mathrm{wor}}(\delta) > \delta$, see also E 2.8.11.)

Lemma 2.8.2 also applies for the problem considered in Subsection 2.8.1, i.e., when F and G are Hilbert spaces, E is the unit ball of F, the solution operator $S : F \to G$ is compact, and Λ is the class of continuous linear functionals with norm bounded by 1. Taking h^* as the eigenvector corresponding to the largest eigenvalue of the operator S^*S, we obtain

$$r_n^{\mathrm{wor}}(\delta) \ \geq \ \min\{1, \delta\} \cdot \|S\|_F.$$

(Here also the inequality '$\geq$' can be replaced by '$>$'.) This observation should be contrasted to the case of noise bounded by δ in the Euclidean norm where the radius always converges to zero as $n \to +\infty$, see (2.61).

Notes and remarks

NR 2.8.1 Some parts of Subsection 2.8.1 (e.g. Lemma 2.8.1) have been taken from Plaskota (1993a), where the corresponding problem in the average case setting was solved, see also Subsection 3.8.1. The other results of Subsection 2.8 are new.

NR 2.8.2 In the case of exact linear information, the minimal radius $r_n^{\mathrm{wor}} = r_n^{\mathrm{wor}}(0)$ is closely related to the Gelfand n-widths and s-numbers from classical approximation theory. If one allows only linear algorithms, there are relations to the linear n-widths. These relations are discussed in Mathé (1990), Novak (1988), Traub and Woźniakowski (1980, Sect. 6 of Chap. 2 and Sect. 5 of Chap. 3), Traub et al. (1988, Sect. 5 of Chap. 4), and Kowalski et al. (1995). A survey of the theory of n-widths and many other references are presented in Pinkus (1985).

We note that for noisy information such close relations do not hold any longer. Indeed, as we convinced ourselves, the minimal radius $r_n^{\mathrm{wor}}(\delta)$ may for $\delta > 0$ tend to zero arbitrarily more slowly than $r_n^{\mathrm{wor}}(0)$ (or it may not converge at all), and consequently the ratio of the n-width and $r_n^{\mathrm{wor}}(\delta)$ may be arbitrary.

NR 2.8.3 For exact data, optimal nonadaptive information that uses n observations is usually called nth optimal information and its radius the nth minimal radius, see e.g. Traub et al. (1988, Sect. 5.3 of Chap. 4). If observations are always performed with the same precision δ, the notion of nth minimal radius and nth optimal information can be carried over to the noisy case in a natural way.

NR 2.8.4 We now present an example of a problem for which the results of Subsection 2.8.1 can be applied.

Let $d \geq 1$ and $r_i \geq 1$, $1 \leq i \leq d$. Let $F = W^{0...0}_{r_1...r_d}$ be the r.k.h.s. defined in NR 2.6.7. That is, F is the r.k.h.s. of multivariate functions $f : [0,1]^d \to \mathbb{R}$ with r.k. $R = \bigotimes_{i=1}^n R_{r_i}$ where R_{r_i} is the r.k. of the r_i-fold Wiener measure. Define the solution operator as $S : F \to G = \mathcal{L}_2([0,1]^d)$, $S(f) = f$. That is, we want to approximate functions in the $\mathcal{L}_2$-norm. It is known (see e.g. Papageorgiou and Wasilkowski, 1990) that in this case the eigenvalues of the operator S^*S satisfy

$$\lambda_j \asymp \left(\frac{\ln^{k-1} j}{j} \right)^{2r}$$

where $r = \min\{r_1, \ldots, r_d\}$ and k is the number of indices i for which $r_i = r$. Observe that the exponent $2r \geq 2$. Hence owing to (2.62) we have $r_n^{\text{wor}}(\delta) \asymp \delta / \sqrt{n}$ for $\delta > 0$, and $r_n^{\text{wor}}(0) \asymp (\ln^{k-1} n / n)^r$.

NR 2.8.5 It would be interesting to know the radius and optimal information in the Hilbert case for a restricted class Λ of permissible functionals. For instance, for the problem of NR 2.8.4 it is natural to assume that only noisy function values can be observed. Much is known in the exact information case, see e.g. Lee and Wasilkowski (1986), Woźniakowski (1991, 1992), Wasilkowski and Woźniakowski (1995). Unfortunately, finding optimal *noisy* information turns out to be a very difficult problem. Some results can be obtained from the average case analysis of Chapter 3, see NR 3.8.5.

Optimal information in the Hilbert case with noise bounded in the sup-norm is also unknown, even when $\delta_i = \delta$, $\forall i$.

NR 2.8.6 The fact used in (2.52) is a special case of the following well known theorem, see e.g. Marcus and Minc (1964).

Let A be a compact, self-adjoint and nonnegative definite operator acting in a separable Hilbert space X with an inner product $\langle \cdot, \cdot \rangle$. Let $\{\xi_i\}_{i \geq 1}$ be the orthonormal basis of eigenelements of A, and $\lambda_1 \geq \lambda_2 \geq \cdots \geq 0$ the corresponding eigenvalues. Then for any $1 \leq m \leq \dim X$ and orthonormal elements $\{x_i\}_{i=1}^m$ we have

$$\sum_{i=1}^m \langle Ax_i, x_i \rangle \leq \sum_{i=1}^m \lambda_i. \tag{2.67}$$

Indeed, since $x_i = \sum_{j \geq 1} \langle x_i, \xi_j \rangle \xi_j$ with $\sum_{j \geq 1} \langle x_i, \xi_j \rangle^2 = 1$, we have

$$
\begin{aligned}
\langle Ax_i, x_i \rangle &= \left\langle \sum_{j \geq 1} \langle x_i, \xi_j \rangle A\xi_j, \sum_{k \geq 1} \langle x_i, \xi_k \rangle \xi_k \right\rangle \\
&= \sum_{j,k \geq 1} \langle x_i, \xi_j \rangle \langle x_i, \xi_k \rangle \langle A\xi_j, \xi_k \rangle \\
&= \sum_{j \geq 1} \lambda_j \langle x_i, \xi_j \rangle^2.
\end{aligned}
$$

Hence

$$
\begin{aligned}
\sum_{i=1}^{m}\langle Ax_i, x_i\rangle &= \sum_{i=1}^{m}\sum_{j\geq 1}\lambda_j\langle x_i, \xi_j\rangle^2 \\
&\leq \sum_{i=1}^{m}\left(\sum_{j=1}^{m}(\lambda_j - \lambda_{m+1})\langle x_i, \xi_j\rangle^2 + \sum_{j\geq 1}\lambda_{m+1}\langle x_i, \xi_j\rangle^2\right) \\
&= \sum_{j=1}^{m}(\lambda_j - \lambda_{m+1})\sum_{i=1}^{m}\langle x_i, \xi_j\rangle^2 + \lambda_{m+1}\sum_{i=1}^{m}\sum_{j\geq 1}\langle x_i, \xi_j\rangle^2 \\
&\leq \sum_{j=1}^{m}(\lambda_j - \lambda_{m+1}) + m\,\lambda_{m+1} = \sum_{j=1}^{m}\lambda_j
\end{aligned}
$$

(for $m = \dim X$ we let $\lambda_{m+1} = 0$), as claimed.

If $d = \dim X < +\infty$ then (2.67) can be equivalently written as

$$
\sum_{i=r}^{d}\langle Ax_i, x_i\rangle \geq \sum_{i=r}^{d}\lambda_i, \qquad 1 \leq r \leq d,
$$

for any orthonormal x_is.

Exercises

E 2.8.1 Let F and G be normed spaces and the solution operator $S : F \to G$ be continuous and linear. Let $\|\cdot\|_Y$ be a norm in $\mathbb{R}^n$. Consider the problem of approximating $S(f)$ for $f \in E$ (E arbitrary), based on information $y \in \mathbb{R}^n$ such that $\|y - N(f)\|_Y \leq \delta$, where $N = [L_1, \ldots, L_n]$ consists of continuous linear functionals from a class Λ. Let $r_n^{\mathrm{wor}}(\delta)$ be the minimal radius of information consisting of n functionals. Show that if Λ satisfies

$$
L \in \Lambda \implies cL \in \Lambda, \quad \forall c \in \mathbb{R},
$$

then $r_n^{\mathrm{wor}}(\delta) = r_n^{\mathrm{wor}}(0)$.

E 2.8.2 Show that at least $(n-2)(n-1)/2$ elements of the matrix W from Lemma 2.8.1 are zero.

E 2.8.3 How will the formula for $r_n^{\mathrm{wor}}(\Delta)$ in the Hilbert case change if E is the ball of radius b and the class Λ consists of functionals whose norm is bounded by M?

E 2.8.4 Consider the minimal radius in the Hilbert case. Let $n_0 = \max\{1 \leq i \leq n \mid \delta_i = 0\}$. Let

$$
\begin{aligned}
s &= \min\{1 \leq i \leq n+1 \mid \lambda_i = \lambda_{n+1}\}, \\
t &= \max\{1 \leq i \leq n+1 \mid \lambda_i = \lambda_1\}.
\end{aligned}
$$

Show that $r_n^{\mathrm{wor}}(\Delta) = \sqrt{\lambda_{n+1}}$ iff $s \leq n_0 + 1$, and also $r_n^{\mathrm{wor}}(\Delta) = \sqrt{\lambda_1}$ iff $\sum_{j=n_0+1}^{n}\delta_j^{-2} \leq n - t$.

E 2.8.5 Let δ be such that

$$\delta^{-2} \geq \frac{1}{n} \sum_{i=1}^{n} \delta_i^{-2}.$$

Show then that in the Hilbert case $r_n^{\text{wor}}(\underbrace{\delta, \ldots, \delta}_{n}) \leq r_n^{\text{wor}}(\delta_1, \ldots, \delta_n)$.

E 2.8.6 Let η_i', $n_0 + 1 \leq i \leq n$, minimize

$$\Omega'(\eta_{n_0+1}, \ldots, \eta_n) = \max_{n_0+1 \leq i \leq n+1} \frac{\lambda_i}{1 + \eta_i}$$

over all $\eta_{n_0+1} \geq \cdots \geq \eta_n \geq 0$ satisfying (2.49). Let N_Δ' be the information operator constructed as in Theorem 2.8.1 with η_i^* replaced by η_i'. Show that in the Hilbert case $\text{rad}^{\text{wor}}(N_\Delta', \Delta) \leq \sqrt{2} \cdot r_n^{\text{wor}}(\Delta)$.

E 2.8.7 Show in the Hilbert case that if the solution operator S is not compact then the radius $r_n^{\text{wor}}(\delta)$ does not converge to zero with n, and that an optimal information does not necessarily exist.

E 2.8.8 Discuss the existence of optimal linear algorithms for the problems App and Int, for an arbitrary precision vector Δ.

E 2.8.9 Analyze when the optimal points t_i^* in Theorem 2.8.3 are uniquely determined.

E 2.8.10 Let $\Delta = [\delta_1, \ldots, \delta_n]$ and $\delta = \left(\sum_{i=1}^{n} \delta_i \right) / n$. Show that for $S \in \{\text{App}, \text{Int}\}$ we have $r_n^{\text{wor}}(S; \delta) \geq r_n^{\text{wor}}(S; \Delta)$.

E 2.8.11 Suppose that the element h^* in Lemma 2.8.2 satisfies

$$\max \{ \|S(h^*) + g\|, \|S(h^*) - g\| \} > \|S(h^*)\|, \quad \forall g \neq 0.$$

Show that if, in addition, $r_n^{\text{wor}}(0) > 0$, $\forall n \geq 1$, then

$$r_n^{\text{wor}}(\delta) > \delta \|S(h^*)\|, \qquad \forall \delta < \|h^*\|_F^{-1}.$$

Apply this result to the concrete problems considered in this section.

E 2.8.12 Let F be the class of functions $f : [0,1] \to \mathbb{R}$ for which the rth derivatives exist and are Lipschitz functions. Let

$$E = \{ f \in E \mid \ |f^{(r)}(t_1) - f^{(r)}(t_2)| \leq |t_1 - t_2| \}.$$

Consider the solution operator $S : F \to C([0,1])$ given as $S(f) = f^{(k)}$ where $0 \leq k \leq r$. Show that if the information consists of noisy function values with noise bounded in the sup-norm, then

$$r_n^{\text{wor}}(\delta) \geq 2\delta \frac{r!}{(r-k)!}, \qquad 1 \leq k \leq r,$$

and $r_n^{\text{wor}}(\delta) \geq \delta$ for $k = 0$.

2.9 Complexity

Up to now we have analyzed only the error of algorithms. It is clear that in practical computations we are interested not only in the error but also in the cost of obtaining approximations. In this section, we explain what we mean by the cost of approximation and discuss the concept of complexity. Then we derive some general bounds on the complexity of a problem. We assume that we are given

- a solution operator $S : F \rightarrow G$ where F is a linear space and G is a normed space,
- a set $E \subset F$ of elements f for which we want to construct approximations of $S(f)$,
- a class Λ of permissible information functionals,
- sets $B(\Delta, z)$ of all possible values of noise corresponding to the precision vector Δ and exact information z.

2.9.1 Computations over the space G

In order to be able to analyze the cost of obtaining approximations, we first present a *model of computation*. Roughly speaking, this model is based on the following two postulates. First, we assume that we can gain information about f by noisy observations of functionals of f. Second, using some primitive permissible operations, the information can be combined to obtain an approximation. These primitive operations are arithmetic operations and comparisons over the reals, linear operations over the space G, and logical operations over the Boolean values.

To describe the computational process leading to obtaining an approximation, we shall use the concept of a *program*. To define the program precisely, we adopt notation from the programming language *Pascal*.

Any program consists of two main parts:

- description of objects that are to be used, and
- description of actions that are to be performed.

The objects used in programs are called *constants* and *variables*. A constant is a fixed real number, an element of the space G, a functional from the class Λ, or a Boolean value ('true' or 'false'). A variable can assume an arbitrary value from a given nonempty set T. This set determines the *type* of the variable. We have four basic types: *real* (i.e., $T = \mathbb{R}$), *G-type* ($T = G$), *Λ-type* ($T = \Lambda$), and *Boolean*

($T = \{\text{'true'}, \text{'false'}\}$). We also allow T to be a subset of one of the basic types. The description of constants and variables is called a *declaration*.

The actions are described by *statements*. We have two *simple* statements (information statement, assignment statement) and three *structured* statements (compound statement, conditional statement, repetitive statement). We now define all of the statements in turn.

• The information statement

$$\mathcal{I}(y; L, \delta)$$

where y is a real variable, and $L \in \Lambda$, $\delta \geq 0$ are constants or variables with specified values. This statement describes the action which allows us to gain data—the noisy value of $L(f)$ where $f \in F$ is the (unknown) element for which we want to compute an approximation. We 'ask' for this noisy value. The 'answer' is a real number y which is then assigned to the variable y. We assume that by the ith question we obtain a value y_i such that

$$[y_1, \ldots, y_i] \in B([\delta_1, \ldots, \delta_i], [L_1(f), \ldots, L_i(f)]).$$

• The assignment statement

$$v := \mathcal{E}$$

where v is a variable and $\mathcal{E}$ is an *expression*. This is the second fundamental statement. It specifies that the value of the expression $\mathcal{E}$ be evaluated for the current values of variables, and that this value be assigned to the variable v.

Expressions are constructs denoting rules of computation for evaluating values of functions of some variables using only permissible *primitive operations* over the reals, elements of the space G, and Boolean values, which are represented by constants and current values of variables. The primitive operations are as follows:

arithmetic operations over the reals $\mathbb{R}$: sign inversion ($x \mapsto -x$), addition ((x, y) $\mapsto x+y$), subtraction ((x, y) $\mapsto x-y$), multiplication ((x, y) $\mapsto x * y$), division ((x, y) $\mapsto x/y$, $y \neq 0$);

comparisons over $\mathbb{R}$: equality ((x, y) $\mapsto x = y$), inequality ((x, y) $\mapsto x \neq y$), ordering ((x, y) $\mapsto x < y$, (x, y) $\mapsto x \leq y$);

linear operations over the space G: sign inversion ($g \mapsto -g$), addition ((g_1, g_2) $\mapsto g_1 + g_2$), subtraction ((g_1, g_2) $\mapsto g_1 - g_2$), multiplication by a scalar ((x, g) $\mapsto x * g$);

Boolean operations: negation ($b \mapsto$ not b), union $((b_1, b_2) \mapsto b_1$ or b_2), intersection $((b_1, b_2) \mapsto b_1$ and b_2).

To be more precise, an expression is a single constant or variable, or is a construct of the form $f(w)$ or $f(w, z)$, where f stands for a primitive operation (of one or two arguments), and w, z are previously defined expressions. In the following three examples, a, b, x, y are real constants or variables and g, h are constants or variables of G-type.

$$(x - a)(b - x)/(b - a) \qquad \text{(real expression)},$$
$$g + y\,h \qquad \text{(G-type expression)},$$
$$(y < a) \text{ or } (y \leq 3) \qquad \text{(Boolean expression)}.$$

Those are simple statements. Structured statements contain other statements in their definitions.

• The compound statement

$$\textbf{begin} \quad S_1;\ S_2;\ \dots\ ; S_n \quad \textbf{end}$$

where $S_1, S_2, \dots, S_n$ are statements. This specifies the successive execution of $S_1, S_2, \dots, S_n$.

• The conditional statement

$$\textbf{if} \ \ \mathcal{E} \ \ \textbf{then} \ \ S_1 \ \ \textbf{else} \ \ S_2$$

where $\mathcal{E}$ is a Boolean expression and S_1, S_2 are statements or *empty* (i.e., do nothing). This corresponds to the following action. First the value of $\mathcal{E}$ is evaluated. If this value is 'true', the action S_1 is executed. If 'false', we perform S_2.

• The repetitive statement

$$\textbf{while} \ \ \mathcal{E} \ \ \textbf{do} \ \ S$$

where $\mathcal{E}$ is a Boolean expression and S is a statement. The action described by this statement relies on repetitive execution of S until the value of $\mathcal{E}$ is 'false'. If $\mathcal{E}$ is 'false' at the beginning, S is not executed at all.

Summarizing, the program consists of one declaration and one compound statement. We make an additional assumption that the set of variables contains a special variable g of G-type. An approximation is obtained by executing the program. The result of computation, i.e., approximation of $S(f)$, is the value of the variable g. The initial values of all variables are undefined. In order that the result be always well defined, we assume that for any data y a finite number of simple statements is executed, including at least one assignment to g.

2.9.2 Cost and complexity, general bounds

We now present the notions of cost and complexity. The basic assumption is that we must charge for gaining information and performing any primitive operation.

1. Obtaining a noisy value of $L(f)$ with precision δ costs $c(\delta)$ where $c : [0, +\infty) \to [0, +\infty)$ is a given *cost function*. It is nonnegative, nonincreasing, and positive for sufficiently small but positive δ.

Observe that the cost of obtaining a single datum d depends on the precision δ. The smaller δ, the larger the cost. Theoretically, c can assume even infinite values. However, $c(\delta) = +\infty$ will mean that the precision δ cannot be used. Examples of cost functions include $c(\delta) = \delta^{-2}$ or $c(\delta) = \max\{0, -\log_2 \delta\}$. The function

$$c(\delta) = c_{\text{fix}}(\delta) = \begin{cases} +\infty & 0 \leq \delta < \delta_0, \\ c_0 & \delta \geq \delta_0, \end{cases} \tag{2.68}$$

corresponds to the case when any observation is performed with fixed precision δ_0. In particular, taking $\delta_0 = 0$ we obtain the exact information case.

2. We assign the following costs to the primitive operations:

arithmetic operations over $\mathbb{R}$:	1
comparisons over $\mathbb{R}$:	1
linear operations over G:	g $(g \geq 1)$
Boolean operations:	0.

Let $\mathcal{P}$ be a program. The total cost of executing $\mathcal{P}$ is given by the sum of costs of gaining information (information cost) and performing all primitive operations (combinatory cost). Observe that the total cost depends only on the information (data) y obtained. We denote this cost by $\text{cost}(\mathcal{P}; y)$. The *(worst case) cost* of computing an approximation using the program $\mathcal{P}$ is given as

$$\text{cost}^{\text{wor}}(\mathcal{P}) = \sup_{y \in Y_0} \text{cost}(\mathcal{P}; y),$$

where Y_0 is the set of all possible values of information that can be obtained by executing $\mathcal{P}$.

Example 2.9.1   Consider the following simple program:

> **constants:** $L_1, \ldots, L_n \in \Lambda$, $\quad \delta_1, \ldots, \delta_n \in \mathbb{R}_+$, $\quad g_1, \ldots, g_n \in G$;
> **variables:** $y_1, \ldots, y_n$: *real,* $\quad g$: G-*type;*
> **begin** $\quad \mathcal{I}(y_1; L_1, \delta_1); \ \ldots ; \mathcal{I}(y_n; L_n, \delta_n);$
> $\qquad\qquad g := y_1\, g_1 + \cdots + y_n\, g_n$
> **end.**

In this program, information $y = [y_1, \ldots, y_n]$ is collected nonadaptively and approximation is obtained by taking a linear combination of y_is. The cost of executing it is independent of y and equal to

$$\text{cost}^{\text{wor}}(\mathcal{P}) \;=\; \sum_{i=1}^{n} \mathbf{c}(\delta_i) + (2n-1)\mathbf{g},$$

where the first component is the information cost and the second component is the combinatory cost.

We now define the complexity of an algorithm. Observe first that for any program $\mathcal{P}$ there exist unique (in general adaptive) information operator $\mathbb{N} = \{N, \Delta\}$ and algorithm φ with the following properties:

(a) for any $f \in E$, the set of all possible values of information obtained by executing $\mathcal{P}$ coincides with $\mathbb{N}(f)$, and

(b) if the information obtained is y, then the result of computation is $\varphi(y)$.

We say that $\mathcal{P}$ is a *realization* of the algorithm φ using the information $\mathbb{N}$. For instance, the program in Example 2.9.1 realizes the linear algorithm $\varphi(y_1, \ldots, y_n) = \sum_{i=1}^{n} y_i g_i$ using nonadaptive information with $N = [L_1, \ldots, L_n]$ and $\Delta = [\delta_1, \ldots, \delta_n]$.

It is clear that not all algorithms φ using some information $\mathbb{N}$ can be realized. On the other hand, if an algorithm has at least one realization then it also has many other realizations. We are interested in such realizations $\mathcal{P}$ that have minimal $\text{cost}^{\text{wor}}(\mathcal{P})$. This minimal cost will be called the *algorithm complexity* and denoted by $\text{comp}^{\text{wor}}(\mathbb{N}, \varphi)$. That is,

$$\text{comp}^{\text{wor}}(\mathbb{N}, \varphi) \;=\; \inf \{\, \text{cost}^{\text{wor}}(\mathcal{P}) \mid \ \mathcal{P} \text{ is a realization of } \varphi \text{ using } \mathbb{N} \,\}.$$

(If φ and $\mathbb{N}$ cannot be realized then $\text{comp}^{\text{wor}}(\mathbb{N}, \varphi) = +\infty$.) Observe that

$\text{comp}^{\text{wor}}(\mathsf{N},\varphi)$ is independent of any realization, i.e., this is a property of the operators N and φ only.

We are now ready to define the problem complexity. Let $\varepsilon \geq 0$. Suppose we want to compute ε-approximations to $S(f)$ for $f \in E$. That is, we want the (worst case) error to be at most ε. By the ε-*complexity* of this problem, $\text{Comp}^{\text{wor}}(\varepsilon)$, we mean the minimal $\text{cost}^{\text{wor}}(\mathcal{P})$ over all programs $\mathcal{P}$ which compute approximations with error at most ε. Clearly, such approximations can be computed only when the corresponding information and algorithm satisfy $e^{\text{wor}}(\mathsf{N},\varphi) \leq \varepsilon$. Hence

$$\text{Comp}^{\text{wor}}(\varepsilon) \;=\; \inf\{\,\text{comp}^{\text{wor}}(\mathsf{N},\varphi) \mid e^{\text{wor}}(\mathsf{N},\varphi) \leq \varepsilon\,\}.$$

Information N_ε and an algorithm φ_ε such that $e^{\text{wor}}(\mathsf{N}_\varepsilon,\varphi_\varepsilon) \leq \varepsilon$ and $\text{comp}^{\text{wor}}(\mathsf{N}_\varepsilon,\varphi_\varepsilon) = \text{Comp}^{\text{wor}}(\varepsilon)$ will be called ε-*complexity optimal*, or simply *optimal* if it is known from the context which optimality concept is being used.

Clearly, the ε-complexity depends not only on ε but also on the other parameters of the problem. Therefore we shall sometimes write $\text{Comp}^{\text{wor}}(S;\varepsilon)$, $\text{Comp}^{\text{wor}}(S,\mathbf{c};\varepsilon)$, etc. To make the notation shorter, the superscript 'wor' in comp^{wor} and Comp^{wor} will often be omitted.

We now give some useful general bounds on the ε-complexity. The results will be oriented towards approximating linear problems and will be used in the next section.

For an information operator $\mathsf{N} = \{N_y, \Delta_y\}_{y \in Y}$ where

$$\Delta_y = [\delta_1, \delta_2(y_1), \ldots, \delta_n(y_1, \ldots, y_{n(y)-1})],$$

the cost of N is given as

$$\text{cost}^{\text{wor}}(\mathsf{N}) \;=\; \sup_{y \in Y_0} \sum_{i=1}^{n(y)} \mathbf{c}(\delta_i(y_1, \ldots, y_{i-1})),$$

where $Y_0 = \bigcup_{f \in E} \mathsf{N}(f) \subset Y$ and $y = [y_1, \ldots, y_{n(y)}]$. For nonadaptive N we obviously have $\text{cost}^{\text{wor}}(\mathsf{N}) = \sum_{i=1}^{n} \mathbf{c}(\delta_i)$. A *(nonadaptive) information* ε-*complexity* is defined as

$$\text{IC}^{\text{non}}(\varepsilon) \;=\; \inf\{\,\text{cost}^{\text{wor}}(\mathsf{N}) \mid \mathsf{N} \text{ nonadaptive, and there exists } \varphi$$
$$\text{such that } e^{\text{wor}}(\mathsf{N},\varphi) \leq \varepsilon\,\}.$$

Hence $\text{IC}^{\text{non}}(\varepsilon)$ is the minimal cost of nonadaptive information from which it is possible (at least theoretically) to obtain approximation with error at most ε.

In what follows, we shall use the concept of a κ-hard element which was introduced in Section 2.7. We assume without loss of generality that if f^* is a κ-hard element then for any nonadaptive N there is an algorithm φ such that

$$e^{\text{wor}}(\mathbb{N}, \varphi) \leq \kappa \cdot r(A_{\mathbb{N}}(N(f^*))).$$

(Otherwise we can replace κ by a slightly larger number and the above condition will hold.)

Lemma 2.9.1 *(i) If a κ-hard element exists then*

$$\text{Comp}^{\text{wor}}(\varepsilon) \geq \text{IC}^{\text{non}}(\kappa \varepsilon).$$

(ii) Let $\rho \geq 1$. Suppose that there exist nonadaptive information $\mathbb{N}_\varepsilon$ using $n(\varepsilon)$ observations, and a linear algorithm φ_ε such that

$$\text{cost}^{\text{wor}}(\mathbb{N}_\varepsilon) \leq \rho \cdot \text{IC}^{\text{non}}(\varepsilon) \quad \text{and} \quad e^{\text{wor}}(\mathbb{N}_\varepsilon, \varphi_\varepsilon) \leq \varepsilon.$$

Then

$$\text{Comp}^{\text{wor}}(\varepsilon) \leq \rho \cdot \text{IC}^{\text{non}}(\varepsilon) + (2\, n(\varepsilon) - 1)\, \mathbf{g}.$$

Proof (i) Let $\mathbb{N}^{\text{ad}}$ be arbitrary, in general adaptive, information with radius $\text{rad}^{\text{wor}}(\mathbb{N}^{\text{ad}}) \leq \varepsilon$. Let $\mathbb{N}^{\text{non}}$ be the nonadaptive information from Theorem 2.7.1 corresponding to $\mathbb{N}^{\text{ad}}$. Then $\text{cost}(\mathbb{N}^{\text{non}}) \leq \text{cost}(\mathbb{N}^{\text{ad}})$ and there is an algorithm φ such that

$$e^{\text{wor}}(\mathbb{N}^{\text{non}}, \varphi) \leq \kappa \cdot \text{rad}^{\text{wor}}(\mathbb{N}^{\text{ad}}) \leq \kappa \varepsilon.$$

Hence $\text{Comp}(\varepsilon) \geq \text{IC}^{\text{non}}(\kappa \varepsilon)$.

(ii) Since the algorithm φ_ε is linear, for given information y it requires at most $2\, n(\varepsilon) - 1$ linear operations in the space G to compute $\varphi_\varepsilon(y)$, see Example 2.9.1. Hence

$$\begin{aligned}
\text{comp}(\mathbb{N}_\varepsilon, \varphi_\varepsilon) &\leq \text{cost}(\mathbb{N}_\varepsilon) + (2\, n(\varepsilon) - 1)\, \mathbf{g} \\
&\leq \rho \cdot \text{IC}^{\text{non}}(\varepsilon) + (2\, n(\varepsilon) - 1)\, \mathbf{g},
\end{aligned}$$

as claimed. $\qquad\qquad\qquad\qquad\qquad\qquad\qquad\qquad\qquad\qquad\qquad\square$

Lemma 2.9.1 immediately gives the following theorem, which is the major result of this section.

Theorem 2.9.1 *Suppose that the assumptions of Lemma 2.9.1 are fulfilled for all ε and some ρ independent of ε. If, in addition,*

$$\text{IC}^{\text{non}}(\varepsilon) = O(\text{IC}^{\text{non}}(\kappa \varepsilon)) \quad \text{and} \quad n(\varepsilon) = O(\text{IC}^{\text{non}}(\varepsilon)),$$

then

$$\text{Comp}^{\text{wor}}(\varepsilon) \asymp \text{IC}^{\text{non}}(\varepsilon),$$

as $\varepsilon \to 0^+$. [1]

Hence, for problems satisfying the assumptions of Theorem 2.9.1, the ε-complexity, $\text{Comp}(\varepsilon)$, is essentially equal to the information ε-complexity $\text{IC}^{\text{non}}(\varepsilon)$. Note that the condition $\text{IC}^{\text{non}}(\varepsilon) = O(\text{IC}^{\text{non}}(\kappa \varepsilon))$ means that $\text{IC}^{\text{non}}(\varepsilon)$ does not increase too fast as $\varepsilon \to 0$. It is satisfied if, for instance, $\text{IC}^{\text{non}}(\varepsilon)$ behaves polynomially in $1/\varepsilon$. The condition $n(\varepsilon) = O(\text{IC}^{\text{non}}(\varepsilon))$ holds if the information operators N_ε use observations with costs bounded uniformly from below by a positive constant. Indeed, if $c(\delta) \geq c_0 > 0$, $\forall \delta \geq 0$, then $n(\varepsilon) \leq \text{IC}^{\text{non}}(\varepsilon)/c_0$.

It turns out that the information complexity is closely related to the minimal radius of information. More precisely, let

$$R(T) \;=\; \inf\left\{\, r_n^{\text{wor}}(\delta_1,\dots,\delta_n) \;\Big|\; n \geq 1,\; \sum_{i=1}^{n} c(\delta_i) \leq T \right\}$$

be the Tth *minimal radius* of nonadaptive information. Then we have the following relation.

Lemma 2.9.2 *Suppose that the function*

$$R^{-1}(\varepsilon) \;=\; \inf\{\, T \mid R(T) \leq \varepsilon \,\}$$

is semicontinuous. That is, there exist a continuous function $\psi(\varepsilon)$ and constants $0 < \alpha \leq \beta < +\infty$ such that for small ε, $0 < \varepsilon \leq \varepsilon_0$,

$$\alpha\,\psi(\varepsilon) \;\leq\; R^{-1}(\varepsilon) \;\leq\; \beta\,\psi(\varepsilon).$$

Then

$$R^{-1}(\varepsilon) \;\leq\; \text{IC}^{\text{non}}(\varepsilon) \;\leq\; \frac{\beta}{\alpha}\cdot R^{-1}(\varepsilon), \qquad \forall\, 0 < \varepsilon \leq \varepsilon_0.$$

Proof For $\beta > 0$, take information N_β and an algorithm φ_β such that $e^{\text{wor}}(N_\beta, \varphi_\beta) \leq \varepsilon$ and $\text{cost}(N_\beta) \leq \text{IC}^{\text{non}}(\varepsilon) + \beta$. Then $R^{-1}(\varepsilon) \leq \text{IC}^{\text{non}}(\varepsilon) + \beta$. Since this holds for arbitrary β, we obtain $R^{-1}(\varepsilon) \leq \text{IC}^{\text{non}}(\varepsilon)$.

We now show the second inequality. Let $0 < \alpha < \varepsilon$ and $\beta > 0$. Then

---

[1] For two functions, $a(\varepsilon) \asymp b(\varepsilon)$ as $\varepsilon \to 0^+$ means the *weak* equivalence of functions. That is, there exist $\varepsilon_0 > 0$ and $0 < K_1 \leq K_2 < +\infty$ such that $K_1 \leq a(\varepsilon)/b(\varepsilon) \leq K_2$ for all $\varepsilon \leq \varepsilon_0$.

$R(R^{-1}(\varepsilon-\alpha)+\beta) \leq \varepsilon-\alpha$ and there are information N_β and an algorithm φ_β such that $\text{cost}(N_\beta) \leq R^{-1}(\varepsilon - \alpha) + \beta$ and $e^{\text{wor}}(N_\beta, \varphi_\beta) \leq \varepsilon$. Then $\text{IC}^{\text{non}}(\varepsilon) \leq \text{cost}(N_\beta)$. Since β can be arbitrarily small, we get

$$\text{IC}^{\text{non}}(\varepsilon) \leq R^{-1}(\varepsilon - \alpha) \leq \beta\psi(\varepsilon - \alpha).$$

Letting $\alpha \to 0^+$ and using continuity of ψ we finally obtain

$$\text{IC}^{\text{non}}(\varepsilon) \leq \beta\psi(\varepsilon) \leq \frac{\beta}{\alpha}R^{-1}(\varepsilon),$$

as claimed. $\qquad\square$

Thus the information ε-complexity is roughly the inverse function to the Tth minimal radius. Note that the minimal radii $r_n^{\text{wor}}(\delta_1, \ldots, \delta_n)$ have already been determined for some problems, see Section 2.8. For those problems we can find $R(T)$. Then $\text{IC}^{\text{non}}(\varepsilon)$ can be evaluated using Lemma 2.9.2.

We end this section with some additional remarks. For fixed precision (2.68), the complexity of information N_ε from Lemma 2.9.1 is equal to $\text{cost}(N_\varepsilon) = c_0 \, n(\varepsilon)$. Hence, in this case, the bounds in Lemma 2.9.1 can be rewritten as

$$c_0 \, n(\kappa\varepsilon) \leq \text{Comp}(\varepsilon) \leq n(\varepsilon)(c_0 + 2\mathbf{g}) - 2\mathbf{g}.$$

Observe that the case of fixed precision establishes an upper bound on the information ε-complexity of a problem with arbitrary cost function $\mathbf{c}$. Indeed, if we set δ_0 in (2.68) to be such that $\mathbf{c}(\delta_0) > 0$, and $c_0 = \mathbf{c}(\delta_0)$, then

$$\text{IC}^{\text{non}}(\mathbf{c};\varepsilon) \leq \text{IC}^{\text{non}}(\mathbf{c}_{\text{fix}};\varepsilon).$$

On the other hand, if the cost function $\mathbf{c}$ is bounded from below by a positive constant c_0, the information ε-complexity is not smaller than $\text{IC}(\varepsilon)$ of the same problem with exact information, where the cost function $\mathbf{c}_{\text{exa}} \equiv c_0$.

Notes and remarks

NR 2.9.1 In the case of exact information or information with fixed noise level, our model of computation corresponds to that of Traub *et al.* (1983, Chap. 5, and 1988, Chap. 3). As far as we know, the model with cost dependent on the noise level was first studied in Kacewicz and Plaskota (1990).

NR 2.9.2 Some researchers define a model of computation using the concept of a *machine*. The most widely known is the *Universal Turing Machine* which can be used to study discrete problems. Another example is the *Unlimited Register Machine* (URM) discussed in Cutland (1980). Machines and complexity over the reals are presented in Blum *et al.* (1989, 1995). Recently, Novak (1995b) generalized these concepts and defined a machine that can be used to study complexity of problems with partial information. For other models, see also Ko (1986, 1991), Schönhage (1986) and Weihrauch (1987).

NR 2.9.3 The choice of a model of computation and, in particular, the set of primitive operations is in general a delicate question. We believe that this choice should depend on the class of problems we want to solve. For instance, for discrete problems the Turing machine seems to be a good choice. For problems defined on the reals it seems that a real number model should be used. We study problems defined on linear spaces. Hence to obtain nontrivial results we have to assume that at least linear operations on the space G are possible.

NR 2.9.4 In view of the previous remark, we can say that we use the basic version of the model of computation over linear spaces. However, natural generalizations of this model are sometimes possible. We now give one example.

Suppose that G is a Cartesian product of some other linear spaces over $\mathbb{R}$, $G = G_1 \times G_2 \times \cdots \times G_s$. For instance, $G = \mathbb{R}^s = \underbrace{\mathbb{R} \times \cdots \times \mathbb{R}}_{s}$. Or, if G is a space of functions $g : \mathbb{R}^d \to \mathbb{R}^s$, then any element $g \in G$ can be represented as $g(x) = (g_1(x), \ldots, g_s(x))$ with $g_i : \mathbb{R}^d \to \mathbb{R}$. In these cases it is natural to assume that we can perform linear operations over each 'coordinate' G_i. Clearly, we would also be able to perform linear operations over G (via the identification $g = (g_1, \ldots, g_s) \in G$, $g_i \in G_i$) with the cost $\mathbf{g} = \sum_{i=1}^{s} \mathbf{g}_i$, where $\mathbf{g}_i$ is the cost of linear operations over G_i.

For our purposes any such 'generalization' is, however, not necessary. As will turn out, for problems considered in this monograph the complexity essentially equals the information complexity. Hence using a 'more powerful' model will not lead to appreciably different results.

NR 2.9.5 The assumption that we can use arbitrary elements of $\mathbb{R}$ or G corresponds in practice to the fact that *precomputation* is possible. This may be sometimes a too idealized assumption. For instance, even if we know theoretically that the optimal algorithm is linear, $\varphi_{\mathrm{opt}}(y) = \sum_{i=1}^{n} y_i g_i$, the elements g_i may sometimes not be known exactly, or may be very difficult to precompute. We believe, however, that such examples are exceptional.

We also stress that the 'precomputed' elements *can* depend on ε. One may assume that precomputing is independent of ε. This leads to another, also useful, model, in which one wants to have a 'good' single program which allows one to produce an ε-approximation to $S(f)$ for any $\varepsilon > 0$. Some examples on this can be found in Kowalski (1989), Novak (1995b), and Paskov (1993).

NR 2.9.6 Clearly, our model also assumes other idealizations. One of them is that the cost of observing a noisy value of a functional depends on the noise level only. That is, we neglect the dependence on the element for which information is obtained. Errors that may occur when the value of $\varphi(y)$ is computed are also neglected.

NR 2.9.7 One can argue that the assumption that linear operations over G are allowed is not very realistic. In practice digital computers are usually used to perform calculations, and they can only manipulate with bits. This is certainly true. On the other hand, computers have been successfully used for solving some very complicated problems including, in particular, continuous and high dimensional problems which require at least computations over the reals. This paradox is possible only because computer arithmetic (which is in fact discrete) can imitate computations in the real number model very well. Similarly, by using an appropriate discrete model, we can make computations over an arbitrary linear space G possible.

This point can also be expressed as follows. Even if it is true that the real world is discrete in nature, it is often more convenient (and simpler!) to use a continuous model to describe, study, and understand some natural phenomena. We believe that the same applies to scientific computations.

NR 2.9.8 We consider a *sequential* model of computation, where only one instruction can be performed at each step. It would also be interesting to study a *parallel* model, see, e.g., Heinrich and Kern (1991), Kacewicz (1990), Nemirovski (1994).

NR 2.9.9 We note that the assertion of Theorem 2.9.1 does not always hold if all the assumptions are not satisfied. That is, there are linear problems for which the ε-complexity is much larger than information ε-complexity (or even infinite), see e.g. Wasilkowski and Woźniakowski (1993).

NR 2.9.10 Information about the programming language Pascal can be found, e.g., in Jensen and Wirth (1975).

Exercises

E 2.9.1 Show that if the conditional and repetitive statements were not allowed then only algorithms using nonadaptive information would be realizable and the cost of computing $\varphi(y)$ would be independent of y.

E 2.9.2 Give an example of an algorithm φ and information N that cannot be realized.

E 2.9.3 Let N be an information operator with $Y = \mathbb{R}^n$, and let φ be an algorithm of the form

$$\varphi(y) = \sum_{i=1}^{n} q_i(y) \, g_i,$$

where $g_i \in G$ and q_i are some real rational functions of n variables $y_1, \ldots, y_n$. Show that then there exists a realization of φ using N.

E 2.9.4 Let φ_1 and φ_2 be two algorithms that use the same information N. Show that if $\varphi_2 = A\varphi_1$, where $A : G \to G$ is a linear transformation, then $\mathrm{comp}(N, \varphi_2) \leq \mathrm{comp}(N, \varphi_1)$. If, in addition, A is one-to-one then $\mathrm{comp}(N, \varphi_1) = \mathrm{comp}(N, \varphi_2)$.

E 2.9.5 Give an example of a problem for which optimal information is nonadaptive and the upper bound in Lemma 2.9.1 is not sharp, i.e., $\mathrm{Comp}(\varepsilon) < \mathrm{IC}^{\mathrm{non}}(\varepsilon) + (2n(\varepsilon) - 1)\mathbf{g}$.

E 2.9.6 Prove that
$$\lim_{\alpha \to 0^+} R^{-1}(\varepsilon - \alpha) \geq IC^{\mathrm{non}}(\varepsilon) \geq R^{-1}(\varepsilon).$$

2.10 Complexity of special problems

In this section, we derive the ε-complexity for several classes of problems. To this end, we use the general bounds given in the previous section. Special attention will be devoted to the dependence of $\mathrm{Comp}(\varepsilon)$ on the cost function.

2.10.1 Linear problems in Hilbert spaces

We begin with the problem defined in Subsection 2.8.1. That is, we assume that S is a compact operator acting between separable Hilbert spaces F and G, and E is the unit ball in F. The class Λ of permissible information functionals consists of all continuous linear functionals with norm bounded by 1. The noise x satisfies $\sum_{i=1}^{n}(x_i/\delta_i)^2 \leq 1$, where n is the length of x and $[\delta_1, \ldots, \delta_n]$ is the precision vector used.

In this case, it is convenient to introduce the function
$$\tilde{c}(x) = c(x^{-2}), \qquad 0 < x < +\infty,$$

where c is the cost function. We assume that $\tilde{c}$ is concave or convex.

We first show how in general the Tth minimal radius can be evaluated. As in Subsection 2.8.1, we denote by ξ_j, $j \geq 1$, the orthonormal basis of eigenvectors of the operator S^*S, and by λ_j the corresponding eigenvalues, $\lambda_1 \geq \lambda_2 \geq \cdots$. We shall also use the function Ω which was defined in Subsection 2.8.1,

$$\Omega = \Omega(\alpha; \eta_1, \ldots, \eta_n) = \max_{1 \leq i \leq n+1} \frac{\lambda_i}{\alpha + (1 - \alpha)\,\eta_i}$$

(with the convention $\lambda_i/0 = +\infty$ for $\lambda_i > 0$, and $0/0 = 0$).

Lemma 2.10.1 *The Tth minimal radius is equal to*
$$R(T) = \inf \sqrt{\Omega(\alpha; \eta_1, \ldots, \eta_n)},$$

where the infimum is taken over all $0 \leq \alpha \leq 1$, n, and $\eta_i \geq 0$, $1 \leq i \leq n$, satisfying
(a1) for concave $\tilde{c}$

$$\sum_{i=1}^{n} \tilde{c}(\eta_i) \leq T,$$

(b1) for convex c̃

$$n\tilde{c}\left(\frac{1}{n}\sum_{i=1}^{n}\eta_i\right) \leq T.$$

Moreover, if the infimum is attained for n^* and $\eta^* = (\eta_1^*, \ldots, \eta_{n^*}^*)$, then

$$R(T) = \text{rad}^{\text{wor}}(\{N_T, \Delta_T\})$$

where
(a2) for concave c̃

$$\Delta_T = \left[1/\sqrt{\eta_1^*}, \ldots, 1/\sqrt{\eta_{n^*}^*}\right], \qquad N_T = [\langle \cdot, \xi_1 \rangle_F, \ldots, \langle \cdot, \xi_{n^*} \rangle_F],$$

(b2) for convex c̃

$$\Delta_T = \left[\underbrace{1/\sqrt{\eta_0^*}, \ldots, 1/\sqrt{\eta_0^*}}_{n^*}\right], \qquad N_T = [\langle \cdot, \xi_1^\Delta \rangle_F, \ldots, \langle \cdot, \xi_{n^*}^\Delta \rangle_F],$$

where $\eta_0^* = (1/n^*)\sum_{i=1}^{n^*} \eta_i^*$ and the ξ_i^Δs are as in Theorem 2.8.1 with $\delta_i = \sqrt{1/\eta_0^*}$, $\forall i$.

Proof We first prove (a1) and (b1). Let the function c̃ be concave. Then for any n and $\eta_1, \ldots, \eta_n$ satisfying (2.49) we have

$$\sum_{i=1}^{n}\tilde{c}(\eta_i) \leq \sum_{i=1}^{n}\tilde{c}(\delta_i^{-2}). \tag{2.69}$$

Denoting by $\eta^*(\delta)$ the vector minimizing Ω over all $0 \leq \alpha \leq 1$ and η satisfying (2.49), we obtain from Theorem 2.8.1 and (2.69) that

$$R^2(T) = \inf\left\{(r_n^{\text{wor}}(\delta_1, \ldots, \delta_n))^2 \,\middle|\, n \geq 1, \sum_{i=1}^{n}c(\delta_i^2) \leq T\right\}$$

$$= \inf\left\{\Omega(\alpha; \eta^*(\delta)) \,\middle|\, 0 \leq \alpha \leq 1, \delta = (\delta_1, \ldots, \delta_n),\right.$$

$$\left. n \geq 1, \sum_{i=1}^{n}\tilde{c}(\delta_i^{-2}) \leq T\right\}$$

$$= \inf\left\{\Omega(\alpha; \eta) \,\middle|\, 0 \leq \alpha \leq 1, \eta = (\eta_1, \ldots, \eta_n),\right.$$

$$\left. n \geq 1, \sum_{i=1}^{n}\tilde{c}(\eta_i) \leq T\right\}.$$

Let $\tilde{c}$ be convex. Then for any n and $\eta_1, \ldots, \eta_n$ we have

$$\sum_{i=1}^{n} \tilde{c}(\eta_i) \geq n\,\tilde{c}(\eta_0)$$

where $\eta_0 = (1/n)\sum_{i=1}^{n} \eta_i$. Since for $\delta_i^2 = 1/\eta_0$, $1 \leq i \leq n$, the condition (2.49) holds for any $\eta_1 \geq \cdots \geq \eta_n$, we obtain

$$R^2(T) \;=\; \inf \left\{ (r_n^{\mathrm{wor}}(\underbrace{\delta,\ldots,\delta}_{n}))^2 \;\middle|\; n \geq 1,\, n\,c(\delta) \leq T \right\}$$

$$=\; \inf \left\{ \Omega(\alpha;\eta) \;\middle|\; 0 \leq \alpha \leq 1,\, \eta = (\eta_1,\ldots,\eta_n), \right.$$

$$\left. n \geq 1, n\,\tilde{c}\left(n^{-1}\sum_{i=1}^{n} \eta_i\right) \leq T \right\}.$$

To show (a2) and (b2) it is enough to apply (a1), (a2), and Theorem 2.8.1. $\qquad\square$

We now comment on the lemma above. Observe first that the Tth minimal radius depends only on the cost function and eigenvalues of the operator S^*S. The second comment is about information for which $R(T)$ is achieved. In the case of convex $\tilde{c}$, optimal information uses observations with fixed precision δ. This is no longer true for concave functions $\tilde{c}$. However, in this case we can restrict ourselves to observations of the functionals $\langle \cdot, \xi_i \rangle_F$.

To give an illustration of how Lemma 2.10.1 can be used to evaluate $\mathrm{Comp}(\varepsilon)$, suppose that the cost function is given by

$$c(\delta) \;=\; c_{\mathrm{lin}}(\delta) \;=\; \begin{cases} \delta^{-2} & \delta > 0, \\ +\infty & \delta = 0. \end{cases}$$

This cost function possesses the following property. The error of approximating the value of a functional from several observations depends only on the total cost of observations and not on their number or the precisions used. Indeed, if we observe the value $L(f)$ n times with accuracy $\Delta = [\delta_1, \ldots, \delta_n]$, then the minimal error in approximating $L(f)$ is $(\sum_{i=1}^{n} \delta_i^{-2})^{-1/2} = \sum_{i=1}^{n} c_{\mathrm{lin}}(\delta_i)$.

Note that in this case the function $\tilde{c}_{\mathrm{lin}}(x) = x$. Hence it is convex and concave. After some calculations we obtain

$$R(c_{\mathrm{lin}}; T)^2 \;=\; \lambda_{n+1} + \frac{1}{T}\sum_{j=1}^{n}(\lambda_j - \lambda_{n+1}) \qquad (2.70)$$

where $n = n(T) = \lfloor T \rfloor$. Observe now that for $0 \leq T \leq 1$ we have

$R(c_{lin}; T)^2 = R(0)^2 = \lambda_1$, while for $T \geq c_0$, $R(c_{lin}; T)^2$ is linear in T on each interval $[n, n + 1]$ and $R(c_{lin}; n)^2 = (1/n) \sum_{j=1}^{n} \lambda_j$, $j \geq 1$. Hence the Tth minimal radius is a continuous function of T and $\lim_{T \to \infty} R(c_{lin}; T) = 0$. Moreover, since $\lambda_1 \geq \lambda_2 \geq \cdots \to 0$, for sufficiently large T (i.e., for $T > \min\{j \mid \lambda_j < \lambda_1\}$) it is also decreasing. In view of Lemma 2.9.2, for small ε we have

$$IC^{non}(c_{lin}; \varepsilon) = R^{-1}(\varepsilon) \approx \min \left\{ n \geq 1 \; \middle| \; \frac{1}{n} \sum_{j=1}^{n} \lambda_j \leq \varepsilon^2 \right\}.^{1}$$

To get the ε-complexity of our problem, we can use Theorem 2.9.1. We have that 0 is a 1-hard element. Furthermore, $IC^{non}(c_{lin}; \varepsilon)$ can be achieved by information that uses $n(\varepsilon) = \lfloor IC^{non}(c_{lin}; \varepsilon) \rfloor$ observations, and there exists an optimal linear algorithm. Hence,

$$Comp(c_{lin}; \varepsilon) \asymp \min \left\{ n \geq 1 \; \middle| \; \frac{1}{n} \sum_{j=1}^{n} \lambda_j \leq \varepsilon^2 \right\}.$$

It turns out that the cost function c_{lin} is in some sense 'worst' possible. That is, we have the following fact.

Lemma 2.10.2 *Let* c *be an arbitrary cost function. Let* δ_0 *be such that* $c(\delta_0) < +\infty$. *Then*

$$Comp^{wor}(c; \varepsilon) \leq M \cdot Comp^{wor}(c_{lin}, \varepsilon), \qquad \forall \varepsilon > 0,$$

where $M = M(c, \delta_0) = \lceil 2\delta_0^2 \rceil (c(\delta_0) + 2g)$.

Proof Since $R(c_{lin}; T)^2 \geq \lambda_1 / \max\{1, T\}$, we have

$$IC^{non}(c_{lin}; \varepsilon) \begin{cases} = 0 & \varepsilon \geq \sqrt{\lambda_1}, \\ > 1 & \varepsilon < \sqrt{\lambda_1}. \end{cases}$$

In the first case, zero is the best approximation and the lemma is true.

Let $\varepsilon < \sqrt{\lambda_1}$. Let N be such that $rad^{wor}(N) = \varepsilon$ and $cost(c_{lin}; N) = IC^{non}(c_{lin}; \varepsilon)$. We can assume that N uses $n = \lfloor IC^{non}(c_{lin}; \varepsilon) \rfloor$ observations with the same precision δ satisfying $\delta^{-2} = IC^{non}(c_{lin}; \varepsilon)/n$. Let $k = k(\delta_0) = \lceil 2\delta_0^2 \rceil$. Consider the information operator $\tilde{N}$ which repeats, k times, observations of the same functionals as in N, but with precisions $\tilde{\delta}$ where $\tilde{\delta}^{-2} = \delta^{-2}/k$. We obviously have $rad^{wor}(\tilde{N}) = rad^{wor}(N)$ and

$$cost(c; \tilde{N}) = k n \tilde{c} \left(\frac{IC^{non}(c_{lin}; \varepsilon)}{k n} \right)$$

---

[1] $a(\varepsilon) \approx b(\varepsilon)$ means the *strong* equivalence of functions, i.e., $\lim_{\varepsilon \to 0+} (a(\varepsilon)/b(\varepsilon)) = 1$ $(0/0 = \infty/\infty = 1)$.

$$\leq \; k\, n\, \tilde{c}(2/k) \; \leq \; k\, c(\delta_0)\, \mathrm{IC}^{\mathrm{non}}(c_{\mathrm{lin}}; \varepsilon).$$

Since the optimal algorithm $\tilde{\varphi}$ for information $\tilde{\mathrm{N}}$ is linear, we finally obtain

$$\begin{aligned}
\mathrm{Comp}^{\mathrm{wor}}(c; \varepsilon) \; &\leq \; \mathrm{comp}(c; \tilde{\mathrm{N}}, \tilde{\varphi}) \\
&\leq \; k\, c(\delta_0)\mathrm{Comp}(c_{\mathrm{lin}}; \varepsilon) + (2\, k\, n - 1)\mathbf{g} \\
&\leq \; k\, (c(\delta_0) + 2\mathbf{g})\, \mathrm{Comp}(c_{\mathrm{lin}}; \varepsilon),
\end{aligned}$$

as claimed. $\square$

Lemma 2.10.2 can be used for deriving the complexity for some other cost functions. For instance, consider the case of observations with fixed noise level, where the cost function $c_{\mathrm{fix}}(\delta) = c_0$ for $\delta \geq \delta_0$, and $c_{\mathrm{fix}}(\delta) = +\infty$ for $\delta < \delta_0$, with $c_0, \delta_0 > 0$. Since $c_{\mathrm{fix}}(\delta) \geq c_0\, \delta_0^2\, c_{\mathrm{lin}}(\delta)$, we have $\mathrm{IC}^{\mathrm{non}}(c_{\mathrm{fix}}; \varepsilon) \geq c_0\, \delta_0^2\, \mathrm{IC}^{\mathrm{non}}(c_{\mathrm{lin}}; \varepsilon)$. Hence c_{fix} is also the 'worst' cost function and $\mathrm{Comp}(c_{\mathrm{fix}}; \varepsilon) \asymp \mathrm{Comp}(c_{\mathrm{lin}}; \varepsilon)$.

We now consider the exact information case where the cost function is constant, e.g., $c_{\mathrm{exa}} \equiv 1$. In this case $r_n^{\mathrm{wor}}(0) = \sqrt{\lambda_{n+1}}$. Hence $\mathrm{R}(c_{\mathrm{exa}}; T) = \sqrt{\lambda_{n+1}}$ where $n = n(T) = \lfloor T \rfloor$, and

$$\mathrm{Comp}(c_{\mathrm{exa}}; \varepsilon) \; \asymp \; \min\left\{ n \geq 1 \;\middle|\; \lambda_{n+1} \leq \varepsilon^2 \right\}.$$

Clearly, $\mathrm{Comp}(c_{\mathrm{exa}}; \varepsilon)$ gives a lower bound for complexity corresponding to a cost function that is bounded from below by a positive constant. That is, if $c(\delta) \geq c_0 > 0$ for all $\delta \geq 0$, then

$$\mathrm{Comp}(c; \varepsilon) \; \geq \; c_0 \cdot \mathrm{Comp}(c_{\mathrm{exa}}; \varepsilon).$$

Let us see more precisely how the complexity depends on the cost function c and eigenvalues λ_j. Consider

$$c_q(\delta) \; = \; \begin{cases} (1 + \delta^{-2})^q & \delta > 0, \\ +\infty & \delta = 0, \end{cases}$$

where $q \geq 0$. Note that for $q \geq 1$ the function $\tilde{c}_q$ is convex, while for $0 < q \leq 1$ it is concave. The case $q = 0$ corresponds to exact information.

Since for all q we have $\mathrm{Comp}(q; \varepsilon) = O(\mathrm{Comp}(1; \varepsilon))$, we can restrict ourselves to $0 \leq q \leq 1$. To obtain the formula for the Tth minimal radius we set, for simplicity, $\alpha = 1/2$ in the α-smoothing spline algorithm and use Lemma 2.10.1. The minimum $\min_{1 \leq i \leq n+1}(\lambda_i/(1 + \eta_i))$ over all

$\eta_1 \geq \cdots \geq \eta_n \geq \eta_{n+1} = 0$ such that $\sum_{i=1}^{n}(1+\eta_i)^q \leq T$ is attained at

$$\eta_j = \frac{T^{1/q}}{(\sum_{i=1}^{n}\lambda_i^q)^{1/q}} \cdot \lambda_j - 1, \qquad 1 \leq j \leq n,$$

where n is the largest integer satisfying

$$\sum_{j=1}^{n}\lambda_j^q \leq \lambda_n^q T.$$

Furthermore,

$$R(q;T)^2 = b \cdot \left(\frac{1}{T}\sum_{i=1}^{n}\lambda_i^q\right)^{1/q}$$

where $1/2 \leq b \leq 1$. Assume now that the eigenvalues of the operator S^*S satisfy

$$\lambda_j \asymp \left(\frac{\ln^s j}{j}\right)^p$$

with $p > 0$ and $s \geq 0$. As we know, this corresponds to function approximation in tensor product spaces, see NR 2.8.4. In this case we have

$$R(q,p,s;T) \asymp R(1,pq,s;T)^{1/q}.$$

The formulas for $R(1,pq,s;T)$ can be derived based on (2.70). We obtain that for all q

$$R(q,p,s;T) \asymp \begin{cases} (1/T)^{1/\tilde{q}} & p\tilde{q} > 1, \\ (\ln^{s+1}T/T)^p & p\tilde{q} = 1, \\ (\ln^s T/T)^p & 0 \leq p\tilde{q} < 1, \end{cases}$$

as $T \to +\infty$, where $\tilde{q} = \min\{1,q\}$. This together with Lemma 2.9.2 and Theorem 2.9.1 gives the ε-complexity. That is, we have the following.

Theorem 2.10.1

$$\mathrm{Comp}^{\mathrm{wor}}(q,p,s;\varepsilon) \asymp \begin{cases} (1/\varepsilon)^{2\tilde{q}} & p\tilde{q} > 1, \\ (1/\varepsilon)^{2/p}\ln^{s+1}(1/\varepsilon) & p\tilde{q} = 1, \\ (1/\varepsilon)^{2/p}\ln^{sp}(1/\varepsilon) & 0 \leq p\tilde{q} < 1, \end{cases}$$

as $\varepsilon \to 0^+$.

We see that the dominating factor which determines the complexity is the exponent of $1/\varepsilon$. Suppose first that $p > 1$. Then this exponent is $2/p$

for $0 \le q \le 1/p$, $2q$ for $1/p < q < 1$, and 2 for $q \ge 2$. On the other hand, if $0 < p \le 1$ then the exponent is $2/p$ and is independent of q. This means that for 'difficult' problems, i.e., for the eigenvalues λ_j tending to zero sufficiently slowly ($p < 1$), the behavior of the ε-complexity does not depend on the cost function.

2.10.2 Approximation and integration of Lipschitz functions

We pass to approximation, App, and integration, Int, of real valued Lipschitz functions $f : [0,1] \to \mathbb{R}$, based on noisy values of f at some points. The noise $x = y - N_y(f)$ is assumed to be bounded in the weighted sup-norm, $x \in B(\Delta_y)$, where

$$B(\Delta_y) = \{\, x \in \mathbb{R}^n \mid \; |x_i| \le \delta_i(y_1,\dots,y_{i-1}),\, 1 \le i \le n(y) \,\}.$$

These problems were precisely defined in Subsection 2.8.2.

Theorem 2.10.2 *Let the cost function* **c** *be convex. Then*

$$\mathrm{IC}^{\mathrm{non}}(\mathrm{App};\varepsilon) = \inf_{0 \le \delta < \varepsilon} \mathbf{c}(\delta) \left\lceil \frac{1}{2(\varepsilon - \delta)} \right\rceil$$

and

$$\inf_{0 \le \delta < 2\varepsilon} \mathbf{c}(\delta) \left\lceil \frac{1}{2(2\varepsilon - \delta)} \right\rceil \le \mathrm{IC}^{\mathrm{non}}(\mathrm{Int};\varepsilon) \le \inf_{0 \le \delta < \varepsilon} \mathbf{c}(\delta) \left\lceil \frac{1}{4(\varepsilon - \delta)} \right\rceil.$$

Furthermore,

$$\mathrm{Comp}^{\mathrm{wor}}(\mathrm{App};\varepsilon) \asymp \mathrm{IC}^{\mathrm{non}}(\mathrm{App};\varepsilon)$$

and

$$\mathrm{Comp}^{\mathrm{wor}}(\mathrm{Int};\varepsilon) \asymp \mathrm{IC}^{\mathrm{non}}(\mathrm{App};\alpha(\varepsilon)\,\varepsilon),$$

where $\alpha(\varepsilon) \in [1,2]$.

Proof For both problems we have

$$\mathrm{IC}^{\mathrm{non}}(\varepsilon) = \inf \left\{\, \sum_{i=1}^{n} \mathbf{c}(\delta_i) \;\middle|\; r_n^{\mathrm{wor}}(\delta_1,\dots,\delta_n) \le \varepsilon \,\right\},$$

where $r_n^{\mathrm{wor}}(\delta_1,\dots,\delta_n)$ is the minimal radius of information using observations with precisions δ_i. The formulas for $r_n^{\mathrm{wor}}(\delta_1,\dots,\delta_n)$ are given in Theorem 2.8.3.

Consider first the function approximation problem. Observe that for δ_is such that $\sum_{i=1}^{n} \delta_i = A$, the radius is minimized at $\delta_i = \delta = A/n$, $\forall\, i$. Using the convexity of $\mathbf{c}$ we also have $\sum_{i=1}^{n} \delta_i \geq n\,\mathbf{c}(\delta)$. Hence

$$\mathrm{IC}^{\mathrm{non}}(\mathrm{App}; \varepsilon) = \inf\left\{ n\,\mathbf{c}(\delta) \mid n \geq 1, \frac{1}{2n} + \delta \leq \varepsilon \right\}$$

$$= \inf_{0 \leq \delta < \varepsilon} \mathbf{c}(\delta) \left\lceil \frac{1}{2(\varepsilon - \delta)} \right\rceil.$$

We now turn to the integration. The upper bound for $\mathrm{IC}^{\mathrm{non}}(\mathrm{Int}; \varepsilon)$ can be obtained by again letting $\delta_i = \delta$, $\forall\, i$. Then

$$\mathrm{IC}^{\mathrm{non}}(\mathrm{Int}; \varepsilon) \leq \inf\left\{ n\,\mathbf{c}(\delta) \mid n \geq 1, \frac{1}{4n} + \delta \leq \varepsilon \right\}$$

$$= \inf_{0 \leq \delta < \varepsilon} \mathbf{c}(\delta) \left\lceil \frac{1}{4(\varepsilon - \delta)} \right\rceil.$$

To get the lower bound, we first observe that for all $n \geq 1$ and $A \geq 0$, the maximum

$$M(A, n) = \max\left\{ \sum_{i=1}^{n} \delta_i^2 \;\middle|\; \sum_{i=1}^{n} \delta_i = A,\ \delta_j \leq \frac{1}{n}\left(\frac{1}{2} + A\right), \forall\, j \right\}$$

is attained at

$$\delta_j^* = \begin{cases} (1/2 + A)/n & 1 \leq j \leq k = \lfloor nA/(1/2 + A) \rfloor, \\ A - (1/2 + A)k/n & j = k + 1, \\ 0 & k + 2 \leq j \leq n, \end{cases}$$

and therefore

$$M(A, n) = \sum_{i=1}^{n} (\delta_i^*)^2 \leq \left(\frac{nA}{1/2 + A} \right)\left(\frac{1/2 + A}{n} \right)^2 = \frac{A}{n}\left(\frac{1}{2} + A \right).$$

This yields that for all δ_is such that $\sum_{i=1}^{n} \delta_i = A$, we have

$$r_n^{\mathrm{wor}}(\delta_1, \ldots, \delta_n) \geq \frac{1}{n}\left(\frac{1}{2} + A \right)^2 - \frac{A}{n}\left(\frac{1}{2} + A \right) = \frac{1}{4n} + \frac{A}{2n}.$$

Hence

$$\mathrm{IC}^{\mathrm{non}}(\mathrm{Int}; \varepsilon) \geq \inf\left\{ n\,\mathbf{c}(\delta) \;\middle|\; \frac{1}{4n} + \frac{\delta}{2} \leq \varepsilon \right\}$$

$$= \inf_{0 \leq \delta < 2\varepsilon} \mathbf{c}(\delta) \left\lceil \frac{1}{2(2\varepsilon - \delta)} \right\rceil.$$

To show the remaining part of the theorem, observe that the bounds for $\mathrm{IC}^{\mathrm{non}}(\mathrm{Int}; \varepsilon)$ proven above yield

$$\mathrm{IC}^{\mathrm{non}}(\mathrm{App}; 2\varepsilon) \leq \mathrm{IC}^{\mathrm{non}}(\mathrm{Int}; \varepsilon) \leq \mathrm{IC}^{\mathrm{non}}(\mathrm{App}; \varepsilon). \tag{2.71}$$

Moreover, $IC^{non}(App; \varepsilon)$ and the upper bound for $IC^{non}(Int; \varepsilon)$ are attained by information that uses $n(\varepsilon)$ observations of the same precision $\delta(\varepsilon)$, and $\delta(\varepsilon) \to 0$ as $\varepsilon \to 0$. For such information, the linear algorithms based on natural splines of order 1 interpolating the data are optimal. Hence, for sufficiently small ε, we have $\mathbf{c}(\delta(\varepsilon)) \geq \mathbf{c}_0$ for some $\mathbf{c}_0 > 0$, and consequently $n(\varepsilon) \leq IC^{non}(\varepsilon)/\mathbf{c}_0$. The formulas for $Comp(\varepsilon)$ now follow from (2.71) and Theorem 2.9.1. $\square$

Clearly, if $IC^{non}(App; 2\varepsilon) \asymp IC^{non}(App; \varepsilon)$ (which holds when $\mathbf{c}(\delta)$ tends to infinity not too fast as $\delta \to 0$, see E 2.10.4), then the factor $\alpha(\varepsilon)$ in Theorem 2.10.2 can be omitted.

To give concrete examples, suppose that the cost function is given as

$$\mathbf{c}_q(\delta) = \delta^{-q}, \qquad \delta > 0,$$

where $q > 0$, and $\mathbf{c}_q(0) = +\infty$. Then we have

$$IC^{non}(App, q; \varepsilon) \approx \left(\frac{1}{\varepsilon}\right)^{q+1} \frac{(q+1)^{q+1}}{2\, q^q}.$$

The best information uses $n(\varepsilon) \approx (1+q)/(2\varepsilon)$ observations with precision $\delta(\varepsilon) \approx q(1+q)^{-1}\varepsilon$. Thus

$$Comp(App, q; \varepsilon) \asymp Comp(Int, q; \varepsilon) \asymp IC^{non}(App, q; \varepsilon). \qquad (2.72)$$

Note that letting $q \to 0$ we get results for exact information with $\mathbf{c} \equiv 1$.

If $\mathbf{c}(\delta) = \max\{0, \log_2 \delta^{-1}\}$ for $\delta > 0$, and $\mathbf{c}(0) = +\infty$, then

$$IC^{non}(App; \varepsilon) \approx \frac{\log_2(1/\varepsilon)}{2\, \varepsilon},$$

and $n(\varepsilon) \approx 1/(2\varepsilon)$, $\delta(\varepsilon) \approx \varepsilon/(\ln \varepsilon^{-1})$. Clearly, (2.72) also holds.

Observe that for any cost function we have the following bounds on the information complexity:

$$\mathbf{c}(\varepsilon) \lceil 1/(2\varepsilon) \rceil \leq IC^{non}(App; \varepsilon) \leq \mathbf{c}(\varepsilon/2) \lceil 1/\varepsilon \rceil.$$

Hence the ε-complexity tends to infinity roughly as $\mathbf{c}(\varepsilon)/\varepsilon$ ($\varepsilon \to 0$). This means, in particular, that for problems with fixed noise level the complexity is infinite, if ε is sufficiently small. Actually, this is the consequence of Lemma 2.8.2 which says that the radius of information cannot be arbitrarily small. We now translate that general result into the language of complexity.

We consider the general linear solution operator $S : F \to G$. The set E is the unit ball of F with respect to a seminorm $\| \cdot \|_F$. We wish to approximate $S(f)$ from noisy adaptive observations of linear functionals from a class Λ, with the noise level δ bounded from below by $\delta_0 > 0$. Recall that this corresponds to the cost function which assumes $+\infty$ on the interval $[0, \delta_0)$.

Theorem 2.10.3 *Suppose there exists an element $h^* \in F$ such that $h^* \notin \ker S$ and*

$$|L(h^*)| \leq 1, \qquad \forall L \in \Lambda.$$

Then for all $\varepsilon < \min\{\delta_0, \|h^*\|_F^{-1}\} \|S(h^*)\|$ we have

$$\mathrm{Comp}^{\mathrm{wor}}(S; \varepsilon) = +\infty.$$

Proof It was shown in Lemma 2.8.2 that for any nonadaptive information $\mathbb{N}$ that uses observations with noise not smaller than δ_0 we have $\mathrm{rad}^{\mathrm{wor}}(\mathbb{N}) \geq \min\{\delta_0, \|h^*\|_F^{-1}\} \|S(h^*)\|$. Repeating the same proof we find that the same bound holds for any adaptive information $\mathbb{N}$. Hence, the theorem follows. $\square$

Recall that for the problems App and Int we can take $h^* \equiv 1$. Then Theorem 2.10.3 says that $\mathrm{Comp}(\mathrm{App}; \varepsilon) = \mathrm{Comp}(\mathrm{Int}; \varepsilon) = +\infty$, for all $\varepsilon < \delta_0$ (actually, this is also true for $\varepsilon = \delta_0$). For approximation of a compact operator S in Hilbert spaces as in Subsection 2.10.1, we find that the ε-complexity is infinite if $\varepsilon < \min\{1, \delta_0\} \|S\|_F$.

2.10.3 Multivariate approximation in a Banach space

For the problems App and Int, the ε-complexity is achieved by nonadaptive information that uses observations with precisions $\delta_i \asymp \varepsilon$. In this subsection we show that this result can be generalized to a class of problems where the information noise is bounded in the absolute or relative sense. The results will be oriented towards approximation of multivariate functions from noisy data about function values. This particular problem will be defined later. Now we consider a general problem.

We assume that F is a linear space equipped with a norm $\| \cdot \|_F$ and G is a normed space. The solution operator $S : F \to G$ is linear. We want to approximate $S(f)$ for all f from the ball $\|f\|_F \leq 1$, based on noisy observations of some functionals $L \in \Lambda$ at f. Two types of information noise are considered: absolute and relative. More precisely, exact information is given as

$$N(f) = [L_1(f), \ldots, L_n(f))]$$

where $L_i \in \Lambda$, $1 \le i \le n$. In the case of noise bounded in the *absolute* sense, the information $y \in \mathbb{R}^n$ obtained satisfies

$$|y_i - L_i(f)| \le \delta_i,$$

while for noise bounded in the *relative* sense we have

$$|y_i - L_i(f)| \le \delta_i \cdot |L_i(f)|,$$

$1 \le i \le n$. We stress that the functionals L_i, the precisions δ_i, and the number n of observations can adaptively depend on the y_js. That is, we deal in general with adaptive information.

To distinguish the absolute and relative noise, we shall sometimes use the subscripts 'abs' and 'rel'.

We start with the analysis of noise bounded in the absolute sense. Let d_n be the minimal diameter of nonadaptive information that uses n exact observations,

$$d_n = \inf \{ \operatorname{diam}(N, 0) \mid N = [L_1, \ldots, L_n],\ L_i \in \Lambda,\ 1 \le i \le n \}.$$

We also let $d_0 = 2\,\|S\|_F = 2\,\sup_{\|h\|_F \le 1}\|S(h)\|$. Define the number

$$n^*(\varepsilon) = \min \{ n \ge 0 \mid d_n(0) \le 2\varepsilon \}$$

($\min \emptyset = +\infty$).

We first show a lower bound on $\operatorname{Comp}_{\mathrm{abs}}(\varepsilon)$. To this end, assume that the following condition is satisfied. There exists a constant K, $0 < K < +\infty$, such that

$$|L(h)| \le K \cdot \|S(h)\|, \qquad \forall L \in \Lambda,\ \forall h \in F. \tag{2.73}$$

Lemma 2.10.3 *Suppose that a κ-hard element exists. If the condition (2.73) is satisfied then*

$$\operatorname{Comp}_{\mathrm{abs}}^{\mathrm{wor}}(\varepsilon) \ge n^*(\kappa\,\varepsilon) \cdot \mathbf{c}(K\,\kappa\,\varepsilon).$$

Proof We first show that

$$\operatorname{IC}_{\mathrm{abs}}^{\mathrm{non}}(\varepsilon) \ge n^*(\varepsilon) \cdot \mathbf{c}(K\,\varepsilon). \tag{2.74}$$

If $\varepsilon \ge \|S\|_F$ then the zero approximation is optimal. Hence $n^*(\varepsilon) = 0$ and (2.74) follows.

Let $\varepsilon < \|S\|_F$. Let $\mathbb{N} = \{N, \Delta\}$ where $N = [L_1, \ldots, L_n]$ and $\Delta =$

$[\delta_1, \ldots, \delta_n]$, $0 \leq \delta_1 \leq \cdots \leq \delta_n$, be an arbitrary information operator with radius $\mathrm{rad}^{\mathrm{wor}}_{\mathrm{abs}}(\mathbb{N}) \leq \varepsilon$. Let

$$k = \max\left\{ i \leq n \mid \delta_i \leq \tfrac{1}{2} K \operatorname{diam}_{\mathrm{abs}}(\mathbb{N}) \right\}.$$

(If $\delta_1 > K \operatorname{diam}_{\mathrm{abs}}(\mathbb{N})/2$ then $k = 0$.) We claim that

$$k \geq n^*(\varepsilon). \qquad (2.75)$$

To show this, it suffices that for information $\mathbb{N}' = \{N', \Delta'\}$ where $N' = [L_1, \ldots, L_k]$ and $\Delta' = [\delta_1, \ldots, \delta_k]$ (or for information $\mathbb{N}' \equiv \{0\}$ if $k = 0$), we have $\operatorname{diam}_{\mathrm{abs}}(\mathbb{N}') \leq 2\varepsilon$.

Indeed, suppose to the contrary that $\operatorname{diam}_{\mathrm{abs}}(\mathbb{N}') > 2\varepsilon$. Then there is $h \in F$ such that $\|h\|_F \leq 1$, $|L_i(h)| \leq \delta_i$, $1 \leq i \leq k$, and $2\|S(h)\| > 2\varepsilon \geq \operatorname{diam}_{\mathrm{abs}}(\mathbb{N})$. Let

$$h' = \min\left\{ 1, \frac{\delta_{k+1}}{K\|S(h)\|} \right\} \cdot h.$$

Then $\|h'\|_F \leq 1$, and for all $k + 1 \leq j \leq n$ the following holds:

$$|L_j(h')| \leq K \cdot \|S(h')\| \leq \min\{ K\|S(h)\|, \delta_j \} = \delta_j.$$

Since for $1 \leq i \leq k$ we also have $|L_i(h')| \leq |L_i(h)| \leq \delta_i$, we find that

$$\begin{aligned}
\operatorname{diam}_{\mathrm{abs}}(\mathbb{N}) &\geq 2\|S(h')\| \\
&= 2\min\left\{ 1, \frac{\delta_{k+1}}{K\|S(h)\|} \right\} \|S(h)\| \\
&= \min\left\{ 2\|S(h)\|, 2\frac{\delta_{k+1}}{K} \right\} > \operatorname{diam}_{\mathrm{abs}}(\mathbb{N}),
\end{aligned}$$

which is a contradiction. Hence $\operatorname{diam}_{\mathrm{abs}}(\mathbb{N}') < 2\varepsilon$. Since the information $\mathbb{N}'$ uses k observations, (2.75) follows.

Observe that (2.75) also yields $k \geq 1$. Hence we have

$$\begin{aligned}
\operatorname{cost}(\mathbb{N}) &= \sum_{i=1}^{n} \mathbf{c}(\delta_i) \geq \sum_{i=1}^{k} \mathbf{c}(\delta_i) \geq k \cdot \mathbf{c}\left(\tfrac{1}{2} K \operatorname{diam}(\mathbb{N})\right) \\
&\geq k\,\mathbf{c}(K\varepsilon) \geq n^*(\varepsilon) \cdot \mathbf{c}(K\varepsilon).
\end{aligned}$$

Since $\mathbb{N}$ was arbitrary, the proof of (2.74) is complete.

Now Lemma 2.9.1 together with (2.74) yields

$$\operatorname{Comp}_{\mathrm{abs}}(\varepsilon) \geq \mathrm{IC}^{\mathrm{non}}_{\mathrm{abs}}(\kappa\varepsilon) \geq n^*(\kappa\varepsilon) \cdot \mathbf{c}(\kappa\varepsilon)$$

which proves the lemma. $\qquad \square$

To show an upper bound, we assume that for any $n \geq 1$ and $\delta > 0$, there exist information $\mathbb{N}$ that uses n observations with the precision vector $\Delta = \underbrace{[\delta, \ldots, \delta]}_{n}$, and a linear algorithm φ, such that

$$e_{\text{abs}}^{\text{wor}}(\mathbb{N}, \varphi) \leq M \cdot (d_n + \delta). \qquad (2.76)$$

Here M is an absolute positive constant independent of n and δ.

Lemma 2.10.4 *If the condition (2.76) is satisfied then*

$$\text{Comp}_{\text{abs}}^{\text{wor}}(\varepsilon) \leq n^*(m\varepsilon)\,(\mathbf{c}(m\varepsilon) + 2\,\mathbf{g})$$

where $m = (3M)^{-1}$.

Proof Let $\delta = m\varepsilon$ and $n = n^*(\delta)$. Let $\mathbb{N}$ be information that uses n observations with precision δ, and let φ be an algorithm such that $e_{\text{abs}}^{\text{wor}}(\mathbb{N}, \varphi) \leq M(d_n + \delta)$. Since $d_n \leq 2\,\delta$, we have

$$e_{\text{abs}}^{\text{wor}}(\mathbb{N}, \varphi) \leq 3\delta M \leq 3M m\varepsilon = \varepsilon.$$

Hence

$$\begin{aligned}
\text{Comp}_{\text{abs}}(\varepsilon) &\leq \text{comp}(\mathbb{N}, \varphi) \leq n\,\mathbf{c}(\delta) + (2n-1)\mathbf{g} \\
&\leq n\,(\mathbf{c}(\delta) + 2\mathbf{g}) = n\,(m\varepsilon)\,(\mathbf{c}\,(m\varepsilon) + 2\mathbf{g}),
\end{aligned}$$

as claimed.   □

The upper and lower bounds on $\text{Comp}_{\text{abs}}(\varepsilon)$ give the following theorem.

Theorem 2.10.4 *Assume that for any $\alpha > 0$,*

$$n^*(\alpha\varepsilon) \asymp n^*(\varepsilon) \quad \text{and} \quad \mathbf{c}(\alpha\varepsilon) \asymp \mathbf{c}(\varepsilon),$$

as $\varepsilon \to 0^+$. If the conditions (2.73) and (2.76) are satisfied and a κ-hard element exists, then

$$\text{Comp}_{\text{abs}}^{\text{wor}}(\varepsilon) \asymp n^*(\varepsilon) \cdot \mathbf{c}(\varepsilon).$$

Furthermore, optimal information uses $n \asymp n^*(\varepsilon)$ observations with the same precision $\delta \asymp \varepsilon$.

This theorem has a very useful interpretation. It states that the ε-complexity is proportional to the cost $\mathbf{c}(\varepsilon)$ of obtaining the value of a functional with precision ε, and to the complexity in the exact information case with $\mathbf{c} \equiv 1$. We stress that Theorem 2.10.4 applies *only* to problems for which $c(\varepsilon)$ and $n^*(\varepsilon)$ tend to infinity at most polynomially in $1/\varepsilon$, as $\varepsilon \to 0^+$. It also seems worth while to mention that we obtained the complexity results without knowing exact formulas for the minimal radii $r_n^{wor}(\Delta)$.

We now pass to the case of relative noise. We assume that all functionals $L \in \Lambda$ satisfy $\|L\|_F \leq 1$, and there exists h_0 such that $\|h_0\|_F \leq 1$ and

$$\inf_{L \in \Lambda} |L(h_0)| = A > 0. \tag{2.77}$$

Theorem 2.10.5 *Suppose that the assumptions of Theorem 2.10.4 and the condition (2.77) are satisfied. Then*

$$\mathrm{Comp}_{rel}^{wor}(\varepsilon) \asymp \mathrm{Comp}_{abs}^{wor}(\varepsilon) \asymp n^*(\varepsilon) \cdot c(\varepsilon).$$

Proof Observe first that if $|y_i - L_i(f)| \leq \delta_i |L_i(f)|$ then $|y_i - L_i(f)| \leq \delta_i \|L_i\|_F \|f\|_F \leq \delta_i$. This means that for any information $\mathbb{N}$ and an element f with $\|f\|_F \leq 1$, we have $\mathbb{N}_{rel}(f) \subset \mathbb{N}_{abs}(f)$. Hence

$$e_{rel}^{wor}(\mathbb{N}, \varphi) \leq e_{abs}^{wor}(\mathbb{N}, \varphi), \quad \forall \mathbb{N}, \forall \varphi,$$

and consequently

$$\mathrm{Comp}_{rel}(\varepsilon) \leq \mathrm{Comp}_{abs}(\varepsilon).$$

This shows the upper bound for $\mathrm{Comp}_{rel}(\varepsilon)$.

As in Subsection 2.7.2, we can show that for any adaptive information $\mathbb{N}$ we have

$$\mathrm{rad}_{rel}^{wor}(\mathbb{N}) \geq \tfrac{1}{2} \min\{1 - \|\alpha h_0\|_F, \alpha A/2\} \cdot \mathrm{rad}_{abs}^{wor}(\mathbb{N}).$$

Taking $\alpha = (1 + A/2)^{-1}$ we obtain

$$\mathrm{rad}_{rel}^{wor}(\mathbb{N}) \geq \frac{1}{2} \frac{A}{A+2} \mathrm{rad}_{abs}^{wor}(\mathbb{N}).$$

Hence for any $B > 2(A+2)/A$ we have

$$\begin{aligned} \mathrm{Comp}_{rel}(\varepsilon) &\geq \mathrm{IC}_{rel}^{non}(\varepsilon) \geq \mathrm{IC}_{abs}^{non}(B\varepsilon) \\ &\asymp \mathrm{IC}_{abs}^{non}(\varepsilon) \asymp \mathrm{Comp}_{abs}(\varepsilon), \end{aligned}$$

which shows the lower bound for $\mathrm{Comp}_{rel}(\varepsilon)$ and completes the proof. $\square$

Thus, under some assumptions, the cases of relative and absolute noise are (almost) equivalent. We note that such an equivalence does not always hold. For instance, for the problems App and Int of Subsection 2.10.2 and information N using n observations of function values with precision $\delta \in (0,1)$, we have $\mathrm{rad}^{\mathrm{wor}}_{\mathrm{rel}}(N) = +\infty$. Indeed, the vector $y = \underbrace{[a, \ldots, a]}_{n}$, $a > 0$, is noisy information about $f_1 \equiv a/(1 - \delta)$ and $f_{-1} \equiv a/(1 + \delta)$. We also have $f_1, f_{-1} \in E$. Hence, for $S \in \{\mathrm{App}, \mathrm{Int}\}$,

$$\mathrm{rad}^{\mathrm{wor}}_{\mathrm{rel}}(N) \; \geq \; \tfrac{1}{2}\,\|S(f_1) - S(f_{-1})\|$$

$$= \; a\,\frac{2\delta}{1 - \delta^2} \; \longrightarrow \; +\infty \qquad \text{as } a \to +\infty.$$

(See also E 2.10.8.)

Multivariate approximation

We now apply the results obtained above to a concrete problem. We consider approximation of multivariate functions from noisy data.

Let $F = F_s^r$ be the space of all real valued functions defined on the s dimensional unit cube $D = [0,1]^s$ that possess all continuous partial derivatives of order r, $r \geq 1$. The norm in F_s^r is given as

$$\|f\|_F \; = \; \max_{0 \leq k_1 + \cdots + k_s = i \leq r} \; \sup_{t \in D} \left| \frac{\partial^i f(t)}{(\partial x^1)^{k_1} \ldots (\partial x^s)^{k_s}} \right|, \qquad f \in F,$$

where $t = (t^1, \ldots, t^s)$. Information about f is given by noisy values of f at some points, i.e., exact information is of the form

$$N(f) \; = \; [\,f(t_1), f(t_2), \ldots, f(t_n)\,],$$

where $t_i \in D$, $1 \leq i \leq n$. We want to approximate $S(f) = f$ in the sup-norm. That is, formally $S : F \to G$ where G is the space of continuous functions $f : D \to \mathbb{R}$ with the norm

$$\|g\| \; = \; \|g\|_\infty \; = \; \sup_{t \in D} |g(t)|.$$

We shall show that the assumptions of Theorems 2.10.4 and 2.10.5 are satisfied. Clearly, there exists a κ-hard element for all $\kappa > 2$. Since for any $t \in D$ and $f \in F_s^r$ we have

$$|f(t)| \; \leq \; \|f\|_\infty \; \leq \; \|f\|_F,$$

the condition (2.73) holds with $K = 1$, and $\|L\|_F \leq 1$ for any functional L of the form $L(f) = f(t)$. It is also easily seen that (2.77) is satisfied with the function $f(t) = 1$, $\forall t$, and with $A = 1$. Hence it remains to show (2.76). We do this in two steps.

Lemma 2.10.5 *For multivariate approximation we have*

$$d_n \geq \gamma \cdot n^{-r/s},$$

where γ is positive and independent of n.

Proof Let $\psi : \mathbb{R} \to \mathbb{R}$ be an arbitrary nonzero function such that
(i) $\psi(x) = 0$ for all $|x| \geq 1/2$, and
(ii) the rth derivative $\psi^{(r)}$ exists and is continuous.
Let $\Psi : \mathbb{R}^s \to \mathbb{R}$,

$$\Psi(t) = \alpha \psi(t^1) \cdots \psi(t^s),$$

where $\alpha \neq 0$ is chosen in such a way that $\|\Psi\|_F \leq 1$.

Let $n \geq 1$ and $\mathbb{N}(f) = [f(t_1), \ldots, f(t_n)]$, $t_i \in D$, be arbitrary exact nonadaptive information. Define $m \geq 1$ such that $(m/2)^s \leq n < m^s$, along with a set $\mathcal{K} \subset D$

$$\mathcal{K} = \left\{ x \in \mathbb{R}^s \;\middle|\; x^j = \frac{2i_j - 1}{m}, 1 \leq i_j \leq m, 1 \leq j \leq s \right\}$$

of m^s points. The set $\mathcal{K} \subset D$ determines the collection

$$\Psi_x(t) = m^{-r} \Psi(m(t - x)), \qquad x \in \mathcal{K},$$

of m^s functions. These functions are linearly independent and, moreover, they have pairwise disjoint supports. Since $n < m^s$, there exist real coefficients β_x, $x \in \mathcal{K}$, not all equal to zero, such that the function

$$f_N = \sum_{x \in \mathcal{K}} \beta_x \Psi_x$$

is in ker N. We can also assume $\max_{x \in \mathcal{K}} |\beta_x| = 1$ so that $\|f_N\|_F \leq 1$. Hence

$$d_n \geq \|S(f_N)\| = \|f_N\|_\infty = m^{-r} \|\Psi\|_\infty = n^{-r/s} 2^{-r} \alpha \|\psi\|_\infty^s,$$

and the lemma holds with $\gamma = 2^{-r} \alpha \|\psi\|_\infty^s$. $\qquad\square$

We now exhibit exact nonadaptive information N_n and a linear algorithm φ_n such that

$$e^{\mathrm{wor}}(N_n, \underbrace{[\delta, \ldots, \delta]}_{n}, \varphi_n) \leq M(n^{-r/s} + \delta),$$

for all δ and $n \geq (r-1)^s$, where M is independent of n and δ.

Assume first that $r \geq 2$. Let $n \geq r^s$. Let $k \geq 1$ be the largest integer such that $(k(r-1)+1)^s = m \leq n$. Information N_n consists of function evaluations at m equispaced points, i.e., $N(f) = \{f(t)\}_{t \in \mathcal{K}}$, where

$$\mathcal{K} = \left\{ t \in \mathbb{R}^s \;\middle|\; t^i = \frac{i_j}{k(r-1)}, \, 0 \leq i_j \leq k(r-1), \, 1 \leq i \leq s \right\}.$$

Let $h = 1/k$. Divide the cube $D = [0,1]^s$ into k^s subcubes

$$D_{i_1 \dots i_k} = [(i_1-1)h, i_1 h] \times \cdots \times [(i_s-1)h, i_s h],$$

$1 \leq i_j \leq k$, $1 \leq j \leq s$. Observe that each subcube contains exactly r^s points from $\mathcal{K}$. For given information $y = \{y_x\}_{x \in \mathcal{K}}$ about $f \in F_s^r$, the approximation $\varphi_n(y)$ is given as a function $w = w_y$ such that

(i) on each subcube w is a polynomial of the form

$$w(t) = \sum a_{i_1 \dots i_s} (t^1)^{i_1} \cdots (t^s)^{i_s},$$

where the summation is taken over all $0 \leq i_j \leq r-1$, $1 \leq j \leq s$,

(ii) w interpolates the data y, i.e.,

$$w(x) = y_x, \qquad \forall x \in \mathcal{K}.$$

Note that w exists and is determined uniquely for any information y. Moreover, w depends linearly on y.

Lemma 2.10.6 *If $|y_x - f(x)| \leq \delta$, $\forall x \in \mathcal{K}$, then for all $t \in D$ we have*

$$|f(t) - w(t)| \leq \frac{h^r}{r!} \left(\sum_{i=0}^{s-1} A^i \right) + \delta A^s$$

where

$$A = \sup_{0 \leq x \leq r-1} \sum_{i=0}^{r-1} \left| \prod_{j=0, \neq i}^{r-1} \frac{x-j}{i-j} \right|.$$

Proof We prove the lemma by induction on s. We assume without loss of generality that $t \in [0, h]^s$.

Let $s = 1$. Let w_f be the polynomial of degree at most $r-1$ that interpolates f at the points $t_i = ih/(r-1)$, $0 \leq i \leq r-1$, i.e.,

$$w_f(x) = \sum_{i=0}^{r-1} f(t_i) \left(\prod_{j=0, \neq i}^{r-1} \frac{x-t_j}{t_i-t_j} \right).$$

From the well known formula for the error of Lagrange interpolation we get

$$f(t) - w(t) = (f(t) - w_f(t)) + (w_f(t) - w(t))$$

$$= \frac{f^{(r)}(u(t))}{r!} \prod_{i=0}^{r-1}(t - t_i) + \sum_{i=0}^{r-1}(y_i - f(t_i))\left(\prod_{j=0,\neq i}^{r-1} \frac{t - t_j}{t_i - t_j}\right),$$

where $0 \leq u(t) \leq h$. Hence

$$|f(t) - w(t)| \leq (r!)^{-1}h^r + \delta A.$$

Let $s > 1$. Let $t = [t^1, \ldots, t^s] \in [0, h]^s$. Consider the function $f_{t^1 \ldots t^{s-1}}(x) = f(t^1, \ldots, t^{s-1}, x)$ of one variable, and the corresponding polynomial $w_{t^1 \ldots t^{s-1}}(x) = w(t^1, \ldots, t^{s-1}, x)$, $0 \leq x \leq h$. From the induction hypothesis it follows that for all $x = ih/(r-1)$, $0 \leq i \leq r-1$, we have

$$|f_{t^1 \ldots t^{s-1}}(x) - w_{t^1 \ldots t^{s-1}}(x)| \leq \frac{h^r}{r!}\left(\sum_{i=0}^{s-2} A^i\right) + \delta A^{s-1}.$$

As in the case $s = 1$, let w_f be the polynomial of one variable that interpolates $f_{t^1 \ldots t^{s-1}}$ at $x = ih/(r-1)$, $0 \leq i \leq r-1$. Then

$$
\begin{aligned}
|f(t) - w(t)| &\leq |f_{t^1 \ldots t^{s-1}}(t^s) - w_f(t^s)| + |w_f(t^s) - w_{t^1 \ldots t^{s-1}}(t^s)| \\
&\leq \frac{h^r}{r!} + \left(\frac{h^r}{r!}\left(\sum_{i=0}^{s-2} A^i\right) + \delta A^{s-1}\right) A \\
&= \frac{h^r}{r!}\left(\sum_{i=0}^{s-1} A^i\right) + \delta A^s,
\end{aligned}
$$

as claimed. $\qquad\qquad\qquad\qquad\qquad\qquad\qquad\qquad\qquad\qquad\qquad\square$

Observe now that $h \approx (r-1)n^{-1/s}$. Thus Lemmas 2.10.5 and 2.10.6 yield $d_n \asymp n^{-r/s}$, and there exists a positive constant M such that for any information y about f, we have

$$\|f - \varphi_n(y)\|_\infty \leq M(d_n + \delta).$$

This is also true for $r = 1$, since we can then use the same information and algorithm as for $r = 2$.

We summarize our analysis in the following theorem.

Theorem 2.10.6 *If the cost function* **c** *satisfies*

$$\mathbf{c}(\alpha\,\delta) \asymp \mathbf{c}(\delta), \qquad \forall\,\alpha > 0,$$

then for multivariate approximation we have

$$\mathrm{Comp}_{\mathrm{abs}}^{\mathrm{wor}}(\varepsilon) \asymp \mathrm{Comp}_{\mathrm{rel}}^{\mathrm{wor}}(\varepsilon) \asymp \mathbf{c}(\varepsilon)\cdot\varepsilon^{-s/r}.$$

Furthermore, optimal information uses $n \asymp \varepsilon^{-s/r}$ *equispaced observations with precision* $\delta \asymp \varepsilon$, *and piecewise-polynomial approximation is the optimal algorithm.*

Notes and remarks

NR 2.10.1   Subsections 2.10.1 and 2.10.2 are original, while Subsection 2.10.3 is based on Kacewicz and Plaskota (1990).

NR 2.10.2   Using results from the average case analysis of Chapter 3, one can also obtain some complexity results for integration in the r.k.h.s. $W_r^0(0,1)$ when only observations of function values are allowed. See NR 3.10.4 for details.

NR 2.10.3   Approximation of smooth functions of a single variable in the case of noise bounded in the absolute sense by a fixed constant, was also studied by Lee *et al.* (1987). In that paper the complexity of information is measured by the memory needed to store it. Consequently, the information ε-complexity can be interpreted as the minimal amount of memory sufficient to store information from which it is possible to recover a function with given accuracy. With such an interpretation, the case of absolute noise corresponds to the fact that the *fixed* point representation of y_i is used with roughly $\max\{0, -\log_2 \delta_i\}$ bits. Relative noise in turn corresponds to the *floating* point representation using the same number of bits. In both cases the cost function is $\mathbf{c}(\delta) = \max\{0, -\log_2 \delta\}$. A more detailed discussion on this subject can be found in Kacewicz and Plaskota (1990).

NR 2.10.4   The techniques used in the proofs of Lemmas 2.10.5 and 2.10.6 are well known and often applied to evaluate diameters of problems with exact information, and also some n-widths in approximation theory (see also NR 2.8.2). The fact that we have $r_n^{\mathrm{wor}}(\delta) \leq M(d_n + \delta)$ for multivariate approximation can be derived from Babenko (1979).

Exercises

E 2.10.1   Consider the Hilbert case. Suppose that the cost function **c** satisfies the following condition: there exist x_0 and $d > 0$ such that $x\mathbf{c}(x) > d, \forall x \geq x_0$. Prove then that

$$\mathrm{IC}^{\mathrm{non}}(\mathbf{c};\varepsilon) \geq \frac{d}{x_0}\cdot\mathrm{IC}^{\mathrm{non}}\left(\mathbf{c}_0; \sqrt{1+\frac{1}{x_0}}\,\varepsilon\right), \qquad \forall\,\varepsilon > 0.$$

Show also that if the condition is not satisfied then $\mathrm{IC}^{\mathrm{non}}(\mathbf{c};\varepsilon) = 0, \forall\,\varepsilon > 0$.

E 2.10.2 Let the cost function $c_{\ln}(\delta) = \ln(1 + \delta^{-2})$. Prove that then in the Hilbert case we have

$$R(T)^2 = d \cdot \left(\frac{\prod_{j=1}^n \lambda_j}{e^T} \right)^{1/n},$$

where $n = n(T)$ is the largest integer for which $\lambda_n \geq (\prod_{j=1}^n \lambda_j)^{1/n} e^{-T/n}$, and $1/2 \leq d \leq 1$.

E 2.10.3 Use the previous exercise to show that for $\lambda_j = j^{-p}$, $j \geq 1$, we have $\mathrm{Comp}(c_{\ln}; \varepsilon) \asymp \mathrm{Comp}(c_0; \varepsilon)$ for all $p > 0$, while for $\lambda_j = e^{-j}$ we have $\mathrm{Comp}(c_{\ln}; \varepsilon) \asymp \ln(1/\varepsilon)^2$ and $\mathrm{Comp}(c_0; \varepsilon) \asymp \ln(1/\varepsilon)$.

E 2.10.4 Show that the equivalence $\mathrm{IC}^{\mathrm{non}}(\mathrm{App}; 2\varepsilon) \asymp \mathrm{IC}^{\mathrm{non}}(\mathrm{App}; \varepsilon)$ holds iff $c(\delta)$ tends to infinity at most polynomially in $1/\delta$, as $\delta \to 0$.

E 2.10.5 Show that Theorem 2.10.4 can be applied for the problems App and Int.

E 2.10.6 (Kacewicz and Plaskota, 1990) Let $F = F_s^r$ be the space defined as in the multivariate approximation problem. Let Λ be the class of functionals $L : F \to \mathbb{R}$ of the form

$$L(f) = \frac{\partial^i f(t)}{(\partial x^1)^{k_1} \dots (\partial x^s)^{k_s}}, \quad \text{for some} \quad t \in [0,1]^s,$$

for any integers $k_1, \dots, k_s$ and i such that $0 \leq k_1 + \dots + k_s = i \leq k$, where $0 \leq k \leq r$. Show that

$$\sup_{\|f\|_F \leq 1} \inf_{L \in \Lambda} |L(f)| \geq e^{-\min\{s,k\}} (\min\{1, k/s\})^k$$

(with the convention that $0^0 = 1$).

E 2.10.7 (Kacewicz and Plaskota, 1990) Show that if the space F and the class Λ are as in the previous exercise, then for any solution operator S, nonadaptive information N, and precision vector Δ, we have

$$\frac{\mathrm{diam}_{\mathrm{abs}}(N, \Delta)}{1 + 2 e^{\min\{k,s\}} (\min\{1, k/s\})^{-k}} \leq \mathrm{diam}_{\mathrm{rel}}(N, \Delta) \leq \mathrm{diam}_{\mathrm{abs}}(N, \Delta).$$

E 2.10.8 (Kacewicz and Plaskota, 1990) For given $p \geq 1$, define $F = \{f \in \mathbb{R}^\infty \mid \|f\|_p < +\infty\}$, where $\|f\|_p = (\sum_{i=1}^\infty |f_i|^p)^{1/p}$, $f = [f_1, f_2, \dots] \in \mathbb{R}^\infty$. For $\|f\|_p \leq 1$, we approximate values $S(f)$ of the operator $S : F \to F$,

$$S(f) = [\alpha_1 f_1, \alpha_2 f_2, \dots],$$

where $\alpha_i = 2^{(1-i)/p}$. Exact information is given as $N_n(f) = [f_1, f_2, \dots, f_n]$. Show that

$$\sup_{\|f\|_p \leq 1} \min_{1 \leq i \leq n} |f_i| = n^{-1/p},$$

and for $\delta_i = \alpha_{n+1}/\alpha_i$, $1 \leq i \leq n$, and $\Delta_n = [\delta_1, \dots, \delta_n]$, we have

$$\frac{\mathrm{diam}_{\mathrm{rel}}(N_n, \Delta_n)}{\mathrm{diam}_{\mathrm{abs}}(N_n, \Delta_n)} \leq n^{-1/p}.$$

E 2.10.9 Although Theorem 2.10.4 can be applied to the approximation problem $S(f) = f$, it cannot be applied to multivariate integration $S(f) = \int_D f(t)dt$. Why not?

3

Average case setting

3.1 Introduction

This chapter deals with the average case setting. In this setting, we are interested in the *average* error and cost of algorithms. The structure of this chapter is similar to that of the previous chapter. That is, we first deal with optimal algorithms, then we analyze the optimal information, and finally, we present some complexity results.

To study the average error and/or cost, we have to replace the deterministic assumptions of the worst case setting by stochastic assumptions. That is, we assume some probability distribution μ on the space F of problem elements as well as some distribution of the information noise. The latter means that information is corrupted by *random noise*. Basically, we consider Gaussian distributions (measures) which seem to be most natural and are most often used in modeling.

In Section 3.2, we give a general formulation of the average case setting. We also introduce the concept of the (average) radius of information which, as in the worst case, provides a sharp lower bound on the (average) error of algorithms.

Then we pass to linear problems with Gaussian measures. These are problems where the solution operator is linear, μ is a Gaussian measure, and information is linear with Gaussian noise. In Section 3.3, we recall the definition of a Gaussian measure on a Banach space, listing some important properties. In Sections 3.4 to 3.6 we study optimal algorithms. Formulas for the optimal algorithm and radius of information are presented in Subsection 3.4.2. The optimal algorithm turns out to be linear and uniquely determined. In Section 3.5, we specialize the results obtained to the case where the solution operator is a linear functional.

In particular, we show that in this case the problem is as difficult as an appropriately chosen one dimensional subproblem.

As we know, in the worst case setting optimal algorithms are smoothing splines with appropriately chosen parameter α. It turns out that a similar fact holds in the average case. More precisely, in Section 3.6 we show that for linear problems with Gaussian measures, the optimal algorithm can be interpreted as a $(1/2)$-smoothing spline algorithm. This smoothing spline corresponds to Hilbert norms $\|\cdot\|_H$ and $\|\cdot\|_Y$ which are induced by the distribution μ on F and the distribution of noise, respectively. Note that, unlike in the worst case, the optimal parameter $\alpha = 1/2$ is constant and the optimal regularization parameter γ equals the variance σ^2 of the noise.

The fact that smoothing splines are optimal in the worst and average case settings enables us to establish a relation between the two settings, namely, the optimal algorithm for the average case is almost optimal for a corresponding problem in the worst case, where the set $E \subset F$ is the unit ball in $\|\cdot\|_H$ and the noise is bounded uniformly in the norm $\|\cdot\|_Y$. Moreover, for approximating a linear functional, the corresponding worst and average radii of the same linear information may differ only by a factor of $\sqrt{2}$.

Next, we allow information to vary. In Section 3.7 we carefully define nonadaptive and adaptive information. Then we show that for linear problems with Gaussian measures, adaptive information cannot reduce the minimal average error given by nonadaptive information. That is, adaption does not help with respect to the error.

The problem of optimal information is studied in Section 3.8. Using a similar technique to that of the worst case setting with Hilbert norms, in Subsection 3.8.1 we show the optimal selection of functionals forming information, for n independent observations with given variances σ_i^2 of noise. The formulas for optimal information and minimal radius are given in terms of σ_i^2s and the eigenvalues of the correlation operator of the a priori Gaussian distribution on the space G. It turns out that for independent observations with the same variances, the minimal radius converges to zero as $n \to \infty$, but not faster than $\sigma/\sqrt{n}$. We also show relations between optimal information in the average and the corresponding worst case settings. We construct information which is almost optimal for both settings.

Tight bounds on the minimal error for function approximation and integration on the Wiener space can be found in Subsection 3.8.2. For these problems, independent noisy observations of function values with the same variances are assumed. Observations at equidistant points turn out to be almost optimal.

In the last two sections we study average case complexity. In Section 3.9 we present the second theorem on adaption. It says that, under some assumptions, adaption cannot help, not only with respect to error but also with respect to average cost of information. That is, for any adaptive information there exists nonadaptive information whose radius and cost are not (much) larger than the radius and cost of the adaptive information. This holds when the minimal cost of information with radius not greater than $\sqrt{\varepsilon}$ is a semiconvex function of ε. This fact and the linearity of optimal algorithms imply that the ε-complexity essentially equals the information complexity, similarly to the worst case setting.

In Section 3.10 we apply the general complexity results to two special problems. We first consider a linear continuous problem with Gaussian measures and information consisting of functionals bounded by 1 in a norm induced by the measure μ. We find sharp bounds on the ε-complexity depending on the cost function. We note that the situation here reminds us of that in the worst case setting with Hilbert norms.

Finally, we show some complexity bounds for function approximation and integration on the Wiener space, based on information about noisy function values.

3.2 Information and its radius

Let $S : F \to G$, where F is a linear space and G is a normed space, be a given solution operator. As in the worst case setting, we wish to construct approximations to $S(f)$ for $f \in F$. Basically, the approximations are obtained as before, i.e., by means of an algorithm that uses some information. However, the deterministic assumptions on the problem elements $f \in F$ and information y about f are now replaced by stochastic assumptions.

More specifically, we assume that the space F is equipped with a probability measure μ defined on a σ-field of F, with respect to which S is a measurable mapping. The measure μ gives a priori information about the probability of occurrence of elements $f \in F$. Note that the exact solution $S(f)$ can be viewed as a random variable distributed according to the measure $\nu = \mu S^{-1}$ induced by μ and S, i.e.,

$$\nu(B) \;=\; \mu(S^{-1}(B)) \;=\; \mu(\{\, f \in F \mid \; S(f) \in B \,\}),$$

for all Borel sets B of G.

In the worst case setting, information y about f was in general an element of a specified subset $\mathbb{N}(f) \subset Y$, where Y consisted of some finite real sequences. In the average case setting, the assumption $y \in \mathbb{N}(f)$ is replaced by the assumption that y is distributed randomly on Y according to some probability measure π_f, i.e., $y \sim \pi_f$, $f \in F$. The family of measures

$$\mathbb{\Pi} = \{\pi_f\}_{f \in F}$$

will be called an *information distribution*, or simply *information*, for brevity.

The Borel structure on Y is given in a natural way. That is, we assume that $Y \cap \mathbb{R}^n$ are Borel sets of $\mathbb{R}^n$. A set $B \subset Y$ is measurable iff $B \cap \mathbb{R}^n$ are measurable for all n. We also assume that the maps $f \mapsto \pi_f(B)$ are measurable for any measurable $B \subset Y$.

Information about f is any sequence $y \in Y$ that is a realization of the random variable distributed according to π_f. If π_f is a Dirac (atomic) measure for a.e. (almost everywhere) $f \in F$, i.e., if there are elements $N(f) \in Y$ such that for any measurable B

$$\pi_f(B) = \left\{ \begin{array}{ll} 0 & N(f) \notin B, \\ 1 & N(f) \in B, \end{array} \right.$$

then information is called *exact*. In this case, the sequence $y = N(f)$ is observed with probability one, and $\mathbb{\Pi}$ can be identified with the operator $N : F \to Y$. Otherwise, information is *noisy*.

We now give two examples.

Example 3.2.1 Suppose we want to approximate a one dimensional random variable f (parameter) with normal distribution, $f \sim \mathcal{N}(0, \lambda)$, based on information $y = f + x$ with $x \sim \mathcal{N}(f, \sigma^2)$. Here , $\lambda > 0$ and $\sigma^2 \geq 0$. In this case, $F = G = \mathbb{R}$ and $S(f) = f$. The measure μ on F is defined as

$$\mu(B) = \frac{1}{\sqrt{2\pi\lambda}} \int_B e^{-x^2/(2\lambda)} \, dx, \quad \forall \, \text{Borel sets } B \text{ of } \mathbb{R}.$$

Furthermore, the set $Y = \mathbb{R}$ and the measures $\pi_f = \mathcal{N}(f, \sigma^2)$. That is, for $\sigma > 0$ we have

$$\pi_f(B) = \frac{1}{\sqrt{2\pi\sigma^2}} \int_B e^{-(y-f)^2/(2\sigma^2)} \, dy,$$

while for $\sigma = 0$ we have $\pi_f(B) = 0$ if $f \notin B$, and $\pi_f(B) = 1$ otherwise. Hence for $\sigma = 0$ information is exact, while for $\sigma > 0$ it is noisy.

Example 3.2.2 Suppose we wish to approximate the value of the integral $S(f) = \int_0^1 f(t)\, dt$ of a continuous function $f : [0,1] \to \mathbb{R}$. In this case, as μ we take the classical *Wiener measure*, $\mu = w$. Recall that w is defined on the σ-field of Borel sets of the space

$$F = \{\, f : [0,1] \to \mathbb{R} \mid f \text{ continuous}, \ f(0) = 0 \,\},$$

with the sup-norm, $\|f\| = \sup_{x \in [0,1]} |f(x)|$. It is uniquely determined by the following condition. Let $m \geq 1$ and B be a Borel set of $\mathbb{R}^m$. Let $B^{t_1 \cdots t_m} = \{\, f \in F \mid (f(t_1), \ldots, f(t_m)) \in B \,\}$ where $0 < t_1 < t_2 < \cdots < t_n \leq 1$. Then

$$w(B^{t_1 \cdots t_m}) = \{\, (2\pi)^n t_1 (t_2 - t_1) \ldots (t_n - t_{n-1}) \,\}^{-1/2}$$
$$\times \int_B \exp\left\{ -\frac{1}{2}\left(\frac{x_1^2}{t_1} + \frac{(x_2 - x_1)^2}{t_2 - t_1} + \cdots + \frac{(x_n - x_{n-1})^2}{t_n - t_{n-1}} \right) \right\}$$
$$dx_1\, dx_2 \ldots dx_n.$$

Information about f may be given by independent noisy observations of f at n points. That is, in the ith observation we obtain $y_i = f(t_i) + x_i$, where $x_i \sim \mathcal{N}(0, \sigma^2)$, $1 \leq i \leq n$, and $\sigma > 0$. This corresponds to $Y = \mathbb{R}^n$ and

$$\pi_f(B) = (2\pi\sigma^2)^{-n/2} \int_{\mathbb{R}^n} \exp\left\{ -\frac{1}{2\sigma^2} \sum_{i=1}^{n} (y_i - f(t_i))^2 \right\} dy_1 \ldots dy_n.$$

Let $\mathbb{II} = \{\pi_f\}$ be a given information distribution. The *average case error* of an algorithm φ that uses information $y \sim \pi_f$ is given as

$$e^{\text{ave}}(\mathbb{II}, \varphi) = \sqrt{ \int_F \int_Y \|S(f) - \varphi(y)\|^2\, \pi_f(dy)\, \mu(df) }.$$

That is, we average with respect to the joint distribution (measure) $\tilde{\mu}$ on the product space $F \times Y$,

$$\tilde{\mu}(B) = \int_F \pi_f(B_f)\, \mu(df), \quad \forall \text{ Borel sets } B \text{ of } F \times Y,$$

where $B_f = \{\, y \in Y \mid (f, y) \in B \,\}$. In order that the error be well defined, we assume measurability of φ with respect to the measure μ_1 defined by (3.1) below. (Note that by slightly redefining the error, this assumption can be relaxed, see NR 3.2.2.)

An algorithm φ_{opt} is *optimal* iff

$$e^{\text{ave}}(\mathbb{II}, \varphi_{\text{opt}}) = \inf_{\varphi} e^{\text{ave}}(\mathbb{II}, \varphi).$$

Let μ_1 be the a priori distribution of information values y on Y,

$$\mu_1(B) = \int_F \pi_f(B)\,\mu(df), \qquad \forall\,\text{Borel sets } B \text{ of } Y. \qquad (3.1)$$

We assume that there exists a unique (up to a set of μ_1-measure zero) family $\{\mu_2(\cdot|y)\}_{y \in Y}$ of probability measures that satisfy the following conditions:

(i) $\mu_2(\cdot|y)$ are for a.e. y probability measures on the σ-field of F,
(ii) the maps $y \mapsto \mu_2(B|y)$ are μ_1-measurable for all measurable sets $B \subset F$, and
(iii) $\tilde{\mu}(B) = \int_Y \mu_2(B_y|y)\,\mu_1(dy)$, for any Borel set $B \subset F$, where $B_y = \{\,f \in F \mid (f,y) \in B\,\}$.

Such a family is called a *regular conditional probability distribution*. It exists under some mild assumptions, e.g., if F is a separable Banach space and $Y = \mathbb{R}^n$; see NR 3.2.3. We interpret $\mu_2(\cdot|y)$ as the a posteriori (or conditional) distribution on F, after information y has been observed.

The most important will be property (iii). It says that the joint measure $\tilde{\mu}$ can be equivalently defined by the right hand side of the first equality in (iii). Hence the error of an algorithm φ can be rewritten as

$$e^{\text{ave}}(\mathbb{II}, \varphi) = \sqrt{\int_Y \int_F \|S(f) - \varphi(y)\|^2\,\mu_2(df|y)\,\mu_1(dy)}. \qquad (3.2)$$

For a probability measure ω on G, let

$$r(\omega) = \inf_{a \in G} \sqrt{\int_G \|g - a\|^2\,\omega(dg)}.$$

We call $r(\omega)$ a *radius* of the measure ω. An element $g_\omega \in G$ is a *center* of ω iff $r(\omega) = \sqrt{\int_G \|g - g_\omega\|^2\omega(dg)}$.

Example 3.2.3   Suppose that the measure ω is centrosymmetric. That is, there exists $g^* \in G$ such that $\omega(B) = \omega(\{\,2g^* - g \mid g \in B\,\})$ holds for any measurable set $B \subset G$. Then g^* is a center of ω and $r(\omega) = \sqrt{\int_G \|g - g^*\|^2\,\omega(dg)}$. Indeed, since

$$\|x + y\|^2 + \|x - y\|^2 \geq \tfrac{1}{2}\,(\,\|x + y\| + \|x - y\|\,)^2 \geq 2\,\|x\|^2,$$

for any $a \in G$ we have

$$\int_G \|g - a\|^2\,\omega(dg) = \int_G \|2g^* - g - a\|^2\,\omega(dg)$$

$$= \frac{1}{2} \int_G \left(\|(g^* - p) + (g^* - a)\|^2 + \|(g - g^*) - (g^* - a)\|^2 \right) \omega(dg)$$

$$\geq \int_G \|g - g^*\|^2 \, \omega(dg).$$

For $y \in Y$, define the measures $\nu_2(\cdot|y) = \mu_2(S^{-1}(\cdot)|y)$. That is, $\nu_2(\cdot|y)$ is the a posteriori distribution of the elements $S(f)$ after information y has been observed. Assuming the mapping $y \mapsto r(\nu_2(\cdot|y))$ is μ_1-measurable, an *(average) radius of the information distribution* Π is given as

$$\mathrm{rad}^{\mathrm{ave}}(\Pi) = \sqrt{\int_Y (r(\nu_2(\cdot|y)))^2 \, \mu_1(dy)}.$$

Hence, in other words, $\mathrm{rad}^{\mathrm{ave}}(\Pi)$ is the average radius of the conditional distributions in G.

Lemma 3.2.1 *If the space G is separable then the function*

$$\psi(y) = \inf_{a \in G} \int_G \|a - g\|^2 \, \nu_2(dg|y), \qquad y \in Y,$$

is μ_1-measurable.

Proof It suffices to show that the set

$$B = \{ y \in Y \mid \psi(y) \geq a \}$$

is μ_1-measurable for any $a \in \mathbb{R}$. Let

$$\psi(x, y) = \int_G \|x - g\|^2 \, \nu_2(dg|y), \qquad x \in G, \, y \in Y.$$

Then ψ is continuous with respect to x and measurable with respect to y, and $\psi(y) = \inf_{x \in G} \psi(x, y)$. Choosing a countable set A dense in G, we obtain

$$
\begin{aligned}
B &= \{ y \in Y \mid \forall x \in G, \, \psi(x, y) \geq a \} \\
&= \{ y \in Y \mid \forall x \in A, \, \psi(x, y) \geq a \} \\
&= \bigcap_{x \in A} \{ y \in Y \mid \psi(x, y) \geq a \}.
\end{aligned}
$$

Hence $B(a)$ is a countable intersection of measurable sets, which implies that B is also measurable. □

From now on we assume that the space G is separable. As we have just shown, separability of G makes the radius of information well defined. We are ready to show the main result of this section.

Theorem 3.2.1 *For any information distribution* Π *we have*

$$\inf_\varphi e^{ave}(\Pi, \varphi) = rad^{ave}(\Pi).$$

If $rad^{ave}(\Pi) < +\infty$ *then a necessary and sufficient condition for the existence of an optimal algorithm is that for a.e.* $y \in Y$, *there exists a center* g_y *of the measure* $\nu_2(\cdot|y)$. *In particular, the algorithm*

$$\varphi_{ctr}(y) = g_y$$

is optimal.

Proof We first show that for any $\varepsilon > 0$ there is an algorithm with error at most $rad^{ave}(\Pi) + \varepsilon$. We can assume that $rad^{ave}(\Pi) < +\infty$. Then the set

$$A = \{ y \in Y \mid r(\nu_2(\cdot|y)) = +\infty \}$$

is of μ_1-measure zero. Let $\psi(x, y)$ be as in the proof of Lemma 3.2.1. We have already mentioned that ψ is continuous with respect to x. We also have $\sup_{x \in G} \psi(x, y) = +\infty$. Indeed, there exists $t > 0$ such that the ball $B_t = \{ g \in G \mid \|g\| \le t \}$ has positive $\nu_2(\cdot|y)$-measure. Then, for $x \in G$ such that $\|x\| > t$, we have

$$\psi(x, y) \ge \int_{B_t} \|x - g\|^2 \, \nu_2(dg|y) \ge \nu_2(B_t|y) \cdot (\|x\| - t)^2,$$

and consequently $\psi(x, y) \to +\infty$ as $x \to +\infty$.

Thus, for fixed $y \in Y \setminus A$, the function $\psi(x, y)$ assumes all values from the interval $(r(\nu_2(\cdot|y)), +\infty)$. Hence for any $\varepsilon > 0$ we can find an element $a_y \in G$ such that

$$\psi(a_y, y) = \int_G \|g - a_y\|^2 \, \nu_2(dg|y) = (r(\nu_2(\cdot|y)))^2 + \varepsilon^2. \qquad (3.3)$$

We now define $\varphi_\varepsilon(y) = a_y$ for $y \in Y \setminus A$, and $\varphi_\varepsilon(y) = 0$ for $y \in A$. Then the algorithm φ_ε is μ_1-measurable and, using (3.2) and (3.3), we have

$$e^{ave}(\Pi, \varphi_\varepsilon) = \sqrt{\int_Y (r(\nu_2(\cdot|y)))^2 \, \mu_1(dy) + \varepsilon^2} \le rad^{ave}(\Pi) + \varepsilon,$$

as claimed.

On the other hand, for an arbitrary algorithm φ we have

$$
\begin{aligned}
(e^{\mathrm{ave}}(\mathbb{II}, \varphi))^2 &= \int_Y \int_F \|S(f) - \varphi(y)\|^2 \, \mu_2(df|y) \, \mu_1(dy) \\
&= \int_Y \int_G \|g - \varphi(y)\|^2 \, \nu_2(dg|y) \, \mu_1(dy) \\
&\geq \int_Y (r(\nu_2(\cdot|y)))^2 \, \mu_1(dy) = (\mathrm{rad}^{\mathrm{ave}}(\mathbb{II}, \varphi))^2,
\end{aligned}
$$

which proves the first part of the theorem.

Let φ be an algorithm such that $e^{\mathrm{ave}}(\mathbb{II}, \varphi) = \mathrm{rad}^{\mathrm{ave}}(\mathbb{II})$. Let $\psi_1(y) = \int_G \|g - \varphi(y)\|^2 \nu_2(dg|y)$ and $\psi_2(y) = (r(\nu_2(\cdot|y)))^2$. Then $\psi_1(y) \geq \psi_2(y)$, $\forall y \in Y$, and $\int_Y \psi_1(y) \, \mu_1(dy) = \int_Y \psi_2(y) \, \mu_1(dy)$. This can hold if and only if $\psi_1(y) = \psi_2(y)$, for a.e. y. Since the last equality means that $\varphi(y)$ is the center of $\nu_2(\cdot|y)$, the proof is complete. $\qquad\square$

Following the terminology of the worst case setting, we can call φ_{ctr} a *central algorithm*. Unlike in the worst case, we see that in the average case setting there is not much difference between the central and the optimal algorithm. Indeed, they can only differ from each other on a set of μ_1-measure zero.

In some cases, the optimal algorithms turn out to be mean elements of conditional distributions. Recall that m_ω is the *mean element* of a measure ω defined on a separable Banach space G iff for any continuous linear functional $L : G \to \mathbb{R}$ we have

$$
\int_G L(g) \, \omega(dg) = L(m_\omega).
$$

We also recall that by ν we denote the a priori distribution of $S(f) \in G$, i.e., $\nu = \mu S^{-1}$.

Lemma 3.2.2 *Let G be a separable Hilbert space and $m(y)$ the mean element of the measure $\nu_2(\cdot|y)$, $y \in Y$. Then the unique (up to a set of μ_1-measure zero) central algorithm is $\varphi_{\mathrm{ctr}}(y) = m(y)$ and*

$$
\mathrm{rad}^{\mathrm{ave}}(\mathbb{II}) = e^{\mathrm{ave}}(\mathbb{II}, \varphi_{\mathrm{ctr}}) = \sqrt{\int_G \|g\|^2 \, \nu(dg) - \int_Y \|m(y)\|^2 \, \mu_1(dy)} .
$$

Proof For any $y \in Y$ and $a \in G$ we have

$$
\int_G \|g - a\|^2 \, \nu_2(dg|y)
$$

$$= \|a\|^2 - 2\langle a, m(y)\rangle + \int_G \|g\|^2 \nu_2(dg|y)$$

$$= \|a - m(y)\|^2 + \int_G \|g\|^2 \nu_2(dg|y) - \|m(y)\|^2.$$

The minimum of this quantity is attained only at $a = m(y)$. Hence $\varphi_{\mathrm{opt}}(y) = m(y)$, a.e. y, and

$$(\mathrm{rad}^{\mathrm{ave}}(\mathbb{I}))^2 = (\mathrm{e}^{\mathrm{ave}}(\mathbb{I}, \varphi_{\mathrm{opt}}))^2$$

$$= \int_Y \int_G \|g\|^2 \nu_2(dg|y)\,\mu_1(dy) - \int_Y \|m(y)\|^2\,\mu_1(dy).$$

To complete the proof, observe that

$$\int_G \|g\|^2 \nu_2(dg|y) = \int_F \|S(f)\|^2 \mu_2(df|y),$$

and consequently

$$\int_Y \int_G \|g\|^2 \nu_2(dg|y)\,\mu_1(dy) = \int_Y \int_F \|S(f)\|^2 \mu_2(df|y)\,\mu_1(dy)$$

$$= \int_F \|S(f)\|^2 \mu(df) = \int_G \|g\|^2 \nu(dg).$$

$\square$

Notes and remarks

NR 3.2.1　Neglecting some details, the results of this section have been adopted from Traub *et al.* (1988, Sect. 2.3 of Chap. 6) (see also Wasilkowski (1983)), where exact information is considered. The concepts of the radius and center of a measure were introduced in Novak and Ritter (1989).

NR 3.2.2　We assume that the algorithm is a measurable mapping. One can allow arbitrary algorithms and define the error $\mathrm{e}^{\mathrm{ave}}(\mathbb{I}, \varphi)$ as the upper integral, as in the papers cited in NR 3.2.1 (see also Novak, 1988, where even nonmeasurable S and N are allowed). As it will turn out, for problems considered in this monograph, optimal algorithms are the same in the two cases.

NR 3.2.3　We now give a general theorem on existence of the regular conditional probability distribution. Let X and Y be two separable Banach spaces, and ω a probability measure on Borel sets of X. Let $\psi : X \to Y$ be a measurable mapping and $\omega_1 = \omega\psi^{-1}$. Then there exists a family of probability measures $\{\omega_2(\cdot|y)\}_{y \in Y}$ such that

(i) $\omega_2(\psi^{-1}(y)|y) = 1$, a.e. y,

(ii) for any Borel set B the mapping $y \mapsto \omega_2(B|y)$ is measurable, and

(iii) $\omega(B) = \int_Y \omega_2(B|y)\,\omega_1(dy)$.

Moreover, any other family satisfying (i)–(iii) can differ from $\{\mu_2(\cdot|y)\}_{y\in Y}$ only on a set of μ_1-measure zero. For a proof, see Parthasarathy (1967) or Varadarajan (1961).

Observe that this theorem tells us about decomposition of the measure ω with respect to the 'exact' mapping ψ. The 'noisy' version can be derived as follows. We set $X = F \times Y$, $\omega = \tilde{\mu}$, and $\psi(f, y) = y$, $\forall f \in F$, $\forall y \in Y$. Then $\omega\psi^{-1} = \mu_1$. Hence there exists a family $\{\tilde{\mu}_2(\cdot|y)\}_{y\in Y}$ of measures defined on $F \times Y$ such that the $\tilde{\mu}_2(\cdot|y)$ are a.e. concentrated on $F \times \{y\}$, the maps $y \mapsto \tilde{\mu}_2(B|y)$ are measurable and $\tilde{\mu}(B) = \int_Y \tilde{\mu}_2(B|y)\mu_1(dy)$. Letting $\mu_2(\cdot|y) = \tilde{\mu}_2(\cdot \times \{y\}|y)$, $\forall y \in Y$, we obtain that the $\mu_2(\cdot|y)$ are a.e. y concentrated on F, the maps $\mu_2(B|\cdot)$ are measurable and

$$\tilde{\mu}(B) = \int_Y \tilde{\mu}_2(B|y)\,\mu_1(dy) = \int_Y \mu_2(B_y|y)\,\mu_1(dy),$$

as claimed. We also note that if F is a Banach space and $Y = \mathbb{R}^n$, then $F \times Y$ is also a Banach space and the regular conditional distribution exists.

NR 3.2.4 In the exact information case with linear information N, the radius of N is closely related to average widths, see e.g. Magaril-Il'yaev (1994), Maiorov (1993, 1994), Sun and Wang (1994).

Exercises

E 3.2.1 Give an example of a measure ω for which
1. The center does not exist.
2. The center is not unique.

E 3.2.2 The diameter of a measure ω on G is defined as

$$d(\omega) = \sqrt{\int_G \int_G \|g_1 - g_2\|^2\, \omega(dg_1)\, \omega(dg_2)}\,.$$

Consequently, the (average) diameter of information II is given as

$$\text{diam}^{\text{ave}}(\text{II}) = \sqrt{\int_Y (d(\mu_2(\cdot|y)))^2\, \mu_1(dy)}\,.$$

Show that $r(\omega) \leq d(\omega) \leq 2\,r(\omega)$ and $\text{rad}^{\text{ave}}(\text{II}) \leq \text{diam}^{\text{ave}}(\text{II}) \leq 2\,\text{rad}^{\text{ave}}(\text{II})$.

E 3.2.3 Let G be a separable Hilbert space. Show that then $d(\omega) = \sqrt{2}\,r(\omega)$ and $\text{diam}^{\text{ave}}(\text{II}) = \sqrt{2}\,\text{rad}^{\text{ave}}(\text{II})$.

E 3.2.4 Let $F = \mathbb{R}^m$ and μ be the weighted Lebesgue measure,

$$\mu(A) = \int_A \alpha(f)\, d_m f,$$

for some positive $\alpha : \mathbb{R}^m \to \mathbb{R}_+$ such that $\int_{\mathbb{R}^m} \alpha(f)\, d_m f = 1$, where d_m is the m dimensional Lebesgue measure. Consider the information distribution II with $Y = \mathbb{R}^n$ and

$$\pi_f(B) = \int_B \beta(y - N(f))\, d_n y,$$

where $N : \mathbb{R}^m \to \mathbb{R}^n$, $\beta : \mathbb{R}^n \to \mathbb{R}_+$, and $\int_{\mathbb{R}^n} \beta(y) \, d_n y = 1$. Show that in this case

$$\mu_1(B) = \int_B \gamma(y) \, d_n y$$

and

$$\mu_2(A|y) = \frac{1}{\gamma(y)} \int_A \alpha(f) \, \beta(y - N(f)) \, d_m f,$$

where $\gamma(y) = \int_{\mathbb{R}^m} \alpha(f) \beta(y - N(f)) \, d_m f$, $\forall y \in Y$.

E 3.2.5 Let the solution operator $S : F \to G$, measure μ on F and information Π with $Y = \mathbb{R}^n$ be given. Define the space $\tilde{F} = F \times Y$, solution operator $\tilde{S} : \tilde{F} \to G$, measure $\tilde{\mu}$ on $\tilde{F}$ and exact information $\tilde{N} : F \to Y$ as

$$\tilde{S}(f, y) = S(f),$$
$$\tilde{\mu}(B) = \int_F \pi_f(B_f) \, \mu(df),$$
$$\tilde{N}(f, y) = y.$$

Show that for any algorithm $\varphi : Y \to G$ we have

$$e^{\mathrm{ave}}(\Pi, \varphi; S, \mu) = \tilde{e}^{\mathrm{ave}}(\tilde{N}, \varphi; \tilde{S}, \tilde{\mu}),$$

where the second quantity stands for the average error of φ with respect to $\tilde{\mu}$, for approximating $\tilde{S}(f, y)$ based on exact information $y = \tilde{N}(f, y)$.

3.3 Gaussian measures on Banach spaces

Gaussian measures defined on Banach spaces will play a crucial role in our studies. In this section, we recall what a Gaussian measure is and cite those properties of Gaussian measures that will be needed later.

3.3.1 Basic properties

Assume first that F is a finite dimensional space, $F = \mathbb{R}^d$, where $d < +\infty$. A *Gaussian measure* μ on $\mathbb{R}^d$ is uniquely defined by its *mean element* $m \in \mathbb{R}^d$ and its *correlation operator* (matrix) $\Sigma : \mathbb{R}^d \to \mathbb{R}^d$, which is symmetric and nonnegative definite, i.e., $\Sigma = \Sigma^* \geq 0$. If $m = 0$ and Σ is positive definite ($\Sigma > 0$) then

$$\mu(B) = \frac{1}{(2\pi)^{d/2}(\det \Sigma)^{1/2}} \int_B \exp\left\{-\tfrac{1}{2} \langle \Sigma^{-1} f, f \rangle_2\right\} df. \qquad (3.4)$$

(Here df stands for the Lebesgue measure on $\mathbb{R}^d$.) In the case of $m \neq 0$ and/or singular Σ, the Gaussian measure μ is concentrated on $m + X_1$ where $X_1 = \Sigma(X)$, and given as follows. Let $\Sigma_1 : X_1 \to X_1$, $\Sigma_1(x) =$

$\Sigma(x)$, $\forall x \in X_1$, let $d_1 = \dim X_1$. Then, for any $B = m + B_1$ where B_1 is a Borel subset of X_1, the measure $\mu(B_1)$ is given by the right hand side of (3.4) with Σ, d and B replaced by Σ_1, d_1 and B_1, respectively, and with the Lebesgue measure df on X_1.

If $m = 0$ and $\Sigma = I$ is the identity then μ is called the *standard d dimensional Gaussian distribution*.

Let μ be a Gaussian measure on $\mathbb{R}^d$. Then for any $x, x_1, x_2 \in \mathbb{R}^d$ we have $\int_{\mathbb{R}^n} \langle x, f \rangle_2 \, \mu(df) = \langle x, m \rangle_2$ and

$$\int_{\mathbb{R}^d} \langle x_1, f - m \rangle_2 \langle x_2, f - m \rangle_2 \, \mu(df) = \langle \Sigma x_1, x_2 \rangle_2 = \langle \Sigma x_2, x_1 \rangle_2.$$

Consider now the more general case of a separable Banach space F. A Borel measure μ on F is *Gaussian* iff for any n and continuous linear mapping $N : F \to \mathbb{R}^n$, the measure $\mu_N = \mu N^{-1}$, given as

$$\mu(N^{-1}(B)) = \mu\{ f \in F \mid N(f) \in B \}, \quad \forall \text{ Borel sets } B \text{ of } \mathbb{R}^n,$$

is Gaussian.

As in the finite dimensional case, any Gaussian measure μ defined on a separable Banach space F is determined by its *mean element $m_\mu \in F$* and *correlation operator $C_\mu : F^* \to F$*. [1] These are characterized by the relations

$$L(m_\mu) = \int_F L(f) \, \mu(df), \quad \forall L \in F^*,$$

and

$$L_1(C_\mu L_2) = \int_F L_1(f - m_\mu) L_2(f - m_\mu) \, \mu(df), \quad \forall L_1, L_2 \in F^*.$$

That is, for any mapping $N(f) = [L_1(f), \ldots, L_n(f)]$ where $L_i \in F^*$, $1 \leq i \leq n$, the Gaussian measure μN^{-1} has mean element $m = N(m_\mu)$ and correlation matrix $\Sigma = \{L_i(C_\mu L_j)\}_{i,j=1}^n$.

The correlation operator is always symmetric, $L_1(C_\mu L_2) = L_2(C_\mu L_1)$, and nonnegative definite, $L(C_\mu L) \geq 0$. It is positive definite, i.e., $L(C_\mu L) > 0$, $\forall L \neq 0$, iff μ has full support, $\operatorname{supp} \mu = F$. In general, μ is concentrated on the hyperplane $m_\mu + \overline{C_\mu(F^*)}$.

Let F be a separable Hilbert space. Then $C_\mu : F^* = F \to F$ is the correlation operator of a Gaussian measure on F iff it is symmetric,

---

[1] For $F = \mathbb{R}^d$ or, more generally, for the case of F being a Hilbert space we have $F^* = F$. Then C_μ can be considered as an operator in F, $C_\mu : F \to F$.

nonnegative definite and has finite trace, i.e.,

$$\mathrm{tr}(C_\mu) \;=\; \int_F \|f\|^2\,\mu(df) \;=\; \sum_{i=1}^\infty \langle C_\mu \eta_i, \eta_i \rangle \;<\; +\infty,$$

where the $\{\eta_i\}$ are a complete orthonormal system in F.

The complete characterization of correlation operators of Gaussian measures on Banach spaces is not known. However, in this case we have the following fact. Let C_μ be the correlation operator of a Gaussian measure on F. Let $a \in F$ and $C' : F^* \to F$ be a symmetric operator, $L_1(C'L_2) = L_2(C'L_1)$, such that

$$0 \;\leq\; L(C'L) \;\leq\; L(C_\mu L), \qquad \forall\, L_1, L_2, L \in F^*.$$

Then there exists a (unique) Gaussian measure on F with mean element a and correlation operator C'.

The *characteristic functional* $\psi_\mu : F^* \to \mathbb{C}$ (where $\mathbb{C}$ stands for complex numbers) of a measure μ is given as

$$\psi_\mu(L) \;=\; \int_F e^{\mathrm{i}\,L(f)}\,\mu(df) \qquad (\mathrm{i} = \sqrt{-1}).$$

Any measure is uniquely determined by its characteristic functional. If μ is Gaussian with mean m_μ and correlation operator C_μ then

$$\psi_\mu(L) \;=\; \exp\left\{\,\mathrm{i}\,L(m_\mu) - \tfrac{1}{2}\,L(C_\mu L)\,\right\}.$$

The correlation operator C_μ generates a μ-semi–inner–product on the space F^*. This is defined as $\langle \cdot, \cdot \rangle_\mu : F^* \times F^* \to \mathbb{R}$,

$$\begin{aligned}
\langle L_1, L_2 \rangle_\mu \;&=\; L_1(C_\mu L_2) \;=\; L_2(C_\mu L_1) \\
&=\; \int_F L_1(f)\,L_2(f)\,\mu(df), \qquad L_1, L_2 \in F^*.
\end{aligned}$$

We denote by $\|\cdot\|_\mu$ the corresponding seminorm, $\|L\|_\mu = \sqrt{\langle L, L \rangle_\mu}$. If supp $\mu = F$ then C_μ is one-to-one, so that $\langle \cdot, \cdot \rangle_\mu$ is an inner product and $\|\cdot\|_\mu$ is a norm. The space F^* with the norm $\|\cdot\|_\mu$ is complete only if $\dim F < +\infty$. μ-orthogonality in F^* means orthogonality with respect to $\langle \cdot, \cdot \rangle_\mu$.

3.3.2 Gaussian measures as abstract Wiener spaces

We noticed that any Gaussian measure μ is determined by its mean element and correlation operator. Sometimes it is convenient to define μ in another way.

Let H be a separable Hilbert space. For any (cylindrical) set $B \subset H$ of the form $B = \{ g \in H \mid P(g) \in A \}$, where P is the H-orthogonal projection onto a finite dimensional subspace of H, and A is a Borel set of $P(H)$, we let

$$\mu'(B) = \frac{1}{(\sqrt{2\pi})^n} \int_A e^{-\|g\|_H^2/2} \, dg \tag{3.5}$$

where $n = \dim P(H)$ and dg is the Lebesgue measure on $P(H)$. That is, μ' is the standard *weak* distribution on the algebra of cylindrical sets. Note that μ' is an additive measure but, in the case $\dim H = +\infty$, it cannot be extended to a σ-additive measure on the Borel σ-field of F. Let $\|\cdot\|_*$ be another norm on H which is weaker than the original norm $\|\cdot\|_H$, i.e., $\|\cdot\|_* \leq K\|\cdot\|_H$ for some constant $K > 0$. Let F be the closure of H with respect to $\|\cdot\|_*$. It turns out that if $\|\cdot\|_F$ possesses some additional properties (it is in some sense measurable, see NR 3.3.2), then there exists a unique σ-additive measure μ defined on the Borel sets of F such that the following holds. For any n and continuous linear functionals $L_i \in F^*$, $1 \leq i \leq n$, we have

$$\mu(\{ f \in F \mid (L_1(f), \dots, L_n(f)) \in B \})$$
$$= \mu'(\{ g \in H \mid (\langle g_{L_1}, g \rangle_H, \dots, \langle g_{L_n}, g \rangle_H) \in B \}),$$

for all Borel sets $B \subset \mathbb{R}^n$. Here g_L is the representer of L in H, i.e., $L(f) = \langle g_L, f \rangle_H$ for $f \in H$. The pair $\{H, F\}$ is called an *abstract Wiener space*.

Such an extension of μ' to a Gaussian measure μ always exists. For instance, we can take $\|g\|_* = \sqrt{\langle Ag, g \rangle_H}$ where $A : H \to H$ is an arbitrary symmetric, positive definite operator with finite trace. Then the resulting space F is a separable Hilbert space and the correlation operator of μ is given by the continuous extension of A to the operator $A : F \to F$.

On the other hand, for any separable Banach space F equipped with a zero-mean Gaussian measure μ, there exists a unique separable Hilbert space H, such that $C_\mu(F^*) \subset H \subset \overline{C_\mu(F^*)}$ and $\{H, F_1\}$ with $F_1 = \operatorname{supp} \mu = \overline{C_\mu(F^*)}$ is an abstract Wiener space. The space H is given as follows. Let $H_0 = C_\mu(F^*)$. For $f_2, f_2 \in H_0$, we define $\langle f_1, f_2 \rangle_H = \langle L_1, L_2 \rangle_\mu$ where the L_i for $i = 1, 2$ are arbitrary functionals satisfying $C_\mu L_i = f_i$. Since $\langle f_1, f_2 \rangle_H$ does not depend on the choice of L_i, it is a well defined inner product on H_0. Then H is the closure of H_0 with respect to the norm $\|\cdot\|_H = \sqrt{\langle \cdot, \cdot \rangle_H}$. Clearly, (3.5) also holds.

Thus any zero-mean Gaussian measure on a separable Banach space can be viewed as an abstract Wiener space (and, of course, vice versa).

Let μ be the Gaussian measure for an abstract Wiener space $\{H, F\}$. Then for $L, L_1, L_2 \in F^*$ we have

$$\int_F L(f)\,\mu(df) = (2\pi\|g_L\|_H^2)^{-1/2} \int_R x \exp\{-x^2/(2\|g_L\|_H^2)\}\,dx = 0$$

and

$$L_1(C_\mu L_2) = \int_F L_1(f)L_2(f)\,\mu(df) = \langle g_{L_1}, g_{L_2}\rangle_H. \qquad (3.6)$$

Hence μ has mean element zero and positive definite correlation operator $C_\mu(L) = g_L, \forall L \in F^*$.

Finally, consider the case when H is an r.k.h.s. with r.k. $R : T \times T \to \mathbb{R}$ (see Subsection 2.6.4). Suppose that function evaluations $L_t(f) = f(t)$, $f \in F$, are continuous functionals in F for all $t \in T$. In this case, by (3.6) we have

$$L_t(C_\mu L_s) = \langle R_t, R_s\rangle_H = R(t, s), \qquad \forall s, t \in T.$$

For this reason, the reproducing kernel R is also called the *covariance kernel*. The measure μ is uniquely determined by its covariance kernel.

Example 3.3.1 Let $r \geq 0$. Let $H = W_{r+1}^0$ be the reproducing kernel Hilbert space of Example 2.6.3 with $(a, b) = (0, 1)$. That is,

$$W_{r+1}^0 = \{f : [0, 1] \to \mathbb{R} \mid$$
$$f^{(r)} \text{ is abs. cont., } f^{(i)} = 0, 0 \leq i \leq r, f^{(r+1)} \in \mathcal{L}_2([0, 1])\}.$$

Let $\|f\|_{C_r} = \sup_{0 \leq x \leq 1} |f^{(r)}(x)|$. Then $\|f\|_{C_r} \leq \|f\|_{W_{r+1}}$. The space W_{r+1}^0 can be completed with respect to the norm $\|\cdot\|_{C_r}$. The resulting space is a separable Banach space,

$$C_r^0 = \{f : [0, 1] \to \mathbb{R} \mid f^{(r)} \text{ continuous, } f^{(i)}(0) = 0, 0 \leq i \leq r\}.$$

Then $\{W_{r+1}^0, C_r^0\}$ is an abstract Wiener space. That is, μ constructed based on the weak distribution on W_{r+1}^0 is a well defined Gaussian measure on the Borel sets of C_r^0. In the case $r = 0$ we obtain the *classical Wiener measure* w of Example 3.2.2, where the covariance kernel $R_0(s, t) = \min\{s, t\}$. For $r \geq 1$ we have the r-*fold Wiener measure* w_r whose covariance kernel is

$$R_r(s, t) = \int_0^1 \frac{(s - u)_+^r}{r!} \frac{(t - u)_+^r}{r!}\,du,$$

see Example 2.6.3.

The name for w_r is justified by the following property. For a Borel set $B \subset C_r^0$, let $D^r(B) = \{\, f^{(r)} \mid f \in B \,\}$. Then $w_r = wD^r$. To see this, observe that $\tilde{w}_r = wD^r$ is a well defined Borel measure on C_r^0. Since $w = w_0$ is uniquely determined by its covariance kernel $R(s,t) = \min\{s,t\}$, $\tilde{w}_r$ is uniquely determined by the equation $\int_{C_r^0} f^{(r)}(s) f^{(r)}(t)\, w_r(df) = \min\{s,t\}$, $s,t \in [0,1]$. On the other hand, the representer of the functional $f^{(r)}(t)$ in W_{r+1}^0 is $G_r(t,\cdot) = (t - \cdot)_+^r/(r!)$. Hence

$$\int_{C_r^0} f^{(r)}(s) f^{(r)}(t)\, w_r(df) = \int_0^1 G_r^{(r)}(s,u)\, G_r^{(r)}(t,u)\, du$$

$$= \int_0^1 G_0(s,u)\, G_0(t,u)\, du = \min\{s,t\},$$

and $\tilde{w}_r = w_r$.

Notes and remarks

NR 3.3.1 For references on Gaussian measures on separable Hilbert and Banach spaces see, e.g., Kuo (1975), Parthasarathy (1967), Skorohod (1974), Vakhania (1981), Vakhania *et al.* (1987). The classical Wiener measure was introduced in Wiener (1923).

Gaussian measures as abstract Wiener spaces are studied in Kuo (1975).

NR 3.3.2 A norm $\|\cdot\|_*$ in a Hilbert space H is called *measurable* iff for any $\varepsilon > 0$ there exists a finite dimensional orthogonal projection P_0, such that for any finite dimensional orthogonal projection $P \perp P_0$ we have

$$\mu'(\{\, g \in H \mid \ \|Pg\|_* > \varepsilon \,\}) \leq \varepsilon.$$

If $\|\cdot\|_*$ is measurable then the weak measure μ' can be extended to a measure μ defined on the closure F of H with respect to $\|\cdot\|_*$. For details, see Kuo (1975).

NR 3.3.3 Some useful properties of Gaussian measures on the space $C([0,1])$ can be found in Parthasarathy (1967). In particular, he gives a sufficient condition for a covariance kernel $R : [0,1]^2 \to \mathbb{R}$ to determine a unique probability measure μ on $C([0,1])$, namely, it suffices that there exist constants α, β, $K > 0$, such that for all $t_1, t_2 \in [0,1]$

$$\int_{\mathbb{R}^2} |x_1 - x_2|^\alpha\, \mu_{t_1 t_2}(dx) \leq K\, |t_1 - t_2|^{1+\beta}.$$

Here $x = (x_1, x_2)$ and $\mu_{t_1 t_2}$ is the Gaussian measure in $\mathbb{R}^2$ with correlation matrix $\{R(t_i, t_j)\}_{i,j=1}^2$.

NR 3.3.4 Let F^{all} be the space of all functions $f : [a,b] \to \mathbb{R}$. Then any function $f(t)$, $a \leq t \leq b$, can be viewed as a realization of the stochastic process corresponding to a covariance kernel $R(s,t)$, $a \leq s, t \leq b$. For instance, the process corresponding to the kernel $R(s,t) = \min\{s,t\}$ is called a *Brownian motion*. The reader interested in stochastic processes is referred to, e.g., Gikhman and Skorohod (1965).

NR 3.3.5 In the case of multivariate functions, Gaussian measures may be defined based on Gaussian distributions on univariate functions. An example is provided by the *Wiener sheet measure* which is given as follows.

Let $d \geq 1$ and $r_i \geq 0$, $1 \leq i \leq d$. Let F be the Banach space of functions $f : [0,1]^d \to \mathbb{R}$ that are r_i times continuously differentiable with respect to the ith variable,

$$
F = C^{0...0}_{r_1...r_d} = \Big\{ f : [0,1]^d \to \mathbb{R} \ \Big| \ D^{r_1...r_d} f \text{ cont.,}
$$
$$
(D^{r_1...r_d}f)(t) = 0, \ 0 \leq i_j \leq r_j, \ 1 \leq j \leq d,
$$
$$
\text{when at least one } t_i \text{ is zero} \Big\},
$$

with the norm $\|f\| = \sup_{t \in [0,1]^d} |(D^{r_1...r_d}f)(t)|$. The Wiener sheet measure on F is defined as

$$
w_{r_1...r_d}(B) = w_{0...0}(D^{r_1...r_d}(B)), \qquad \forall \text{Borel sets } B \text{ of } F,
$$

where $w_{0...0}$ is the classical Wiener measure on $C^{0...0}_{0...0}$. Its covariance kernel is given as

$$
R_{0...0}(s,t) = \int_{C^{0...0}_{0...0}} f(s)f(t) = \prod_{j=1}^d \min\{s_j, t_j\},
$$

where $s = (s_1, \ldots, s_d)$, $t = (t_1, \ldots, t_d)$.

It is easy to see that $w_{r_1...r_d}$ is the zero-mean Gaussian measure with covariance kernel

$$
R_{r_1...r_d}(s,t) = \prod_{j=1}^d R_{r_j}(s_j, t_j),
$$

where R_{r_j} is the covariance kernel of the r_j-fold Wiener measure on $C^0_{r_j}$. Hence the abstract Wiener space for $w_{r_1...r_d}$ is $\{W^{0...0}_{r_1+1...r_d+1}, C^{0...0}_{r_1...r_d}\}$, where $W^{0...0}_{r_1+1...r_d+1}$ is the r.k.h.s. defined in NR 2.6.7.

Another example of a Gaussian distribution on multivariate functions is the *isotropic Wiener measure* (or the Brownian motion in Lévy's sense) which is defined on the space $C([0,1]^d)$. Its mean is zero and its covariance kernel is given as

$$
R(s,t) = \tfrac{1}{2}(\|s\|_2 + \|t\|_2 - \|s-t\|_2), \qquad s, t \in [0,1]^d,
$$

see, e.g., Ciesielski (1975) for more details.

Exercises

E 3.3.1 Let H be a separable Hilbert space. Let the $\{e_i\}$ be a complete orthonormal system in H, and let $P_n : H \to \mathbb{R}^n$, $n \geq 1$, be defined as $P_n(x) = \{\langle x, e_i \rangle\}_{i=1}^n$. Prove that there is no a Gaussian measure μ on H such that for all n, μP_n^{-1} is the n dimensional zero-mean Gaussian measure with identity correlation operator.

E 3.3.2 The space l_2 can be treated as the space of functions $f : \{1, 2, \ldots\} \to \mathbb{R}$, such that $\|f\|^2 = \sum_{i=1}^{\infty} f^2(i) < +\infty$. Show that $R(i, j) = \lambda_i \delta_{ij}$, $i, j \geq 1$, is the covariance kernel of a Gaussian measure on l_2 iff $\sum_{i=1}^{\infty} \lambda_i < +\infty$.

E 3.3.3 Let H and F be separable Hilbert spaces with the same elements and equivalent norms. Show that $\{H, F\}$ is an abstract Wiener space if and only if $\dim H = \dim F < +\infty$.

E 3.3.4 Let $\{H, F\}$ be an abstract Wiener space with $\dim H = +\infty$, and μ the corresponding Gaussian measure. Show that $\mu(H) = 0$.

E 3.3.5 Show that the r-fold Wiener measures w_r satisfy $w_r = w_s D^{r-s}$, where D^k is the differential operator of order k, and $r \geq s \geq 0$.

E 3.3.6 Let R_r be the covariance kernel of the r-fold Wiener measure. Check that

$$R_r(s, t) = \int_0^s \int_0^t R_{r-1}(u_1, u_2) \, du_1 \, du_2.$$

3.4 Linear problems with Gaussian measures

We start the study of linear problems with Gaussian measures. These are problems for which

- F is a separable Banach space, G is a separable Hilbert space, and the solution operator $S : F \to G$ is continuous and linear,
- the a priori distribution μ on F is a zero-mean Gaussian measure,
- information is *linear with Gaussian noise*.

The latter assumption means that the information distribution $\Pi = \{\pi_f\}$ is given as

$$\pi_f = \mathcal{N}(N(f), \sigma^2 \Sigma), \tag{3.7}$$

where $N : F \to \mathbb{R}^n$ is a continuous linear operator,

$$N(f) = [L_1(f), L_2(f), \ldots, L_n(f)], \quad f \in F,$$

$\Sigma : \mathbb{R}^n \to \mathbb{R}^n$ is a symmetric and nonnegative operator (matrix), and $\sigma \geq 0$. That is, information y about f is obtained by noisy observation of the value $N(f)$, and noise $x = y - N(f)$ is the zero-mean Gaussian random variable with covariance matrix $\sigma^2 \Sigma$.

The parameter σ is interpreted as *noise level*. Hence it plays a similar role to δ in the worst case setting. If $\sigma \to 0^+$ then noisy information approaches exact information, which is obtained by letting $\sigma = 0$.

Note that independent observations of L_is correspond to a diagonal matrix Σ. If Σ is the identity, $\Sigma = I$, then the noise $x = y - N(f)$ is said to be *white*. In this case $x \sim \mathcal{N}(0, \sigma^2 I)$. For instance, in Example 3.2.2 we have

$$N(f) = [f(t_1), f(t_2), \ldots, f(t_n)]$$

and the information noise is white.

The goal of this section is to find optimal algorithms and radii of information for linear problems with Gaussian measures. To this end, we first give formulas for induced and conditional distributions.

3.4.1 Induced and conditional distributions

The following lemma is well known. For completeness, we provide it with a proof.

Lemma 3.4.1 *Let ω be the Gaussian measure on F with mean element m_ω and correlation operator C_ω. Then the induced measure ωS^{-1} is also Gaussian. The mean element of ωS^{-1} is $S(m_\omega)$, and the correlation operator equals $S(C_\omega S^*)$, where $S^* : G = G^* \to F^*$ is the adjoint operator to S, i.e., $S^*(g) = \langle S(\cdot), g \rangle$.*

Proof Indeed, the characteristic functional of ωS^{-1} is given as

$$
\begin{aligned}
\psi_{\omega S^{-1}}(g) &= \int_G e^{i\langle x, g \rangle} \, \omega S^{-1}(dx) \\
&= \int_F e^{i\langle S(f), g \rangle} \, \omega(df) = \int_F e^{i(S^* g)(f)} \, \omega(df) \\
&= \exp\left\{ i(S^* g)(m_\omega) - \tfrac{1}{2}(S^* g)(C_\omega(S^* g)) \right\} \\
&= \exp\left\{ i\langle S(m_\omega), g \rangle - \tfrac{1}{2}\langle SC_\omega(S^* g), g \rangle \right\}.
\end{aligned}
$$

Hence $S(m_\omega)$ is the mean element and $S(C_\omega S^*)$ is the correlation operator of ω. $\qquad\square$

For given information (3.7), let

$$G_N = \{ \langle L_j, L_k \rangle_\mu \}_{j,k=1}^n$$

be the $(\mu\text{-})$Gram matrix for the functionals L_i. Clearly, G_N is symmetric and nonnegative definite. Let $Y_1 = (\sigma^2 \Sigma + G_N)(\mathbb{R}^n)$. Then for any $y \in Y_1$ there is exactly one element $z \in Y_1$ satisfying $(\sigma^2 \Sigma + G_N)z = y$.

Lemma 3.4.2 *For $L \in F^*$ we have $N(C_\mu L) \in Y_1$.*

Proof Indeed, any $L \in F^*$ can be decomposed as $L = L_0 + \sum_{j=1}^{n} \alpha_j L_j$, where $L_0 \perp_\mu \text{span}\{L_1, \ldots, L_n\}$. Then $N(C_\mu L) = G_N(\alpha)$ with the vector $\alpha = (\alpha_1, \ldots, \alpha_n)$. Since both matrices Σ and G_N are symmetric and nonnegative definite, we have $G_N(\mathbb{R}^n) \subset (\sigma^2 \Sigma + G_N)(\mathbb{R}^n) = Y_1$ and $N(C_\mu L) \in Y_1$. □

We now show formulas for the regular conditional distribution. Recall that the distribution of information y on $\mathbb{R}^n$ is denoted by μ_1, and the conditional distribution on F with respect to y is denoted by $\mu_2(\cdot|y)$.

Theorem 3.4.1 *For the linear information with Gaussian noise, μ_1 is a zero-mean Gaussian measure and its correlation matrix is $\sigma^2 \Sigma + G_N$. Furthermore, the conditional measure $\mu_2(\cdot|y)$, $y \in Y_1$, is also Gaussian. Its mean element equals*

$$m(y) = \sum_{j=1}^{n} z_j (C_\mu L_j),$$

where $z = z(y) = (z_1, \ldots, z_n) \in Y_1$ satisfies $(\sigma^2 \Sigma + G_N) z = y$. The correlation operator of $\mu_2(\cdot|y)$ is independent of y and given as

$$C_{\mu_2}(L) = C_\mu(L) - m(N(C_\mu L)), \qquad \forall L \in F^*.$$

Observe that the measure μ_1 is concentrated on the subspace Y_1. Therefore it suffices to define $\mu_2(\cdot|y)$ only for $y \in Y_1$.

Proof The characteristic functional of the measure μ_1 is given as ($a \in \mathbb{R}^n$ and $i = \sqrt{-1}$)

$$\psi_{\mu_1}(a) = \int_{\mathbb{R}^n} e^{i \langle y, a \rangle_2} \mu_1(dy) = \int_F \int_{\mathbb{R}^n} e^{i \langle y, a \rangle_2} \pi_f(dy) \, \mu(df)$$

$$= \int_F \exp\left\{ i \langle N(f), a \rangle_2 - \tfrac{1}{2}\sigma^2 \langle \Sigma a, a \rangle_2 \right\} \mu(df).$$

Since for $L_a(\cdot) = \langle N(\cdot), a \rangle_2$ we have $L_a(C_\mu L_a) = \langle G_N a, a \rangle_2$, we find that

$$\psi_{\mu_1}(a) = \exp\left\{ -\tfrac{1}{2} \langle (\sigma^2 \Sigma + G_N) a, a \rangle_2 \right\}.$$

Hence μ_1 is the zero-mean Gaussian measure with correlation matrix $\sigma^2 \Sigma + G_N$.

We now pass to the conditional distribution. Observe first that owing to Lemma 3.4.2 the element $m(N(C_\mu L))$ in the definition of C_{μ_2} is well defined. For $y \in Y_1$, let $\mu_2'(\cdot|y)$ be the Gaussian measure on F with mean $m'(y) = \sum_{j=1}^{n} z_j(C_\mu L_j)$, where $(\sigma^2\Sigma + G_N)z = y$, and correlation operator $C'(\cdot) = C_\mu(\cdot) - m'(NC_\mu(\cdot))$. Then the $\mu'_2(\cdot|y)$s are well defined Gaussian measures. Indeed, for $y \in Y_1$ we have

$$
\begin{aligned}
L(m'(y)) &= L\Big(\sum_{j=1}^{n} z_j C_\mu L_j \Big) = \langle (\sigma^2\Sigma + G_N)^{-1}y, NC_\mu L\rangle_2 \\
&= \langle y, (\sigma^2\Sigma + G_N)^{-1}NC_\mu L\rangle_2.
\end{aligned}
$$

Hence, for any $L, L' \in F^*$, we have

$$
\begin{aligned}
L(C'L') &= L(C_\mu L') - L(m'(NC_\mu L')) \\
&= L(C_\mu L') - \langle NC_\mu L', (\sigma^2\Sigma + G_N)^{-1}NC_\mu L\rangle_2 \\
&= L'(C_\mu L) - \langle NC_\mu L, (\sigma^2\Sigma + G_N)^{-1}NC_\mu L'\rangle_2 \\
&= L'(C'L),
\end{aligned}
$$

and $0 \le L(C'L) \le L(C_\mu L)$.

We need to show that the characteristic functional of the measure $\tilde{\mu}$ is equal to the characteristic functional of the measure $\tilde{\mu}'$ defined as

$$
\tilde{\mu}'(B) = \int_Y \mu'_2(B_y|y)\,\mu_1(dy), \quad \forall \text{Borel sets } B \text{ of } \tilde{F} = F \times \mathbb{R}^n.
$$

To this end, let $\tilde{L} \in \tilde{F}^*$. Then there exist $L \in F^*$ and $w \in \mathbb{R}^n$ such that $\tilde{L}(\tilde{f}) = L(f) + \langle y, w\rangle_2, \forall \tilde{f} = (f, y) \in \tilde{F}$. We have

$$
\begin{aligned}
\psi_{\tilde{\mu}'}(\tilde{L}) &= \int_{\mathbb{R}^n} \Big(\int_F \exp\{i(L(f) + \langle y, w\rangle_2)\}\mu'_2(df|y) \Big)\,\mu_1(dy) \\
&= \int_{\mathbb{R}^n} \exp\{i\langle y, w\rangle_2\} \Big(\int_F \exp\{iL(f)\}\,\mu'_2(df|y) \Big)\,\mu_1(dy) \\
&= \int_{\mathbb{R}^n} \exp\big\{i(\langle y, w\rangle_2 + L(m'(y))) \\
&\qquad\qquad - \tfrac{1}{2}(L(C_\mu L) - L(m'(NC_\mu L)))\big\}\,\mu_1(dy).
\end{aligned}
$$

Recall that for $y \in Y_1$ we have $L(m'(y)) = \langle y, (\sigma^2\Sigma + G_N)^{-1}NC_\mu L\rangle_2$. Hence $L(m'(NC_\mu L)) = \langle NC_\mu L, (\sigma^2\Sigma + G_N)^{-1}NC_\mu L\rangle_2$, and

$$
\begin{aligned}
\psi_{\tilde{\mu}'}(\tilde{L}) &= \exp\big\{-\tfrac{1}{2}(L(C_\mu L) - \langle NC_\mu L, (\sigma^2\Sigma + G_N)^{-1}NC_\mu L\rangle_2)\big\} \\
&\qquad \times \int_{\mathbb{R}^n} \exp\{i\langle y, w + (\sigma^2\Sigma + G_N)^{-1}NC_\mu L\rangle_2\}\,\mu_1(dy) \\
&= \exp\big\{-\tfrac{1}{2}(L(C_\mu L) - \langle NC_\mu L, (\sigma^2\Sigma + G_N)^{-1}NC_\mu L\rangle_2)\big\} \\
&\qquad \times \exp\big\{-\tfrac{1}{2}(\langle(\sigma^2\Sigma + G_N)w, w\rangle_2 \\
&\qquad\qquad + \langle NC_\mu L, (\sigma^2\Sigma + G_N)NC_\mu L\rangle_2 + 2\langle w, NC_\mu L\rangle_2)\big\}
\end{aligned}
$$

$$= \exp\left\{ -\tfrac{1}{2}(L(C_\mu L) + 2\langle w, NC_\mu L\rangle_2 + \langle(\sigma^2\Sigma + G_N)w, w\rangle_2)\right\}.$$

On the other hand, for the characteristic functional $\psi_{\tilde\mu}$ of the measure $\tilde\mu$ we have

$$
\begin{aligned}
\psi_{\tilde\mu}(\tilde L) &= \int_F \int_{\mathbb{R}^n} \exp\{i(L(f) + \langle y, w\rangle_2)\}\, \pi_f(dy)\, \mu(df) \\
&= \int_F \exp\{iL(f)\} \left(\int_{\mathbb{R}^n} \exp\{i\langle y, w\rangle_2\}\, \pi_f(dy) \right) \mu(df) \\
&= \exp\{-\tfrac{1}{2}\langle(\sigma^2\Sigma + G_N)w, w\rangle_2\} \\
&\quad \times \int_F \exp\{i(L(f) + \langle N(f), w\rangle_2)\}\, \mu(df) \\
&= \exp\left\{ -\tfrac{1}{2}(L(C_\mu L) + 2\langle w, NC_\mu L\rangle_2 + \langle(\sigma^2\Sigma + G_N)w, w\rangle_2)\right\}.
\end{aligned}
$$

Thus $\psi_{\tilde\mu} = \psi_{\tilde\mu'}$ which completes the proof. $\qquad\square$

3.4.2 Optimal algorithms

We are now ready to give formulas for the optimal algorithm φ_{opt} and radius of information $\mathrm{rad}^{\mathrm{ave}}(\mathbb{II})$. These can be easily found using the formulas for induced and conditional distributions.

Indeed, Lemma 3.2.2 states that φ_{opt} is determined uniquely (up to a set of y having μ_1-measure zero), and that $\varphi_{\mathrm{opt}}(y)$ ($y \in Y_1$) is the mean element of the measure $\nu_2(\cdot|y) = \mu_2(S^{-1}(\cdot)|y)$. By Lemma 3.4.1, $\varphi_{\mathrm{opt}}(y) = S(m(y))$ where $m(y)$ is the mean element of $\mu_2(\cdot|y)$. Theorem 3.4.1 yields in turn that $m(y) = \sum_{j=1}^n z_j(C_\mu L_j)$ where $z = (\sigma^2\Sigma + G_N)^{-1}y \in Y_1$. Furthermore, by Lemma 3.2.2, the radius of information $\mathbb{II}$ is given as

$$
\begin{aligned}
(\mathrm{rad}^{\mathrm{ave}}(\mathbb{II}))^2 &= (\mathrm{e}^{\mathrm{ave}}(\mathbb{II}, \varphi_{\mathrm{opt}}))^2 \\
&= \int_G \|g\|^2\, \nu(dg) - \int_Y \|\varphi_{\mathrm{opt}}(y)\|^2\, \mu_1(dy) \\
&= \mathrm{tr}\,(SC_\mu S^*) - \mathrm{tr}\,(\varphi_{\mathrm{opt}}(\sigma^2\Sigma + G_N)\varphi_{\mathrm{opt}}^*),
\end{aligned}
$$

where $\varphi_{\mathrm{opt}}^* : G \to Y_1$ is the adjoint operator to φ_{opt}, i.e., it is defined by $\langle \varphi_{\mathrm{opt}}(y), g\rangle = \langle y, \varphi_{\mathrm{opt}}^*(g)\rangle_2$. Observe now that $\varphi_{\mathrm{opt}}^* = (\sigma^2\Sigma + G_N)^{-1}NC_\mu(S^*g)$. Indeed, for any $y \in Y_1$ and $g \in G$ we have

$$\langle\varphi_{\mathrm{opt}}(y), g\rangle = \left\langle \sum_{j=1}^n z_j S(C_\mu L_j), g \right\rangle = \sum_{j=1}^n z_j\langle S(C_\mu L_j), g\rangle$$

$$= \sum_{j=1}^{n} z_j (S^* g)(C_\mu L_j) = \sum_{j=1}^{n} z_j L_j (C_\mu S^* g)$$

$$= \langle z, N C_\mu (S^* g) \rangle_2 = \langle y, (\sigma^2 \Sigma + G_N)^{-1} N C_\mu (S^* g) \rangle_2$$

$$= \langle y, \varphi_{\text{opt}}^* (g) \rangle.$$

Thus $\varphi_{\text{opt}}(\sigma^2 \Sigma + G_N) \varphi_{\text{opt}}^* g = \varphi_{\text{opt}}(N C_\mu (S^* g))$, $\forall g \in G$.

We summarize this in the following theorem.

Theorem 3.4.2 *Let the solution operator S be continuous and linear, and let information $\mathrm{I\!I\!I}$ be linear with Gaussian noise. Then the optimal algorithm is linear and is given by*

$$\varphi_{\text{opt}}(y) = \sum_{j=1}^{n} z_j S(C_\mu L_j), \qquad y \in Y_1,$$

where $z = z(y) \in Y_1$ satisfies $(\sigma^2 \Sigma + G_N) z = y$. Furthermore,

$$\text{rad}^{\text{ave}}(\mathrm{I\!I\!I}) = \text{e}^{\text{ave}}(\mathrm{I\!I\!I}, \varphi_{\text{opt}})$$

$$= \sqrt{\text{tr}(S C_\mu S^*) - \text{tr}(\varphi_{\text{opt}}(N C_\mu S^*))}.$$

The above formulas can be simplified if we assume a special form of N and Σ. That is, suppose that information consists of independent observations of n functionals that are μ-orthonormal. That is, the matrix $\Sigma = \text{diag}\{\eta_1, \ldots, \eta_n\}$ and $N = [L_1, \ldots, L_n]$ with $\langle L_i, L_j \rangle_\mu = \delta_{ij}$. (Here δ_{ij} stands for the Kronecker delta.)

In this case, the Gram matrix G_N is the identity and $\sigma^2 \Sigma + G_N = \text{diag}\{1 + \sigma^2 \eta_1, \ldots, 1 + \sigma^2 \eta_n\}$. Hence

$$\varphi_{\text{opt}}(y) = \sum_{j=1}^{n} (1 + \sigma^2 \eta_j)^{-1} y_j S(C_\mu L_j).$$

If we replace y above by $N(C_\mu L)$, $L \in F^*$, then

$$\varphi_{\text{opt}}(N C_\mu L) = \sum_{j=1}^{n} \frac{\langle L, L_j \rangle_\mu}{1 + \sigma^2 \eta_j},$$

so that for $g \in G$ we have

$$\langle \varphi_{\text{opt}}(N C_\mu (S^* g)), g \rangle = \sum_{j=1}^{n} \frac{\langle S^* g, L_j \rangle_\mu}{1 + \sigma^2 \eta_j} \langle S(C_\mu L_j), g \rangle$$

$$= \sum_{j=1}^{n} \frac{\langle S(C_\mu L_j), g \rangle^2}{1 + \sigma^2 \eta_j}.$$

Choosing an orthonormal basis $\{g_i\}_{i=1}^{\infty}$ in G, we obtain

$$
\begin{aligned}
\mathrm{tr}\left(\varphi_{\mathrm{opt}}(NC_{\mu}S^*)\right) &= \sum_{i=1}^{\infty}\sum_{j=1}^{n}\frac{\langle S(C_{\mu}L_j), g_i\rangle^2}{1+\sigma^2\eta_j} \\
&= \sum_{j=1}^{n}\frac{1}{1+\sigma^2\eta_j}\sum_{i=1}^{\infty}\langle S(C_{\mu}L_j), g_i\rangle^2 = \sum_{j=1}^{n}\frac{\|S(C_{\mu}L_j)\|^2}{1+\sigma^2\eta_j}.
\end{aligned}
$$

Thus we have the following corollary.

Corollary 3.4.1 *If the functionals L_i are μ-orthonormal, $\langle L_i, L_j\rangle_{\mu} = \delta_{ij}$ for $1 \le i, j \le n$, and observations of $L_i(f)$ are independent, $\Sigma = \mathrm{diag}\{\eta_1, \ldots, \eta_n\}$, then the optimal algorithm*

$$
\varphi_{\mathrm{opt}}(y) = \sum_{j=1}^{n}\frac{S(C_{\mu}L_j)}{1+\sigma^2\eta_j}\, y_j
$$

and the radius of information

$$
\mathrm{rad}^{\mathrm{ave}}(\mathbb{II}) = \sqrt{\mathrm{tr}\,(SC_{\mu}S^*) - \sum_{j=1}^{n}\frac{\|S(C_{\mu}L_j)\|^2}{1+\sigma^2\eta_j}}.
$$

It turns out that the assumptions of Corollary 3.4.1 are not restrictive. More precisely, any linear information with Gaussian noise can be linearly transformed to information of the same radius, and consisting of independent observations of μ-orthonormal functionals. Moreover, this transformation does not depend on the noise level σ. The proof is given in NR 3.4.3.

Let us see how the radius of information depends on the noise level σ. As explained above, we can assume without loss of generality that $\Sigma = D = \mathrm{diag}\{\eta_1, \ldots, \eta_n\}$ and $\langle L_i, L_j\rangle_{\mu} = \delta_{ij}$, $1 \le i, j \le n$. Let $r(\sigma)$ be the radius of information $y \sim \mathcal{N}(N(\cdot), \sigma^2 D)$. Then

$$
r^2(\sigma) = r^2(0) + \sigma^2\sum_{j=1}^{n}\frac{\eta_j}{1+\sigma^2\eta_j}\,\|S(C_{\mu}L_j)\|^2.
$$

Letting $\sigma \to 0^+$, for $r(0) > 0$ we have

$$
r(\sigma) - r(0) \approx \sigma^2 \cdot \frac{\sum_{j=1}^{n}\eta_j\|S(C_{\mu}L_j)\|^2}{2\left(\mathrm{tr}(SC_{\mu}S^*) - \sum_{j=1}^{n}\|S(C_{\mu}L_j)\|^2\right)^{1/2}},
$$

while for $r(0) = 0$ we have

$$r(\sigma) - r(0) = r(\sigma) \approx \sigma \cdot \sqrt{\sum_{j=1}^{n} \eta_j \|S(C_\mu L_j)\|^2}.$$

Thus the radius $r(\sigma)$ is a constant or increasing function of σ. If $r(0) = 0$ then the radius of noisy information converges to the radius of exact information linearly in σ. Otherwise we have quadratic convergence in σ. For S a functional, this is in contrast to results of the worst case setting, where we always have linear convergence of $r(\delta)$ to $r(0)$; see Theorem 2.4.2.

Notes and remarks

NR 3.4.1 This section is based mainly on Plaskota (1990), where the case of white noise $\Sigma = I$ is considered. Exact information is treated, e.g., in Traub *et al.* (1988).

NR 3.4.2 It is worth while to mention that the space G in Theorem 3.4.2 need not be a Hilbert space. That is, the algorithm $\varphi(y) = S(m(y))$, where $m(y)$ is mean element of $\mu_2(\cdot|y)$, is still optimal when G is a separable Banach space. Indeed, observe that in this case the measure $\nu_2(\cdot|y) = \mu_2(S^{-1}(\cdot)|y)$ remains Gaussian with the mean element $S(m(y))$ (see E 3.4.3). Any Gaussian measure is centrosymmetric with respect to its mean element (see e.g. Vakhania *et al.* , 1987). Hence, owing to Example 3.2.3, the element $S(m(y))$ is the center of $\nu_2(\cdot|y)$ and the algorithm $\varphi(y) = S(m(y))$ is optimal.

NR 3.4.3 We now show the result already announced that any linear information with Gaussian noise can be linearly transformed to information of the same radius and consisting of independent observations of μ-orthonormal functionals.

Let $\Pi = \{\pi_f\}$ with $\pi_f = \mathcal{N}(N(f), \sigma^2\Sigma)$ and $N : F \to \mathbb{R}^n$. Suppose first that the matrix Σ is nonsingular. Denote by L'_i the functionals which form the operator $\Sigma^{-1/2}N$, i.e., $\Sigma^{-1/2}N = [L'_1, \ldots, L'_n]$. Let $G' = \{\langle L'_i, L'_j\rangle_\mu\}_{i,j=1}^n$ and $\{q^{(i)}\}_{i=1}^n$ be the orthonormal basis of eigenvectors of the matrix G', $G'q^{(i)} = \eta_i q^{(i)}$ where $\eta_1 \geq \cdots \geq \eta_m > 0 = \eta_{m+1} = \ldots = \eta_n$. Letting Q be the (orthogonal) $n \times n$ matrix of vectors $q^{(i)}$, and D_1 the $m \times n$ diagonal matrix $\mathrm{diag}\{\eta_1^{-1/2}, \ldots, \eta_m^{-1/2}\}$, we define the linear transformation $T = D_1 Q^* \Sigma^{-1/2} : \mathbb{R}^n \to \mathbb{R}^m$.

The problem of approximating $S(f)$ from the data $y = N(f) + x$ where $x \sim \mathcal{N}(0, \sigma^2\Sigma)$ can be translated to the problem of approximating $S(f)$ from $\tilde{y} = Ty = \tilde{N}(f) + \tilde{x}$, where $\tilde{N} = TN$ and $\tilde{x} = Tx$. The functionals forming $\tilde{N}$ are μ-orthonormal. Indeed, let $\tilde{N} = [\tilde{L}_1, \ldots, \tilde{L}_m]$. Then $\tilde{L}_i = \sum_{j=1}^m \eta_j^{-1/2} q_j^{(i)} L'_j$ and

$$\langle \tilde{L}_i, \tilde{L}_j\rangle_\mu = \eta_i^{-1/2} \eta_j^{-1/2} \sum_{s,t=1}^n q_s^{(i)} q_t^{(j)} \langle L'_i, L'_j\rangle_\mu$$

$$= \eta_i^{-1/2} \eta_j^{-1/2} \langle G' q^{(i)}, q^{(j)} \rangle_2 = \delta_{ij}.$$

Moreover, the random variable $\tilde{y}$ is Gaussian with mean $\tilde{N}(f)$ and correlation matrix

$$\sigma^2 \tilde{\Sigma} = \sigma^2 (D_1 Q^* \Sigma^{-1/2}) \Sigma (D_1 Q^* \Sigma^{-1/2})^* = \sigma^2 \operatorname{diag}\{\eta_1^{-1}, \ldots, \eta_m^{-1}\}.$$

Thus information $\tilde{y}$ is obtained by independent observations of μ-orthonormal functionals.

We show that the information $\mathrm{I\!I}$ and $\tilde{\mathrm{I\!I}} = \{\tilde{\pi}_f\}$ with $\tilde{\pi}_f = \mathcal{N}(\tilde{N}(f), \sigma^2 D)$, $D = \operatorname{diag}\{\eta_1^{-1}, \ldots, \eta_m^{-1}\}$, are of the same radius, i.e., $\operatorname{rad}^{\mathrm{ave}}(\mathrm{I\!I}) = \operatorname{rad}^{\mathrm{ave}}(\tilde{\mathrm{I\!I}})$. To this end, it suffices that the conditional measures with respect to information $\mathrm{I\!I}$ and $\tilde{\mathrm{I\!I}}$ have the same correlation operator. This in turn holds iff the functionals $\sum_{j=1}^n z_j L_j$ where $(\sigma^2 \Sigma + G_N) z = N C_\mu L$, and $\sum_{j=1}^n \tilde{z}_j \tilde{L}_j$ where $(\sigma^2 D + I) \tilde{z} = \tilde{N} C_\mu L$, coincide for all $L \in F^*$. Indeed, simple calculations show that z and $\tilde{z}$ satisfy $Q^* \Sigma^{1/2} z = (D^{1/2} \tilde{z}, \underbrace{0, \ldots, 0}_{n-m})$. Hence

$$
\begin{aligned}
\sum_{j=1}^m \tilde{z}_j \tilde{L}_j(f) &= \langle \tilde{z}, \tilde{N}(f) \rangle_2 = \langle \tilde{z}, D_1 Q^* \Sigma^{-1/2} N(f) \rangle_2 \\
&= \langle Q^* \Sigma^{1/2} z, Q^* \Sigma^{1/2} N(f) \rangle_2 = \langle \Sigma^{-1/2} Q Q^* \Sigma^{-1/2} z, N(f) \rangle_2 \\
&= \sum_{j=1}^n z_j L_j(f).
\end{aligned}
$$

Consider now the case when Σ is singular, $\dim \Sigma N(\mathbb{R}^n) = k < n$. Then there exists a nonsingular and symmetric matrix V such that $V \Sigma V$ is diagonal with $n - k$ zeros and k ones. Let $V N = [L_1', \ldots, L_n']$. We can assume that the functionals L_i' and L_j' are μ-orthogonal for $1 \le i \le n - k < j \le n$, since otherwise L_j' can be replaced by their μ-orthogonal projections onto $(\operatorname{span}\{L_1', \ldots, L_{n-k}'\})^\perp$. Let $N_0 = [L_1', \ldots, L_{n-k}']$ and $N_1 = [L_{n-k+1}', \ldots, L_n']$. Let 0 be the zero matrix in $\mathbb{R}^{n-k}$ and I the identity matrix in $\mathbb{R}^k$. Now we can use the procedure above to transform $y^{(0)} \sim \mathcal{N}(N_0(\cdot), 0)$ and $y^{(1)} \sim \mathcal{N}(N_1(\cdot), \sigma^2 I)$ into equivalent information $\tilde{y}^{(0)}$ and $\tilde{y}^{(1)}$, where $\tilde{y}^{(0)}$ is exact and both consist of independent observations of μ-orthonormal functionals. Then $\tilde{y} = [\tilde{y}^{(0)}, \tilde{y}^{(1)}]$ also consists of independent observations of μ-orthonormal functionals, and y is equivalent to $\tilde{y}$.

Exercises

E 3.4.1 Prove that $N(C_\mu(F^*)) = G_N(\mathbb{R}^n)$, and for $\sigma > 0$

$$N(C_\mu(F^*)) + \Sigma(\mathbb{R}^n) = (\sigma^2 \Sigma + G_N)(\mathbb{R}^n).$$

E 3.4.2 Show that the joint measure $\tilde{\mu}$ defined on $F \times \mathbb{R}^n$ is Gaussian, and that the mean element of $\tilde{\mu}$ is zero and the correlation operator is given as

$$C_{\tilde{\mu}}(\tilde{L}) = \big(C_\mu(L) + C_\mu(\langle N(\cdot), w \rangle_2), \ N(C_\mu L) + (\sigma^2 \Sigma + G_N) w \big) \in F \times \mathbb{R}^n,$$

where $\tilde{L}(f, y) = L(f) + \langle y, w \rangle_2$, $f \in F$, $y \in \mathbb{R}^n$.

E 3.4.3 Let F and G be separable Banach spaces and $S : F \to G$ a continuous linear operator. Let ω be a Gaussian measure on F with mean element m_ω and correlation operator C_ω. Show that then the measure ωS^{-1} on G is also Gaussian, and that its mean element is $S(m_\omega)$ and its correlation operator $C_{\omega S^{-1}}(L) = S(C_\mu(LS))$, $L \in G^*$.

E 3.4.4 Suppose that the functionals L_j, $1 \le j \le n$, are orthonormal and $\Sigma = \operatorname{diag}\{\eta_1, \ldots, \eta_n\}$. Let $P_N : F^* \to F^*$ be the μ-orthogonal projection onto the subspace $V = \operatorname{span}\{L_1, \ldots, L_n\}$, and let $D : V \to V$ be defined by $D(L_j) = (1 + \sigma^2\eta_j)L_j$, $1 \le j \le n$. Show that then the correlation operator C_{μ_2} of the conditional distribution $\mu_2(\cdot|y)$ can be rewritten as $C_{\mu_2} = C_\mu(I - D^{-1}P_N)$, and that for small σ the operator C_{μ_2} is roughly the superposition of the 'almost' μ-orthogonal projection onto $V^\perp$, and C_μ.

E 3.4.5 Show that $\varphi_{\mathrm{opt}}(y) = \varphi_0(y - \sigma^2\Sigma z)$ where $(\sigma^2\Sigma + G_N)z = y$ and φ_0 is the optimal algorithm for exact information ($\sigma = 0$).

E 3.4.6 Let $S : F \to G$ be a given solution operator, and let Π be a given linear information with Gaussian noise. Let μ_m be a Gaussian measure on F with mean element m, not necessarily equal to zero. Let φ_m and $\operatorname{rad}_m^{\mathrm{ave}}(\Pi)$ denote the optimal algorithm and radius of information with respect to μ_m. Show that for all $m \in F$ we have $\operatorname{rad}_m^{\mathrm{ave}}(\Pi) = \operatorname{rad}_0^{\mathrm{ave}}(\Pi)$ and $\varphi_m(y) = S(m) + \varphi_0(y - N(m))$.

E 3.4.7 Let Π be linear information with Gaussian noise, $\pi_f = \mathcal{N}(N(f), \Sigma)$, with $Y = \mathbb{R}^n$. Let $B : \mathbb{R}^n \to \mathbb{R}^n$ be a linear mapping. Show that for information $\tilde{\Pi}$ given as $\tilde{\pi}_f = \mathcal{N}(BN(f), B\Sigma B^*)$ we have $\operatorname{rad}^{\mathrm{ave}}(\Pi) \le \operatorname{rad}^{\mathrm{ave}}(\tilde{\Pi})$. If B is nonsingular then $\operatorname{rad}^{\mathrm{ave}}(\Pi) = \operatorname{rad}^{\mathrm{ave}}(\tilde{\Pi})$ and the corresponding optimal algorithms satisfy $\tilde{\varphi}_{\mathrm{opt}}(y) = \varphi_{\mathrm{opt}}(B^{-1}y)$.

E 3.4.8 Suppose we approximate $S(f)$ from information $y = [N(f) + x, t] \in \mathbb{R}^n$, where $N : F \to \mathbb{R}^n$ is a continuous linear operator and the noise $(x, t) \in \mathbb{R}^n$ has mean zero and is Gaussian. Prove that if the random variables x and t are independent then the 'pure noise' data t do not count. That is, the radius of information corresponding to y is equal to the radius of $y^{(1)} = N(f) + x$, and the optimal algorithm uses only $y^{(1)}$.

3.5 The case of linear functionals

In this section we make an additional assumption that

- the solution operator S is a continuous linear functional.

In this case, the formulas for φ_{opt} and $\operatorname{rad}^{\mathrm{ave}}(\Pi)$ in Theorem 3.4.2 can be expressed in a simple way. That is, we have

$$
\begin{aligned}
\varphi_{\mathrm{opt}}(y) &= \sum_{j=1}^n z_j S(C_\mu L_j) = \sum_{j=1}^n z_j L_j(C_\mu S) \\
&= \langle z, N(C_\mu S)\rangle_2
\end{aligned}
$$

where $(\sigma^2 \Sigma + G_N)z = y$, or equivalently,

$$\varphi_{\text{opt}}(y) = \langle y, w \rangle_2$$

where w satisfies $(\sigma^2 \Sigma + G_N)w = N(C_\mu S)$. To find the radius, observe that $\text{tr}(S(C_\mu S^*)) = \|S\|_\mu^2$ and $\text{tr}(\varphi_{\text{opt}}(NC_\mu S^*)) = \varphi_{\text{opt}}(NC_\mu S)$. Hence

$$\text{rad}^{\text{ave}}(\mathbb{I}) = \sqrt{\|S\|_\mu^2 - \varphi_{\text{opt}}(NC_\mu S)}.$$

For independent observations μ-orthonormal functionals, i.e., for $\Sigma = D = \text{diag}\{\eta_1, \ldots, \eta_n\}$ and $\langle L_i, L_j \rangle_\mu = \delta_{ij}$, we have

$$\varphi_{\text{opt}}(y) = \sum_{j=1}^n \frac{\langle S, L_j \rangle_\mu}{1 + \sigma^2 \eta_j} y_j$$

and

$$\text{rad}^{\text{ave}}(\mathbb{I}) = \sqrt{\|S\|_\mu^2 - \sum_{j=1}^n \frac{\langle S, L_j \rangle_\mu^2}{1 + \sigma^2 \eta_j}}.$$

Observe that $\sum_{j=1}^n \langle S, L_j \rangle_\mu L_j$ is the μ-orthogonal projection of S onto $V = \text{span}\{L_1, \ldots, L_n\}$. Denoting this projection by P_N, the above formulas can be rewritten as

$$\varphi_{\text{opt}}(y) = (P_N S)(f) + \sum_{j=1}^n \frac{\langle S, L_j \rangle_\mu}{1 + \sigma^2 \eta_j} x_j$$

$(y = N(f) + x)$, and

$$\text{rad}^{\text{ave}}(\mathbb{I}) = \sqrt{\|S - P_N S\|_\mu^2 + \sigma^2 \sum_{j=1}^n \frac{\eta_j}{1 + \sigma^2 \eta_j} \langle S, L_j \rangle_\mu^2}.$$

Hence, for small noise level σ, the optimal algorithm is close to the μ-orthogonal projection of S onto V, and the radius is close to the μ-distance of S from V. In particular, for exact information $\varphi_{\text{opt}}(N(f)) = (P_N S)(f)$ is the exact projection and $\text{rad}^{\text{ave}}(\mathbb{I})$ is the exact μ-distance.

In Subsection 2.4.2, we noticed that in the worst case setting the problem of approximating a linear functional based on linear information with uniformly bounded noise is as difficult as the hardest one dimensional subproblem contained in the original problem. E 2.3.5 shows that this holds not only for functionals but also for all linear solution operators. We shall see that in the average case setting the corresponding property is preserved only for S a linear functional.

We first explain what we mean by one dimensional subproblems in the average case setting. For a functional $K \in F^*$ with $\|K\|_\mu > 0$, let $P_K : F \to F$ be given as

$$P_K(f) = f - \frac{K(f)}{\|K\|_\mu^2} C_\mu K.$$

Note that for any $L \in F^*$ we have

$$P_K(C_\mu L) = C_\mu \left(L - \frac{\langle K, L \rangle_\mu}{\|K\|_\mu^2} K \right).$$

That is, $P_K C_\mu : F^* \to F$ is the superposition of the μ-orthogonal projection onto the subspace μ-orthonormal to K, and C_μ. We also have that $\ker P_K = \mathrm{span}\{C_\mu K\}$ and $P_K(F) = \ker K$.

The a priori Gaussian measure μ on F can be decomposed with respect to P_K, i.e.,

$$\mu = \int_{\ker K} \mu_K(\cdot | g) \, \mu P_K^{-1}(dg)$$

where $\mu_K(\cdot | g)$ is the conditional measure on F given $g = P_K(f)$. Obviously, $\mu_K(\cdot | g)$ is concentrated on the line

$$P_K^{-1}(g) = \{ g + \alpha C_\mu K \mid \alpha \in \mathbb{R} \}.$$

We also formally allow $K \in F^*$ with $\|K\|_\mu = 0$. In this case, we set $P_K(f) = f$, $\forall f$. Then $\mu P_K^{-1} = \mu$ and $\mu_K(\cdot | g)$ is the Dirac measure concentrated on $\{g\}$, $\forall g \in F$.

Lemma 3.5.1 *Let $\|K\|_\mu > 0$. Then for a.e. g the measure $\mu_K(\cdot | g)$ is Gaussian with mean $m(g) = g$ and correlation operator*

$$A_K(L) = \frac{\langle L, K \rangle_\mu}{\|K\|_\mu^2} C_\mu K.$$

Proof Consider the characteristic functional ψ_ω of the measure $\omega = \mu P_K^{-1}$. We have

$$\psi_\omega(L) = \int_{\ker K} \exp\{iL(g)\} \, \mu P_K^{-1}(dg) = \int_F \exp\{iL(P_K f)\} \, \mu(df)$$
$$= \exp\left\{ -\tfrac{1}{2} \left(L \, P_K \left(C_\mu(L P_K) \right) \right) \right\}.$$

Hence the measure ω is a zero-mean Gaussian and its correlation operator is given as

$$C_\omega(L) = P_K(C_\mu(L P_K)) = C_\mu L - \frac{\langle K, L \rangle_\mu}{\|K\|_\mu^2} C_\mu K.$$

Now let $\mu'_K(\cdot\,|g)$ be the Gaussian measure with mean g and correlation operator A_K. Then the characteristic functional of the measure $\mu' = \int_{\ker K} \mu'_K(\cdot\,|g)\,\mu P_K^{-1}(dg)$ is given as

$$
\begin{aligned}
\psi_{\mu'}(L) &= \int_{\ker K}\int_F \exp\{iL(f)\}\,\mu'_K(\,df\,|g)\,\mu P_K^{-1}(dg)\\[4pt]
&= \int_{\ker K} \exp\left\{i\,L(g) - \frac{\langle K,L\rangle_\mu^2}{2\,\|K\|_\mu^2}\right\}\,\mu P_K^{-1}(dg)\\[4pt]
&= \exp\left\{-\frac{\langle K,L\rangle_\mu^2}{2\,\|K\|_\mu^2}\right\}\int_{\ker K} \exp\{iL(g)\}\,\mu P_K^{-1}(dg)\\[4pt]
&= \exp\left\{-\tfrac12\langle L,L\rangle_\mu\right\}.
\end{aligned}
$$

This shows that $\mu = \mu'$. Since conditional distribution is determined uniquely (up to a set of μ_1-measure zero), the lemma follows. $\qquad\square$

Any functional $K \in F^*$ determines a *family* of one dimensional sub-problems which is indexed by $g \in \ker K$ and given as follows. For $g \in \ker K$, the subproblem relies on minimizing the average error

$$
\mathrm{e}^{\mathrm{ave}}(\mathrm{I\!I\!I},\varphi;\mu_K(\cdot|g)) = \sqrt{\int_F\int_{\mathbb{R}^n} |S(f) - \varphi(y)|^2\,\pi_f(dy)\,\mu_K(df|g)}
$$

over all algorithms φ. That is, in the subproblem g we use additional (exact) information that $P_K(f) = g$ or, in other words, that f is in the line $P_K^{-1}(g)$.

Since the measures $\mu_K(\cdot|g)$ have the same correlation operator, the radius $\mathrm{rad}^{\mathrm{ave}}(\mathrm{I\!I\!I};\mu_K(\cdot|g))$ is independent of g (compare with E 3.4.6). We denote this radius by $\mathrm{rad}_K^{\mathrm{ave}}(\mathrm{I\!I\!I})$. It is clear that

$$
\mathrm{rad}_K^{\mathrm{ave}}(\mathrm{I\!I\!I}) \leq \mathrm{rad}^{\mathrm{ave}}(\mathrm{I\!I\!I}). \tag{3.8}
$$

Indeed, we have

$$
\begin{aligned}
\left(\mathrm{rad}_K^{\mathrm{ave}}(\mathrm{I\!I\!I};\mu)\right)^2 &= \int_{\ker K}\left(\mathrm{rad}^{\mathrm{ave}}(\mathrm{I\!I\!I};\mu_K(\cdot|g))\right)^2\,\mu P_K^{-1}(dg)\\[4pt]
&= \int_{\ker K}\inf_\varphi\left(\mathrm{e}^{\mathrm{ave}}(\mathrm{I\!I\!I},\varphi;\mu_K(\cdot|g))\right)^2\,\mu P_K^{-1}(dg)\\[4pt]
&\leq \inf_\varphi\int_{\ker K}\left(\mathrm{e}^{\mathrm{ave}}(\mathrm{I\!I\!I},\varphi;\mu_K(\cdot|g))\right)^2\,\mu P_K^{-1}(dg)\\[4pt]
&= \inf_\varphi\left(\mathrm{e}^{\mathrm{ave}}(\mathrm{I\!I\!I},\varphi;\mu)\right)^2\\[4pt]
&= \left(\mathrm{rad}^{\mathrm{ave}}(\mathrm{I\!I\!I};\mu)\right)^2.
\end{aligned}
$$

We now prove that for a special choice of K we have equality in (3.8).

Theorem 3.5.1 *Consider the family of one dimensional subproblems determined by the functional*

$$K_* = S - \varphi_{\mathrm{opt}} N = S - \sum_{j=1}^{n} w_j L_j,$$

where $(\sigma^2 \Sigma + G_N)w = N(C_\mu S)$. Then for a.e. g the algorithm

$$\varphi_{\mathrm{opt}}(y) = \langle y, w \rangle_2$$

is optimal not only for the original problem, but also for the subproblem indexed by $g \in \ker K_*$. Moreover,

$$\mathrm{rad}_{K_*}^{\mathrm{ave}}(\mathrm{II}) = \mathrm{rad}^{\mathrm{ave}}(\mathrm{II}).$$

Proof If $\|K_*\|_\mu = 0$ then $S(f) = \varphi_{\mathrm{opt}}(N(f))$, $\forall f \in \overline{C_\mu(F^*)}$. In this case $P_K = I$, the measure $\mu_{K_*}(\cdot | g)$ is concentrated on $\{g\}$, and any algorithm with the property $\varphi(N(g)) = S(g)$ is optimal for the subproblem indexed by g. Hence optimality of φ_{opt} for all subproblems (a.e.) follows from the fact that $P_{K_*}(F) = \ker K_* \subset \overline{C_\nu(F^*)}$. We also have

$$\mathrm{rad}^{\mathrm{ave}}(\mathrm{II}) = \sqrt{S(C_\mu K_*)} = 0 = \mathrm{rad}_{K_*}^{\mathrm{ave}}(\mathrm{II}).$$

Assume now that $\|K_*\|_\mu > 0$. Let ω be the zero-mean Gaussian measure with correlation operator $A = A_{K_*}$, where A_{K_*} is defined in Lemma 3.5.1. We need to show that the algorithm $\varphi_{\mathrm{opt}} = \langle \cdot, w \rangle_2$ is optimal if the average error over f is taken with respect to ω, i.e.,

$$\mathrm{rad}^{\mathrm{ave}}(\mathrm{II}; \omega) = \inf_\varphi e^{\mathrm{ave}}(\mathrm{II}, \varphi; \omega) = e^{\mathrm{ave}}(\mathrm{II}, \varphi_{\mathrm{opt}}; \omega)$$

where

$$e^{\mathrm{ave}}(\mathrm{II}, \varphi; \omega) = \sqrt{\int_F \int_{\mathbb{R}^n} \|S(f) - \varphi(y)\|^2 \, \pi_f(dy) \, \omega(df)}.$$

Owing to Theorem 3.4.2, the optimal algorithm with respect to ω is given by $\varphi_\omega(y) = \sum_{j=1}^{n} z_j S(A L_j)$, where $(\sigma^2 \Sigma + H_N)z = y$, $H_N = \{L_i(A L_j)\}_{i,j=1}^{n}$, and $z, y \in (\sigma^2 \Sigma + H_N)(\mathbb{R}^n)$. We have $L_i(A L_j) = \langle K_*, L_i \rangle_\mu \langle K_*, L_j \rangle_\mu \|K_*\|_\mu^{-2}$ and $S(A L_j) = \langle K_*, S \rangle_\mu \langle K_*, L_j \rangle_\mu \|K_*\|_\mu^{-2}$. Hence, letting $a = N(C_\mu K_*)$, we obtain

$$\varphi_\omega(y) = \frac{\langle K_*, S \rangle_\mu}{\|K_*\|_\mu^2} \langle z, a \rangle_2 \tag{3.9}$$

where z satisfies

$$\sigma^2 \Sigma z + \frac{\langle a, z \rangle_2}{\|K_*\|_\mu^2} a = y. \tag{3.10}$$

Observe now that

$$a = N(C_\mu K_*) = N(C_\mu S) - \sum_{j=1}^n w_j N(C_\mu L_j)$$

$$= N(C_\mu S) - G_N w = \sigma^2 \Sigma w.$$

This and (3.10) yield

$$\langle y, w \rangle_2 = \sigma^2 \langle \Sigma z, w \rangle_2 + \langle a, z \rangle_2 \langle a, w \rangle_2 \|K_*\|_\mu^{-2}$$

$$= \langle z, a \rangle_2 (1 + \sigma^2 \langle \Sigma w, w \rangle_2 \|K_*\|_\mu^{-2}),$$

so that

$$\langle z, a \rangle_2 = \frac{\|K_*\|_\mu^2 \langle y, w \rangle_2}{\|K_*\|_\mu^2 + \sigma^2 \langle \Sigma w, w \rangle_2}. \tag{3.11}$$

We also have

$$\langle S, K_* \rangle_\mu = \|S\|_\mu^2 - \langle w, N(C_\mu S) \rangle_2$$

$$= \left(\|S\|_\mu^2 - 2 \langle w, N(C_\mu S) \rangle_2 + \langle G_N w, w \rangle_2 \right)$$

$$+ \left(\langle w, (\sigma^2 \Sigma + G_N) w \rangle_2 - \langle G_N w, w \rangle_2 \right)$$

$$= \|K_*\|_\mu^2 + \sigma^2 \langle \Sigma w, w \rangle_2. \tag{3.12}$$

Taking (3.9), (3.11) and (3.12) together we finally obtain

$$\varphi_\omega(y) = \frac{\langle S, K_* \rangle_\mu}{\|K_*\|_\mu^2 + \sigma^2 \langle \Sigma w, w \rangle_2} \langle y, w \rangle_2 = \langle y, w \rangle_2,$$

as claimed.

Now let ω_g be the Gaussian measure with mean $g \in \ker K_*$ and correlation operator A. By E 3.4.6, the optimal algorithm for ω_g is given as

$$\varphi_g(y) = S(g) + \langle y - N(g), w \rangle_2 = S(g) - \langle N(g), w \rangle_2 + \langle y, w \rangle_2$$

$$= K_*(g) + \langle y, w \rangle_2 = \langle y, w \rangle_2 = \varphi_{\text{opt}}(y).$$

Since $\mu_{K_*}(\cdot|g) = \omega_g$ a.e. g, the algorithm φ_{opt} is optimal for all subproblems almost everywhere.

To prove the equality $\mathrm{rad}_{K_*}^{\mathrm{ave}}(\mathrm{II}) = \mathrm{rad}^{\mathrm{ave}}(\mathrm{II})$, observe that

$$
\begin{aligned}
\left(\mathrm{rad}_{K_*}^{\mathrm{ave}}(\mathrm{II})\right)^2 &= \int_{\ker K_*} \left(\mathrm{rad}^{\mathrm{ave}}(\mathrm{II}; \mu_{K_*}(\cdot|g))\right)^2 \mu P_{K_*}^{-1}(dg) \\
&= \int_{\ker K_*} \int_F \left(\int_{\mathbb{R}^n} \|S(f) - \varphi_{\mathrm{opt}}(y)\|^2 \pi_f(dy)\right) \\
&\qquad\qquad\qquad \mu_{K_*}(df|g) \, \mu P_{K_*}^{-1}(dg) \\
&= \int_F \int_{\mathbb{R}^n} \|S(f) - \varphi_{\mathrm{opt}}(y)\|^2 \pi_f(dy) \, \mu(df) \\
&= (\mathrm{rad}^{\mathrm{ave}}(\mathrm{II}))^2.
\end{aligned}
$$

This completes the proof of the theorem. $\qquad\qquad\qquad\qquad\qquad\square$

Theorem 3.5.1 together with (3.8) immediately yields the following corollary.

Corollary 3.5.1 *If the solution operator S is a linear functional then for any information II we have*

$$
\mathrm{rad}^{\mathrm{ave}}(\mathrm{II}) = \sup_{K \in F^*} \mathrm{rad}_K^{\mathrm{ave}}(\mathrm{II}) = \mathrm{rad}_{K_*}^{\mathrm{ave}}(\mathrm{II}),
$$

where the functional K_* is given as $K_*(f) = S(f) - \varphi_{\mathrm{opt}}(N(f))$, $f \in F$.

That is, the difficulty of the original problem is determined by the difficulty of the *hardest one dimensional subproblems*, and these subproblems are determined by the functional K_*.

If S is not a functional then Corollary 3.5.1 is no longer true. For an example, see E 3.5.4.

Notes and remarks

NR 3.5.1 This section is based on Plaskota (1994).

Exercises

E 3.5.1 Suppose we want to estimate a real random variable f, where $f \sim \mathcal{N}(0, \lambda)$ for $\lambda > 0$, based on the data $y = f + x$ where $x \sim \mathcal{N}(0, \sigma^2)$. Show that in this case the radius equals

$$
r(\sigma^2) = \sqrt{\frac{\sigma^2 \lambda}{\sigma^2 + \lambda}},
$$

and the optimal algorithm

$$\varphi_{\text{opt}}(y) \;=\; \frac{\lambda}{\sigma^2 + \lambda}\, y, \qquad y \in \mathbb{R}.$$

E 3.5.2   Consider the problem of the previous exercise but with information $y = [y_1, \ldots, y_n]$ where $y_i \sim \mathcal{N}(f, \sigma_i^2)$ and $\sigma_j^2 > 0$, $1 \le i \le n$. Show that the radius of information is given as

$$r(\sigma_1^2, \ldots, \sigma_n^2) \;=\; \sqrt{\frac{\lambda}{1 + \lambda \sum_{i=1}^n \sigma_i^{-2}}}$$

and

$$\varphi_{\text{opt}}(y) \;=\; \frac{\lambda}{1 + \lambda \sum_{i=1}^n \sigma_i^{-2}} \sum_{i=1}^n \frac{y_i}{\sigma_i^2}.$$

In particular, show that n observations of f with variances σ_i^2 are as good as one observation of f with the variance $\sigma^2 = \left(\sum_{i=1}^n \sigma_i^{-2} \right)^{-1}$.

E 3.5.3   Consider the one dimensional linear problem with the correlation operator $C_\mu(L) = \lambda L(f_0) f_0$, $\forall L \in F^*$, where $\lambda > 0$ and $f_0 \in F$, and information $y \sim \mathcal{N}(N(\cdot), \sigma^2 \Sigma)$. Let $g_0 = S(f_0) \in \mathbb{R}$ and $y_0 = N(f_0) \in \mathbb{R}^n$. Show that for $y_0 \in \Sigma(\mathbb{R}^n)$ we have

$$\text{rad}^{\text{ave}}(\Pi) \;=\; |g_0| \sqrt{\frac{\sigma^2 \lambda}{\sigma^2 + \lambda \langle \Sigma^{-1} y_0, y_0 \rangle_2}},$$

$$\varphi_{\text{opt}}(y) \;=\; g_0\, \frac{\lambda \langle \Sigma^{-1} y_0, y \rangle_2}{\sigma^2 + \lambda \langle \Sigma^{-1} y_0, y_0 \rangle_2},$$

while for $y_0 \notin \Sigma(\mathbb{R}^n)$ we have $\text{rad}^{\text{ave}}(\Pi) = 0$ and

$$\varphi_{\text{opt}}(y) \;=\; g_0\, \frac{\langle P y_0, y \rangle_2}{\langle P y_0, y_0 \rangle_2},$$

where P is the orthogonal projection in $\mathbb{R}^n$ onto $(\Sigma(\mathbb{R}^n))^\perp$.

E 3.5.4   Let $F = G = \mathbb{R}^d$ and S be the identity. Let μ be the standard Gaussian measure on $\mathbb{R}^d$, $\mu = \mathcal{N}(0, I)$. Consider information Π consisting of $n < d$ noisy observations. Show that $\text{rad}^{\text{ave}}(\Pi) \ge d - n$, while for any functional $K \in F^*$ we have $\text{rad}_K^{\text{ave}}(\Pi) \le 1$. Hence show that

$$\text{rad}^{\text{ave}}(\Pi) \;\ge\; (d - n) \sup_{K \in F^*} \text{rad}_K^{\text{ave}}(\Pi)$$

and that any one dimensional subproblem is at least $d - n$ times as difficult as the original problem.

3.6 Optimal algorithms as smoothing splines

Recall that in the worst case setting we defined an α-smoothing spline algorithm as $\varphi_\alpha(y) = S(\mathbf{s}_\alpha(y))$. Here $\mathbf{s}_\alpha(y)$ is the α-smoothing spline element, which minimizes the functional

$$\Gamma_\alpha(f, y) \;=\; \alpha \cdot \|f\|_F^2 + (1 - \alpha) \cdot \delta^{-2} \|y - N(f)\|_Y^2, \tag{3.13}$$

where $\| \cdot \|_F$ and $\| \cdot \|_Y$ are extended Hilbert seminorms. Moreover, if the set of problem elements is the unit ball with respect to $\| \cdot \|_F$ and the noise is uniformly bounded in $\| \cdot \|_Y$ by δ, then for appropriately chosen α, the algorithm φ_α turns out to be optimal; see Subsection 2.5.2.

In this section, we show that in the average case setting optimal algorithms can also be viewed as smoothing spline algorithms.

3.6.1 A general case

We consider the linear problem with Gaussian noise of Section 3.4. That is, the measure μ on F is Gaussian with zero mean and correlation operator C_μ. Information $\mathrm{II} = \{\pi_f\}$ is linear with Gaussian noise, $\pi_f = \mathcal{N}(N(f), \sigma^2 \Sigma)$ with $\sigma^2 > 0$. The operator N consists of functionals $L_i \in F^*$,

$$N = [L_1, L_2, \ldots, L_n].$$

Let H be the separable Hilbert space such that the pair $(H, \overline{C_\mu(F^*)})$ is an abstract Wiener space, see Subsection 3.3.2. Recall that $C_\mu(F^*) \subset H \subset \overline{C_\mu(F^*)}$. Let $\| \cdot \|_Y$ be the extended norm in $\mathbb{R}^n$ defined as

$$\|x\|_Y = \begin{cases} \sqrt{\langle \Sigma^{-1} x, x \rangle_2} & x \in \Sigma(\mathbb{R}^n), \\ +\infty & x \notin \Sigma(\mathbb{R}^n). \end{cases}$$

We denote by $s(y) \in H$ the smoothing spline that minimizes

$$\Gamma(f, y) = \|f\|_H^2 + \sigma^{-2} \|y - N(f)\|_Y^2$$

over all $f \in H$. That is, in the average case setting, Γ corresponds to $2\Gamma_{1/2}$ with δ replaced by σ in (3.13). For instance, in the case of independent observations, $\Sigma = \mathrm{diag}\{\sigma_1^2, \ldots, \sigma_n^2\}$ and $\sigma^2 = 1$, $s(y)$ is the minimizer of

$$\|f\|_H^2 + \sum_{j=1}^{n} \sigma_j^{-2}(y_j - L_j(f))^2$$

(with the convention that $0/0 = 0$). As usual, the smoothing spline algorithm is given as

$$\varphi_{\mathrm{spl}}(y) = S(s(y)), \qquad y \in \mathbb{R}^n.$$

Let $f_j = C_\mu L_j \in H$, $1 \le j \le n$. Then f_j is the representer of L_j in H, and for all $f \in H$ we have

$$N(f) = [\langle f_1, f \rangle_H, \langle f_2, f \rangle_H, \ldots, \langle f_n, f \rangle_H].$$

Applying Lemma 2.6.1 we immediately obtain that $\Gamma(y) = \inf_{f \in F} \Gamma(f, y)$ is finite if and only if $y \in Y_2 = N(H) + \Sigma(\mathbb{R}^n)$. For $y \in Y_2$, the smoothing spline is unique and given as

$$\mathbf{s}(y) = \sum_{j=1}^{n} z_j f_j$$

where $z \in Y_2$ satisfies $(\gamma \Sigma + G_N)z = y$ and $\gamma = \sigma^2$. Comparing this with Theorem 3.4.1 and noting that $Y_2 = Y_1 = (\sigma^2 \Sigma + G_N)(\mathbb{R}^n)$ we obtain that $\mathbf{s}(y)$ is the mean element $m(y)$ of the conditional distribution for information y. Hence $\varphi_{\mathrm{spl}}(y) = S(\mathbf{s}(y)) = S(m(y))$ is the optimal algorithm.

Theorem 3.6.1 *In the average case setting, the smoothing spline algorithm φ_{spl} is optimal.*

We stress that, unlike in the worst case, this time we have no problems with the optimal choice of the parameters α and γ. That is, we have $\alpha^* = 1/2$ and $\gamma^* = \sigma^2$.

3.6.2 Special cases

The formulas for α-smoothing splines in some special cases were given in Section 2.6. Clearly, the formulas can be applied to obtain optimal algorithms in the average case. It suffices to set $\alpha = 1/2$ and replace δ^2 and γ by σ^2, and the norm $\| \cdot \|_F$ by $\| \cdot \|_H$.

We now discuss relations between the smoothing spline algorithm and regularized approximation as well as analyzing the least squares algorithm in the average case setting.

Consider the linear problem of Subsection 3.6.1 with a positive definite matrix Σ. Then $\| \cdot \|_Y$ is a Hilbert norm. We denote by Y the Hilbert space of vectors in $\mathbb{R}^n$ with inner product $\langle \cdot, \cdot \rangle_Y = \langle \Sigma^{-1}(\cdot), \cdot \rangle_2$. Let $N_H : H \to Y$ be the restriction of $N : F \to Y$ to the subspace $H \subset F$, i.e., $N_H(f) = N(f)$, $\forall f \in H$. Let $N_H^* : Y \to H$ be the adjoint operator to N_H. That is, N_H^* is defined by $\langle N_H(f), y \rangle_Y = \langle f, N_H^*(y) \rangle_H$, $\forall f \in H$, $\forall y \in Y$. Similarly, we define the operators $S_H : H \to G$ and $S_H^* : G \to H$.

Recall that the regularized approximation $\varphi_\gamma(y) = S(u_\gamma(y))$, where $u_\gamma(y) \in H$ is the solution of the equation

$$(\gamma I_H + N_H^* N_H)f = N_H^* y.$$

Here $\gamma > 0$ is the regularization parameter and I_H is the identity in H; compare with Subsection 2.6.2. In view of Lemma 2.6.3 and Theorem 3.6.1, we immediately obtain the following result.

Corollary 3.6.1 *The regularized solution*

$$u_\gamma(y) = (\gamma I_H + N_H^* N_H)^{-1} N_H^* y$$

is the smoothing spline, $u_\gamma(y) = s(y)$, if and only if the regularization parameter $\gamma = \sigma^2$. Hence the regularization algorithm $\varphi_{\sigma^2}(y) = S(u_{\sigma^2}(y))$ is optimal.

Let us now consider the case where the space F is finite dimensional, $\dim F = d < +\infty$. Recall that the worst case error is then minimized by the least squares algorithm, provided that the noise level δ is small, see Theorem 2.6.2. We want to see whether a similar result holds in the average case setting.

We assume that the correlation operator C_μ of the a priori Gaussian measure μ is positive definite. Information about f is given as $y = N(f) + x \in \mathbb{R}^n$, where $\dim N(F) = d$ and $x \sim \mathcal{N}(0, \sigma^2 \Sigma)$. Recall that the (generalized) least squares algorithm is defined as $\varphi_{ls} = S(N^*N)^{-1}N^*$, or equivalently, $\varphi_{ls} = SN^{-1}P_N$ where P_N is the orthogonal projection onto $N(F)$ with respect to $\langle \cdot, \cdot \rangle_Y$.

Since, in the average case setting, the optimal value of the regularization parameter is $\gamma = \sigma^2$, the least squares algorithm is optimal only for exact information ($\sigma = 0$), and then its error is zero. It turns out, however, that for small noise level σ as well, this algorithm is nearly optimal. That is, we have the following theorem.

Theorem 3.6.2 *For the (generalized) least squares algorithm φ_{ls} we have*

$$e^{\mathrm{ave}}(\mathrm{III}, \varphi_{ls}) = \sigma \cdot \sqrt{\mathrm{tr}(S(N^*N)^{-1}S^*)}$$

and

$$e^{\mathrm{ave}}(\mathrm{III}, \varphi_{ls}) = \mathrm{rad}^{\mathrm{ave}}(\mathrm{III})\,(1 + O(\sigma^2)) \qquad as \quad \sigma \to 0^+.$$

Proof The formula for $e^{\mathrm{ave}}(\mathrm{III}, \varphi_{ls})$ follows from the fact that for any f

$$\int_{\mathbb{R}^n} \|S(f) - \varphi_{ls}(N(f) + x)\|^2\, \pi(dx)$$

$$= \int_{\mathbb{R}^n} \|SN^{-1}P_N(x)\|^2\, \pi(dx) = \sigma^2\, \mathrm{tr}((SN^{-1})(SN^{-1})^*)$$

$$= \sigma^2 \operatorname{tr}(S(N^*N)^{-1}S^*).$$

We now derive a formula for the radius $\operatorname{rad}^{\mathrm{ave}}(\mathbb{II})$. Let $\{\xi_i\}_{i=1}^d$ be the orthonormal basis in H (which is now equal to F with inner product $\langle \cdot, \cdot \rangle_H = \langle C^{-1}(\cdot), \cdot \rangle_F)$ of eigenelements of $N_H^*N_H$, and let the η_is be the corresponding eigenvalues, $N_H^*N_H\xi_i = \eta_i\xi_i$. Since $\dim N(F) = \dim F$, all η_is are positive. Theorem 3.4.2 and the equalities $N_H^* = C_\mu N^*$ and $S_H^* = C_\mu S^*$ yield

$$
\begin{aligned}
(\operatorname{rad}^{\mathrm{ave}}(\mathbb{II}))^2 &= \operatorname{tr}(SC_\mu S^*) - \operatorname{tr}(\varphi_{\mathrm{opt}}(NC_\mu S^*)) \\
&= \operatorname{tr}(SC_\mu S^*) - \operatorname{tr}(S(\sigma^2 I_H + N_H^*N_H)^{-1}N_H^*(NC_\mu S^*)) \\
&= \operatorname{tr}(S_H S_H^*) - \operatorname{tr}(S_H(\sigma^2 I_H + N_H^*N_H)^{-1}N_H^*N_H S_H^*) \\
&= \sum_{i=1}^d \|S_H(\xi_i)\|^2 - \sum_{i=1}^d \|S_H((\sigma^2 I_H + N_H^*N_H)^{-1}N_H^*N_H)^{1/2}\xi_i\|^2 \\
&= \sigma^2 \cdot \sum_{i=1}^d \frac{\|S(\xi_i)\|^2}{\sigma^2 + \eta_i}. \qquad (3.14)
\end{aligned}
$$

Since $S(N^*N)^{-1}S^* = S_H(N_H^*N_H)^{-1}S_H^*$,

$$(\mathrm{e}^{\mathrm{ave}}(\mathbb{II}, \varphi_{\mathrm{ls}}))^2 = \sigma^2 \operatorname{tr}(S_H(N_H^*N_H)^{-1}S_H^*) = \sigma^2 \cdot \sum_{i=1}^d \frac{\|S(\xi_i)\|^2}{\eta_i}.$$

Comparing this with (3.14) we have $\mathrm{e}^{\mathrm{ave}}(\mathbb{II}, \varphi_{\mathrm{ls}}) = \operatorname{rad}^{\mathrm{ave}}(\mathbb{II})(1+O(\sigma^2))$, as claimed. $\qquad\square$

3.6.3 Relations to worst case setting

The fact that smoothing spline algorithms are optimal in the worst and average case settings enables us to show a relation between the two settings. That is, consider the following two problems.

(WW) Approximate $S(f)$ for $f \in E \subset F$, based on information $y = N(f) + x \in \mathbb{R}^n$ where $x \in \Sigma(\mathbb{R}^n)$ and $\|x\|_Y = \sqrt{\langle \Sigma^{-1}x, x \rangle_2} \le \delta$.

(AA) Approximate $S(f)$, where $f \in F$ is distributed according to a zero-mean Gaussian measure μ on F, based on information $y = N(f) + x \in \mathbb{R}^n$ such that $x \sim \mathcal{N}(0, \sigma^2\Sigma)$.

Then we have the following correspondence theorem.

Theorem 3.6.3 *Suppose that $\{H, F\}$ is the abstract Wiener space for the measure μ, and the set E is the unit ball of H. If $\delta = \sigma$ then the algorithm $\varphi_{\mathrm{spl}}(y) = S(\mathbf{s}(y))$ is optimal for the problem (AA) in the average* case, $e^{ave}(\Pi, \varphi_{spl}; \mu) = rad^{ave}(\Pi; \mu)$, and almost optimal for the problem (WW) in the worst case, $e^{wor}(\mathbb{N}, \varphi_{spl}; E) \leq \sqrt{2} \cdot rad^{wor}(\mathbb{N}, \varphi_{spl}; E)$. Furthermore,

$$rad^{wor}(\mathbb{N}; E) \leq \sqrt{2} \cdot rad^{ave}(\Pi; \mu).$$

If S is a functional then

$$rad^{ave}(\Pi; \mu) \leq rad^{wor}(\mathbb{N}; E) \leq \sqrt{2} \cdot rad^{ave}(\Pi; \mu).$$

Proof Optimality or almost optimality of φ_{spl} follows from Theorem 3.6.1, Lemma 2.5.1, and the fact that $s(y)$ is the $(1/2)$-smoothing spline for (WW).

To obtain the formulas for the radii, we proceed as follows. Assume first that $\Sigma > 0$. Let $\{f_i\}_{i=1}^{\dim H}$ be the complete and H-orthonormal basis consisting of eigenelements of the operator $N_H^* N_H : H \to H$, i.e., $N_H^* N_H f_i = \eta_i f_i$, $i \geq 1$. Owing to NR 3.6.3 we have

$$(e^{ave}(\Pi, \varphi_{spl}))^2 = (rad^{ave}(\Pi))^2 = \sigma^2 \sum_{i=1}^{\dim H} \frac{\|S(f_i)\|^2}{\sigma^2 + \eta_i}. \qquad (3.15)$$

On the other hand, in view of Lemma 2.5.1 and Theorem 2.6.2 we have

$$\begin{aligned}
(e^{wor}(\mathbb{N}, \varphi_{spl}))^2 &\leq 2\delta^2 \|S(\delta^2 I_H + N_H^* N_H)^{-1/2}\|^2 \\
&\leq 2(rad^{wor}(\mathbb{N}))^2.
\end{aligned}$$

Note that any operator $T : H \to G$ satisfies $\|T\|^2 \leq tr(T^*T)$ with equality if T is a functional. This and (3.15) yield

$$\begin{aligned}
(e^{wor}(\mathbb{N}, \varphi_{spl}))^2 &\leq 2\delta^2 \sum_{i=1}^{\dim H} \|S(\delta^2 I_H + N_H^* N_H)^{-1/2} f_i\|^2 \\
&= 2\delta^2 \sum_{i=1}^{\dim H} \frac{\|S(f_i)\|^2}{\delta^2 + \eta_i} = 2(rad^{ave}(\Pi))^2,
\end{aligned}$$

which proves $rad^{wor}(\mathbb{N}) \leq \sqrt{2}\, rad^{ave}(\Pi)$. If S is a functional then

$$rad^{ave}(\Pi) = \frac{1}{\sqrt{2}}\, e^{wor}(\mathbb{N}, \varphi_{spl}) \leq \frac{1}{\sqrt{2}}(\sqrt{2}\, rad^{wor}(\mathbb{N})) = rad^{wor}(\mathbb{N}),$$

as claimed.

If Σ is singular then we repeat the proof with H replaced by $H_1 = \{ f \in H \mid N(f) \in \Sigma(\mathbb{R}^n) \}$. $\qquad\square$

Notes and remarks

NR 3.6.1 Optimality of spline algorithms in the average case setting and for exact information was shown in Traub *et al.* (1988, Sect. 5.4 of Chap. 6). Optimality properties of smoothing splines in reproducing kernel Hilbert spaces and for $\Sigma = \sigma^2 I$ are well known in Bayesian statistics. We mention only Kimeldorf and Wahba (1970) and Wahba (1990), where many other references can be found. The general result of Theorem 3.6.1 (together with Lemma 2.6.1) is, however, new.

NR 3.6.2 The correspondence theorem of Subsection 3.6.3 is well known in the case of exact information and the solution operator S being a functional. In that case the algorithm φ_{spl} is optimal in both settings and $\mathrm{rad}^{\mathrm{wor}}(\mathbb{N}) = \mathrm{rad}^{\mathrm{ave}}(\mathbb{II})$ ($\delta = \sigma$). The generalization of those results to the noisy case and arbitrary S is new.

NR 3.6.3 The formula for the radius $\mathrm{rad}^{\mathrm{ave}}(\mathbb{II})$ evaluated in the proof of Theorem 3.6.2 can be easily generalized to the case where the Hilbert space F is infinite dimensional. Denote, as before, by $\{\xi_i\}_{i\geq 1}$ the complete H-orthonormal basis of eigenvectors of $N_H^* N_H$, and by η_i the corresponding eigenelements, $\eta_1 \geq \cdots \geq \eta_k > 0$ where $k = \dim N(F)$. Repeating the corresponding part of the proof of Theorem 3.6.2, we obtain

$$\mathrm{rad}^{\mathrm{ave}}(\mathbb{II}) = \sqrt{\sigma^2 \cdot \sum_{i=1}^{k} \frac{\|S(\xi_i)\|^2}{\sigma^2 + \eta_i} + \sum_{j\geq k+1} \|S(\xi_i)\|^2}.$$

Note that if the matrix Σ is singular, then the formula above holds with the space H replaced by $H_1 = \{f \in H \mid N(f) \in \Sigma(\mathbb{R}^n)\}$ with the norm $\|\cdot\|_{H_1} = \|\cdot\|_H$ (compare with the proof of Theorem 2.6.2). If the operators $S_H^* S_H$ and $N_H^* N_H$ possess a common orthonormal basis of eigenelements $\{\xi_i\}$ and $S_H^* S_H \xi_i = \lambda_i \xi_i$, then

$$\mathrm{rad}^{\mathrm{ave}}(\mathbb{II}) = \sqrt{\sigma^2 \sum_{i=1}^{k} \frac{\lambda_i}{\sigma^2 + \eta_i} + \sum_{j=1}^{\dim H} \lambda_j}.$$

NR 3.6.4 If the solution operator S in Theorem 3.6.3 is not a functional, then the relation $\mathrm{rad}^{\mathrm{ave}}(\mathbb{II}; \mu) \leq \mathrm{rad}^{\mathrm{wor}}(\mathbb{N}; E)$ does not hold in general. To see this, consider an infinite dimensional separable Hilbert space F with complete orthonormal basis $\{\xi_i\}$. Let the correlation operator of the measure μ be given by $C_\mu \xi_i = \lambda_i \xi_i$, $\lambda_1 \geq \lambda_2 \geq \cdots > 0$. Consider the approximation problem, i.e., $S(f) = f$, with exact information

$$N_n(f) = [\langle f, \xi_1 \rangle_F, \dots, \langle f, \xi_n \rangle_F].$$

In this case,

$$E = \left\{ f \in F \ \middle| \ \sum_{i=1}^{\infty} \lambda_i^{-1} \langle f, \xi_i \rangle_F^2 \leq 1 \right\}$$

$(0^{-1} \cdot 0 = 0)$. Hence $\mathrm{rad}^{\mathrm{wor}}(N_n) = \sqrt{\lambda_{n+1}}$, $\mathrm{rad}^{\mathrm{ave}}(N_n) = \sqrt{\sum_{i=n+1}^{\infty} \lambda_i}$, and

$$\frac{\mathrm{rad}^{\mathrm{ave}}(N_n; \mu)}{\mathrm{rad}^{\mathrm{wor}}(N_n; E)} = \sqrt{\sum_{i=n+1}^{\infty} \frac{\lambda_i}{\lambda_{n+1}}}.$$

The ratio above can be arbitrarily large. For instance, for $\lambda_i = i^{-p}$ with $p > 1$ we obtain

$$\frac{\mathrm{rad}^{\mathrm{ave}}(N_n; \mu)}{\mathrm{rad}^{\mathrm{wor}}(N_n; E)} \asymp n \qquad \text{as} \qquad n \to \infty.$$

Exercises

E 3.6.1 Show that for exact information, $\sigma = 0$, the optimal algorithms in the worst and average case settings are the same and given as $\varphi_{\mathrm{opt}}(y) = S(\mathbf{s}(y))$, $y \in N(F)$, where $\mathbf{s}(y) \in H$ is such an element that $N(\mathbf{s}(y)) = y$ and $\|\mathbf{s}(y)\|_H = \inf \{ \|f\|_H \mid f \in H, N(f) = y \}$. Moreover, show that if S is a functional then for exact informaton we have $\mathrm{rad}^{\mathrm{wor}}(N) = \mathrm{rad}^{\mathrm{ave}}(N)$.

E 3.6.2 Consider approximation of a parameter $f \in \mathbb{R}$ based on information $y = f + x$, where
(a) $|f| \le 1$ and $|x| \le \delta$,
(b) $f \sim \mathcal{N}(0, 1)$ and $x \sim \mathcal{N}(0, \sigma^2)$.
Let $r^w(\gamma)$ and $r^a(\gamma)$ be the worst and average radii of information for the problems (a) and (b) with $\delta = \gamma$ and $\sigma = \gamma$, respectively. Show that

$$\frac{r^w(\gamma)}{r^a(\gamma)} = \begin{cases} (1 + \gamma^2)^{1/2} & 0 \le \gamma \le 1, \\ (1 + \gamma^{-2})^{1/2} & \gamma > 1. \end{cases}$$

Thus show that the ratio $r^w(\gamma)/r^a(\gamma)$, $\gamma \ge 0$, assumes all values from the interval $[1, \sqrt{2}]$.

E 3.6.3 Suppose that the solution operator S in Theorem 3.6.3 is finite dimensional, i.e., $\dim S(F) = d < +\infty$. Show that then

$$d^{-1} \cdot \mathrm{rad}^{\mathrm{ave}}(\mathbb{N}) \le \mathrm{rad}^{\mathrm{wor}}(\mathbb{N}) \le \sqrt{2} \cdot \mathrm{rad}^{\mathrm{ave}}(\mathbb{N}).$$

3.7 Varying information

With this section we start the study of varying information, which will be continued in the following sections. Basically, we assume that information can be obtained as in the worst case setting. The only difference is in the interpretation of noise, which is now a random variable.

3.7.1 Nonadaptive and adaptive information

A nonadaptive information distribution Π is uniquely determined by exact information $N : F \to \mathbb{R}^n$,

$$N(f) = [L_1(f), L_2(f), \ldots, L_n(f)], \qquad \forall f \in F,$$

where the L_is are continuous linear functionals belonging to some class $\Lambda \subset F^*$, and by a diagonal correlation matrix

$$\Sigma = \mathrm{diag}\{\sigma_1^2, \sigma_2^2, \ldots, \sigma_n^2\},$$

where $\sigma_i \geq 0$, $1 \leq i \leq n$. Using N and Σ we obtain information $y = [y_1, \ldots, y_n]$, where $y_i = L_i(f) + x_i$ and the x_is are independent random variables with $x_i \sim \mathcal{N}(0, \sigma_i^2)$. That is, $\Pi = \{\pi_f\}$ is identified with the pair $\{N, \Sigma\}$,

$$\Pi = \{N, \Sigma\},$$

and given by

$$\pi_f = \mathcal{N}(N(f), \Sigma).$$

We now define adaptive information. As in the worst case, we assume that the set Y of possible information values satisfies the condition:

for any $(y_1, y_2, \ldots) \in \mathbb{R}^\infty$ there exists exactly one index n

such that $(y_1, y_2, \ldots, y_n) \in Y$.

(Recall that we also assume measurability of the sets $Y_i = Y \cap \mathbb{R}^i$.) An adaptive information distribution Π is determined by a family $N = \{N_y\}_{y \in Y}$ of exact nonadaptive information,

$$N_y = [L_1(\cdot), L_2(\cdot; y_1), \ldots, L_{n(y)}(\cdot; y_1, \ldots, y_{n(y)-1})],$$

where $L_i(\cdot; y_1, \ldots, y_{n-1}) \in \Lambda$, $1 \leq i \leq n$, and $n(y)$ is the length of y, $y = (y_1, \ldots, y_{n(y)})$, and by a family $\Sigma = \{\Sigma_y\}_{y \in Y}$ of diagonal matrices,

$$\Sigma_y = \mathrm{diag}\{\sigma_1^2, \sigma_2^2(y_1), \ldots, \sigma_{n(y)}^2(y_1, \ldots, y_{n(y)-1})\}.$$

To complete the definition, we have to specify the distributions π_f on Y, for $f \in F$. These are defined as follows. We let $W_1 = \mathbb{R}$, and

$$W_m = \{(y_1, \ldots, y_m) \in \mathbb{R}^m \mid (y_1, \ldots, y_j) \notin Y, \ 1 \leq j \leq m-1\}$$

for $m \geq 2$. (In words, $y \in W_m$ iff $y \in \mathbb{R}^m$ and y can be extended to a sequence belonging to Y.) Note that the W_m are measurable. Indeed, so is W_1, and for arbitrary $m \geq 2$ we have $W_m = (W_{m-1} \setminus Y_{m-1}) \times \mathbb{R}$. Observe also that W_{m-1} is the domain of $L_m(f; \cdot)$ and $\sigma_m^2(\cdot)$.

Assuming that the maps $L_i(f;\cdot): W_{i-1} \to \mathbb{R}$ and $\sigma_i(\cdot): W_{i-1} \to \mathbb{R}_+$ are Borel measurable, the distribution $\omega_{m,f}$ on W_m is as follows. Let $\mathcal{N}(\cdot\,|\,t, \sigma^2)$ be the one dimensional Gaussian measure with mean $t \in \mathbb{R}$ and variance $\sigma^2 \geq 0$. Then

$$\omega_{1,f}(B) = \mathcal{N}(B|L_1(f), \sigma_1^2),$$

$$\omega_{m+1,f}(B) = \int_{W_m \setminus Y_m} \mathcal{N}(B^{(t)}|L_{m+1}(f;t), \sigma_{m+1}^2(t))\, \omega_{m,f}(dt),$$

where $t \in \mathbb{R}^m$ and $B^{(t)} = \{u \in \mathbb{R}\,|\, (t, u) \in B\}$. That is, the conditional distribution of y_{m+1} given $(y_1, \ldots, y_m)$ is Gaussian with mean $L_{m+1}(f; y_1, \ldots, y_m)$ and variance $\sigma_m^2(y_1, \ldots, y_m)$.

The distribution π_f is now given as

$$\pi_f(\cdot) = \sum_{m=1}^{\infty} \omega_{m,f}(\cdot \cap Y_m).$$

Lemma 3.7.1 π_f *is a well defined probability measure on* Y.

Proof The σ-field on Y is generated by the cylindrical sets of the form

$$B = \left(\bigcup_{i=1}^{m-1} B_i \right) \cup \{y \in Y\,|\, y^m \in A_m\},$$

where the B_i are Borel sets of Y_i, A_m is a Borel set of W_m, and y^m is the sequence consisting of the first m components of y, $m \geq 1$. For any such set, we let

$$\tilde{\pi}_f(B) = \sum_{i=1}^{m-1} \omega_i(B_i) + \omega_m(A_m).$$

Observe that $\tilde{\pi}_f(B)$ is well defined since it does not depend on the representation of B. Indeed, a representation of the same set B with m replaced by $m+1$ is given as

$$B = \left(\left(\bigcup_{i=1}^{m-1} B_i \right) \cup (A_m \cap Y_m) \right) \cup \{y \in Y\,|\, y^{m+1} \in (A_m \setminus Y_m) \times \mathbb{R}\}.$$

Then

$$\sum_{i=1}^{m-1} \omega_i(B_i) + \omega_m(A_m \cap Y_m) + \omega_{m+1}((A_m \setminus Y_m) \times \mathbb{R})$$

$$= \sum_{i=1}^{m-1} \omega_i(B_i) + \omega_m(A_m \cap Y_m) + \omega_m(A_m \setminus Y_m)$$

$$= \sum_{i=1}^{m-1} \omega_i(B_i) + \omega_m(A_m).$$

$\tilde{\pi}_f$ is an additive measure defined on the cylindrical sets. Hence it can be uniquely extended to a σ-additive measure defined on the Borel sets of Y. Since $\tilde{\pi}(Y) = \omega_1(W_1) = 1$, this is a probability measure.

Now, for any $B = \bigcup_{i=1}^{\infty} B_i$ where $B_i = B \cap Y_i$, we have

$$\tilde{\pi}_f(B) = \lim_{m \to \infty} \tilde{\pi}_f\left(\bigcup_{i=1}^{m} B_i\right) = \lim_{m \to \infty} \sum_{i=1}^{m} \omega_i(B_i) = \pi_f(B).$$

Thus $\pi_f = \tilde{\pi}_f$ and π_f is well defined. □

Clearly, nonadaptive information can also be treated as adaptive information. Then $Y = \mathbb{R}^n$ and the maps $L_i(\cdot; y_1, \ldots, y_{i-1}) = L_i$ and $\sigma_i^2(y_1, \ldots, y_{i-1}) = \sigma_i^2$ are independent of $y_1, \ldots, y_{i-1} \in \mathbb{R}^{i-1}$, $1 \le i \le n$.

3.7.2 Adaption versus nonadaption

In the worst case setting, for adaptive information $\mathbb{N}$ it is often possible to select $y^* \in Y$ in such a way that the radius of nonadaptive information $\mathbb{N}_{y^*}$ is not much larger than the radius of $\mathbb{N}$, see Theorem 2.7.1. Our aim now is to show a corresponding result in the average case setting for linear problems with Gaussian measures. That is, we assume that F is a separable Banach space, G is a separable Hilbert space, and the solution operator $S : F \to G$ is continuous and linear. The measure μ is zero-mean and Gaussian with correlation operator $C_\mu : F^* \to F$.

Let $\mathbb{I} = \{\mathbb{I}_y\}_{y \in Y}$ be arbitrary information. Recall that for $y = (y_1, \ldots, y_n) \in Y$ the nonadaptive information $\mathbb{I}_y = \{N_y, \Sigma_y\}$ is given by

$$N_y = [L_{1,y}, L_{2,y}, \ldots, L_{n,y}]$$

and

$$\Sigma_y = \mathrm{diag}\{\sigma_{1,y}^2, \sigma_{2,y}^2, \ldots, \sigma_{n,y}^2\}$$

where, for brevity, $L_{i,y} = L_i(\cdot; y_1, \ldots, y_{i-1})$ and $\sigma_{i,y}^2 = \sigma_i^2(y_1, \ldots, y_{i-1})$, $1 \le i \le n$. Recall also that μ_1 denotes the a priori distribution of information y in Y, i.e.,

$$\mu_1 = \int_F \pi_f(\cdot)\,\mu(df),$$

and μ_1 is in general not Gaussian even when $Y = \mathbb{R}^n$. For any $f \in F$, the measure π_f is supported on $Y_{1,f} = \{\, y \in Y \mid y \in N_y(f) + \Sigma_y(\mathbb{R}^{n(y)})\,\}$. Hence μ_1 is supported on $Y_1 = \{\, y \in Y \mid y \in N_y(F_1) + \Sigma_y(\mathbb{R}^{n(y)})\}$ where $F_1 = \overline{C_\mu(F^*)} = \operatorname{supp}\mu$, or equivalently, $Y_1 = \{\, y \in Y \mid y \in (\Sigma_y + G_{N_y})(\mathbb{R}^{n(y)})\}$.

We need a theorem about the conditional distribution of a Gaussian measure with respect to adaptive information.

Theorem 3.7.1 *For adaptive information $\mathrm{I\!I\!I} = \{N_y, \Sigma_y\}_{y \in Y}$ the conditional distribution $\mu_2(\cdot|y)$, $y \in Y_1$, is Gaussian. Its mean element is given as*

$$m(y) = \sum_{j=1}^{n(y)} z_j (C_\mu L_{j,y}),$$

where z is the solution of $(\Sigma_y + G_{N_y})z = y$, $\Sigma_y = \operatorname{diag}\{\sigma_{1,y}^2, \ldots, \sigma_{n(y),y}^2\}$, $G_{N_y} = \{\langle L_{i,y}, L_{j,y}\rangle_\mu\}_{i,j=1}^{n(y)}$, and $y = [y_1, \ldots, y_{n(y)}]$. The correlation operator of $\mu_2(\cdot|y)$ is given as

$$C_{\mu_2,y}(L) = C_\mu(L) - m(N_y(C_\mu L)), \qquad L \in F^*.$$

Proof We first give a proof for adaptive information $\mathrm{I\!I\!I}$ with $n(y) \equiv n$, i.e., $Y = \mathbb{R}^n$.

Let $\tilde{F} = F \times \mathbb{R}^n$ and $\tilde{\mu}$ be the joint probability on $\tilde{F}$,

$$\tilde{\mu}(B) = \int_F \pi_f(B^{(f)})\,\mu(df),$$

where $B^{(f)} = \{\, y \in Y \mid (f,y) \in B\,\}$. Let χ_B be the characteristic function of B, i.e., $\chi_B(\tilde{f}) = 1$ for $\tilde{f} \in B$, and $\chi_B(\tilde{f}) = 0$ for $\tilde{f} \notin B$. We denote by $\mu_1(\cdot|\mathrm{I\!I\!I}_1)$ the a priori distribution of information values with respect to (adaptive or nonadaptive) information $\mathrm{I\!I\!I}_1$, and by $\mu_2(\cdot|y, \mathrm{I\!I\!I}_1)$ the conditional distribution on F given y.

In view of Theorem 3.4.1, we only need to show that $\mu_2(\cdot|y, \mathrm{I\!I\!I}) = \mu_2(\cdot|y, \mathrm{I\!I\!I}_y)$. To this end, we shall use induction on n.

If $n = 1$ then any adaptive information is also nonadaptive and the proof is obvious. Suppose that $n > 1$. Let $\mathbb{N}^{n-1}$ be the adaptive information consisting of noisy evaluations of the first $(n-1)$ functionals of

III. For $y \in \mathbb{R}^n$, we write $y = (y^{n-1}, y_n)$ where $y^{n-1} \in \mathbb{R}^{n-1}$ and $y_n \in \mathbb{R}$. Then we have

$$
\begin{aligned}
\tilde{\mu}(B) &= \int_F \int_{\mathbb{R}^n} \chi_B(f,y)\, \pi_f(dy)\, \mu(df) \\
&= \int_F \int_{\mathbb{R}^{n-1}} \chi_B(f,y)\, \mathcal{N}\big(dy_n \big| L_{n,y^{n-1}}(f), \sigma_{y^{n-1}}^2\big) \\
&\qquad\qquad\qquad \omega_{n-1,f}(dy^{n-1})\, \mu(df) \\
&= \int_{\mathbb{R}^{n-1}} \int_F \int_{\mathbb{R}} \chi_B(f,y)\, \mathcal{N}\big(dy_n \big| L_{n,y^{n-1}}(f), \sigma_{y^{n-1}}^2\big) \\
&\qquad\qquad\qquad \mu_2(df|y^{n-1}, \mathbb{N}^{n-1})\, \mu_1(dy^{n-1}|\mathbb{N}^{n-1}).
\end{aligned}
$$

Using the inductive assumption and Theorem 3.4.1, $\mu_2(\cdot|y^{n-1}, \mathbb{N}^{n-1})$ can be interpreted as the conditional distribution on F with respect to the nonadaptive information $\mathbb{N}_{y^{n-1}}^{n-1}$. Hence, denoting by ρ the distribution of y_n given y^{n-1}, and using decomposition of $\mu_2(\cdot|y^{n-1}, N^{n-1})$ with respect to y_n, we have

$$
\begin{aligned}
&\int_F \int_{\mathbb{R}} \mathcal{N}\big(dy_n \big| L_{n,y^{n-1}}(f), \sigma_{y^{n-1}}^2\big)\, \mu_2(df|y^{n-1}, N^{n-1}) \\
&\qquad = \int_{\mathbb{R}} h(y)\, \rho(dy_n)
\end{aligned}
$$

where $h(y) = \int_F \chi_B(f,y)\, \mu_2(df|y, \mathbb{II}_y)$. As a consequence, we obtain

$$
\begin{aligned}
\tilde{\mu}(B) &= \int_{\mathbb{R}^{n-1}} \int_{\mathbb{R}} h(y)\, \rho(dy_n)\, \mu_1(dy^{n-1}|\mathbb{N}^{n-1}) \\
&= \int_{\mathbb{R}^{n-1}} \int_{\mathbb{R}} \int_F h(y)\, \mu_2(df|y, \mathbb{II}_y)\, \rho(dy_n)\, \mu_1(dy^{n-1}|\mathbb{N}^{n-1}) \\
&= \cdots = \int_F \int_{\mathbb{R}^n} h(y)\, \pi_f(dy)\, \mu(df) = \int_{\mathbb{R}^n} h(y)\, \mu_1(dy) \\
&= \int_{\mathbb{R}^n} \int_F \chi_B(f,y)\, \mu_2(df|y, \mathbb{II}_y)\, \mu_1(dy).
\end{aligned}
$$

On the other hand, $\tilde{\mu}(B) = \int_{\mathbb{R}^n} \int_F \chi_B(f,y) \mu_2(df|y, \mathbb{II}) \mu_1(dy)$. Thus

$$
\mu_2(\cdot|y, \mathbb{II}) = \mu_2(\cdot|y, N_y), \qquad \text{a.e. } y
$$

as claimed.

In the general case $(Y \subset \mathbb{R}^\infty)$, we have

$$
\tilde{\mu}(B) = \int_F \int_Y \chi_B(f,y)\, \pi_f(dy)\, \mu(df)
$$

$$= \sum_{m=1}^{\infty} \int_F \int_{Y_m} \chi_B(f, y)\, \omega_{m,f}(dy)\, \mu(df)$$

$$= \sum_{m=1}^{\infty} \int_{Y_m} \int_F \chi_B(f, y)\, \mu_2(df|y, \mathbb{II}_y)\, \mu_1(dy)$$

$$= \int_Y \int_F \chi_B(f, y)\, \mu_2(df|y, \mathbb{II}_y)\, \mu_1(dy).$$

The proof is complete. $\qquad\qquad\qquad\qquad\qquad\qquad\qquad\qquad\qquad\square$

Thus the conditional distribution $\mu_2(\cdot|y)$ with respect to adaptive information $\mathbb{II}$ is equal to the conditional distribution with respect to nonadaptive information $\mathbb{II}_y$ and the same y. This should be intuitively clear. Indeed, in both cases, the information y is obtained by using the same functionals $L_{i,y}$ and precisions $\sigma_{i,y}^2$.

Theorem 3.7.1 gives almost immediately the following result corresponding to Theorem 2.7.1 of the worst case setting.

Theorem 3.7.2 *For any adaptive information* $\mathbb{II} = \{\mathbb{II}_y\}_{y \in Y}$ *there exists* $y^* \in Y$ *such that for the nonadaptive information* $\mathbb{II}_{y^*}$ *we have*

$$\mathrm{rad}^{\mathrm{ave}}(\mathbb{II}_{y^*}) \le \mathrm{rad}^{\mathrm{ave}}(\mathbb{II}).$$

Proof There exists $y^* \in Y_1$ such that

$$\mathrm{rad}^{\mathrm{ave}}(\mathbb{II}) = \sqrt{\int_Y \left(r(\nu_2(\cdot|y))\right)^2 \mu_1(dy)} \ge r(\nu_2(\cdot|y^*)) \qquad (3.16)$$

where, as in Section 3.2, $\nu_2(\cdot|y) = \mu_2(S^{-1}(\cdot)|y)$ and $r(\nu_2(\cdot|y))$ is the radius of $\nu_2(\cdot|y)$. By Theorem 3.4.1, the measures $\mu_2(\cdot|y, \mathbb{II}_{y^*})$ have the same correlation operator. Hence $r(\nu_2(\cdot|y, \mathbb{II}_{y^*})) = r(\nu_2(\cdot|y^*, \mathbb{II}_{y^*}))$ a.e. y. This, Theorem 3.7.1, and (3.16) yield

$$\mathrm{rad}^{\mathrm{ave}}(\mathbb{II}_{y^*}) = \sqrt{\int_{\mathbb{R}^{n(y^*)}} r(\nu_2(\cdot|y, \mathbb{II}_{y^*}))\, \mu_1(dy|\mathbb{II}_{y^*})}$$

$$= r(\nu_2(\cdot|y^*, \mathbb{II}_{y^*})) = r(\nu_2(\cdot|y^*)) \le \mathrm{rad}^{\mathrm{ave}}(\mathbb{II}),$$

as claimed. $\qquad\qquad\qquad\qquad\qquad\qquad\qquad\qquad\qquad\qquad\qquad\square$

Observe that Theorem 3.7.1 does not say anything about the construction of y^*. Actually, y^* can assume arbitrary values, see E 3.7.2. Thus the situation differs from that in the worst case in which for linear problems with uniformly bounded noise we have $y^* = 0$ and $\mathrm{rad}^{\mathrm{wor}}(N_0) \leq 2\,\mathrm{rad}^{\mathrm{wor}}(N)$.

We also stress that it is only with respect to the radius that non-adaptive information $\mathrm{I\!I}_{y^*}$ is not worse than adaptive information $\mathrm{I\!I}$. It would be interesting to know whether it is possible to select such a y that not only $\mathrm{rad}^{\mathrm{ave}}(\mathrm{I\!I}_y) \leq \mathrm{rad}^{\mathrm{ave}}(\mathrm{I\!I})$, but also $\mathrm{I\!I}_y$ does not require a larger number and more precise observations than does $\mathrm{I\!I}$ for an 'average' y. To this issue will be devoted Subsection 3.9.1.

Notes and remarks

NR 3.7.1 This section is based on Plaskota (1990, 1995a).

NR 3.7.2 Adaptive information with fixed, but not necessarily Gaussian, information noise was studied in Kadane *et al.* (1988). They give examples that adaption can generally be much more powerful than nonadaption and show, under some additional assumptions, a result corresponding to Theorem 3.7.1; see also E 3.7.3.

Exercises

E 3.7.1 Let $\mathrm{I\!I} = \{N, \Sigma\}$ be adaptive information such that $\sigma_i^2(y_1, \ldots, y_{i-1})$ is positive for all i and $y_1, \ldots, y_{i-1}$. Show that then the measure π_f is given as

$$
\begin{aligned}
\pi_f(B) &= \sum_{m=1}^{\infty} (2\pi)^{-m/2} \int_{B_m} (\sigma_1 \sigma_2(t_1) \cdots \sigma_m(t_1, \ldots, t_{m-1}))^{-1} \\
&\quad \times \exp\left\{ -\frac{1}{2} \sum_{i=1}^{m} \frac{(t_i - L_i(f; t_1, \ldots, t_{i-1}))^2}{\sigma_i^2(t_1, \ldots, t_{i-1})} \right\} dt_m dt_{m-1} \ldots dt_1.
\end{aligned}
$$

E 3.7.2 Let $y \in \mathbb{R}^n$. Give an example of adaptive information $\mathrm{I\!I}$ with $y \in Y$ such that
1. y is the only element for which $\mathrm{rad}^{\mathrm{ave}}(\mathrm{I\!I}) = \mathrm{rad}^{\mathrm{ave}}(\mathrm{I\!I}_y)$.
2. $\mathrm{rad}^{\mathrm{ave}}(\mathrm{I\!I}) = 0$, but $\mathrm{rad}^{\mathrm{ave}}(\mathrm{I\!I}_y) > 0$.

E 3.7.3 (Kadane *et al.*, 1988) Let $F = \mathbb{R}^2$ be equipped with the Euclidean norm and standard Gaussian measure μ, and S be the identity in F. Consider adaptive information $\mathrm{I\!I}$ with $Y = \mathbb{R}^n$, consisting of noisy observations of n adaptively chosen functionals L_i,

$$
L_i(f) = L_i(f; y_1, \ldots, y_{i-1}) = \begin{cases} f_1 & y_1 = y_2 = \cdots = y_{i-1}, \\ f_2 & \text{otherwise}, \end{cases}
$$

with noise x_i such that $x_i = -1$ or $x_i = 1$ with probability $1/2$. Show that

$$
\lim_{n \to +\infty} \frac{\inf_{y \in \mathbb{R}^n} \mathrm{rad}^{\mathrm{ave}}(\mathrm{I\!I}_y)}{\mathrm{rad}^{\mathrm{ave}}(\mathrm{I\!I})} = +\infty.
$$

3.8 Optimal nonadaptive information

In this section, we study the minimal radius of (nonadaptive) information, as well as the choice of optimal information. Recall that these are defined as follows. Let $\mathcal{N}_n$ be the class of exact nonadaptive information operators N consisting of n functionals from the class Λ, $N = [L_1, \ldots, L_n]$, $L_i \in \Lambda$. Then the minimal (average) radius corresponding to a correlation matrix $\Sigma = \mathrm{diag}\{\sigma_1^2, \sigma_2^2, \ldots, \sigma_n^2\}$ is given as

$$r_n^{\mathrm{ave}}(\Sigma) = \inf_{N \in \mathcal{N}_n} \mathrm{rad}^{\mathrm{ave}}(N, \Sigma).$$

Information $N_\Sigma \in \mathcal{N}_n$ is optimal iff

$$r_n^{\mathrm{ave}}(\Sigma) = \mathrm{rad}^{\mathrm{ave}}(N_\Sigma, \Sigma).$$

We shall find the minimal radius and optimal information for approximating a continuous solution operator with Gaussian measures and also for function approximation and integration on the classical Wiener space.

3.8.1 Linear problems with Gaussian measures

Here we consider a continuous solution operator $S : F \to G$ and a zero-mean Gaussian measure μ on F. The class Λ of permissible functionals consists of functionals whose μ-norm is bounded by 1,

$$\Lambda = \Lambda^{\mathrm{all}} = \left\{ L \in F^* \ \middle| \ \|L\|_\mu = \sqrt{L(C_\mu L)} \le 1 \right\}.$$

Observe that Λ^{all} can be equivalently defined as

$$\Lambda^{\mathrm{all}} = \left\{ L \in F^* \ \middle| \ \|L_H\|_H = \sup_{\|f\|_H = 1} |L(f)| \le 1 \right\}$$

where $\{H, \overline{C_\mu(F)}\}$ is the abstract Wiener space for the measure μ, and L_H is the restriction of L to the Hilbert space H. Without loss of generality we assume that

$$0 = \sigma_1 = \cdots = \sigma_{n_0} < \sigma_{n_0+1} \le \cdots \le \sigma_n$$

(if all the σ_is are nonzero then $n_0 = 0$).

We shall see that the method of finding optimal information in this case is similar to that used in Subsection 2.8.1, where the problem of optimal information in the worst case setting was studied for a compact solution operator and noise bounded in the weighted Euclidean norm.

Recall that $\nu = \mu S^{-1}$ is the a priori distribution on the space G, induced by the measure μ and the operator S. By Lemma 3.4.1, ν is the zero-mean Gaussian measure with correlation operator $C_\nu = SC_\mu S^*$: $G \to G$ where $S^* : G \to F^*$ is the adjoint operator to S, $S^*g = \langle S(\cdot), g \rangle$, $\forall g \in G$. Moreover, C_ν is self-adjoint, nonnegative definite, and has finite trace, see Subsection 3.3.1.

Let $\{\xi_i\}_{i=1}^{\dim G} \subset G$ be the complete orthonormal system of eigenelements of C_ν. Let $\lambda_1 \geq \lambda_2 \geq \lambda_3 \geq \cdots \geq 0$ be the corresponding eigenvalues, $C_\nu \xi_i = \lambda_i \xi_i$. We may assume that the sequence $\{\lambda_i\}$ is infinite by letting, if necessary, $\lambda_i = 0$ for $i > \dim G$. For $\lambda_i > 0$, define the functionals

$$K_i = \lambda_i^{-1/2} S^* \xi_i = \lambda_i^{-1/2} \langle S(\cdot), \xi_i \rangle.$$

Clearly, these functionals are μ-orthonormal,

$$\begin{aligned}
\langle K_i, K_j \rangle_\mu &= (\lambda_i \lambda_j)^{-1/2} \langle S_H^* \xi_i, S_H^* \xi_j \rangle_H \\
&= (\lambda_i \lambda_j)^{-1/2} \langle S_H S_H^* \xi_i, \xi_j \rangle = \delta_{ij}.
\end{aligned}$$

For $\lambda_i = 0$ we set $K_i^* = 0$.

Since $C_\nu = S_H S_H^*$, the λ_is are also eigenvalues of the compact operator $S_H^* S_H : H \to H$, and the corresponding H-orthonormal eigenelements are $\xi_{H,i} = C_\mu K_i \in H$, $i \geq 1$.

Recall that in the worst case setting the problem of optimal information was related to some minimization problem. The corresponding problem in the average case is as follows:

Problem (MP)   *Minimize*

$$\Omega(\eta_{n_0+1}, \ldots, \eta_n) = \sum_{i=n_0+1}^{n} \frac{\lambda_i}{1 + \eta_i} \tag{3.17}$$

over all $\eta_{n_0+1} \geq \cdots \geq \eta_n \geq 0$ *satisfying*

$$\sum_{i=r}^{n} \eta_i \leq \sum_{i=r}^{n} \sigma_i^{-2}, \qquad n_0 + 1 \leq r \leq n, \tag{3.18}$$

and $\sum_{i=n_0+1}^{n} \eta_i = \sum_{i=n_0+1}^{n} \sigma_i^{-2}$.

Theorem 3.8.1 *Let* $\eta_{n_0+1}^* \geq \cdots \geq \eta_n^*$ *be the solution of* (MP). *Then*

$$r_n^{\mathrm{ave}}(\Sigma) = \sqrt{\Omega(\eta_{n_0+1}^*, \ldots, \eta_n^*) + \sum_{i=n+1}^{\infty} \lambda_i}.$$

Furthermore, the optimal information is given as

$$N_\Sigma = [K_1, \ldots, K_{n_0}, L_{n_0+1}^\Sigma, \ldots, L_n^\Sigma],$$

where

$$L_{n_0+i}^{\Sigma} = \sigma_{n_0+i} \sum_{j=1}^{n-n_0} w_{ij} K_{n_0+j},$$

and $W = \{w_{ij}\}_{i,j=1}^{n-n_0}$ *is the matrix from Lemma 2.8.1 with*

$$\eta_i = \eta_{n_0+i}^* \qquad and \qquad \beta_i = \sigma_{n_0+i}^{-2},$$

$1 \le i \le n - n_0$.

Proof Assume first that all σ_is are positive, i.e., $n_0 = 0$. Let $N = [L_1, \ldots, L_n]$ be arbitrary information from $\mathcal{N}_n$. We can assume that $\|L_i\|_{\mu} = 1$, $1 \le i \le n$.

We start with the lower bound on $\text{rad}^{\text{ave}}(N, \Sigma)$. Let the matrix

$$G_{\Pi} = \Sigma^{-1/2} G_N \Sigma^{-1/2} = \{(\sigma_i \sigma_j)^{-1} \langle L_i, L_j \rangle_{\mu}\}_{i,j=1}^n,$$

and let $\{q^{(i)}\}_{i=1}^n$ be an orthonormal basis of its eigenvectors, $G_{\Pi} q^{(i)} = \eta_i q^{(i)}$ where $\eta_1 \ge \cdots \ge \eta_m > 0 = \eta_{m+1} = \cdots = \eta_n$. We know from NR 3.4.3 that the radius of $\Pi = \{N, \Sigma\}$ is equal to the radius of information $\tilde{\Pi} = \{\tilde{N}, \tilde{\Sigma}\}$ where $\tilde{N}$ consists of m μ-orthonormal functionals $\tilde{L}_i$,

$$\tilde{L}_i = \frac{1}{\eta_i} \sum_{j=1}^n \frac{q_j^{(i)}}{\sigma_j} L_j, \qquad 1 \le i \le m,$$

and $\tilde{\Sigma} = \text{diag}\{\eta_1^{-1}, \ldots, \eta_m^{-1}\}$. That is,

$$(\text{rad}^{\text{ave}}(N, \Sigma))^2 = (\text{rad}^{\text{ave}}(\tilde{N}, \tilde{\Sigma}))^2 = \text{tr}(SC_{\mu}S^*) - \sum_{i=1}^m \frac{\|SC_{\mu}\tilde{L}_i\|^2}{1 + \eta_i^{-1}}.$$

Note that for any H-orthonormal elements f_i we have (see NR 2.8.6) $\sum_{i=1}^k \langle S_H^* S_H f_i, f_i \rangle_H \le \sum_{i=1}^k \lambda_i$. Letting $f_i = C_{\mu} \tilde{L}_i$ we get $\langle f_i, f_j \rangle_H = \delta_{ij}$ and

$$\sum_{i=1}^k \|S(C_{\mu} \tilde{L}_i)\|^2 = \sum_{i=1}^k \|S_H f_i\|^2 = \sum_{i=1}^k \langle S_H^* S_H f_i, f_i \rangle_H \le \sum_{i=1}^k \lambda_i.$$

This and $\eta_1 \ge \cdots \ge \eta_m$ yield

$$\sum_{i=1}^m \frac{\eta_i}{1 + \eta_i} \|S(C_{\mu} \tilde{L}_i)\|^2 \le \sum_{i=1}^n \frac{\eta_i}{1 + \eta_i} \lambda_i$$

(compare with E 3.8.1), which implies the following lower bound on $\mathrm{rad}^{\mathrm{ave}}(N, \Sigma)$:

$$(\mathrm{rad}^{\mathrm{ave}}(N, \Sigma))^2 \geq \sum_{i=1}^{\infty} \lambda_i - \sum_{j=1}^{n} \frac{\eta_j}{1 + \eta_j} \lambda_j = \Omega(\eta_1, \ldots, \eta_n) + \sum_{j=n+1}^{\infty} \lambda_j.$$

Observe that for all $1 \leq r \leq n$ we also have (see again NR 2.8.6)

$$\sum_{i=r}^{n} \eta_i \leq \sum_{i=r}^{n} \langle G_{\Pi} e_i, e_i \rangle_2 = \sum_{i=r}^{n} \sigma_i^{-2}$$

(e_i stands for the ith versor), and $\sum_{i=1}^{n} \eta_i = \sum_{i=1}^{n} \sigma_i^{-2}$. Thus we finally obtain

$$r_n^{\mathrm{ave}}(\Sigma) \geq \sqrt{\Omega(\eta_1^*, \ldots, \eta_n^*) + \sum_{i=n+1}^{\infty} \lambda_i}. \tag{3.19}$$

We now show that $\mathrm{rad}^{\mathrm{ave}}(N_\Sigma, \Sigma)$ is equal to the right hand side of (3.19). Indeed, since

$$\langle L_i^\Sigma, L_j^\Sigma \rangle_\mu = \left\langle \sigma_i \sum_{s=1}^{n} w_{is} K_s, \sigma_j \sum_{t=1}^{n} w_{jt} K_t \right\rangle_\mu = \sigma_i \sigma_j \sum_{s=1}^{n} w_{ij} w_{js}, \tag{3.20}$$

the corresponding matrix G_{Π} equals WW^*, the eigenvectors $q^{(i)}$ of G_{Π} are the columns $w^{(i)}$ of W, and $G_{\Pi} w^{(i)}$ equals $\eta_i^* w^{(i)}$, $1 \leq i \leq n$. Furthermore, for $1 \leq i \leq m$, the functionals $\tilde{L}_i$ are equal to

$$\begin{aligned}
\tilde{L}_i &= \frac{1}{\eta_i} \sum_{s=1}^{n} q_s^{(i)} \sigma_s^{-1} \left(\sigma_s \sum_{j=1}^{n} w_{sj} K_j \right) \\
&= \frac{1}{\eta_i} \sum_{s=1}^{n} w_{si} \sum_{j=1}^{n} w_{sj} K_j = \frac{1}{\eta_i} \sum_{j=1}^{n} K_j \sum_{s=1}^{n} w_{si} w_{sj} \\
&= \frac{1}{\eta_i} \eta_i K_i = K_i.
\end{aligned}$$

Hence

$$\begin{aligned}
\mathrm{rad}^{\mathrm{ave}}(N_\Sigma, \Sigma) &= \sqrt{\sum_{i=1}^{\infty} \lambda_i - \sum_{j=1}^{m} \frac{\eta_i^*}{1 + \eta_i^*} \|S(C_\mu \tilde{L}_j)\|^2} \\
&= \sqrt{\sum_{i=1}^{\infty} \lambda_i - \sum_{j=1}^{n} \frac{\eta_j^*}{1 + \eta_j^*} \lambda_j} = \sqrt{\Omega(\eta_1^*, \ldots, \eta_n^*) + \sum_{j=n+1}^{\infty} \lambda_j}.
\end{aligned}$$

Since, in view of (3.20), we also have $\|L_i^\Sigma\|_\mu = \sigma_i^2 \sum_{s=1}^n w_{is}^2 = 1$, the information N_Σ is in $\mathcal{N}_n$. This completes the proof for the case $n_0 = 0$.

Suppose now that $n_0 \geq 1$. Then the a posteriori Gaussian measure on F with respect to exact information $N^{(0)} = [L_1, \ldots, L_{n_0}]$ has the correlation operator $C_{\mu, N^{(0)}} = C_\mu(I - P_{N^{(0)}})$, where $P_{N^{(0)}} : F^* \to F^*$ is the μ-orthogonal projection onto span$\{L_1, \ldots, L_{n_0}\}$. For the dominating eigenvalues $\tilde{\lambda}_i$ of $SC_{\mu, N^{(0)}}S^*$ (which is the correlation operator of the a posteriori measure on G with respect to $N^{(0)}$) we have $\tilde{\lambda}_i \geq \lambda_{n_0+i}$, $\forall i \geq 1$. Moreover, if $N^{(0)} = N_0 = [K_1, \ldots, K_{n_0}]$ then $\tilde{\lambda}_i = \lambda_{n_0+i}$, and the corresponding eigenelements are $\tilde{\xi}_i = \xi_{n_0+i}$, $\forall i \geq 1$. Hence we obtain the desired result by reducing our problem to that of finding optimal $N^{(1)} = [L_{n_0+1}, \ldots, L_n]$, for the correlation matrix $\Sigma^{(1)} = \text{diag}\{\sigma_{n_0+1}^2, \ldots, \sigma_n^2\}$ and the Gaussian a priori distribution on F with correlation operator $C_\mu(I - P_{N_0})$. $\square$

We now give an explicit formula for the solution of the minimization problem (MP) as well as for the minimal radius $r_n^{\text{ave}}(\Sigma)$. For $n_0 \leq q < r \leq n$, define the following auxiliary minimization problem.

Problem $P(q, r)$ *Minimize*

$$\Omega_{qr}(\eta_{q+1}, \ldots, \eta_r) = \sum_{j=q+1}^r \frac{\lambda_j}{1 + \eta_j}$$

over all $\eta_{q+1} \geq \cdots \geq \eta_r \geq 0$ *satisfying* $\sum_{i=q+1}^r \eta_i = \sum_{i=q+1}^r \sigma_i^{-2}$.

The solution $\eta^* = (\eta_{q+1}^*, \ldots, \eta_r^*)$ of $P(q, r)$ is as follows. Let $k = k(q, r)$ be the largest integer satisfying $q + 1 \leq k \leq r$ and

$$\frac{\sum_{j=q+1}^k \lambda_j^{1/2}}{\sum_{j=q+1}^r \sigma_j^{-2} + (k - q)} \leq \lambda_k^{1/2}. \tag{3.21}$$

Then

$$\eta_i^* = \frac{\sum_{j=q+1}^r \sigma_j^{-2} + (k - q)}{\sum_{j=q+1}^k \lambda_j^{1/2}} \cdot \lambda_i^{1/2} - 1 \quad \text{for } q + 1 \leq i \leq k, \tag{3.22}$$

and $\eta_i^* = 0$ for $k + 1 \leq i \leq r$. Furthermore,

$$\Omega_{qr}(\eta^*) = \frac{\left(\sum_{j=q+1}^k \lambda_j^{1/2}\right)^2}{\sum_{j=q+1}^r \sigma_j^{-2} + (k - q)} + \sum_{j=k+1}^r \lambda_j.$$

We shall say that the solution $\eta^* = (\eta_{q+1}, \ldots, \eta_r^*)$ of $P(q, r)$ is *acceptable* iff

$$\sum_{j=s}^{r} \eta_j^* \leq \sum_{j=s}^{r} \sigma_j^{-2}, \qquad \text{for } q + 1 \leq s \leq r.$$

Let the number p, $0 \leq p < n$, and the sequence $0 \leq n_0 < n_1 < \cdots < n_p < n_{p+1} = n$ be defined (uniquely) by the condition

$$n_i = \min\{ s \geq n_0 \mid \text{solution of } P(s, n_{i+1}) \text{ is acceptable } \}, \qquad (3.23)$$

$0 \leq i \leq p$.

Theorem 3.8.2 *Let p and the sequence $n_0 < n_1 < \cdots < n_{p+1} = n$ be defined by (3.23). Then the optimal η^* is given as*

$$\eta^* = (\eta^{(0)}, \eta^{(1)}, \ldots, \eta^{(p)})$$

where $\eta^{(i)} = (\eta_{n_i+1}^*, \ldots, \eta_{n_{i+1}}^*)$ is the solution of $P(n_i, n_{i+1})$, $0 \leq i \leq p$.

Proof Let $t = \max\{n_0 + 1 \leq i \leq n \mid \eta_i^* > 0\}$. For $n_0 + 1 \leq i \leq t$, the function

$$\psi_i(\tau) = \Omega(\eta_{n_0+1}^*, \ldots, \eta_{i-2}^*, \eta_{i-1}^* + \eta_i^* - \tau, \tau, \eta_{i+1}^*, \ldots, \eta_n^*)$$

is continuous, convex, and attains the minimum at τ_0 such that

$$\lambda_{i-1}(1 + \eta_{i-1}^* + \eta_i^* - \tau_0)^{-2} = \lambda_i(1 + \tau_0)^{-2}.$$

From this and the definition of (MP) it follows that

$$\frac{\lambda_{i-1}}{(1 + \eta_{i-1}^*)^2} \leq \frac{\lambda_i}{(1 + \eta_i^*)^2} . \qquad (3.24)$$

Moreover, if $\lambda_{i-1}(1 + \eta_{i-1}^*)^{-2} < \lambda_i(1 + \eta_i^*)^{-2}$ then $\sum_{j=i}^{n} \eta_j^* = \sum_{j=i}^{n} \sigma_j^{-2}$. If $t < n$ then, using the same argument with $i = t + 1$, we find that

$$\frac{\lambda_t}{(1 + \eta_t^*)^2} \geq \lambda_{t+1}. \qquad (3.25)$$

Let $m_1 < \cdots < m_s$ be the sequence of all indices i, $n_0 < i < t$, for which $\lambda_i(1 + \eta_i^*)^{-2} < \lambda_{i+1}(1 + \eta_{i+1}^*)^{-2}$. Set $m_0 = n_0$ and $m_{s+1} = n$. From (3.24) it follows that $\sum_{j=m_i+1}^{m_{i+1}} \eta_j^* = \sum_{j=m_i+1}^{m_{i+1}} \sigma_j^{-2}$, $0 \leq i \leq s$. This and (3.25) yield that the numbers $\eta_{m_i+1}^*, \ldots, \eta_{m_{i+1}}^*$ are the solution of $P(m_i, m_{i+1})$ for all $0 \leq i \leq s$. To complete the proof, it is now enough to show that the sequences $\{m_i\}_{i=0}^{s+1}$ and $\{n_i\}_{i=0}^{p+1}$ are the same, i.e., $\{m_i\}_{i=0}^{q+1}$ satisfies (3.23). Indeed, suppose to the contrary that for some

i there is j_0, $0 \leq j_0 < m_i$, such that the solution $\tilde{\eta}^*_{j_0+1}, \ldots, \tilde{\eta}^*_{m_{i+1}}$ of $P(j_0, m_{i+1})$ is acceptable. Then

$$\sum_{j=m_i+1}^{m_{i+1}} \tilde{\eta}^*_j \leq \sum_{j=m_i+1}^{m_{i+1}} \sigma_j^{-2} = \sum_{j=m_i+1}^{m_{i+1}} \eta^*_j .$$

This and the formulas (3.21), (3.22) yield $\tilde{\eta}^*_j \leq \eta^*_j$ for all $m_i + 1 \leq j \leq m_{i+1}$. Similarly, for $j_0 \leq j \leq m_i$ we have

$$\frac{\lambda_j}{(1+\eta^*_j)^2} < \frac{\lambda_{m_i+1}}{(1+\eta^*_{m_i+1})^2} \leq \frac{\lambda_{m_i+1}}{(1+\tilde{\eta}^*_{m_i+1})^2} = \frac{\lambda_j}{(1+\tilde{\eta}^*_j)^2} ,$$

and consequently $\tilde{\eta}^*_j < \eta^*_j$. Hence

$$\sum_{j=j_0+1}^{m_{i+1}} \sigma_j^{-2} = \sum_{j=j_0+1}^{m_{i+1}} \tilde{\eta}^*_j < \sum_{j=j_0+1}^{m_{i+1}} \eta^*_j ,$$

which is a contradiction. $\square$

Knowing the optimal η^*, we can write an explicit formula for $r^{\mathrm{ave}}_n(\Sigma)$.

Corollary 3.8.1 *Let p and the sequence $\{n_i\}_{i=0}^{p+1}$ be defined by (3.23), and $k = k(n_p, n)$ be given by (3.21). Then*

$$r^{\mathrm{ave}}_n(\Sigma) = \sqrt{Z + \sum_{j=k+1}^{\infty} \lambda_j},$$

where

$$Z = \sum_{i=0}^{p-1} \frac{\left(\sum_{j=n_i+1}^{n_{i+1}} \lambda_j^{1/2}\right)^2}{\sum_{j=n_i+1}^{n_{i+1}} \sigma_j^{-2} + (n_{i+1}-n_i)} + \frac{\left(\sum_{j=n_p+1}^{k} \lambda_j^{1/2}\right)^2}{\sum_{j=n_p+1}^{n} \sigma_j^{-2} + (k-n_p)} .$$

As we see, the formula for the minimal radius given in terms of the eigenvalues λ_i and variances σ_i^2 is rather complicated. Let, for simplicity, all σ_is be nonzero. Then we have the following bounds on $r^{\mathrm{ave}}_n(\Sigma)$:

$$\sqrt{\frac{\left(\sum_{i=1}^{k} \lambda_i^{1/2}\right)^2}{\sum_{i=1}^{n} \sigma_i^{-2} + k} + \sum_{i=k+1}^{\infty} \lambda_i} \leq r^{\mathrm{ave}}_n(\Sigma) \leq \sqrt{\sum_{i=1}^{n} \frac{\lambda_i}{\sigma_i^{-2} + 1} + \sum_{i=n+1}^{\infty} \lambda_i},$$

$$\tag{3.26}$$

where k is the largest integer satisfying $1 \leq k \leq n$ and

$$\frac{\sum_{j=1}^{k} \lambda_j^{1/2}}{\sum_{j=1}^{n} \sigma_j^{-2} + k} \leq \lambda_k^{1/2} .$$

Clearly, we always have $\sqrt{\sum_{i=n+1}^{\infty} \lambda_i} \leq r_n^{\text{ave}}(\Sigma) \leq \sqrt{\sum_{i=1}^{\infty} \lambda_i}$.

Let us see what happens when all n observations are performed with the same variance, $\sigma_i^2 = \sigma^2 > 0$, $\forall i$. It is easy to verify that then

$$r_n^{\text{ave}}(\Sigma) = r_n^{\text{ave}}(\sigma^2) = \sqrt{\sigma^2 \cdot \frac{\left(\sum_{i=1}^{k} \lambda_i^{1/2}\right)^2}{n + \sigma^2 k} + \sum_{j=1}^{\infty} \lambda_j}, \qquad (3.27)$$

where $k = k(\sigma^2, n)$ is the largest integer satisfying $1 \leq k \leq n$ and

$$\sigma^2 \cdot \frac{\sum_{j=1}^{k} \lambda_j^{1/2}}{n + \sigma^2 k} \leq \lambda_k^{1/2}.$$

The optimal information $N_{n,\sigma} = [L_1^*, \dots, L_n^*]$ is given by Theorem 3.8.1 with

$$\eta_i^* = \frac{n\sigma^{-2} + k}{\sum_{j=1}^{k} \lambda_j^{1/2}} \cdot \lambda_i^{1/2} - 1, \qquad 1 \leq i \leq k,$$

and $\eta_i^* = 0$ for $k+1 \leq i \leq n$. The optimal algorithm is the smoothing spline (or regularization) algorithm with $\gamma = \sigma^2$.

Let us look at the behavior of $r_n^{\text{ave}}(\sigma^2)$. Suppose first that $\sigma \to 0^+$. Then, for $r_n^{\text{ave}}(0) = \sqrt{\sum_{i=n+1}^{\infty} \lambda_i} > 0$, we have

$$r_n^{\text{ave}}(\sigma^2) - r_n^{\text{ave}}(0) \approx \frac{\sigma^2 \left(\sum_{i=1}^{n} \lambda_i^{1/2}\right)^2}{2n(1+\sigma^2)\sqrt{\sum_{j=1}^{\infty} \lambda_j}},$$

while for $r_n^{\text{ave}}(0) = 0$ we have

$$r_n^{\text{ave}}(\sigma^2) - r_n^{\text{ave}}(0) \approx \frac{\sigma \sum_{i=1}^{n} \lambda_i^{1/2}}{\sqrt{n + \sigma^2 m}}$$

where m is the largest integer such that $\lambda_m > 0$.

For fixed σ and $n \to +\infty$, the radius converges to zero, but not faster than $\sigma/\sqrt{n}$. Suppose that the eigenvalues λ_j satisfy

$$\lambda_j \asymp \left(\frac{\ln^s j}{j}\right)^p \qquad \text{as} \quad j \to +\infty, \qquad (3.28)$$

where $p > 1$ and $s \geq 0$. After some calculations we find that for $\sigma > 0$

$$r_n^{\text{ave}}(\sigma^2) \asymp \begin{cases} \sigma \left(\ln^{sp} n/n^{p-1}\right)^{1/2} & 1 < p < 2, \\ \sigma \left(\ln^{2(s+1)} n/n\right)^{1/2} & p = 2, \\ \sigma \left(1/n\right)^{1/2} & p > 2, \end{cases}$$

where the constants in the '$\asymp$' notation do not depend on σ. For exact information we have

$$r_n^{\text{ave}}(0) \asymp \left(\frac{\ln^{sp} n}{n^{p-1}}\right)^{1/2}.$$

Hence for $1 < p < 2$ the radius of noisy information behaves as $r_n^{\text{ave}}(0)$, while for $p > 2$ it achieves the best possible rate of convergence which is $\sigma/\sqrt{n}$.

Note that the eigenvalues (3.28) correspond to the multivariate function approximation in $\mathcal{L}_2((0,1)^d)$ with respect to the Wiener sheet measure, see NR 3.8.4.

Relations to worst case setting

We now discuss the relations mentioned previously between the optimal information in the average case and the worst case settings of Subsection 2.8.1.

Consider the pair of problems defined as in Subsection 3.6.3. That is, assume that $\{H, F\}$ is the abstract Wiener space for a zero-mean Gaussian measure μ. We approximate values $S(f)$ of a continuous linear operator $S : F \to G$, based on noisy information $y = N(f) + x$, where $N = [L_1, \ldots, L_n]$ and the functionals $\|L_i\|_\mu = \|(L_i)_H\|_H \leq 1$. In view of Theorem 3.6.3. for fixed N the optimal algorithms in the worst and average case settings are (almost) the same. We now want to see whether a similar result holds with respect to optimal information. More precisely, suppose we want to choose information $N \in \mathcal{N}_n$ and algorithm φ so as to minimize

(WW) Worst case error $e^{\text{wor}}(\mathbb{N}, \varphi)$ for the set $E = \{ f \in H \mid \|f\|_H \leq 1 \}$ and noise $\|x\|_Y = \sqrt{\langle \Sigma^{-1}x, x\rangle_2} \leq \delta$,

(AA) Average case error $e^{\text{ave}}(\mathbb{II}, \varphi)$ for the Gaussian measure μ and noise $x \sim \mathcal{N}(0, \sigma^2\Sigma)$,

where Σ is an $n \times n$ diagonal matrix.

Observe first that in both problems the minimal radii are determined by n dominating eigenvalues of the operator $S_H^* S_H = S C_\mu S^*$, and the optimal functionals are linear combinations of the functionals K_i, $1 \leq i \leq n$. Furthermore, in the case $\Sigma = I$ and $\delta = \sigma > 0$, the radii $r_n^{\text{wor}}(\delta)$ and $r_n^{\text{ave}}(\sigma^2)$ decrease to zero as $n \to +\infty$; however, their convergence may be different and is not faster than $n^{-1/2}$.

It turns out that an even stronger correspondence between the two problems holds, similar to that of Theorem 3.6.3. That is, there exists information N_* which is almost optimal in both the worst and average case settings. To show this, assume additionally that $\delta = \sigma$ and $0 = \gamma_1^2 = \cdots = \gamma_{n_0}^2 < \gamma_{n_0+1}^2 \leq \cdots \leq \gamma_n^2$ are the diagonal elements of the matrix Σ. Let α^w and $\eta_{n_0+1}^w \geq \cdots \geq \eta_n^w \geq \eta_{n+1}^w = 0$ be the solution of the minimization problem (MP) of Subsection 2.8.1 with $\delta_i = \gamma_i$, and let $\eta_1^a \geq \cdots \geq \eta_n^a \geq 0$ be the solution of the minimization problem (MP) of the present section with $\sigma_i = \gamma_i$. Next, let the information N_* be given as in Theorem 3.8.1 (or in Theorem 2.8.1) with $\sigma_i = \gamma_i/\sqrt{2}$ (or $\delta_i = \gamma_i/\sqrt{2}$) and $\eta_i^* = (\eta_i^w + \eta_i^a)/2$, $n_0 + 1 \leq i \leq n$. Observe that N^* is well defined since for any $n_0 + 1 \leq r \leq n$ we have

$$\sum_{i=r}^{n} \eta_i^* = \sum_{i=r}^{n} (\eta_i^w + \eta_i^a)/2 \leq \sum_{i=r}^{n} \gamma_i^{-2},$$

and the assumptions of Lemma 2.8.1 are satisfied. Also, $N_* \in \mathcal{N}_n$. We have the following theorem.

Theorem 3.8.3 *For information N_* and the spline algorithm φ_{spl} we have*

$$e^{\mathrm{wor}}\left(\{N_*, \Delta\}, \varphi_{\mathrm{spl}}\right) \leq 2 \cdot r_n^{\mathrm{wor}}(\Delta)$$

and

$$e^{\mathrm{ave}}\left(\{N_*, \Sigma\}, \varphi_{\mathrm{spl}}\right) \leq \sqrt{2} \cdot r_n^{\mathrm{ave}}(\Sigma),$$

where $\Delta = [\gamma_1, \ldots, \gamma_n]$ *and* $\Sigma = [\gamma_1^2, \ldots, \gamma_n^2]$.

Proof Indeed, the formulas for the worst and average case errors of the algorithm φ_{spl} using information N_* can be obtained as in the proofs of Theorems 2.8.1 and 3.8.1, respectively. Hence

$$
\begin{aligned}
\left(e^{\mathrm{wor}}\left(\{N_*, \Delta\}, \varphi_{\mathrm{spl}}\right)\right)^2 &\leq \max_{n_0+1 \leq i \leq n+1} \frac{2\lambda_i}{1 + \eta_i^*} \\
&\leq \max_{n_0+1 \leq i \leq n+1} \frac{2\lambda_i}{1 + \eta_i^w/2} \\
&\leq 4 \cdot \max_{n_0+1 \leq i \leq n+1} \frac{\lambda_i}{\alpha^w + (1 - \alpha^w)\eta_i^w} \\
&= 4 \cdot (r_n^{\mathrm{wor}}(\Delta))^2.
\end{aligned}
$$

Similarly,

$$
\left(e^{\mathrm{ave}}\left(\{N_*, \Sigma\}, \varphi_{\mathrm{spl}}\right)\right)^2 = \sum_{i=n_0+1}^{n} \frac{\lambda_i}{1 + \eta_i^*} + \sum_{j=n+1}^{\infty} \lambda_j
$$

$$\leq \sum_{i=n_0+1}^{n} \frac{\lambda_i}{1+\eta_i^a/2} + \sum_{j=n+1}^{\infty} \lambda_j$$

$$\leq 2 \cdot \left(\sum_{i=n_0+1}^{n} \frac{\lambda_i}{1+\eta_i^a} + \sum_{j=n+1}^{\infty} \lambda_j \right)$$

$$= 2 \cdot (r_n^{\text{ave}}(\Sigma))^2,$$

as claimed.   □

We stress that Theorem 3.8.3 does not say anything about a correspondence between $r_n^{\text{wor}}(\Delta)$ and $r_n^{\text{ave}}(\Sigma)$. Owing to Theorem 3.6.3, we have $r_n^{\text{wor}}(\Delta) \leq \sqrt{2}\, r_n^{\text{ave}}(\Sigma)$. However, the ratio $r_n^{\text{ave}}(\Sigma)/r_n^{\text{wor}}(\Delta)$ can be arbitrarily large. For instance, consider $\Delta = \underbrace{[\delta, \ldots, \delta]}_{n}$, $\Sigma = \underbrace{[\sigma^2, \ldots, \sigma^2]}_{n}$,

and the eigenvalues as in (3.28). Then, using results of this section and Subsection 2.8.1, for $\sigma = \delta > 0$ we obtain

$$\frac{r_n^{\text{ave}}(\sigma^2)}{r_n^{\text{wor}}(\delta)} \asymp \begin{cases} n^{1-p/2} \ln^{sp/2} n & 1 < p < 2, \\ \ln^{s+1} n & p = 2, \\ 1 & p > 2, \end{cases}$$

as $n \to +\infty$. For exact information we have $r_n^{\text{ave}}(0)/r_n^{\text{wor}}(0) \asymp \sqrt{n}$.

3.8.2 Approximation and integration on the Wiener space

In this subsection, we study optimal information for approximation and integration of continuous scalar functions, based on noisy observations of function values at n points. More precisely, we let F be the space of functions defined as

$$F = C^0 = \{ f : [0,1] \to \mathbb{R} \mid f \text{ continuous}, f(0) = 0 \},$$

equipped with the classical Wiener measure w. Recall that w is uniquely determined by its mean element zero and covariance kernel

$$R(s,t) = \int_{C^0} f(s)f(t)\, w(df) = \min\{s,t\}, \qquad 0 \leq s, t \leq 1.$$

The solution operator corresponding to the function approximation is given as

$$\text{App} : C^0 \to \mathcal{L}_2(0,1), \qquad \text{App}(f) = f, \quad \forall f \in C^0,$$

while the integration operator is defined as

$$\text{Int} : C^0 \to \mathbb{R}, \qquad \text{Int}(f) = \int_0^1 f(x)\, dx, \quad \forall f \in C^0.$$

We assume that $\Lambda = \Lambda^{\text{std}}$. That is, information about $f \in C^0$ is supplied by n noisy values of f at arbitrary points from $[0, 1]$,

$$N(f) = [f(t_1), f(t_2), \ldots, f(t_n)] \tag{3.29}$$

where $0 = t_0 \leq t_1 \leq t_2 \leq \cdots \leq t_n \leq 1$. The information noise is assumed to be white, i.e., $x \sim \mathcal{N}(0, \sigma^2 I)$. Hence information is determined by N and the noise level σ.

We start with a remark about the radius of information. Let $S \in \{\text{App}, \text{Int}\}$, the variance be σ^2, and exact information N of the form (3.29) be given. We know that the radius $\text{rad}^{\text{ave}}(S, N, \sigma^2)$ is attained by the algorithm $\varphi_{\text{opt}}(y) = S(m(y))$, $y \in \mathbb{R}^n$, where $m(y)$ is the mean of the conditional measure $w(\cdot|y)$ with respect to the observed vector y. Furthermore,

$$\text{rad}^{\text{ave}}(S, N, \sigma^2) = \left(\int_{C^0} \|S(f)\|^2\, w(df|0) \right)^{1/2}. \tag{3.30}$$

Let $R_N : [0, 1]^2 \to \mathbb{R}$ denote the covariance kernel of the conditional measure $w(\cdot|y)$ (it is independent of y). Applying (3.30) and the Fubini theorem we obtain

$$
\begin{aligned}
\left(\text{rad}^{\text{ave}}(\text{App}, N, \sigma^2) \right)^2
&= \int_{C^0} \left(\int_0^1 f^2(x)\, dx \right) w(df|0) \\
&= \int_0^1 \left(\int_{C^0} f^2(x)\, w(df|0) \right) dx \\
&= \int_0^1 R_N(x, x)\, dx \tag{3.31}
\end{aligned}
$$

and

$$
\begin{aligned}
\left(\text{rad}^{\text{ave}}(\text{Int}, N, \sigma^2) \right)^2
&= \int_{C^0} \left(\int_0^1 f(x)\, dx \right)^2 w(df|0) \\
&= \int_{C^0} \left(\int_0^1 \int_0^1 f(s) f(t)\, ds\, dt \right) w(df|0) \\
&= \int_0^1 \int_0^1 R_N(s, t)\, ds\, dt. \tag{3.32}
\end{aligned}
$$

Hence the problem of finding the minimal error $r_n^{\mathrm{ave}}(S, \sigma^2)$ can be reduced to minimizing (3.31) for function approximation and (3.32) for integration, over all N of the form (3.29).

We shall find the optimal information in three steps. We first give formulas for R_N. Then, using these formulas, we estimate the radius of information N_n consisting of observations at equidistant points. Finally, we present lower bounds on $r_n^{\mathrm{ave}}(S, \sigma^2)$, $S \in \{\mathrm{App}, \mathrm{Int}\}$, from which it will follow that information N_n is almost optimal.

Covariance kernel of the conditional distribution

Recall that the mean element $m(y)$ of $w(\cdot|y)$ is the natural linear spline interpolating the data $\{t_i, z_i\}_{i=0}^n$ where the z_is are obtained by smoothing the original data $\{y_i\}_{i=1}^n$, see Subsection 2.6.4. We now find formulas for the covariance kernel R_N of $w(\cdot|y)$.

Define the sequences $\{a_i\}_{i=0}^n$, $\{c_i\}_{i=0}^n$, $\{d_i\}_{i=0}^n$, and $\{b_i\}_{i=1}^n$, as follows.

$$
\begin{aligned}
a_0 = c_0 &= 0, \\
c_i &= \frac{\sigma^2 (t_i - a_{i-1})}{\sigma^2 + (t_i - a_{i-1})}, \\
a_i &= t_i - c_i,
\end{aligned}
\tag{3.33}
$$

$i = 1, 2, \ldots, n$, and

$$
\begin{aligned}
d_n &= c_n, \\
b_i &= a_{i-1} + \frac{(t_i - a_{i-1})^2}{(t_i - a_{i-1}) - d_i}, \\
d_{i-1} &= \frac{(t_{i-1} - a_{i-1})(b_i - t_{i-1})}{b_i - a_{i-1}},
\end{aligned}
\tag{3.34}
$$

$i = n, n-1, \ldots, 1$. (To make these and the next formulas well defined for all σs and t_is, we use the convention that $0/0 = 0$.) Note that the numbers b_i, $b_i \geq t_i$, are defined in such a way that for the parabola

$$
p_i(t) = \frac{(b_i - t)(t - a_{i-1})}{b_i - a_{i-1}}
$$

we have $p_i(t_{i-1}) = d_{i-1}$. If the information is exact, $\sigma = 0$, then $a_i = b_i = t_i$, while for $\sigma > 0$ we have

$$
0 \leq a_{i-1} \leq t_{i-1} \leq t_i \leq b_i, \qquad 1 \leq i \leq n.
$$

Theorem 3.8.4 *The covariance kernel R_N is given as*

$$R_N(s,t) = \begin{cases} s - a_n & t_n \le s \le t \le 1, \\ \frac{(s-a_{i-1})(b_i-t)}{b_i-a_{i-1}} & t_{i-1} \le s \le t \le t_i, \ 1 \le i \le n, \\ \frac{s-a_{i-1}}{t_i-a_{i-1}} R_N(t_i,t) & t_{i-1} \le s \le t_i < t, \ 1 \le i \le n, \end{cases}$$

where a_i, $0 \le i \le n$, and b_i, $1 \le i \le n$, are defined by (3.33) and (3.34).

Proof We start the proof with the following observation. Let μ be a Gaussian measure on a separable Banach space F of functions $f :$ $[0,1] \to \mathbb{R}$ whose covariance kernel is K_0. Let $L(f) = f(u)$, $\forall f \in F$, where $0 \le u \le 1$. Then the conditional distribution of μ with respect to information $N = L : F \to \mathbb{R}$ and variance σ^2 is Gaussian with covariance kernel

$$K_1(s,t) = K_0(s,t) - \frac{K_0(s,u) K_0(t,u)}{K_0(u,u) + \sigma^2}, \qquad 0 \le s,t \le 1. \quad (3.35)$$

Indeed, from the general formulas for conditional distributions given in Subsection 3.4.1 it follows that $K_1(s,t) = K_0(s,t) - (m_1(K_0(s,u)))(t)$, where $(m_1(y))(t) = (\sigma^2 + K_0(u,u))^{-1}K_0(t,u)y$, $\forall y \in \mathbb{R}$, $0 \le t \le 1$. This gives (3.35).

We now use (3.35) to prove the theorem by induction with respect to the number n of observations. Clearly, the theorem holds for $n = 0$. Assume that the theorem holds for some $n \ge 0$. We shall show that it also holds for any information consisting of $n + 1$ function evaluations,

$$N_1(f) = [f(t_1), \dots, f(t_n), f(t_{n+1})],$$

$0 = t_0 \le t_1 \le \cdots \le t_{n+1} \le 1$. That is, we show that the function $\tilde{R} : [0,1]^2 \to \mathbb{R}$,

$$\tilde{R}(s,t) = \begin{cases} s - \tilde{a}_{n+1} & t_{n+1} \le s \le t \le 1, \\ \frac{(s-\tilde{a}_{i-1})(\tilde{b}_i-t)}{\tilde{b}_i-\tilde{a}_{i-1}} & t_{i-1} \le s \le t \le t_i, \ 1 \le i \le n+1, \\ \frac{s-\tilde{a}_{i-1}}{t_i-\tilde{a}_{i-1}}\tilde{R}(t_i,t) & t_{i-1} \le s \le t_i \le t, \ 1 \le i \le n+1, \end{cases}$$

where $\{\tilde{a}_i\}_{i=0}^{n+1}$ and $\{\tilde{b}_i\}_{i=1}^{n+1}$ are defined by (3.33), (3.34), for information N_1, is equal to the covariance kernel R_1 of the measure $w(\cdot|0, N_1)$. To this end, let the information $N(f) = [f(t_1), \dots, f(t_n)]$, and R_0 be the covariance kernel of $w(\cdot|0, N)$. Then (3.35) is valid with $u = t_{n+1}$ and

$$\tilde{a}_i = a_i, \qquad 0 \le i \le n. \quad (3.36)$$

We have three cases:

1. $t_{n+1} \leq s \leq t \leq 1$.

Then, in view of (3.35), (3.36), and the inductive assumption we have

$$R_1(s,t) = (s-a_n) - \frac{(t_{n+1}-a_n)^2}{\sigma^2+(t_{n+1}-a_n)}$$

$$s - \left(t_{n+1} - \frac{\sigma^2(t_{n+1}-a_n)}{\sigma^2+(t_{n+1}-a_n)}\right) = s - \tilde{a}_{n+1} = R_2(s,t).$$

2. $t_{i-1} \leq s \leq t \leq t_i, \quad 1 \leq i \leq n+1$.

To show that for such s,t it is the case that $R_2(s,t) = R_1(s,t)$, we use induction on i with $i = n+1, n, \ldots, 1$. For $i = n+1$ we have

$$R_1(s,t) = (s-a_n) - \frac{(s-a_n)(t-a_n)}{\sigma^2+(t_{n+1}-a_n)} = \frac{(s-a_n)(\sigma^2+t_{n+1}-t)}{\sigma^2+t_{n+1}-a_n}$$

$$= \frac{(s-\tilde{a}_n)(\tilde{b}_{n+1}-t)}{\tilde{b}_{n+1}-\tilde{a}_n} = R_2(s,t).$$

Suppose that $1 \leq i \leq n$. Then from (3.35) we obtain

$$R_1(s,t) = \frac{(s-a_{i-1})(b_i-t)}{b_i-a_{i-1}}$$
$$- \frac{(s-a_{i-1})(t-a_{i-1})}{(t-a_{i-1})^2} \cdot \frac{R_0^2(t_i,t_{n+1})}{\sigma^2+R_0(t_{n+1},t_{n+1})} \quad (3.37)$$

and

$$R_1(t_i,t_i) = \frac{(t_i-a_{i-1})(b_i-t_i)}{b_i-a_{i-1}} - \frac{R_0^2(t_i,t_{n+1})}{\sigma^2+R_0(t_{n+1},t_{n+1})}. \quad (3.38)$$

On the other hand, we have

$$R_1(t_i,t_i) = \frac{(\tilde{b}_{i+1}-t_i)(t_i-\tilde{a}_i)}{\tilde{b}_{i+1}-\tilde{a}_i} = \frac{(\tilde{b}_i-t_i)(t_i-a_{i-1})}{\tilde{b}_i-a_{i-1}}. \quad (3.39)$$

Combining (3.37), (3.38), (3.39) and performing some elementary calculations, we finally get

$$R_1(s,t) = \frac{(s-a_{i-1})(b_i-t)}{b_i-a_{i-1}} + \frac{(s-a_{i-1})(t-a_{i-1})}{(t_i-a_{i-1})^2}$$

$$\times \left(\frac{(t_i-a_{i-1})(b_i-t_i)}{b_i-a_{i-1}} - \frac{(\tilde{b}_i-t_i)(t_i-a_{i-1})}{\tilde{b}_i-a_{i-1}}\right)$$

$$= \cdots = \frac{(s-a_{i-1})(\tilde{b}_i-t)}{\tilde{b}_i-a_{i-1}} = R_2(s,t).$$

3. $t_{i-1} \leq s \leq t_i \leq t, \quad 1 \leq i \leq n+1$.

In this case,

$$R_1(s,t) = \frac{s - a_{i-1}}{t_i - a_{i-1}} R_0(t_i, t) - \frac{(s - a_{i-1})R_0(t_i, t_{n+1})}{t_i - a_{i-1}}$$

$$\times \frac{R_0(t, t_{n+1})}{\sigma^2 + R_0(t_{n+1}, t_{n+1})} = \frac{s - \tilde{a}_{i-1}}{t_i - \tilde{a}_{i-1}} R_1(t_i, t).$$

This completes the induction on n and the proof of the theorem. $\qquad\square$

Note that in the case of exact information, $\sigma = 0$, the formulas for R_N reduce to

$$R_N(s,t) = \begin{cases} s - t_n & t_n \le s \le t \le 1, \\ \frac{(s - t_{i-1})(t_i - t)}{t_i - t_{i-1}} & t_{i-1} \le s \le t \le t_i, \ 1 \le i \le n, \\ 0 & \text{otherwise.} \end{cases}$$

Equidistant sampling

We now consider information consisting of observations at equidistant points. That is, we assume that

$$N(f) = N_n(f) = [f(t_1^*), f(t_2^*), \ldots, f(t_n^*)], \qquad \forall f \in C^0,$$

where $t_i^* = i/n$, $1 \le i \le n$. Such information is of practical importance since observing function values at equidistant points is often more convenient than observing them at other points.

Using (3.40) and (3.31), (3.32), we find that

$$\operatorname{rad}^{\mathrm{ave}}(\mathrm{App}, N_n, 0) = \frac{1}{\sqrt{6n}}$$

and

$$\operatorname{rad}^{\mathrm{ave}}(\mathrm{Int}, N_n, 0) = \frac{1}{2\sqrt{3}\, n}.$$

Theorem 3.8.5 *For $\sigma > 0$ and $n \to +\infty$ we have*

$$\operatorname{rad}^{\mathrm{ave}}(\mathrm{App}, N_n, \sigma^2) \approx \left(\frac{\sigma^2}{4n}\right)^{1/4}$$

and

$$\operatorname{rad}^{\mathrm{ave}}(\mathrm{Int}, N_n, \sigma^2) \approx \left(\frac{\sigma^2}{n}\right)^{1/2}.$$

The proof will be based on the following two lemmas. Let the sequences $\{c_i^*\}_{i=0}^n$ and $\{d_i^*\}_{i=0}^n$ be defined by (3.33) and (3.34) for the information N_n. That is,

$$c_0^* = 0, \qquad c_i^* = \frac{\sigma^2(c_{i-1}^* + 1/n)}{\sigma^2 + c_{i-1}^* + 1/n}, \qquad 1 \le i \le n,$$

$$d_n^* = c_n^*, \qquad d_{i-1}^* = d_i^* \left(\frac{c_{i-1}^*}{c_{i-1}^* + 1/n}\right)^2 + \frac{c_{i-1}^*/n}{c_{i-1}^* + 1/n}, \qquad n \ge i \ge 1.$$

Lemma 3.8.1 *(i)*

$$0 \le c_i^* < \frac{\sigma}{\sqrt{n}}, \qquad \forall i \ge 0.$$

(ii) Let $0 < \alpha < 1$ and $K > \alpha/(1 - \alpha^2)$. Then for sufficiently large n we have

$$c_i^* \ge \frac{\alpha\sigma}{\sqrt{n}}, \qquad \forall i \ge K\sigma\sqrt{n}.$$

Proof Observe that the function

$$\xi(x) = \frac{\sigma^2(x + 1/n)}{\sigma^2 + x + 1/n} - x = -\frac{x^2 + x/n - \sigma^2/n}{\sigma^2 + x + 1/n}, \qquad x \ge 0,$$

is decreasing and is zero at

$$g = \frac{\sigma}{\sqrt{n}}\sqrt{1 + \frac{1}{4\sigma^2 n}} - \frac{1}{2n}.$$

Moreover, if $0 \le x < g$ then $x + \xi(x) < g$. Hence the sequence $\{c_i^*\}$ is increasing and $c_i^* < g < \sigma n^{-1/2}$, $\forall i \ge 0$, which proves (i).

To show (ii) observe that for $c_s^* < h < g$ we have

$$c_s^* = \sum_{j=0}^{s-1}(c_{j+1}^* - c_j^*) = \sum_{j=0}^{s-1}\xi(c_j^*) \ge s\,\xi(c_s^*) \ge s\,\xi(h).$$

Hence, for any $0 < h < g$ and $s \ge 0$,

$$c_s^* \ge \min\{h, s\,\xi(h)\} = \min\left\{h, -\frac{s(h^2 + h/n - \sigma^2/n)}{\sigma^2 + h + 1/n}\right\}. \qquad (3.40)$$

Letting $h = \alpha\sigma n^{-1/2}$ and using (3.40) we get that the inequality $c_i^* \ge \alpha\sigma n^{-1/2}$ is satisfied for

$$i \ge \frac{\alpha\sigma\sqrt{n}\,(1 + \alpha(\sigma\sqrt{n})^{-1} + (\sigma\sqrt{n})^{-2})}{1 - \alpha^2 - \alpha(\sigma\sqrt{n})^{-1}} \approx \frac{\alpha}{1 - \alpha^2}\sigma\sqrt{n}.$$

Hence, (ii) follows. $\square$

Lemma 3.8.2 (i) *Let* $0 < \alpha < 1$ *and* $K > \alpha/(1 - \alpha^2)$. *Then for sufficiently large* n

$$d_i^* > \frac{\alpha\sigma}{2\sqrt{n}}, \qquad \forall i \geq K\sigma\sqrt{n}.$$

(ii) *Let* $\beta > 1$ *and* $L > -\frac{1}{2}\ln(\beta - 1)$. *Then for sufficiently large* n

$$d_{n-i}^* \leq \frac{\beta\sigma}{2\sqrt{n}}, \qquad \forall i \geq L\sigma\sqrt{n}.$$

Proof Let

$$A_i = \left(\frac{c_i^*}{c_i^* + 1/n}\right)^2, \qquad B_i = \frac{c_i^*/n}{c_i^* + 1/n}, \qquad 0 \leq i \leq n.$$

Let α_1 be such that $\alpha < \alpha_1 < 1$ and $\alpha/(1 - \alpha^2) < \alpha_1/(1 - \alpha_1^2) < K$. Owing to Lemma 3.8.1, for large n and $i \geq K\sigma\sqrt{n}$ we have $c_i^* \geq \alpha_1\sigma/\sqrt{n}$. Hence, for such i and n,

$$
\begin{aligned}
d_i^* &= A_i d_{i+1} + B_i \geq A d_{i+1}^* + B \\
&\geq \cdots \geq A^{n-i} d_n^* + B \sum_{j=0}^{n-i-1} A^j \\
&= A^{n-i}\left(c_n^* - \frac{B}{1-A}\right) + \frac{B}{1-A},
\end{aligned}
$$

where

$$A = \left(\frac{\alpha_1\sigma\sqrt{n}}{1 + \alpha_1\sigma\sqrt{n}}\right)^2, \qquad B = \frac{\alpha_1\sigma}{\alpha_1\sigma n + \sqrt{n}}.$$

Since $c_n^* \approx \sigma/\sqrt{n}$ and

$$\frac{B}{1-A} = \frac{\alpha_1\sigma}{2\sqrt{n}} \cdot \frac{2 + 2\alpha_1\sigma\sqrt{n}}{1 + 2\alpha_1\sigma\sqrt{n}} \approx \frac{\alpha_1\sigma}{2\sqrt{n}},$$

(i) is proven.

To show (ii), let

$$C = \left(\frac{\sigma\sqrt{n}}{1 + \sigma\sqrt{n}}\right)^2, \qquad D = \frac{\sigma}{\sigma n + \sqrt{n}}.$$

Then, owing to Lemma 3.8.1(i), we have $A_i \leq C$ and $B_i \leq D$, $\forall i$. Hence

$$d_{n-i} \leq C^i\left(d_n^* - \frac{D}{1-C}\right) + \frac{D}{1-C}$$

$$\leq \frac{\sigma}{2\sqrt{n}} \cdot \frac{2+2\sigma\sqrt{n}}{1+2\sigma\sqrt{n}} \left(1 + \frac{\sigma\sqrt{n}}{1+\sigma\sqrt{n}} \left(1 + \frac{1}{\sigma\sqrt{n}}\right)^{-2i}\right).$$

For $i \geq L\sigma\sqrt{n}$ we have

$$\left(1 + \frac{1}{\sigma\sqrt{n}}\right)^{-2i} \leq e^{-2L} < \beta - 1,$$

and (ii) follows.   □

Proof of Theorem 3.8.5 It follows from Theorem 3.8.4 that for $t_{i-1}^* \leq t \leq t_i^*$ we have

$$\min\{d_{i-1}^*, d_i^*\} \leq R_N(t,t) \leq \max\{d_{i-1}^*, d_i^*\} + \frac{1}{4n}. \qquad (3.41)$$

Consider first the approximation problem. Let $0 < \alpha < 1 < \beta$ and K, L be as in Lemma 3.8.2. Using (3.31) and (3.41) we obtain that for sufficiently large n,

$$\left(\text{rad}^{\text{ave}}(\text{App}, N_n, \sigma^2)\right)^2$$
$$= \int_0^{1-\frac{L\sigma}{\sqrt{n}}-\frac{1}{n}} R_N(t,t)\,dt + \int_{1-\frac{L\sigma}{\sqrt{n}}-\frac{1}{n}}^1 R_N(t,t)\,dt$$
$$\leq \left(1 - \frac{L\sigma}{\sqrt{n}} - \frac{1}{n}\right)\left(\frac{\beta\sigma}{2\sqrt{n}} + \frac{1}{4n}\right) + \left(\frac{L\sigma}{\sqrt{n}} + \frac{1}{n}\right)\left(\frac{\sigma}{\sqrt{n}} + \frac{1}{4n}\right)$$
$$\approx \frac{\beta\sigma}{2\sqrt{n}}. \qquad (3.42)$$

On the other hand,

$$\left(\text{rad}^{\text{ave}}(\text{App}, N_n, \sigma^2)\right)^2 \geq \int_{\frac{K\sigma}{\sqrt{n}}+\frac{1}{n}}^1 R_N(t,t)\,dt$$
$$\geq \left(1 - \frac{K\sigma}{\sqrt{n}} - \frac{1}{n}\right)\frac{\alpha\sigma}{2\sqrt{n}} \approx \frac{\alpha\sigma}{2\sqrt{n}}. \qquad (3.43)$$

Since (3.42) and (3.43) hold for arbitrary α and β satisfying $0 < \alpha < 1 < \beta$, (a) follows.

We now turn to the integration problem. Let $0 \leq s \leq t \leq 1$, $t_{j-1}^* \leq s \leq t_j^*$, $t_{i-1}^* \leq t \leq t_i^*$, $1 \leq j \leq i \leq n$. In view of Theorem 3.8.4 we have that $R_N(s,t)$ is given by

$$\begin{cases} \frac{s-a_{j-1}^*}{t-a_{j-1}^*} R_N(t,t) & j=i, \\ \frac{s-a_{j-1}^*}{t_j^*-a_{j-1}^*} \frac{t_{i-1}^*-a_{i-1}^*}{t-a_{i-1}^*} R_N(t,t) & j=i+1, \quad (3.44) \\ \frac{s-a_{j-1}^*}{t_j^*-a_{j-1}^*} \frac{t_{i-1}^*-a_{i-1}^*}{t-a_{i-1}^*} \prod_{k=j+1}^{i-1} \frac{t_{k-1}^*-a_{k-1}^*}{t_k^*-a_{k-1}^*} R_N(t,t) & \text{otherwise,} \end{cases}$$

where the sequence $\{a_i^*\}_{i=0}^n$ is defined by (3.33) for information N_n. By Lemma 3.8.1(i)

$$\frac{t_i^*-a_i^*}{t_{i+1}^*-a_i^*} = \frac{c_i^*}{c_k^*+1/n} \le \gamma = \frac{\sigma\sqrt{n}}{1+\sigma\sqrt{n}}, \qquad \forall i. \qquad (3.45)$$

Using (3.41), (3.44), (3.45), Lemmas 3.8.1(i) and 3.8.2(ii), we get that for $\beta > 1$ and $L > -(1/2)\ln(\beta-1)$, for sufficiently large n,

$$\begin{aligned} R_N(s,t) &\le \gamma^{i-j-1} R_N(t,t) \\ &\le \gamma^{n(t-s)} \times \begin{cases} \frac{\beta\sigma}{2\sqrt{n}} + \frac{1}{4n} & 0 \le t \le 1 - \frac{L\sigma}{\sqrt{n}} - \frac{1}{n}, \\ \frac{\sigma}{\sqrt{n}} + \frac{1}{4n} & 1 - \frac{L\sigma}{\sqrt{n}} - \frac{1}{n} \le t \le 1. \end{cases} \end{aligned}$$

Hence, for large n,

$$\begin{aligned} \left(\text{rad}^{\text{ave}}(\text{Int}, N_n, \sigma^2)\right)^2 &= 2 \int_0^1 \int_0^t R(s,t)\, ds\, dt \\ &\le 2\left(\frac{\beta\sigma}{2\sqrt{n}} + \frac{1}{4n}\right) \int_0^{1-\frac{L\sigma}{\sqrt{n}}-\frac{1}{n}} \int_0^t \gamma^{n(t-s)}\, ds\, dt \\ &\quad + 2\left(\frac{\sigma}{\sqrt{n}} + \frac{1}{4n}\right) \int_{1-\frac{L\sigma}{\sqrt{n}}-\frac{1}{n}}^1 \int_0^t \gamma^{n(t-s)}\, ds\, dt \\ &= 2\left(\frac{\beta\sigma}{2\sqrt{n}} + \frac{1}{4n}\right) \frac{1}{n\ln(1/\gamma)} \left\{ 1 - \frac{L\sigma}{\sqrt{n}} - \frac{1}{n} + \frac{\gamma^{(n-L\sigma\sqrt{n}-1)}-1}{n\ln(1/\gamma)} \right\} \\ &\quad + 2\left(\frac{\sigma}{\sqrt{n}} + \frac{1}{4n}\right) \frac{1}{n\ln(1/\gamma)} \left\{ \frac{L\sigma}{\sqrt{n}} + \frac{1}{n} + \frac{\gamma^n - \gamma^{(n-L\sigma\sqrt{n}-1)}}{n\ln(1/\gamma)} \right\}. \end{aligned}$$

Since

$$\frac{1}{n\ln(1/\gamma)} = \frac{1}{n\ln\left(1 + (\sigma\sqrt{n})^{-1}\right)} \approx \frac{\sigma}{\sqrt{n}}$$

and $\gamma^{n-L\sigma\sqrt{n}-1} \to 0$ as $n \to +\infty$, we have

$$\left(\text{rad}^{\text{ave}}(\text{Int}, N_n, \sigma^2)\right)^2 \approx \frac{\beta\sigma^2}{n} + \frac{2\sigma^3 L}{n\sqrt{n}} \approx \frac{\beta\sigma^2}{n},$$

which gives the upper bound on $\text{rad}^{\text{ave}}(\text{Int}, N_n, \sigma^2)$.

To show the lower bound, we use Lemma 3.8.1(ii) and Lemma 3.8.2(i). Let $0 < \alpha < 1$ and $K > \alpha/(1 - \alpha^2)$. Then for sufficiently large n we have

$$\frac{t_{i-1}^* - a_{i-1}^*}{t_i^* - a_{i-1}^*} \geq \delta = \frac{\alpha\sigma\sqrt{n}}{1 + \alpha\sigma\sqrt{n}}, \qquad \forall i \geq K\sigma\sqrt{n} + 1,$$

and

$$R_N(t, t) \geq \frac{\alpha\sigma}{2\sqrt{n}}, \qquad \forall t \geq \frac{K\sigma}{\sqrt{n}} + \frac{1}{n}.$$

This and (3.44) yield that for large n

$$R_N(s, t) \geq \delta^{n(t-s)} \frac{\alpha\sigma}{2\sqrt{n}}, \qquad t \geq s \geq \frac{K\sigma}{\sqrt{n}} + \frac{2}{n},$$

and, as a consequence,

$$\left(\mathrm{rad}^{\mathrm{ave}}(\mathrm{Int}, N_n, \sigma^2)\right)^2 \geq \frac{\sigma}{\sqrt{n}} \int_{\frac{K\sigma}{\sqrt{n}} + \frac{2}{n}}^{1} \int_0^t \delta^{n(t-s)} \, ds \, dt$$

$$= \frac{\alpha\sigma}{\sqrt{n}} \frac{1}{n\ln(1/\delta)} \left\{ 1 - \frac{K\sigma}{\sqrt{n}} - \frac{2}{n} + \frac{1}{n\ln(1/\delta)} \left(\delta^n - \delta^{(K\sigma\sqrt{n}+2)} \right) \right\}$$

$$\approx \frac{\alpha^2\sigma^2}{n}.$$

This shows the lower bound on $\mathrm{rad}^{\mathrm{ave}}(\mathrm{Int}, N_n, \sigma^2)$ and completes the proof of the theorem. $\qquad\qquad\qquad\qquad\qquad\qquad\qquad\qquad\qquad\qquad\square$

Lower bounds

Using (3.33), (3.34), and the formulas (3.40) we can easily show that for exact information the actual values of the minimal errors are equal to

$$r_n^{\mathrm{ave}}(\mathrm{App}, 0) = \frac{1}{\sqrt{2(3n+1)}} \approx \frac{1}{\sqrt{6n}}, \qquad (3.46)$$

$$r_n^{\mathrm{ave}}(\mathrm{Int}, 0) = \frac{1}{\sqrt{3(2n+1)}} \approx \frac{1}{2\sqrt{3n}}. \qquad (3.47)$$

Furthermore, the optimal sample points are given by $t_i = 3i/(3n+1)$ for function approximation and $t_i = 2i/(2n+1)$ for integration, $1 \leq i \leq n$. This shows that in the exact information case equidistant sampling N_n is nearly optimal.

We now turn to the 'noisy' case, $\sigma > 0$, in which N_n will be proven to be almost optimal. We first find lower bounds for the average radii.

Theorem 3.8.6 *For any σ and $n \to +\infty$ we have*

$$r_n^{\text{ave}}(\text{App}, \sigma^2) \geq \left(\frac{\sigma}{6\sqrt{n}} - \frac{\sigma^2}{3n} \right)_+^{1/2} \approx \frac{1}{\sqrt{6}} \left(\frac{\sigma^2}{n} \right)^{1/4}$$

and

$$r_n^{\text{ave}}(\text{Int}, \sigma^2) \geq \left(\frac{\sigma^2}{3(n + \sigma^2)} \right)^{1/2} \approx \frac{1}{\sqrt{3}} \left(\frac{\sigma^2}{n} \right)^{1/2}.$$

To prove the bound on $r_n^{\text{ave}}(\text{App}, \sigma^2)$, we need the following lemma.

Lemma 3.8.3 *Let N be arbitrary information of the form $N(f) = [f(t_1), \ldots, f(t_n)]$. Then for any $0 \leq a < t < b \leq 1$ we have*

$$R_N(t, t) \geq \frac{\sigma^2 \psi(t)}{\sigma^2 + s\psi(t)},$$

where

$$\psi(t) = \frac{(t - a)(b - t)}{b - a}$$

and s is the number of points t_i satisfying $a < t_i < b$.

Proof Let $\{a_i\}$ and $\{b_i\}$ be the sequences defined by (3.33) and (3.34). Observe first that for any k we have

$$a_k \leq t_k - \frac{\sigma^2(t_k - a)}{\sigma^2 + s_1(t_k - a)}, \tag{3.48}$$

where $s_1 = s_1(k)$ is the number of points t_i, $i \leq k$, satisfying $a < t_i$. Indeed, (3.48) can be easily shown by induction on s_1. If $s_1 = 0$ then $t_k \leq a$ and $a_k \leq a$. For $s_1 \geq 1$ we have from (3.33) and the inductive assumption applied to a_{k-1} that

$$a_k = t_k - \frac{\sigma^2(t_k - a_{k-1})}{\sigma^2 + t_k - a_{k-1}} \leq t_k - \frac{\sigma^2(t_k - a)}{\sigma^2 + s_1(t_k - a)}.$$

Similarly we can show that for any k

$$b_k \geq t_k + \frac{\sigma^2(b - t_k)}{\sigma^2 + s_2(b - t_k)}, \tag{3.49}$$

where $s_2 = s_2(k)$ is the number of points t_i, $i \geq k$, satisfying $t_i < b$.

Now let $r = \max\{i \geq 0 \,|\, t_i \leq t\}$. Owing to (3.48) we have

$$a_r \leq t - \frac{\sigma^2(t - a)}{\sigma^2 + s_1(t - a)} =: a_{\max} \tag{3.50}$$

where $s_1 = s_1(r)$. Hence for $r = n$ we have $s_1 = s$ and

$$R_N(t,t) \geq t - a_{\max} \geq \frac{\sigma^2 \psi(t)}{\sigma^2 + s\psi(t)} .$$

For $r < n$, (3.49) implies

$$b_{r+1} \geq t - \frac{\sigma^2(b-t)}{\sigma^2 + s_2(b-t)} =: b_{\min} \qquad (3.51)$$

where $s_2 = s_2(r+1)$. Since $s_1 + s_2 = s$, (3.50) and (3.51) yield

$$R_N(t,t) \geq \frac{(t - a_{\max})(b_{\min} - t)}{b_{\min} - a_{\max}} = \frac{\sigma^2 \psi(t)}{\sigma^2 + s\psi(t)} ,$$

as claimed.   □

Proof of Theorem 3.8.6 We start with the problem App. Let N be arbitrary information consisting of observations at t_i, $1 \leq i \leq n$. Divide the unit interval into k equal subintervals (u_{i-1}, u_i), $1 \leq i \leq k$, where $u_i = i/k$. Let s_i be the number of the points t_j belonging to the ith interval, and let $\psi_i(t) = (t - u_{i-1})(u_i - t)/(u_i - u_{i-1})$. Then, for $u_{i-1} < t < u_i$, we have $\psi_i(t) \leq 1/4(u_i - u_{i-1}) = 1/(4k)$. This, (3.31), and Lemma 3.8.3 yield that the radius of N can be estimated as follows:

$$\begin{aligned}
\left(\mathrm{rad}^{\mathrm{ave}}(\mathrm{App}, N, \sigma^2)\right)^2 &\geq \sum_{i=1}^{k} \int_{u_{i-1}}^{u_i} \frac{\sigma^2 \psi_i(t)}{\sigma^2 + s_i/(4k)} dt \\
&= \frac{2\sigma^2}{3k} \sum_{i=1}^{k} \frac{1}{s_i + 4k\sigma^2} =: \Omega(s_1, \ldots, s_k).
\end{aligned}$$

The function Ω, restricted to the set

$$\{(s_1, \ldots, s_k) \mid s_1, \ldots, s_k \geq 0, \sum_{i=1}^{k} s_i \leq n\},$$

has its minimum at $s_i = n/k$, $\forall i$. Hence

$$\Omega(s_1, \ldots, s_k) \geq \Omega(\underbrace{n/k, \ldots, n/k}_{k}) = \frac{2\sigma^2 k}{3(n + 4\sigma^2 k^2)} .$$

Letting $k_1 = \max\{1, l\}$, where l is the largest integer satisfying $l \leq k_{\mathrm{opt}} = \sqrt{n}/(2\sigma)$, we obtain

$$\left(\mathrm{rad}^{\mathrm{ave}}(\mathrm{App}, N, \sigma^2)\right)^2 \geq \frac{2\sigma^2 k_1}{3(n + 4\sigma^2 k_1^2)} \geq \frac{2\sigma^2(k_{\mathrm{opt}} - 1)}{3(n + 4\sigma^2 k_{\mathrm{opt}}^2)}$$

$$= \frac{\sigma}{6\sqrt{n}} - \frac{\sigma^2}{3n},$$

which proves the desired lower bound on $r_n^{\text{ave}}(\text{App}, \sigma^2)$.

To show the bound on $r_n^{\text{ave}}(\text{Int}, \sigma^2)$, we use the general results of Subsection 3.8.1. When applied to the integration problem on the Wiener space, those results read as follows.

Suppose that the class of permissible functionals consists of all L with $\|L\|_w^2 = \int_{C^0} L^2(f) \, w(df) \leq 1$, i.e., $\Lambda = \Lambda^{\text{all}}$. Then the minimal radius corresponding to observations with variance σ^2 equals

$$\left(r_n^{\text{ave}}(\text{Int}, \Lambda^{\text{all}}\sigma^2)\right)^2 = \frac{\sigma^2}{n + \sigma^2} \int_F \text{Int}^2(f) \, w(df).$$

For $L_t(f) = f(t)$ we have $\|L_t\|_w^2 = t$ which inplies $\Lambda^{\text{std}} \subset \Lambda^{\text{all}}$. This, (3.32), and

$$\int_{C^0} \text{Int}^2(f) \, w(df) = \int_0^1 \int_0^1 \min\{s, t\} \, ds \, dt = \tfrac{1}{3},$$

yield

$$\left(r_n^{\text{ave}}(\text{Int}, \Lambda^{\text{std}}\sigma^2)\right)^2 \geq \left(r_n^{\text{ave}}(\text{Int}, \Lambda^{\text{all}}\sigma^2)\right)^2 = \frac{\sigma^2}{3(n + \sigma^2)},$$

as claimed. $\qquad\square$

Theorems 3.8.5, 3.8.6, and the formulas (3.46), (3.47) yield that information N_n consisting of noisy observations of function values at equidistant points is almost optimal, for both the approximation and integration problems. That is, the errors obtained by applying N_n together with the smoothing spline algorithm are at most $\sqrt{3}$ times as large as optimal. We summarize this in the following corollary.

Corollary 3.8.2 *For any $\sigma \geq 0$ and $n \to +\infty$ we have*

$$r_n^{\text{ave}}(\text{App}, \sigma^2) \approx \frac{1}{\sqrt{6n}} + p_n \left(\frac{\sigma^2}{4n}\right)^{1/4}$$

and

$$r_n^{\text{ave}}(\text{Int}, \sigma^2) \approx \frac{1}{2\sqrt{3n}} + q_n \left(\frac{\sigma^2}{n}\right)^{1/2},$$

where $p_n, q_n \in [1/\sqrt{3}, 1]$.

It seems interesting to compare these results with those of Subsection 3.8.1. More precisely, we want to see whether the class Λ^{std} is as powerful as Λ^{all}. Clearly, $\Lambda^{\text{std}} \subset \Lambda^{\text{all}}$.

As we noticed in the proof of Theorem 3.8.6, for the integration problem we have $r_n^{\text{ave}}(\text{Int}, \Lambda^{\text{all}}, \sigma^2) \asymp \sigma/\sqrt{n}$ $(\sigma \geq 0)$. Hence for $\sigma > 0$ the classes Λ^{std} and Λ^{all} give similar minimal errors, while for exact information Λ^{all} is obviously much more powerful than Λ^{std}.

Owing to NR 3.8.4, the corresponding radius for approximation satisfies $r_n^{\text{ave}}(\text{App}, \Lambda^{\text{all}}, \sigma^2) \asymp 1/\sqrt{n} + \sigma \ln n/\sqrt{n}$. The situation is then quite the opposite. We have $r_n^{\text{ave}}(\text{App}, \Lambda^{\text{all}}, 0) \asymp r_n^{\text{ave}}(\text{App}, \Lambda^{\text{std}}, 0)$, while for $\sigma > 0$

$$\frac{r_n^{\text{ave}}(\text{App}, \Lambda^{\text{all}}, \sigma^2)}{r_n^{\text{ave}}(\text{App}, \Lambda^{\text{std}}, \sigma^2)} \asymp \left(\frac{\sigma^2}{n}\right)^{1/4} \ln n.$$

Notes and remarks

NR 3.8.1 Most of Subsection 3.8.1 is based on Plaskota (1990) and (1993a). Theorem 3.8.3 is new. Subsection 3.8.2 is based on Plaskota (1992).

NR 3.8.2 There are many papers dealing with integration or approximation in Wiener type spaces, based on exact information. The first papers on this subject are due to Suldin (1959, 1960) who analyzed integration with respect to the classical Wiener measure on C^0. Other contributions include, e.g., Lee (1986) (who showed the formulas (3.46) and (3.47)), Lee and Wasilkowski (1986), Sacks and Ylvisaker (1966, 1968, 1970), Wahba (1971). The multivariate case with exact information was studied, e.g., by Papageorgiou and Wasilkowski (1990), Ritter *et al.* (1995), Wasilkowski (1994), Wasilkowski and Woźniakowski (1995), Woźniakowski (1991, 1992, 1994).

NR 3.8.3 In the average case setting, we assume that noise of different observations is uncorrelated, e.g., $x \sim \mathcal{N}(0, \sigma^2 I)$. As we already mentioned, in the worst case the uncorrelated noise corresponds to noise bounded in the maximum norm, e.g., $\|x\|_Y = \|x\|_\infty \leq \delta$. Lemma 2.8.2 says that for such noise the worst case radius does not tend to zero with n. This stands in contrast to the average case where the radius can be reduced to an arbitrary small value.

NR 3.8.4 Consider the problem of approximating multivariate functions $f \in F = C^{0...0}_{r_1...r_d}$ in the norm of $G = \mathcal{L}_2((0,1)^d)$, with respect to the Wiener sheet measure $\mu = w_{r_1...r_d}$. That is, $S : C^{0...0}_{r_1...r_d} \to \mathcal{L}_2((0,1)^d)$, $S(f) = f$. As mentioned in NR 3.3.5, the abstract Wiener space corresponding to $w_{r_1...r_d}$ is $\{H, F\}$ with $H = W^{0...0}_{r_1+1...r_d+1}$. Recall that $SC_\mu S^* = S_H S_H^*$. Owing to NR 2.8.4, the eigenvalues of $S_H S_H^*$ are given as

$$\lambda_j \asymp \left(\frac{\ln^{k-1} j}{j}\right)^{2(r+1)} \qquad \text{as} \quad j \to +\infty,$$

where $r = \min\{r_1, \dots, r_d\}$ and k is the number of i such that $r_i = r$. The results of Subsection 3.8.1 yield that for $\sigma^2 > 0$ we have

$$r_n^{\text{ave}}(\sigma^2) \asymp \begin{cases} \sigma \ln^k n/\sqrt{n} & r = 0, \\ \sigma/\sqrt{n} & r \geq 1, \end{cases}$$

and $r_n^{\text{ave}}(0) \asymp n^{-(r+1/2)} \ln^{(k-1)(r+1)} n$.

NR 3.8.5 We now give a concrete application of the correspondence theorem of Subsection 3.6.3. We let F be the Hilbert space,

$$F = W^0 = \{ f : [0,1] \to \mathbb{R} \mid f(0) = 0, f \text{ is abs. cont.}, f' \in \mathcal{L}_2(0,1) \},$$

with inner product $\langle f_1, f_2 \rangle_F = \int_0^1 f_1'(t) f_2'(t) \, dt$. Consider the problem of approximating the integral $\text{Int}(f)$ in the worst case setting with E the unit ball of F. Information consists of n function evaluations and noise is bounded in the Euclidean norm, $\sum_{i=1}^n x_i^2 \leq \delta^2$. As we know, $\{W^0, C^0\}$ is an abstract Wiener space and the classical Wiener measure w is the corresponding Gaussian measure on C^0. Hence we can apply Theorem 3.6.3 and Corollary 3.8.2 to get that the minimal radius for this problem is given as

$$r_n^{\text{wor}}(\text{Int}, \delta) \approx \frac{1}{2\sqrt{3n}} + \tilde{q}_n \frac{\delta}{\sqrt{n}}$$

where $\tilde{q}_n \in [1/\sqrt{3}, \sqrt{2}]$. These bounds are attained by the $(1/2)$-smoothing spline algorithm using noisy function values at equidistant points.

NR 3.8.6 We assume that each value $f(t_i)$ is observed with the same variance σ^2. One may consider a model in which $f(t_i)$ is observed with variance σ_i^2 where the σ_is may be different. It is easy to verify that in this case Theorem 3.8.4 remains valid provided that σ^2 in the formulas (2.5) and (2.6) is replaced by σ_i^2. However, formulas for the minimal radii are in this case unknown.

NR 3.8.7 The problems App and Int with $F = C_r^0$ and μ the r-fold Wiener measure w_r ($r \geq 1$) were studied in Plaskota (1992). It was shown that if the class Λ consists of function values or derivatives of order at most r, then

$$r_n^{\text{ave}}(\text{App}, r, \sigma^2) \asymp \frac{\sigma}{\sqrt{n}} + \left(\frac{1}{n}\right)^{r+1/2}$$

and

$$r_n^{\text{ave}}(\text{Int}, r, \sigma^2) \asymp \frac{\sigma}{\sqrt{n}} + \left(\frac{1}{n}\right)^{r+1}.$$

These bounds are attained by information

$$N_n^r(f) = [f^{(r)}(t_1^*), f^{(r)}(t_2^*), \ldots, f^{(r)}(t_n^*)], \tag{3.52}$$

where $t_i^* = i/n$, $1 \leq i \leq n$; see E 3.8.9.

One can show that for integration the same bound can be obtained using only function values. However, this fact does not apply to the function approximation which follows from more general results of Ritter (1994). He considered numerical differentiation, $S(f) = \text{Diff}_k(f) = f^{(k)}$ ($0 \leq k \leq r$), with respect to the same r-fold Wiener measure. Assuming that only observations of function values are allowed, he showed that

$$r_n^{\text{ave}}(\text{Diff}_k, r, \sigma^2) \asymp \left(\frac{\sigma}{\sqrt{n}}\right)^{(2(r-k)+1)/(2r+2)} + \left(\frac{1}{n}\right)^{r+1/2}.$$

In particular, for approximation from noisy function values ($\sigma > 0$), the minimal radius has the exponent $(2r + 1)/(2r + 2)$ which is worse than $(1/2)$. Hence, for function approximation, noisy information about rth derivatives is much more powerful than information about function values.

Exercises

E 3.8.1 Let $a_1 \geq a_2 \geq \cdots \geq a_m \geq 0$ and let λ_i', λ_i, $1 \leq i \leq m$, be such that $\sum_{i=1}^{r} \lambda_i' \leq \sum_{i=1}^{r} \lambda_i$, for all $1 \leq r \leq n$. Show that then $\sum_{i=1}^{m} a_i \lambda_i' \leq \sum_{i=1}^{m} a_i \lambda_i$.

E 3.8.2 Show that the lower bound in (3.26) is achieved if

$$\sum_{i=s}^{n} \eta_i^{**} \leq \sum_{i=s}^{n} \frac{1}{\sigma_i^2}, \qquad 1 \leq s \leq n,$$

where $\eta^{**} = (\eta_1^{**}, \ldots, \eta_n^{**})$ is the solution (3.22) of the problem $P(0, n)$. On the other hand, show that the upper bound in (3.26) is achieved if for all $0 \leq q < r \leq n$ the solution η^* of $P(q, r)$ satisfies

$$\sum_{j=s}^{r} \eta_j^* \geq \sum_{j=s}^{r} \frac{1}{\sigma_j^2}, \qquad q + 1 \leq s \leq r.$$

E 3.8.3 Show that $r_n^{\mathrm{ave}}(\mathrm{diag}\{\sigma_1^2, \ldots, \sigma_n^2\})$ is a strictly increasing function of each σ_i.

E 3.8.4 Show that the sequence $r_n^{\mathrm{ave}}(\sigma^2)$ of the minimal radii given by (3.27) is convex, i.e.,

$$r_n^{\mathrm{ave}}(\sigma^2) \leq \tfrac{1}{2}\left(r_{n-1}^{\mathrm{ave}}(\sigma^2) + r_{n+1}^{\mathrm{ave}}(\sigma^2)\right), \qquad \forall n \geq 1.$$

E 3.8.5 Consider the pair of problems (WW) and (AA) on page 178 with $\Sigma = I$ and $\delta = \sigma$. Suppose that the eigenvalues λ_i of the operator $S_H^* S_H$ are $\lambda_i = i^{-2}$, $i \geq 1$. Show that then

$$\frac{\mathrm{rad}^{\mathrm{wor}}(N_\Sigma, \Delta)}{r_n^{\mathrm{wor}}(\delta)} \asymp \ln n \qquad \text{and} \qquad \frac{\mathrm{rad}^{\mathrm{ave}}(N_\Delta, \Sigma)}{r_n^{\mathrm{ave}}(\sigma^2)} \asymp \frac{\sqrt{n}}{\ln n},$$

where N_Σ is the optimal information in the worst case (WW), and N_Δ is the optimal information in the average case (AA). Hence show that Theorem 3.8.3 does not hold if information N_* is replaced by N_Σ or N_Δ.

E 3.8.6 Suppose that for $f \in C^0$ the values $f(t_i)$ are observed with variances σ_i^2, $1 \leq i \leq n$, where the σ_is may be different. Show that then the formula for the conditional distribution in Theorem 3.8.4 remains valid provided that σ^2 in the formulas (3.33) is replaced by σ_i^2.

E 3.8.7 Consider the approximation problem on the Wiener space with the class $\tilde{\Lambda}^{\mathrm{std}}$ consisting of functionals of the form $L(f) = t^{-1/2} f(t)$, $t \in [0, 1]$ (or equivalently, assuming that only observations of $f(t)$ with the variance $t\sigma^2$ are allowed). Show that then

$$r_n^{\mathrm{ave}}(\mathrm{App}, \tilde{\Lambda}^{\mathrm{std}}, \sigma^2) \asymp r_n^{\mathrm{ave}}(\mathrm{App}, \Lambda^{\mathrm{std}}, \sigma^2) \asymp \frac{1}{\sqrt{n}} + \left(\frac{\sigma^2}{n}\right)^{1/4}.$$

Hint: Consider the solution operator $S_a : C^0 \to \mathcal{L}_2(a,1)$, $(S_a(f))(t) = f(t)$, where $a \in (0,1)$. Observe that for any $\mathbb{II}$ and φ we have $e^{\text{ave}}(S_a, \mathbb{II}, \varphi) \leq e^{\text{ave}}(\text{App}, \mathbb{II}, \varphi)$. To find a lower bound on $e^{\text{ave}}(S_a, \mathbb{II}, \varphi)$, use the technique from the proof of Theorem 3.8.6.

E 3.8.8 Let w_r be the r-fold Wiener measure and $L(f) = f^{(k)}(t)$, $f \in C_r^0$, with $0 \leq k \leq r$. Show that

$$\|L\|_{w_r}^2 = \int_{C_r^0} L^2(f)\, w_r(df) = \frac{t^{2(r-k)+1}}{((r-k)!)^2 \, (2(r-k)+1)} \leq 1.$$

E 3.8.9 Let $F = C_r^0$, $\mu = w_r$, and N_n^r be information defined by (3.52). Show the inequalities

$$\text{rad}^{\text{ave}}(\text{App}, r+1, N_n^{r+1}) \leq \text{rad}^{\text{ave}}(\text{Int}, r, N_n^r) \leq \text{rad}^{\text{ave}}(\text{App}, r, N_n^r).$$

Use this and the previous exercise to obtain that for Λ consisting of function values and derivatives of order at most r we have

$$r_n^{\text{ave}}(\text{App}, r, \sigma^2) \asymp \frac{\sigma}{\sqrt{n}} \asymp r_n^{\text{ave}}(\text{Int}, r, \sigma^2),$$

for all $r \geq 1$ and $\sigma > 0$.

3.9 Complexity

In this section we deal with the problem complexity in the average case setting. Recall that the problem is defined by the solution operator $S : F \to G$, the probability measure μ on F, and the class Λ of permissible functionals.

As in the worst case setting, we assume that approximations are obtained by executing a program. The program is defined in Section 2.9. The only difference is in the interpretation of the information statement. That is,

$$\mathcal{I}(y; L, \sigma)$$

now means that the real variable d takes a value of the real Gaussian random variable whose mean element is $L(f)$ and variance is σ^2. The cost of executing this statement is $c(\sigma^2)$ where, as before, c is a non-negative and nonincreasing cost function with positive values for small $\sigma > 0$.

We recall that the program specifies not only how information is collected, but also which primitive operations are to be performed. The operations are arithmetic operations and comparisons over $\mathbb{R}$, elementary linear operations over G, and logical operations over the Boolean values.

Let $\mathcal{P}$ be a program which is a realization of an algorithm φ using information $y \sim \pi_f$. The (average) cost of computing an approximation with the program $\mathcal{P}$ equals

$$\mathrm{cost}^{\mathrm{ave}}(\mathcal{P}) = \int_Y \mathrm{cost}(\mathcal{P}; y)\, \mu_1(dy)$$

where, as before, $\mathrm{cost}(\mathcal{P}; y)$ is the cost of computing $\varphi(y)$, and μ_1 is the a priori distribution of noisy information y on Y,

$$\mu_1(B) = \int_F \pi_f(B)\, \mu(df) \qquad (3.53)$$

(compare with Section 3.2).

The definition of the cost of approximation yields the algorithm complexity, $\mathrm{comp}^{\mathrm{ave}}(\mathbb{II}, \varphi)$, and the problem ε-complexity, $\mathrm{Comp}^{\mathrm{ave}}(\varepsilon)$, in the average case setting. That is,

$$\mathrm{comp}^{\mathrm{ave}}(\mathbb{II}, \varphi) = \inf\{\, \mathrm{cost}^{\mathrm{ave}}(\mathcal{P}) \mid \mathcal{P} \text{ is a realization of } \varphi \text{ using } \mathbb{N} \,\},$$

and for $\varepsilon \geq 0$,

$$\mathrm{Comp}^{\mathrm{ave}}(\varepsilon) = \inf\{\, \mathrm{comp}^{\mathrm{ave}}(\mathbb{II}, \varphi) \mid \mathrm{e}^{\mathrm{ave}}(\mathbb{II}, \varphi) \leq \varepsilon \,\}$$

($\inf \emptyset = +\infty$).

Our aim now is to obtain tight bounds on the average complexity of linear problems with Gaussian measures. That is, we assume that

- S is a continuous linear operator acting between a separable Banach space F and a separable Hilbert space G, and
- μ is a zero-mean Gaussian measure on F.

To establish complexity bounds, we need further relations between nonadaptive and adaptive information in terms of the cost function $\mathbf{c}(\cdot)$.

3.9.1 Adaption versus nonadaption

In Subsection 3.7.2 we compared the radii of adaptive and nonadaptive information. Theorem 3.7.2 says that for any adaptive information $\mathbb{II}$ there exists $y \in Y$ such that the average radius of the nonadaptive information $\mathbb{II}_y$ is not larger than the average radius of $\mathbb{II}$. However, it is not excluded that the cost of observations in $\mathbb{II}_y$ could be much larger than the average cost of observations in $\mathbb{II}$. In the present section we study this issue.

Let $\Pi = \{N_y, \Sigma_y\}_{y \in Y}$ with $\Sigma_y = \mathrm{diag}\{\sigma_1^2, \ldots, \sigma_{n(y)}^2 (y_1, \ldots, y_{n(y)-1})\}$ be arbitrary information. The average cost of Π is given as

$$\mathrm{cost}^{\mathrm{ave}}(\Pi) = \int_Y \sum_{i=1}^{n(y)} \mathbf{c}(\sigma_i^2(y_1, \ldots, y_{i-1})) \, dy.$$

Clearly, if Π is nonadaptive then we have $\mathrm{cost}^{\mathrm{ave}}(\Pi) = \sum_{i=1}^{n} \mathbf{c}(\sigma_i^2)$.

For $a \in \mathbb{R}$ and $y^{(1)}, y^{(2)} \in Y$, let $\Pi' = \Pi'(y^{(1)}, y^{(2)}, a)$ be information defined in the following way. Denote by n_i the length of $y^{(i)}$ and by y_1 the first component of y. Let

$$Y' = \{y \in \mathbb{R}^{n_1} \mid y_1 \le a\} \cup \{y \in \mathbb{R}^{n_2} \mid y_1 > a\},$$

and for $y \in Y'$,

$$\{N_y', \Sigma_y'\} = \begin{cases} \{N_{y^{(1)}}, \Sigma_{y^{(1)}}\} & y_1 \le a, \\ \{N_{y^{(2)}}, \Sigma_{y^{(2)}}\} & y_1 > a. \end{cases}$$

We set $\Pi' = \{N_y', \Sigma_y'\}_{y \in Y'}$. Observe that the information Π' is almost nonadaptive since it uses only at most two nonadaptive sequences of observations. It turns out that the class of such information is as powerful as the class of adaptive information. That is, we have the following theorem.

Theorem 3.9.1 *Let $\Pi = \{N_y, \Sigma_y\}_{y \in Y}$ be adaptive information. Then there exist $y^{(1)}, y^{(2)} \in Y$ and $a \in \mathbb{R}$ such that for the information $\Pi' = \Pi'(y^{(1)}, y^{(2)}, a)$ we have*

$$\mathrm{cost}^{\mathrm{ave}}(\Pi') \le \mathrm{cost}^{\mathrm{ave}}(\Pi) \qquad and \qquad \mathrm{rad}^{\mathrm{ave}}(\Pi') \le \mathrm{rad}^{\mathrm{ave}}(\Pi).$$

Proof Let ω be the a priori distribution of the variable $y \mapsto \mathrm{cost}(\Pi_y) = \sum_{i=1}^{n(y)} \mathbf{c}(\sigma_i^2(y_1, \ldots, y_{i-1}))$ on $\mathbb{R}_+$, i.e.,

$$\omega(B) = \mu_1(\{y \in Y \mid \mathrm{cost}(\Pi_y) \in B\}), \qquad \forall \text{ Borel sets } B \text{ of } \mathbb{R},$$

where μ_1 is given by (3.53). Clearly,

$$\mathrm{cost}(\Pi) = \int_{\mathbb{R}_+} T \, \omega(dT). \tag{3.54}$$

The measure μ_1 can be decomposed with respect to the mapping $y \mapsto \mathrm{cost}(\Pi_y)$ as

$$\mu_1(\cdot) = \int_{\mathbb{R}_+} \mu_1(\cdot | T) \, \omega(dT),$$

where $\mu_1(\cdot|T)$ is a probability measure on Y which is supported on the set $Y_T = \{y \mid \text{cost}(\mathbb{I}_y) = T\}$, for all T such that $Y_T \neq \emptyset$. This, (3.2) and Theorem 3.4.1 yield

$$(\text{rad}^{\text{ave}}(\mathbb{I}))^2 = \int_Y (r(\nu_2(\cdot|y)))^2 \, \mu_1(dy) = \int_{\mathbb{R}_+} \psi(T) \, \omega(dT) \quad (3.55)$$

where

$$\psi(T) = \begin{cases} \int_Y (r(\nu_2(\cdot|y)))^2 \, \mu_1(dy|T) & Y_T \neq \emptyset, \\ +\infty & \text{otherwise.} \end{cases} \quad (3.56)$$

Here $\nu_2(\cdot|y) = \mu_2(S^{-1}(\cdot)|y)$ is the conditional distribution of $S(f)$ given y, and $r(\cdot)$ is the radius of a measure, see Section 3.2.

We now show that it is possible to select real numbers $0 \leq T_1 \leq T_2 < +\infty$ and $0 \leq \alpha^* \leq 1$ such that

$$\alpha^* T_1 + (1 - \alpha^*) T_2 \leq \int_{\mathbb{R}_+} T \, \omega(dT) \quad (3.57)$$

and

$$\alpha^* \psi(T_1) + (1 - \alpha^*) \psi(T_2) \leq \int_{\mathbb{R}_+} \psi(T) \, \omega(dT). \quad (3.58)$$

To this end, let $T_0 = \int_{\mathbb{R}_+} T \, \omega(dT)$ and $\psi_0 = \int_{\mathbb{R}_+} \psi(T) \, \omega(dT)$. If such numbers did not exist, for any $T > T_0$ the graph of ψ on the interval $[0, T_0]$ would lie above the line passing through the points (T_0, ψ_0) and $(T, \psi(T))$, i.e.,

$$\psi(R) > \tilde{\psi}_{\beta_T}(R) = \beta_T(R - T_0) + \psi_0, \quad \forall R \in [0, T_0],$$

where $\beta_T = (\psi(T) - \psi_0)/(T - T_0)$. Let $\beta = \inf_{T > T_0} \beta_T$. Then $\beta > -\infty$ and for all $T \geq 0$ we have $\psi(T) \geq \tilde{\psi}_\beta(T)$. Moreover, the last inequality '$\geq$' can be replaced by '$>$' on the interval $[0, T_0]$ or on $[T_0, +\infty)$. Hence we obtain

$$\int_{\mathbb{R}_+} \psi(T) \, \omega(dT) > \int_{\mathbb{R}_+} \tilde{\psi}_\beta(T) \, \omega(dT) = \psi_0 = \int_{\mathbb{R}_+} \psi(T) \, \omega(dT),$$

which is a contradiction.

Let T_1, T_2 and α^* satisfy (3.57) and (3.58). We now choose two sequences $y^{(j)}$, $j = 1, 2$, in such a way that $\text{cost}(\mathbb{I}_{y^{(j)}}) = T_j$ and

$$\int_F (r(\nu_2(\cdot|y^{(j)})))^2 \, \mu_2(df|z^{(j)}) \leq \psi(T_j),$$

as well as the number a such that

$$\frac{1}{\sqrt{2\pi\sigma_*^2}} \int_{-\infty}^{a} \exp\left\{\frac{-x^2}{2\sigma_*^2}\right\} dx = \alpha^*,$$

where $\sigma_*^2 = L_1(C_\mu L_1) + \sigma_1^2$ is the variance of the Gaussian random variable y_1. From (3.54) to (3.58) it now follows that for the information $\mathbb{II}' = \mathbb{II}'(y^{(1)}, y^{(2)}, a)$ we have

$$\begin{aligned}
\text{cost}(\mathbb{II}') &= \alpha^* \text{cost}(\mathbb{II}_{y^{(1)}}) + (1 - \alpha^*)\text{cost}(\mathbb{II}_{y^{(2)}}) \\
&\leq \int_{\mathbb{R}_+} T\,\omega(dT) = \text{cost}(\mathbb{II})
\end{aligned}$$

and

$$\begin{aligned}
\left(\text{rad}^{\text{ave}}(\mathbb{II}')\right)^2 &= \alpha^*\left(\text{rad}^{\text{ave}}(\mathbb{II}_{y^{(1)}})\right)^2 + (1 - \alpha^*)\left(\text{rad}^{\text{ave}}(\mathbb{II}_{y^{(2)}})\right)^2 \\
&\leq \alpha^* \psi(T_1) + (1 - \alpha^*)\psi(T_2) \leq \int_{\mathbb{R}} \psi(T)\,\omega(dT) \\
&= \left(\text{rad}^{\text{ave}}(\mathbb{II})\right)^2,
\end{aligned}$$

as claimed. $\qquad\qquad\square$

We now make the following observation. Assume without loss of generality that $\text{cost}(\mathbb{II}_{y^{(1)}}) \leq \text{cost}(\mathbb{II})$ and $\text{rad}^{\text{ave}}(\mathbb{II}_{y^{(2)}}) \leq \text{rad}^{\text{ave}}(\mathbb{II})$ (if this were not true, it would be possible to select $y^{(1)} = y^{(2)}$). Let $0 < p < 1$. Then for $\alpha^* \geq p$ we have

$$\text{cost}(\mathbb{II}_{y^{(1)}}) \leq \text{cost}(\mathbb{II}) \quad \text{and} \quad \text{rad}^{\text{ave}}(\mathbb{II}_{y^{(1)}}) \leq \frac{1}{\sqrt{p}}\text{rad}^{\text{ave}}(\mathbb{II}),$$

while for $\alpha^* < p$,

$$\text{rad}^{\text{ave}}(\mathbb{II}_{y^{(2)}}) \leq \text{rad}^{\text{ave}}(\mathbb{II}) \quad \text{and} \quad \text{cost}(\mathbb{II}_{y^{(2)}}) \leq \frac{1}{1-p}\text{cost}(\mathbb{II}).$$

This yields the following corollary.

Corollary 3.9.1 *Let* $0 < p < 1$. *For any adaptive information* $\mathbb{II} = \{\mathbb{II}_y\}_{y \in Y}$ *there exists* $y^* \in Y$ *such that*

$$\text{cost}(\mathbb{II}_{y^*}) \leq \frac{1}{1-p}\text{cost}(\mathbb{II}) \quad \text{and} \quad \text{rad}^{\text{ave}}(\mathbb{II}_{y^*}) \leq \frac{1}{\sqrt{p}}\text{rad}^{\text{ave}}(\mathbb{II}).$$

In particular, one can take $p = (3 - \sqrt{5})/2$ *to get*

$$\text{cost}(\mathbb{II}_{y^*}) \leq q \cdot \text{cost}(\mathbb{II}) \quad \text{and} \quad \text{rad}^{\text{ave}}(\mathbb{II}_{y^*}) \leq q \cdot \text{rad}^{\text{ave}}(\mathbb{II}),$$

where $q = (p - 1)^{-1} = 1/\sqrt{p} = 2/(\sqrt{5} - 1) = 1.6....$

3.9.2 Complexity bounds

We are now ready to present bounds on the average ε-complexity of linear problems with Gaussian measures. Let

$$\mathrm{IC}^{\mathrm{non}}(\varepsilon) \; = \; \inf\left\{\,\mathrm{cost}(\mathbb{II}) \;\middle|\; \mathbb{II} \text{ nonadaptive and } \mathrm{rad}^{\mathrm{ave}}(\mathbb{II}) \le \varepsilon \,\right\}$$

be the (nonadaptive) information ε-complexity. The following lemma corresponds to Lemma 2.9.1 of the worst case setting.

Lemma 3.9.1 *(i) For any $0 < p < 1$ we have*

$$\mathrm{Comp}(\varepsilon) \; \ge \; (1-p)\cdot\mathrm{IC}^{\mathrm{non}}\left(\frac{\varepsilon}{\sqrt{p}}\right).$$

(ii) Let $\rho \ge 1$. Suppose there exists nonadaptive information $\mathbb{II}_\varepsilon$ using $n(\varepsilon)$ observations such that $\mathrm{cost}(\mathbb{II}_\varepsilon) \le \rho\cdot\mathrm{IC}^{\mathrm{non}}(\varepsilon)$. Then

$$\mathrm{Comp}(\varepsilon) \; \le \; \rho\cdot\mathrm{IC}^{\mathrm{non}}(\varepsilon) + (2\,n(\varepsilon) - 1)\,\mathbf{g}.$$

Proof Part (i) follows immediately from Corollary 3.9.1. To see (ii) observe that for the spline algorithm we have $\mathrm{e}^{\mathrm{ave}}(\mathbb{II}_\varepsilon, \varphi_{\mathrm{spl}}) = \mathrm{rad}^{\mathrm{ave}}(\mathbb{II}_\varepsilon)$. Since φ_{spl} is linear, the complexity of φ_{spl} using $\mathbb{II}_\varepsilon$ is at most $\mathrm{cost}(\mathbb{II}_\varepsilon) + (2\,n(\varepsilon) - 1)\mathbf{g}$. $\qquad\square$

Lemma 3.9.1 immediately yields the following theorem.

Theorem 3.9.2 *Suppose the assumptions of Lemma 3.9.1 are fulfilled for all ε and some ρ independent of ε. If, in addition,*

$$\mathrm{IC}^{\mathrm{non}}(\varepsilon) \; = \; O(\mathrm{IC}^{\mathrm{non}}(p^{-1/2}\varepsilon)) \quad\text{and}\quad n(\varepsilon) \; = \; O(\mathrm{IC}^{\mathrm{non}}(\varepsilon)),$$

then

$$\mathrm{Comp}(\varepsilon) \; \asymp \; \mathrm{IC}^{\mathrm{non}}(\varepsilon)$$

as $\varepsilon \to 0^+$.

Recall that the assumption $n(\varepsilon) = O(\mathrm{IC}^{\mathrm{non}}(\varepsilon))$ is satisfied when the cost function is bounded from below by a positive constant, $\mathbf{c}(\sigma^2) \ge c_0 > 0$. The second assumption, $\mathrm{IC}^{\mathrm{non}}(\varepsilon) = O(\mathrm{IC}^{\mathrm{non}}(p^{-1/2}\varepsilon))$, means that $\mathrm{IC}^{\mathrm{non}}(\varepsilon)$ increases at most polynomially in $1/\varepsilon$ as $\varepsilon \to 0^+$. This condition can often be replaced by the semiconvexity of $\mathrm{IC}^{\mathrm{non}}(\sqrt{\varepsilon})$. That is, we have the following lemma.

Lemma 3.9.2 Let $\varepsilon_0 = \int_F \|S(f)\|^2 \mu(df)$. Suppose that $\mathrm{IC}^{\mathrm{non}}(\sqrt{\varepsilon})$ is a semiconvex function of ε on the interval $[0, \varepsilon_0]$, i.e., there exist $0 < \alpha \leq \beta$ and a convex function $h : [0, \varepsilon_0] \to [0, +\infty]$ such that

$$\alpha \cdot h(\varepsilon) \leq \mathrm{IC}^{\mathrm{non}}(\sqrt{\varepsilon}) \leq \beta \cdot h(\varepsilon), \qquad \forall 0 \leq \varepsilon \leq \varepsilon_0.$$

Then

$$\mathrm{Comp}(\varepsilon) \geq \frac{\alpha}{\beta} \cdot \mathrm{IC}^{\mathrm{non}}(\varepsilon), \qquad \forall 0 \leq \varepsilon \leq \varepsilon_0.$$

Proof Let $\mathbb{II} = \{\mathbb{II}_y\}_{y \in Y}$ be arbitrary adaptive information with radius $\mathrm{rad}^{\mathrm{ave}}(\mathbb{II}) \leq \varepsilon \leq \varepsilon_0$. Let

$$\psi(y) = (r(\mu_2(\cdot | y)))^2.$$

Clearly, $\psi(y) \leq \varepsilon_0$. Define the probability measure ω on $\mathbb{R}$ as

$$\omega(B) = \mu_1(\{y \in Y \mid \psi(y) \in B\}), \qquad \forall \text{ Borel sets } B \text{ of } \mathbb{R}.$$

The convexity of h and the inequality

$$\mathrm{cost}(\mathbb{II}_y) \geq \mathrm{IC}^{\mathrm{non}}\left(\sqrt{\psi(y)}\right) \geq \alpha \cdot h(\psi(y)),$$

yield

$$\begin{aligned}
\mathrm{cost}(\mathbb{II}) &= \int_Y \mathrm{cost}(\mathbb{II}_y)\,\mu_1(dy) \geq \alpha \cdot \int_Y h(\psi(y))\,\mu_1(dy) \\
&= \alpha \cdot \int_{\mathbb{R}_+} h(x)\,\omega(dx) \geq \alpha \cdot h\left(\int_{\mathbb{R}_+} x\,\omega(dx)\right) \\
&= \alpha \cdot h\left((\mathrm{rad}^{\mathrm{ave}}(\mathbb{II}))^2\right) \geq \frac{\alpha}{\beta} \cdot \mathrm{IC}^{\mathrm{non}}(e^{\mathrm{ave}}(\mathbb{II})) \\
&\geq \frac{\alpha}{\beta} \cdot \mathrm{IC}^{\mathrm{non}}(\varepsilon).
\end{aligned}$$

Since $\mathbb{II}$ was arbitrary and

$$\mathrm{Comp}(\varepsilon) \geq \inf\{\,\mathrm{cost}(\mathbb{II}) \mid \mathrm{rad}^{\mathrm{ave}}(\mathbb{II}) \leq \varepsilon\,\},$$

the lemma follows. $\qquad\square$

The essence of the proven estimates is that it is enough to know the information ε-complexity to obtain bounds on the problem complexity. As in the worst case setting, $\mathrm{IC}^{\mathrm{non}}(\varepsilon)$ can be derived as the inverse of the Tth minimal radius. More precisely, the Tth minimal (average) radius is defined as

$$\mathrm{R}(T) = \inf\left\{r_n^{\mathrm{ave}}(\mathrm{diag}\{\sigma_1^2, \ldots, \sigma_n^2\}) \,\Big|\, n \geq 1,\ \sum_{i=1}^n \mathrm{c}(\sigma_i^2) \leq T\right\}.$$

Knowing $R(T)$ we can find its inverse

$$R^{-1}(\varepsilon) = \inf\{T \mid R(T) \le \varepsilon\}.$$

If this function is semicontinuous then, similarly to Lemma 2.9.2,

$$IC^{non}(\varepsilon) \asymp R^{-1}(\varepsilon) \qquad \text{as} \quad \varepsilon \to 0.$$

Notes and remarks

NR 3.9.1 First results on adaption versus nonadaption in the average case setting were obtained by Wasilkowski (1986) who studied exact information, see also Traub *et al.* (1988, Sect. 5.6 of Chap. 6). The results on adaptive information with noise have been taken mainly from Plaskota (1995a).

NR 3.9.2 Let

$$IC^{ad}(\varepsilon) = \inf\{\,\text{cost}(\Pi) \mid \Pi \text{ adaptive and } rad^{ave}(\Pi) \le \varepsilon\,\} \qquad (3.59)$$

be the adaptive information ε-complexity. In terms of $IC^{ad}(\varepsilon)$ and $IC^{non}(\varepsilon)$, the results of Theorem 3.9.1 mean that for any ε and $0 < p < 1$, at least one of the two following inequalities holds:

$$IC^{ad}(\varepsilon) \ge IC^{non}\left(\frac{\varepsilon}{\sqrt{p}}\right)$$

or

$$IC^{ad}(\varepsilon) \ge (1-p)\,IC^{non}(\varepsilon).$$

It turns out that this estimate is sharp. More precisely, it was proven by Plaskota (1993b) that for exact information (i.e. for the cost function $c \equiv const > 0$) the following theorem holds.

Let the nonzero solution operator $S : F \to G$ and the Gaussian measure μ with $\dim(\text{supp}\,\mu) = +\infty$ be given. Then there exists a class $\Lambda \subset F^*$ of permissible information functionals such that:

(i) For any $\alpha, \beta > 0$ satisfying $\alpha + \beta > 1$, and for any $\varepsilon_0 > 0$, there exists $\varepsilon < \varepsilon_0$ such that

$$IC^{ad}(\varepsilon) < IC^{non}\left(\frac{\varepsilon}{\sqrt{\alpha}}\right) \qquad \text{and} \qquad IC^{ad}(\varepsilon) < \beta \cdot IC^{non}(\varepsilon).$$

(ii) For any $\gamma > 0$ and $\varepsilon_0 > 0$ there exists $\varepsilon < \varepsilon_0$ such that

$$IC^{ad}(\varepsilon) < IC^{non}\left(\frac{\varepsilon}{\gamma}\right).$$

(iii) For any $\gamma > 0$ and $\varepsilon_0 > 0$ there exists $\varepsilon < \varepsilon_0$ such that

$$IC^{ad}(\varepsilon) < \gamma \cdot IC^{non}(\varepsilon).$$

Exercises

E 3.9.1 Show that the adaptive information ε-complexity defined in (3.59) satisfies

$$IC^{ad}(\varepsilon) = \inf\{\alpha\,IC^{non}(\varepsilon_1) + (1-\alpha)\,IC^{non}(\varepsilon_2)\mid$$
$$0 \le \varepsilon_1 \le \varepsilon \le \varepsilon_2,\ \alpha\varepsilon_1^2 + (1-\alpha)\varepsilon_2^2 = \varepsilon^2\,\},$$

and that $IC^{ad}(\sqrt{\varepsilon})$ is a convex function of ε.

E 3.9.2 Suppose that the function $T \to R^2(T)$ is semiconvex, i.e., there exist $T_0 \ge 0$, $0 < \alpha \le \beta$, and a convex function $h : [0,+\infty) \to [0,+\infty)$ such that

$$\alpha \cdot h(T) \le R^2(T), \qquad \forall T \ge 0,$$

and

$$R^2(T) \le \beta \cdot h(T), \qquad \forall T \ge T_0.$$

Show that then for any information Π with $\mathrm{cost}(\Pi) \le T$ we have

$$\mathrm{rad}^{ave}(\Pi) \ge \sqrt{\frac{\alpha}{\beta}} \cdot R(T), \qquad \forall T \ge T_0.$$

3.10 Complexity of special problems

In this section we analyze the ε-complexity of the problems considered in Section 3.8.

3.10.1 Linear problems with Gaussian measures

We begin with the problem defined in Subsection 3.8.1. That is, $S : F \to G$ is an arbitrary continuous linear operator, μ is a zero-mean Gaussian measure, and the class Λ consists of linear functionals bounded by 1 in the μ-norm. The technique of evaluating $\mathrm{Comp}(\varepsilon)$ will be similar to that used in Subsection 2.10.1 where the corresponding problem in the worst case setting is studied. Therefore we only sketch some proofs.

For a given cost function $\mathbf{c}$, we let $\tilde{c}(x) = c(x^{-1})$, $0 < x < +\infty$. We assume that the function $\tilde{c}$ is concave or convex, and $c(0) = +\infty$.

Recall that $\{\xi_i\}_{i=1}^{\dim G}$ is the complete orthonormal system of eigenelements of $SC_\mu S^*$, $\lambda_1 \ge \lambda_2 \ge \cdots \ge 0$ are the corresponding eigenvalues, and $K_i^* = \lambda_i^{-1/2} S^* \xi_i$. The function Ω is given by (3.17).

Lemma 3.10.1 *The Tth minimal radius is equal to*

$$R(T) = \sqrt{\inf \Omega(\eta_1, \ldots, \eta_n)},$$

where the infimum is taken over all n and $\eta_i \ge 0$, $1 \le i \le n$, satisfying *(a1) for concave $\tilde{c}$*

$$\sum_{i=1}^{n} \tilde{c}(\eta_i) \leq T,$$

(b1) for convex $\tilde{c}$

$$n\,\tilde{c}\left(\frac{1}{n}\sum_{i=1}^{n}\eta_i\right) \leq T.$$

Moreover, if the infimum is achieved for n^* and $\eta^* = (\eta_1^*, \ldots, \eta_{n^*}^*)$, then

$$R(T) = \mathrm{rad}^{\mathrm{ave}}(\{N_T, \Sigma_T\})$$

where
(a2) for concave $\tilde{c}$

$$\Sigma_T = \left[1/\sqrt{\eta_1^*}, \ldots, 1/\sqrt{\eta_{n^*}^*}\right], \qquad N_T = [K_1^*, \ldots, K_{n^*}^*],$$

(b2) for convex $\tilde{c}$

$$\Sigma_T = \left[\underbrace{1/\sqrt{\eta_0^*}, \ldots, 1/\sqrt{\eta_0^*}}_{n^*}\right], \qquad N_T = [L_1^\Sigma, \ldots, L_{n^*}^\Sigma],$$

where $\eta_0^* = (1/n^*)\sum_{i=1}^{n^*}\eta_i^*$ and the L_i^Σs are as in Theorem 3.8.1 with $\sigma_i^2 = 1/\eta_0^*$, $\forall i$.

Proof The proof goes like the proof of Lemma 2.10.1. If $\tilde{c}$ is concave then for any n and $\eta_1, \ldots, \eta_n$ satisfying (3.18) we have $\sum_{i=1}^{n}\tilde{c}(\eta_i) \leq \sum_{i=1}^{n}\tilde{c}(\sigma_i^{-2})$. This yields

$$R^2(T) = \inf\left\{(r_n^{\mathrm{ave}}(\mathrm{diag}\{\sigma_1^2, \ldots, \sigma_n^2\}))^2 \,\Big|\, n \geq 1, \sum_{i=1}^{n}c(\sigma_i^2) \leq T\right\}$$

$$= \inf\left\{\Omega(\eta_1, \ldots, \eta_n) \,\Big|\, n \geq 1, \sum_{i=1}^{n}\tilde{c}(\eta_i) \leq T\right\}.$$

On the other hand, for convex $\tilde{c}$ we have $\sum_{i=1}^{n}\tilde{c}(\eta_i) \geq n\,\tilde{c}(\eta_0)$ where $\eta_0 = (1/n)\sum_{i=1}^{n}\eta_i$. Hence

$$R^2(T) = \inf\left\{(r_n^{\mathrm{ave}}(\sigma^2 I))^2 \,\Big|\, n \geq 1, n\,c(\sigma^2) \leq T\right\}$$

$$= \inf\left\{\Omega(\eta_1, \ldots, \eta_n) \,\Big|\, n \geq 1, n\,\tilde{c}\left(\frac{1}{n}\sum_{i=1}^{n}\eta_i\right) \leq T\right\}.$$

The rest of the lemma follows from Theorem 3.8.1. $\square$

Consider the cost function $\mathbf{c} = \mathbf{c}_{\text{lin}}$. That is, $\mathbf{c}_{\text{lin}}(\sigma^2) = \sigma^{-2}$ for $\sigma^2 > 0$, and $\mathbf{c}_{\text{lin}}(0) = +\infty$. This cost function possesses a property similar to that of the worst case, i.e., the quality of n observations of $L(f)$ with precisions σ_i^2 depends only on the total cost $\sum_{i=1}^{n} \sigma_i^{-2}$, and not on their number n. Owing to Lemma 3.10.1 we have

$$R^2(\mathbf{c}_{\text{lin}}; T) = \frac{\left(\sum_{i=1}^{n} \lambda_i^{1/2}\right)^2}{T + n} + \sum_{j=n+1}^{\infty} \lambda_j, \tag{3.60}$$

where $n = n(T)$ is the largest integer satisfying

$$\sum_{i=1}^{n} \lambda_i^{1/2} \leq \lambda_n^{1/2} (T + n). \tag{3.61}$$

Observe that $R(\mathbf{c}_{\text{lin}}; T)$ is well defined, since for large n the inequality (3.61) is not satisfied. We also have that $\psi(T) = R^2(\mathbf{c}_{\text{lin}}; T)$ is a strictly convex function. To see this, for $n \geq 1$ we let

$$T_n = \sum_{j=1}^{n} \left(\frac{\lambda_j^{1/2}}{\lambda_n^{1/2}} - 1\right) \tag{3.62}$$

(if $\lambda_n = 0$ then $T_n = +\infty$). Then $n = n(T)$ iff $T \in [T_n, T_{n+1})$. On each interval (T_n, T_{n+1}) the function $\psi(T)$ is convex. Hence for convexity of ψ on $[0, +\infty)$ it suffices that ψ and $d\psi/dT$ are continuous at T_n. Indeed, in view of (3.62) we have

$$\psi(T_n^+) = \lambda_n(n + T_n) + \sum_{j=n+1}^{\infty} \lambda_j$$

$$= \lambda_n(n - 1 + T_n) + \sum_{j=n}^{\infty} \lambda_j = \psi(T_n^-)$$

and

$$\frac{d\psi}{dT}(T_n^+) = -\lambda_n = \frac{d\psi}{dT}(T_n^-).$$

Convexity of $R^2(\mathbf{c}_{\text{lin}}; T)$ implies convexity of $\text{IC}^{\text{non}}(\mathbf{c}_{\text{lin}}; \sqrt{\varepsilon})$. Hence owing to Theorem 3.9.2 we have

$$\text{IC}^{\text{non}}(\mathbf{c}_{\text{lin}}; \varepsilon) = \inf\{T \geq 0 \mid R(T) \leq \varepsilon\}.$$

If the number $n = n(T)$ defined by (3.61) satisfies $n(T) = O(T)$ as $T \to +\infty$, then $\text{IC}(\mathbf{c}_{\text{lin}}; \varepsilon)$ is attained by information that uses $O(T)$ observations, and the ε-complexity behaves as $\text{IC}(\mathbf{c}_{\text{lin}}; \varepsilon)$.

Observe that the condition $n(T) = O(T)$ means that zero is not an attraction point of the sequence $(1/n) \sum_{j=1}^{n} \left(\lambda_j^{1/2} / \lambda_n^{1/2} - 1 \right)$. When this is the case, we can show that c_{lin} is the 'worst' cost function—the result corresponding to Lemma 2.10.2 of the worst case setting.

Lemma 3.10.2 *Let* c *be an arbitrary cost function. Let* σ_0^2 *be such that* $c(\sigma_0^2) < +\infty$. *If there exists* $a > 0$ *such that for sufficiently large* n

$$\frac{1}{n} \sum_{j=1}^{n} \left(\frac{\lambda_j^{1/2}}{\lambda_n^{1/2}} - 1 \right) \geq a, \tag{3.63}$$

then for small $\varepsilon > 0$ *we have*

$$\text{Comp}(c; \varepsilon) \leq M \cdot \text{Comp}(c_{\text{lin}}; \varepsilon)$$

where $M = M(c, \sigma_0^2) = a^{-1} \lceil 2 a \sigma_0^2 \rceil (c(\sigma_0^2) + 2g)$.

Proof Let n_0 be such that (3.63) holds for all $n \geq n_0$. Let ε_0 satisfy $\varepsilon_0 \leq R(c_{\text{lin}}; a n_0)$ and $\text{IC}^{\text{non}}(c_{\text{lin}}; \varepsilon_0) \geq a$. We shall show that the required inequality holds for all $\varepsilon < \varepsilon_0$. To this end, we proceed similarly to the proof of Lemma 2.10.2.

We choose information $\mathbb{N}$ for which $\text{rad}^{\text{ave}}(\mathbb{N}) = \varepsilon$ and $\text{cost}(c_{\text{lin}}; \mathbb{N}) = \text{IC}^{\text{non}}(c_{\text{lin}}; \varepsilon)$. Owing to (3.63), we can assume that the number of observations in $\mathbb{N}$ is $n = \lfloor \text{IC}^{\text{non}}(c_{\text{lin}}; \varepsilon)/a \rfloor$ and they are performed with the same variance $\sigma^{-2} = \text{IC}^{\text{non}}(c_{\text{lin}}; \varepsilon)/n$. Let $k = \lfloor 2a\sigma_0^2 \rfloor$. Then for the information $\tilde{\mathbb{N}}$ which repeats the same observations as $\mathbb{N}$ k times but with variance $\tilde{\sigma}^2$, $\tilde{\sigma}^{-2} = \sigma^{-2}/k$, we have $\text{rad}^{\text{ave}}(\tilde{\mathbb{N}}) = \text{rad}^{\text{ave}}(\mathbb{N})$ and

$$\text{cost}(c; \tilde{\mathbb{N}}) \leq K n \tilde{c} \left(\frac{\text{IC}^{\text{non}}(c_{\text{lin}}; \varepsilon)}{k n} \right)$$
$$\leq k n \tilde{c}(2a/k) \leq a^{-1} k c(\sigma_0^2) \text{IC}^{\text{non}}(c_{\text{lin}}; \varepsilon).$$

Hence

$$\text{Comp}(c; \varepsilon) \leq a^{-1} k c(\sigma_0^2) \text{Comp}(c_{\text{lin}}; \varepsilon) + (2 k n - 1)g$$
$$\leq a^{-1} k (c(\sigma_0^2) + 2g) \text{Comp}(c_{\text{lin}}; \varepsilon),$$

as claimed.   □

We note that the condition (3.63) holds for many sequences $\{\lambda_j\}$ of eigenvalues. For instance, for $\lambda_j = j^{-p}$ with $p > 1$ we have

$$\lim_{n \to \infty} \frac{1}{n} \sum_{j=1}^{n} \left(\frac{\lambda_j^{1/2}}{\lambda_n^{1/2}} - 1 \right) = \begin{cases} p/(2-p) & 1 < p < 2, \\ +\infty & p \geq 2. \end{cases}$$

Hence we can take $a = 1$. This means, in particular, that $\mathrm{Comp}(\mathbf{c}_{\mathrm{lin}}; \varepsilon)$ can be achieved by using no more than $\lfloor \mathrm{Comp}(\mathbf{c}_{\mathrm{lin}}; \varepsilon) \rfloor$ observations.

There are, however, sequences $\{\lambda_j\}$ for which (3.63) is not satisfied, and consequently the Tth minimal radius cannot be achieved by information using $O(T)$ observations. An example is given in E 3.10.2.

Clearly, when the cost function is bounded from below by a positive constant, the lower bound (up to a constant) on the ε-complexity is provided by $\mathrm{Comp}^{\mathrm{non}}(\mathbf{c}_{\mathrm{exa}}; \varepsilon)$ where $\mathbf{c}_{\mathrm{exa}} \equiv 1$ is the cost function for exact information. In this case, letting $n = n(\varepsilon) \geq 0$ be the minimal n for which

$$\sum_{i=n+1}^{\infty} \lambda_i \leq \varepsilon^2,$$

we have

$$\mathrm{IC}^{\mathrm{non}}(\mathbf{c}_{\mathrm{exa}}; \varepsilon) = n(\varepsilon).$$

Note that $\mathrm{IC}^{\mathrm{non}}(\mathbf{c}_{\mathrm{exa}}; \sqrt{\varepsilon})$ is a semiconvex, but *not* a strictly convex function.

Assume now that the cost function is given as

$$\mathbf{c}_q(\sigma^2) = \begin{cases} (1 + \sigma^{-2})^q & \sigma^2 > 0, \\ +\infty & \sigma^2 = 0, \end{cases}$$

where $q \geq 0$. Note that for $q = 0$ we have exact information. Assuming (3.63), for $q > 1$ we have $\mathrm{Comp}(q; \varepsilon) \asymp \mathrm{Comp}(1; \varepsilon)$. Therefore in the following calculations we restrict ourselves to $0 < q \leq 1$. Using Lemma 3.10.1 we obtain

$$R(q; T)^2 = \left(\frac{1}{T}\right)^{1/q} \left(\sum_{i=1}^{n} \lambda_i^r\right)^{1/r} + \sum_{j=n+1}^{\infty} \lambda_j \qquad (3.64)$$

where $r = q/(1 + q)$ and $n = n(T)$ is the largest integer satisfying

$$\left(1 + \sum_{i=1}^{n-1} \left(\frac{\lambda_i}{\lambda_n}\right)^r\right)^{1/r} - \left(\sum_{i=1}^{n-1} \left(\frac{\lambda_i}{\lambda_n}\right)^r\right)^{1/r} \leq T^{1/q}.$$

Furthermore, $R(q; T)$ is attained by observing $K_1^*, \ldots, K_n^*$ with variances

$$\sigma_i^2 = \left(\lambda_i^{1/(1+q)} \left(\frac{T}{\sum_{j=1}^{n} \lambda_j^r}\right)^{1/q} - 1\right)^{-1}, \qquad 1 \leq i \leq n.$$

Consider now a problem for which the eigenvalues

$$\lambda_j \asymp \left(\frac{\ln^s j}{j}\right)^p$$

where $p > 1$ and $s \geq 0$. Recall that such behavior of the eigenvalues can be observed for the function approximation with respect to the Wiener sheet measure, see NR 3.3.5. Then we have

$$R(q, p, s; T) \asymp \begin{cases} (1/T)^{1/\tilde{q}} & (p-1)\tilde{q} > 1, \\ (1/T)^{p-1} \ln^{(s+1)p} T & (p-1)\tilde{q} = 1, \\ (1/T)^{p-1} \ln^{sp} T & 0 \leq (p-1)\tilde{q} < 1, \end{cases}$$

as $T \to +\infty$, where $\tilde{q} = \min\{1, q\}$. We check that $R(q, p, s; T)^2$ is a semiconvex function of T and that the sequence $\{\lambda_j\}$ satisfies (3.63). Hence $\mathrm{Comp}^{\mathrm{non}}(q, p, s; \sqrt{\varepsilon})$ is also semiconvex and we obtain the following formulas for the ε-complexity.

Theorem 3.10.1

$$\mathrm{Comp}^{\mathrm{ave}}(q, p, s; \varepsilon)$$

$$\asymp \begin{cases} (1/\varepsilon)^{2\tilde{q}} & (p-1)\tilde{q} > 1, \\ (1/\varepsilon)^{2/(p-1)} (\ln(1/\varepsilon))^{(s+1)p/(p-1)} & (p-1)\tilde{q} = 1, \\ (1/\varepsilon)^{2/(p-1)} (\ln(1/\varepsilon))^{sp/(p-1)} & 0 \leq (p-1)\tilde{q} < 1, \end{cases}$$

as $\varepsilon \to 0$.

Thus the dominating factor of the complexity is the exponent of $1/\varepsilon$. If $p > 2$ then this exponent is $2/(p-1)$ for $0 \leq q \leq 1/(p-1)$, $2q$ for $1/(p-1) < q < 1$, and 2 for $q \geq 2$. If $0 < p \leq 2$ then the exponent is $2/p$ and does not depend on q. In the latter case, the complexity behaves independently of the cost function. The situation is then similar to that in the corresponding problem of the worst case setting, see Theorem 2.10.1. The only difference is that p is replaced by $p-1$.

3.10.2 Approximation and integration on the Wiener space

We pass to the approximation and integration problems of Subsection 3.8.2. Recall that both problems are defined on the Wiener space of continuous functions and information consists of noisy observations of function values. In that subsection we proved tight bounds on the minimal errors $r_n^{\mathrm{ave}}(\mathrm{App}, \sigma^2)$ and $r_n^{\mathrm{ave}}(\mathrm{Int}, \sigma^2)$ with $\sigma \geq 0$. They allow us to find complexity for fixed observations with variance σ_0^2 or, in other words, when the cost function is $c_{fix}(\sigma^2) = c_0 > 0$ for $\sigma^2 \geq \sigma_0^2$, and $c_{fix}(\sigma^2) = +\infty$ for $\sigma^2 < \sigma_0^2$. That is, we have $R(c_{fix}; T) = r_n^{ave}(\sigma_0^2)$ with $n = n(T) = \lfloor T/c_0 \rfloor$, and owing to Corollary 3.8.2,

$$IC^{non}(App, c_{fix}; \varepsilon) \approx c_0 \left(\frac{1}{6\varepsilon^2} + p_n^4 \frac{\sigma_0^2}{4\varepsilon^4} \right)$$

and

$$IC^{non}(Int, c_{fix}; \varepsilon) \approx c_0 \left(\frac{1}{2\sqrt{3}\,\varepsilon} + q_n^2 \frac{\sigma_0^2}{\varepsilon^2} \right)$$

where $p_n, q_n \in [1/\sqrt{3}, 1]$. Since for both problems $IC^{non}(c_{fix}; \sqrt{\varepsilon})$ is a semiconvex function, the last estimates with '$\approx$' replaced by '$\asymp$' also hold for the problem complexity.

It turns out that similar bounds can be proven for the cost function $c_{lin}(\sigma^2) = \sigma^{-2}$. Indeed, the upper bound on $Comp(c_{lin}; \varepsilon)$ is provided by $Comp(c_{fix}; \varepsilon)$ with $\sigma_0 = 1 = c_0$, while the lower bound follows from the following lemma.

Lemma 3.10.3 *For all T we have*

$$(R(App, c_{lin}; T))^2 \geq \frac{1}{6\sqrt{T}} - \frac{1}{6T}$$

and

$$(R(Int, c_{lin}; T))^2 \geq \frac{1}{3(1 + T)}.$$

Proof Let Π be arbitrary nonadaptive information using observations at t_is with variances σ_i^2, $1 \leq i \leq n$, such that

$$cost(c_{lin}; \Pi) = \sum_{i=1}^n \sigma_i^{-2} \leq T.$$

Consider first the approximation problem. Proceeding exactly as in the proof of Lemma 3.8.3 we can show the following generalization of that lemma: namely, for any $0 \leq a < t < b \leq 1$, the covariance kernel of the conditional distribution, $R_N(t, t)$, satisfies

$$R_N(t, t) \geq \frac{\psi(t)}{1 + T_{ab}\psi(t)}, \tag{3.65}$$

where $\psi(t) = (t - a)(b - t)/(b - a)$, $T_{ab} = \sum \sigma_i^{-2}$, and the summation is taken over all i such that $t_i \in (a, b)$.

We now use (3.65) to obtain a lower bound on $R(App, c_{lin}; T)$. To this end, we divide the unit interval into k equal subintervals (u_{i-1}, u_i), $1 \leq i \leq k$. For $1 \leq i \leq n$, let $T_i = \sum_{j \in A_i} \sigma_j^2$ where

$$A_i = \{j \mid 1 \leq j \leq n, t_j \in (u_{i-1}, u_i)\}.$$

Denoting $\psi_i(t) = (t - u_{i-1})(u_i - t)/(u_i - u_{i-1})$ and applying (3.31) and (3.65) we obtain

$$(\mathrm{rad}^{\mathrm{ave}}(\mathrm{App}, \mathrm{II}))^2 \geq \sum_{i=1}^{k} \int_{u_{i-1}}^{u_i} \frac{\psi_i(t)}{1 + T_i/(4k)} \, dt = \frac{2}{3k} \sum_{i=1}^{k} \frac{1}{T_i + 4k}.$$

The last quantity, as a function of the nonnegative arguments $T_1, \ldots, T_k$, $\sum_{i=1}^{k} T_i \leq T$, is minimized for $T_i = T/k$. Hence, for any k,

$$(\mathrm{rad}^{\mathrm{ave}}(\mathrm{App}, \mathrm{II}))^2 \geq \frac{2k}{3(T + 4k^2)}.$$

Taking $k = \lfloor \sqrt{T/4} \rfloor$ we obtain the desired bound.

For integration we have

$$(\mathrm{rad}^{\mathrm{ave}}(\mathrm{Int}, \mathrm{II}))^2 \geq \frac{\lambda_1}{1 + T}$$

where $\lambda_1 = \int_F \mathrm{Int}^2(f) \, w(df) = 1/3$. This completes the proof. $\square$

Thus we have proven the following theorem.

Theorem 3.10.2 *For the cost function* c_{lin} *and* c_{fix} *with* $\sigma_0 > 0$ *we have*

$$\mathrm{Comp}^{\mathrm{ave}}(\mathrm{App}, c_{\mathrm{fix}}; \varepsilon) \asymp \mathrm{Comp}^{\mathrm{ave}}(\mathrm{App}, c_{\mathrm{lin}}; \varepsilon) \asymp \varepsilon^{-4}$$

and

$$\mathrm{Comp}^{\mathrm{ave}}(\mathrm{Int}, c_{\mathrm{fix}}; \varepsilon) \asymp \mathrm{Comp}^{\mathrm{ave}}(\mathrm{Int}, c_{\mathrm{lin}}; \varepsilon) \asymp \varepsilon^{-2},$$

as $\varepsilon \to 0^+$.

Notes and remarks

NR 3.10.1   Most of Subsection 3.10.1 is based on Plaskota (1995a). Subsection 3.10.2 is new.

NR 3.10.2   We can apply Theorem 3.10.1 to the multivariate approximation with respect to the Wiener sheet measure, i.e., to the problem formally defined in NR 3.8.4. We obtain

$$\text{Comp}^{\text{ave}}(\varepsilon)$$
$$\asymp \begin{cases} (1/\varepsilon)^{2\tilde{q}} & \tilde{q} > (r + 1/2)^{-1}, \\ (1/\varepsilon)^{1/(r+1/2)} \left(\ln(1/\varepsilon)\right)^{k(r+1)/(r+1/2)} & \tilde{q} = (r + 1/2)^{-1}, \\ (1/\varepsilon)^{1/(r+1/2)} \left(\ln(1/\varepsilon)\right)^{(k-1)(r+1)/(r+1/2)} & \tilde{q} < (r + 1/2)^{-1}, \end{cases}$$

where k and r are as in NR 3.8.4, and $\tilde{q}$ is as in Theorem 3.10.1.

NR 3.10.3 Complexity for the function approximation and integration with respect to the r-fold Wiener measure with $r \geq 1$ can be derived from Plaskota (1992, 1995b) and Ritter (1994), see also NR 3.8.7. That is, suppose that the class Λ consists of function values and derivatives of order at most r, and the cost function $\mathbf{c} = \mathbf{c}_{\text{fix}}$, i.e., observations are performed with the same variance $\sigma_0^2 \geq 0$ and cost c_0. Then

$$\text{Comp}^{\text{ave}}(\text{App}; \varepsilon) \asymp \frac{\sigma_0^2}{\varepsilon^2} + \left(\frac{1}{\varepsilon}\right)^{1/(r+1/2)}$$

and

$$\text{Comp}^{\text{ave}}(\text{Int}; \varepsilon) \asymp \frac{\sigma_0^2}{\varepsilon^2} + \left(\frac{1}{\varepsilon}\right)^{1/(r+1)},$$

where the constants in the '$\asymp$' notation do not depend on σ_0. Suppose now that only observations of function values are allowed. Then

$$\text{Comp}^{\text{ave}}(\text{App}; \varepsilon) \asymp \sigma_0^2 (1/\varepsilon)^{2+1/(r+1/2)},$$

while $\text{Comp}^{\text{ave}}(\text{Int}; \varepsilon)$ remains unchanged.

NR 3.10.4 We recall that in the case of the solution operator S being a functional we have the correspondence Theorem 3.6.3. It says that for the corresponding problems, the worst case and average case radii of the same information are equal up to the constant factor $\sqrt{2}$. We can formulate an analogous correspondence theorem about the worst and average case complexities.

Let $\{H, F\}$ be an abstract Wiener space μ for a Gaussian measure on F. Let the solution operator $S : F \to \mathbb{R}$ be a continuous linear functional and the class Λ of permissible functionals be given. Consider the problem of finding the ε-complexity in the two settings:

(WW) The worst case setting with respect to $E = \{f \in H \mid \|f\|_H \leq 1\}$, noise bounded in the weighted Euclidean norm, $\sum_{i=1}^n ((y_i - L_i(f))/\delta_i)^2 \leq 1$, and a cost function $\mathbf{c}_w(\delta)$,

(AA) The average case setting with respect to the measure μ, independent noise with $(y_i - L_i(f)) \sim \mathcal{N}(0, \sigma_i^2)$, and a cost function $\mathbf{c}_a(\sigma^2)$.

If $\mathbf{c}_w(x) = \mathbf{c}_a(x^2)$ then

$$(\text{IC}^{\text{non}})^{\text{wor}}(\sqrt{2}\,\varepsilon) \leq (\text{IC}^{\text{non}})^{\text{ave}}(\varepsilon) \leq (\text{IC}^{\text{non}})^{\text{wor}}(\varepsilon).$$

If, additionally, $(\text{IC}^{\text{non}})^{\text{ave}}(\sqrt{\varepsilon})$ is semiconvex and $(\text{IC}^{\text{non}})^{\text{ave}}(\sqrt{2}\,\varepsilon)$ behaves as $(\text{IC}^{\text{non}})^{\text{ave}}(\varepsilon)$, then

$$\text{Comp}^{\text{wor}}(\varepsilon) \asymp \text{Comp}^{\text{ave}}(\varepsilon) \qquad \text{as} \quad \varepsilon \to 0^+.$$

For instance, the results of Subsection 3.10.2 can be applied to get complexity results for the corresponding problem in the worst case setting (compare also with NR 3.8.5).

Exercises

E 3.10.1 Show that the condition $\sum_{j=1}^{\infty} \lambda_j^{1/2} < +\infty$ implies

$$\lim_{n \to \infty} \frac{1}{n} \sum_{j=1}^{n} \left(\frac{\lambda_j^{1/2}}{\lambda_n^{1/2}} - 1 \right) = +\infty.$$

That is, Lemma 3.10.2 can be applied to such eigenvalues.

E 3.10.2 Let $1/2 < p < 1$. Let $a_n = n^{-p}$ and $P_n = n^{-1} \sum_{i=1}^{n} a_i / a_n$, $n \geq 1$. For $\alpha_1 > \alpha_2 > \cdots \to 0$, let $0 = n_0 < n_1 < \cdots$ be the sequence of integers defined inductively by the condition

$$P_{n_i - 1} \left(\frac{n_{i-1}}{n_i} \right)^{1-p} - \frac{n_{i-1}}{n_i} < \alpha_i,$$

with $P_0 = 0$. For $n \geq 1$ we let $\lambda_n = a_{n_i}^2$, where i is the unique positive integer such that $n_{i-1} < n \leq n_i$. Show that for any n satisfying

$$\sum_{i=1}^{n} \lambda_i^{1/2} \geq \lambda_n^{1/2} (T_i + n)$$

with $T_i = \alpha_i n_i$, we have $n/T_i \geq 1/\alpha_i \to +\infty$ as $i \to +\infty$.

E 3.10.3 Let $0 < q \leq 1$. Show that $\mathrm{Comp}^{\mathrm{non}}(q, p, s; \sqrt{\varepsilon})$ is *not* a strictly convex function of ε.

E 3.10.4 Show that for the cost function

$$c_1(\sigma^2) = \begin{cases} 1 + \sigma^{-2} & \sigma^2 > 0, \\ +\infty & \sigma^2 = 0, \end{cases}$$

we have

$$R(c_1; T)^2 = \frac{1}{T} \cdot \left(\sum_{i=1}^{n} \lambda_i^{1/2} \right)^2 + \sum_{j=n+1}^{\infty} \lambda_j$$

where $n = n(T)$ is the largest integer satisfying

$$\sum_{i=1}^{n} \lambda_i^{1/2} \leq \lambda_n^{1/2} \left(\frac{T+1}{2} \right).$$

4

Worst-average case setting

4.1 Introduction

In the previous two chapters, we studied settings in which we made exclusively deterministic assumptions on problem elements f and information noise x (the worst case setting), or exclusively stochastic assumptions (the average case setting). In the first setting we analyzed the worst performance of algorithms, while in the other we analyzed the average performance. The deterministic and stochastic assumptions can be combined, and this leads to *mixed settings*.

In this chapter, we study the first mixed setting in which we have deterministic assumptions on the problem elements and stochastic assumptions on noise. We call it the *worst-average case setting*. More precisely, we want to approximate values $S(f)$ for elements f belonging to a set $E \subset F$. Information about f is given with random noise. That is, nonadaptive or adaptive information $\mathbb{N}$ is defined as in the average case setting of Chapter 3. The error of an algorithm φ that uses information $\mathbb{N}$ is given as

$$e^{\mathrm{w-a}}(\mathbb{N}, \varphi) = \sup_{f \in E} \sqrt{\int_Y \|S(f) - \varphi(y)\|^2 \, \pi_f(dy)}, \qquad (4.1)$$

where Y is the set of all possible values y of noisy information, and π_f is the distribution of y for the element f, i.e., $\mathbb{N} = \{\pi_f\}_{f \in F}$.

This setting has been studied extensively in statistics. It is often called *statistical estimation*, and the problem of minimizing the error over a class of algorithms is called the *minimax (statistical) problem*.

In the mixed settings, the complexity results are not as complete as in the worst and average case settings. The reason for this lies in the technical difficulty. For instance, even for apparently simple one dimen-

215

sional problems, optimal algorithms are not linear (or not affine), and they are actually not known explicitly.

The body of this chapter consists of three sections. In Section 4.2, we study approximation of a linear functional over a convex set E. We consider nonadaptive linear information with Gaussian noise. It turns out that, although optimal algorithms are not affine, we lose about 11% by using affine algorithms. Hence, affine approximations prove once more to be (almost) optimal. Optimal affine algorithms are constructed. These results are obtained by using the concept of a hardest one dimensional subproblem, and by establishing a relation between the worst-average and worst case settings. In particular, it turns out that appropriately calibrating the levels of random noise in one setting and deterministic noise in the other setting, we get the same optimal affine algorithm.

If E is the unit ball in a Hilbert norm, there are also close relations between the worst-average and the corresponding average case settings. This enables us to show that these three settings are almost equivalent. The same smoothing spline algorithms are almost optimal in any of them.

The situation becomes much more complicated when the solution operator is not a functional. This case is considered in Section 4.3. We only present some special results about optimal algorithms when, roughly speaking, information is given 'coordinatewise'. In particular, we show optimality of the least squares algorithm when $E = \mathbb{R}^d$. For arbitrary information, optimal algorithms are unknown even for problems defined on Hilbert spaces.

4.2 Affine algorithms for linear functionals

Optimal algorithms often turn out to be linear or affine for approximating a linear functional in the worst or average case setting. In this section, we investigate whether a similar result holds in the mixed worst-average case setting.

To begin with, we consider a one dimensional problem. We shall see that even in this simple case the situation is complicated.

4.2.1 The one dimensional problem

Consider the problem of approximating a real parameter $f \in [-\tau, \tau]$, $\tau > 0$, from data $y = f + x$ where x is distributed according to the zero-mean one dimensional Gaussian measure with variance $\sigma^2 \geq 0$. That is, we formally have $S : \mathbb{R} \to \mathbb{R}$, $S(f) = f$, and $\pi_f = \mathcal{N}(f, \sigma^2)$.

Clearly, for $\sigma = 0$ we have exact information. In this case, the algorithm $\varphi(y) = y$ gives the exact value of $S(f)$ with probability 1 and its error is zero. For $\sigma > 0$, the error of any algorithm $\varphi : \mathbb{R} \to \mathbb{R}$ is positive and given as

$$e^{\mathrm{w-a}}(\mathrm{II}, \varphi) = e^{\mathrm{w-a}}(\tau, \sigma^2; \varphi)$$

$$= \sup_{|f| \leq \tau} \sqrt{\frac{1}{\sqrt{2\pi\sigma^2}} \int_{\mathbb{R}} |f - \varphi(f + x)|^2 \exp\{-x^2/(2\sigma^2)\}\, dx}.$$

First consider linear algorithms. That is, φ is of the form $\varphi(y) = cy$ for all $y \in \mathbb{R}$. Let

$$r_{\mathrm{lin}}(\tau, \sigma^2) = \inf \{ e^{\mathrm{w-a}}(\tau, \sigma^2; \varphi) \mid \varphi \text{ linear} \}$$

be the minimal error of linear algorithms.

Lemma 4.2.1 *For all $\tau > 0$ and $\sigma \geq 0$ we have*

$$r_{\mathrm{lin}}(\tau, \sigma^2) = \sigma \cdot \sqrt{\frac{\tau^2}{\tau^2 + \sigma^2}}.$$

The optimal linear algorithm $\varphi(y) = c_{\mathrm{opt}}\, y$ is uniquely determined and its coefficient is given as

$$c_{\mathrm{opt}} = c_{\mathrm{opt}}(\tau, \sigma^2) = \frac{\tau^2}{\tau^2 + \sigma^2}.$$

Proof We have already noticed that the lemma is true for $\sigma = 0$. Let $\sigma > 0$. Then for any linear algorithm $\varphi(y) = cy$ and $f \in \mathbb{R}$ we have

$$(e^{\mathrm{w-a}}(\tau, \sigma^2; \varphi))^2 = \sup_{|f| \leq \tau} \frac{1}{\sqrt{2\pi\sigma^2}} \int_{\mathbb{R}} |f - \varphi(f + x)|^2 e^{-x^2/(2\sigma^2)}\, dx$$

$$= \sup_{|f| \leq \tau} f^2(1 - c)^2 + \sigma^2 c^2 = \tau^2(1 - c)^2 + \sigma^2 c^2.$$

The lemma now follows by taking the minimum of the last expression over $c \in \mathbb{R}$. □

Hence the optimal coefficient c_{opt} depends only on the ratio σ/τ, i.e., $c_{\mathrm{opt}}(\tau, \sigma^2) = c_{\mathrm{opt}}(1, \sigma^2/\tau^2)$. For the minimal error we have

$$r_{\mathrm{lin}}(\tau, \sigma^2) = \tau \cdot r_{\mathrm{lin}}(1, \sigma^2/\tau^2). \tag{4.2}$$

Furthermore, for $\sigma \to 0$ we have $r_{\mathrm{lin}}(\tau, \sigma^2) \approx \sigma$, and for $\sigma \to \infty$ we have $r_{\mathrm{lin}}(\tau, \sigma^2) \to \tau$.

Obviously, the linear algorithm $\varphi_{\mathrm{opt}}(y) = c_{\mathrm{opt}}y$ is also optimal in the class of affine algorithms. However, if we consider arbitrary algorithms, then it is not difficult to see that we can do better.

Example 4.2.1 Observe that for $|y| > \tau + \sigma^2/\tau$ we have $c_{\mathrm{opt}}y \notin [-\tau, \tau]$, and $\tau y/|y|$ provides a better approximation to any f from $[-\tau, \tau]$ than $c_{\mathrm{opt}}y$. Hence, for the nonlinear algorithm

$$\varphi_{\mathrm{non}}(y) = \begin{cases} c_{\mathrm{opt}}(\tau, \sigma^2)\, y & |y| \le \tau + \sigma^2/\tau, \\ \tau \cdot y/|y| & |y| > \tau + \sigma^2/\tau, \end{cases}$$

we have $e^{\mathrm{w-a}}(\tau, \sigma^2; \varphi_{\mathrm{non}}) < r_{\mathrm{lin}}(\tau, \sigma^2)$.

The fact that nonlinear algorithms are better than linear ones (in the mixed setting) should be contrasted with the results of the worst and average case settings where linear algorithms are optimal, see E 2.4.4 and E 3.5.1.

It turns out, however, that we never gain much. Thus let

$$r_{\mathrm{non}}(\tau, \sigma^2) = \inf\{\, e^{\mathrm{w-a}}(\tau, \sigma^2; \varphi) \mid \varphi \text{ nonlinear} \,\}$$

be the minimal error of arbitrary nonlinear algorithms.

Theorem 4.2.1 *For all $\tau > 0$ and $\sigma \ge 0$ we have*

$$1 \le \frac{r_{\mathrm{lin}}(\tau, \sigma^2)}{r_{\mathrm{non}}(\tau, \sigma^2)} < 1.5.$$

Furthermore,

$$\lim_{\sigma/\tau \to 0} \frac{r_{\mathrm{lin}}(\tau, \sigma^2)}{r_{\mathrm{non}}(\tau, \sigma^2)} = 1 = \lim_{\sigma/\tau \to \infty} \frac{r_{\mathrm{lin}}(\tau, \sigma^2)}{r_{\mathrm{non}}(\tau, \sigma^2)}$$

(0/0 = 1 by convention).

Proof Without loss of generality we can restrict ourselves to the case $\tau = 1$. Indeed, letting $\tilde{f} = f/\tau$, $\tilde{x} = x/\tau$, and $\tilde{\varphi}(y) = \varphi(\tau y)/\tau$ for arbitrary φ, we get $e^{\mathrm{w-a}}(\tau, \sigma^2; \varphi) = \tau\, e^{\mathrm{w-a}}(1, \sigma^2/\tau^2; \tilde{\varphi})$. Hence

$$r_{\mathrm{non}}(\tau, \sigma^2) = \tau \cdot r_{\mathrm{non}}(1, \sigma^2/\tau^2).$$

This and (4.2) yield

$$\frac{r_{\mathrm{lin}}(\tau, \sigma^2)}{r_{\mathrm{non}}(\tau, \sigma^2)} = \frac{r_{\mathrm{lin}}(1, \sigma^2/\tau^2)}{r_{\mathrm{non}}(1, \sigma^2/\tau^2)}.$$

Observe that the error of an arbitrary nonlinear algorithm φ satisfies

$$(e^{w-a}(1,\sigma^2;\varphi))^2 \geq \frac{1}{2}\frac{1}{\sqrt{2\pi\sigma^2}}$$
$$\times \int_{\mathbb{R}} (f - \varphi(y))^2 e^{-\frac{(y-f)^2}{2\sigma^2}} + (f + \varphi(y))^2 e^{-\frac{(y+f)^2}{2\sigma^2}} dy, \quad (4.3)$$

where f is arbitrarily chosen from $[-1, 1]$. This is minimized by

$$\varphi_1(y) = \frac{a_- - a_+}{a_- + a_+} f, \qquad a_{\pm} = e^{-\frac{(y\pm f)^2}{2\sigma^2}}. \quad (4.4)$$

Putting $\varphi = \varphi_1$ in (4.3) we obtain

$$(e^{w-a}(1,\sigma^2;\varphi))^2 \geq f^2 \psi(f/\sigma) \quad (4.5)$$

where

$$\psi(x) = e^{-x^2/2} \sqrt{\frac{2}{\pi}} \int_0^\infty \frac{e^{-u^2/2}}{\cosh(ux)} du.$$

For $\sigma \geq 1$ we have $r_{\text{lin}}(1,\sigma^2) \leq 1$ and $r_{\text{non}}(1,\sigma^2) \geq \sqrt{\psi(1)}$, where the last inequality follows from (4.5) by taking $f = 1$ and using the monotonicity of ψ. On the other hand, for $\sigma < 1$ we have $r_{\text{lin}}(1,\sigma^2) \leq \sigma$ and $r_{\text{non}}(1,\sigma^2) \geq \sigma\sqrt{\psi(1)}$, where now the last inequality follows from (4.5) by taking $f = \sigma$. Thus for any σ we have

$$\frac{r_{\text{lin}}(1,\sigma^2)}{r_{\text{non}}(1,\sigma^2)} \leq \frac{1}{\sqrt{\psi(1)}}.$$

By numerical computation we find that $\psi^{-1/2}(1) = 1.49... < 1.5$.

Since $r_{\text{lin}}(1,\sigma^2) \approx \sigma$ as $\sigma \to 0$, to obtain the first limit in the theorem it suffices to show that $r_{\text{non}}(1,\sigma^2) \approx \sigma$ as $\sigma \to 0$. To this end, observe that for any φ we have

$$(e^{w-a}(1,\sigma^2;\varphi))^2$$
$$\geq \frac{1}{2}\int_{-1}^1 \left(\frac{1}{\sqrt{2\pi\sigma^2}} \int_{\mathbb{R}} (f - \varphi(y))^2 e^{-\frac{(y-f)^2}{2\sigma^2}} dy\right) df$$
$$= \frac{1}{2}\frac{1}{\sqrt{2\pi\sigma^2}} \int_{\mathbb{R}} \left(\int_{-1}^1 (f - \varphi(y))^2 e^{-\frac{(y-f)^2}{2\sigma^2}} df\right) dy. \quad (4.6)$$

The inner integral in (4.6) is minimized by

$$\varphi_2(y) = \frac{\int_{-1}^1 x e^{-\frac{(y-x)^2}{2\sigma^2}} dx}{\int_{-1}^1 e^{-\frac{(y-x)^2}{2\sigma^2}} dx} = y - \sigma \frac{\int x e^{-x^2/2} dx}{\int e^{-x^2/2} dx}$$

where the last integrals are taken from $(y-1)/\sigma$ to $(y+1)/\sigma$. Put $\varphi = \varphi_2$ and change variables in (4.6), $y = f + \sigma u$. After some calculations we get

$$(e^{w-a}(1,\sigma^2;\varphi))^2 \ge \sigma^2 \cdot \frac{1}{2} \int_{-1}^{1} \left(\frac{1}{\sqrt{2\pi}} \int_{\mathbb{R}} \psi_1^2(f,u,\sigma^2) e^{-u^2/2} \, du \right) df,$$

where

$$\psi_1(f,u,\sigma^2) = \frac{\int (u-x) e^{-x^2/2} dx}{\int e^{-x^2/2} dx}$$

and the integrals are taken from $u+(f-1)/\sigma$ to $u+(f+1)/\sigma$. Observe now that for $|f| \le a < 1$ and $|u| < A < +\infty$, the function $\psi_1(f,u,\sigma^2)$ converges uniformly to u as $\sigma \to 0$. Hence

$$\lim_{\sigma \to 0} \frac{1}{2} \int_{-1}^{1} \left(\frac{1}{\sqrt{2\pi}} \int_{\mathbb{R}} \psi_1^2(f,u,\sigma^2) e^{-u^2/2} du \right) df$$

$$= \frac{1}{2} \int_{-1}^{1} \left(\frac{1}{\sqrt{2\pi}} \int_{\mathbb{R}} u^2 e^{-u^2/2} du \right) df = 1.$$

Consequently, $r_{\mathrm{non}}(1,\sigma^2) \approx \sigma$, as claimed.

To prove the second limit, observe that by taking $f = 1$ in (4.5) we obtain

$$(e^{w-a}(1,\sigma^2;\varphi))^2 \ge \psi(1/\sigma) \ge \frac{e^{-1/(2\sigma^2)}}{\cosh(1/\sqrt{\sigma})} \sqrt{\frac{2}{\pi}} \int_{0}^{\sqrt{\sigma}} e^{-u^2/2} \, du$$

which tends to 1 as $\sigma \to +\infty$. Since $\lim_{\sigma \to \infty} r_{\mathrm{lin}}(1,\sigma^2) = 1$, the proof is complete. $\qquad\square$

The upper bound 1.5 in Theorem 4.2.1 can be improved. Actually, the best bound is known. Thus let us define the constant

$$\kappa_1^* = \sup_{\tau,\sigma} \frac{r_{\mathrm{lin}}(\tau,\sigma^2)}{r_{\mathrm{non}}(\tau,\sigma^2)}. \tag{4.7}$$

Then $\kappa_1^* = 1.11...$, see NR 4.2.2.

4.2.2 Almost optimality of affine algorithms

We pass to the general problem. We assume that the functional S is defined on a linear space F. We want to approximate $S(f)$ for f belonging to a convex set $E \subset F$, based on linear information with Gaussian noise. That is, we have at our disposal information $y = N(f) + x \in \mathbb{R}^n$, where $N : F \to Y = \mathbb{R}^n$ is a linear operator and the noise $x \sim \mathcal{N}(0,\sigma^2\Sigma)$.

The symmetric matrix $\Sigma \in \mathbb{R}^{n \times n}$ is assumed to be positive definite. It induces an inner product $\langle \cdot, \cdot \rangle_Y$ in $\mathbb{R}^n$ defined by $\langle y, z \rangle_Y = \langle \Sigma^{-1} y, z \rangle_2$. The error $e^{w-a}(\mathbb{II}, \varphi)$ is given by (4.1).

We denote by $\mathrm{rad}_{\mathrm{aff}}^{w-a}(\mathbb{II}; E)$ and $\mathrm{rad}_{\mathrm{non}}^{w-a}(\mathbb{II}; E)$ the minimal errors of affine and arbitrary nonlinear algorithms over E,

$$\mathrm{rad}_{\mathrm{aff}}^{w-a}(\mathbb{II}; E) = \inf \{ e^{w-a}(\mathbb{II}, \varphi; E) \mid \varphi \text{ affine} \},$$
$$\mathrm{rad}_{\mathrm{non}}^{w-a}(\mathbb{II}; E) = \inf \{ e^{w-a}(\mathbb{II}, \varphi; E) \mid \varphi \text{ arbitrary} \}.$$

Algorithms that attain the first and second infimum will be called optimal affine algorithms and optimal algorithms, respectively.

Consider first the case where the set E is an interval. That is,

$$E = I(f_{-1}, f_1) = \{ \alpha f_{-1} + (1 - \alpha) f_1 \mid 0 \le \alpha \le 1 \}$$

for some $f_{-1}, f_1 \in F$.

Lemma 4.2.2 *Let E be the one dimensional set $E = I(f_{-1}, f_1)$. Let $h = (f_1 - f_{-1})/2$ and $f_0 = (f_1 + f_{-1})/2$.*
(i) If $N(h) = 0$ then

$$\mathrm{rad}_{\mathrm{aff}}^{w-a}(\mathbb{II}; I) = \mathrm{rad}_{\mathrm{non}}^{w-a}(\mathbb{II}; I) = |S(h)|$$

and the optimal algorithm is $\varphi \equiv S(f_0)$.
(ii) If $N(h) \ne 0$ then

$$\mathrm{rad}_{\mathrm{aff}}^{w-a}(\mathbb{II}; I) = |S(h)| \, r_{\mathrm{lin}}\left(1, \frac{\sigma^2}{\|N(h)\|_Y^2} \right),$$

$$\mathrm{rad}_{\mathrm{non}}^{w-a}(\mathbb{II}; I) = |S(h)| \, r_{\mathrm{non}}\left(1, \frac{\sigma^2}{\|N(h)\|_Y^2} \right),$$

and the optimal affine algorithm is given as

$$\varphi_{\mathrm{aff}}(y) = S(f_0)$$
$$+ c_{\mathrm{opt}}\left(1, \frac{\sigma^2}{\|N(h)\|_Y^2} \right) \frac{S(h)}{\|N(h)\|_Y} \left\langle y - N(f_0), \frac{N(h)}{\|N(h)\|_Y} \right\rangle_Y,$$

where $r_{\mathrm{lin}}(\cdot, \cdot)$, $r_{\mathrm{non}}(\cdot, \cdot)$ and $c_{\mathrm{opt}}(\cdot, \cdot)$ are as in Lemma 4.2.1.

Proof (i) Since for any $f \in I$ we have $N(f) = N(f_0)$, information consists of pure noise only. Hence, in view of NR 4.2.4, such information is useless. The optimal algorithm is the center $S(f_0)$ of $S(I)$ and the formula for the minimal error follows.

(ii) For $f \in I$, let $\alpha = \alpha(f)$ be defined by $f = f_0 + \alpha h$. Clearly, $f \in I$ iff $|\alpha| \leq 1$. Transform the data $y = N(f) + x$ to

$$z = \frac{\Sigma^{-1/2}(y - N(f_0))}{\|N(h)\|_Y} = \alpha w + x',$$

where $w = (\Sigma^{-1/2}N(h))/\|N(h)\|_Y$ and

$$x' = \frac{\Sigma^{-1/2}x}{\|N(h)\|_Y} \sim \mathcal{N}\left(0, \frac{\sigma^2}{\|N(h)\|_Y} I\right).$$

We now choose Q to be an orthogonal matrix such that $Qw = e_1$ (the first versor). Then the problem of approximating $S(f)$ from data y is equivalent to that of approximating $s(\alpha) = S(f_0) + \alpha S(h)$, $-1 \leq \alpha \leq 1$, from data

$$\tilde{y} = Qz = [\alpha + \tilde{x}_1, \tilde{x}_2, \ldots, \tilde{x}_n] \in \mathbb{R}^n,$$

where the $\tilde{x}_i$s are independent, $\tilde{x}_i \sim \mathcal{N}(0, \sigma^2/\|N(h)\|_Y^2)$, $1 \leq i \leq n$. We see that only the first component of $\tilde{y}$ is not pure noise. Owing to NR 4.2.4, we cannot make use of $\tilde{x}_2, \ldots, \tilde{x}_n$ to reduce the error, and we can restrict ourselves to data $\tilde{y}_1 = \alpha + \tilde{x}_1$.

Thus we have reduced the original problem to the one dimensional problem of approximating $s(\alpha)$ from $\tilde{y}_1 = \alpha + \tilde{x}_1$. The formulas for the minimal errors now follow from Lemma 4.2.1. The optimal affine algorithm is given as

$$\varphi_{\text{aff}}(y) = S(f_0) + S(h)\, c_{\text{opt}}\left(1, \frac{\sigma^2}{\|N(h)\|_Y^2}\right) \tilde{y}_1.$$

To complete the proof, observe that

$$
\begin{aligned}
\tilde{y}_1 &= \langle Qz, e_1 \rangle_2 = \langle z, Q^{-1}e_1 \rangle_2 = \langle z, w \rangle_2 \\
&= \left\langle \frac{\Sigma^{-1/2}(y - N(f_0))}{\|N(h)\|_Y}, \frac{\Sigma^{-1/2}N(h)}{\|N(h)\|_Y} \right\rangle_2 \\
&= \frac{1}{\|N(h)\|_Y} \left\langle y - N(f_0), \frac{N(h)}{\|N(h)\|_Y} \right\rangle_Y.
\end{aligned}
$$

$\square$

We now find optimal affine algorithms for an arbitrary convex set E. For $\delta \geq 0$, let $r(\delta)$ be the worst case radius of information

$$\mathbb{N}_\delta(f) = \{N(f) + x \mid \|x\|_Y \leq \delta\}$$

with respect to E. That is,

$$r(\delta) = \sup\{S(h) \mid h \in \text{bal}(E), \|N(h)\|_Y \leq \delta\} \qquad (4.8)$$

where $\text{bal}(E) = (E - E)/2$, see Section 2.3.

Recall that an optimal affine algorithm for information $\mathbb{N}_\delta$ exists in the worst case setting. This algorithm is also optimal among all nonlinear algorithms, i.e., $\text{rad}^{\text{wor}}(\mathbb{N}_\delta; E) = e^{\text{wor}}(\mathbb{N}_\delta, \varphi_\delta; E)$, and given as

$$\varphi_\delta = g_\delta + d_\delta \langle \cdot, w_\delta \rangle_Y,$$

where $g_\delta \in \mathbb{R}$, $w_\delta \in \mathbb{R}^n$ with $\|w_\delta\|_Y = 1$, and $d_\delta \geq 0$ is any number such that $r(\gamma) \leq r(\delta) + d_\delta(\gamma - \delta)$, $\forall \gamma$, see Section 2.4. The set of all such d_δ will be denoted by $\partial r(\delta)$.

Observe that by taking $\delta = \sigma$ we obtain an algorithm which is close to an optimal affine one in the mixed worst-average case setting. Indeed, for any affine $\varphi = g + d\langle \cdot, w \rangle_Y$ with $\|w\|_Y = 1$, we have

$$|S(f) - \varphi(N(f) + x)|^2$$
$$= |S(f) - \varphi(N(f))|^2 - 2\,d\,S(f)\,\langle w, \Sigma^{-1}x \rangle_2 + d^2 \langle w, \Sigma^{-1}x \rangle_2^2.$$

If we integrate this over $x \sim \pi = \mathcal{N}(0, \sigma^2\Sigma)$, the second component will vanish and the third one will become $\sigma^2 d^2$. Hence

$$e^{\text{w}-\text{a}}(\Pi, \varphi; E) = \sup_{f \in E} \sqrt{\int_{\mathbb{R}^n} |S(f) - \varphi(N(f) + x)|^2\, \pi(dx)}$$

$$= \sqrt{\sup_{f \in E} |S(f) - \varphi(N(f))|^2 + \sigma^2\,d^2}.$$

Since $e^{\text{wor}}(\mathbb{N}, \varphi; E) = \sup_{f \in E} |S(f) - \varphi(N(f))| + \delta\, d$, for $\delta = \sigma$ we have

$$\frac{1}{\sqrt{2}}\, e^{\text{wor}}(\mathbb{N}, \varphi; E) \leq e^{\text{w}-\text{a}}(\Pi, \varphi; E) \leq e^{\text{wor}}(\mathbb{N}, \varphi; E).$$

In particular, this implies

$$e^{\text{w}-\text{a}}(\Pi, \varphi_\delta; E) \leq \sqrt{2} \cdot \text{rad}_{\text{non}}^{\text{w}-\text{a}}(\Pi; E) \qquad (\delta = \sigma).$$

It turns out that for appropriately chosen δ, φ_δ is an optimal affine algorithm. Obviously, if $\sigma = 0$ then information is exact and we can take $\delta = 0$.

Theorem 4.2.2 *Let $\sigma > 0$.*

(i) If $r(\delta)$ is a homogeneous function, i.e., $r(\delta) = \delta\, r'(0^+)$, then $\varphi_\delta = \varphi_0$, $\forall \delta$, and φ_0 is an optimal affine algorithm. Furthermore,

$$\text{rad}_{\text{aff}}^{\text{w}-\text{a}}(\Pi; E) = e^{\text{w}-\text{a}}(\mathbb{N}, \varphi_0; E) = \sigma\, r'(0^+).$$

(ii) If $r(\delta)$ is not homogeneous, then there exist $\delta = \delta(\sigma)$ and $d_\delta \in \partial r(\delta)$ such that

$$d_\delta = \frac{\delta\, r(\delta)}{\sigma^2 + \delta^2},\tag{4.9}$$

and φ_δ is an optimal affine algorithm in the mixed worst-average case setting. Furthermore,

$$\mathrm{rad}_{\mathrm{aff}}^{\mathrm{w-a}}(\mathrm{II}; E) = \mathrm{e}^{\mathrm{w-a}}(\mathrm{II}, \varphi_\delta; E) = \frac{\sigma\, r(\delta)}{\sqrt{\sigma^2 + \delta^2}}.$$

Proof (i) In this case, the worst case error of φ_0 with information N_δ is given as

$$\begin{aligned}
\mathrm{e}^{\mathrm{wor}}(\mathrm{N}_\delta, \varphi_0; E) &= \sup_{f \in E} |S(f) - \varphi_0(N(f))| + \delta\, d_0 \\
&= r(0) + \delta\, d_0 = \delta\, r'(0^+) = r(\delta),
\end{aligned}$$

which shows the optimality of φ_0 in the worst case setting for all δ. Similarly, we show that

$$\mathrm{e}^{\mathrm{w-a}}(\mathrm{II}, \varphi_0; E) = \sigma\, r'(0^+).$$

For $\varepsilon > 0$, let $h = (f_1 - f_{-1})/2 \in \mathrm{bal}(E)$, $f_1, f_{-1} \in E$, be such that $\|N(h)\|_Y \le \delta$ and $S(h) \ge r(\delta) - \varepsilon$. Let $I = I(f_{-1}, f_1)$. Then the error over E is not smaller than the error over the interval I. The formula for $\mathrm{rad}^{\mathrm{w-a}}(\mathrm{II}; I)$ given in Lemma 4.2.2 yields

$$\mathrm{rad}_{\mathrm{aff}}^{\mathrm{w-a}}(\mathrm{II}; E) \ge \mathrm{rad}_{\mathrm{aff}}^{\mathrm{w-a}}(\mathrm{II}; I) \ge \frac{\sigma\, (r(\delta) - \varepsilon)}{\sqrt{\sigma^2 + \delta^2}},$$

and since ε is arbitrary,

$$\mathrm{rad}_{\mathrm{aff}}^{\mathrm{w-a}}(\mathrm{II}; E) \ge \frac{\sigma\, r(\delta)}{\sqrt{\sigma^2 + \delta^2}}.\tag{4.10}$$

Now, replacing $r(\delta)$ by $\delta\, r'(0^+)$ and letting $\delta \to +\infty$, we obtain

$$\mathrm{rad}_{\mathrm{aff}}^{\mathrm{w-a}}(\mathrm{II}; E) \ge \sigma\, r'(0^+),$$

which proves the optimality of φ_0.

(ii) We first show the existence of $\delta = \delta(\sigma)$ and $d_\delta \in \partial r(\delta)$. Since $r(\gamma)$ is a concave function of γ (see E 2.4.6), the set

$$\{\, (\gamma, d) \mid \gamma \ge 0,\, d \in \partial r(\gamma) \,\}$$

forms a continuous and nonincreasing curve. We also have that the function $\psi(\gamma) = \gamma r(\gamma)(\sigma^2 + \gamma^2)^{-1}$ is nonnegative, continuous and takes the value zero for $\gamma = 0$. Hence $d_0 \geq \psi(0)$ and it suffices to show that for large γ we have $d_\gamma \leq \psi(\gamma)$. Indeed, assume without loss of generality that $d_\gamma > 0$, $\forall \gamma$. Then, owing to the concavity of $r(\gamma)$, there exists $\gamma_0 > 0$ such that

$$\frac{r(\gamma_0)}{\gamma_0 d_{\gamma_0}} = a > 1.$$

This and the inequality

$$d_\gamma \leq \frac{r(\gamma) - r(\gamma_0)}{\gamma - \gamma_0} \leq d_{\gamma_0}, \qquad \forall \gamma > \gamma_0,$$

yield

$$\frac{r(\gamma)}{d_\gamma} \geq \frac{r(\gamma_0)}{d_{\gamma_0}} + (\gamma - \gamma_0) \geq \gamma + \gamma_0(a - 1).$$

Consequently

$$\frac{\psi(\gamma)}{d_\gamma} \geq \frac{\gamma^2 + \gamma \gamma_0(a - 1)}{\gamma^2 + \sigma^2},$$

which is larger than 1 for $\gamma > \sigma^2/(\gamma_0(a - 1))$. Hence $\delta = \delta(\sigma)$ exists.

In view of (4.9), the (squared) error of φ_δ is equal to

$$
\begin{aligned}
(e^{\mathrm{w-a}}(\mathrm{II}, \varphi_\delta; E))^2 &= \sup_{f \in E} |S(f) - \varphi_\delta(N(f))|^2 + \sigma^2 d_\delta^2 \\
&= (r(\delta) - \delta d_\delta)^2 + \sigma^2 d_\delta^2 = \frac{\sigma^2 r^2(\delta)}{\sigma^2 + \delta^2}.
\end{aligned}
$$

This together with (4.10) proves the optimality of φ_δ and completes the proof. □

Thus the optimal algorithm in the mixed setting turns out to be optimal in the worst case setting with appropriately chosen δ.

Observe that in the proof we also showed that the minimal affine worst-average error over E equals the minimal affine worst-average error over the hardest one dimensional subset $I \subset E$. We emphasize this important fact in the following corollary.

Corollary 4.2.1 *For approximating linear functionals over convex sets E we have*

$$\mathrm{rad}_{\mathrm{aff}}^{\mathrm{w-a}}(\mathrm{II}; E) = \sup_{I \subset E} \mathrm{rad}_{\mathrm{aff}}^{\mathrm{w-a}}(\mathrm{II}; I).$$

Furthermore, if the worst case radius $r(\delta)$ is attained at $h^* = (f_1^* - f_{-1}^*)/2 \in \mathrm{bal}(E)$, $f_1^*, f_{-1}^* \in E$, then $I^* = I(f_{-1}^*, f_1^*)$ is the hardest one dimensional subproblem, i.e., $\mathrm{rad}_{\mathrm{aff}}^{\mathrm{w-a}}(\mathrm{II}; E) = \mathrm{rad}_{\mathrm{aff}}^{\mathrm{w-a}}(\mathrm{II}; I^*)$.

We note that if E is not only convex but also balanced, then the optimal affine algorithm φ_δ is linear and the hardest one dimensional subproblem is symmetric about zero.

We now give two simple illustrations of Theorem 4.2.2 and Corollary 4.2.1.

Example 4.2.2 For the one dimensional problem of Subsection 4.2.1 with $\tau = +\infty$, the radius $r(\delta) = \delta$ is a homogeneous function. Then the optimal linear algorithm in the worst and worst-average case settings is independent of the noise level and given as $\varphi_{\mathrm{opt}}(y) = y$. The hardest subproblem does not exist, however:

$$r_{\mathrm{lin}}(+\infty, \sigma^2) = \sigma = \lim_{\tau \to \infty} r_{\mathrm{lin}}(\tau, \sigma^2).$$

Example 4.2.3 Consider the integration problem over the class E of 1-Lipschitz periodic functions $f : [0, 1] \to \mathbb{R}$, as in Example 2.4.2. The information is given as $y_i = f(i/n) + x_i$, $1 \le i \le n$, where the x_i are independent and $x_i \sim \mathcal{N}(0, \sigma^2)$.

Recall that in this case $r(\gamma) = \gamma/\sqrt{n} + 1/(4n)$. The worst case optimal algorithm is independent of γ and equals $\varphi_{\mathrm{lin}}(y) = n^{-1} \sum_{i=1}^{n} y_i$. We check that (4.9) holds for $\delta = \delta(\sigma) = 4\sigma^2\sqrt{n}$. Hence Theorem 4.2.2 yields that φ_{lin} is also the optimal linear algorithm in the mixed case for any σ and

$$\mathrm{rad}_{\mathrm{aff}}^{\mathrm{w-a}}(\mathbb{I}; E) = \sqrt{\frac{\sigma^2}{n} + \frac{1}{16\,n^2}}.$$

The hardest one dimensional subproblem is $[-h^*, h^*]$ where

$$h^* = 4\sigma^2 + \frac{1}{2n} - \left| t - \frac{2i-1}{2n} \right|, \quad \frac{i-1}{n} \le t \le \frac{i}{n}, \ 1 \le i \le n.$$

We now pass to arbitrary nonlinear algorithms. The relations just proven between the mixed and worst case settings for affine algorithms enable us to show the following result.

Theorem 4.2.3 *For approximating linear functionals over convex sets E we have*

$$1 \le \frac{\mathrm{rad}_{\mathrm{aff}}^{\mathrm{w-a}}(\mathbb{I}; E)}{\mathrm{rad}_{\mathrm{non}}^{\mathrm{w-a}}(\mathbb{I}; E)} \le \kappa_1^* = 1.11\ldots. \tag{4.11}$$

Furthermore,

$$\mathrm{rad}_{\mathrm{aff}}^{\mathrm{w-a}}(\mathbb{I}; E) \approx \mathrm{rad}_{\mathrm{non}}^{\mathrm{w-a}}(\mathbb{I}; E) \qquad as \quad \sigma \to 0^+.$$

Proof Owing to Lemma 4.2.2, (4.11) holds for the case of E being an interval. This and Corollary 4.2.1 yield

$$\mathrm{rad}_{\mathrm{aff}}^{\mathrm{w-a}}(\mathrm{I\!I}; E) = \sup_{I \subset E} \mathrm{rad}_{\mathrm{aff}}^{\mathrm{w-a}}(\mathrm{I\!I}; I)$$
$$\leq \kappa_1^* \cdot \sup_{I \subset E} \mathrm{rad}_{\mathrm{non}}^{\mathrm{w-a}}(\mathrm{I\!I}; I) \leq \kappa_1^* \cdot \mathrm{rad}_{\mathrm{non}}^{\mathrm{w-a}}(\mathrm{I\!I}; E).$$

We now prove the remaining part of the theorem. We can assume without loss of generality that $r'(\delta) > 0$, since otherwise the information is useless. Then, in view of Lemma 4.2.2 and Theorem 4.2.1, we have to show that it is possible to select $\delta = \delta(\sigma^2)$ and d_δ in such a way that σ/δ converges to 0 or to $+\infty$, as $\sigma \to 0^+$. Indeed, if this were not true, we would have $\delta \to 0^+$. However,

$$\frac{\sigma^2}{\delta^2} = \frac{r(\delta)}{\delta \, d_\delta} - 1,$$

and so the limit

$$\lim_{\delta \to 0^+} \frac{\sigma^2}{\delta^2} = \begin{cases} 0 & \text{if } r(0) = 0, \\ +\infty & \text{if } r(0) > 0, \end{cases}$$

as claimed. $\qquad\qquad\qquad\qquad\qquad\qquad\qquad\qquad\qquad\qquad\square$

Thus we have shown that nonaffine algorithms can only be slightly better than affine algorithms. Moreover, the optimal affine algorithm 'becomes' optimal among arbitrary nonlinear algorithms, as the noise level σ decreases to zero.

The Hilbert case

We end this subsection by considering a special case where E is the unit ball in a separable Hilbert space. We first show the following lemma.

Lemma 4.2.3 *Suppose that $\{H, F\}$ is an abstract Wiener space and μ the corresponding Gaussian measure. If $E \subset F$ is the unit ball with respect to the H-norm, then for any linear algorithm φ_{lin} we have*

$$e^{\mathrm{w-a}}(\mathrm{I\!I}, \varphi_{\mathrm{lin}}; E) = e^{\mathrm{ave}}(\mathrm{I\!I}, \varphi_{\mathrm{lin}}; \mu).$$

Hence

$$\mathrm{rad}_{\mathrm{lin}}^{\mathrm{w-a}}(\mathrm{I\!I}; E) = \mathrm{rad}^{\mathrm{ave}}(\mathrm{I\!I}; \mu).$$

Proof Indeed, writing $\varphi_{\text{lin}} = d\langle \cdot, w \rangle_Y$ with $\|w\|_Y = 1$, we obtain

$$
\begin{aligned}
(e^{\text{ave}}(\mathbb{I\!I}, \varphi_{\text{lin}}; \mu))^2 &= \int_F \int_{\mathbb{R}^n} (S(f) - \varphi_{\text{lin}}(N(f) + x))^2 \, \pi(dx) \, \mu(df) \\
&= \int_F (\tilde{S}(f) - \varphi_{\text{lin}}(N(f)))^2 \mu(df) + \sigma^2 d^2.
\end{aligned}
$$

Recall that for any continuous linear functional L defined on F we have $\int_F L^2(f)\mu(df) = \|f_L\|_H^2$, where $f_L \in H$ is the representer of L in H, see Subsection 3.3.2. Since $K = S(\cdot) - \varphi_{\text{lin}}(N(\cdot))$ is a continuous functional on F and $f_K = f_S - d \sum_{i=1}^n w_i f_i$, we have

$$
\begin{aligned}
(e^{\text{ave}}(\mathbb{I\!I}, \varphi_{\text{lin}}; \mu))^2 &= \left\| f_S - d \sum_{i=1}^n w_i f_i \right\|_H^2 + \sigma^2 d^2 \\
&= \sup_{\|f\|_H \le 1} (S(f) - \varphi_{\text{lin}}(N(f)))^2 + \sigma^2 d^2 \\
&= (e^{\text{w}-\text{a}}(\mathbb{I\!I}, \varphi_{\text{lin}}; E))^2,
\end{aligned}
$$

as claimed. $\square$

We now use Lemma 4.2.3 to obtain explicit formulas for optimal linear algorithms in the case when F itself is a Hilbert space.

Theorem 4.2.4 *Let F be a separable Hilbert space and E the unit ball in F. Let the solution operator be given as $S(f) = \langle f, f_S \rangle_F$, and information $y = N(f) + x$, where*

$$
N = [\langle \cdot, f_1 \rangle_F, \langle \cdot, f_2 \rangle_F, \dots, \langle \cdot, f_n \rangle_F]
$$

and $x \sim \mathcal{N}(0, \sigma^2 \Sigma)$. Then, in the worst-average case setting, the optimal affine algorithm is linear, uniquely determined, and given as

$$
\varphi_{\text{lin}}(y) = \langle y, w \rangle_2,
$$

where w is the solution of $(\sigma^2 \Sigma + G_N)w = N(f_S)$ and the matrix $G_N = \{\langle f_i, f_j \rangle_F\}_{i,j=1}^n$. Furthermore,

$$
\text{rad}_{\text{aff}}^{\text{w}-\text{a}}(\mathbb{I\!I}; E) = \sqrt{\|f_S\|_F^2 - \varphi_{\text{lin}}(N(f_S))}.
$$

Proof In view of Lemma 4.2.3 and the formulas for the optimal algorithm in the average case setting given at the beginning of Section 3.5, it suffices to show that there exists a separable Hilbert space $\tilde{F}$ satisfying the following conditions.

(i) $\{F, \tilde{F}\}$ is an abstract Wiener space.

(ii) S and N can be extended to a continuous linear functional $\tilde{S}$ and an operator $\tilde{N}$ on $\tilde{F}$.

Indeed, $\tilde{F}$ can be constructed as follows. Let W be the space spanned by $f_S, f_1, \ldots, f_n$ and $W^\perp$ be the orthogonal complement of W in F. Let $\{f_j\}_{j>n}$ be a complete orthonormal basis of $W^\perp$. Define $\tilde{F}$ as the closure of F with respect to the norm

$$\|f\|_{\tilde{F}}^2 = \|f_W\|_F^2 + \sum_{j=n+1}^{\infty} \lambda_j \alpha_j^2, \quad f = f_W + \sum_{j=n+1}^{\infty} \alpha_j f_j, \ f_W \in W,$$

where $\{\lambda_j\}$ is a positive sequence with $\sum_{j=n+1}^{\infty} \lambda_j < +\infty$. Then $\{F, \tilde{F}\}$ is an abstract Wiener space. (And the corresponding zero-mean Gaussian measure μ has correlation operator given by $C_\mu f = f$ for $f \in W$, and $C_\mu f_j = \lambda_j f_j$.) Furthermore, it is easy to see that we can take $\tilde{S}(f) = S(f_W)$ and $\tilde{N}(f) = N(f_W)$. $\qquad\square$

In the Hilbert case, the hardest one dimensional subproblem can also be shown explicitly. Indeed, we know from Theorem 3.5.1 that the average case approximation of $S(f)$ with respect to the measure μ is as difficult as the average case approximation with respect to the zero-mean Gaussian measure μ_{K_*}. Here $K_* = S - \varphi_{\text{lin}} N$ and the correlation operator of μ_{K_*} is given by

$$A_{K_*}(L) = \frac{\langle L, K_* \rangle_\mu}{\|K_*\|_\mu^2} C_\mu K_*, \qquad L \in F^*.$$

Furthermore, the algorithm φ_{lin} is optimal in both cases. Note that μ_{K_*} is concentrated on the one dimensional subspace $V = \text{span}\{C_\mu K_*\}$. Hence, owing to Lemma 4.2.3, φ_{lin} is also the optimal linear algorithm in the mixed setting for the set

$$E_{K_*} = \{\alpha C_\mu K_* \in V \mid |\alpha| \|K_*\|_{\mu_{K_*}} \leq 1\},$$

and $e^{w-a}(\mathrm{III}, \varphi_{\text{lin}}; E_{K_*}) = e^{w-a}(\mathrm{III}, \varphi_{\text{lin}}; E)$. Since

$$\|K_*\|_{\mu_{K_*}}^2 = K_*(A_{K_*} K^*) = \|K_*\|_\mu^2 = \|C_\mu K_*\|_F^2,$$

we have $E_{K_*} = [-h^*, h^*]$, where

$$h^* = \frac{C_\mu K_*}{\|C_\mu K_*\|_F} = \frac{f_S - \sum_{j=1}^{n} w_j f_j}{\|f_S - \sum_{j=1}^{n} w_j f_j\|_F}$$

and $E_{K_*} \subset E$. Hence $[-h^*, h^*]$ is the hardest one dimensional subproblem.

4.2.3 Relations to other settings

We summarize relations between the mixed worst-average and other settings discussed in Subsection 4.2.2.

Let S be a linear functional on a linear space F. Let information about f be given as $y = N(f) + x$. Consider the problem of approximating $S(f)$ from data y in the following three settings.

(WA) Mixed worst-average case setting with a convex set $E \subset F$ and the noise $x \sim \mathcal{N}(0, \sigma^2 \Sigma)$.

(WW) Worst case setting with a convex set $E \subset F$ and the noise bounded by $\|x\|_Y = \sqrt{\langle \Sigma^{-1} x, x \rangle_2} \le \delta$.

(AA) Average case setting with a Gaussian measure μ defined on F and $x \sim \mathcal{N}(0, \sigma^2 \Sigma)$.

We denote the optimal affine algorithm in the mixed setting (WA) by φ_σ.

Theorem 4.2.5 *(i) If $\sigma = \delta$ then the algorithm φ_σ is almost optimal in the worst case setting* (WW), $e^{\mathrm{wor}}(N, \varphi_\sigma; E) \le \sqrt{2}\, \mathrm{rad}^{\mathrm{wor}}(N; E)$, *and*

$$q_1 \cdot \mathrm{rad}^{\mathrm{wor}}(N; E) \le \mathrm{rad}^{\mathrm{w-a}}_{\mathrm{non}}(\mathbb{I}; E) \le \mathrm{rad}^{\mathrm{wor}}(N; E),$$

where $q_1 = \sqrt{2}/(2\kappa_1^*) = 0.63\ldots$.

(ii) Let $\{H, F\}$ be the abstract Wiener space for the measure μ and let E be the unit ball with respect to the norm in H. Then the algorithm φ_σ is optimal in the average case setting (AA), $e^{\mathrm{ave}}(\mathbb{I}, \varphi_\sigma; \mu) = \mathrm{rad}^{\mathrm{ave}}(\mathbb{I}; \mu)$, *and*

$$q_2 \cdot \mathrm{rad}^{\mathrm{ave}}(\mathbb{I}; \mu) \le \mathrm{rad}^{\mathrm{w-a}}_{\mathrm{non}}(\mathbb{I}; E) \le \mathrm{rad}^{\mathrm{ave}}(\mathbb{I}; \mu),$$

where $q_2 = 1/\kappa_1^* = 0.90\ldots$.

We can say even more. For any $\sigma \in [0, +\infty]$ we can find $\delta = \delta(\sigma) \in [0, +\infty]$ such that φ_δ is an optimal affine algorithm in the mixed setting (WA) and in the worst case setting (WW). Moreover, the inverse is true. For any $\delta \in [0, +\infty]$ there exists $\sigma = \sigma(\delta) \in [0, +\infty]$ ($\sigma^2 = \delta(r(\delta)/d_\delta - \delta)$) such that the algorithm φ_σ is optimal affine for (WA) and (WW). Since φ_σ is also an optimal affine algorithm in the average case setting (AA), similar relations hold between the worst and average case settings.

Example 4.2.4 Consider the abstract Wiener space $\{H, F\}$ where $H = W^0_{r+1}$ and $F = C^0_r$ ($r \ge 0$), and its r-fold Wiener measure w_r (see

Example 3.3.1). Suppose we want to approximate a functional $S \in F^*$, e.g., $S(f) = \int_0^1 f(t) \, dt$, from noisy information $y = N(f) + x$, where

$$N(f) = [f(t_1), f(t_2), \ldots, f(t_n)]$$

and the noise x is white. We know that in the average case (AA) with $\mu = w_r$, the unique optimal algorithm is the smoothing spline algorithm. It is given as $\varphi_\sigma(y) = S(\mathbf{s}(y))$ where $\mathbf{s}(y)$ is the natural polynomial spline of order r which belongs to W_{r+1}^0 and minimizes

$$\int_0^1 (f^{(r+1)}(t))^2 \, dt + \frac{1}{\sigma^2} \cdot \sum_{j=1}^n (y_j - f(t_j))^2$$

(for $\sigma = 0$, $\mathbf{s}(y)$ interpolates the data y_i exactly, i.e., $\mathbf{s}(y)(t_i) = y_i$, $\forall i$). Hence this is the unique optimal affine algorithm in the mixed setting (WA) with E the unit ball in H, and close to optimal among all algorithms in the mixed and worst case settings (WA) and (WW).

Let $\{\varphi_\sigma\}$ be the family of smoothing spline algorithms for $0 \le \sigma \le +\infty$. Then each φ_σ is an optimal affine algorithm in any of the three settings for appropriately chosen noise levels.

Notes and remarks

NR 4.2.1 The one dimensional problem of Subsection 4.2.1 has been studied by many authors. Bickel (1981), Casella and Strawderman (1981), Levit (1980) looked for optimal nonlinear algorithms. It is known that the optimal algorithm is the Bayes estimator with respect to the least favorable distribution on $[-\tau, \tau]$. This least favorable distribution is concentrated on a finite number of points. Moreover, for $\tau/\sigma < 1.05$, this distribution assigns mass $1/2$ each to $\pm\tau$. Hence in this case the algorithm φ_1 defined by (4.4) with $f = \tau$ is optimal and

$$(r_{\text{non}}(\tau, \sigma^2))^2 = \tau^2 e^{-\frac{1}{2}(\tau/\sigma)^2} \frac{1}{\sqrt{2\pi}} \int_0^\infty \frac{e^{-u^2/2}}{\cosh(u\tau/\sigma)} \, du.$$

As τ/σ increases, the number of points also increases and the least favorable distribution 'tends' to uniform distribution.

NR 4.2.2 The fact that the ratio $r_{\text{lin}}(\tau, \sigma^2)/r_{\text{non}}(\tau, \sigma^2)$ is bounded from above by a finite constant was pointed out by Ibragimov and Hasminski (1984) who studied the case of $N = I$ and convex balanced E. Donoho et al. (1990) and Brown and Feldman (1990) independently calculated the value of $\kappa_1^* = 1.11\ldots$.

NR 4.2.3 Li (1982) and Speckman (1979) showed optimality properties of smoothing splines for approximating functionals defined on Hilbert spaces. The results of Subsection 4.2.2 (under some additional assumptions) were first obtained by Donoho (1994) who also considered other error criteria. The generalization to an arbitrary convex set E and an arbitrary linear S and N, as well as the results about asymptotic optimality of affine algorithms (as $\sigma \to 0$) and the special results for the Hilbert case, is new. Lemma 4.2.3 was pointed out to me by K. Ritter in a conversation.

NR 4.2.4 In the proof of Lemma 4.2.2 we used the fact that for the one dimensional problem the 'pure noise' data are useless. This is the consequence of a more general theorem giving us a sufficient condition under which randomized algorithms using noisy but fixed information are not better than nonrandomized algorithms.

More precisely, let information $\Pi = \{\pi_f\}$ where the π_f are distributions on Y, and a set T with probability distribution ω on T, be given. Suppose that approximations to $S(f)$, for $f \in E$, are constructed using an algorithm φ_t which is chosen randomly according to ω. The family $\{\varphi_t\}$ with $t \sim \omega$ is called a *randomized algorithm*. The error of $\{\varphi_t\}$ is defined as

$$e^{\mathrm{ran}}(\Pi, \{\varphi_t\}) = \sup_{f \in E} \sqrt{\int_T \int_Y \|S(f) - \varphi_t(y)\|^2 \, \pi_f(dy) \, \omega(dt)}.$$

(We note that randomized algorithms are a special case of the well known and extensively studied *Monte Carlo* methods which, in general, use a random choice of algorithms as well as information. Usually exact information is studied, see e.g. Heinrich (1993), Mathé (1994), Novak (1988).)

Let $\mathcal{A}$ be a given class of permissible algorithms. Assume that, for the information Π, there exists a probability distribution μ on the set E such that the average and worst-average case radii of Π are the same, i.e.,

$$\mathrm{rad}^{\mathrm{ave}}(\Pi; \mathcal{A}, \mu) = \mathrm{rad}^{\mathrm{w-a}}(\Pi; \mathcal{A}, E). \tag{4.12}$$

Then randomized algorithms are not better than nonrandomized algorithms. Indeed, denote by

$$e^2(f, t) = \int_Y (S(f) - \varphi_t(y))^2 \, \pi_f(dy)$$

the squared average error of the (nonrandomized) algorithm φ_t at f. Using the mean value theorem and assumption (4.12) we obtain

$$\begin{aligned}
(e^{\mathrm{ran}}(\Pi, \{\varphi_t\}))^2 &= \sup_{f \in E} \int_T e^2(f, t) \, \omega(dt) \geq \int_E \int_T e^2(f, t) \, \omega(dt) \, \mu(df) \\
&= \int_T \int_E e^2(f, t) \, \mu(df) \, \omega(dt) \geq \int_E e^2(f, t^*) \, \mu(df) \\
&\geq (\mathrm{rad}^{\mathrm{ave}}(\Pi; \mathcal{A}, \mu))^2 = (\mathrm{rad}^{\mathrm{w-a}}(\Pi; \mathcal{A}, E))^2,
\end{aligned}$$

as claimed.

For instance, for the one dimensional problem of Subsection 4.2.1, the measure μ satisfying (4.12) exists for the class of linear algorithms as well as for the class of nonlinear algorithms. For linear algorithms this measure puts equal mass at $\pm\tau$, $\mu(\{-\tau\}) = \mu(\{\tau\}) = 1/2$, which follows from the fact that the error of any linear algorithm is attained at the endpoints. For nonlinear algorithms, μ is concentrated on a finite set of points, see NR 4.2.1.

To see that pure noise data are useless for one dimensional problems, it now suffices to observe that any algorithm using such data can be interpreted as a randomized algorithm. Indeed, suppose that information $y = [f + x_1, x_2, \ldots, x_n]$ where the x_is are independent. Then, for any algorithm $\varphi : \mathbb{R}^n \to \mathbb{R}$, we can define a randomized algorithm

$$\varphi_t(y_1) = \varphi(y), \qquad t = [x_2, \ldots, x_n],$$

whose 'randomized' error is equal to the worst-average case error of φ. Existence of μ gives the desired result.

Exercises

E 4.2.1 Suppose we want to approximate $f \in [-\tau, \tau]$ based on n independent observations of f, $y_i = f + x_i$ where $x_i \sim \mathcal{N}(0, \sigma^2)$. Show then that the sample mean, $\varphi_n(y) = n^{-1} \sum_{j=1}^{n} y_j$, is an asymptotically optimal algorithm,

$$e^{\text{w-a}}(\varphi_n) = \frac{\sigma}{\sqrt{n}} \approx \text{rad}_{\text{non}}^{\text{w-a}}(n) \qquad \text{as } n \to +\infty,$$

where $\text{rad}_{\text{non}}^{\text{w-a}}(n)$ is the corresponding nth minimal error of arbitrary algorithms.

E 4.2.2 Consider the problem of E 4.2.1 with $f \in \mathbb{R}$ ($\tau = +\infty$) and observations with possibly different variances, $x_i \sim \mathcal{N}(0, \sigma_i^2)$, $1 \le i \le n$. Show that then the algorithm

$$\varphi(y) = \frac{\sum_{i=1}^{n} \sigma_i^{-2} y_i}{\sum_{i=1}^{n} \sigma_i^{-2}}$$

is optimal among nonlinear algorithms and its error equals $(\sum_{i=1}^{n} \sigma_i^{-2})^{-1/2}$.

E 4.2.3 Suppose we approximate values $S(f)$ of a linear functional for f belonging to a convex and balanced set E. Let information $y = S(f) + x$, $x \sim \mathcal{N}(0, \sigma^2)$. Show that

$$\text{rad}_{\text{lin}}^{\text{w-a}}(\Pi; E) = r_{\text{lin}}(\tau, \sigma^2) \quad \text{and} \quad \text{rad}_{\text{non}}^{\text{w-a}}(\Pi; E) = r_{\text{non}}(\tau, \sigma^2),$$

where $\tau = \sup_{f \in E} S(f)$. Moreover, the optimal linear algorithm is $\varphi_{\text{opt}}(y) = c_{\text{opt}}(\tau, \sigma^2) y$.

E 4.2.4 Consider approximation of a linear functional S with $F = \mathbb{R}^n$, based on information $y = f + x$, $x \sim \mathcal{N}(0, \sigma^2 I)$. Show that for a convex and balanced set $E \subset \mathbb{R}^n$ we have

$$\text{rad}_{\text{aff}}^{\text{w-a}}(\Pi; E) = \sigma \cdot \sup_{f \in E} \sqrt{\frac{S^2(f)}{\sigma^2 + \|f\|_F^2}}.$$

E 4.2.5 Prove the uniqueness of the optimal affine algorithm $\varphi_{\delta(\sigma^2)}$ from Theorem 4.2.2 (if it exists).
Hint: Consider first the case of E being an interval.

E 4.2.6 Consider the problem defined on a Hilbert space as in Theorem 4.2.4, but with uniformly bounded information noise, $\langle \Sigma^{-1} x, x \rangle_2 \le \delta$. Show that then the optimal value of the regularization parameter γ is equal to

$$\gamma(\delta) = \sigma^2(\delta) = \delta \left(\frac{r(\delta)}{d_\delta} - \delta \right) \qquad (a/0 = +\infty).$$

E 4.2.7 Let F be a separable Hilbert space. Consider approximation of a nonzero functional $S = \langle \cdot, s \rangle_F$ from information $y = N(f) + x$ where

$$N = [\langle \cdot, f_1 \rangle_F, \ldots, \langle \cdot, f_n \rangle_F],$$

$\langle f_i, f_j \rangle_F = \delta_{ij}$, and $x \sim \mathcal{N}(0, \sigma^2 I)$. Denote by s_1 the orthogonal projection of s onto $\mathrm{span}\{f_1, \ldots, f_n\}$ and by s_2 its orthogonal complement. Show that

$$\delta(\sigma) = \frac{\left(\frac{\sigma^2}{1+\sigma^2}\right) \|s_1\|_F}{\sqrt{\left(\frac{\sigma^2}{1+\sigma^2}\right)^2 \|s_1\|_F^2 + \|s_2\|_F^2}} \qquad \text{for } 0 \le \sigma \le +\infty,$$

and

$$\sigma^2(\delta) = \frac{\delta \|s_2\|_F}{\sqrt{1 - \delta^2} \, \|s_1\|_F - \delta \|s_2\|_2} \qquad \text{for } 0 \le \delta < \frac{\|s_1\|_F}{\|s\|_F},$$

$\sigma(\delta) = +\infty$ for $\delta \ge \|s_1\|_F / \|s\|_F$. Hence, in particular, the regularization parameter $\gamma(\delta) = \sigma^2(\delta) \approx \delta \|s_2\|_F / \|s_1\|_F$ as $\delta \to 0^+$.

E 4.2.8 Show that in the general case $\sigma(\delta) \to 0$ as $\delta \to 0^+$ and the convergence is at least linear.

E 4.2.9 Prove Corollary 4.2.1 (and consequently also Theorem 4.2.3) in the Hilbert case, using only Lemma 4.2.3 and Theorem 3.5.1.

4.3 Approximation of operators

In this section, we present some results about approximation of linear operators in the mixed worst-average case setting.

4.3.1 Ellipsoidal problems in $\mathbb{R}^n$

Suppose we want to approximate a vector $f = (f_1, \ldots, f_n) \in \mathbb{R}^n$ which is known to belong to a rectangle

$$E = \mathcal{R}(\tau) = \{ f \in \mathbb{R}^n \mid |f_i| \le \tau_i, \ 1 \le i \le n \},$$

where $\tau = (\tau_1, \ldots, \tau_n) \in \mathbb{R}^n$ with $\tau_i \ge 0$, $\forall i$. Information y about f is given coordinatewise, i.e., $y_i = f_i + x_i$, $1 \le i \le n$, where the x_i are independent and $x_i \sim \mathcal{N}(0, \sigma_i^2)$.

Lemma 4.3.1 *For the rectangular problem above we have*

$$\mathrm{rad}_{\mathrm{lin}}^{\mathrm{w-a}}(\mathrm{III}, \mathcal{R}(\tau)) = \sqrt{\sum_{i=1}^n r_{\mathrm{lin}}^2(\tau_i, \sigma_i^2)} = \sqrt{\sum_{i=1}^n \frac{\sigma_i^2 \tau_i^2}{\sigma_i^2 + \tau_i^2}},$$

$$\mathrm{rad}_{\mathrm{non}}^{\mathrm{w-a}}(\mathrm{III}, \mathcal{R}(\tau)) = \sqrt{\sum_{i=1}^n r_{\mathrm{non}}^2(\tau_i, \sigma_i^2)},$$

and the (unique) optimal linear algorithm is $\varphi_\tau(y) = (c_1 y_1, \ldots, c_n y_n)$ where

$$c_i = c_{opt}(\tau_i, \sigma_i^2) = \frac{\tau_i^2}{\sigma_i^2 + \tau_i^2}, \quad 1 \le i \le n.$$

Proof Indeed, in this case the error of any algorithm $\varphi = (\varphi_1, \ldots, \varphi_n)$, $\varphi_i : \mathbb{R}^n \to \mathbb{R}$, can be written as

$$(e^{w-a}(\mathbb{II}, \varphi; \mathcal{R}(\tau)))^2 = \sup_{f \in \mathcal{R}(\tau)} \int_{\mathbb{R}^n} \sum_{i=1}^n (f_i - \varphi_i(f+x))^2 \, \pi(dx)$$

$$= \sum_{i=1}^n \left(\sup_{|f_i| \le \tau_i} \int_{\mathbb{R}} (f_i - \varphi_i(f+x))^2 \, \pi_i(dx) \right)$$

where $\pi_i = \mathcal{N}(0, \sigma_i^2)$. Hence the optimal (linear or nonlinear) approximation is coordinatewise. Moreover, as the y_is are independent, optimal φ_is use only y_i. The lemma now follows from results about the one dimensional problem given in Lemma 4.2.1.   □

It turns out that such a 'coordinatewise' algorithm is an optimal linear one over a larger set than the rectangle. Indeed, observe that the squared error of φ_τ at any $f \in \mathbb{R}^n$ is $\sum_{i=1}^n ((1-c_i)^2 f_i^2 + \sigma_i^2 c_i^2)$. Since for $f \in \mathcal{R}(\tau)$ this error is maximized at $f = \tau$, the algorithm φ_τ is also optimal over the set of f satisfying the inequality

$$\sum_{i=1}^n (1 - c_i)^2 f_i^2 \le \sum_{i=1}^n (1 - c_i)^2 \tau_i^2.$$

Taking into account the formulas for c_i we get that this set is ellipsoidal,

$$\mathcal{E}(\tau) = \left\{ f \in \mathbb{R}^n \;\middle|\; \sum_{i=1}^n (f_i^2 / a_i^2) \le 1 \right\}$$

where

$$a_i^2 = a_i^2(\tau) = (1 + \tau_i^2 / \sigma_i^2)^2 \cdot \sum_{j=1}^n \frac{\tau_j^2}{(1 + \tau_j^2 / \sigma_j^2)^2}, \quad 1 \le i \le n.$$

Hence we have the following corollary.

Corollary 4.3.1 *Let $E \subset \mathbb{R}^n$. Suppose there exists $\tau^* \in \mathbb{R}^n$ such that*

$$\mathcal{R}(\tau^*) \subset \overline{E} \subset \mathcal{E}(\tau^*). \tag{4.13}$$

Then φ_{τ^*} is the optimal linear algorithm over E and

$$\text{rad}_{\text{lin}}^{\text{w}-\text{a}}(\text{II}; \mathcal{R}(\tau^*)) = \text{rad}_{\text{lin}}^{\text{w}-\text{a}}(\text{II}; E) = \text{rad}_{\text{lin}}^{\text{w}-\text{a}}(\text{II}; \mathcal{E}(\tau^*)).$$

Observe that there exists at most one τ^* satisfying (4.13). If it exists then

$$\text{rad}_{\text{lin}}^{\text{w}-\text{a}}(\text{II}; E) = \sup_{\mathcal{R}(\tau) \subseteq E} \text{rad}_{\text{lin}}^{\text{w}-\text{a}}(\text{II}; \mathcal{R}(\tau)).$$

The condition (4.13) is satisfied by many sets. The most important examples are ellipsoids. For such ellipsoidal problems, the formulas for τ^*, and consequently for the minimal error, can be found explicitly. That is, we have the following theorem.

Theorem 4.3.1 *Let E be an ellipsoid,*

$$E = \left\{ f \in \mathbb{R}^n \,\middle|\, \sum_{i=1}^n (f_i^2/b_i^2) \leq 1 \right\}$$

where $b_1 \geq b_2 \geq \cdots \geq b_n > b_{n+1} = 0$. Let

$$\tau_i^* = \sigma_i \sqrt{b_i \left(\frac{1 + \sum_{j=1}^k (\sigma_j^2/b_j^2)}{\sum_{j=1}^k (\sigma_j^2/b_j)} \right) - 1}$$

for $1 \leq i \leq k$, and $\tau_i^* = 0$ for $k+1 \leq i \leq n$, where k is the smallest positive integer satisfying

$$b_{k+1} \leq \frac{\sum_{j=1}^k (\sigma_j^2/b_j)}{1 + \sum_{j=1}^k (\sigma_j^2/b_j^2)}.$$

Then the 'coordinatewise' algorithm φ_{τ^*} is the (unique) optimal linear one, and

$$\text{rad}_{\text{lin}}^{\text{w}-\text{a}}(\text{II}; E) = \text{e}^{\text{w}-\text{a}}(\text{II}, \varphi_{\tau^*}; E) = \sqrt{\sum_{j=1}^k \sigma_j^2 - \frac{(\sum_{j=1}^k (\sigma_j^2/b_j))^2}{1 + \sum_{j=1}^k (\sigma_j^2/b_j^2)}}.$$

Furthermore,

$$\text{rad}_{\text{lin}}^{\text{w}-\text{a}}(\text{II}; E) \leq \kappa_1^* \cdot \text{rad}_{\text{non}}^{\text{w}-\text{a}}(\text{II}; E) \qquad (\kappa_1^* = 1.11...)$$

and

$$\text{rad}_{\text{lin}}^{\text{w}-\text{a}}(\text{II}; E) \approx \text{rad}_{\text{non}}^{\text{w}-\text{a}}(\text{II}; E) \qquad as \quad \sigma_i \to 0^+, \quad 1 \leq i \leq n.$$

Proof Observe first that τ^* is well defined. Indeed, the definition of k implies

$$\frac{1 + \sum_{j=1}^{k}(\sigma_j^2/b_j^2)}{\sum_{j=1}^{k}(\sigma_j^2/b_j)} > \frac{1 + \sum_{j=1}^{k}(\sigma_j^2/b_j^2)}{b_k\left(1 + \sum_{j=1}^{k-1}(\sigma_j^2/b_j^2)\right) + \sigma_k^2/b_k} = \frac{1}{b_k},$$

which means that $b_i(1 + \sum_{j=1}^{k}(\sigma_j^2/b_j^2))/(\sum_{j=1}^{k}(\sigma_j^2/b_j)) - 1 > 0, \ \forall i$.

Obviously $\mathcal{R}(\tau^*) \subset E$. We can also easily check that $E \subset \mathcal{E}(\tau^*)$. Indeed, for $1 \leq i \leq k$ we have $a_i(\tau^*) = b_i$, while for $k + 1 \leq i \leq n$ we have

$$a_i(\tau^*) = \frac{\sum_{j=1}^{k}(\sigma_j^2/b_j)}{1 + \sum_{j=1}^{k}(\sigma_j^2/b_j^2)} \geq b_{k+1} \geq b_i.$$

Hence $\mathcal{R}(\tau^*)$ is the hardest rectangular subproblem contained in E and we can apply Corollary 4.3.1. We obtain that φ_{τ^*} is the unique optimal linear algorithm, and the radius $\mathrm{rad}_{\mathrm{lin}}^{\mathrm{w-a}}(\Pi; E) = \mathrm{e}^{\mathrm{w-a}}(\Pi, \varphi_{\tau^*}; E)$ can be easily calculated.

As $r_{\mathrm{lin}}(\tau_i, \sigma_i^2) \leq \kappa_1^* r_{\mathrm{non}}(\tau_i, \sigma_i^2)$, in view of Lemma 4.3.1 we have

$$\begin{aligned}
\mathrm{rad}_{\mathrm{lin}}^{\mathrm{w-a}}(\Pi; E) &= \mathrm{rad}_{\mathrm{lin}}^{\mathrm{w-a}}(\Pi; \mathcal{R}(\tau^*)) \\
&\leq \kappa_1^* \cdot \mathrm{rad}_{\mathrm{non}}^{\mathrm{w-a}}(\Pi; \mathcal{R}(\tau^*)) \leq \kappa_1^* \cdot \mathrm{rad}_{\mathrm{non}}^{\mathrm{w-a}}(\Pi; E).
\end{aligned}$$

We also have $r_{\mathrm{lin}}(\tau_i, \sigma_i^2) \approx r_{\mathrm{non}}(\tau_i, \sigma_i^2)$ as $\sigma_i/\tau_i \to 0$. Hence to complete the proof it suffices to observe that $\sigma_i/\tau_i^* \to 0$ as all σ_is decrease to zero. $\qquad\square$

Another characterization of problems whose difficulty is determined by the difficulty of rectangular subproblems is given as follows.

We shall say that a set E is *orthosymmetric* iff $(f_1, \ldots, f_n) \in E$ implies $(s_1 f_2, \ldots, s_n f_n) \in E$ for all choices of $s_i \in \{+1, -1\}$. A set E is *quadratically convex* iff

$$Q(E) = \{(f_1^2, \ldots, f_n^2) \mid (f_1, \ldots, f_n) \in E\}$$

is convex. Examples of orthosymmetric and quadratically convex sets include rectangles, ellipsoids, and l_p-bodies with $p \geq 2$, i.e.,

$$E = \left\{ f \in \mathbb{R}^n \ \middle| \ \sum_{i=1}^{n}(|f_i|^p/|a_i|^p) \leq 1 \right\}.$$

Lemma 4.3.2 *Let E be a bounded convex set of $\mathbb{R}^n$. If E is orthosymmetric and quadratically convex then the condition (4.13) holds, i.e.,*

$$\mathrm{rad}_{\mathrm{lin}}^{\mathrm{w-a}}(\mathbb{II}; E) \;=\; \sup_{\mathcal{R}(\tau) \subseteq E} \; \mathrm{rad}_{\mathrm{lin}}^{\mathrm{w-a}}(\mathbb{II}; \mathcal{R}(\tau)).$$

Proof Let τ^* be the maximizer of $\mathrm{rad}_{\mathrm{lin}}^{\mathrm{w-a}}(\mathbb{II}; \mathcal{R}(\tau))$ over $\tau \in \overline{E}$. As E is orthosymmetric and convex, $\mathcal{R}(\tau^*) \subset \overline{E}$. We now show that $\overline{E} \subset \mathcal{E}(\tau^*)$. For $x_i \geq 0$, $\forall i$, let

$$\psi(x_1, \ldots, x_n) \;=\; (\mathrm{rad}_{\mathrm{lin}}^{\mathrm{w-a}}(\mathbb{II}; \mathcal{R}(\sqrt{x_1}, \ldots, \sqrt{x_n})))^2 \;=\; \sum_{i=1}^{n} \frac{\sigma_i^2 x_i}{\sigma_i^2 + x_i}.$$

Denoting by ∂A the boundary of a set A, we have that $P = Q(\,\partial \mathcal{E}(\tau^*))$ is a hyperplane which is adjacent to the set

$$B \;=\; \{\, x \mid\; \psi(x) \geq (\mathrm{rad}_{\mathrm{lin}}^{\mathrm{w-a}}(\mathbb{II}; \mathcal{R}(\tau^*)))^2 \,\}.$$

As $Q(E)$ is convex and the interiors of $Q(E)$ and $Q(B)$ have empty intersection, both sets are separated by P. Hence $Q(E) \subset Q(\mathcal{E}(\tau^*))$ which implies $\overline{E} \subset \mathcal{E}(\tau^*)$. Now we can apply Corollary 4.3.1, completing the proof.   □

4.3.2 The Hilbert case

We now apply the results obtained above to get optimal algorithms for some problems defined on Hilbert spaces. We assume that S is a compact operator acting between separable Hilbert spaces F and G. We want to approximate $S(f)$ for f from the unit ball E of F. Information is linear with Gaussian noise, i.e., $y = N(f) + x$ where $N = [\langle \cdot, f_1 \rangle_F, \ldots, \langle \cdot, f_n \rangle_F]$ and $x \sim \mathcal{N}(0, \sigma^2 \Sigma)$, $\Sigma > 0$. As always, $\langle \cdot, \cdot \rangle_Y = \langle \Sigma^{-1}(\cdot), \cdot \rangle_2$.

We also assume that the operators S^*S and N^*N (where N^* is meant with respect to the inner products $\langle \cdot, \cdot \rangle_F$ and $\langle \cdot, \cdot \rangle_Y$) have a common orthonormal basis of eigenelements. Write this basis as $\{\xi_i\}_{i \geq 1}$ and the corresponding eigenvalues as λ_i and η_i,

$$S^*S\,\xi_i \;=\; \lambda_i\,\xi_i, \qquad N^*N\,\xi_i \;=\; \eta_i\,\xi_i, \qquad i \geq 1,$$

where $\lambda_1 \geq \lambda_2 \geq \lambda_3 \geq \cdots \geq 0$ and $\lim_{j \to \infty} \lambda_j = 0$.

Our aim is to find the optimal linear algorithm and its error. It is clear that we can restrict our considerations to φ such that $\varphi(\mathbb{R}^n) \subset \overline{S(F)}$ since otherwise we would project φ onto $\overline{S(F)}$ to obtain a better algorithm. We write φ in the form

$$\varphi(y) = \sum_j \varphi_j(y) S(\xi_j),$$

where $\varphi_j : \mathbb{R}^n \to \mathbb{R}$ and the summation is taken over all $j \geq 1$ with $\lambda_j > 0$. As the elements $S(\xi_j)$ are orthogonal and $\|S(\xi_j)\|^2 = \lambda_j$, for such φ we have

$$(e^{w-a}(\mathrm{III}, \varphi))^2$$

$$= \sup_{\|f\|_F \leq 1} \int_{\mathbb{R}^n} \left\| \sum_j (\langle f, \xi_j \rangle_F - \varphi_j(y)) S(\xi_j) \right\|^2 \pi_f(dy)$$

$$= \sup_{\sum_i \langle f, \xi_i \rangle_F^2 \leq 1} \sum_j \int_{\mathbb{R}^n} \lambda_j(\langle f, \xi_j \rangle_F - \varphi_j(y))^2 \pi_f(dy).$$

We now change variables as follows. Let $\mathcal{I} = \{i_1, i_2, \ldots, i_m\}$ ($i_1 < i_2 < \cdots < i_m$) be the set of all indices $i \geq 1$ such that $\eta_i > 0$. Clearly, $m \leq n$. For $j \in \mathcal{I}$, let $q_j = N\xi_j/\sqrt{\eta_j}$. Then the vectors q_j are orthonormal in $\mathbb{R}^n$ with respect to the inner product $\langle \cdot, \cdot \rangle_Y$, and the $\Sigma^{-1/2} q_j$ are orthonormal with respect to $\langle \cdot, \cdot \rangle_2$. Let Q be an orthogonal $n \times n$ matrix whose first m columns are $\Sigma^{-1/2} q_{i_j}$, and

$$D_1 = \mathrm{diag}\Big\{ \eta_{i_1}^{-1/2}, \ldots, \eta_{i_m}^{-1/2}, \underbrace{1, \ldots, 1}_{n-m} \Big\}.$$

Letting $\tilde{y} = D_1 Q^T \Sigma^{-1/2} y$ we transform the data $y = N(f) + x$ to $\tilde{y} = M(f) + \tilde{x}$, where

$$M(f) = \Big[\langle f, \xi_{i_1} \rangle_F, \ldots, \langle f, \xi_{i_m} \rangle_F, \underbrace{0, \ldots, 0}_{n-m} \Big]$$

and the $\tilde{x}_j$ are independent,

$$\tilde{x} \sim \tilde{\pi} = \mathcal{N}\Big(0, \sigma^2 \mathrm{diag}\Big\{ \eta_{i_1}^{-1}, \ldots, \eta_{i_m}^{-1}, \underbrace{1, \ldots, 1}_{n-m} \Big\} \Big).$$

(Compare with the analogous transformation in Subsection 3.4.2.) Writing $\tilde{\varphi}(\tilde{y}) = \varphi(y)$ and $f_j = \langle f, \xi_j \rangle_F$ we obtain

$$(e^{w-a}(\mathrm{III}, \varphi))^2 = \sup_{\sum_i f_i^2 \leq 1} \sum_j \int_{\mathbb{R}^n} \lambda_j (f_j - \tilde{\varphi}_j(M(f) + \tilde{x}))^2 \tilde{\pi}(d\tilde{x}).$$

Changing the variables once more to $h_j = \sqrt{\lambda_j} f_j$, $t_j = \sqrt{\lambda_j} \tilde{x}_j$ for

$1 \leq j \leq m$, $t_j = \tilde{x}_j$ for $m + 1 \leq j \leq n$, and letting

$$\psi_j(y_1, \ldots, y_n) = \sqrt{\lambda_j} \cdot \tilde{\varphi}_j \left(y_1 / \sqrt{\lambda_{i_1}}, \ldots, y_m / \sqrt{\lambda_{i_m}}, y_{m+1}, \ldots, y_n \right),$$

we finally get that the squared error $(e^{w-a}(\mathbb{II}, \varphi))^2$ equals

$$\sup_{\sum_i (h_i^2/\lambda_i) \leq 1} \sum_j \int_{\mathbb{R}^n} (h_j - \psi_j(h_{i_1} + t_1, \ldots, h_{i_m} + t_m, t_{m+1}, \ldots, t_n)) \, \omega(dt)$$

where

$$\omega = \mathcal{N}\left(0, \sigma^2 \operatorname{diag}\left\{ \lambda_{i_1} \eta_{i_1}^{-1}, \ldots, \lambda_{i_m} \eta_{i_m}^{-1}, \underbrace{1, \ldots, 1}_{n-m} \right\} \right).$$

Observe that information about $h = (h_1, h_2, \ldots) \in l_2$ is now given coordinatewise. Thus we can apply the whole machinery of Subsection 4.3.1 for rectangular subproblems, which are now given as $\mathcal{R}(\tau) = \{ h \in l_2 \mid |h_i| \leq \tau_i, i \geq 1 \}$ where $\tau \in l_2$ is in the ellipsoid $\sum_i (\tau_i^2/\lambda_i) \leq 1$.

It is not difficult to see that the parameter τ^* is given as follows. Let

$$s = \min\{ i \geq 0 \mid \eta_{i+1} = 0 \text{ or } \lambda_{i+1} = 0 \}. \tag{4.14}$$

Then $\tau_i^* = 0$ for $i \geq s + 2$, and $\tau_1^*, \ldots, \tau_{s+1}^*$ are the maximizer of

$$\sum_{j=1}^{s} \frac{\sigma_j^2 \tau_j^2}{\sigma_j^2 + \tau_j^2} + \tau_{s+1}^2$$

over the ellipsoid $\sum_{i=1}^{s+1} (\tau_i^2/\lambda_i) \leq 1$ (if $\lambda_{s+1} = 0$ then $\tau_{s+1} = 0$ and the last summation is taken from 1 to s), where the noise levels $\sigma_j^2 = \sigma^2 \lambda_j / \eta_j$. Solving this maximization problem, we obtain the following formulas.

Let k be the smallest integer satisfying $k \in \{1, 2, \ldots, s\}$ and

$$\sqrt{\lambda_{k+1}} \leq \frac{\sigma^2 \sum_{j=1}^{k} \sqrt{\lambda_j} \eta_j^{-1}}{1 + \sigma^2 \sum_{j=1}^{k} \eta_j^{-1}}, \tag{4.15}$$

or $k = s + 1$ if such a number does not exist. We have two cases:
(i) If $1 \leq k \leq s$ then

$$(\tau_i^*)^2 = \begin{cases} \frac{\lambda_i}{\eta_i} \left(\sqrt{\lambda_i} \left(\frac{1 + \sigma^2 \sum_{j=1}^{k} \eta_j^{-1}}{\sigma^2 \sum_{j=1}^{k} \sqrt{\lambda_j} \eta_j^{-1}} \right) - \sigma^2 \right) & 1 \leq i \leq k, \\ 0 & i \geq k + 1. \end{cases}$$

$$\tag{4.16}$$

(ii) If $k = s + 1$ then

$$(\tau_i^*)^2 = \begin{cases} \sigma^2 \frac{\lambda_i}{\eta_i} \left(\frac{\sqrt{\lambda_i}}{\sqrt{\lambda_{s+1}}} - 1 \right) & 1 \leq i \leq s, \\ \lambda_{s+1} - \sigma^2 \sqrt{\lambda_{s+1}} \sum_{j=1}^s \left(\frac{\sqrt{\lambda_j} - \sqrt{\lambda_{s+1}}}{\eta_j} \right) & i = s + 1, \\ 0 & i \geq s + 2. \end{cases}$$
(4.17)

Now we can check that the 'coordinatewise' algorithm φ_{τ^*} is optimal not only for the rectangular subproblem $\mathcal{R}(\tau^*)$, but also for the ellipsoid $\sum_{j=1}^{s+1} (h_j^2/\lambda_j) \leq 1$. The minimal linear error is then equal to the error of φ_{τ^*} and nonlinear algorithms can only be slightly better. We summarize our analysis in the following theorem.

Theorem 4.3.2 *Suppose the operators S^*S and N^*N have a common orthonormal basis of eigenelements $\{\xi_i\}$ and the corresponding eigenvalues are λ_i and η_i, respectively, $\lambda_1 \geq \lambda_2 \geq \cdots \geq 0$. Let s and k be defined by (4.14) and (4.15).*

(i) If $1 \leq k \leq s$ then

$$\mathrm{rad}_{\mathrm{lin}}^{\mathrm{w-a}}(\mathbb{II}) = \sigma \cdot \sqrt{\sum_{i=1}^k \frac{\lambda_i}{\eta_i} - \sigma^2 \frac{\left(\sum_{j=1}^k \sqrt{\lambda_j} \eta_j^{-1} \right)^2}{1 + \sigma^2 \sum_{j=1}^k \eta_j^{-1}}}$$

and the optimal linear algorithm is given as

$\varphi_{\mathrm{lin}}(y)$

$$= \sum_{i=1}^k \left(1 - \sigma^2 \frac{\sum_{j=1}^k \sqrt{\lambda_j} \eta_j^{-1}}{\sqrt{\lambda_i}(1 + \sigma^2 \sum_{j=1}^k \eta_j^{-1})} \right) \eta_i^{-1} \langle N(\xi_i), \Sigma^{-1} y \rangle_2 \, S(\xi_i).$$

(ii) If $k = s + 1$ then

$$\mathrm{rad}_{\mathrm{lin}}^{\mathrm{w-a}}(\mathbb{II}) = \sqrt{\lambda_{s+1} + \sigma^2 \sum_{i=1}^s \frac{(\sqrt{\lambda_i} - \sqrt{\lambda_{s+1}})^2}{\eta_i}}.$$

and the optimal linear algorithm is given as

$$\varphi_{\mathrm{lin}}(y) = \sum_{i=1}^s \left(1 - \frac{\sqrt{\lambda_{s+1}}}{\sqrt{\lambda_i}} \right) \eta_i^{-1} \langle N(\xi_i), \Sigma^{-1} y \rangle_2 \, S(\xi_i).$$

In both cases, for nonlinear algorithms we have

$$\mathrm{rad}_{\mathrm{non}}^{\mathrm{w-a}}(\mathbb{II}) \leq \kappa_1^* \, \mathrm{rad}_{\mathrm{lin}}^{\mathrm{w-a}}(\mathbb{II}) \qquad (\kappa_1^* = 1.11...).$$

Let us see more carefully what happens when $\sigma \to 0$. We have two cases. Assume first that $\lambda_{s+1} = 0$, i.e., the radius of exact information is zero. Then we fall into (i),

$$\mathrm{rad}_{\mathrm{lin}}^{\mathrm{w-a}}(\mathbb{II}) \approx \sigma \sqrt{\sum_{i=1}^{s} \frac{\lambda_i}{\eta_i}}$$

$$= \sigma \sqrt{\mathrm{tr}(S(N^*N)^{-1}S^*)} \approx \mathrm{rad}_{\mathrm{non}}^{\mathrm{w-a}}(\mathbb{II})$$

(where the last equivalence follows from the fact that $\sigma_j/\tau_j^* \to 0$ as $\sigma \to 0$, $1 \le j \le s$), and the algorithm φ_{lin} 'tends' to

$$\varphi_*(y) = \sum_{i=1}^{s} \eta_i^{-1} \langle N(\xi_i), \Sigma^{-1}y \rangle_2 \, S(\xi_i).$$

Observe that if $F = \mathrm{span}\{\xi_1, \ldots, \xi_s\}$ then φ_* is nothing else but the least squares algorithm $\varphi_{\mathrm{ls}} = SN^{-1}P_N$ (where P_N is the orthogonal projection in the space Y onto $N(F)$ with respect to $\langle \cdot, \cdot \rangle_Y$). Indeed, for $y = N(f) + x$ with $P_N x = 0$, we have

$$\varphi_*(y) = \sum_{i=1}^{s} \langle f, \xi_i \rangle_F \, S(\xi_i) = S(f) = \varphi_{\mathrm{ls}}(y).$$

Suppose now that $\lambda_{s+1} > 0$ which means that the radius of exact information is positive. Then

$$\lim_{\sigma \to 0} \mathrm{rad}_{\mathrm{lin}}^{\mathrm{w-a}}(\mathbb{II}) = \sqrt{\lambda_{s+1}} = \lim_{\sigma \to 0} \mathrm{rad}_{\mathrm{non}}^{\mathrm{w-a}}(\mathbb{II})$$

and the optimal linear algorithm is independent of the noise level σ, provided that it is small,

$$\sigma^2 \le \left(\sum_{j=1}^{s} \eta_j^{-1} \left(\sqrt{\frac{\lambda_j}{\lambda_{s+1}}} - 1 \right) \right)^{-1}.$$

Example 4.3.1 Suppose we approximate a vector $f \in \mathbb{R}^d$, $\|f\|_2 \le 1$, from information $y_i = \langle f, f_i \rangle_2 + x_i$, $1 \le i \le n$, where $x \sim \mathcal{N}(0, \sigma^2 \Sigma)$ and the vectors f_i span the space $\mathbb{R}^d$. (If the last assumption is not satisfied then $\mathrm{rad}^{\mathrm{w-a}}(\mathbb{II}) = 1$.) Then $S = I$ and $\lambda_i = 1$, $\forall i$. From Theorem 4.3.2(i) we obtain that the minimal error depends only on σ and $\sum_{i=1}^{d} \eta_i^{-1} = \mathrm{tr}((N^*N)^{-1})$, and is equal to

$$\mathrm{rad}_{\mathrm{lin}}^{\mathrm{w-a}}(\mathbb{II}) = \sigma \cdot \sqrt{\frac{\mathrm{tr}((N^*N)^{-1})}{1 + \sigma^2 \, \mathrm{tr}((N^*N)^{-1})}}.$$

The optimal linear algorithm is

$$\varphi_{\text{lin}}(y) = \left(1 + \sigma^2 \operatorname{tr}((N^*N)^{-1})\right)^{-1} \varphi_{\text{ls}}(y),$$

where, as always, φ_{ls} denotes the least squares algorithm.

A simple comparison shows that in this case the optimal linear algorithm φ_{lin} is in general *not* an α-smoothing spline. Thus in the mixed worst-average case the situation changes as compared to the worst and average case settings, in which α-smoothing splines are optimal algorithms in the Hilbert case.

The assumption that S^*S and N^*N have a common orthonormal basis of eigenelements is essential. When this is not satisfied, optimal (or almost optimal) algorithms are known only for some special problems. We now present one such problem; for other examples see NR 4.3.3.

Suppose we approximate values of a linear operator S defined on $F = \mathbb{R}^d$, for all elements $f \in \mathbb{R}^d$, i.e., $E = \mathbb{R}^d$. Information $\mathbb{II}$ is assumed to be arbitrary. It turns out that in this case the least squares algorithm is optimal even in the class of arbitrary algorithms. Indeed, from the proof of Theorem 3.6.2 we know that for any f

$$\int_{\mathbb{R}^n} \|S(f) - \varphi_{\text{ls}}(N(f) + x)\|^2 \, \pi(dx) = \sigma^2 \operatorname{tr}(S(N^*N)^{-1}S^*).$$

Hence $(e^{\text{w-a}}(\mathbb{II}, \varphi_{\text{ls}}))^2 = \sigma^2 \operatorname{tr}(S(N^*N)^{-1}S^*)$. On the other hand, a lower bound on $\operatorname{rad}^{\text{w-a}}(\mathbb{II}; \mathbb{R}^d)$ can be obtained by calculating the average radius of the same information with respect to the measure $\mu_\lambda = \mathcal{N}(0, \lambda I)$. Using Corollary 3.4.1 we obtain

$$(\operatorname{rad}^{\text{ave}}(\mathbb{II}; \mu_\lambda))^2 = \lambda \cdot \operatorname{tr}(SS^*) - \sum_{j=1}^{d} \frac{\lambda \|S(\xi_j)\|^2}{1 + \sigma^2/(\eta_j \lambda)}$$

$$= \sum_{j=1}^{d} \frac{\sigma^2 \lambda}{\sigma^2 + \eta_j \lambda} \|S(\xi_j)\|^2.$$

Now letting $\lambda \to +\infty$ we get

$$(\operatorname{rad}_{\text{non}}^{\text{w-a}}(\mathbb{II}; \mathbb{R}^d))^2 \geq \lim_{\lambda \to \infty} (\operatorname{rad}^{\text{ave}}(\mathbb{II}; \mu_\lambda))^2$$

$$= \sigma^2 \sum_{j=1}^{d} \frac{\|S(\xi_j)\|^2}{\eta_j} = \sigma^2 \sum_{j=1}^{d} \|SN^{-1}(N\xi_j/\sqrt{\eta_j})\|^2$$

$$= \sigma^2 \operatorname{tr}(S(N^*N)^{-1}S^*).$$

Hence we have proven the following theorem.

Theorem 4.3.3 *Let $E = F = \mathbb{R}^d$ and $\dim N(F) = d$. Then the generalized least squares algorithm φ_{ls} is optimal among arbitrary nonlinear algorithms and*

$$\mathrm{rad}_{non}^{w-a}(\mathrm{I\!I}; \mathbb{R}^d) = \mathrm{e}^{w-a}(\mathrm{I\!I}, \varphi_{ls}; \mathbb{R}^d) = \sigma \sqrt{\mathrm{tr}(S(N^*N)^{-1}S^*)}.$$

Notes and remarks

NR 4.3.1 Subsection 4.3.1 is based on the results of Donoho *et al.* (1990), where the model with infinitely many observations is studied. However, Corollary 4.3.1 and Theorem 4.3.1 are new. The formulas for the optimal linear algorithms obtained in Subsection 4.3.2 are also new.

Asymptotic optimality of linear algorithms for ellipsoidal problems was first shown by Pinsker (1980).

NR 4.3.2 It is interesting that if the set E in Lemma 4.3.2 is orthosymmetric and convex, but *not* quadratically convex, then this lemma need not be true and nonlinear algorithms can significantly outperform optimal linear algorithms.

Consider, for instance, the problem of estimating an n dimensional vector from noisy observations of its coefficients, as in Subsection 4.3.1. Let E be the unit ball in the l_p-norm, $E = \{f \in \mathbb{R}^n \mid \sum_{i=1}^n |f_i|^p \le 1\}$, where $p \ge 1$. Note that E is not quadratically convex for $1 \le p < 2$. Assuming that the variance of noise satisfies $\sigma^2 = \sigma^2(n) = 1/n$, we have

$$\lim_{n \to \infty} \frac{\mathrm{rad}_{lin}^{w-a}(\mathrm{I\!I}, E)}{\mathrm{rad}_{non}^{w-a}(\mathrm{I\!I}, E)} = \begin{cases} 1 & p \ge 2, \\ +\infty & 1 \le p < 1. \end{cases}$$

Furthermore, an (almost) optimal nonlinear approximation relies on a shrinkage of the experimental coefficients y_i of f towards the origin, i.e.,

$$\varphi_{non}(y) = (\mathrm{sgn}(y_i)(|y_i| - \lambda)_+)_{i=1}^n,$$

where the parameter $\lambda = \lambda(n, \sigma, p)$. For results of this type, see Donoho and Johnstone (1994), and also NR 4.3.4.

NR 4.3.3 The model with 'coordinatewise' observations turns out to be the limiting model in curve estimation (function approximation). This fact together with results of Subsection 4.3.1 can be used to derive results about optimal algorithms for some other problems. We now give one example.

Suppose we want to approximate a function $f : [0, 1] \to \mathbb{R}$ in the $\mathcal{L}_2$-norm belonging to the set $E = E_P = \{f \in W_r \mid \int_0^1 (f^{(r)}(t))^2\, dt \le P^2\}$, based on noisy values of f at equidistant points, $y_i = f(i/n) + x_i$, $0 \le i \le n$, and $x \sim \mathcal{N}(0, \sigma^2 I)$ ($\sigma > 0$). In the statistical literature, this is called a *nonparametric regression* model, and it was studied, e.g., in Golubev and Nussbaum (1990), Nussbaum (1985), Speckman (1985), Stone (1982) (see also the book of Eubank, 1988). It is known that for this problem the radius of information is asymptotically (as $n \to \infty$) achieved by a smoothing spline algorithm and that this radius satisfies

$$\mathrm{rad}_{non}^{w-a}(\mathrm{I\!I}; n) \approx \left(\frac{\sigma}{\sqrt{n}}\right)^{2r/(2r+1)} \gamma^{1/2}(r) P^{1/(2r+1)}, \qquad (4.18)$$

where $\gamma(r) = (2r+1)^{1/(2r+1)}(r/\pi(r+1))^{2r/(2r+1)}$ is *Pinsker's constant*, see Nussbaum (1985). The main idea for proving this result is as follows. For large n, the $\mathcal{L}_2$-norm of a function f roughly equals $\|f\|_n = (n^{-1}\sum_{i=1}^n f^2(i/n))^{1/2}$. So we can consider the error with respect to the seminorm $\|\cdot\|_n$ instead of the $\mathcal{L}_2$-norm. The set $E_n = \{(f(0), f(1/n), \ldots, f((n-1)/n), f(1)) \mid f \in E_P\}$ is an ellipsoid. Hence the original problem can be reduced to that of approximating a vector $v \in E_n \subset \mathbb{R}^n$ from information $y = v + x$ where $x \sim \mathcal{N}(0, \sigma^2 I)$. If we find the coordinates of E_n (which is the main difficulty in this problem), results of Subsection 4.3.1 can be applied.

Golubev and Nussbaum (1990) showed that we cannot do better by allowing observations at arbitrary points. That is, the estimate (4.18) holds also for the nth minimal radius and equidistant observations are asymptotically optimal.

NR 4.3.4 Recently, Donoho and Johnstone (1992) (see also Donoho, 1995, and Donoho *et al.*, 1995) developed a new algorithm for approximating functions from their noisy samples at equidistant points. The algorithm is nonlinear. It uses the wavelet transform and relies on translating the empirical wavelet coefficients towards the origin by $\sqrt{2\log(n)}\sigma/\sqrt{n}$. Surprisingly enough, such a simple algorithm turns out to be nearly optimal for estimating many classes of functions, in standard Hölder and Sobolev spaces as well as in more general Besov and Triebel spaces.

More precisely, suppose that f is in the unit ball of the Besov space $B_{p,q}^s$ or the Triebel space $F_{p,q}^s$. Then the minimal errors of arbitrary and linear algorithms using n noisy samples are given as

$$\mathrm{rad}_{\mathrm{non}}^{\mathrm{w-a}}(n) \asymp n^{-k} \quad \text{and} \quad \mathrm{rad}_{\mathrm{lin}}^{\mathrm{w-a}}(n) \asymp n^{-k'},$$

where

$$k = \frac{s}{s+1/2} \quad \text{and} \quad k' = \frac{s + (1/p_- - 1/p)}{s + 1/2 + (1/p_- - 1/p)},$$

with $p_- = \max\{p, 2\}$. Hence, for $p < 2$, no linear algorithm can achieve the optimal rate of convergence.

For information on Besov and Triebel spaces see, e.g., Triebel (1992). An introduction to wavelets may be found in Daubechies (1992) or Meyer (1990).

NR 4.3.5 As far as we know, the computational complexity in the mixed worst-average case setting has not been studied so far. There are two main difficulties that have to be overcome before finding concrete complexity formulas.

The first difficulty lies in obtaining optimal information. As optimal algorithms are not known exactly even for problems defined in Hilbert spaces, results on optimal information are limited. (For some special cases see NR 4.3.3 and E 4.3.6, 4.3.7.)

The second difficulty is adaption. In the mixed worst-average case setting, the situation seems to be much more complicated than in the worst and average case settings, even for problems defined on convex and balanced sets. For instance, Ibragimov and Hasminski (1982) and Golubev (1992) proved that in the nonparametric regression model the (nonadaptive) equidistant design is asymptotically optimal in the class of adaptive designs. This is, however, no longer true for integration. Recently, Plaskota (1995b) gave an example where adaption helps significantly for multivariate integration for a convex and balanced class of functions.

More precisely, let

$$F = \{f : D = [0,1]^d \to \mathbb{R} \mid |f(x) - f(y)| \le \|x - y\|_\infty\}$$

with $d \ge 2$. Suppose we want to approximate the integral $S(f) = \int_D f(u)du$ from observations of the function values. Let $r_{\text{non}}(n,\sigma)$ and $r_{\text{ad}}(n,\sigma)$ be the minimal errors that can be achieved using exactly n nonadaptive and adaptive observations with variance σ^2, respectively. Then, for any $\sigma \ge 0$, we have $r_{\text{non}}(n,\sigma) \asymp n^{-1/d}$, but

$$r_{\text{ad}}(n,\sigma) \asymp \begin{cases} n^{-1/d} & \sigma = 0, \\ n^{-1/2} & \sigma > 0. \end{cases}$$

Thus, for large d, adaptive information can be much better than nonadaptive information. Moreover, using adaptive information one can obtain much better approximations for noisy data than for exact data. These results hold because adaption and noisy information make the Monte Carlo simulation possible.

Exercises

E 4.3.1 Show that the number k in Theorem 4.3.1 can be equivalently defined as the largest integer satisfying $1 \le k \le n$ and

$$b_k < \frac{\sum_{j=1}^{k}(\sigma_j^2/b_j)}{1 + \sum_{j=1}^{k}(\sigma_j^2/b_j^2)}.$$

E 4.3.2 Let E be the l_p-body with $1 \le p < 2$. Show that then the condition (4.13) is not satisfied and, in particular, E is not quadratically convex.

E 4.3.3 Consider the 'coordinatewise' problem of Subsection 4.3.1 with E the l_p-ball,

$$E = \left\{ f \in \mathbb{R}^n \,\middle|\, \sum_{i=1}^{n} |f_i|^p \le 1 \right\},$$

where $0 < p < +\infty$. Show that the minimal error of linear algorithms equals

$$\text{rad}_{\text{lin}}^{\text{w-a}}(\mathbb{I}, E) = \begin{cases} \sigma(n/(1+\sigma^2 n))^{1/2} & 0 < p \le 2, \\ \sigma(n/(1+\sigma^2 n^{2/p}))^{1/2} & p > 2. \end{cases}$$

Furthermore, show that the optimal linear algorithm is given as $\varphi_{\text{lin}}(y) = c_{\text{opt}} y$ where

$$c_{\text{opt}} = \begin{cases} (1+\sigma^2 n)^{-1} & 0 < p \le 2, \\ (1+\sigma^2 n^{2/p})^{-1} & p > 2. \end{cases}$$

E 4.3.4 Suppose that the least squares algorithm φ_{ls} is applied for $S = I$ and E the unit ball of $\mathbb{R}^d$. Show that

$$e^{\text{w-a}}(\mathbb{I}, \varphi_{\text{ls}}) \approx \text{rad}_{\text{non}}^{\text{w-a}}(\mathbb{I}) \qquad \text{as} \quad \text{tr}((N^*N)^{-1}) \to 0.$$

E 4.3.5 Let $E \subset F$ and $\mathbb{II} = \{\pi_f\}$ be an arbitrary set and linear information with Gaussian noise, $\pi_f = \mathcal{N}(N(f), \Sigma)$. For $\sigma > 0$ we define

$$E_\sigma = \sigma E = \{\sigma f \in F \mid f \in E\}$$

and information $\mathbb{II}_\sigma$ with $\pi_{\sigma,f} = \mathcal{N}(N(f), \sigma^2 \Sigma)$. Show that for an arbitrary linear solution operator S, the minimal linear, affine, or nonlinear errors satisfy

$$\mathrm{rad}^{\mathrm{w-a}}(\mathbb{II}_\sigma; E) = \sigma \cdot \mathrm{rad}^{\mathrm{w-a}}(\mathbb{II}; E_{1/\sigma}).$$

E 4.3.6 Consider the problem of approximating a vector f from the unit ball of $\mathbb{R}^d$. Let $r_n(\sigma_1, \ldots, \sigma_n)$ $(0 < \sigma_1 \leq \cdots \leq \sigma_n)$ be the minimal error that can be attained by linear algorithms that use n $(n \geq d)$ independent observations $y_i = \langle f, f_i \rangle_2 + x_i$ with Gaussian noise, $x_i \sim \mathcal{N}(0, \sigma_i^2)$, where $\|f_i\|_2 \leq 1$, $1 \leq i \leq n$. Show that

$$r_n(\sigma_1, \ldots, \sigma_n) = \min \sqrt{\frac{\sum_{i=1}^d \eta_i^{-1}}{1 + \sum_{i=1}^d \eta_i^{-1}}}$$

where the minimum is taken over all $\eta_i \geq 0$ such that

$$\sum_{j=r}^n \eta_j \leq \sum_{j=r}^n \sigma_j^{-2}, \qquad 1 \leq r \leq n. \tag{4.19}$$

In particular, for $n = d$ we have

$$r_n(\sigma_1, \ldots, \sigma_n) = \sqrt{\frac{\sum_{i=1}^d \sigma_i^2}{1 + \sum_{i=1}^d \sigma_i^2}}.$$

What is the optimal information?
Hint: Use Lemma 2.8.1 to obtain the upper bound and optimal information.

E 4.3.7 Consider the optimal information problem as in E 4.3.6, but with $E = \mathbb{R}^d$ and an arbitrary solution operator $S : \mathbb{R}^d \to G$. Let $\lambda_1 \geq \cdots \geq \lambda_d \geq 0$ be the eigenvalues of S^*S. Show that

$$r_n(\sigma_1, \ldots, \sigma_n) = \min \sqrt{\sum_{i=1}^d \frac{\lambda_i}{\eta_i}}$$

where the minimum is taken over all $\eta_i \geq 0$ satisfying (4.19). In particular, show that for equal variances $\sigma_i^2 = \sigma^2$ we have

$$r_n(\sigma) = \frac{\sigma}{\sqrt{n}} \cdot \sum_{i=1}^d \lambda_i^{1/2}.$$

Find the optimal information.

5

Average-worst case setting

5.1 Introduction

In the previous chapter, we studied the mixed worst-average case setting in which we have deterministic assumptions on the problem elements and stochastic assumptions on noise. In the present chapter, we analyze the second mixed setting called the *average-worst case setting*. It is obtained by exchanging the assumptions of the previous chapter. More precisely, we assume some (Gaussian) distribution μ on the elements f. The information operator is defined as in the worst case setting of Chapter 2. That is, $N(f)$ is a set of finite real sequences. The error of an algorithm φ that uses information N is given as

$$e^{a-w}(N, \varphi) = \sqrt{\int_F \sup_{y \in N(f)} \|S(f) - \varphi(y)\|^2 \, \mu(df)}.$$

The average-worst case setting seems to be new and its study has been initiated only recently. Nevertheless, as a counterpart of the widely studied worst-average case setting, it is also important and leads to interesting and nontrivial results.

The main results of this chapter concern approximating linear functionals, and are presented in Section 5.2. It turns out that in this case the average-worst case setting can be analyzed similarly to the worst-average case setting, although they seem to be quite different. Assuming that the information noise is bounded in a Hilbert norm, we establish a close relation between the average-worst setting and the corresponding average case setting. That is, in both settings, optimal linear algorithms belong to the same class of smoothing spline algorithms. Moreover, the minimal errors are (almost) attained by the same algorithm, and the ratio of the minimal errors is bounded by at most 1.5. Using once more the concept

248

of hardest one dimensional subproblems, we show that nonlinear algorithms cannot be much better than linear algorithms for approximating linear functionals.

The relation between the average-worst and average settings, together with relations established in the previous sections, enables us to formulate a theorem about (almost) equivalence of all four corresponding settings for linear functionals.

In Section 5.3, we present some results for operators. In particular, we show optimality properties of the least squares algorithm.

5.2 Linear algorithms for linear functionals

In this section, we construct almost optimal algorithms for the case when the solution operator S is a linear functional. To do this, we use ideas similar to those in the worst-average case setting.

5.2.1 The one dimensional problem

Suppose we want to approximate a real random variable f which has zero-mean normal distribution with variance $\lambda > 0$, $f \sim \mathcal{N}(0, \lambda)$. We assume that instead of f we know only its noisy value $y = f + x$ where $|x| \le \delta$. That is, the information operator $\mathbb{N}(f) = [f - \delta, f + \delta]$. In this case, the error of an algorithm φ is given as

$$
\begin{aligned}
e^{a-w}(\mathbb{N}, \varphi) \;&=\; e^{a-w}(\lambda, \delta; \varphi) \\
&=\; \sqrt{\frac{1}{\sqrt{2\pi\lambda}} \int_{\mathbb{R}} \sup_{|x| \le \delta} |f - \varphi(f + x)|^2 \exp\{-f^2/(2\lambda)\} \, df} \; .
\end{aligned}
$$

First, we consider linear algorithms. Let

$$
r_{\mathrm{lin}}(\lambda, \delta) \;=\; \inf\{\, e^{a-w}(\lambda, \delta; \varphi) \mid \varphi \text{ linear }\}.
$$

Lemma 5.2.1 *For all $\lambda > 0$ and $\delta \ge 0$ we have*

$$
r_{\mathrm{lin}}(\lambda, \delta) \;=\;
\begin{cases}
\delta & \delta^2 \le 2\lambda/\pi, \\[2mm]
\sqrt{\dfrac{\lambda\delta^2(1 - 2/\pi)}{\lambda + \delta^2 - 2\delta(2\lambda/\pi)^{1/2}}} & 2\lambda/\pi < \delta^2 < \pi\lambda/2, \\[2mm]
\sqrt{\lambda} & \pi\lambda/2 \le \delta^2 \,.
\end{cases}
$$

The optimal linear algorithm $\varphi(y) = c_{\mathrm{opt}} y$ is uniquely determined and *its coefficient is given as*

$$
c_{\mathrm{opt}} \; = \; c_{\mathrm{opt}}(\lambda, \delta) \;\; = \;\;
\begin{cases}
1 & \delta^2 \le 2\lambda/\pi, \\[2mm]
\dfrac{\lambda - \delta\sqrt{2\lambda/\pi}}{\lambda + \delta^2 - 2\delta\sqrt{2\lambda/\pi}} & 2\lambda/\pi < \delta^2 < \pi\lambda/2, \\[2mm]
0 & \pi\lambda/2 \le \delta^2.
\end{cases}
$$

Proof For a linear algorithm $\varphi(y) = cy$ and $f \in \mathbb{R}$ we have

$$
\begin{aligned}
\sup_{|x| \le \delta} |f - \varphi(f + x)|^2 \;\; &= \;\; \sup_{|x| \le \delta} |(1 - c)f - cx|^2 \\
&= \;\; (1 - c)^2 f^2 + c^2 \delta^2 + 2\delta \,|(1 - c)\,c|\,|f|.
\end{aligned}
$$

Taking the integral over f we get

$$
e^{\mathrm{a-w}}(\lambda, \delta; \varphi) \;\; = \;\; (1 - c)^2 \lambda + c^2 \delta^2 + 2\delta |(1 - c)c|\sqrt{\dfrac{2\lambda}{\pi}}.
$$

To obtain the desired result it is now enough to minimize the expression obtained with respect to c. $\qquad\square$

Observe that the optimal coefficient c_{opt} is a function of $\delta/\sqrt{\lambda}$, i.e., $c_{\mathrm{opt}}(\lambda, \delta) = c_{\mathrm{opt}}(1, \delta/\sqrt{\lambda})$. Furthermore,

$$
r_{\mathrm{lin}}(\lambda, \delta) \;\; = \;\; \sqrt{\lambda} \cdot r_{\mathrm{lin}}(1, \delta/\sqrt{\lambda}). \tag{5.1}
$$

It is clear that we can do better by using nonlinear algorithms.

Example 5.2.1 Let $\lambda > 0$ and $\delta^2 \ge \lambda\pi/2$. Then the nonlinear algorithm

$$
\varphi_{\mathrm{non}}(y) \;\; = \;\;
\begin{cases}
y + \delta & y < -\delta, \\
0 & -\delta \le y \le \delta, \\
y - \delta & \delta < y,
\end{cases}
$$

has smaller error than the optimal linear algorithm $\varphi_{\mathrm{lin}} \equiv 0$. Indeed, it is easy to check that for any f we have

$$
\sup_{|x| \le \delta} |f - \varphi_{\mathrm{non}}(f + x)|^2 \;\; = \;\; \min\{\,|f|^2,\, 4\delta^2\,\},
$$

while for $\varphi \equiv 0$ the quantity above equals $|f|^2$. Hence $e^{\mathrm{a-w}}(\lambda, \delta; \varphi_{\mathrm{non}})$ is less than $e^{\mathrm{a-w}}(\lambda, \delta; 0)$.

However, as in the first mixed setting, we never gain much. Indeed, let

$$
r_{\mathrm{non}}(\lambda, \delta) \;\; = \;\; \inf\{\, e^{\mathrm{a-w}}(\lambda, \delta; \varphi) \mid \varphi \text{ arbitrary}\,\}.
$$

Theorem 5.2.1 *For all $\lambda > 0$ and $\delta \geq 0$ we have*

$$1 \leq \frac{r_{\mathrm{lin}}(\lambda, \delta)}{r_{\mathrm{non}}(\lambda, \delta)} < 1.5.$$

Furthermore,

$$\lim_{\delta/\sqrt{\lambda} \to 0} \frac{r_{\mathrm{lin}}(\lambda, \delta)}{r_{\mathrm{non}}(\lambda, \delta)} = 1 = \lim_{\delta/\sqrt{\lambda} \to \infty} \frac{r_{\mathrm{lin}}(\lambda, \delta)}{r_{\mathrm{non}}(\lambda, \delta)}$$

(0/0 = 1)

Proof Owing to the same argument as in the proof of Theorem 4.2.1, we can assume without loss of generality that $\lambda = 1$.

To obtain a lower bound on the error of φ, note that

$$\sup_{|x| \leq \delta} |f - \varphi(f + x)|^2 \geq \tfrac{1}{2} \left(|f - \varphi(f + \delta)|^2 + |f - \varphi(f - \delta)|^2 \right).$$

This yields

$$(e^{\mathrm{a-w}}(1, \delta; \varphi))^2$$

$$\geq \frac{1}{\sqrt{2\pi}} \int_{\mathbb{R}} \tfrac{1}{2} \left(|f - \varphi(f + \delta)|^2 + |f - \varphi(f - \delta)|^2 \right) e^{-f^2/2} \, df$$

$$= \frac{1}{\sqrt{8\pi}} \int_{\mathbb{R}} (y - \varphi(y) - \delta)^2 e^{-(y-\delta)^2/2} + (y - \varphi(y) + \delta)^2 e^{-(y+\delta)^2/2} \, df.$$

For each y, the last integrand is minimized by

$$\varphi^*(y) = y - \delta \frac{a_- - a_+}{a_- + a_+}$$

where $a_- = e^{-(y-\delta)^2/2}$ and $a_+ = e^{-(y+\delta)^2/2}$. Hence, letting $\varphi = \varphi^*$ and performing some elementary transformations, we arrive at the following bound:

$$(e^{\mathrm{a-w}}(1, \delta; \varphi))^2 \geq \delta^2 \, \psi(\delta) \tag{5.2}$$

where

$$\psi(\delta) = e^{-\delta^2/2} \sqrt{\frac{2}{\pi}} \int_0^{+\infty} \frac{\exp\{-y^2/2\}}{\cosh\{\delta y\}} \, dy.$$

The inequality $r_{\mathrm{non}}(1, \delta) \leq r_{\mathrm{lin}}(1, \delta)$ is obvious. To show the reverse inequality, observe that the function ψ is decreasing. This, (5.2) and Lemma 5.2.1 yield that for $\delta \in [0, 1]$

$$\frac{r_{\mathrm{lin}}(1, \delta)}{r_{\mathrm{non}}(1, \delta)} \leq \frac{\delta}{\delta \sqrt{\psi(\delta)}} \leq \frac{1}{\sqrt{\psi(1)}}.$$

On the other hand, for $\delta \in (1, +\infty)$ we have

$$\frac{r_{\text{lin}}(1,\delta)}{r_{\text{non}}(1,\delta)} \leq \frac{1}{r_{\text{non}}(1,1)} \leq \frac{1}{\sqrt{\psi(1)}},$$

which, as in the proof of Theorem 4.2.1, is less than 1.5.

To prove the first limit of the theorem, observe that for all δ

$$\psi(\delta) \geq \sqrt{\frac{2}{\pi}} \int_{\delta}^{+\infty} \exp\{-y^2/2\}\, dy.$$

This, (5.2) and Lemma 5.2.1 yield

$$\lim_{\delta \to 0} \frac{r_{\text{lin}}(1,\delta)}{r_{\text{non}}(1,\delta)} = 1.$$

The second limit follows from the fact that for any φ and $|f| \leq \delta$ we have $\sup_{|x| \leq \delta} |f - \varphi(f + x)| \geq |f - \varphi(0)|$. This yields

$$(e^{a-w}(1,\delta;\varphi))^2 \geq \frac{1}{\sqrt{2\pi}} \int_{-\delta}^{\delta} (f - \varphi(0))^2\, e^{-f^2/2}\, df$$

$$\geq \frac{1}{\sqrt{2\pi}} \int_{-\delta}^{\delta} f^2\, e^{-f^2/2}\, df \longrightarrow 1,$$

as $\delta \to +\infty$, and completes the proof. $\qquad\qquad\square$

Now define the constant

$$\kappa_2^* = \sup_{\lambda,\delta} \frac{r_{\text{lin}}(\lambda,\delta)}{r_{\text{non}}(\lambda,\delta)}. \qquad\qquad (5.3)$$

From the proof of Theorem 5.2.1 we have $\kappa_2^* \leq \psi^{-1/2}(1) = 1.49\ldots$. However, unlike in the first mixed setting, the exact value of κ_2^* is not known.

5.2.2 Almost optimality of linear algorithms

We now consider the case of a general linear functional. That is, we assume that S is an arbitrary continuous linear functional defined on a separable Banach space F, and μ is a zero-mean Gaussian measure on F with correlation operator $C_\mu : F^* \to F$. Information about $f \in F$ is linear with noise bounded uniformly in a Hilbert norm. That is, $y = N(f) + x \in \mathbb{R}^n$, where $N = [L_1,, \ldots, L_n]$ $(L_i \in F^*)$ and $\|x\|_Y = \sqrt{\langle \Sigma^{-1}x, x \rangle_2} \leq \delta$, $\Sigma = \Sigma^* > 0$. Let

$$\text{rad}_{\text{lin}}^{a-w}(N; \mu) = \inf\{e^{a-w}(N, \varphi; \mu) \mid \varphi \text{ linear}\},$$

$$\text{rad}_{\text{non}}^{a-w}(N; \mu) = \inf\{e^{a-w}(N, \varphi; \mu) \mid \varphi \text{ arbitrary}\},$$

be the minimal errors of linear and arbitrary nonlinear algorithms.

Consider first the case when the measure μ is concentrated on a one dimensional subspace.

Lemma 5.2.2   *Let $h \in F$ and μ be the zero-mean Gaussian measure with correlation operator*

$$C_\mu(L) = L(h)\, h, \qquad \forall L \in F^*.$$

(i) If $N(h) = 0$ then

$$\mathrm{rad}_{\mathrm{lin}}^{\mathrm{a-w}}(\mathbb{N}; \mu) = \mathrm{rad}_{\mathrm{non}}^{\mathrm{a-w}}(\mathbb{N}, \mu) = |S(h)|$$

and $\varphi \equiv 0$ is the optimal algorithm.

(ii) If $N(h) \neq 0$ then

$$\mathrm{rad}_{\mathrm{lin}}^{\mathrm{a-w}}(\mathbb{N}; \mu) = |S(h)|\, r_{\mathrm{lin}}\left(1, \frac{\delta}{\|N(h)\|_Y}\right),$$

$$\mathrm{rad}_{\mathrm{non}}^{\mathrm{a-w}}(\mathbb{N}; \mu) = |S(h)|\, r_{\mathrm{non}}\left(1, \frac{\delta}{\|N(h)\|_Y}\right),$$

and the optimal linear algorithm is given as

$$\varphi(y) = c_{\mathrm{opt}}\left(1, \frac{\delta}{\|N(h)\|_Y}\right) \frac{S(h)}{\|N(h)\|_Y} \left\langle y, \frac{N(h)}{\|N(h)\|_Y} \right\rangle_Y$$

where $r_{\mathrm{lin}}(\cdot, \cdot)$, $r_{\mathrm{non}}(\cdot, \cdot)$ and $c_{\mathrm{opt}}(\cdot, \cdot)$ are as in Lemma 5.2.1.

Proof   (i) Since $N(f)$ vanishes on span$\{h\}$, information consists of pure noise only. Let $\varphi : \mathbb{R}^n \to \mathbb{R}$ be an arbitrary algorithm. Then, for any $a \in \mathbb{R}^n$ with $\|a\|_Y \leq \delta$, the error of the constant algorithm $\varphi_a \equiv \varphi(a)$ is not larger than the error of φ. Hence zero provides the best approximation and the minimal error equals $\sqrt{S(C_\mu S)} = |S(h)|$, as claimed.

(ii) Define the random variable $\alpha = \alpha(f)$ by $f = \alpha h$. Then α has standard Gaussian distribution. Similarly to the proof of Lemma 4.2.2, letting $z = \Sigma^{-1/2} y / \|N(h)\|_Y$, we can transform the data $y = N(f) + x$ to $z = \alpha w + x'$ where $w = \Sigma^{-1/2} N(h) / \|N(h)\|_Y$ and $\|x'\|_2 \leq \delta / \|N(h)\|_Y$. Using an orthogonal matrix Q with $Qw = e_1$ we get that the original problem of approximating $S(f)$ from data y is equivalent to that of approximating $s(\alpha) = \alpha S(h)$, $\alpha \sim \mathcal{N}(0, 1)$, from data

$$\tilde{y} = Qz = [\alpha + \tilde{x}_1, \tilde{x}_2, \ldots, \tilde{x}_n]$$

where $\|x'\|_2 \leq \delta / \|N(h)\|_Y$.

It is now easily seen that we cannot use the 'pure noise' data $\tilde{y}_2, \ldots, \tilde{y}_n$

to reduce the error. Indeed, for an arbitrary algorithm $\varphi : \mathbb{R}^n \to \mathbb{R}$ we can define another algorithm $\varphi_0(\tilde{y}) = \varphi(\tilde{y}_1, \underbrace{0, \ldots, 0}_{n-1})$ which uses only $\tilde{y}_1$.

Then, for any $\alpha \in \mathbb{R}$, we have $(\delta_h = \delta / \|N(h)\|_Y)$

$$\sup_{\|\tilde{x}\|_2 \leq \delta_h} |s(\alpha) - \varphi(\tilde{y})| \geq \sup_{|\tilde{x}_1| \leq \delta_h} |s(\alpha) - \varphi(\tilde{y}_1, \underbrace{0, \ldots, 0}_{n-1})|$$

$$= \sup_{\|\tilde{x}\|_2 \leq \delta_h} |s(\alpha) - \varphi_0(\tilde{y})|,$$

and hence $e^{a-w}(\varphi) \geq e^{a-w}(\varphi_0)$.

Thus we have reduced the original problem to that of approximating $s(\alpha)$ from $\tilde{y}_1 = \alpha + \tilde{x}_1$ where $\alpha \sim \mathcal{N}(0, 1)$ and $|\tilde{x}_1| \leq \delta / \|N(h)\|_Y$. The formulas for the minimal errors and optimal linear algorithm now follow from Lemma 5.2.1 and the fact that $\tilde{y}_1 = \langle y, N(h) \rangle_Y / \|N(h)\|_Y^2$. $\square$

Assume now that the Gaussian measure μ is arbitrary. Let φ_σ be the optimal algorithm in the average case setting with the measure μ and information $y = N(f) + x$ where the noise $x \sim \mathcal{N}(0, \sigma^2 \Sigma)$. Recall that φ_σ is given as

$$\varphi_\sigma(y) = \langle y, w_\sigma \rangle_2,$$

where w_σ is the only solution of $(\sigma^2 \Sigma + G_N) w_\sigma = N(C_\mu S)$ belonging to $(\sigma^2 \Sigma + G_N)(\mathbb{R}^n)$, and the matrix $G_N = \{L_i(C_\mu L_j)\}_{i,j}$; see Section 3.5.

It is easy to see that for $\sigma = \delta$, φ_σ is an almost optimal linear algorithm in the mixed average-worst case setting. Indeed, let $\varphi = d \langle \cdot, w \rangle_Y$ with $\|w\|_Y = 1$ and $d \geq 0$ be a linear algorithm. Then the worst case error for $f \in F$ equals

$$\sup_{\|x\|_Y \leq \delta} |S(f) - \varphi(N(f) + x)|^2 = (|S(f) - d\langle N(f), w \rangle_Y| + \delta d)^2,$$

while the average case error for f equals

$$\int_{\mathbb{R}^n} |S(f) - \varphi(N(f) + x)|^2 \pi(dx) = |S(f) - d\langle N(f), w \rangle_Y|^2 + \delta^2 d^2.$$

Hence

$$e^{wor}(\mathbb{N}, \varphi; \mu) \leq e^{a-w}(\mathbb{N}, \varphi; \mu) \leq \sqrt{2} \cdot e^{ave}(\mathbb{N}, \varphi; \mu),$$

and consequently

$$e^{a-w}(\mathbb{N}, \varphi_\sigma; \mu) \leq \sqrt{2} \cdot rad^{a-w}(\mathbb{N}; \mu) \qquad (\sigma = \delta).$$

(Compare this with the corresponding discussion in the worst-average case setting of Subsection 4.2.2.)

For an appropriately chosen σ, φ_σ turns out to be an optimal linear algorithm. To show this, we first need some preliminary facts.

Let $K_\sigma = S - \varphi_\sigma(N(\cdot))$. Recall that in the average case setting the functional K_σ determines the family of one dimensional subproblems which are as difficult as the original problem, see Theorem 3.5.1. Define the function $\rho : [0, +\infty) \to (0, +\infty]$ as

$$\rho(\sigma) = \frac{\|K_\sigma\|_\mu}{\|N(C_\mu K_\sigma)\|_Y}$$

for $\sigma > 0$, and $\rho(0) = \lim_{\sigma \to 0^+} \rho(\sigma)$.

Lemma 5.2.3 *If $N(C_\mu S) \neq 0$ then the function $\rho(\sigma)$ is well defined for all $\sigma \geq 0$.*

Proof We first show that $N(C_\mu K_\sigma) \neq 0$ for $\sigma > 0$. Indeed, using the formula for φ_σ we obtain

$$N(C_\mu K_\sigma) = N(C_\mu S) - \sum_{j=1}^n w_{\sigma,j} N(C_\mu L_j)$$
$$= N(C_\mu S) - G_N w_\sigma = \sigma^2 \Sigma w_\sigma.$$

Since $N(C_\mu S) \neq 0$, we have $w_\sigma \neq 0$ and consequently $N(C_\mu K_\sigma) \neq 0$, as claimed.

Now let us see what happens when $\sigma \to 0^+$. If the average radius of exact information ($\sigma = 0$) is positive then $N(C_\mu K_\sigma) = \sigma^2 \Sigma w_\sigma \to 0$ and $\|K_\sigma\|_\mu \to \|K_0\|_\mu = \|S - \varphi_0 N\|_\mu > 0$, which means that $\lim_{\sigma \to 0^+} \rho(\sigma) = +\infty$. Otherwise we have $\|K_0\|_\mu = 0$ and $S = \sum_{j=1}^n w_{0,j} L_j$ a.e. on F. This yields

$$\|K_\sigma\|_\mu^2 = \sum_{i,j=1}^n (w_0 - w_\sigma)_i (w_0 - w_\sigma)_j L_i(C_\mu L_j)$$
$$= \langle G_N(w_0 - w_\sigma), (w_0 - w_\sigma) \rangle_2 = \sigma^2 \langle \Sigma w_\sigma, w_0 - w_\sigma \rangle_2.$$

Since $\|N(C_\mu K_\sigma)\|_Y^2 = \sigma^4 \|\Sigma w_\sigma\|_Y^2 = \sigma^4 \langle \Sigma w_\sigma, w_\sigma \rangle_2$, in this case ρ takes the form

$$\rho^2(\sigma) = \frac{\langle \Sigma w_\sigma, (w_0 - w_\sigma) \rangle_2}{\sigma^2 \langle \Sigma w_\sigma, w_\sigma \rangle_2}.$$

Let P_N be the orthogonal projection in $\mathbb{R}^n$ onto $X = G_N(\mathbb{R}^n)$ with respect to the Euclidean inner product. Since $\Sigma w_\sigma \in X$, we have $(\sigma^2 P_N \Sigma + G_N) w_\sigma = N(C_\mu S) = G_N w_0$ which yields $(w_0 - w_\sigma) = \sigma^2 G_N^{-1} P_N \Sigma w_\sigma$. (For $x \in X$, $G_N^{-1} x$ is the only element $y \in X$ such that $G_N y = x$.) Thus we finally obtain

$$\rho^2(\sigma) = \frac{\langle \Sigma w_\sigma, G_N^{-1} P_N \Sigma w_\sigma \rangle_2}{\langle \Sigma w_\sigma, w_\sigma \rangle_2} \longrightarrow \frac{\langle \Sigma w_0, G_N^{-1} P_N \Sigma w_0 \rangle_2}{\langle \Sigma w_0, w_0 \rangle_2}$$

as $\sigma \to 0^+$.   □

We are ready to state the following theorem about optimal linear algorithms.

Theorem 5.2.2 *Let $\delta > 0$.*

(i) If $\delta \|S\|_\mu \geq \sqrt{\pi/2}\,\|N(C_\mu S)\|_Y$ then $\varphi \equiv 0$ is the optimal linear algorithm and

$$\operatorname{rad}_{\mathrm{lin}}^{\mathrm{a-w}}(\mathbb{N}; \mu) = \|S\|_\mu.$$

(ii) If $\delta \|S\|_\mu < \sqrt{\pi/2}\,\|N(C_\mu S)\|$ then the optimal linear algorithm is φ_σ, where $\sigma = \sigma(\delta) \geq 0$ is the solution of

$$c_{\mathrm{opt}}(1, \delta \rho(\sigma)) = \frac{1}{1 + \sigma^2 \rho^2(\sigma)}, \tag{5.4}$$

such a solution being known to exist. Furthermore, for $\sigma(\delta) > 0$ we have

$$\operatorname{rad}_{\mathrm{lin}}^{\mathrm{a-w}}(\mathbb{N}; \mu) = \left(\|K_\sigma\|_\mu + \rho^{-1}(\sigma)\sqrt{\langle \Sigma w_\sigma, w_\sigma \rangle_2} \right) r_{\mathrm{lin}}(1, \delta \rho(\sigma)),$$

while for $\sigma(\delta) = 0$ we have

$$\operatorname{rad}_{\mathrm{lin}}^{\mathrm{a-w}}(\mathbb{N}; \mu) = \delta \sqrt{\langle \Sigma w_0, w_0 \rangle_2}.$$

Proof (i) We can assume that $N(C_\mu S) \neq 0$ (and consequently $\|S\|_\mu \neq 0$) since otherwise the theorem is obvious. Let $\mu_S(\cdot|g)$ be the conditional distribution of μ given $g = P_S(f) = f - S(f)C_\mu S/\|S\|_\mu^2$. Owing to Lemma 3.5.1, $\mu_S(\cdot|g)$ has mean element g and correlation operator

$$A_S(L) = \frac{L(C_\mu S)}{\|S\|_\mu^2} C_\mu S, \qquad \text{a.e. } g$$

This and Lemmas 5.2.2 and 5.2.1 yield

$$\operatorname{rad}_{\mathrm{lin}}^{\mathrm{a-w}}(\mathbb{N}; \mu_S(\cdot|g)) \geq \frac{S(C_\mu S)}{\|S\|_\mu} r_{\mathrm{lin}}\left(1, \frac{\delta \|S\|_\mu}{\|N(C_\mu S)\|_Y}\right) = \|S\|_\mu.$$

Hence

$$\mathrm{rad}_{\mathrm{lin}}^{\mathrm{a-w}}(\aleph;\mu) \geq \sqrt{\int_{P_S(F)} \left(\mathrm{rad}_{\mathrm{lin}}^{\mathrm{a-w}}(\aleph;\mu_S(\cdot|g))\right)^2 \mu P_S^{-1}(dg)} \geq \|S\|_\mu.$$

On the other hand, the error $\|S\|_\mu$ is achieved by $\varphi \equiv 0$. Hence $\varphi \equiv 0$ is the optimal linear algorithm.

(ii) We first show that there exists $\sigma = \sigma(\delta)$ satisfying (5.4). Let ψ_l and ψ_r denote the left and right hand sides of (5.4), respectively. Since w_σ depends continuously on σ, ψ_l and ψ_r are continuous functions of σ on $(0, +\infty)$. If $\rho(0) < +\infty$, we also have continuity at 0. Hence, to prove the existence of $\sigma(\delta)$, it suffices to show that the function $(\psi_l - \psi_r)(\sigma)$ takes positive and nonpositive values. Indeed, for $\sigma \to +\infty$ we have $w_\sigma \to 0$ and $\rho(\sigma) \to \|S\|_\mu / \|N(C_\mu S)\|_Y$. Hence

$$\lim_{\sigma \to \infty} c_{\mathrm{opt}}(1, \delta \rho(\sigma)) = c_{\mathrm{opt}}\left(1, \frac{\delta \|S\|_\mu}{\|N(C_\mu S)\|_Y}\right) > c_{\mathrm{opt}}\left(1, \sqrt{\pi/2}\right) = 0.$$

On the other hand $\lim_{\sigma \to \infty}(1 + \sigma^2 \rho^2(\sigma))^{-1} = 0$, which means that for large σ we have $\psi_l(\sigma) > \psi_r(\sigma)$. If $\rho(0) = +\infty$ then for small positive σ we have $\psi_l(\sigma) = 0 < \psi_r(\sigma)$. If $\rho(0) < +\infty$ then $\psi_l(0) \leq 1 = \psi_r(0)$.

Hence there always exists $\sigma = \sigma(\delta) \geq 0$ such that $\psi_l(\sigma) = \psi_r(\sigma)$. Note that $\sigma(\delta) = 0$ only if $\rho(0) < +\infty$ and $c_{\mathrm{opt}}(1, \delta\rho(0)) = 1$.

We now prove the optimality of φ_σ. Assume first that $\sigma(\delta) > 0$. Then

$$\mathrm{rad}_{\mathrm{lin}}^{\mathrm{a-w}}(\aleph;\mu) \geq \sqrt{\int_{P_{K_\sigma}(F)} \left(\mathrm{rad}_{\mathrm{aff}}^{\mathrm{a-w}}(\aleph;\mu_{K_\sigma}(\cdot|g))\right)^2 \mu P_{K_\sigma}^{-1}(dg)}$$

where $P_{K_\sigma}(f) = f - K_\sigma(f)C_\mu K_\sigma / \|K_\sigma\|_\mu^2$. Since the measures $\mu_{K_\sigma}(\cdot|g)$ have the same (independent of g) correlation operator

$$A_{K_\sigma}(L) = \frac{L(C_\mu K_\sigma)}{\|K_\sigma\|_\mu^2} C_\mu K_\sigma, \qquad \text{a.e. } g,$$

and they differ only in the mean g, the minimal error of affine algorithms with respect to $\mu_{K_\sigma}(\cdot|g)$ is independent of g. That is,

$$\mathrm{rad}_{\mathrm{aff}}^{\mathrm{a-w}}(\aleph;\mu_{K_\sigma}(\cdot|g)) = \mathrm{rad}_{\mathrm{lin}}^{\mathrm{a-w}}(\aleph;\mu_{K_\sigma})$$

where $\mu_{K_\sigma} = \mu_{K_\sigma}(\cdot|0)$. Now we can use Lemma 5.2.2 to obtain the affine algorithm φ_g with error equal to $\mathrm{rad}_{\mathrm{aff}}^{\mathrm{a-w}}(\aleph;\mu_{K_\sigma}(\cdot|g))$. We have

$$\varphi_g(y) = S(g)$$
$$+ c_{\mathrm{opt}}\left(1, \frac{\delta}{\|N(h_\sigma)\|_Y}\right) \frac{S(h_\sigma)}{\|N(h_\sigma)\|_Y} \left\langle y - N(g), \frac{N(h_\sigma)}{\|N(h_\sigma)\|_Y} \right\rangle_Y$$

where $h_\sigma = C_\mu K_\sigma / \|K_\sigma\|_\mu$. We find that

$$N(h_\sigma) = \frac{N(C_\mu K_\sigma)}{\|K_\sigma\|_\mu} = \frac{\sigma^2 \Sigma w_\sigma}{\|K_\sigma\|_\mu},$$

$\|N(h_\sigma)\|_Y = \rho^{-1}(\sigma)$, and

$$S(h_\sigma) = \frac{S(C_\mu K_\sigma)}{\|K_\sigma\|_\mu} = \frac{\|K_\sigma\|^2 + \sigma^{-2}\|N(C_\mu K_\sigma)\|_Y^2}{\|K_\mu\|_\mu}$$

(compare with the proof of Theorem 3.5.1). Hence

$$\varphi_g(y) = S(g) + c_{\mathrm{opt}}(1, \delta\rho(\sigma))\,(1 + \sigma^2\rho^2(\sigma))\,\langle y, w_\sigma \rangle_2.$$

Since σ satisfies (5.4) and $S(g) - \langle w_\sigma, N(g)\rangle_2 = K_\sigma(g) = 0$ for all $g \in P_{K_\sigma}(F)$, we finally obtain

$$\varphi_g = \langle \cdot, w_\sigma \rangle_2 = \varphi_\sigma.$$

Thus the same (linear) algorithm φ_σ minimizes the errors over $\mu_{K_\sigma}(\cdot|g)$ a.e. g. Hence this is the optimal linear algorithm.

To find the error of φ_σ, observe that $S(h_\sigma)$ can be written as

$$S(h_\sigma) = \left(\|K_\sigma\|_\mu + \rho^{-1}(\sigma) \right) \sqrt{\langle \Sigma w_\sigma, w_\sigma \rangle_2}.$$

This and Lemma 5.2.2 give

$$\begin{aligned}
e^{\mathrm{a-w}}(\mathbb{N}, \varphi_\sigma; \mu) &= \mathrm{rad}_{\mathrm{lin}}^{\mathrm{a-w}}(\mathbb{N}; \mu) = \mathrm{rad}_{\mathrm{lin}}^{\mathrm{a-w}}(\mathbb{N}; \mu_{K_\sigma}) \\
&= |S(h_\sigma)|\, r_{\mathrm{lin}}(1, \delta\,\rho(\sigma)) \\
&= \left(\|K_\sigma\|_\mu + \rho^{-1}(\sigma) \sqrt{\langle \Sigma w_\sigma, w_\sigma \rangle_2} \right) r_{\mathrm{lin}}(1, \delta\rho(\sigma)).
\end{aligned}$$

Consider now the case when $\sigma(\delta) = 0$. Proceeding as for $\sigma(\delta) > 0$ we get that for any $\gamma > 0$

$$\begin{aligned}
\mathrm{rad}_{\mathrm{lin}}^{\mathrm{a-w}}(\mathbb{N}; \mu) &\geq \mathrm{rad}_{\mathrm{lin}}^{\mathrm{a-w}}(\mathbb{N}; \mu_{K_\gamma}) \\
&= \left(\|K_\gamma\|_\mu + \rho^{-1}(\gamma) \right) \sqrt{\langle \Sigma w_\gamma, w_\gamma \rangle_2}.
\end{aligned}$$

We have already noticed that in the case $\sigma(\delta) = 0$ we have $\rho(0) < +\infty$ and $c_{\mathrm{opt}}(1, \delta\rho(0)) = 1$. In view of Lemma 5.2.1, this means that $r_{\mathrm{lin}}(1, \delta\rho(0)) = \delta\rho(0)$. We also have $\|K_0\|_\mu = 0$ which follows from the proof of Lemma 5.2.3. Hence, letting $\gamma \to 0^+$ and using continuity arguments, we get

$$\begin{aligned}
\mathrm{rad}_{\mathrm{lin}}^{\mathrm{a-w}}(\mathbb{N}; \mu) &\geq \left(\|K_0\|_\mu + \rho^{-1}(0)\sqrt{\langle \Sigma w_0, w_0 \rangle_2} \right) r_{\mathrm{lin}}(1, \delta\rho(0)) \\
&= \delta \sqrt{\langle \Sigma w_0, w_0 \rangle_2}. \qquad (5.5)
\end{aligned}$$

On the other hand, in the case $\sigma(\delta) = 0$ we have $S(f) = \varphi_0(Nf)$ a.e. f. Hence

$$\sup_{\|x\|_Y \le \delta} |S(f) - \varphi_0(Nf)| = \sup_{\|x\|_Y \le \delta} |\langle w_0, x \rangle_2| = \delta \sqrt{\langle \Sigma w_0, w_0 \rangle_2}.$$

This and (5.5) give the optimality of φ_0 and complete the proof. $\qquad \square$

Similarly to the average case setting, we can introduce the concept of a family of one dimensional subproblems. Any such family is determined by a functional $K \in F^*$ and indexed by $g \in P_K(F)$ where $P_K(f) = f - K(f)C_\mu K/\|K\|_\mu^2$. For given g, the subproblem relies on minimizing the average-worst case error of linear algorithms with respect to the conditional measure $\mu(\cdot|g)$ whose mean is g and correlation operator $A_K(L) = L(C_\mu K)C_\mu(K)/\|K\|_\mu^2$. (Equivalently, the subproblem relies on minimizing the error with respect to μ using additional information that $P_K(f) = g$.) From the proof of Theorem 5.2.2 it follows that the subproblems determined by the functional K_σ are as difficult as the original problem. Writing as before $\mu_K = \mu(\cdot|0)$, we have the following corollary.

Corollary 5.2.1 *Let $\sigma = \sigma(\delta)$ be defined by the equation (5.4). Then*

$$\mathrm{rad}_{\mathrm{lin}}^{\mathrm{a-w}}(\mathbb{N}; \mu) = \sup_{K \in F^*} \mathrm{rad}_{\mathrm{lin}}^{\mathrm{a-w}}(\mathbb{N}; \mu_K) = \mathrm{rad}_{\mathrm{lin}}^{\mathrm{a-w}}(\mathbb{N}; \mu_{K_\sigma}).$$

For arbitrary algorithms, we can show a result corresponding to Theorem 4.2.3 of the worst-average case setting.

Theorem 5.2.3 *We have*

$$1 \le \frac{\mathrm{rad}_{\mathrm{lin}}^{\mathrm{a-w}}(\mathbb{N}; \mu)}{\mathrm{rad}_{\mathrm{non}}^{\mathrm{a-w}}(\mathbb{N}; \mu)} \le \kappa_2^* < 1.5,$$

where κ_2^* is defined by (5.3). Furthermore,

$$\mathrm{rad}_{\mathrm{lin}}^{\mathrm{a-w}}(\mathbb{N}; \mu) \approx \mathrm{rad}_{\mathrm{non}}^{\mathrm{a-w}}(\mathbb{N}; \mu) \qquad as \quad \delta \to 0^+.$$

Proof Take $\sigma = \sigma(\delta)$ such that φ_σ is the optimal linear algorithm. In view of Lemma 5.2.2 we have

$$\frac{\mathrm{rad}_{\mathrm{lin}}^{\mathrm{a-w}}(\mathbb{N}; \mu_{K_\sigma}(\cdot|g))}{\mathrm{rad}_{\mathrm{non}}^{\mathrm{a-w}}(\mathbb{N}; \mu_{K_\sigma}(\cdot|g))} \le \kappa_2^* \qquad \text{a.e. } g.$$

This and Theorem 5.2.2 yield that for an arbitrary algorithm φ

$$
\begin{aligned}
e^{a-w}(N, \varphi; \mu) &= \sqrt{\int_{P_{K_\sigma}(F)} (e^{a-w}(N, \varphi; \mu_{K_\sigma}(\cdot|g)))^2 \, \mu P_{K_\sigma}^{-1}(dg)} \\
&\geq \frac{1}{\kappa_2^*} \sqrt{\int_{P_{K_\sigma}(F)} (\mathrm{rad}_{\mathrm{lin}}^{a-w}(N; \mu_{K_\sigma}(\cdot|g)))^2 \, \mu P_{K_\sigma}^{-1}(dg)} \\
&= \frac{1}{\kappa_2^*} \, \mathrm{rad}_{\mathrm{lin}}^{a-w}(N; \mu),
\end{aligned}
$$

which proves the first part of the theorem.

Let r_0 be the error of exact information. To show $\mathrm{rad}_{\mathrm{lin}}^{a-w}(N; \mu) \approx \mathrm{rad}_{\mathrm{non}}^{a-w}(N; \mu)$, it suffices to consider $r_0 = 0$ since otherwise $\mathrm{rad}_{\mathrm{non}}^{a-w}(N; \mu)$ goes to r_0 and $\mathrm{rad}_{\mathrm{lin}}^{a-w}(N; \mu)$ to r_0 as $\delta \to 0$. However, $r_0 = 0$ implies $\rho(0) < +\infty$ and consequently $\delta\rho(\sigma(\delta)) \to 0$ as $\delta \to 0^+$. Using Lemma 5.2.2 and Theorem 5.2.1 again we obtain

$$
\frac{\mathrm{rad}_{\mathrm{lin}}^{a-w}(N; \mu)}{\mathrm{rad}_{\mathrm{non}}^{a-w}(N; \mu)} \leq \frac{r_{\mathrm{lin}}(1, \delta\rho(\sigma(\delta)))}{r_{\mathrm{non}}(1, \delta\rho(\sigma(\delta)))} \to 1 \quad \text{as} \quad \delta \to 0^+,
$$

completing the proof.   □

Thus nonlinear algorithms can only be slightly better than linear algorithms.

5.2.3 Relations to other settings

In Subsection 4.2.3 we established close relations between optimal approximation of functionals in the mixed worst-average case setting and in the other settings. In this subsection we show similar relations for the mixed average-worst case setting. These follow from the results of Subsection 5.2.2.

Let μ be a zero-mean Gaussian measure on F and $H \subset F$ a separable Hilbert space such that $\{H, F_1\}$ with $F_1 = \mathrm{supp}\,\mu$ is the abstract Wiener space for μ. We consider the problem of approximating a continuous linear functional $S(f)$ from noisy information $y = N(f) + x$ in the following four settings.

(AW) Average-worst case setting with the measure μ on F and the noise $\|x\|_Y = \sqrt{\langle \Sigma^{-1}x, x \rangle_2} \leq \delta$.

(WW) Worst case setting with E the unit ball in H and $\|x\|_Y = \sqrt{\langle \Sigma^{-1}x, x \rangle_2} \leq \delta$.

(AA) Average case setting with the measure μ and $x \sim \mathcal{N}(0, \sigma^2\Sigma)$.

(WA) Mixed worst-average setting with E the unit ball in H and $x \sim \mathcal{N}(0, \sigma^2 \Sigma)$.

As before, we denote by φ_σ the optimal (linear) algorithm in the average case setting. Recall that φ_σ can be interpreted as the smoothing spline algorithm, $\varphi_\sigma(y) = S(\mathbf{s}(y))$ where $\mathbf{s}(y)$ is the minimizer of $\|f\|_H^2 + \sigma^{-2}\|y - N(f)\|_Y^2$ in H.

Theorem 5.2.4 *Let $\sigma = \delta$. Then we have*

$$e^{\mathrm{a-w}}(\mathbb{N}, \varphi_\sigma; \mu) \leq \sqrt{2}\, \mathrm{rad}_{\mathrm{lin}}^{\mathrm{a-w}}(\mathbb{N}; \mu) \leq \kappa_2^* \sqrt{2}\, \mathrm{rad}_{\mathrm{non}}^{\mathrm{a-w}}(\mathbb{N}; \mu)$$

($\kappa_2^* < 1.5$) and

$$\frac{1}{\kappa_2^* \sqrt{2}}\, \mathrm{rad}^{\mathrm{wor}}(\mathbb{N}; E) \leq \mathrm{rad}_{\mathrm{non}}^{\mathrm{a-w}}(\mathbb{N}; \mu) \leq \sqrt{2}\, \mathrm{rad}^{\mathrm{wor}}(\mathbb{N}; E),$$

$$\frac{1}{\kappa_2^*}\, \mathrm{rad}^{\mathrm{ave}}(\mathbb{N}; \mu) \leq \mathrm{rad}_{\mathrm{non}}^{\mathrm{a-w}}(\mathbb{N}; \mu) \leq \sqrt{2}\, \mathrm{rad}^{\mathrm{ave}}(\mathbb{N}; \mu),$$

$$\frac{1}{\kappa_2^*}\, \mathrm{rad}_{\mathrm{non}}^{\mathrm{w-a}}(\mathbb{N}; E) \leq \mathrm{rad}_{\mathrm{non}}^{\mathrm{a-w}}(\mathbb{N}; \mu) \leq \sqrt{2}\, \mathrm{rad}_{\mathrm{non}}^{\mathrm{w-a}}(\mathbb{N}; E).$$

We also showed that for any $\delta \in [0, +\infty]$ we can find $\sigma = \sigma(\delta) \in [0, +\infty]$ such that the (smoothing spline) algorithm φ_σ (with convention $\varphi_\infty \equiv 0$) is optimal linear in the mixed setting (AW) and in the average case setting (AA). Clearly, the inverse relation is also true. For any $\sigma \in [0, +\infty]$ there is $\delta = \delta(\sigma) \in [0, +\infty]$ such that φ_σ is optimal in both settings.

Taking Theorems 5.2.4, 4.2.5, and 3.6.3 together, we obtain an almost equivalence of *all* four settings for approximating linear functionals: namely, if the set E is the unit ball in H (induced by the measure μ), and $\delta = \sigma$, then in all four settings

(i) the minimal errors are almost the same,
(ii) the same linear algorithm φ_σ is almost optimal in the class of arbitrary nonlinear algorithms, and
(iii) the optimal linear algorithms are smoothing spline algorithms.

Notes and remarks

NR 5.2.1 This section is based on Plaskota (1994). Theorem 5.2.4 is new.

Exercises

E 5.2.1 Suppose we want to approximate a real parameter $f \sim \mathcal{N}(0, \lambda)$ based on n observations $y_i = f + x_i$ with noise satisfying $\|x\|_2 = \sqrt{\sum_{j=1}^n x_j^2} \leq \delta$. Show that the sample mean, $\varphi_n(y) = n^{-1} \sum_{j=1}^n y_j$, is an asymptotically optimal algorithm,

$$e^{\mathrm{a-w}}(\varphi_n) = \frac{\delta}{\sqrt{n}} \approx \mathrm{rad}_{\mathrm{non}}^{\mathrm{a-w}}(n) \qquad \text{as} \quad n \to +\infty,$$

where $\mathrm{rad}_{\mathrm{non}}^{\mathrm{a-w}}(n)$ is the corresponding nth minimal radius.

E 5.2.2 Suppose that the noise in E 5.2.1 satisfies $\sum_{j=1}^n (x_j^2/\delta_j^2) \leq 1$. Show that for the algorithm

$$\varphi(y) = \frac{\sum_{i=1}^n \delta_i^{-2} y_i}{\sum_{i=1}^n \delta_i^{-2}}$$

we have

$$e^{\mathrm{a-w}}(\varphi) = \sqrt{\frac{1}{\sum_{i=1}^n \delta_i^{-2}}} \approx \mathrm{rad}^{\mathrm{a-w}}(\mathbb{N})$$

as $\lambda \to +\infty$.

E 5.2.3 Consider the problem of approximating $S(f)$ from information $y = S(f) + x$, $|x| \leq \delta$. Show that

$$\mathrm{rad}_{\mathrm{lin}}^{\mathrm{a-w}}(\mathbb{N}; \mu) = r_{\mathrm{lin}}(\lambda, \delta) \qquad \text{and} \qquad \mathrm{rad}_{\mathrm{non}}^{\mathrm{w-a}}(\mathbb{N}; \mu) = r_{\mathrm{non}}(\lambda, \delta),$$

where $\lambda = S(C_\mu S)$ and C_μ is the correlation operator of μ.

E 5.2.4 Prove the uniqueness of the optimal linear algorithm of Theorem 5.2.2.
Hint: Consider first the case when μ is concentrated on a one dimensional subspace.

E 5.2.5 Show that the solution $\sigma = \sigma(\delta)$ of (5.4) is uniquely determined.

E 5.2.6 Let μ be the standard Gaussian distribution on $F = \mathbb{R}^n$, $\mu = \mathcal{N}(0, I)$. Consider approximation of a functional S from information $y = f + x \in \mathbb{R}^n$ where $\|x\|_2 \leq \delta$. Show that for $\delta \geq \sqrt{\pi/2}$ the optimal linear algorithm is $\varphi_\infty \equiv 0$, while for $\delta < \sqrt{\pi/2}$ it is given as $\varphi_\sigma(y) = (1+\sigma^2)^{-1} S(y)$ where $\sigma = \sigma(\delta) = \sqrt{1/c_{\mathrm{opt}}(1, \delta) - 1}$. Furthermore, show that the error of φ_σ equals $\|S\|_2\, r_{\mathrm{lin}}(1, \delta)$.

E 5.2.7 Let $\delta > 0$. Show that the necessary and sufficient condition for the algorithm φ_0 to be optimal is that $K_0 = S - \varphi_0 N = 0$ a.e. on F, and

$$\delta^2\, \frac{\pi}{2}\, \frac{\langle \Sigma w_0, G_N^{-1} P_N \Sigma w_0 \rangle_2}{\langle \Sigma w_0, w_0 \rangle_2} \leq 1,$$

where w_0, G_N and P_N are as in the proof of Lemma 5.2.3.

5.3 Approximation of operators

As we have already noticed, we know very little about approximation of operators which are not functionals. Here we present some very specific results.

Suppose we approximate a vector $f = (f_1, \ldots, f_n) \in \mathbb{R}^n$ whose coordinates f_i have independent normal distributions, $f_i \sim \mathcal{N}(0, \lambda_i)$ with $\lambda_i > 0$, $1 \leq i \leq n$. That is, the joint probability distribution μ on $\mathbb{R}^n$ is the zero-mean Gaussian measure with diagonal correlation matrix. Information about f is given coordinatewise, $y_i = f_i + x_i$ where $|x_i| \leq \delta_i$, $1 \leq i \leq n$.

Lemma 5.3.1 *We have*

$$\mathrm{rad}_{\mathrm{lin}}^{\mathrm{a-w}}(\mathbb{N}) = \sqrt{\sum_{i=1}^{n} r_{\mathrm{lin}}^2(\lambda_i, \delta_i)},$$

$$\mathrm{rad}_{\mathrm{non}}^{\mathrm{a-w}}(\mathbb{N}) = \sqrt{\sum_{i=1}^{n} r_{\mathrm{non}}^2(\lambda_i, \delta_i)},$$

and the (unique) optimal linear algorithm is given as $\varphi(c_1 y_1, \ldots, c_n y_n)$ *where* $c_i = c_{\mathrm{opt}}(\lambda_i, \delta_i)$, $1 \leq i \leq n$.

Proof Let $\mu_i = \mathcal{N}(0, \lambda_i)$. Owing to the independence of the f_is and x_is, the error of any algorithm $\varphi = (\varphi_1, \ldots, \varphi_n)$ equals

$$\left(e^{\mathrm{a-w}}(\mathbb{N}, \varphi) \right)^2 = \sum_{i=1}^{n} \left(\int_{\mathbb{R}} \sup_{|x_i| \leq \delta_i} (f_i - \varphi_i(f_i + x_i))^2 \, \mu_i(df_i) \right).$$

Hence the lemma follows from Lemma 5.2.1 about optimal algorithms for the one dimensional problems. $\square$

Recall that for $\delta_i \leq \sqrt{2\lambda_i/\pi}$ we have $c_i = 1$ and $r_{\mathrm{lin}}(\lambda_i, \delta_i) = \delta_i$. Hence, for sufficiently small noise level (or for sufficiently large λ_is), $\varphi(y) = y$ is the optimal linear algorithm and its error is $(\sum_{i=1}^{n} \delta_i^2)^{1/2}$. This observation can be generalized as follows.

Consider the same problem but with noise x belonging to a set $B \subset \mathbb{R}^n$, i.e., $\mathbb{N}(f) = \{ f + x \mid x \in B \}$. Write

$$\rho(B) = \sup_{x \in B} \|x\|_2.$$

Lemma 5.3.2 *Suppose that the set B is convex and orthosymmetric. If there exists $\bar{x} \in \overline{B}$ such that $\|\bar{x}\|_2 = \rho(B)$ and $|\bar{x}_i| \leq \sqrt{2\lambda_i/\pi}$, $1 \leq i \leq n$, then $\varphi(y) = y$ is the optimal linear algorithm and*

$$\mathrm{rad}_{\mathrm{lin}}^{\mathrm{a-w}}(\mathbb{N}) = \rho(B) \approx \mathrm{rad}_{\mathrm{non}}^{\mathrm{a-w}}(\mathbb{N})$$

as $\rho(B) \to 0$.

Proof Owing to convexity and orthosymmetry, $\overline{B}$ includes the rectangle $\mathcal{R} = \{\, x \in \mathbb{R}^n \mid |x_i| \leq |\bar{x}_i|, \ 1 \leq i \leq n \,\}$. Hence Lemma 5.3.1 yields

$$\mathrm{rad}_{\mathrm{lin}}^{\mathrm{a-w}}(\mathbb{N}) \geq \sqrt{\sum_{i=1}^{n} |\bar{x}_i|^2} = \rho(B).$$

On the other hand, for the identity algorithm we have $e^{\mathrm{a-w}}(\mathbb{N}, \varphi; E) = \rho(B)$.

To show the remaining part of the lemma, observe that for $\rho(B) \to 0^+$,

$$
\begin{aligned}
\mathrm{rad}_{\mathrm{non}}^{\mathrm{a-w}}(\mathbb{N}) &\geq \sqrt{\sum_{i=1}^{n} r_{\mathrm{non}}^2(\lambda_i, |\bar{x}_i|)} \\
&\approx \sqrt{\sum_{i=1}^{n} r_{\mathrm{lin}}^2(\lambda_i, |\bar{x}_i|)} = \mathrm{rad}_{\mathrm{lin}}^{\mathrm{a-w}}(\mathbb{N}).
\end{aligned}
$$

Hence $\mathrm{rad}_{\mathrm{non}}^{\mathrm{a-w}}(\mathbb{N}) \approx \mathrm{rad}_{\mathrm{lin}}^{\mathrm{a-w}}(\mathbb{N})$, as claimed. $\qquad\square$

Thus the identity is the optimal linear algorithm if the noise belongs to a convex and orthosymmetric set B with small radius. If E is an ellipsoid $\sum_{i=1}^{n}(x_i^2/\delta_i^2) \leq 1$ with $\delta_1 \geq \cdots \geq \delta_n > 0$, then $\bar{x} = (\delta_1, \underbrace{0, \dots, 0}_{n-1})$. In this case, the condition $\delta_1 \leq \sqrt{2\lambda_1/\pi}$ is sufficient for the identity algorithm to be optimal linear.

We end this chapter with analysis of the (generalized) least squares algorithm $\varphi_{\mathrm{ls}}(y)$ for linear problems S defined on $\mathbb{R}^d$. We assume that information $\mathbb{N}$ is linear with $N : \mathbb{R}^d \to Y = \mathbb{R}^n$, $\dim N(\mathbb{R}^d) = d$, and that the noise x is bounded in a Hilbert norm, $\|x\|_Y = \sqrt{\langle x, x \rangle_Y} \leq \delta$. The Gaussian measure μ on $\mathbb{R}^d$ has mean element zero and positive definite correlation operator C_μ.

Recall that $\varphi_{\mathrm{ls}} = SN^{-1}P_N$ (where P_N is the orthogonal projection onto $N(\mathbb{R}^d)$ with respect to $\langle \cdot, \cdot \rangle_Y$). For a small noise level, in all three

Theorems 2.6.2, 3.6.2 and 4.3.3. The following theorem shows optimality properties of φ_{ls} in the average-worst case setting. This theorem can be viewed as a generalization of Lemma 5.3.2 for ellipsoidal B.

Theorem 5.3.1 *Let $\bar{g} \in G$ be such that $\|\bar{g}\| = 1$ and*

$$\|S(N^*N)^{-1}S^*\bar{g}\| = \|S(N^*N)^{-1}S^*\|.$$

Let δ be chosen so that

$$\delta^2 \cdot \langle S(N^*N)^{-1}C_\mu^{-1}(N^*N)^{-1}S^*\bar{g},\, \bar{g} \rangle \leq \frac{2}{\pi}\,\|S(N^*N)^{-1}S^*\|. \quad (5.6)$$

Then the generalized least squares φ_{ls} is an optimal linear algorithm and

$$\operatorname{rad}_{\text{lin}}^{\text{a-w}}(\mathbb{N}) = \delta \cdot \sqrt{\|S(N^*N)^{-1}S^*\|}.$$

Furthermore, $\operatorname{rad}_{\text{lin}}^{\text{a-w}}(\mathbb{N}) \approx \operatorname{rad}_{\text{non}}^{\text{a-w}}(\mathbb{N})$ as $\delta \to 0^+$.

Proof We shall use once more the concept of the one dimensional sub-problem. Suppose that we have additional information that f is in the subspace span $\{\bar{h}\}$ where $\bar{h} = (N^*N)^{-1}S^*\bar{g}$. Owing to Lemma 3.5.1, this corresponds to changing the measure μ to $\tilde{\mu}$ which is zero-mean and Gaussian and its correlation operator

$$A = \frac{\langle \cdot, \bar{h}\rangle_2\, \bar{h}}{\|C_\mu^{-1}\bar{h}\|_\mu^2} = \langle \cdot, h\rangle_2\, h,$$

where $h = \bar{h}/\|C_\mu^{-1}\bar{h}\|_\mu$. Obviously, $\operatorname{rad}_{\text{lin}}^{\text{a-w}}(\mathbb{N}; \mu) \geq \operatorname{rad}_{\text{lin}}^{\text{a-w}}(\mathbb{N}; \tilde{\mu})$, and from Lemma 5.2.2,

$$\operatorname{rad}_{\text{lin}}^{\text{a-w}}(\mathbb{N}; \tilde{\mu}) = \|S(h)\|\, r_{\text{lin}}\left(1,\, \frac{\delta}{\|N(h)\|_Y}\right).$$

Since

$$\|N(\bar{h})\|_Y^2 = \langle S(N^*N)^{-1}S^*\bar{g}, \bar{g}\rangle = \|S(N^*N)^{-1}S^*\|$$

and

$$\|C_\mu^{-1}\bar{h}\|_\mu^2 = \langle \bar{h}, C_\mu^{-1}\bar{h}\rangle_2 = \langle S(N^*N)^{-1}C_\mu^{-1}(N^*N)^{-1}S^*\bar{g}, \bar{g}\rangle,$$

the condition (5.6) is equivalent to $\delta/\|N(h)\|_Y \leq \sqrt{2/\pi}$. This means that

$$\operatorname{rad}_{\text{lin}}^{\text{a-w}}(\mathbb{N}; \tilde{\mu}) = \delta\,\frac{\|S(h)\|}{\|N(h)\|_Y} = \delta \cdot \|S(N^*N)^{-1}S^*\|^{1/2}.$$

On the other hand, for the least squares algorithm we have

$$\sup_{\|x\|_Y \leq \delta} \|S(f) - \varphi_{\mathrm{ls}}(N(f) + x)\|^2 = \delta^2 \cdot \|S(N^*N)^{-1}S^*\|.$$

(Compare this with the corresponding part of the proof of Theorem 2.6.2.) Hence $e^{\mathrm{a-w}}(\mathbb{N}, \varphi_{\mathrm{ls}}; \mu) = \delta \|S(N^*N)^{-1}S^*\|$, and consequently $\mathrm{rad}_{\mathrm{lin}}^{\mathrm{a-w}}(\mathbb{N}; \mu) = e^{\mathrm{a-w}}(\mathbb{N}, \varphi_{\mathrm{ls}}; \mu)$.

To complete the proof, observe that for $\delta \to 0^+$ we have

$$\mathrm{rad}_{\mathrm{lin}}^{\mathrm{a-w}}(\mathbb{N}; \mu) = \mathrm{rad}_{\mathrm{lin}}^{\mathrm{a-w}}(\mathbb{N}; \tilde{\mu}) \approx \mathrm{rad}_{\mathrm{non}}^{\mathrm{a-w}}(\mathbb{N}; \tilde{\mu}) \leq \mathrm{rad}_{\mathrm{non}}^{\mathrm{a-w}}(\mathbb{N}; \mu).$$

Thus $\mathrm{rad}_{\mathrm{lin}}^{\mathrm{a-w}}(\mathbb{N}; \mu) \approx \mathrm{rad}_{\mathrm{non}}^{\mathrm{a-w}}(\mathbb{N}; \mu)$, as claimed. $\square$

Notes and remarks

NR 5.3.1 Section 5.3 is new.

Exercises

E 5.3.1 Suppose we approximate an operator $S : F \to G$ from information $y = [N(f) + x, t]$ where the noise $(x, t) \in B$. Prove that if B satisfies

$$(x, t) \in B \quad \Longrightarrow \quad (x, 0) \in B, \tag{5.7}$$

then the 'pure noise' data t do not count. That is, the optimal algorithm uses $y^{(1)} = N(f) + x$ only. Give an example showing that the condition (5.7) is essential.

E 5.3.2 Consider approximation of $f = (f_1, \ldots, f_n) \in \mathbb{R}^n$ where the f_i are independent and $f_i \sim \mathcal{N}(0, \lambda_i)$, based on information $y = f + x$, $x \in B$. Show that if the set B is sufficiently large, i.e., if

$$B \supset \{x \in \mathbb{R}^n \mid |x_i|^2 \leq \lambda_i \pi/2, 1 \leq i \leq n\},$$

then zero is the best linear algorithm. In particular, if E is an ellipsoidal set, $E = \{x \in \mathbb{R}^n \mid \sum_{j=1}^n (x_j^2/\delta_j^2) \leq 1\}$, then the condition $\sum_{j=1}^n (\lambda_j/\delta_j^2) \leq 2/\pi$ is sufficient for the zero algorithm to be an optimal linear one.

E 5.3.3 Consider the problem of approximating a vector $f \in \mathbb{R}^d$ whose distribution is zero-mean Gaussian with full support. Let $r_n(\delta_1, \ldots, \delta_n)$ $(0 < \delta_1 \leq \cdots \leq \delta_n)$ be the minimal error that can be attained by linear algorithms using n $(n \geq d)$ observations $y_i = \langle f, f_i \rangle_2 + x_i$ with noise $\sum_{j=1}^n (x_j^2/\delta_j^2) \leq 1$, where $\|f_i\|_2 \leq 1$, $1 \leq i \leq n$. Denote by $\lambda_1 \geq \cdots \geq \lambda_d \geq 0$ the eigenvalues of S^*S. Show that for sufficiently small δ_is we have

$$r_n(\delta_1, \ldots, \delta_n) = \min \max_{1 \leq i \leq d} \sqrt{\frac{\lambda_i}{\eta_i}},$$

where the minimum is taken over all $\eta_i \geq 0$ satisfying

$$\sum_{j=r}^{n} \eta_j \leq \sum_{j=r}^{n} \delta_j^{-2}, \qquad 1 \leq r \leq n.$$

In particular, for fixed noise levels, $\delta_i = \delta$, $\forall i$, and large n we have

$$r_n(\delta) = \frac{\delta}{\sqrt{n}} \cdot \sqrt{\sum_{j=1}^{d} \lambda_j}.$$

Find the optimal information.
Hint: Use Lemma 2.8.1 to obtain the optimal information.

6

Asymptotic setting

6.1 Introduction

In Chapters 2 to 5, we *fixed* the set of problem elements and were interested in finding *single* information and algorithm which minimize an error or cost of approximation. Depending on the deterministic or stochastic assumptions on the problem elements and information noise, we studied the four different settings: worst, average, worst-average, and average-worst case settings.

In this chapter, we study the asymptotic setting in which a problem element f is *fixed* and we wish to analyze asymptotic behavior of algorithms. The aim is to construct a *sequence* of information and algorithms such that the error of successive approximations vanishes as fast as possible, as the number of observations increases to infinity.

The asymptotic setting is often studied in computational practice. We mention only the Romberg algorithm for computing integrals, and finite element methods (FEM) for solving partial differential equations with the meshsize tending to zero. When dealing with these and other numerical algorithms, we are interested in how fast they converge to the solution.

One might hope that it will be possible to construct a sequence $\varphi^n(y^n)$ of approximations such that for the element f the error $\|S(f) - \varphi^n(y^n)\|$ vanishes much faster than the error over the whole set of problem elements (or, equivalently, faster than the corresponding radius of information). It turns out, however, that in many cases any attempts to construct such algorithms would fail. We show this by establishing relations between the asymptotic and other settings.

We present two types of results dependent on whether we have deterministic or stochastic assumptions on the problem elements and information noise. In the first type, we establish relations between the asymptotic and worst case settings, in the other type between the asymptotic and average case settings. This is done under linearity of both the solution operator and information.

The body of this chapter consists of two sections. In Section 6.2 we use deterministic assumptions on the problem elements and noise. We show that an upper bound on the rate of convergence of algorithms is provided by the worst case radii $\text{rad}^{\text{wor}}(\mathbb{N}^n)$ taken over the unit ball of F. It turns out that if F is a Banach space, this convergence essentially cannot be improved by any algorithm. More precisely, in any ball of F, we can find an element f such that for some information $y^n \in \mathbb{N}^n(f)$ the error $\|S(f) - \varphi^n(y^n)\|$ behaves essentially as $\text{rad}^{\text{wor}}(\mathbb{N}^n)$. Hence optimal algorithms in the worst case setting are also optimal in the asymptotic setting. The assumption that F is a Banach space is crucial. We also consider the optimal information. Under mild assumptions we show that, as for optimal algorithms, optimal information in the worst case setting is also optimal in the asymptotic setting.

In Section 6.3 we use stochastic assumptions on the problem elements and noise. More precisely, we assume that information noise is Gaussian and we have some Gaussian measure on F. In this case, we show relations between the asymptotic and average case settings. That is, we first prove that the spline algorithm (which is optimal in the average case setting) gives the best possible convergence. Any other algorithm can converge better only on a set of measure zero. Then we investigate the rate of convergence of the spline algorithm. We show that this convergence can be characterized by the sequence of average radii $\text{rad}^{\text{ave}}(\mathrm{III}^n)$. Finally, we show that optimal information in the average case setting is often optimal in the asymptotic setting.

Notes and remarks

NR 6.1.1 A more detailed discussion of the asymptotic setting can be found in Traub *et al.* (1988, Chap. 10) .

6.2 Asymptotic and worst case settings

We start with the formal definition of the asymptotic setting with deterministic information noise. Then we show a close relation between the asymptotic and worst case settings.

6.2.1 Information, algorithm and error

In the asymptotic setting, we are interested in the behavior of algorithms as the number of observations increases to infinity. Therefore it is convenient to define both information and algorithm as infinite sequences. That is, nonadaptive information $\mathbb{N}$ is a pair $\mathbb{N} = \{N, \Delta\}$, where $N : F \to \mathbb{R}^\infty$ is exact information,

$$N = [L_1, L_2, L_3, \ldots],$$

and $\Delta \in \mathbb{R}^\infty$ is a precision vector,

$$\Delta = [\delta_1, \delta_2, \delta_3, \ldots].$$

For given $\mathbb{N}$, let N^n and Δ^n denote the first n components of N and Δ. In particular,

$$N^n(f) = [L_1(f), L_2(f), \ldots, L_n(f)].$$

We say that an infinite sequence $y = [y_1, y_2, y_3, \ldots] \in \mathbb{R}^\infty$ is (noisy) information about $f \in F$ and write $y \in \mathbb{N}(f)$ iff for all $n \geq 1$ the vector $x^n = y^n - N^n(f)$ is in a given set $B(\Delta^n, N^n(f)) \subset \mathbb{R}^n$ of all possible values of the nth information noise corresponding to exact information $N^n(f)$. Here $y^n = [y_1, \ldots, y_n]$ and $B(\Delta^n, N^n(f))$ satisfy conditions (i)-(iii) of Subsection 2.7.1. That is,

(i) $B(0, z) = \{0\}$,
(ii) If $\Delta^n \leq \bar{\Delta}^n$ then $B(\Delta^n, z) \subset B(\bar{\Delta}^n, z)$,
(iii) $B(\Delta^n, z^n) = \{ x \in \mathbb{R}^n \mid \exists a \in \mathbb{R}, \ [x, a] \in B(\Delta^{n+1}, z^{n+1}) \}$.

Defining the nth information $\mathbb{N}^n = \{N^n, \Delta^n\}$ as

$$\mathbb{N}^n(f) = \{y^n \in \mathbb{R}^n \mid y^n - N^n(f) \in B(\Delta^n, N^n(f))\},$$

we can equivalently say that $y \in \mathbb{R}^n$ is information about f iff for all $n \geq 1$ the vector y^n is the nth noisy information about f, $y^n \in \mathbb{N}^n(f)$.

We now pass to adaptive information. It is given by a family $\mathbb{N} = \{\mathbb{N}_y\}_{y \in \mathbb{R}^\infty}$, where $\mathbb{N}_y = \{N_y, \Delta_y\}$ is nonadaptive information with

$$N_y = [L_1, L_2(\cdot; y_1), \ldots, L_n(\cdot; y_1, \ldots, y_{n-1}), \ldots]$$

and

$$\Delta_y = [\delta_1, \delta_2(y_1), \ldots, \delta_n(y_1, \ldots, y_{n-1}), \ldots].$$

For adaptive $\mathbb{N}$, a sequence y is called (noisy) information about f ($y \in \mathbb{N}(f)$) iff $y^n \in \mathbb{N}_y^n(f)$, $\forall n \geq 1$.

For a given solution operator $S : F \to G$, where G is a normed space, an approximation to $S(f)$ is provided by an algorithm. The algorithm is a sequence of transformations, i.e., $\varphi = \{\varphi^n\}_{n \geq 0}$, where $\varphi^n : \mathbb{R}^n \to G$. ($\varphi^0$ is a fixed element of G.) The nth error of the algorithm φ at $f \in F$ with information $y \in \mathbb{N}(f)$ is given by the distance

$$\|S(f) - \varphi^n(y^n)\|.$$

We shall only consider the case where

- the solution operator S is linear,
- the functionals L_i are linear, and
- the sets $B(\Delta^n, z^n) = B(\Delta^n)$ are unit balls in some extended norms $\|\cdot\|_{\Delta^n}$ of $\mathbb{R}^n$.

Recall that the last assumption and the conditions (i)–(iii) imply that (see E 2.7.1)

$$\|x\|_{\Delta^n} = \min_{t \in \mathbb{R}} \|[x, t]\|_{\Delta^{n+1}}, \qquad n \geq 1, \ x \in \mathbb{R}^n. \tag{6.1}$$

6.2.2 Optimal algorithms

Our first goal is to characterize the best possible behavior of the error $\|S(f) - \varphi^n(y^n)\|$ for fixed (adaptive) information $\mathbb{N}$. The nth (worst case) radii of nonadaptive information $\mathbb{N}_y$ will play a crucial role. These radii are given as the usual worst case radii of $\mathbb{N}_y^n$ with respect to the unit ball of F, i.e.,

$$\operatorname{rad}_n^{\text{wor}}(\mathbb{N}_y) = \operatorname{rad}^{\text{wor}}(\mathbb{N}_y^n) = \inf_{\varphi^n} \sup_{\|f\|_F \leq 1} \sup_{z \in \mathbb{N}_y(f)} \|S(f) - \varphi^n(z^n)\|.$$

Recall that in this case

$$\operatorname{rad}_n^{\text{wor}}(\mathbb{N}_y) = \alpha \cdot \sup \{ \|S(h)\| \mid \|h\|_F \leq 1, \|N_y^n(h)\|_{\Delta_y^n} \leq 1 \} \tag{6.2}$$

where $\alpha \in [1, 2]$, see Theorem 2.3.2.

Given $\mathbb{N}$, it is not difficult to construct an algorithm for which the error converges to zero at least as fast as the sequence $\operatorname{rad}_n^{\text{wor}}(\mathbb{N}_y)$, for all $f \in F$ and $y \in \mathbb{N}(f)$. Indeed, it suffices to consider the (ordinary) spline algorithm $\varphi_o = \{\varphi_o^n\}$. This was first defined in Subsection 2.5.1 for nonadaptive information. A natural generalization of this algorithm for adaptive $\mathbb{N}$ is as follows:

$$\varphi_o^n(y^n) = S(\mathbf{s}_o^n(y^n)), \qquad y^n \in \mathbb{N}^n(F),$$

where $\mathbf{s}_o^n(y^n)$ is the ordinary spline, i.e.,

(i) $y^n \in \mathbb{N}^n(\mathbf{s}_o^n(y^n))$,

(ii) $\|\mathbf{s}_o^n(y^n)\|_F \leq \rho \cdot \inf\{\|f\|_F \mid y^n \in \mathbb{N}^n(f)\}$ $(\rho > 0)$.

Proceeding as in the proof of Theorem 2.5.1 we show that

$$\|S(f) - \varphi_o^n(y^n)\| \leq c(f) \cdot \text{diam}(\mathbb{N}_y^n) \leq 2\,c(f) \cdot \text{rad}_n^{\text{wor}}(\mathbb{N}_y) \quad (6.3)$$

where $c(f) = \max\{1, (1/2)(1+\rho)\|f\|_F\}$.

Corollary 6.2.1 *For the algorithm φ_o, the error $\|S(f) - \varphi_o^n(y^n)\|$ converges to zero at least as fast as the nth worst case radii $\text{rad}_n^{\text{wor}}(\mathbb{N}_y)$, for all $f \in F$ and $y \in \mathbb{N}(f)$.*

As we know, the ordinary spline algorithm is usually nonlinear. It would be nice to have a linear algorithm for which Corollary 6.2.1 also holds. More precisely, we shall say that an algorithm $\varphi = \{\varphi^n\}$ is linear iff the mappings $\varphi^n : \mathbb{R}^n \to G$ are linear for all $n \geq 1$.

Lemma 6.2.1 *Let information $\mathbb{N}$ be nonadaptive. Suppose that there exist a linear algorithm φ_{lin} and $M \geq 1$ such that for all n*

$$e^{\text{wor}}(\mathbb{N}^n, \varphi_{\text{lin}}^n) \leq M \cdot \text{rad}_n^{\text{wor}}(\mathbb{N}).$$

Then for all $f \in F$ and $y \in \mathbb{N}(f)$ we have

$$\|S(f) - \varphi_{\text{lin}}^n(y^n)\| \leq M \cdot \max\{1, \|f\|_F\} \cdot \text{rad}_n^{\text{wor}}(\mathbb{N}).$$

Proof The lemma is obviously true for $\|f\|_F \leq 1$. For $\|f\|_F > 1$, we have that $y' = y/\|f\|_F$ is noisy information about $f' = f/\|f\|_F$, and $\|f'\|_F = 1$. Hence

$$\|S(f) - \varphi_{\text{lin}}^n(y^n)\| = \|f\|_F\,\|S(f') - \varphi_{\text{lin}}^n((y')^n)\| \leq M\,\|f\|_F\,\text{rad}_n^{\text{wor}}(\mathbb{N}),$$

as claimed. $\square$

Lemma 6.2.1 can be applied, for instance, in the case when F is a Hilbert space and the noise is bounded uniformly in a Hilbert norm. Owing to Lemma 2.5.1, in this case the α-smoothing spline algorithm φ_α (with any $\alpha \in (0,1)$) is almost optimal, and $M = \max\{\alpha^{-1/2}, (1-\alpha)^{-1/2}\}$.

Are there algorithms for which convergence is better than $\text{rad}_n^{\text{wor}}(\mathbb{N}_y)$? We now give two examples showing that the answer depends on the particular problem.

Example 6.2.1 Let dim $F \geq 1$, S be a continuous embedding, $S(f) = f$, and $\mathbb{N}$ be the zero information, $N = [0, 0, \ldots]$. Then $\mathrm{rad}_n^{\mathrm{wor}} = \|S\|_F > 0$, $\forall n$. Since we always have $y = 0$, any algorithm φ is just a sequence $\{\varphi^n\}$ of elements in G. Hence the error can converge to zero for at most one element of F.

Example 6.2.2 Let $F = G$ be the space of Lipschitz functions $f : [0,1] \to \mathbb{R}$ with the sup-norm. Let S be the identity. Suppose the nth approximation to f is based on data $y^n = [y_1, \ldots, y_n]$ where $y_i = f(t_i) + x_i$ and $|x_i| \leq \delta_i$, $1 \leq i \leq n$. It is easy to see that for any choice of the points t_n, precisions δ_n and mappings φ^n, the nth worst case error, $\mathrm{e}^{\mathrm{wor}}(\mathbb{N}^n, \varphi^n)$, is at least 1.

Now let t_n and δ_n be given as

$$t_n = (2i + 1)/2^{k+1}, \qquad \delta_n = 2^{-(k+1)}, \qquad n \geq 1,$$

where $n = 2^k + i$, $0 \leq i \leq 2^k - 1$. Let the nth approximation $\varphi^n(y^n)$ be given by the linear spline interpolating the data y^n. Then for any $f \in F$ and $y^n \in \mathbb{N}^n(f)$ we have

$$\|f - \varphi^n(y^n)\|_\infty \leq M/n,$$

where $M = M(f)$ depends only on the Lipschitz constant for f. Hence for all f we have at least linear convergence of the successive approximations to f, while the radii $\mathrm{rad}_n^{\mathrm{wor}}(\mathbb{N})$ do not converge at all.

In the last example, the space F is *not* complete. The completeness of F and continuity of information turn out to be crucial assumptions. If these conditions are met, $\{\mathrm{rad}_n^{\mathrm{wor}}(\mathbb{N}_y)\}$ also establishes a lower bound on the speed of convergence of the error $\|S(f) - \varphi^n(y^n)\|$. More precisely, we have the following theorem.

Theorem 6.2.1 *Suppose that the domain F of the linear solution operator S is a Banach space, and information consists of continuous linear functionals $L_i(\,\cdot\,; y_1, \ldots, y_{n-1})$. Let $\tau(y)$, $y \in \mathbb{R}^\infty$, be arbitrary nonnegative sequences such that*

$$\tau(y) = [\tau_1, \tau_2(y^1), \ldots, \tau_n(y^{n-1}), \ldots]$$

and $\lim_{n \to \infty} \tau_n(y) = 0$. Then the set

$$A = \left\{ f \in F \;\middle|\; \limsup_{n \to \infty} \frac{\|S(f) - \varphi^n(y^n)\|}{\tau_n(y)\, \mathrm{rad}_n^{\mathrm{wor}}(\mathbb{N}_y)} < +\infty, \quad \forall y \in \mathbb{N}(f) \right\}$$

is boundary, i.e., it does not contain any ball in F. (Here $0/0 = +\infty$.)

Proof Suppose to the contrary that A contains a closed ball B of radius r, $0 < r \leq 1$. We shall show that then it is possible to find an element $f^* \in B$ and information y^* about f^* such that

$$\limsup_{n \to \infty} \frac{\|S(f^*) - \varphi((y^*)^n)\|}{\tau_n(y^*) \, \mathrm{rad}_n^{\mathrm{wor}}(\mathbb{N}_{y^*})} = +\infty. \tag{6.4}$$

We first construct by induction a sequence $\{f_k\}_{k \geq 1} \subset B$, a sequence of integers $0 = n_0 < n_1 < \cdots$, and $y_k \in \mathbb{N}_{y_k}(f_k)$, $k \geq 1$, which satisfy the following conditions:

$$y_{k+1}^{n_k} = y_k^{n_k},$$

$$\|y_k^{n_k} - N_{y_k}^{n_k}(f_{k+1})\|_{\Delta_{y_k}^{n_k}} \leq \sum_{j=1}^{k} 2^{-j},$$

$$\|f_{k+1} - f_k\|_F \leq (r/2)^k,$$

for all $k \geq 1$.

Let f_1 be the center of B. Suppose that for some $k \geq 1$ we have constructed $f_1, \ldots, f_k$, $n_0 < \cdots < n_{k-1}$, and $y_1, \ldots, y_{k-1}$. We select $y_k = [y_{k,1}, y_{k,2}, \ldots]$ in such a way that $y_{k,i} = y_{k-1,i}$ for $1 \leq i \leq n_{k-1}$, and

$$\|y_k^{i+1} - N_{y_k}^{i+1}(f_k)\|_{\Delta_{y_k}^{i+1}} = \|y_k^i - N_{y_k}^i(f_k)\|_{\Delta_{y_k}^i}, \quad i \geq n_{k-1} + 1.$$

Note that in view of (6.1) this selection is possible. (For $k = 1$ we set $y_{1,i} = L_i(f_k; y_1^{i-1})$ so that $y_1 = N_{y_1}(f_1)$.) Clearly, y_k is noisy information about f_k.

Now we choose $r_k > 0$ such that for $\|f - f_k\| \leq r_k$ we have $\|S(f) - S(f_k)\| \leq (1/3)\|S(f_k) - S(f_{k-1})\|$. (For $k = 1$ we choose r_1 such that $\|S(f) - S(f_1)\| \leq (1/3)$ for $\|f - f_1\| \leq r_1$.) Since $f_k \in B$, there is an integer $n_k > n_{k-1}$ for which

$$\sqrt{\tau_{n_k}(y_k)} \leq \min\{r_k, (r/2)^k\}$$

and

$$\frac{\|S(f_k) - \varphi^{n_k}(y_k^{n_k})\|}{\tau_{n_k}(y_k) \, \mathrm{rad}_{n_k}^{\mathrm{wor}}(\mathbb{N}_{y_k})} \leq \frac{1}{10\sqrt{\tau_{n_k}(y_k)}}.$$

Owing to (6.2) there exists $h_k \in F$ such that

(i) $\|N_{y_k}^{n_k}(h_k)\|_{\Delta_{y_k}^{n_k}} \leq \sqrt{\tau_{n_k}(y_k)}$,

(ii) $\|h_k\|_F \leq \sqrt{\tau_{n_k}(y_k)}$, and

(iii) $\|S(h_k)\| \geq (1/4)\sqrt{\tau_{n_k}(y_k)} \, \mathrm{rad}_{n_k}^{\mathrm{wor}}(\mathbb{N}_{y_k})$.

We now set $f_{k+1} = f_k + h_k$. Observe that for $k = 1$ we have

$$\|y_1^{n_1} - N_{y_1}^{n_1}(f_2)\|_{\Delta_{y_1}^{n_1}} = \|N_{y_1}^{n_1}(h_1)\|_{\Delta_{y_1}^{n_1}} \leq \sqrt{\tau_{n_1}(y_1)} \leq \tfrac{1}{2},$$

while for $k \geq 2$ we have

$$
\begin{aligned}
\|y_k^{n_k} - N_{y_k}^{n_k}(f_{k+1})\|_{\Delta_{y_k}^{n_k}} &\leq \|y_k^{n_k} - N_{y_k}^{n_k}(f_k)\|_{\Delta_{y_k}^{n_k}} + \|N_{y_k}^{n_k}(h_k)\|_{\Delta_{y_k}^{n_k}} \\
&\leq \|y_{k-1}^{n_{k-1}} - N_{y_{k-1}}^{n_{k-1}}(f_k)\|_{\Delta_{y_{k-1}}^{n_{k-1}}} + \sqrt{\tau_{n_k}(y_{n_k})} \\
&\leq \sum_{j=1}^{k} 2^{-j}.
\end{aligned}
$$

Furthermore, $\|f_{k+1} - f_1\|_F \leq \sum_{j=1}^{k} \|f_{j+1} - f_j\|_F \leq r$, so that $f_{k+1} \in B$. This completes the construction of $\{f_k\}$, $\{n_k\}$ and $\{y_k\}$.

The sequence $\{f_k\}$ satisfies the Cauchy condition. Indeed, for any $m > k$ we have

$$\|f_m - f_k\|_F \leq \sum_{j=k}^{m-1} \|f_{j+1} - f_j\|_F \leq \sum_{j=1}^{m-1} (r/2)^j \leq 2\,(r/2)^k.$$

Hence there exists the limit $f^* = \lim_{k \to \infty} f_k \in B$.

We now show a property of f^*. Since $\|f_{k+1} - f_k\|_F \leq r_k$, we have $\|S(f_{k+1}) - S(f_k)\| \leq (1/3)\|S(f_k) - S(f_{k-1})\|$, $k \geq 2$. This gives for $m > k$

$$
\begin{aligned}
\|S(f_m) - S(f_k)\| &\geq \|S(f_{k+1}) - S(f_k)\| - \sum_{j=k+1}^{m-1} \|S(f_{j+1}) - S(f_j)\| \\
&\geq \left(1 - \sum_{j=k+1}^{m-1} (\tfrac{1}{3})^{j-k}\right) \|S(f_{k+1}) - S(f_k)\| \\
&\geq \tfrac{1}{2} \cdot \|S(f_{k+1}) - S(f_k)\|.
\end{aligned}
$$

By letting $m \to +\infty$ we get

$$\|S(f^*) - S(f_k)\| \geq \tfrac{1}{2} \cdot \|S(f_{k+1}) - S(f_k)\|, \qquad k \geq 1.$$

Now define the sequence $y^* \in \mathbb{R}^\infty$ as

$$y^* = [y_{1,1}, \ldots, y_{1,n_1}, \ldots, y_{k,n_{k-1}+1}, \ldots, y_{k,n_k}, \ldots].$$

That is, $(y^*)^{n_k} = y_k^{n_k}$, $k \geq 1$, where the $y_k \in \mathbb{R}^\infty$ are as constructed before. We shall show that y^* is noisy information about f^*. Indeed, for $m > k$ we have

$$\|(y^*)^{n_k} - N_{y^*}^{n_k}(f_m)\|_{\Delta_{y^*}^{n_k}}$$

$$\leq \quad \|(y^*)^{n_k} - N_{y^*}^{n_k}(f_{k+1})\|_{\Delta_{y^*}^{n_k}} + \sum_{j=k+1}^{m-1} \|N_{y^*}^{n_k}(f_{j+1} - f_j)\|_{\Delta_{y^*}^{n_k}}$$

$$\leq \quad \sum_{j=1}^{k} 2^{-j} + \sum_{j=k+1}^{m-1} \|N_{y^*}^{n_j}(h_j)\|_{\Delta_{y^*}^{n_j}} \leq \sum_{j=1}^{m-1} 2^{-j} \leq 1.$$

Letting $m \to +\infty$ and using the continuity of $N_{y^*}^{n_k}$, we find that $\|(y^*)^{n_k} - N_{y^*}^{n_k}(f^*)\|_{\Delta_{y^*}^{n_k}} \leq 1$. This in turn yields $y^* \in N_{y^*}^n(f^*)$ for all $n \geq 1$, i.e., y^* is noisy information about f^*.

Finally, for $k \geq 1$ we obtain

$$\|S(f^*) - \varphi^{n_k}((y^*)^{n_k})\|$$

$$\geq \quad \|S(f^*) - S(f_k)\| - \|S(f_k) - \varphi^{n_k}((y^*)^{n_k})\|$$

$$\geq \quad \tfrac{1}{2} \cdot \|S(f_{k+1}) - S(f_k)\| - \tfrac{1}{10} \cdot \sqrt{\tau_{n_k}(y^*)} \, \mathrm{rad}_{n_k}^{\mathrm{wor}}(N_{y^*})$$

$$\geq \quad \tfrac{1}{40} \cdot \sqrt{\tau_{n_k}(y^*)} \, \mathrm{rad}_{n_k}^{\mathrm{wor}}(N_{y^*}),$$

which implies (6.4) and contradicts the fact that $f^* \in B$. The proof is complete. □

Observe that the sequences $\tau(y)$ can be selected in such a way that they converge to zero arbitrarily slowly. This means that the speed of convergence of the radii $\{\mathrm{rad}_n^{\mathrm{wor}}(N_y)\}$ essentially cannot be beaten by any algorithm φ. In this sense, the optimal convergence rate is given by that of the radii, and the (ordinary) spline algorithm φ_o is optimal.

Observe that the sequences $\tau(y)$ cannot be eliminated from the formulation of Theorem 6.2.1. Indeed, for the spline algorithm φ_o we have

$$\left\{ f \in F \;\middle|\; \limsup_{n \to \infty} \frac{\|S(f) - \varphi_o^n(y^n)\|}{\mathrm{rad}_n^{\mathrm{wor}}(N_y)} < +\infty, \quad \forall y \in N(f) \right\} = F.$$

For further discussion on Theorem 6.2.1, see NR 6.2.2.

6.2.3 Optimal nonadaptive information

In this subsection we consider the problem of optimal information. We wish to select the functionals L_i in such a way that the speed of convergence is maximized. In view of Theorem 6.2.1, we can restrict ourselves to nonadaptive information, since adaption does not help. (The behavior of the error $\|S(f) - \varphi^n(y^n)\|$ is characterized by that of the nth radii of the nonadaptive information $\mathbb{N}_y$.)

More precisely, let $\mathcal{N}$ be the class of nonadaptive (exact) information operators $N = [L_1, L_2, \ldots]$, where the functionals $L_i \in \Lambda$ belong to a given class $\Lambda \subset F^*$. Suppose the precision vector is fixed,

$$\Delta = [\delta_1, \delta_2, \delta_3, \ldots].$$

It is clear that the error cannot tend to zero essentially faster than the sequence of the nth minimal worst case radii $\{r_n^{\text{wor}}(\Delta)\}$ defined by

$$r_n^{\text{wor}}(\Delta) = \inf_{N \in \mathcal{N}} \text{rad}_n^{\text{wor}}(N^n, \Delta^n), \qquad n \geq 1$$

(compare with the corresponding definition in Section 2.8). We shall show that it is often possible to construct information $N \in \mathcal{N}$ for which that convergence is achieved.

We assume that the extended norms $\| \cdot \|_{\Delta^n}$ satisfy the following condition. For any $n \geq 1$ and permutation $\{p_i\}_{i=1}^n$ of $\{1, 2, \ldots, n\}$ we have

$$\| (x_1, \ldots, x_n) \|_{[\delta_1, \ldots, \delta_n]} = \| (x_{p_1}, \ldots, x_{p_n}) \|_{[\delta_{p_1}, \ldots, \delta_{p_n}]}, \qquad (6.5)$$

for all $(x_1, \ldots, x_n) \in \mathbb{R}^n$. This condition expresses the property that the power of information does not depend on the order of performing observations. Indeed, for information $\mathbb{N}_1 = \{[L_1, \ldots, L_n], [\delta_1, \ldots, \delta_n]\}$ and $\mathbb{N}_2 = \{[L_{p_1}, \ldots, L_{p_n}], [\delta_{p_1}, \ldots, \delta_{p_n}]\}$ we have $[y_1, \ldots, y_n] \in \mathbb{N}_1(f)$ iff $[y_{p_1}, \ldots, y_{p_n}] \in \mathbb{N}_2(f)$. Clearly, (6.5) holds, for instance, for the weighted sup-norm and Euclidean norm.

Let $\eta > 1$. For any $n \geq 1$, let information $N_n \in \mathcal{N}$ be such that

$$\text{rad}_n^{\text{wor}}(N_n, \Delta) \leq \eta \cdot r_n^{\text{wor}}(\Delta).$$

Define

$$N_\Delta = [N_1^1, N_2^2, N_4^4, \ldots, N_{2^k}^{2^k}, \ldots]$$

where, as always, N_n^n denotes the first n functionals of N_n.

Lemma 6.2.2 *Suppose that*

$$\delta_1 \geq \delta_2 \geq \delta_3 \geq \cdots \geq 0. \qquad (6.6)$$

Then for information $\mathbb{N}_\Delta = \{N_\Delta, \Delta\}$ and the ordinary spline algorithm φ_o we have

$$\|S(f) - \varphi_o^n(y^n)\| \leq K(f) \cdot r_{\lceil (n+1)/4 \rceil}^{\text{wor}}(\Delta), \qquad f \in F, \quad y \in \mathbb{N}_\Delta(f),$$

where $K(f) = \eta \cdot \max\{2, (1+\rho)\|f\|_F\}$.

Proof For $n \geq 1$, let $k = k(n)$ be the largest integer satisfying $n \geq \sum_{i=0}^{k} 2^i = 2^{k+1} - 1$. Then all the functionals of $N_{2^k}^{2^k}$ are contained in N_Δ^n and, in view of (6.6), these functionals are observed with smaller noise bounds using information $\mathbb{N}_\Delta$ than using $\{N_{2^k}^{2^k}, \Delta^{2^k}\}$. This, (6.1) and (6.5) yield

$$\text{rad}_n^{\text{wor}}(\mathbb{N}_\Delta) \leq \text{rad}_{2^k}^{\text{wor}}(\{N_{2^k}^{2^k}, \Delta^{2^k}\}) \leq \eta \cdot r_{2^k}^{\text{wor}}(\Delta).$$

Using (6.3), for any $f \in F$ and $y \in \mathbb{N}_\Delta(f)$ we obtain

$$\begin{aligned}
\|S(f) - \varphi_o^n(y^n)\| &\leq \max\{2, (1+\rho)\|f\|_F\}\,\text{rad}_n^{\text{wor}}(\mathbb{N}_\Delta) \\
&\leq \eta \max\{2, (1+\rho)\|f\|_F\}\,r_{2^k}^{\text{wor}}(\Delta).
\end{aligned}$$

The lemma now follows from the fact that $2^k \geq \lceil (n+1)/4 \rceil$. $\qquad\square$

Lemma 6.2.2 often yields optimality of information N_Δ. Indeed, for many problems the nth minimal radius $r_n^{\text{wor}}(\Delta)$ behaves polynomially in $1/n$, i.e., $r_n^{\text{wor}}(\Delta) \asymp n^{-p}$ for some $p \geq 0$. Then $r_{\lceil(n+1)/4\rceil}^{\text{wor}}(\Delta) \asymp r_n^{\text{wor}}(\Delta)$, the error $\|S(f) - \varphi_o^n(y^n)\|$ achieves the optimal convergence rate, and information N_Δ is optimal.

Corollary 6.2.2 *If the nth minimal radii satisfy*

$$r_n^{\text{wor}}(\Delta) \asymp n^{-p}, \qquad p \geq 0,$$

then information N_Δ is optimal, i.e., for the spline algorithm φ_o we have

$$\|S(f) - \varphi_o^n(y^n)\| = O(n^{-p}), \qquad f \in F, \quad y \in \mathbb{N}_\Delta(f).$$

Notes and remarks

NR 6.2.1 The first results which revealed relations between the asymptotic and worst case settings were obtained by Trojan (1983) who analyzed the linear case with exact information. His results were then generalized by Kacewicz (1987) to the nonlinear case with exact information. The particular nonlinear problems of multivariate global optimization and scalar zero finding were studied in Plaskota (1989) and Sikorski and Trojan (1990), respectively.

The results for noisy information were obtained by Kacewicz and Plaskota (1991, 1992, 1993). This section is based mainly on these last three papers.

NR 6.2.2 One can try to strengthen Theorem 6.2.1 by making the sequences $\tau(y)$ dependent not only on the information y, but also on the problem elements f. That is, we select nonnegative sequences $\tau(f; y)$ such that

and $\lim_{n\to\infty} \tau_n(f;y) = 0$, and replace the set A in Theorem 6.2.1 by

$$B = \left\{ f \in F \mid \limsup_{n\to\infty} \frac{\|S(f) - \varphi^n(y^n)\|}{\tau_n(f;y)\,\mathrm{rad}_n^{\mathrm{wor}}(\mathbb{N}_y)} < +\infty, \quad \forall\, y \in \mathbb{N}(f) \right\}.$$

Then such a 'reformulated' theorem is in general no longer true, as can be illustrated by the following example.

Let $F = G$ be a separable, infinite dimensional Hilbert space with the orthonormal basis $\{\xi_i\}_{i\geq 1}$. Let S be given by $S\xi_i = \lambda_i \xi_i$, $i \geq 1$, where $|\lambda_1| \geq |\lambda_2| \geq \cdots > 0$. Let the information $\mathbb{N}$ be exact with $N = [\langle \cdot, \xi_1\rangle_F, \langle \cdot, \xi_2\rangle_F, \ldots]$. In this case we have $\mathrm{rad}_n^{\mathrm{wor}}(N) = |\lambda_{n+1}|$. On the other hand, for the algorithm $\varphi = \{\varphi^n\}$ where $\varphi^n(y^n) = \sum_{i=1}^n y_i \lambda_i \xi_i$, we have

$$\frac{\|S(f) - \varphi^n(y^n)\|}{|\lambda_{n+1}|} = \frac{1}{|\lambda_{n+1}|} \sqrt{\sum_{i=n+1}^{\infty} \langle f, \xi_i\rangle_F^2 \lambda_i^2} \leq \sqrt{\sum_{i=n+1}^{\infty} \langle f, \xi_i\rangle_F^2}$$

which converges to zero with $n \to +\infty$ for all $f \in F$ and $y \in \mathbb{N}(f)$. Hence, taking $\tau_n(f;y) = \tau_n(f) = \|S(f) - \varphi^n(y^n)\|/|\lambda_{n+1}|$, we have $B = F$.

In this example, the ratio $\|S(f) - \varphi_o^n(y^n)\|/\mathrm{rad}_n^{\mathrm{wor}}(N)$ converges to zero for all f and information y about f. However, owing to Theorem 6.2.1, on a dense set of f this convergence is arbitrarily slow.

NR 6.2.3 In this section we analyzed behavior of algorithms for fixed f as the number of observations increases to infinity. It is also possible to study behavior of the cost of computing an ε-approximation, as $\varepsilon \to 0$. Clearly, we want this cost to grow as slowly as possible. The corresponding computational model would be as follows.

The approximations are obtained by executing a program $\mathcal{P}$. This time, however, the result of computation is a sequence $g_0, g_1, g_2, \ldots$ of approximations rather than a single approximation. That is, the execution consists (at least theoretically) of infinitely many steps. At each (nth) step a noisy value y_n of a functional $L_n(f; y_1, \ldots, y_{n-1})$ is observed and then the nth approximation $g_n = \varphi^n(y_1, \ldots, y_n)$ is computed. Obviously, such an infinite process usually requires infinitely many constants and variables. However, we assume that for any n, the nth approximation is obtained using a finite number of constants and variables, as well as a finite number of primitive operations. In other words, the first n steps of $\mathcal{P}$ constitute a program in the sense of the worst case setting of Subsection 2.9.1.

Let $\mathcal{P}$ be a program that realizes an algorithm φ using information $\mathbb{N}$. For $\varepsilon \geq 0$, let

$$m(\mathcal{P}; f, y)(\varepsilon) = \min\{ k \geq 0 \mid \|S(f) - \varphi^i(y^i)\| \leq \varepsilon, \quad \forall\, i \geq k \} \qquad (6.7)$$

be the minimal number of steps for which all elements $g_m, g_{m+1}, g_{m+2}, \ldots$ are ε-approximations to $S(f)$. (If such a k does not exist we let $m(\mathcal{P}; f, y) = +\infty$.) Then the cost of obtaining an ε-approximation using the program $\mathcal{P}$ is given as

$$\mathrm{cost}(\mathcal{P}; f, y)(\varepsilon) = \mathrm{cost}_m(\mathcal{P}, y), \quad f \in F,\ y \in \mathbb{N}(f),$$

where $m = m(\mathcal{P}; f, y)(\varepsilon)$ is defined by (6.7), and $\mathrm{cost}_m(\mathcal{P}; y)$ is the cost of performing m steps using the program $\mathcal{P}$ with information y. (If $m = +\infty$ then $\mathrm{cost}(\mathcal{P}; f, y)(\varepsilon) = +\infty$.)

A similar model of (asymptotic) cost was studied by Kacewicz and Plaskota (1992, 1993). They showed that, under some additional assumptions, the best behavior of $\mathrm{cost}(\mathcal{P}; f, y)(\varepsilon)$ is essentially determined by the worst case complexity $\mathrm{Comp}^{\mathrm{wor}}(\varepsilon)$. Hence there are close relations between the asymptotic and worst case settings not only with respect to the error but also with respect to the cost of approximation.

NR 6.2.4 In the previous remark we assumed that the computational process is infinite. It is clear that in practice the computation must be terminated. The choice of an adequate termination criterion is an important practical problem. Obviously, (6.7) cannot serve as a computable termination criterion since $m(\mathcal{P}; f, y)(\varepsilon)$ explicitly depends on f which is unknown.

Suppose that we want to compute approximations using a program $\mathcal{P}$ which realizes a linear algorithm φ using nonadaptive information N. Suppose also that we know some bound on the norm of f, say $\|f\|_F \leq K$. Then to obtain an ε-approximation it is enough to terminate after

$$m = \min\{\, i \mid \mathrm{e}^{\mathrm{wor}}(\mathrm{N}^i, \varphi^i) \leq \varepsilon \min\{1, 1/K\} \,\}$$

steps. In view of the results of Kacewicz and Plaskota (1992, 1993), this is the best we can do. On the other hand, if we do not have any additional information about the norm $\|f\|_F$, then any computable termination criterion fails; see E 6.2.5.

Exercises

E 6.2.1 Let $\Delta \in \mathbb{R}^\infty$ be a given precision vector. Show that

$$\|x\|_\Delta = \lim_{n \to \infty} \|x^n\|_{\Delta^n}, \qquad x \in \mathbb{R}^\infty,$$

is a well defined extended norm in $\mathbb{R}^\infty$, and for all $n \geq 1$ we have

$$\|x^n\|_{\Delta^n} = \min_{z \in \mathbb{R}^\infty} \|[x^n, z]\|_\Delta, \qquad x^n \in \mathbb{R}^n.$$

E 6.2.2 Show that Corollary 6.2.1 also holds for the smoothing spline algorithm φ_∞ defined in Subsection 2.5.1.

E 6.2.3 Let N and φ be arbitrary information and algorithm. Show that for the spline algorithm φ_o and $\tau_n(y)$ as in Theorem 6.2.1, the set

$$\left\{ f \in F \;\middle|\; \limsup_{n \to \infty} \frac{\|S(f) - \varphi^n(y^n)\|}{\tau_n(y)\,\|S(f) - \varphi_o^n(y^n)\|} < +\infty, \quad \forall y \in \mathrm{N}(f) \right\}$$

does not contain any ball.

E 6.2.4 Suppose that the solution operator S is compact and acts between separable Hilbert spaces, and that observations of all functionals with norm bounded by 1 are allowed. Let

$$N_0 = [\langle \cdot, \xi_1 \rangle_F, \langle \cdot, \xi_2 \rangle_F, \ldots],$$

where $\{\xi_i\}$ is the complete orthonormal basis of eigenelements of S^*S and the corresponding eigenelements satisfy $\lambda_1 \geq \lambda_2 \geq \cdots \geq 0$. Assuming exact observations, $\Delta = [0, 0, 0, \ldots]$, show that for the spline algorithm φ_{spl} we have

$$\|S(f) - \varphi_{\mathrm{spl}}^n(y^n)\| \leq \|f\|_F \cdot \tau_n^{\mathrm{wor}}(0), \qquad f \in F, \; y = N_0(f).$$

That is, N_0 is the optimal information independently of the behavior of $r_n^{\text{wor}}(0) = \sqrt{\lambda_{n+1}}$.

E 6.2.5 (Kacewicz and Plaskota, 1992) Let $\mathcal{P}$ be a program realizing an algorithm φ using nonadaptive information $\mathbb{N} = \{N, \Delta\}$ such that $r_n^{\text{wor}}(\{N, 0\}) > 0$, $\forall n \geq 1$. Let $t_n : \mathbb{R}^\infty \to \{0, 1\}$ be arbitrary termination functions. That is, for $f \in F$ and $y \in \mathbb{N}(f)$ calculations are terminated after

$$m(y) = \min\{i \geq 0 \mid t_i(y_1, \ldots, y_i) = 1\}$$

steps. Show that for any $\varepsilon > 0$ and $y \in \mathbb{N}(F)$, there exists $f \in F$ such that $y \in \mathbb{N}(f)$ and $\|S(f) - \varphi^{m(y)}(y^{m(y)})\| > \varepsilon$.

6.3 Asymptotic and average case settings

In this section, we assume that information noise has random character. We show close relations between the asymptotic and average case settings. This will be done under the following assumptions:

- F is a separable Banach space equipped with a zero-mean Gaussian measure μ,
- the solution operator S is continuous and linear and acts between F and a separable Hilbert space G, and
- information consists of independent observations of continuous linear functionals with Gaussian noise.

To be more specific, (adaptive) information with Gaussian noise in the asymptotic setting is given as $\Pi = \{N_y, \Sigma_y\}_{y \in \mathbb{R}^\infty}$, where

$$N_y = [L_1(\,\cdot\,), L_2(\,\cdot\,; y_1), \ldots, L_n(\,\cdot\,; y_1, \ldots, y_{n-1}), \ldots]$$

is an infinite sequence of continuous linear functionals, and

$$\Sigma_y = \text{diag}\{\sigma_1^2, \sigma_2^2(y_1), \ldots, \sigma_n^2(y_1, \ldots, y_{n-1}), \ldots\}$$

is an infinite diagonal matrix. By the ith observation we obtain $y_i = L_i(f; y_1, \ldots, y_{i-1}) + x_i$ where $x_i \sim \mathcal{N}(0, \sigma_i^2(y_1, \ldots, y_{i-1}^2))$. That is, for $f \in F$ the probability distribution of information $y = [y_1, y_2, \ldots] \in \mathbb{R}^\infty$ about f is defined on the σ-field generated by the (cylindrical) sets of the form $B = A \times \mathbb{R}^\infty$ where A is a Borel set of $\mathbb{R}^n$ and $n \geq 1$, and given as follows. For any such B we have $\pi_f(B) = \pi_f^n(A)$ where π_f^n is the distribution of $[y_1, \ldots, y_n] \in \mathbb{R}^n$ corresponding to the first n observations. It is defined as in Subsection 3.7.1 for information $\Pi^n = \{N_y^n, \Sigma_y^n\}_{y \in \mathbb{R}^n}$ with

$$N_y^n = [L_1(\,\cdot\,), L_2(\,\cdot\,; y_1), \ldots, L_n(\,\cdot\,; y_1, \ldots, y_{n-1})]$$

and

$$\Sigma_y^n = [\delta_1, \delta_2(y_1), \ldots, \delta_n(y_1, \ldots, y_{n-1})].$$

Now, for an arbitrary Borel set $B \subset \mathbb{R}^\infty$,

$$\pi_f(B) = \lim_{n \to \infty} \pi_f^n(B^n) \qquad (6.8)$$

where $B^n = \{ y^n \in \mathbb{R}^n \mid y \in B \}$ is the projection of B onto $\mathbb{R}^n$.

6.3.1 Optimal algorithms

We now deal with the problem of an optimal algorithm. Recall that in the average case setting the optimal algorithms φ_{opt} are obtained by applying S to the mean of the conditional distribution corresponding to information about f. Also, φ_{opt} can be interpreted as a smoothing spline algorithm, $\varphi_{\mathrm{opt}} = \varphi_{\mathrm{spl}}$. We now show that the same type of algorithms can be successfully used in the asymptotic setting.

More precisely, for $y \in \mathbb{R}^\infty$, let the algorithm $\varphi_{\mathrm{spl}} = \{\varphi_{\mathrm{spl}}^n\}$ be given as $\varphi_{\mathrm{spl}}^n(y^n) = S(m(y^n))$ where

$$m(y^n) = \sum_{j=1}^n z_j^n \left(C_\mu(L_j(\cdot; y^{j-1})) \right),$$

z^n is the solution of

$$\left(\Sigma_y^n + G_{N_y}^n \right) z^n = y^n,$$

$\Sigma_y^n = \mathrm{diag}\,\{\sigma_1^2, \sigma_2^2(y^1), \ldots, \sigma_n^2(y^{n-1})\}$, and $G_{N_y}^n$ is the Gram matrix, $G_{N_y}^n = \{\langle L_i(\cdot; y^{i-1}), L_j(\cdot; y^{j-1})\rangle_\mu\}_{i,j=1}^n$. Let $\{H, F_1\}$ ($F_1 = \mathrm{supp}\,\mu$) be the abstract Wiener space for μ. Then $m(y^n)$ can be equivalently defined as the minimizer in the Hilbert space H of

$$\|f\|_H^2 + \sum_{j=1}^n \sigma_j^{-2}(y^{j-1}) \, (y_j - L_j(f; y^{j-1}))^2$$

(compare with Section 3.6 and Subsection 3.7.2).

In what follows, we shall use the joint distribution $\tilde{\mu}$ on the space $F \times \mathbb{R}^\infty$. This represents the probability of the occurrence of $f \in F$ and information y about f, and is generated by the measure μ and the distributions π_f. That is, for measurable sets $A \subset F$ and $B \subset \mathbb{R}^\infty$, we have

$$\tilde{\mu}(A \times B) = \int_A \pi_f(B) \, \mu(df).$$

Observe that in view of (6.8) we can also write

$$\tilde{\mu}(A \times B) = \lim_{n \to \infty} \tilde{\mu}^n(A \times B^n),$$

where $\tilde{\mu}^n(A \times B^n) = \int_A \pi_f^n(B^n)\,\mu(df)$ is the joint probability on $F \times \mathbb{R}^n$, i.e., the projection of $\tilde{\mu}$ onto $F \times \mathbb{R}^n$. Obviously, $m(y^n)$ is the mean element of the conditional distribution $\mu_2(\cdot|y^n)$ on F. Hence φ_{spl}^n minimizes the average error over $\tilde{\mu}^n$.

The algorithm φ_{spl} is optimal in the asymptotic setting in the following sense.

Theorem 6.3.1 *For any algorithm $\varphi = \{\varphi^n\}$, its error almost nowhere tends to zero faster than the error of φ_{spl}. That is, the set*

$$A = \left\{ (f, y) \in F \times \mathbb{R}^\infty \;\middle|\; \lim_{n \to \infty} \frac{\|S(f) - \varphi^n(y^n)\|}{\|S(f) - \varphi_{\mathrm{spl}}^n(y^n)\|} = 0 \right\}$$

is of $\tilde{\mu}$-measure zero. (By convention, $0/0 = 1$.)

The proof of this theorem is based on the following lemma.

Lemma 6.3.1 *Let ω be a Gaussian measure on G with mean m_ω. Then for any $g_0 \in G$ and $q \in (0,1)$ we have*

$$\omega\left(\{g \in G \mid \|g - g_0\| < q\,\|g - m_\omega\|\}\right) \le \beta \frac{q}{1 - q} \qquad (6.9)$$

where $\beta = \sqrt{2/(\pi e)}$.

Proof Suppose first that $m_\omega = 0$. Let $g = c\,g_0 + g_1$ where $g_1 \perp g_0$. Then $\|g - g_0\| < q\,\|g\|$ is equivalent to

$$(1 - c)^2 c^2 \|g_0\|^2 + \|g_1\|^2 < q^2\left(c^2 \|g_0\|^2 + \|g_1\|^2\right)$$

which, in particular, implies $(1 - c)^2 < c^2 q^2$ and $c \in ((1+q)^{-1}, (1-q)^{-1})$. This in turn means that

$$\frac{\|g_0\|^2}{1 + q} < \langle g, g_0 \rangle < \frac{\|g_0\|^2}{1 - q}. \qquad (6.10)$$

Let B be the set of all g satisfying (6.10). As $\langle g, g_0 \rangle$ is the zero-mean Gaussian random variable with variance $\lambda = \langle C_\omega g_0, g_0 \rangle$ (where $C_\omega : G \to G$ is the correlation operator of ω), for $\lambda = 0$ we have $\omega(B) = 0$, while for $\lambda > 0$

$$\omega(B) = \frac{1}{\sqrt{2\pi\lambda}} \int_{\|g_0\|^2/(1+q)}^{\|g_0\|^2/(1-q)} e^{-x^2/(2\lambda)}\,dx = \frac{1}{\sqrt{2\pi}} \int_{a/(1+q)}^{a/(1-q)} e^{-x^2/2}\,dx,$$

where $a = \|g_0\|^2 \lambda^{-1/2}$. Hence

$$
\begin{aligned}
\omega(B) &\leq \frac{a}{\sqrt{2\pi}} \left(\frac{1}{1-q} - \frac{1}{1+q} \right) \exp\left\{ -\frac{1}{2}\left(\frac{a}{1+q} \right)^2 \right\} \\
&= \sqrt{\frac{2}{\pi}} \frac{q}{1-q} \left(\frac{a}{1+q} \right) \exp\left\{ -\frac{1}{2}\left(\frac{a}{1+q} \right)^2 \right\}.
\end{aligned}
$$

To get (6.9), it suffices to observe that the maximal value of $x\, e^{-x^2/2}$ is $e^{-1/2}$. If $m_\omega \neq 0$ then we let $\omega(\cdot) = \omega_1(\cdot - m_\omega)$ and $\bar{g}_0 = g_0 - m_\omega$. Then zero is the mean element of ω and $\omega(A) = \omega_1(\{g \mid \|g - \bar{g}_0\| < q\|g\|\})$. $\qquad\square$

Proof of Theorem 6.3.1 Choose $q \in (0,1)$. For $n \geq 1$, define the sets

$$
A_n = \left\{ (f,y) \in F \times \mathbb{R}^\infty \mid \ \|S(f) - \varphi^n(y^n)\| < q\,\|S(f) - \varphi^n_{\mathrm{spl}}(y^n)\| \right\}.
$$

Observe that if $(f,y) \in A$ then for all sufficiently large n we have $(f,y) \in A_n$, and consequently

$$
A \subset \bigcup_{j=1}^{\infty} \bigcap_{n=j}^{\infty} A_n.
$$

Hence

$$
\tilde{\mu}(A) \leq \lim_{j \to \infty} \tilde{\mu}\left(\bigcap_{n=j}^{\infty} A_n \right) \leq \limsup_{n \to \infty} \tilde{\mu}(A_n). \tag{6.11}
$$

We now estimate the measure $\tilde{\mu}$ of A_n. Let

$$
A_n^n = \{ (f,y^n) \in F \times \mathbb{R}^n \mid \ (f,y) \in A_n \}.
$$

Then $\tilde{\mu}(A_n) = \tilde{\mu}^n(A_n^n)$. Using decomposition of $\tilde{\mu}^n$ with respect to the nth information y^n we get

$$
\tilde{\mu}^n(A_n^n) = \int_{\mathbb{R}^n} \mu_2(A_n^n|y^n)\,\mu_1(dy^n),
$$

where μ_1 is the a priori distribution of y^n, $\mu_2(\cdot|y^n)$ is the conditional distribution on F given y^n, and

$$
A_n^n(y^n) = \{ f \in F \mid \ (f,y^n) \in A_n^n \}.
$$

Owing to Theorem 3.7.1, the measures $\mu_2(\cdot|y^n)$ are Gaussian. Write $\nu_2(\cdot|y^n) = \mu_2(S^{-1}(\cdot)|y^n)$ and

$$
B_n^n(y^n) = S(A_n^n(y^n)) = \{ g \in G \mid \ \|g - \varphi^n(y^n)\| < q\,\|g - \varphi^n_{\mathrm{spl}}(y^n)\| \}.
$$

Since $\nu_2(\cdot|y^n)$ is also Gaussian and its mean element equals $\varphi_{\mathrm{spl}}^n(y^n)$, Lemma 6.3.1 gives $\nu_2(B_n^n(y^n)) \leq \beta\, q/(1-q)$, and consequently

$$\tilde{\mu}^n(A_n^n) = \int_{\mathbb{R}^n} \nu_2(B_n^n(y^n))\, \mu_1(dy^n) \leq \beta\, \frac{q}{1-q}.$$

Thus the set A_n has $\tilde{\mu}$-measure at most $\beta\, q/(1-q)$. In view of (6.11), this also means that $\tilde{\mu}(A) \leq \beta\, q/(1-q)$. Since q can be arbitrarily close to 0, we finally obtain $\tilde{\mu}(A) = 0$, as claimed. $\quad\square$

Theorem 6.3.1 establishes a close relation between the asymptotic and average case settings. Indeed, the optimal algorithm φ_{spl} in the asymptotic setting is composed of the optimal algorithms in the average case setting, $\varphi_{\mathrm{spl}} = \{\varphi_{\mathrm{spl}}^n\}$. There is no algorithm φ for which the successive approximations $\varphi^n(y^n)$ converge to $S(f)$ faster than $\varphi_{\mathrm{spl}}^n(y^n)$.

6.3.2 Convergence rate

We now discuss the rate of convergence. In view of Theorem 6.3.1, this rate depends on how fast $\varphi_{\mathrm{spl}}^n(y^n)$ goes to $S(f)$.

Recall that for deterministic noise, the best behavior of the error is essentially given by that of the worst case radii. It turns out that for random noise the nth average radii play a similar role. The nth average radius of nonadaptive information $\mathrm{I\!I}_y$ ($y \in \mathbb{R}^\infty$) is given as

$$\mathrm{rad}_n^{\mathrm{ave}}(\mathrm{I\!I}_y) = \mathrm{rad}^{\mathrm{ave}}(\mathrm{I\!I}_y^n) = \sqrt{\int_{\mathbb{R}^n} r^2(\mu_2(\cdot|y^n))},$$

where $\mu_2(\cdot|y^n)$ is the conditional distribution on F given y^n, and $r^2(\cdot)$ is the squared radius of a measure, see Section 3.2.

Before we state theorems about the rate of convergence of φ_{spl}, we first cite some known estimates for Gaussian measures of balls in G. (For completeness, we give proofs in NR 6.3.3 and NR 6.3.4.) In what follows, we denote by $B_r(a)$ the ball with radius r and centered at a.

Lemma 6.3.2 *Let ω be a zero-mean Gaussian measure on G. Then for any $r \geq 0$ and $a \in G$ we have*

$$\omega(B_r(0)) \geq \omega(B_r(a)).$$

Lemma 6.3.3 *Let ω be a Gaussian measure on G and C_ω its correlation operator. Then*

$$\omega(B_r(a)) \leq \frac{4}{3}\psi\left(\frac{2r}{\sqrt{\text{tr}(C_\omega)}}\right)$$

where $\psi(x) = \sqrt{2/\pi}\int_0^x e^{-t^2/2}dt$.

We are now ready to show that the error of any algorithm (and particularly the error of φ_{spl}) cannot converge to zero faster than $\{\text{rad}_n^{\text{ave}}(\mathbb{I}_y)\}$.

Theorem 6.3.2 *For any algorithm φ the set*

$$A_1 = \left\{ (f,y) \in F \times \mathbb{R}^\infty \;\middle|\; \lim_{n\to\infty} \frac{\|S(f) - \varphi^n(y^n)\|}{\text{rad}_n^{\text{ave}}(\mathbb{I}_y)} = 0 \right\}$$

has $\tilde{\mu}$-measure zero.

Proof We choose $q \in (0,1)$ and define

$$A_{1,n} = \{ (f,y) \in F \times \mathbb{R}^\infty \mid \|S(f) - \varphi^n(y^n)\| < q \cdot \text{rad}_n^{\text{ave}}(\mathbb{I}_y)\}$$

and $B_{1,n} = \{ (f,y^n) \in F \times \mathbb{R}^n \mid (f,y) \in A_{1,n} \}$. Similarly to the proof of Theorem 6.3.1, we have $A_1 \subset \bigcup_{i=1}^\infty \bigcap_{n=i}^\infty A_{1,n}$ and $\tilde{\mu}(A_1) \leq \limsup_{n\to\infty} \tilde{\mu}^n(B_{1,n})$. It now suffices to show that the last limit tends to zero as $q \to 0^+$.

Indeed, using the conditional distribution of $\tilde{\mu}^n$ we get

$$\begin{aligned}
&\tilde{\mu}^n(B_{1,n}) \\
&= \int_{\mathbb{R}^n} \mu_2(\{ f \in F \mid (f,y^n) \in B_{1,n} \}\,|\,y^n)\,\mu_1(dy^n) \\
&= \int_{\mathbb{R}^n} \nu_2(\{ g \in G \mid \|g - \varphi^n(y^n)\| < q \cdot \text{rad}_n^{\text{ave}}(\mathbb{I}_y)\}\,|\,y^n)\,\mu_1(dy^n).
\end{aligned}$$

Since $\text{rad}_n^{\text{ave}}(\mathbb{I}_y) = \text{tr}(C_{\nu_2,y^n})$ where C_{ν_2,y^n} is the correlation operator of the Gaussian measure $\nu_2(\cdot|y^n)$, we can use Lemma 6.3.3 to get that

$$\nu_2\left(\{ g \in G \mid \|g - \varphi^n(y^n)\| < q \cdot \text{rad}_n^{\text{ave}}(\mathbb{I}_y)\}\,|\,y^n\right) \leq \tfrac{4}{3}\psi(2q).$$

Thus $\tilde{\mu}^n(B_{1,n}) \leq (4/3)\psi(2q)$. Since this tends to zero with $q \to 0^+$, $\tilde{\mu}(A_1) = 0$. $\qquad\square$

We now show that in some sense the sequence $\{\text{rad}_n^{\text{ave}}(\mathbb{I}_y)\}$ also provides an upper bound on the convergence rate.

Theorem 6.3.3 *For the algorithm φ_{spl} the set*

$$A_2 = \left\{ (f,y) \in F \times \mathbb{R}^\infty \;\Big|\; \lim_{n\to\infty} \frac{\mathrm{rad}_n^{\mathrm{ave}}(\mathrm{I\!I}_y)}{\|S(f) - \varphi_{\mathrm{spl}}^n(y^n)\|} = 0 \right\}.$$

has $\tilde{\mu}$-measure zero.

Proof Choose $q \in (0,1)$ and define

$$A_{2,n} = \{(f,y) \in F \times \mathbb{R}^\infty \mid \|S(f) - \varphi_{\mathrm{spl}}^n(y^n)\| \geq (1/q)\mathrm{rad}_n^{\mathrm{ave}}(\mathrm{I\!I}_y)\}$$

and $B_{2,n} = \{ (f,y^n) \in F \times \mathbb{R}^\infty \mid (f,y) \in A_{2,n}\}$. Then A_2 is a sub-set of $\bigcup_{i=1}^\infty \bigcap_{n=i}^\infty A_{2,n}$ and $\tilde{\mu}(A_2) \leq \limsup_{n\to\infty} \tilde{\mu}^n(B_{2,n})$. Using the decomposition of $\tilde{\mu}$ we have

$$\tilde{\mu}^n(B_{2,n})$$
$$= \int_{\mathbb{R}^n} \nu_2\left(\left\{ g \in G \mid \|g - \varphi_{\mathrm{spl}}^n(y^n)\| \geq (1/q)\sqrt{\mathrm{tr}(C_{\nu,y^n})} \right\} \Big| y^n \right)$$
$$\mu_1(dy^n). \quad (6.12)$$

We now use a slight generalization of the Chebyshev inequality to estimate the Gaussian measure of the set of all g which are not in the ball centered at the mean element. That is, if ω is a Gaussian measure on G then for any $r > 0$

$$\mathrm{tr}(C_\omega) = \int_G \|g - m_\omega\|^2 \,\omega(dg)$$
$$\geq \int_{\|g-m_\omega\|>r} \|g - m_\omega\|^2 \,\omega(dg) \geq r^2\,\omega(G \setminus B_r(m_\omega)),$$

and consequently

$$\omega\left(\{g \in G \mid \|g - m_\omega\| \geq r\}\right) \leq \frac{\mathrm{tr}(C_\omega)}{r^2}.$$

For $r = (1/q)\sqrt{\mathrm{tr}(C_\omega)}$, the right hand side of the last inequality is just q^2. Hence (6.12) is bounded from above by q^2.

Using the same argument as in the proof of Theorem 6.3.2 we conclude that $\tilde{\mu}(A_2) = 0$.   □

Theorem 6.3.3 says that for almost every element (f,y) some subse-quence $\|S(f) - \varphi_{\mathrm{spl}}^{n_k}(y^{n_k})\|$ converges to zero at least as fast as $\mathrm{rad}_{n_k}^{\mathrm{ave}}(\mathrm{I\!I}_y)$ as $k \to \infty$. The word 'subsequence' above cannot be omitted, see NR 6.3.2.

6.3.3 Optimal nonadaptive information

Finally, we consider the problem of optimal information. We restrict ourselves to nonadaptive information since, in view of results of the previous section, adaption does not help. (Convergence is determined by the nth radii of nonadaptive information III_y.) We fix the matrix

$$\Sigma \;=\; \mathrm{diag}\,\{\,\sigma_1^2, \sigma_2^2, \sigma_3^2 \dots\,\}$$

and want to select an infinite sequence of functionals $N = [L_1, L_2, \dots]$ in such a way that the error $\|S(f) - \varphi_{\mathrm{spl}}^n(y^n)\|$ goes to zero as fast as possible. We assume that N belongs to the class $\mathcal{N}$ of all information for which the functionals L_i are in a given class $\Lambda \subset F^*$.

Theorems 6.3.2 and 6.3.3 say that for given information $\mathrm{III} = \{N, \Sigma\}$ the behavior of errors can be essentially characterized by that of the nth average radii of III. Hence it seems natural to call *optimal* the information for which the sequence $\mathrm{rad}_n^{\mathrm{ave}}(N, \Sigma)$ vanishes at the fastest rate.

For $n \geq 1$, let

$$r_n^{\mathrm{ave}}(\Sigma) \;=\; \inf_{N \in \mathcal{N}} \; \mathrm{rad}_n^{\mathrm{ave}}(N^n, \Sigma^n)$$

be the minimal average error that can be achieved using the first n nonadaptive observations. It is clear that for any information $N \in \mathcal{N}$ we have $\mathrm{rad}_n^{\mathrm{ave}}(N, \Sigma) \geq r_n^{\mathrm{ave}}(\Sigma)$, i.e., the radii $\mathrm{rad}_n^{\mathrm{ave}}(N, \Sigma)$ do not converge faster than $r_n^{\mathrm{ave}}(\Sigma)$. Consequently, Theorem 6.3.2 yields that for arbitrary information $N \in \mathcal{N}$ the $\tilde{\mu}$-measure of the set

$$\left\{ (f, y) \in F \times \mathbb{R}^\infty \;\middle|\; \lim_{n \to \infty} \frac{\|S(f) - \varphi_{\mathrm{spl}}^n(y^n)\|}{r_n^{\mathrm{ave}}(\Sigma)} = 0 \right\}$$

is zero. We now establish information N_Σ whose radii behave in many cases as $r_n^{\mathrm{ave}}(\Sigma)$. To this end, we use the construction from Subsection 6.2.3. We let $\eta > 1$ and choose $N_n \in \mathcal{N}$ for $n \geq 1$ in such a way that

$$\mathrm{rad}_n^{\mathrm{ave}}(N_n, \Sigma) \;\leq\; \eta \cdot r_n^{\mathrm{ave}}(\Sigma).$$

Then

$$N_\Sigma \;=\; [N_1^1, N_2^2, N_4^4, \dots, N_{2^k}^{2^k}, \dots].$$

Lemma 6.3.4 *Suppose that*

$$\sigma_1 \geq \sigma_2 \geq \sigma_3 \geq \cdots \geq 0.$$

Then for the information N_Σ and algorithm φ_{spl} the set

$$\left\{ (f, y) \in F \times \mathbb{R}^\infty \ \Big| \ \lim_{n \to \infty} \frac{r^{ave}_{\lceil (n+1)/4 \rceil}(\Sigma)}{\|S(f) - \varphi^n_{spl}(y^n)\|} = 0 \right\}$$

has $\tilde{\mu}$-measure zero.

Proof Proceeding as in the proof of Lemma 6.2.2 we show that

$$\mathrm{rad}^{ave}_n(N_\Sigma, \Sigma) \ \leq \ \eta \cdot r^{ave}_{\lceil (n+1)/4 \rceil}(\Sigma). \tag{6.13}$$

Hence the lemma is a consequence of (6.13) and Theorem 6.3.3. $\qquad\square$

As in Subsection 6.2.2, Lemma 6.3.4 immediately gives the following corollary.

Corollary 6.3.1 *If the nth minimal radii satisfy $r^{ave}_n(\Sigma) \asymp n^{-p}$ for some $p \geq 0$, then the information N_Σ is optimal.*

Notes and remarks

NR 6.3.1 Relations between the asymptotic and average case settings were first established by Wasilkowski and Woźniakowski (1987) who studied exact information. The results for information with random noise are new; however, we adopted techniques from the paper cited to prove Theorems 6.3.1, 6.3.2 and 6.3.3. Lemma 6.3.3 is due to Kwapień.

NR 6.3.2 We cannot claim in general that the sequence $\|S(f) - \varphi^n_{spl}(y^n)\|$ behaves at least as well as $\mathrm{rad}^{ave}_n(\Pi_y)$ with probability one. Actually, the probability that $\|S(f) - \varphi^n_{spl}(y^n)\| = O(\mathrm{rad}^{ave}_n(\Pi_y))$ can even be zero, as illustrated by the following example.

Let $F = G$ be the space of infinite real sequences with $\|f\|^2_F = \sum^\infty_{j=1} f^2_j < +\infty$. We equip F with the zero-mean Gaussian measure μ such that $C_\mu e_i = \lambda_i e_i$, where $\lambda_i = a^j$ and $0 < a < 1$. Consider approximation of $f \in F$ from exact information about coordinates of f, i.e., $N(f) = [f_1, f_2, f_3 \ldots]$ and $\Sigma = \mathrm{diag}\{0, 0, 0, \ldots\}$. We shall see that in this case the set

$$A_3 = \left\{ (f, y) \in F \times \mathbb{R}^\infty \ \Big| \ \limsup_{n \to \infty} \frac{\|S(f) - \varphi^n_{spl}(y^n)\|}{\mathrm{rad}^{ave}_n(\Pi)} < +\infty \right\}$$

has $\tilde{\mu}$-measure zero.

Indeed, as noise is zero, the measure $\tilde{\mu}$ is concentrated on $\{(f, N(f)) \mid f \in F\}$ and $\tilde{\mu}(A_3)$ equals the μ-measure of the set $B = \{f \in F \mid (f, N(f)) \in A_3\}$. Moreover, since in this case $\varphi^n_{spl}(y^n) = [y_1, \ldots, y_n, 0, 0, 0, \ldots]$ and $\mathrm{rad}^{ave}_n(\Pi) = \sqrt{\sum^\infty_{i=n+1} \lambda_i}$, we have $B = \bigcup^\infty_{k=1} B_k$ where

$$B_k = \left\{ f \in F \ \Big| \ \sum^\infty_{i=n} f^2_i \leq k^2 \sum^\infty_{i=n} \lambda_i, \quad \forall n \geq 1 \right\}.$$

Observe now that the condition $\sum_{i=n}^{\infty} f_i^2 \leq k^2 \sum_{i=n}^{\infty} \lambda_i$ implies

$$|f_n| \leq k\sqrt{\sum_{i=n}^{\infty} \lambda_i} = k\sqrt{\frac{a^n}{1-a}} = \frac{k}{\sqrt{1-a}}\sqrt{\lambda_n}.$$

Hence

$$\mu(B_k) \leq \prod_{n=1}^{\infty} \mu\left(\left\{f \in F \,\middle|\, |f_n| \leq \frac{k}{\sqrt{1-a}}\sqrt{\lambda_n}\right\}\right)$$

$$= \prod_{n=1}^{\infty}\left(\sqrt{\frac{2}{\pi}}\int_0^{\frac{k}{\sqrt{1-a}}} e^{-x^2/2}\,dx\right) = 0,$$

and consequently $\tilde{\mu}(A_3) = \mu(B) = \lim_{k\to\infty}\mu(B_k) = 0$.

NR 6.3.3 *Proof of Lemma 6.3.2* Assume first that $G = \mathbb{R}^n$ and the co-ordinates g_i, $1 \leq i \leq n$, are independent random variables. For $n = 1$ the lemma is obvious. Let $n \geq 2$. Let ω^{n-1} be the joint distribution of $g^{n-1} = (g_1, \ldots, g_{n-1})$ and ω_n be the distribution of g_n. Then

$$\omega(B_r(a))$$

$$= \int_{\mathbb{R}^n} \omega_n\left(\left\{g_n \,\middle|\, |g_n - a_n| \leq \sqrt{r^2 - \|g^{n-1} - a^{n-1}\|^2}\right\}\right)\omega^{n-1}(dg^{n-1})$$

$$\leq \int_{\mathbb{R}^n} \omega_n\left(\left\{g_n \,\middle|\, |g_n| \leq \sqrt{r^2 - \|g^{n-1} - a^{n-1}\|^2}\right\}\right)\omega^{n-1}(dg^{n-1})$$

$$= \omega(B_r(a^{n-1}, 0)).$$

Proceeding in this way with successive coordinates we obtain

$$\omega(B_r(a^{n-1}, 0)) \leq \omega(B_r(a^{n-2}, 0, 0)) \leq \cdots \leq \omega(B_r(\underbrace{0, \ldots, 0}_{n})),$$

and consequently $\omega(B_r(a)) \leq \omega(B_r(0))$.

Consider now the general case. Let $\{\xi_j\}_{j\geq 1}$ be the complete orthonormal system of eigenelements of C_ω. Then the $g_j = \langle g, \xi_j\rangle$ are independent zero-mean Gaussian random variables and $B_r(a) = \{g \in G \,|\, \sum_j (g_j - a_j)^2 \leq r^2\}$. Denoting by ω^n the joint distribution of $(g_1, \ldots, g_n)$ and by $B_r^n(a^n)$ the ball in $\mathbb{R}^n$ with center $a^n = (a_1, \ldots, a_n)$ and radius r, we have

$$\omega(B_r(a)) = \lim_{n\to\infty}\omega^n(B_r^n(a^n)) \leq \lim_{n\to\infty}\omega^n(B_r^n(0)) = \omega(B_r(0)),$$

as claimed. $\qquad\qquad\qquad\qquad\qquad\qquad\qquad\qquad\qquad\qquad\qquad\qquad\square$

NR 6.3.4 *Proof of Lemma 6.3.3* We can assume without loss of generality that the mean element of ω is zero, since we can always shift the measure towards the origin. In view of Lemma 6.3.2, we can also assume that the ball is centered at zero. In this case we write, for brevity, B_r instead of $B_r(0)$.

Let $d = \dim G \leq +\infty$. Let $\{\xi_j\}$ be the complete orthonormal system of eigenelements of C_ω, $C_\omega\xi_j = \lambda_j\xi_j$. Then the random variables $g_j = \langle g, \xi_j\rangle$ are independent and $g_j \sim \mathcal{N}(0, \lambda_j)$. Let t_j be independent random variables which take -1 and $+1$ each with probability $1/2$, and $t = (t_j)_{j=1}^d$. Denote by

p the joint probability on $T = \{-1, +1\}^d$, and by $\tilde{\omega}$ the joint probability on $T \times G$. Then

$$\tilde{\omega}\left(\left\{ (t,g) \in T \times G \,\middle|\, \left|\sum_{j=1}^d t_j\, g_j\right| \leq 2r \right\}\right)$$

$$\geq \int_{B_r} p\left(\left\{ t \in T \,\middle|\, \left|\sum_{j=1}^d t_j\, g_j\right| \leq 2r \right\}\right) \omega(dg)$$

$$\geq \gamma \cdot \omega(B_r), \tag{6.14}$$

where

$$\gamma = \inf p\left(\left\{ t \in T \,\middle|\, \left|\sum_{j=1}^d t_j\, c_j\right| \leq 2 \right\}\right),$$

the infimum being taken over all c_j with $\sum_{j=1}^d c_j^2 \leq 1$.

On the other hand, $\{t_j g_j\}$ are independent random variables and $t_j g_j \sim \mathcal{N}(0, \lambda_j)$, which implies that $\sum_{j=1}^d t_j g_j \sim \mathcal{N}(0, \lambda)$ where $\lambda = \mathrm{tr}(C_\omega)$. Hence (6.14) equals

$$\frac{1}{\sqrt{2\pi\lambda}} \int_{-2r}^{2r} e^{-t^2/(2\lambda)}\, dt = \psi\left(\frac{2r}{\sqrt{\lambda}}\right),$$

and consequently

$$\omega(B_r) \leq \frac{1}{\gamma}\, \psi\left(\frac{2r}{\sqrt{\mathrm{tr}(C_\omega)}}\right).$$

We now estimate γ^{-1}. Since for any $c = (c_1, c_2, \dots)$ the random variable $\sum_{j=1}^d t_j c_j$ has mean zero and variance $\sum_{j=1}^d c_j^2$, we can use the well known Chebyshev inequality to get

$$p\left(\left\{ t \in T \,\middle|\, \left|\sum_{j=1}^d t_j c_j\right| > 2 \right\}\right) \leq \tfrac{1}{4} \cdot \sum_{j=1}^d c_j^2 \leq \tfrac{1}{4}.$$

Hence $\gamma \geq 1 - (1/4)$ and $\gamma^{-1} \leq (4/3)$. The proof is complete. $\qquad\square$

Exercises

E 6.3.1   Consider the problem of approximating a parameter $f \in \mathbb{R}$ from information $y = [y_1, y_2, y_3, \dots] \in \mathbb{R}^\infty$, where $y_i = f + x_i$ and the x_is are independent, $x_i \sim \mathcal{N}(0, \sigma^2)$, $i \geq 1$. Show that then for any f

$$\pi_f\left(\left\{ y \in \mathbb{R}^\infty \,\middle|\, \lim_{n \to \infty} \frac{1}{n} \sum_{j=1}^n y_j = f \right\}\right) = 1,$$

where, as always, π_f is the distribution of information y about f, i.e., the algorithm $\varphi^n(y^n) = (1/n)\sum_{j=1}^n y_j$ converges to the 'true' solution f with probability 1.

E 6.3.2 Consider the one dimensional problem of E 6.3.1. For y belonging to the set

$$C = \left\{ y \in \mathbb{R}^\infty \;\middle|\; \text{the limit} \;\; m(y) = \lim_{n\to\infty} \frac{1}{n} \sum_{j=1}^{n} y_j \;\; \text{exists and is finite} \right\},$$

let ω_y be the Dirac measure on $\mathbb{R}$ centered at $m(y)$. Let μ_1 be the distribution of information $y \in \mathbb{R}^\infty$,

$$\mu_1(\cdot) = \int_F \pi_f(\cdot)\,\mu(df).$$

Show that $\mu_1(C) = 1$ and

$$\tilde{\mu}(A \times B) = \int_B \omega_y(A)\,\mu_1(dy),$$

for any measurable sets $A \subset F$ and $B \subset \mathbb{R}^\infty$, i.e., $\{\omega_y\}$ is the regular conditional distribution on $\mathbb{R}$ with respect to the information $y \in \mathbb{R}^\infty$, $\omega_y = \mu_2(\cdot|y)$.

E 6.3.3 Give an example where

$$\tilde{\mu}\left(\left\{(f,y) \in F \times \mathbb{R}^\infty \;\middle|\; \|S(f) - \varphi_{\mathrm{spl}}^n(y^n)\| \asymp \mathrm{rad}_n^{\mathrm{ave}}(\mathrm{II}_y)\right\}\right) = 1.$$

E 6.3.4 Let II be given information. Can we claim that for a.e. (f,y) there exists a subsequence $\{n_k\}$ such that $\|S(f) - \varphi_{\mathrm{spl}}^{n_k}(y^{n_k})\| \asymp \mathrm{rad}_n^{\mathrm{ave}}(\mathrm{II})$?

E 6.3.5 Suppose the class Λ consists of functionals whose μ-norm is bounded by 1. Let

$$N_0 = [\langle \cdot, \xi_1 \rangle, \langle \cdot, \xi_2 \rangle, \dots]$$

where $\{\xi_i\}$ is the complete orthonormal basis of eigenelements of $SC_\mu S^*$ and the corresponding eigenvalues satisfy $\lambda_1 \geq \lambda_2 \geq \cdots \geq 0$. Assuming exact observations, $\Sigma = \mathrm{diag}\{0,0,0,\dots\}$, show that the information N_0 is optimal independently of the behavior of $r_n^{\mathrm{ave}}(0) = \sqrt{\sum_{j \geq n+1} \lambda_j}$.

References

ARESTOV, B.B.
(1990) Best recovery of operators, and related problems. Vol. 189 of *Proc. of the Steklov Inst. of Math.*, pp. 1–20.

ARONSZAJN, N.
(1950) Theory of reproducing kernels. *Trans. AMS*, **68**, 337–404.

BABENKO, K.I.
(1979) *Theoretical Background and Constructing Computational Algorithms for Mathematical-Physical Problems*. Nauka, Moscow. (In Russian.)

BAKHVALOV, N.S.
(1971) On the optimality of linear methods for operator approximation in convex classes. *Comput. Math. Math. Phys.*, **11**, 244–249.

BICKEL, P.J.
(1981) Minimax estimation of the mean of a normal distribution when the parameter space is restricted. *Ann. Statist.*, **9**, 1301–1309.

BJÖRCK, A.
(1990) Least squares methods. In *Handbook of Numerical Analysis*. Ed. by P.G. Ciarlet and J.L. Lions, Elsevier, North-Holland, pp. 465–652.

BLUM, L., CUCKER, F., SHUB, M. AND SMALE, S.
(1995) *Complexity and Real Computation: A Manifesto*. To appear.

BLUM, L., SHUB, M. AND SMALE, S.
(1989) On a theory of computation and complexity over the real numbers: NP-completeness, recursive functions and universal machines. *Bull. AMS (new series)*, **21**, 1–46.

BROWN, L.D. AND FELDMAN, I.
(1990) The minimax risk for estimating a bounded normal mean. Unpublished manuscript.

CASELLA, G. AND STRAWDERMAN, W.E.
(1981) Estimating bounded normal mean. *Ann. Statist.*, **9**, 870–878.

CIESIELSKI, Z.
(1975) On Lévy's Brownian motion with several-dimensional time. In *Probability-Winter School*. Ed. by Z. Ciesielski *et al.* Vol. 472 of *Lecture Notes in Math.*, Springer-Verlag, New York, pp. 29–56.

CUTLAND, N.J.
(1980) *Computability*. Cambridge Univ. Press, Cambridge.

DAUBECHIES, I.
(1992) *Ten Lectures on Wavelets*. Vol. 61 of *CBMS-NSF Ser. in Appl. Math.* SIAM, Philadelphia.

DONOHO, D.L.
(1994) Statistical estimation and optimal recovery. *Ann. Statist.*, **22**, 238–270.

(1995) De-noising by soft-thresholding. *IEEE Trans. on Inform. Th.*, **41**, 613–627.

DONOHO, D.L. AND JOHNSTONE, I.M.
(1994) Minimax risk over l_p-balls for l_q-error. *Probab. Theory Related Fields*, **99**, 277–303.

(1992) Minimax estimation via wavelet shrinkage. To appear in *Ann. Statist.*

DONOHO, D.L., JOHNSTONE, I.M., KERKYACHARIAN, G. AND PICARD. D.
(1995) Wavelet shrinkage: asymptopia? *J. Roy. Stat. Soc., ser. B*, **57**, 301–369.

DONOHO, D.L., LIU, R.C. AND MACGIBBON, K.B.
(1990) Minimax risk over hyperrectangles, and implications. *Ann. of Statist.*, **18**, 1416–1437.

EUBANK, R.L.
(1988) *Spline Smoothing and Nonparametric Regression*. Dekker, New York.

GAL, S. AND MICCHELLI, C.A.
(1980) Optimal sequential and non-sequential procedures for evaluating a functional. *Appl. Anal.*, **10**, 105–120.

GIKHMAN, I.I. AND SKOROHOD, A.V.
(1965) *Introduction to the Theory of Random Processes*. Nauka, Moscow. (In Russian.)

GOLOMB, M. AND WEINBERGER, H.F.
(1959) Optimal approximation and error bounds. In *On Numerical Approximation*. Ed. by R.F. Langer, Univ. of Wisconsin Press, Madison, pp. 117–190.

GOLUB, G.H., HEATH, M.T. AND WAHBA, G.
(1979) Validation as a method for choosing a good ridge parameter. *Technometrics*, **21**, 215–223.

GOLUBEV, G.K.
(1992) On sequential experimental designs for nonparametric estimation of smooth regression functions. *Problems Inform. Transmission*, **28**, 76–79. (In Russian.)

GOLUBEV, G.K. AND M. NUSSBAUM, M.
(1990) A risk bound in Sobolev class regression. *Ann. of Statist.*, **18**, 758–778.

GREVILLE, T.N.E.
(1969) Introduction to spline functions. In *Theory and Applications of Spline Functions*, Ed. by T.N.E. Greville, Academic Press, New York, pp. 1–35.

HANSEN, P.C.
(1992) Analysis of discrete ill-posed problems by means of the L-curve. *SIAM Review*, **34**, 561–580.

HEINRICH, S.
(1993) Random approximation in numerical analysis. In *Proc. of the Functional Analysis Conf.*, Essen 1991, Ed. by K.D. Bierstedt *et al.*. Marcel Dekker, New York, pp. 123–171.

HEINRICH, S. AND KERN, J.D.
(1991) Parallel information-based complexity. *J. Complexity*, **7**, 339–370.

HOLLADAY, J.C.
(1957) Smoothest curve approximation. *Math. Tables Aids Computation*, **11**, 233–243.

IBRAGIMOV, I.A. AND HASMINSKI, R.Z.
(1982) Bounds for the risk of nonparametric regression estimates. *Theory Probab. Appl.*, **28**, 81–94. (In Russian.)

(1984) On the nonparametric estimation of the value of a linear functional in Gaussian white noise. *Theory Probab. Appl.*, **29**, 19–32. (In Russian.)

JENSEN, K. AND WIRTH, N.
(1975) *Pascal. User Manual and Report*. Springer-Verlag, Berlin.

KACEWICZ, B.Z.
(1987) Asymptotic error of algorithms for solving nonlinear problems. *J. Complexity*, **3**, 41–56.

(1990) On sequential and parallel solution of initial value problems. *J. Complexity*, **6**, 136–148.

KACEWICZ, B.Z. AND KOWALSKI, M.A.
(1995a) Approximating linear functionals on unitary spaces in the presence of bounded data errors with applications to signal recovery. *Intern. J. of Adaptive Control and Signal Processing*, **9**, 19–31.

296 References

(1995b) Recovering linear operators from inaccurate data. *J. Complexity*, **11**, 227–239.

KACEWICZ, B.Z., MILANESE, M., TEMPO, R. AND VICINO, A.
(1986) Optimality of central and projection algorithms for bounded uncertainty. *Systems Control Lett.*, **8**, 161–171.

KACEWICZ, B.Z. AND PLASKOTA, L.
(1990) On the minimal cost of approximating linear problems based on information with deterministic noise. *Numer. Funct. Anal. Optimiz.*, **11**, 511–525.

(1991) Noisy information for linear problems in the asymptotic setting. *J. Complexity*, **7**, 35–57.

(1992) Termination conditions for approximating linear problems with noisy information. *Math. of Comp.*, **59**, 503–513.

(1993) The minimal cost of approximating linear operators using perturbed information—the asymptotic setting. *J. Complexity*, **9**, 113–134.

KADANE, J.B., WASILKOWSKI, G.W. AND WOŹNIAKOWSKI, H.
(1988) On adaption with noisy information. *J. Complexity*, **4**, 257–276.

KIEFER, J.
(1953) Sequential minimax search for a maximum. *Proc. AMS*, **4**. 502–505.

KIEŁBASIŃSKI, A. AND SCHWETLICK, H.
(1988) *Numerische Lineare Algebra*. VEB Deutscher Verlag der Wissenschaften, Berlin.

KIMELDORF, G.S. AND WAHBA, G.
(1970) A correspondence between Bayesian estimation of stochastic processes and smoothing by splines. *Ann. Math. Statist.*, **41**, 495–502.

KO, KER-I.
(1986) Applying techniques of discrete complexity theory to numerical computation. In *Studies in Complexity Theory*. Ed. by R.V. Book, Pitman, London, pp. 1–62.

(1991) *Complexity Theory of Real Functions*. Birkhäuser, Boston, Massachusetts.

KON, M.A. AND NOVAK, E.
(1989) On the adaptive and continuous information problems. *J. Complexity*, **5**, 345–362.

(1990) The adaption problem for approximating linear operators. *Bull. AMS*, **23**, 159–165.

KORNEICHUK, N.P.
(1994) Optimization of active algorithms for recovery of monotonic functions from Hölder's class. *J. Complexity*, **10**, 265–269.

KOWALSKI, M.A.
(1989) On approximation of band-limited signals. *J. Complexity*, **5**, 283–302.

KOWALSKI, M.A., SIKORSKI, K. AND STENGER, F.
(1995) *Selected Topics in Approximation and Computation*. Oxford Univ. Press, New York.

KUO, H.H.
(1975) *Gaussian Measures in Banach Spaces*. Vol. 463 of *Lecture Notes in Math.*, Springer-Verlag, Berlin.

LAWSON, C.L. AND HANSON, R.J.
(1974) *Solving Least Squares Problems*. Prentice-Hall, Englewood Cliffs, New Jersey.

LEE, D.
(1986) Approximation of linear operators on a Wiener space. *Rocky Mount. J. Math.*, **16**, 641–659.

LEE, D., PAVLIDIS, T. AND WASILKOWSKI, G.W.
(1987) A note on the trade-off between sampling and quantization in signal processing. *J. Complexity*, **3**, 359–371.

LEE, D. AND WASILKOWSKI, G.W.
(1986) Approximation of linear functionals on a Banach space with a Gaussian measure. *J. Complexity*, **2**, 12–43.

LEVIT, B.Y.
(1980) On asymptotic minimax estimates of the second order. *Theory Probab. Appl.*, **25**, 552–568.

LI, K.-C.
(1982) Minimaxity of the method of regularization on stochastic processes. *Ann. Statist.*, **10**, 937–942.

MAGARIL-IL'YAEV, G.G.
(1994) Average widths of Sobolev classes on $\mathbb{R}^n$. *J. Approx. Th.*, **76**, 65–76.

MAGARIL-IL'YAEV, G.G. AND OSIPENKO, K.YU.
(1991) On optimal recovery of functionals from inaccurate data. *Matem. Zametki*, **50**, 85–93. (In Russian.)

MAIOROV, V.
(1993) Average n-widths of the Wiener space in the $\mathcal{L}_\infty$-norm. *J. Complexity*, **9**, 222–230.

(1994) Linear widths of function spaces equipped with the Gaussian measure. *J. Approx. Th.*, **77**, 74–88.

MARCHUK, A.G. AND OSIPENKO, K.YU.
(1975) Best approximation of functions specified with an error at a finite number of points. *Math. Notes*, **17**, 207–212.

MARCUS, M. AND MINC, H.
(1964) *A Survey of Matrix Theory and Matrix Inequalities.* Allyn and Bacon, Boston, Massachusetts.

MATHÉ, P.
(1990) *s*-Numbers in information-based complexity. *J. Complexity*, **6**, 41–66.

(1994) Approximation theory of stochastic numerical methods. Habilitation thesis. Institut für Angewandte Analysis und Stochastic, Berlin.

MELKMAN, A.A. AND MICCHELLI, C.A.
(1979) Optimal estimation of linear operators in Hilbert spaces from inaccurate data. *SIAM J. Numer. Anal.*, **16**, 87–105.

MEYER, Y.
(1990) *Ondelettes et Opérateurs.* Hermann. Paris.

MICCHELLI, C.A.
(1993) Optimal estimation of linear operators from inaccurate data: a second look. *Numer. Algorithms*, **5**, 375–390.

MICCHELLI, C.A. AND RIVLIN, T.J.
(1977) A survey of optimal recovery. In *Estimation in Approx. Th..* Ed. by C.A. Micchelli and T.J. Rivlin, Plenum, New York, pp. 1–54.

MOROZOV, V.A.
(1984) *Methods for Solving Incorrectly Posed Problems.* Springer-Verlag, New York.

NEMIROVSKI, A.S.
(1994) On parallel complexity of nonsmooth convex optimization. *J. Complexity*, **10**, 451–463.

NEMIROVSKI, A.S. AND YUDIN, D.B.
(1983) *Problem Complexity and Method Efficiency in Optimization.* Wiley and Sons, New York.

NIKOLSKIJ, S.M.
(1950) On the estimation error of quadrature formulas. *Uspekhi Mat. Nauk*, **5**, 165–177. (In Russian.)

NOVAK, E.
(1988) *Deterministic and Stochastic Error Bounds in Numerical Analysis.* Vol. 1349 of *Lecture Notes in Math.*, Springer-Verlag, Berlin.

(1993) Quadrature formulas for convex classes of functions. In H. Brass and G. Hämmerlin, editors, *Numerical Integration IV*, Birkhäuser, Basel.

(1995a) The adaption problem for nonsymmetric convex sets. *J. Approx. Th.*, **82**, 123–134.

(1995b) The real number model in numerical analysis. *J. Complexity*, **11**, 57–73.

(1995c) On the power of adaption. Manuscript.

NOVAK, E. AND RITTER, K.
(1989) A stochastic analog to Chebyshev centers and optimal average case algorithms. *J. Complexity*, **5**, 60–79.

NUSSBAUM, M.
(1985) Spline smoothing in regression model and asymptotic efficiency in $\mathcal{L}_2$. *Ann. Statist.*, **13**, 984–997.

OSIPENKO, K.YU.
(1994) Optimal recovery of periodic functions from Fourier coefficients given with an error. To appear in *J. Complexity*.

PACKEL, E.W.
(1986) Linear problems (with extended range) have linear optimal algorithms. *Aequationes Math.*, **30**, 18–25.

PAPAGEORGIOU, A. AND WASILKOWSKI, G.W.
(1990) Average complexity of multivariate problems. *J. Complexity*, **5**, 1–23.

PARTHASARATHY, K.R.
(1967) *Probability Measures on Metric Spaces*. Academic Press, New York.

PARZEN, E.
(1962) An approach to time series analysis. *Ann. Math. Statist.*, **32**, 951–989.

(1963) Probability density functionals and reproducing kernel Hilbert spaces. In M. Rosenblatt, editor, *Proc. Symposium on Time Series Analysis*, Wiley, New York, pp. 155–169.

PASKOV, S.H.
(1993) Average case complexity of multivariate integration for smooth functions. *J. Complexity*, **9**, 291–312.

PINKUS, A.
(1985) *n-Widths in Approximation Theory*. Springer-Verlag, Berlin.

PINSKER, M.S.
(1980) Optimal filtering of square integrable signals in Gaussian white noise. *Problems Inform. Transmission*, **16**, 52–68. (In Russian.)

PLASKOTA, L.
(1989) Asymptotic error for the global maximum of functions in s-dimensions. *J. Complexity*, **5**, 369–378.

(1990) On average case complexity of linear problems with noisy information. *J. Complexity*, **6**, 199–230.

(1992) Function approximation and integration on the Wiener space with noisy data. *J. Complexity*, **8**, 301–323.

(1993a) Optimal approximation of linear operators based on noisy data on functionals. *J. Approx. Th.*, **73**, 93–105.

(1993b) A note on varying cardinality in the average case setting. *J. Complexity*, **9**, 458–470.

(1994) Average case approximation of linear functionals based on information with deterministic noise. *J. of Comp. and Inform.*, **4**, 21–39.

(1995a) Average complexity for linear problems in a model with varying information noise. *J. Complexity*, **11**, 240–264.

(1995b) On sequential designs in statistical estimation, or, how to benefit from noise. Int. Comp. Sci. Inst. at Berkeley. Report.

RITTER, K.
(1994) Almost optimal differentiation using noisy data. To appear in *J. Approx. Th.*

RITTER, K., WASILKOWSKI, G.W. AND WOŹNIAKOWSKI, H.
(1995) Multivariate integration and approximation for random fields satisfying Sacks-Ylvisaker conditions. *Ann. of Appl. Prob.*, **5**, 518–540.

SACKS, J. AND YLVISAKER, D.
(1966) Designs for regression problems with correlated errors. *Ann. Math. Statist.*, **37**, 66–89.

(1968) Designs for regression problems with correlated errors; many parameters. *Ann. Math. Statist.*, **39**, 49–69.

(1970) Designs for regression problems with correlated errors III. *Ann. Math. Statist.*, **41**, 2057–2074.

SARD, A.
(1949) Best approximate integration formulas: best approximation formulas. *Amer. J. Math.*, **71**, 80–91.

SCHOENBERG, I.J.
(1946) Contributions to the problem of approximation of equidistant data by analytic functions. *Quart. Appl. Math.*, **4**, 44–99, 112–141.

(1964a) On interpolation by spline functions and its minimum properties. *Intern. Ser. Numer. Anal.*, **5**, 109–129.

(1964b) Spline functions and the problem of graduation. *Proc. Nat. Acad. Sci. USA*, **52**, 947–949.

(1973) *Cardinal Spline Interpolation*. Vol. 12 of *CBMS*, SIAM, Philadelphia.

SCHOENBERG, I.J. AND GREVILLE, T.N.E.
(1965) Smoothing by generalized spline functions. *SIAM Rev.*, **7**, 617.

SCHÖNHAGE, A.
(1986) Equation solving in terms of computational complexity. In *Proc. Intern. Congress Math.*, Berkeley, California.

SCHUMAKER, L.
(1981) *Spline Functions: Basic Theory.* Wiley and Sons, New York.

SIKORSKI, K. AND TROJAN, G.M.
(1990) Asymptotic near optimality of the bisection method. *Numer. Math.*, **57**, 421–433.

SKOROHOD, A.V.
(1974) *Integration in Hilbert Spaces.* Springer-Verlag, New York.

SMOLYAK, S.A.
(1965) *On optimal recovery of functions and functionals of them.* PhD thesis, Moscow State Univ.

SPECKMAN, P.
(1979) Minimax estimates of linear functionals in a Hilbert space. Unpublished manuscript.

(1985) Spline smoothing and optimal rates of convergence in nonparametric regression models. *Ann. Statist.*, **13**, 970–983.

STECKIN, S.B. AND SUBBOTIN, YU.N.
(1976) *Splines in Numerical Mathematics.* Nauka, Moscow. (In Russian.)

STONE, C.J.
(1982) Optimal global rates of convergence for nonparametric regression. *Ann. Statist.*, **10**, 1040–1053.

SUKHAREV, A.G.
(1986) On the existence of optimal affine methods for approximating linear functionals. *J. Complexity*, **2**, 317–322.

SULDIN, A.V.
(1959) Wiener measure and its applications to approximation methods, I. *Izv. Vyssh. Uchebn. Zaved. Mat.*, **13**, 145–158. (In Russian.)

(1960) Wiener measure and its applications to approximation methods, II. *Izv. Vyssh. Uchebn. Zaved. Mat.*, **18**, 165–179. (In Russian.)

SUN, Y. AND WANG, C.
(1994) μ-Average n-widths on the Wiener space. *J. Complexity*, **10**, 428–436.

TIKHONOV, A.N.
(1963) On regularization of ill-posed problems. *Dokl. Akad. Nauk SSSR*, **153**, 49–52.

TIKHONOV, A.N. AND ARSENIN, V.JA.
(1979) *Methods for Solving Ill-posed Problems.* Wiley and Sons, New York.

TRAUB, J.F., WASILKOWSKI, G.W. AND WOŹNIAKOWSKI, H.
(1983) *Information, Uncertainty, Complexity.* Addison-Wesley, Reading, Massachusetts.

(1988) *Information-based Complexity.* Academic Press, New York.

TRAUB, J.F. AND WOŹNIAKOWSKI, H.
(1980) *A General Theory of Optimal Algorithms.* Academic Press, New York.

TRIEBEL, H.
(1992) *Theory of Function Spaces II.* Birkhäuser Verlag, Basel.

TROJAN, G.M.
(1983) Asymptotic setting for linear problems. Unpublished manuscript. See also Traub *et al.* (1988), pp. 383–400.

VAKHANIA, N.N.
(1981) *Probability Distributions on Linear Spaces.* North-Holland, New York.

VAKHANIA, N.N., TARIELADZE, V.I. AND CHOBANYAN, S.A.
(1987) *Probability Distributions on Banach Spaces.* Reidel, Netherlands.

VARADARAJAN, V.S.
(1961) Measures on topological spaces. *Mat. Sbornik*, **55**, 35–100. (In Russian.)

WAHBA, G.
(1971) On the regression design problem of Sacks and Ylvisaker. *Ann. Math. Statist.*, 1035–1043.

(1990) *Spline Models for Observational Data.* Vol. 59 of *CBMS-NSF Ser. in Appl. Math.*, SIAM, Philadelphia.

WASILKOWSKI, G.W.
(1983) Local average error. Columbia University Comp. Sc. Report.

(1986) Information of varying cardinality. *J. Complexity*, **2**, 204–228.

(1994) Integration and approximation of multivariate functions: average case complexity with isotropic Wiener measure. *J. Approx. Th.*, **77**, 212–227.

WASILKOWSKI, G.W. AND WOŹNIAKOWSKI, H.
(1987) On optimal algorithms in an asymptotic model with Gaussian measure. *SIAM J. Math. Anal.*, **3**, 632–647.

(1993) There exists a linear problem with infinite combinatory cost. *J. Complexity*, **7**, 326–337.

(1995) Explicit cost bounds of algorithms for solving multivariate problems. *J. Complexity*, **11**, 1–56.

WEIHRAUCH, K.
(1987) *Computability*. Springer-Verlag, Berlin.

WERSCHULZ, A.G.
(1987) An information-based approach to ill-posed problems. *J. Complexity*, **3**, 270–301.

(1991) *The Computational Complexity of Differential and Integral Equations*. Oxford Univ. Press, Oxford.

WERSCHULZ, A.G. AND WOŹNIAKOWSKI, H.
(1986) Are linear algorithms always good for linear problems? *Aequationes Math.*, **30**, 202–212.

WIENER, N.
(1923) Differential space. *J. Math. and Phys.*, **2**, 131–174.

WILANSKY, A.
(1978) *Modern Methods in Topological Vector Spaces*. McGraw-Hill, New York.

WOŹNIAKOWSKI, H.
(1991) Average case complexity of multivariate integration. *Bull. AMS*, **24**, 185–194.

(1992) Average case complexity of multivariate linear problems I, II. *J. Complexity*, **8**, 337–392.

(1994) Tractability of linear multivariate problems. *J. Complexity*, **10**, 96–128.

Author index

Subject index

Printed in the United States
By Bookmasters